Remedies in EC law

Law and Practice in the English and EC Courts

Second Edition

Mark Brealey

of Middle Temple, Barrister

Mark Hoskins

of Gray's Inn, Barrister

With foreword by David Vaughan QC

Sweet & Maxwell

Published by
Sweet & Maxwell Limited of
100 Avenue Road
London NW3 3PF
Set by Tradespools Ltd, Frome, Somerset, United Kingdom
Printed and bound in Great Britain by MPG Books Ltd, Bodmin, Cornwall

A CIP catalogue record for this book
is available from the British Library

ISBN 075200 4697
First published 1994
Second edition 1998

No natural forests were destroyed to make this product, only naturally farmed
timber was used and re-planted

Contents

Foreword to the Second Edition

For someone who has spent a large proportion of his professional life working at the coal-face of the enforcement of Community law rights and remedies, it is a great privilege to have been invited to write the Foreword to the second edition of this important book with its well-established reputation.

One does not need to revert to Latin tags to appreciate the importance of remedies in any legal system, be they interlocutory or final. It was the early recognition by the Court of Justice of rights for individuals (initially with regard to Treaty provisions, then to Regulations and subsequently to Directives, at least vertically) and the need for fully effective remedies (and the subsequent development of those), which distinguishes the Community legal order from traditional international law. It is probably only with recent developments, particularly in interlocutory protection and damages against the State, that Community law can now be recognised as a fully developed legal system. Community law is leading the way. Experience has shown that where Community law leads, the national laws of the Member States tend to follow. It will be surprising if a fully developed tort of State liability, based on the standards set out in *Factortame III* and *Dillenkofer*, does not develop in all Member States to apply in purely national situations (see the statements on this issue in today's Judgment of the Court of Appeal in *Factortame IV*).

In the period since the first edition (early 1994) there have been major advances in remedies provided by Community law, both in the national and in the Community arena. These are extensively covered in this new edition. The authors have extended their treatment of general principles by creating a new chapter to deal with the highly topical subjects of proportionality and legitimate expectations. They have brought up to date and greatly extended the chapter on Interpretation and on Effective Protection of Community Law rights. Inevitably the most significant changes have come in the chapters on Damages and Judicial Review in National Courts. There is extensive treatment of both these subjects which are of critical importance.

The sections on Preliminary References and Remedies in the Community Courts have also been extended and brought up to date, with extensive references to the latest case law.

Rights are nothing without remedies and remedies are worthless if lawyers are not fully aware of their significance. This excellent book (now fully up to date) provides a clear and complete guide for experts and beginners alike. It will be a foolish lawyer who does not consult this book before embarking on EC litigation in either the national or the Community forum. Although in its treatment of national remedies it concentrates on the English (and Welsh) courts, it will also be of significance to lawyers from other jurisdictions, for inevitably courts in one jurisdiction will need to know how similar problems are dealt with in other jurisdictions. Equally for those involved in the development of remedies in the national legal system for purely domestic situations, this book will provide some important indications as to how such remedies are likely to develop.

I have no doubt that this new edition will have the success it deserves.

8 April 1998

David Vaughan QC
Brick Court Chambers,
London

Foreword to the First Edition

Lawyers, whether practitioners or teachers, are increasingly aware of the relevance of Community law in their daily work.

The question of remedies in Community law is becoming more and more important. The general principle is that the question of how Community rights should be protected is to be determined by the national legal systems of the Member States. This is subject to the conditions, first, that the national rules relating to the protection of Community rights should not be less favourable than those relating to purely domestic rights and, second, that the national rules should not make it impossible in practice to protect Community rights.

However, the Court of Justice has, on occasion, indicated the nature of the remedy which must be available to protect a Community right. Thus, in *Rewe* and *Comet*, the Court recognised a right to restitution where charges had been demanded which were contrary to Community law, thus anticipating the decision of the House of Lords in *Woolwich*. In *Factortame*, the Court held that the English courts could not be prevented by a rule of national law from granting an injunction against the Crown where this was necessary to protect rights under Community law. In *Francovich*, the Court held that failure by a Member State to implement a directive may give rise to a right to damages for individuals who have thereby suffered loss. The recent Opinion of the Advocate General in *Banks* suggests that the Court should now set at rest the doubts remaining after *Garden Cottage Foods*.

So lawyers of all disciplines need to find out in greater detail how Community law interacts with national law, and this book will help them to do it. It covers the existing material in a thorough, but accessible, way and provides clear guidance as to the way in which Community law can be used in the English legal system. In addition, it deals with the direct actions which can be brought before the Court of Justice and Court of First Instance and includes a useful analysis of the Rules of Procedure to be followed before these Courts.

I commend this book to all lawyers who take seriously the duty they owe to their clients to be aware of Community law, and I am sure it will have the success it deserves.

28 October 1993   *David Edward*
Judge of the Court of Justice
of the European Communities

Preface

In Scotland, when someone says that a particular task is 'like painting the Forth Rail Bridge', they mean that the task is never-ending. This is because it takes so long to paint the bridge that, by the time the painters reach one end, they need to start again at the place where they began, which has become rusty in the meantime. Writing a law book is like painting the Forth Bridge. Writing a book on remedies in EC law is like painting a very long Forth Bridge because of the high volume of case law from the Court of Justice and the Court of First Instance, and the increasing number of domestic judgments concerning Community law.

We have done a lot of work on this second edition and many sections have been completely reworked. However, we are already aware of potential developments which may need to be dealt with in the third edition. On the question of State liability, the *Factortame* litigation is still taking place in the English courts. Furthermore, there have been a number of first instance decisions dealing with the question of whether a party to an agreement which is in breach of Article 85 may claim damages from a co-contractor. This line of jurisprudence is still at a formative stage and will almost certainly need to be elaborated further by the domestic courts and probably, at some stage, by the Court of Justice. For the purposes of this edition, we have endeavoured to state the law as at September 1997.

Another very important potential development will be the re-numbering of the articles of the EU and EC Treaties by the Amsterdam Treaty. As the Amsterdam Treaty had still to be ratified at the time when the book went to press, we have decided to retain the current (and more familiar) Treaty numbering in the text and to indicate the new re-numbering in square brackets where appropriate. In addition, a complete table setting out the relationship between the old and new numbers is included as one of the Appendices.

We were delighted with the positive response which the first edition received and pleasantly surprised by the large number of copies which were sold outside the United Kingdom. A number of people have suggested to us that it would be a good idea to broaden the scope of the book to deal with the manner in which EC law remedies are dealt with in the legal systems of other Member States, as well as in Scots law. On reflection, we decided not to attempt to expand the coverage of the book in that way as we felt the task would be simply too vast.

We would like to thank Alison Spencer, Paquita Bahr, Helen Davies and Alison Padfield for the work which they have done on the book. We are very grateful for all their efforts. We would also like to thank David Vaughan QC for agreeing to write the foreword, Judge David Edward for allowing us to re-print his foreword from the first edition and our clerks, Ian Moyler and Mark Simpkin, for their patience and encouragement. Finally, we would like to thank Susan Marshall of Sweet & Maxwell who has provided us with excellent support in the preparation of this edition.

The writing of the second edition has coincided in large part with the 1997-1998 football season. MH would like to record his gratitude to Notts County for making him a very happy man by clinching the Third Division Championship in fine style. MB hopes that Spurs' fortunes improve considerably to spare him from continued anguish on Saturday afternoons.

28 March 1998   *Mark Hoskins and Mark Brealey*
                                                   Brick Court Chambers

Table of Cases

EUROPEAN CASES: ALPHABETICAL LIST

TABLE OF CASES

INTERNATIONAL CASES

TABLE OF CASES

Table of Statutes

Table of Statutory Instruments

Table of Treaties

Table of Regulations

Table of Decisions and Directives

Table of Notices

Table of International Conventions

Table of Procedural Rules

Part I

Application of EC Law in the English Courts

Chapter 1

Sources of EC Law

Sources The main sources of European Community law are the EC Treaty and the secondary legislation and administrative acts which are adopted by the Community institutions to implement and give effect to that Treaty. These sources are supplemented by the case-law of the EC courts (the Court of Justice and the Court of First Instance), by the general principles of Community law,[1] by international agreements entered into by the Community and the Member States and by public international law.

1. TREATIES

The Treaties The European Union is founded on the three treaties establishing the European Communities, and the European Union Treaty itself. The first treaty, which entered into force in 1952, was the treaty establishing the European Coal and Steel Community ('ECSC' Treaty).[2] There then followed the treaty establishing the European Economic Community ('EEC' Treaty)[3] and the treaty establishing the European Atomic Energy Community ('EAEC' or 'EURATOM' Treaty),[4] both of which entered into force in 1958. The EEC Treaty is the most important in practice as it is of more general application than the other two, sectoral treaties.

The ECSC, EEC and EAEC Treaties were originally concluded between a Community of six Member States: Belgium, France, Germany, Italy, Luxembourg and the Netherlands. By virtue of successive Treaties of Accession, Denmark, Ireland and the United Kingdom became members in 1973,[5] Greece

---

[1] These are discussed separately in Ch 2.
[2] Treaty of Paris, signed on 18 April 1951.
[3] Treaty of Rome, signed on 25 March 1957.
[4] Treaty of Rome, signed on 25 March 1957.
[5] Act concerning the Conditions of Accession and the Adjustments to the Treaties – Accession to the European Communities of the Kingdom of Denmark, Ireland and the United Kingdom of Great Britain and Northern Ireland, signed on 22 January 1972, entered into force 1 January 1973 (OJ 1972 L73, p 1).

in 1981,[6] Spain and Portugal in 1986,[7] and Austria, Finland and Sweden in 1995.[8]

The EEC Treaty has been subject to notable amendments by the Single European Act[9] and by the Treaty on European Union ('EU' or 'Maastricht' Treaty).[10] Pursuant to the EU Treaty, the European Economic Community ('EEC') has been renamed the European Community ('EC').[11]

The EU Treaty created a new entity called the 'European Union',[12] based on three 'pillars': (a) the existing European Communities (ie the ECSC, EC and EAEC Treaties); (b) a common foreign and security policy;[13] and (c) cooperation in the fields of justice and home affairs.[14] The EU Treaty and the Community Treaties will be further amended provided that the Amsterdam Treaty is ratified by the Member States.[15]

The Court of Justice has jurisdiction in respect of the ECSC, EC and EAEC Treaties. However, it has only limited jurisdiction in respect of the EU Treaty. In particular, the provisions governing foreign/security policy and justice/home affairs fall outside the jurisdiction of the Court.[16] Article M of the EU Treaty [new art 47] provides that, save for the provisions specifically amending the ECSC, EC and EAEC Treaties, nothing in the EU Treaty shall affect the Treaties establishing the European Communities. The Court of Justice therefore has jurisdiction to determine the interface between the EU and the EC Treaties.[17]

In addition, there have been a number of institutional treaties dealing with the operation of the Communities.[18]

---

[6] Act concerning the Conditions of Accession and the Adjustments to the Treaties – Accession to the European Communities of the Hellenic Republic, signed on 28 May 1979, entered into force 1 January 1981 (OJ 1979 L291, p 17).

[7] Act concerning the Conditions of Accession and the Adjustments to the Treaties – Accession to the European Communities of the Kingdom of Spain and the Portuguese Republic, signed on 12 June 1985, entered into force 1 January 1986 (OJ 1985 L302, p 1).

[8] Act concerning the Conditions of Accession and the Adjustments to the Treaties – Accession to the European Union of the Republic of Austria, the Republic of Finland and the Kingdom of Sweden, signed on 24 June 1994, entered into force 1 January 1995 (OJ 1995, L1, p 1).

[9] Signed on 17 February 1986 (OJ 1986 L169 p 1). Entered into force on 1 July 1987.

[10] Signed at Maastricht on 7 February 1992 (OJ 1992 C191 p 1). Entered into force on 1 November 1993. The Treaty on European Union is sometimes referred to by the abbreviation 'TEU'. The text of the EEC Treaty, as amended by the Maastricht Treaty, has been published in OJ 1992 C224, p 1.

[11] EU Treaty, article G(1) [new art 8].

[12] Ibid, article A [new art 1].

[13] Ibid, article J [new arts 1–28].

[14] Ibid, article K [new arts 29–45].

[15] The Amsterdam Treaty was signed by the Member States on 2 October 1997; however, it cannot enter into force until it has been ratified by all of the Member States.

[16] Article L of the EU Treaty [new art 46]. See also Case C-167/94 *Grau Gromis* [1995] ECR I-1023 para 6. This will be subject to alteration by the Amsterdam Treaty (if it is ratified).

[17] Case C-124/95 *R v HM Treasury, ex p Centro-Com* [1997] ECR I-81 paras 23–30.

[18] Treaty establishing a Single Council and a Single Commission of the European Communities ('Merger Treaty', OJ 152, 13 June 1967); Treaty amending Certain Budgetary Provisions of the Treaties establishing the European Communities and of the Treaty establishing a Single Council

The Agreement on the European Economic Area ('EEA Agreement')[19] came into effect on 1 January 1994. It is not, strictly speaking, a Community treaty as it involves certain third countries. The EEA Agreement in effect extended the rules of the Internal Market laid down by the EC Treaty to Austria, Finland, Iceland, Norway and Sweden without those countries being full members of the European Community. Following the accession of Austria, Finland and Sweden to the European Union, the EEA Agreement now applies to the European Union, Iceland, Liechtenstein and Norway.[20]

Status of Community Treaties The Community Treaties are the legal bases upon which the Community operates. They are, in effect, the constitution of the Community,[21] and as such take priority over all other sources of law within the Community. The Treaties define the limits of the EC's competence to act and provide the legal bases for all secondary legislation. No acts can be adopted which are not justified, directly or indirectly, by the provisions of the Treaties.[22] It follows that where there is a conflict between the EC Treaty and secondary legislation, the EC Treaty will prevail.[23] Furthermore, the institutions are not entitled to act outside the scope of the powers granted to them by the Treaties.[24] Thus, the Court of Justice has consistently held that a mere practice on the part of the Community institutions cannot derogate from the rules laid down in the EC Treaty and cannot create a precedent binding on the institutions.[25]

---

and a Single Commission of the European Communities (OJ 1971 L2, 2 January 1971); Act concerning the election of representatives of the Assembly by direct universal suffrage (OJ 1976 L278, 8 October 1976); Treaty amending Certain Financial Provisions of the Treaty establishing the European Communities and of the Treaty establishing a Single Council and a Single Commission of the European Communities (OJ 1977 L359, 31 December 1977); and Treaty amending Certain Provisions of the Protocol on the Statute of the European Investment Bank (OJ 1978 L91, 6 April 1978).

[19] See OJ 1994 L1 p 1 and OJ 1994 L1 p 571.

[20] For analysis of the EEA Agreement, see Norberg, Hökborg, Johansson, Eliasson and Dedichen, *The European Economic Area EEA Law A Commentary on the EEA Agreement*, 1st edn (Fritzes/Kluwer, 1993); Christopher Bright, *Business Law in the European Economic Area* (Clarendon Press, Oxford, 1994); Blanchet, Piipponen and Westman-Clément, *The Agreement on the European Economic Area (EEA)*, 1st edn (Clarendon Press, Oxford, 1994).

[21] Case 294/83 *Parti écologiste 'Les Verts' v Parliament* [1986] ECR 1339 para 23; *Opinion 1/91* [1991] ECR I-6079 para 21 (Opinion concerning the draft Treaty on a European Economic Area).

[22] Article 3b of the EC Treaty [new art 5]; *Opinion 2/94* [1996] ECR I-1759 paras 23–25 and 28–30 (Opinion on the Accession by the Communities to the Convention for the Protection of Human Rights and Fundamental Freedoms).

[23] See, for example, Case 37/70 *Rewe-Zentrale v Hauptzollamt Emmerich* [1971] ECR 23 paras 2–5; Joined Cases 80/77 and 81/77 *Commissionnaires Réunis v Receveur des Douanes* [1978] ECR 927; Case C-21/88 *Du Pont de Nemours Italiana* [1990] ECR I-889 paras 16–17; Joined Cases T-24 to 26/93 and 28/93 *Compagnie Maritime Belge Transports v Commission* [1996] ECR II-1201 para 152.

[24] Article 4(1) of the EC Treaty [new art 7].

[25] Case 68/86 *United Kingdom v Council* [1988] ECR 855 para 24; Case C-327/91 *France v Commission* [1994] ECR I-3641 para 36; Case C-426/93 *Germany v Council* [1995] ECR I-3723 para 21; Case C-271/94 *Parliament v Council* [1996] ECR I-1689 para 24.

Geographical scope The geographical scope of the EC Treaty is defined in article 227 of that Treaty [new art 299].[26] Secondary legislation adopted pursuant to the EC Treaty applies in the same geographical area as the Treaty itself.[27]

Article 227(4) provides that the provisions of the EC Treaty apply to the European territories for whose external relations a Member State is responsible. The United Kingdom is responsible for the external relations of Gibraltar and therefore the provisions of the EC Treaty *prima facie* apply to Gibraltar.[28] The position of the Channel Islands and the Isle of Man is specifically dealt with by article 227(5)(c) of the EC Treaty and Protocol No 3 to the 1973 Act of Accession.

The European Council In Case C-233/94 *Germany v Parliament*[29] the German Government argued that the provision of a directive was unlawful as it conflicted with certain of the conclusions of the European Council in Edinburgh; however, the Court of Justice found that it was not necessary to determine the precise legal value of those conclusions.

2. SECONDARY LEGISLATION/ADMINISTRATIVE ACTS

Community measures The EC Treaty sets out the basic principles upon which the European Community is founded. In practice, further detailed measures are necessary to give effect to the Treaty. The EC Treaty therefore gives the Community institutions law-making and administrative powers.

Article 189 of the EC Treaty [new art 249] defines the characteristics of the five main types of legislative and administrative measures which may be adopted by the Community institutions. These are regulations, directives, decisions, recommendations and opinions.[30] In addition, the Court of Justice has recognised that measures which fall outside article 189 (*sui generis* measures) are capable of producing legal effects.

---

[26] See the Opinion of Advocate-General Légér in Case C-214/94 *Boukhalfa v Germany* [1996] ECR I-2253 paras 23–47 where he discusses the extraterritorial application of the EC Treaty, and paras 14–15 of the judgment of the Court of Justice.

[27] Case 61/77 *Commission v Ireland* [1978] ECR 417 para 46; Case C-214/94 *Boukhalfa v Germany* [1996] ECR I-2253 paras 13–14.

[28] However, see article 28 of the 1973 Act of Accession.

[29] [1997] ECR I-2405 paras 76 and 80. Note that the 'European Council' is distinct from the 'Council of the European Union'. The latter is a Community institution whereas the former is used to connote the summit meetings of the Heads of State or of Government of the Member States and the President of the Commission (see article D of the EU Treaty [new art 4]), which usually take place twice a year.

[30] Note that the terminology used for measures under the ECSC Treaty is different: see article 14 of the ECSC Treaty.

(a) Regulations

Definition Article 189 of the EC Treaty [new art 249] defines regulations as follows:

> A regulation shall have general application. It shall be binding in its entirety and directly applicable in all Member States.

'General application' means that regulations are not addressed to specific Member States or private parties. They are also 'binding in their entirety', which means that their provisions apply in identical terms throughout the Community.

Entry into force A regulation takes effect on the date specified in its text, or, if no such date is specified, on the twentieth day following its publication in the *Official Journal of the European Communities*.[31] A regulation is presumed to be published on the date shown on the issue of the *Official Journal* in which it appears, unless evidence can be produced that the issue was not in fact available until a later date.[32] It is not permissible for a copy of the *Official Journal* to be backdated so as to show a date on its cover which is prior to its actual date of publication.[33]

Directly applicable Regulations are 'directly applicable'. This means that as soon as a regulation comes into force, it takes effect automatically in the national legal systems of the Member States. There is no need for the Member States to pass national implementing legislation.[34] The entry into force of a regulation precludes the application of any national legislative measure—even one adopted subsequently—which is incompatible with the provisions of that regulation.[35] Furthermore, Member States are not permitted to modify the scope of application of a regulation by national measures, for example, by providing for exemptions which are not contained in the regulation.[36] Once a regulation has entered into force, the Member States have an obligation to repeal all existing national legislation which is incompatible with it. It is not sufficient simply to issue administrative instructions waiving the application of the national law.[37]

---

[31] Article 191(1) and (2) of the EC Treaty [new art 254]. Where a specific date for entry into force is laid down in the regulation itself, this may be subject to review by the EC courts, particularly where it would entail retroactive effect: Case 17/67 *Neumann v Hauptzollamt Hof* [1967] ECR 441 at 455–456.

[32] Case 99/78 *Decker v Hauptzollamt Landau* [1979] ECR 101 paras 2–5; Case C-337/88 *SAFA v Amministrazione delle Finanze* [1990] ECRI-1 paras 8, 12.

[33] Case T-115/94 *Opel Austria v Council* [1997] ECR II-39 paras 127–135.

[34] Case 34/73 *Variola v Amministrazione Italiana delle Finanze* [1973] ECR 981 para 10; Case 50/76 *Amsterdam Bulb v Produktschap voor Siergewassen* [1977] ECR 137 paras 4–6; Case 94/77 *Zerbone v Amministrazione delle Finanze* [1978] ECR 99 paras 22–24.

[35] Case 84/71 *Marimex v Italian Ministry for Finance* [1972] ECR 89 paras 4–5; Case 34/73 *Variola v Amministrazione Italiana delle Finanze* [1973] ECR 981 paras 14–15; Case 31/78 *Bussone v Italian Ministry for Agriculture and Forestry* [1978] ECR 2429 paras 30–31.

[36] Case 18/72 *Granaria v Produktschap voor Veevoeder* [1972] ECR 1163 paras 14–18.

[37] Case 167/73 *Commission v France* [1974] ECR 359 para 42; Case C-307/89 *Commission v France* [1991] ECR I-2903 paras 12–13.

Implementation Member States are not permitted to adopt national implementing measures unless this is required, explicitly or implicitly, by the regulation.[38] In particular, Member States are not permitted simply to reproduce the provisions of a regulation in a national law, as this might conceal the Community nature of the rights contained in the regulation.[39]

Member States may adopt national legislative, regulatory, administrative or financial measures where this is expressly required by the regulation[40] or where this is necessary to give effect to the regulation in their national legal system.[41] For example, in Case 31/78 *Bussone v Italian Ministry for Agriculture and Forestry*[42] a regulation required the Member States to designate official agencies to organise the preparation and distribution of bands and labels with which large packs of eggs had to be provided.

The implementing measures need not be identical in all respects throughout the Community.[43] However, Member States are not permitted to amend the scope of the regulation or to add to its provisions, unless this complies with the aim and objectives of the regulation.[44] National implementing measures may reproduce the provisions of a regulation where this is necessary for the sake of coherence and comprehensibility.[45] In addition, the national measures must respect the general principles of Community law.[46] Where a Member State has adopted implementing measures, the national courts are entitled to review those national measures to ascertain whether they are in accordance with the regulation.[47]

---

[38] Case 93/71 *Leonesio v Italian Ministry for Agriculture and Forestry* [1972] ECR 287 paras 5–6 and 22; Case 50/76 *Amsterdam Bulb v Produktschap voor Siergewassen* [1977] ECR 137 paras 4–8.

[39] Case 39/72 *Commission v Italy* [1973] ECR 101 paras 14–18; Case 34/73 *Variola v Amministrazione Italiana delle Finanze* [1973] ECR 981 paras 9–11; Case 272/83 *Commission v Italy* [1985] ECR 1057 para 26.

[40] See, for example, Case 40/69 *Hauptzollamt Hamburg v Bollmann* [1970] ECR 69 paras 2–5; Case 74/69 *Hauptzollamt Bremen v Krohn* [1970] ECR 451 paras 2–6; Case 31/78 *Bussone v Italian Ministry for Agriculture and Forestry* [1978] ECR 2429 paras 30–32; Case 230/78 *Eridania v Minister of Agriculture and Forestry* [1979] ECR 2749 paras 33–35.

[41] Case 94/77 *Zerbone v Amministrazione delle Finanze* [1978] ECR 99 paras 22–27; Joined Cases 146/81, 192/81 and 193/81 *BayWa v BALM* [1982] ECR 1503 paras 26–31.

[42] [1978] ECR 2429 paras 26–36.

[43] Case 111/76 *Van den Hazel* [1977] ECR 901 para 22.

[44] Case 40/69 *Hauptzollamt Hamburg v Bollmann* [1970] ECR 69 paras 2–5; Case 74/69 *Hauptzollamt Bremen v Krohn* [1970] ECR 451 paras 2–6; Case 118/76 *Balkan-Import-Export v Hauptzollamt Berlin-Packhof* [1977] ECR 1177 paras 3–6; Case 31/78 *Bussone v Italian Ministry for Agriculture and Forestry* [1978] ECR 2429 paras 26–36; Case 819/79 *Germany v Commission* [1981] ECR 21 paras 1–11. See also *R v Ministry of Agriculture, Fisheries and Food, ex p National Farmers Union* [1995] 3 CMLR 116 paras 16–20 (QBD).

[45] Case 272/83 *Commission v Italy* [1985] ECR 1057 paras 21–28.

[46] Case 5/88 *Wachauf v Germany* [1989] ECR 2609 para 19. General principles are discussed in Ch 2.

[47] Case 46/75 *IBC v Commission* [1976] ECR 65; Case 230/78 *Eridania v Minister of Agriculture and Forestry* [1979] ECR 2749 para 34.

Effective enforcement Member States are under an obligation to ensure that the rules established by a regulation are effectively applied in practice in their territory. In the absence of common Community rules, they are entitled to do so in accordance with the procedural and substantive rules of their own national law, as long as this does not make it virtually impossible to give effect to the relevant Community regulation. Furthermore, the rules and procedures used to give effect to a Community regulation must not be less favourable than those applied to similar, purely national situations.[48] The obligation of effective enforcement may require a Member State, for example, to take penal or administrative action against individuals who have infringed a regulation,[49] to recover sums wrongly paid pursuant to a regulation as a result of irregularities or negligence,[50] or to impose penalties on individuals for breach of a regulation where there has been fraud affecting the financial interests of the Community.[51]

Where the regulation itself does not provide for any penalty in the event of its infringement, the Member States are competent to adopt such criminal or administrative sanctions as appear to them to be appropriate,[52] save that (a) they must ensure that any infringement is penalised under conditions, both procedural and substantive, which are analogous to those applicable to infringements of national law which are of a similar nature and importance and (b) any penalty imposed must be effective, proportionate and persuasive.[53] A system of strict criminal liability penalising breach of a regulation is not in itself incompatible with Community law.[54]

Hierarchy of norms The scope and binding nature of a regulation cannot be affected, during the period of its validity, by the adoption of a subsequent regulation which has the same objectives and which imposes less stringent requirements on Member States, but which does not expressly repeal or amend the original regulation.[55] Furthermore, an implementing regulation cannot derogate from the rules contained in the basic regulation pursuant to which it was adopted.[56]

---

[48] Joined Cases 205 to 215/82 *Deutsche Milchkontor v Germany* [1983] ECR 2633 paras 17 and 19; Case C-285/93 *Dominikanerinnen-Kloster Altenhohenau v Hauptzollamt Rosenheim* [1995] ECR I-4069 para 26.

[49] Case C-52/95 *Commission v France* [1995] ECR I-4443 paras 32–38.

[50] Joined Cases 89/86 and 91/86 *Étoile commerciale and CNTA v Commission* [1987] ECR 3005 paras 11–12.

[51] Case C-476/93P *Nutral v Commission* [1995] ECR I-4125, Opinion of Advocate-General Ruiz-Jarabo Colomer at para 17.

[52] Case 50/76 *Amsterdam Bulb v Produktschap voor Siergewassen* [1977] ECR 137 paras 31–33.

[53] Case 68/88 *Commission v Greece* [1989] ECR 2965 paras 22–27; Case C-36/94 *Siesse v Director da Alfândega de Alcântara* [1995] ECR I-3573 paras 19–21; Case C-83/94 *Leifer* [1995] ECR I-3231 paras 32–40; Case C-341/94 *Allain* [1996] ECR I-4631 para 24; Case C-29/95 *Pastoors v Belgium* [1997] ECR I-285 paras 24–26.

[54] Case C-177/95 *Ebony Maritime v Prefetto della Provincia* [1997] ECR I-1111 paras 35–38.

[55] Case C-39/88 *Commission v Ireland* [1990] ECR I-4271 para 9. See also Case C-174/89 *Hoche v BALM* [1990] ECR I-2681 para 23.

[56] Case T-64/92 *Chavane de Dalmassy v Commission* [1994] ECR-SC II-723 para 52.

An act of general application, such as a regulation, cannot be altered by an individual decision unless the general measure expressly provides for such a possibility.[57]

The mere fact that a particular measure is a regulation or directive is not conclusive in considering whether it should prevail over a conflicting measure. Thus, in Joined Cases C-246 to 249//94 *Cooperativa Agricola Zootecnica S Antonio*[58] the provisions of a Council directive which was of general application prevailed over the provisions of a Commission regulation which was of limited scope and was adopted pursuant to powers granted by the Council.

Repeal of legal basis An implementing regulation will not lapse automatically when the basic regulation pursuant to which it was adopted is repealed. In particular, the implementing regulation may continue in force where the basic provision is replaced by a new regulation with an identical content, the implementing regulation was adopted by a procedure which is identical to that provided for in the new basic regulation, and there is no contradiction between the implementing regulation and subsequent provisions of Community law.[59]

(b) Directives[60]

Definition Article 189 of the EC Treaty [new art 249] provides:

> A directive shall be binding, as to the result to be achieved, upon each Member State to which it is addressed, but shall leave to the national authorities the choice of form and methods.

A directive imposes an obligation on each Member State to which it is addressed to adopt, in that Member State's national legal system, all the measures necessary to ensure that the provisions of the directive are fully effective, in accordance with its objective, while leaving the choice of the forms and methods used to achieve that objective to the Member State itself.[61]

The main difference between a directive and a regulation is that, under the terms of a directive, a Member State has an obligation to pass national implementing legislation to give effect to the directive in its national legal system.[62] Thus, directives are not directly applicable in the same way as regulations. However, in certain circumstances a directive may create legal effects in the national legal systems of Member States before it has been

---

[57] Case T-2/93 *Air France v Commission* [1994] ECR II-323 para 102; Case T-7/93 *Langnese-Iglo v Commission* [1995] ECR II-1533 para 208; Case T-5/96 *Sveriges Betodlares Centralförening v Commission* [1996] ECR II-1299 para 30.

[58] [1996] ECR I-4373 paras 30–31.

[59] Paragraphs 16 and 18 of the Opinion of Advocate-General Gulmann in Case C-143/93 *van Es Douane Agenten v Inspecteur der Invoerrechten en Accijnzen* [1996] ECR I-431.

[60] See generally Sacha Prechal, *Directives in European Community Law* (Oxford, 1995).

[61] For example, see Case C-271/91 *Marshall v Southampton and South West Hampshire AHA* [1993] ECR I-4367 para 17.

[62] Case 91/79 *Commission v Italy* [1980] ECR 1099 para 6; Case C-287/91 *Commission v Italy* [1992] I-3515 para 7.

implemented by national legislation by virtue of the principles of direct effect[63] or interpretation.[64] In addition, where an individual has suffered loss as a result of a Member State's failure to implement a directive, he may be entitled to recover damages from the State.[65]

Unlike regulations, which are of 'general application', directives may be addressed to particular Member States, although usually they will be addressed to all the Member States.

Entry into force Directives which have been adopted in accordance with the procedure laid down in article 189b of the EC Treaty [new art 251] and Council or Commission directives which are addressed to all Member States must be published in the *Official Journal of the European Communities* and enter into force on the date specified in their text, or, if no such date is specified, on the twentieth day following their publication.[66] Other directives must be notified to those to whom they are addressed and take effect upon such notification.[67]

Implementation period A directive will usually specify a particular date by which the Member States must have adopted the national implementing measures necessary to give effect to its provisions. Member States are entitled to maintain potentially conflicting national legislation in force until the implementation period for the directive has expired.[68] Member States may also adopt conflicting measures during the implementation period provided those measures do not render the attainment of the objectives required by the directive before the expiry of the limitation period impossible or unduly difficult.[69]

Implementation A directive will specify a legislative result which must be achieved by each Member State within a given time-limit. Generally, each Member State has a discretion as to what national legislative measures are necessary to achieve that result, so that the form and content of national implementing legislation for a directive may differ between Member States. However, Member States do not enjoy a complete discretion as to how to implement a directive; they must adopt the most appropriate forms and methods to ensure that a directive is fully effective.[70] In addition, they must respect the general principles of Community law.[71]

---

[63] See Ch 4, pp 64–77

[64] See Ch 5, pp 88–96

[65] See Ch 7, pp 128–148

[66] Article 191(1) and (2) of the EC Treaty [new art 254].

[67] Article 191(3) of the EC Treaty.

[68] Case 244/78 *Union Laitière Normande v French Dairy Farmers* [1979] ECR 2663 paras 13–15.

[69] Paragraphs 37–53 of the Opinion of Advocate-General Jacobs in Case C-129/96 *Inter-Environnement Wallonie v Région Wallonne* (Opinion of 24 April 1997).

[70] Case 48/75 *Royer* [1976] ECR 497 para 75; Case 14/83 *Von Colson and Kamann v Land Nordrhein-Westfalen* [1984] ECR 1891 para 15.

[71] Case 230/78 *Eridania v Ministry of Agriculture and Forestry* [1979] ECR 2749 para 31; Joined Cases C-31 to 44/91 *Lageder v Amministrazione delle Finanze* [1993] ECR I-1761 para 33. See also Case 5/88 *Wachauf v Germany* [1989] ECR 2609 para 19; and *R v MAFF, ex p First City Trading* [1997] 1 CMLR 250, paras 24–45; [1997] EuLR 195 at 205B–212A. General principles are discussed in Ch 2.

As a general rule, a Member State is not obliged to adopt specific implementing legislation which reproduces *verbatim* the provisions of the directive. Furthermore, it may rely on its existing legal framework where this is sufficient to ensure the full application of the directive in a sufficiently clear and precise manner. Where the directive is intended to create rights for individuals, the persons concerned must be able to ascertain the full extent of their rights and, where appropriate, rely on them before the national courts.[72] The Court of Justice has emphasised that the need for clarity and precision is particularly important in implementing exceptions or derogations provided for by a directive.[73] Furthermore, it has held that the ability to rely on their rights before the national courts is of particular importance where the directive is intended to accord rights to nationals of other Member States.[74]

In some instances, given the subject-matter of the directive (eg prevention of pollution, conservation of wild birds) and the nature of the obligations which it imposes, the Court of Justice has departed from the general rule and held that it is necessary for the Member States to reproduce the terms of the directive in their national laws.[75]

A Member State is not entitled to implement a directive by means of administrative circulars or practices, as these can be changed by the authorities as they please and are not publicised widely enough.[76] In order properly to implement a directive, a national measure must be legally binding in the sense that it creates rights and obligations which are enforceable before the national courts.[77] In Case C-197/96 *Commission v France*[78] the Court of Justice held that the provisions of a directive must be implemented with 'unquestionable binding force'.

---

[72] Case 29/84 *Commission v Germany* [1985] ECR 1661 paras 22–23; Case 363/85 *Commission v Italy* [1987] ECR 1733 para 7; Case 131/88 *Commission v Germany* [1991] ECR I-825 para 6; Case C-190/90 *Commission v Netherlands* [1992] ECR I-3265 para 17; Case C-433/93 *Commission v Germany* [1995] ECR I-2303 para 18.

[73] Case C-71/92 *Commission v Spain* [1993] ECR I-5923 paras 23–25.

[74] Case C-365/93 *Commission v Greece* [1995] ECR I-499 para 9; Case C-96/95 *Commission v Germany* [1997] ECR I-1653 para 35.

[75] Case C-131/88 *Commission v Germany* [1991] ECR I-825 paras 6 and 19 (the 'groundwater case'). In relation to the conservation of wild birds, see Case 252/85 *Commission v France* [1988] ECR 2243 para 5; Case C-339/87 *Commission v Netherlands* [1990] ECR I-851 paras 26–28; Case C-118/94 *Associazione Italiana per il WWF v Regione Veneto* [1996] ECR I-1223 paras 20–22.

[76] Case 102/79 *Commission v Belgium* [1980] ECR 1473 para 11; Case 145/82 *Commission v Italy* [1983] ECR 711 para 10; Case 168/85 *Commission v Italy* [1986] ECR 2945; Case C-306/89 *Commission v Greece* [1991] ECR I-5863 paras 18–20; Case 235/91 *Commission v Ireland* [1992] ECR I-5917 para 10. *Cf* Case C-339/87 *Commission v Netherlands* [1990] ECR I-851 paras 6 and 8, where the Court of Justice held that ministerial measures which were published in the Dutch Official Gazette and which were capable of creating rights and obligations for individuals could constitute proper implementation of a directive.

[77] Case C-306/89 *Commission v Greece* [1991] ECR I-5863 paras 18–20; Case C-220/94 *Commission v Luxembourg* [1995] ECR I-1589 para 11; Case C-298/95 *Commission v Germany* [1996] ECR I-6747 paras 15–16.

[78] [1997] ECR I-1489 paras 14–15.

It is not sufficient for a Member State to make a general reference to Community law in its national law. For example, in Case C-96/95 *Commission v Germany*[79] the Court of Justice held that Germany had failed correctly to implement two directives where its national law simply stated that it applied 'save where otherwise provided by Community law'.

A Member State is not absolved from its obligation to adopt national implementing legislation on the basis that a directive has direct effect and therefore can be relied on by individuals in the national courts.[80] Equally, the fact that the national courts have interpreted provisions of domestic law so as to conform with the requirements of a directive does not necessarily constitute proper implementation.[81]

A Member State is free to delegate the task of implementing directives to regional or local authorities. However, the Member State remains responsible for ensuring that directives are correctly implemented.[82]

Effective enforcement It is not sufficient for a Member State merely to transpose the requirements of a directive into national law; it must also ensure the effective application in practice of the rights and obligations contained in the directive. Thus, where the directive itself does not provide for any penalty in the event of its infringement, the Member States must ensure that any infringement is penalised under conditions, both procedural and substantive, which are analogous to those applicable to infringements of national law which are of a similar nature and importance. In addition, the penalty imposed must be effective, proportionate and dissuasive.[83]

Position once a directive has been implemented Once a directive has been properly implemented by national legislation, a private party must rely on the national legislation rather than on the direct effect of the directive.[84] However, a private party may continue to rely on the direct effect of a directive where the legislation introduced by a Member State does not properly implement the directive.[85] Furthermore, where a directive has been implemented into national

---

[79] [1997] ECR I-1653 paras 35–36.

[80] Case 102/79 *Commission v Belgium* [1980] ECR 1473 para 12; Case C-433/93 *Commission v Germany* [1995] ECR I-2303 paras 21 and 24; Case C-96/95 *Commission v Germany* [1997] ECR I-1653 paras 35–40.

[81] Case C-236/95 *Commission v Greece* [1996] ECR I-4459 paras 23–26 of the Opinion of Advocate-General Léger and paras 8–14 of the judgment. See further at Ch 12, p 257.

[82] Case 96/81 *Commission v Netherlands* [1982] ECR 1791 para 12; Joined Cases 227 to 230/85 *Commission v Belgium* [1988] ECR 1 para 9; Case C-131/88 *Commission v Germany* [1991] ECR I-825 para 71.

[83] Case C-382/92 *Commission v United Kingdom* [1994] ECR I-2435 para 55; Case C-383/92 *Commission v United Kingdom* [1994] ECR I-2479 para 40; Joined Cases C-58 and others/95 *Gallotti* [1996] ECR I-4345.

[84] Case 102/79 *Commission v Belgium* [1980] ECR 1473; Case 270/81 *Felicitas v Finanzamt für Verkehrsteuern* [1982] ECR 2771 para 24; Case 222/84 *Johnston v Chief Constable of the Royal Ulster Constabulary* [1986] ECR 1651 para 51.

[85] Case 51/76 *Van Nederlandse Ondernemingen v Inspecteur der Invoerrechten en Accijnzen* [1977] ECR 113 paras 23–24; Case 38/77 *Enka v Inspecteur der Invoerrechten en Accijnzen* [1977] ECR 2203; Case 102/79 *Commission v Belgium* [1980] ECR 1473 para 12; Case C-208/90 *Emmott v Minister for Social Welfare* [1991] ECR I-4269 para 20.

law, a national court may seek a preliminary ruling from the Court of Justice pursuant to article 177 of the EC Treaty [new art 234] as to the interpretation of the directive in order to ensure that the national implementing law is interpreted and applied in accordance with Community law.[86]

Conflict between directive and national law Whenever there is a potential conflict between a directive and a provision of national law, the court should:[87]

(1) first, consider whether it is possible to interpret the national law in conformity with the directive;[88]

(2) if this is not possible, consider whether the directive has direct effect so that it may be relied on as against the conflicting national rule.[89]

Furthermore, failure to implement a directive may give rise to a claim in damages against the State.[90]

(c) Decisions

Definition Article 189 of the EC Treaty [new art 249] defines decisions as follows:

> A decision shall be binding in its entirety upon those to whom it is addressed.

There is no set form which a decision must take.[91] Indeed, the Court of Justice will look at the substance, not the form, of a measure in deciding whether or not it constitutes a decision.[92] For example, a letter sent by a Community institution may be a decision even if it is not expressly stated to constitute a decision.[93] In Case T-3/93 *Air France v Commission*[94] an oral statement by a Commission spokesman that a proposed merger between British Airways and Dan Air did not fall within the scope of Community competence under the Merger Regulation was held by the Court of First Instance to be a decision.

Notification[95] Decisions must be notified to those to whom they are addressed and take effect upon such notification.[96] A decision is duly notified once it has been communicated to the person to whom it is addressed and that person is in a position to take cognisance of it. Notification will usually take place by a registered letter accompanied by a form headed 'Acknowledgement of Receipt'

---

[86] Case C-331/92 *Gestión-Hotelera Internacional v Comunidad Autónoma de Canarias* [1994] ECR I-1329 paras 11–13.

[87] Case C-118/94 *Associazione Italiana per il WWF v Regione Veneto* [1996] ECR I-1223 paras 18–19; Case C-54/96 *Dorsch Consult v Bundesbaugesellschaft Berlin* [1997] ECR I-4961 paras 43–45.

[88] See Ch 5, pp 88–96.

[89] See Ch 4, pp 64–77.

[90] See Ch 7, pp 128–148.

[91] See Ch 13, pp 270–274 and 281–284.

[92] For example, see joined Cases 16/62 and 17/62 *Producteurs de fruits v Council* [1962] ECR 471.

[93] For example, see Joined Cases 8–11/66 *Cimenteries v Commission* [1967] ECR 75 at 90–93.

[94] [1994] ECR II-121 paras 8 and 43–60.

[95] See also at Ch 13, p 326.

[96] Article 191(3) of the EC Treaty [new art 254].

to be completed by the recipient or delivered by hand against receipt.[97] Regardless of the time of day when the measure in question is notified, time does not begin to run until the end of the day of notification.[98] An irregularity in the notification procedure does not invalidate the act notified.[99] Furthermore, an inaccuracy in the name of the addressee as contained in the decision will not invalidate the decision where it is clear which legal or private individual is the intended addressee.[100]

Legal status of decisions[101] The case-law of the Court of Justice may be relied on to support the following propositions:

(1) Where a party has unsuccessfully challenged the substantive conclusions of a decision before the EC courts, he will be bound by that decision in subsequent proceedings before the national courts.

(2) Where a party could undoubtedly have challenged a decision by bringing proceedings in the EC courts under article 173 of the EC Treaty [new art 230], but failed to do so within the two-month time-limit laid down therein, he will be bound by that decision in subsequent proceedings before the national courts.

The leading case is Case C-188/92 *TWD v Germany*.[102] TWD had received state aid from the German Government. The Commission adopted a decision addressed to Germany declaring that the aid was unlawful. The German Government forwarded a copy of the decision to TWD and informed it that it was entitled to challenge the validity of that decision before the EC courts by means of an action under article 173 of the EC Treaty. However, TWD did not bring such an action. When the German Government brought proceedings against TWD in the national courts in order to recover the illegal aid, TWD argued that the Commission decision was invalid. On a preliminary reference, the Court of Justice held that, as TWD was fully aware of the Commission's decision and of the fact that it could without any doubt have challenged it under article 173 of the EC Treaty, the national court was bound by the Commission decision.

In general terms, it follows from the judgment that a party who was not the addressee of a decision but who was aware of it, and who was *undoubtedly* entitled to challenge its validity under article 173 of the EC Treaty but did not do so within the applicable two-month time limit, should be bound by that decision in any subsequent proceedings in the national courts. The case-law on when a private party has *locus standi* to bring an application under article 173 is

---

[97] Case 6/72 *Europemballage and Continental Can v Commission* [1973] ECR 215 paras 9–10; Case 42/85 *Cockerill-Sambre v Commission* [1985] ECR 3749 para 10 (ECSC); Case C-195/91P *Bayer v Commission* [1994] ECR I-5619 paras 1–7 and 16–24.

[98] Case 152/85 *Misset v Council* [1987] ECR 223 (staff case).

[99] Case T-43/92 *Dunlop Slazenger International v Commission* [1994] ECR II-441 para 25.

[100] Joined Cases T-24 to 26 and 28/93 *Compagnie Maritime Belge Transports v Commission* [1996] ECR II-1201 para 36.

[101] For an analysis of the legal effect of decisions, see Rosa Greaves, 'The Nature and Binding Effect of Decisions under Article 189 EC' (1996) 21 ELRev 3 at 10–16.

[102] [1994] ECR I-833.

notoriously opaque[103] and therefore the application of the *TWD* principle to private parties who are not the addressees of decisions will remain relatively restricted.[104]

However, the precise scope of the *TWD* principle is uncertain, particularly as the Court of Justice emphasised that its judgment was limited to considering the issue 'in the factual and legal circumstances of the main proceedings'.[105] In particular, the following aspects remain unclear:

(1) In his Opinion in *TWD*[106] Advocate-General Jacobs raised (without answering) the 'difficult question' as to whether the *TWD* principle should apply whenever a decision has been published in the *Official Journal of the European Communities* even though a party did not have actual knowledge of that decision. It is unlikely that the Court of Justice would apply the *TWD* principle in such circumstances as the judgment in *TWD* was expressly based on *actual* knowledge of the decision by TWD.[107] Furthermore, to hold otherwise would impose a very heavy burden on private parties as they would be obliged to carry out continuous monitoring and assessment of the contents of the *Official Journal* in order to protect their interests.

(2) TWD had been expressly informed by the German authorities of the possibility of bringing an action to challenge the decision under article 173 of the EC Treaty. This leaves open the question as to whether the *TWD* principle can apply only where it is established that the party concerned had actual knowledge of the possibility of bringing an action under article 173. It would be surprising if this were correct. If a party is aware of a decision which adversely affects it, there is no reason why its legal advisers should not be able to advise it as to all possible remedies, including those available under Community law.[108]

(3) In *TWD* the Court of Justice did not distinguish between matters of fact and matters of law in its judgment. It therefore appears to follow that the application of the *TWD* principle will bind a party as to both fact and law.

The reasoning adopted by the Court of Justice in *TWD* applies equally to addressees of a decision as (a) the addressee of a decision will be aware of the decision and (b) the fourth paragraph of article 173 of the EC Treaty expressly provides that addressees of decisions have *locus standi* to challenge them directly before the Court of Justice. Furthermore, article 189 of the EC Treaty [new art 249] provides that decisions are binding in their entirety on addressees.

---

[103] In contrast, Member States are entitled to challenge acts of the Community institutions as of right under article 173 of the EC Treaty: see Ch 13, p 279.

[104] See Case C-241/95 *R v IBAP, ex p Accrington Beef Co Ltd* [1996] ECR I-6699 paras 14–16 and the Opinion of Advocate-General Léger at paras 23–26. The question of *locus standi* under article 173 of the EC Treaty is discussed at Ch 13, pp 280–307.

[105] Paragraphs 10 and 25 of the judgment. For further discussion of the scope of the *TWD* principle, see the Opinion of Advocate-General Jacobs in *TWD*; see also the case notes by Ross in (1994) 19 ELRev 640 and Hoskins in (1994) 31 CMLR 1399.

[106] At para 24.

[107] See para 24 of the judgment.

[108] However, it should be noted that in Case C-241/95 *R v IBAP, ex p Accrington Beef Co Ltd* [1996] ECR I-6699 paras 14–16 the Court of Justice emphasised that TWD had been specifically informed of its right to bring an action pursuant to article 173.

Thus, where the addressee of a decision fails to challenge it directly before the EC courts under article 173 of the EC Treaty within the relevant two-month limitation period, it will be bound by it in any subsequent proceedings before the national courts.[109] In Case 249/85 *Albako v BALM*[110] the Court of Justice held that where a decision is addressed to a Member State it is binding on all the organs of that State, including the national courts.

Finally, it would appear to follow *a fortiori* from the judgment in *TWD* that where a private party is entitled to challenge a decision before the EC courts and does so unsuccessfully, he should be bound by that decision in the national courts.[111]

Competition law decisions The English courts have generally been willing to place a certain amount of reliance on Commission decisions in the context of competition law without carrying out a detailed analysis of their precise legal status. In *British Leyland Motor Corporation Ltd v Wyatt Interpart Company Ltd* [112] Graham J considered, *obiter*, that English courts would be bound by decisions of the Commission which had not been overturned by the Community courts. In *Fyffes plc v Chiquita Brands International Inc*[113] Vinelott J stated that 'the Court will attach very great weight to a decision (even a provisional decision) of the Commission'. Further, in *Inntrepreneur Estates Ltd v Mason*[114]M Barnes QC, sitting as a deputy judge of the High Court, stated that an English court should take into account letters written by the Commission which did not have the formal status of comfort letters.

A detailed analysis was carried out by Laddie J in *Iberian UK Ltd v BPB Industries plc*.[115] Iberian, a Spanish producer of plasterboard, made a complaint to the Commission alleging that BPB and British Gypsum Ltd had abused their dominant position contrary to article 86 of the EC Treaty [new art 82]. Iberian and both defendants participated fully in the proceedings before the Commission, as a result of which the Commission adopted a decision finding that there had been a breach of article 86 of the EC Treaty. The defendants challenged this decision unsuccessfully before the Court of First Instance and the Court of Justice. Iberian then sought to rely on the Commission decision in proceedings for damages which it had commenced against the defendants in the English

---

[109] Case C-178/95 *Wiljo v Belgium* [1997] ECR I-585 paras 19–23 and paras 18–20 of the Opinion of Advocate-General Jacobs. See also para 13 of the Opinion of Advocate-General Jacobs in Case C-188/92 *TWD v Germany* [1994] ECR I-833 para 60; and footnote 175 of the Opinion of Advocate-General van Gerven in Case C-128/92 *Banks v British Coal Corporation* [1994] ECR I-1209; *Coal Authority v HJ Banks & Co Ltd* [1997] EuLR 610 (ECSC) (QBD, Commercial Court).

[110] [1987] ECR 2345 at para 17.

[111] In any event, judgments of the EC courts are binding on the English courts on questions of Community law by virtue of s 3(1) of the European Communities Act 1972.

[112] [1979] 3 CMLR 79 para 14.

[113] [1993] ECC 193 paras 62–63.

[114] [1993] 2 CMLR 293 paras 31–56. In reaching this conclusion, the judge relied on the 'Notice on co-operation between national courts and the Commission in applying Articles 85 and 86 of the EEC Treaty', issued by the Commission and published at OJ 1993 C39 p 6.

[115] [1996] 2 CMLR 601, [1997] EuLR 1 (Ch).

courts. Laddie J held that the Commission decision and the judgments of the Court of First Instance and the Court of Justice were conclusive as to questions of fact[116] and law in the English proceedings. He based his decision on the following principles:[117]

> ...where, as here, the parties have disputed the same issues before the Commission and have had real and reasonable opportunities to appeal from an adverse decision, there is no injustice in obliging them to accept the result obtained in Europe. The position is *a fortiori* when, as here, the opportunities of appeal have been used to the full. Therefore, whether expressed in terms of *res judicata* or abuse of process, it would be contrary to public policy to allow persons who have been involved in competition proceedings in Europe to deny here the correctness of the conclusions reached there. The parties are bound.

On the basis of Laddie J's reasoning, a party who had participated in the proceedings leading to the adoption of a decision by the Commission but had not challenged that decision before the EC courts would also be bound by that decision in the national courts.

The judgment of the Court of Justice in *TWD* was raised before Laddie J; however, he did not consider that it added much given the circumstances of the case before him. The principles established by the Court of Justice in *TWD* are arguably of more general application than those relied on by Laddie J, which were based to a large extent on the specific nature of the competition rules of the EC Treaty. However, any difference in the respective approaches is unlikely to affect the practical result in any particular case.[118]

(d) Recommendations and opinions

Definition   Article 189 of the EC Treaty [new art 249] states:

> Recommendations and opinions shall have no binding force.

Recommendations are generally adopted by the institutions of the Community when they do not have the power under the Treaty to adopt binding measures or when they consider that it is not appropriate to adopt mandatory rules.[119] Although recommendations do not produce binding legal rights which individuals can rely on before national courts, they do have some legal effect. This is clear from Case 322/88 *Grimaldi v Fonds des maladies*[120] where the Court of Justice held that national courts are bound to take recommendations into consideration in deciding disputes submitted to them, in particular where they are capable of casting light on the interpretation of other provisions of national or Community law.

---

[116] Cf *Macarthy v Unichem* [1991] ECC 41 where Scott J held that findings of fact contained in a Monopolies and Mergers Commission Report constituted hearsay.

[117] [1996] 2 CMLR 601 para 72; [1997] EuLR 1 at 21F-G.

[118] Indeed, in *Coal Authority v HJ Banks & Co Ltd* [1997] EuLR 610 (ECSC) (QBD, Commercial Court), Tuckey J based his judgment on both *TWD* and *Iberian* without distinguishing between them.

[119] Case 322/88 *Grimaldi v Fonds des maladies* [1989] ECR 4407 para 13.

[120] Ibid, paras 16–19.

(e) Sui generis *measures*

***Sui generis* measures** The types of measures listed in article 189 [new art 249] are not exhaustive, and certain *sui generis* measures have been accepted as producing legal effects in the Community legal order.[121] Thus, in Case 22/70 *Commission v Council* (the 'ERTA' case)[122] the Court of Justice considered that 'conclusions' reached by the Council regarding the negotiation and conclusion of an international agreement by the Member States was a measure which created legal effects in the Community legal order.[123]

3. CASE–LAW

Precedent Although the EC courts are not bound by a strict doctrine of precedent, they will usually follow the principles established in their own previous judgments.[124] The Court of Justice has, on limited occasions, reconsidered its previous case-law.[125]

The Court of First Instance has held[126] that it is only bound by judgments of the Court of Justice: (a) in the circumstances laid down in the second paragraph of article 54 of the Statute of the Court of Justice (EC) (ie where, following an appeal to the Court of Justice, a case is referred back to the Court of First Instance); and (b) pursuant to the principle of *res judicata*.[127] However, in practice the Court of First Instance will usually follow the case-law of the Court of Justice; if it did not do so, its judgments would be likely to be overturned by the Court of Justice on appeal.

Status of EC courts' judgments in English law Judgments of the EC courts are binding on English courts on matters of Community law. This is the effect of s 3(1) of the European Communities Act 1972[128] which provides that:

---

[121] See further at Ch 13, pp 271–274.

[122] [1971] ECR 263 paras 34–55.

[123] See also Case C-366/88 *France v Commission* [1990] ECR I-3571 in which the Court of Justice annulled a measure adopted by the Commission entitled 'Internal instructions concerning certain administrative and technical procedures to be followed by officials given powers by the Commission concerning sampling and analysis of products for the purposes of the management and control of the European Agricultural Guidance and Guarantee Fund'; Case C-313/90 *CIRFS v Commission* [1993] ECR I-1125 paras 3–5 which concerned, *inter alia,* a Commission communication or 'discipline' concerning State aid.

[124] See the comments of Lord Denning MR in *HP Bulmer Ltd v J Bollinger SA* [1974] 1 Ch 401 at 420C–E; and the comments of Lord Diplock in *Henn and Darby v DPP* [1981] AC 850 at 905B–D. See also Anthony Arnull, 'Owning up to fallibility: Precedent and the Court of Justice' (1993) 30 CMLR 247.

[125] For example, see Case C-10/89 *CNL-Sucal v HAG GF* [1990] ECR I-3711 para 10 ('HAG II'); Joined Cases C-267/91 and 268/91 *Keck and Mithouard* [1993] ECR I-6097 paras 15–16.

[126] Case T-162/94 *NMB v Commission* [1996] ECR II-427 paras 36–40.

[127] The application of the principle of *res judicata* is discussed at Ch 18, p 392.

[128] As amended by s 2 of the European Communities (Amendment) Act 1986. See *Garden Cottage Foods Ltd v Milk Marketing Board* [1984] AC 130 at 141C–D, per Lord Diplock.

> For the purposes of all legal proceedings any question as to the meaning or effect of any of the Treaties, or as to the validity, meaning or effect of any Community instrument, shall be treated as a question of law (and, if not referred to the European Court, be for determination as such in accordance with the principles laid down by and any relevant decision of the European Court or any court attached thereto).

In *Iberian UK Ltd v BPB Industries plc*[129] Laddie J held that judgments of the EC courts could be binding on the English courts in relation to matters of fact where the parties in the national proceedings had participated fully in competition law proceedings before the Commission and the EC courts.

Opinions of Advocates-General The function of the Advocate-General is to prepare 'with complete impartiality and independence...reasoned submissions on the case brought before the Court of Justice' in order to assist the Court in reaching its judgment.[130] The Opinion of an Advocate-General is his own personal view of how the case should be decided. It is not binding in any way on the EC courts, but is of great assistance as it explores the issues and possible solutions to the particular case under consideration.

Opinions of the Advocates-General are not binding in any way upon a national court, but may be of some persuasive value.[131] In general terms, the status of Opinions may be analysed as follows:

(1) Where the EC court has followed the Opinion, there is no need to rely on the Opinion as the judgment of the EC court is binding on the national court.

(2) Where the EC court has taken a conflicting view from that expressed by the Advocate-General in his Opinion, the Opinion will be of little, if any, persuasive value as the national court is bound by the judgment of the EC court.

(3) Where the Advocate-General has expressed a view on an issue which is not then dealt with by the EC court in its judgment, the Opinion will have some persuasive value as it will indicate how the EC court might consider the issue were it to come before it.

4. INTERNATIONAL AGREEMENTS[132]

(a) International agreements entered into by the Community

Competence to enter into international agreements The European Community has legal personality[133] and therefore is prima facie capable of entering into international agreements with third countries and other international

---

[129] [1996] 2 CMLR 601 paras 69–72; [1997] EuLR 1 at 21A–H (Ch). This case is discussed at Ch 1, pp 17–18.

[130] Article 166 of the EC Treaty [new art 222]. The position of the Advocates-General is discussed further at Ch 18, p 390.

[131] For examples of English courts referring to Opinions of Advocates-General, see *WH Smith Do-It-All Ltd v Peterborough City Council* [1991] 1 QB 304 at 327B–328B; *Battersea Leisure Ltd v Commissioners of Customs and Excise* [1992] 3 CMLR 610 para 34.

[132] See, generally, I MacLeod, ID Henry and Stephen Hyett, *The External Relations of the European Communities* (Clarendon Press, Oxford, 1996).

[133] Article 210 of the EC Treaty [new art 281].

organisations in its own right. The Community is competent to enter into such agreements where this is expressly provided for by the EC Treaty itself[134] or under the doctrine of implied or parallel competence. Under this doctrine, the Community has competence to enter into agreements with third countries whenever it has power under the Community Treaties to adopt internal measures regulating the same subject-matter within the European Union.[135]

Exclusive/mixed competence The competence of the Community to enter into international agreements can be either exclusive or mixed.[136] If the Community has exclusive competence in a particular field, the Member States are precluded from entering into their own international agreements. If competence in a particular field is mixed, the Community may only enter into international agreements jointly with the Member States.

Procedure Except where expressly provided otherwise, the procedure to be followed by the European Community for the conclusion of international agreements is that established by article 228 of the EC Treaty [new art 300]. Article 228(6) permits the Council, Commission or a Member State to obtain the Opinion of the Court of Justice as to whether an agreement envisaged is compatible with the provisions of the EC Treaty.[137]

Status of international agreements in Community law Article 228(7) of the EC Treaty [new art 300(7)] provides that agreements concluded pursuant to article 228 are binding on the Community institutions and the Member States. Further, the Court of Justice has consistently held that international agreements concluded by the European Community form an integral part of the Community legal order.[138] International agreements may, in certain circumstances, have

---

[134] See article 109(3) [new art 111] (agreements concerning monetary or foreign exchange regime matters); article 113 [new art 133] (common commercial policy); article 130m [new art 170] (research and technological development); article 130r(4) [new art 174] (environmental policy); article 238 [new art 310] (association agreements); and article 130y [new art 181] (development cooperation). See also article 126(3) [new art 149] (education); article 127(3) [new art 150] (vocational training); article 128(3) [new art 151] (culture); article 129(3) [new art 152] (public health); and article 129c(3) [new art 155] (trans-European networks) which require/permit the Community to cooperate with third countries and international organisations.

[135] Case 22/70 *Commission v Council* [1971] ECR 263 paras 6–32 (the 'ERTA case'); Joined Cases 3/76, 4/76 and 6/76 *Kramer* [1976] ECR 1279 paras 12–45; *Opinion 1/76 (European laying-up fund for inland waterway vessels)* [1977] ECR 741 paras 1–5; *Opinion 2/91 (ILO Convention No 170)* [1993] ECR I-1061 paras 7–12; *Opinion 2/92 (Third Revised Decision of the OECD on national treatment)* [1995] ECR I-521 paras 29–36; *Opinion 1/94 (WTO Agreement)* [1994] ECR I-5267 paras 72–105.

[136] For example, see *Opinion 1/94* [1994] ECR I-5267.

[137] As to the nature of article 228(6) of the EC Treaty (which replaced article 228(1) of the EEC Treaty), see *Opinion 1/75 (OECD Understanding on a Local Cost Standard)* [1975] ECR 1355 at 1359–1361; *Opinion 1/76* [1977] ECR 741 para 20; *Opinion 1/78 (International Agreement on Natural Rubber)* [1979] ECR 2871 paras 28–35; *Opinion 2/91* [1993] ECR I-1061 paras 1–6; *Opinion 2/92* [1995] ECR I-521 paras 8–15; *Opinion 1/94* [1994] ECR I-5267 paras 9–14; *Opinion 1/94* [1996] ECR I-1759 paras 1–22. The relevant procedural rules are at ECJ Rules of Procedure, articles 107–108.

[138] Case 181/73 *Haegeman v Belgium* [1974] ECR 449 paras 2–6; Case 12/86 *Demirel v Stadt Schwäbisch Gmünd* [1987] ECR 3719 para 7; Case C-192/89 *Sevince v Staatssecretaris* [1990] ECR I-3461 para 8; T-115/94 *Opel Austria v Council* [1997] ECR II-39 paras

direct effect so that their provisions can be relied on by private parties in the national courts.[139] Furthermore, Community secondary legislation must be interpreted, as far as possible, in a manner which is consistent with international agreements concluded by the Community.[140]

The EC courts are competent, in certain circumstances, to review the legality of acts of the institutions in light of the obligations imposed on them by international agreements.[141]

(b) International agreements entered into by the Member States

Article 234 Article 234 of the EC Treaty [new art 307] deals with international agreements entered into by the Member States prior to the entry into force of the EC Treaty.[142] The first paragraph of article 234 provides that the rights and obligations arising from agreements concluded before the entry into force of the Treaty between one or more Member States on the one hand, and one or more third countries on the other, shall not be affected by the provisions of the Treaty. The purpose of article 234 is to ensure that the application of the EC Treaty does not affect the duty of a Member State under international law to respect the rights of third countries under a prior agreement and to perform its obligations thereunder.[143] Where a number of Member States and third countries are parties to an agreement entered into prior to the EC Treaty, as between the Member States and the third countries, the prior agreement will continue to apply; however, as between the Member States the provisions of the EC Treaty will prevail.[144]

The second paragraph of article 234 requires the Member States to take all appropriate steps to eliminate any incompatibilities between pre-existing international agreements and the EC Treaty. Furthermore, a Member State may rely on article 234 only to justify a measure which is contrary to Community law where the adoption of such a measure is *required* under a pre-existing international agreement with a third country. Where the international agree-

---

101–102 (EEA Agreement).

[139] See at Ch 4, pp 77–79.

[140] See at Ch 5, p 86.

[141] See at Ch 13, pp 322–323 (GATT).

[142] The various Acts of Accession (see Ch 1, pp 3–4) each contain a provision providing that article 234 of the EC Treaty is to apply for the new Member States to agreements or conventions concluded before their accession (eg see article 5 of the Act of Accession for Denmark, Ireland and the United Kingdom (OJ 1972 L73, 27 March 1972)).

[143] Case 812/79 *A-G v Burgoa* [1980] ECR 2787 paras 5–11. For an application of article 234 by the English courts, see *R v Searle* [1995] 3 CMLR 196 paras 47–60.

[144] Case 10/61 *Commission v Italy* [1962] ECR 1 at 10–11; Case 121/85 *Conegate v HM Customs & Excise* [1986] ECR 1007 paras 24–26; Case 286/86 *Ministère public v Deserbais* [1988] ECR 4907 paras 17–18; Joined Cases C-241/91 and 242/91P *RTE and ITP v Commission* [1995] ECR I-808 paras 72–87. The same principle applies to secondary Community law, see Case 278/82 *Rewe v Hauptzollämter Flensburg, Itzehoe and Lübeck-West* [1984] ECR 721 paras 28–29.

ment merely permits the adoption of such a measure, the Member State must act in conformity with its obligations under the EC Treaty.[145]

5. PUBLIC INTERNATIONAL LAW

Public international law The Court of Justice has recognised and applied principles of public international law in cases before it, for example:

(1) The Court has relied on both the Vienna Convention of 23 May 1969 on the Law of Treaties[146] and the Vienna Convention of 21 March 1986 on the Law of Treaties between States and International Organizations or between International Organizations[147] when considering international agreements entered into by the Community with third countries, even though the Community is not a party to either of these Conventions.

(2) In Case T-115/94 *Opel Austria v Council*[148] the Court of First Instance held that as the principle of good faith is a rule of customary international law whose existence is recognised by the case-law of the International Court of Justice, it is therefore binding on the Community.

(3) In Case C-432/92 *R v MAFF, ex p Anastasiou*[149] the Court of Justice took account of the fact that the 'Turkish Republic of Northern Cyprus' was not recognised as a state by either the Member States or the Community in interpreting the EC–Cyprus Association Agreement and a Community direct-ive concerning plant health.

Furthermore, the Court has been prepared to consider arguments which alleged that Community measures were incompatible with general principles of public international law in cases involving parties from third countries.[150] Indeed, in Case 48/69 *ICI v Commission*[151] Advocate-General Mayras stated that, when the Community exercises powers granted to it by the Community Treaties, 'it must comply with international law'.

Fundamental rights The Court of Justice has consistently held that interna-tional treaties concerning human rights on which the Member States have collaborated or of which they are signatories are a potential source of fundamental rights in the Community legal order, even though the Community is not itself a party to the treaty concerned.[152] The most important source of such

---

[145] Case C-324/93 *R v Secretary of State for the Home Department, ex p Evans Medical* [1995] ECR I-563 paras 23 and 25–32; Case C-124/95 *R v HM Treasury, ex p Centro-Com* [1997] ECR I-81 paras 54–61. See also Case C-158/91 *Levy* [1993] ECR I-4287; Case C-13/93 *ONEM v Minne* [1994] ECR I-371 paras 17–18.

[146] *Opinion 1/91 (European Economic Area Agreement)* [1991] ECR I-6079 para 14; Case C-312/91 *Metalsa* [1993] ECR I-3751 para 12.

[147] Case C-327/91 *France v Commission* [1994] ECR I-3641 para 25.

[148] [1997] ECR II-39 paras 90–91 and 93.

[149] [1994] ECR I-3087.

[150] Case 48/69 *ICI v Commission* [1972] ECR 619; Joined Cases 89 and others/85 *Åhlström v Commission* ('Woodpulp') [1988] ECR 5193 paras 15–23.

[151] [1972] ECR 619, at pp 692–693 of his Opinion.

[152] For example, see Case 4/73 *Nold v Commission* [1974] ECR 491 para 13; Joined Cases 46/87

rights in the Community legal order is the European Convention on Human Rights.[153]

6. PROVING COMMUNITY LAW IN THE NATIONAL COURTS

Judicial notice Section 3 of the European Communities Act 1972 contains specific provisions as to proving Community law in the English courts. In particular, it provides that judicial notice must be taken of the Treaties, the *Official Journal of the European Communities* and decisions of the EC courts.[154] Issues of Community law are to be treated as questions of law.[155] Therefore, in criminal trials any question of Community law is a question for the judge and not a question for the jury.[156]

Precedent—English authority The judgment of Hidden J in *Feehan v HM Commissioners of Customs and Excise*[157] is authority for the proposition that a ruling of a superior English court interpreting a provision of Community law is a precedent which is binding on lower courts, subject to the right of the latter to seek a preliminary ruling from the Court of Justice under article 177 of the EC Treaty [new art 234] on that issue.

Competition law Particular difficulties may arise in the English courts in respect of evidence in competition cases as a result of the House of Lords' decision in *Rio Tinto Zinc Corporation v Westinghouse Electric Corporation*.[158] The House of Lords held that a party may claim privilege against self-incrimination under s 14(1) of the Civil Evidence Act 1968 in respect of documents which, if produced, might expose it to the imposition of fines by the Commission under the Community competition rules. Furthermore, in *Shearson Lehman Hutton Inc v MacLaine Watson & Co Ltd*[159] Webster J indicated that he would require a high degree of probability, but less than the standard of proof in criminal matters, to establish an infringement of article 85 of the EC Treaty [new art 81], as such an infringement could lead to the imposition of fines. However, this approach has generally not been followed in subsequent cases.[160]

---

and 227/88 *Hoechst v Commission* [1989] ECR 2859 para 13.

[153] Fundamental rights are discussed at Ch 2, pp 47–50.

[154] Section 3(2) of the European Communities Act 1972, as amended by s 2 of the European Communities (Amendment) Act 1986.

[155] Section 3(1) of the European Communities Act 1972, as amended by s 2 of the European Communities (Amendment) Act 1986.

[156] *R v Goldstein* [1983] 1 WLR 151 at 156A–E.

[157] [1995] 1 CMLR 193 paras 13–21 (QBD). See further at Ch 11, p 222.

[158] [1978] 1 AC 547. See the comments of Advocate-General Edward as to the difficulties of bringing cases based on Community competition law in the national courts in Case T-24/90 *Automec v Commission* [1992] ECR II-2223 and Case T-28/90 *Asia Motor France v Commission* [1992] ECR II-2285 at paras 109–116 of the Opinion.

[159] [1989] 3 CMLR 429 paras 283–284.

[160] See *Chiron Corporation v Organon Teknika Ltd (No 2)* [1992] 3 CMLR 813 para 11; *Masterfoods Ltd v HB Ice Cream Ltd* [1992] 3 CMLR 830 paras 128–131 (Irish High Court); *Panayiotou v Sony Music Entertainment Ltd* [1994] EMLR 229 (ChD); *The Society of Lloyd's v*

Cooperation with the Commission In Case C-2/88 Imm. *Zwartveld* [161] the
Court of Justice held that the Community institutions are under an obligation to
cooperate with national judicial authorities considering issues of Community
law. In particular, the Court held that the Commission was obliged to produce
documents to the national court and to authorise its officials to give evidence in
the national proceedings unless it could demonstrate that it was justified in
refusing to do so for reasons relating to the functioning and independence of the
Communities.

In the field of competition law, the Commission has published a 'Notice on
co-operation between national courts and the Commission in applying Articles
85 and 86 of the EEC Treaty'.[162] The purpose of this Notice is to encourage the
hearing of cases involving Community competition law in the national courts.
The Notice indicates, *inter alia*, that national courts may, within the limits of
their national procedural law, consult the Commission on points of law and
obtain information regarding factual data, for example statistics, market studies
and economic analyses. A similar notice has been published in the field of state
aid.[163]

Access to Community documents The Council,[164] Commission[165] and European Parliament[166] have each adopted decisions intended to allow the public
wide access to documents held by them. 'Document' means any written text,
whatever its medium. A party requiring access to a particular document must
make an application in writing to the relevant institution. The decisions provide
that access to documents *shall* not be granted where disclosure could undermine
the protection of the public interest, protection of the individual and of privacy,
protection of commercial and industrial secrecy, protection of the Community's
financial interests or protection of confidentiality. In addition, access to
documents *may* be refused in order to protect the institution's interest in the
confidentiality of its proceedings. In exercising its discretion, the institution
must 'genuinely balance the interest of its citizens in gaining access to its
documents against any interest of its own in maintaining the confidentiality of
its deliberations'.[167] A party who has applied and been refused access

---

John Stewart Clementson [1997] ECC 193 paras 28–31.Contrast *Yorkshire Water Services Ltd v
Jarmain & Son Ltd* (nyr, judgment of 14 February 1997) (QBD, Commercial Court).

[161] [1990] ECR I-3365.

[162] OJ 1993 C39 p 6.

[163] Notice on cooperation between national courts and the Commission in the State aid field (OJ
1995 C312 p 8).

[164] Council Decision 93/731 on public access to Council documents (OJ 1993 L340 p 43), as
amended by Council Decision 96/705 (OJ 1996 L325 p 19). The Court of Justice rejected a
challenge to the legality of this decision in Case C-58/94 *Netherlands v Council* [1996] ECR
I-2169.

[165] Commission Decision 94/90 on public access to Commission documents (OJ 1994 L46 p 58), as
amended by Commission Decision 96/567 (OJ 1996 L247 p 45).

[166] European Parliament Decision 97/632 on public access to European Parliament documents (OJ
1997 L263 p 27).

[167] Case T-194/94 *Carvel and Guardian Newspapers v Council* [1995] ECR II-2765 paras 63–67.

to a particular document may challenge that refusal before the EC courts under article 173 of the EC Treaty [new art 230][168] or make a complaint to the Ombudsman under article 138e of the EC Treaty [new art 195].

---

[168] Case T-105/95 *WWF UK v Commission* [1997] ECR II-313 paras 52–66.

Chapter 2

General Principles of Community Law

Introduction The EC courts have recognised certain general principles of law, drawn largely from the national legal systems of the Member States.[1] The Community institutions and the Member States, when acting in areas covered by Community law, are bound to respect these principles. The principles provide grounds for review of Community acts before the Community courts. They are also of direct effect and can therefore be relied on directly by individuals in the national legal order as grounds of review of Community acts and of national acts which are required or permitted by Community law.[2]

1. PROPORTIONALITY[3]

(a) Three-part test

Definition The principle of proportionality has long been recognised as one of the general principles of Community law by the case-law of the Court of Justice and has now been expressly recognised in article 3b of the EC Treaty [new art 5].[4] The Court of Justice has consistently expressed the principle as follows:

> By virtue of that principle, the lawfulness of the prohibition of an economic activity is subject to the condition that the prohibitory measures are appropriate and

---

[1] See, generally, Jürgen Schwarze, *European Administrative Law* (Sweet & Maxwell, 1992); Schermers and Waelbroeck, *Judicial Protection in the European Communities*, 5th edn (Kluwer, 1992), pp 27–94; de Smith, Woolf and Jowell, *Judicial Review of Administrative Action*, 5th edn (Sweet & Maxwell, 1995), Ch 21.

[2] Case C-27/95 *Woodspring District Council v Bakers of Nailsea* [1997] ECR I-1847 para 17 (grounds for reviewing Community acts); Case C-15/95 *EARL de Kerlast v Unicopa* [1997] ECR I-1961 para 36 (grounds for reviewing national acts). As to the circumstances in which Member States must respect these principles, see Ch 10, and *R v MAFF, ex p First City Trading Ltd* [1997] 1 CMLR 250 paras 39–43; [1997] EuLR 195 at 210A–211F.

[3] See de Búrca, 'The Principle of Proportionality and its Application in EC Law' in the *Yearbook of European Law* (Oxford University Press, 1993), p 105. See Ch 10, pp 190–191.

[4] Article 3b was added to the EC Treaty by the Treaty on European Union ('Maastricht Treaty'). The third paragraph provides that 'Any action by the Community shall not go beyond what is necessary to achieve the objectives of this Treaty'.

necessary in order to achieve the objectives legitimately pursued by the legislation in question; when there is a choice between several appropriate measures recourse must be had to the least onerous, and the disadvantages caused must not be disproportionate to the aims pursued.[5]

The application of the principle may be divided into three stages:[6]

(1) Is the relevant measure an appropriate method for the attainment of a legitimate objective?

(2) Are the means employed limited to what is necessary for the attainment of the legitimate objective?

(3) Are the disadvantages caused or restrictions imposed unacceptable given the objective pursued?

(i) Is the relevant measure an appropriate method for the attainment of a legitimate objective?

Legitimate objective Restrictions imposed on individuals must be justified by reference to a legitimate public interest objective. The EC Treaty and the case-law of the EC courts have recognised a large number of legitimate objectives, depending on the context.[7] The Community institutions have, for example, a legitimate interest in the proper functioning of the Common Market and the Community policies (eg the common agricultural policy, transport, the common commercial policy, and social policy). The Member States have a legitimate interest in seeking to protect, *inter alia*, public health and safety, public morality and public security.

Appropriate means This involves an examination as to whether the relevant measure employs means which are 'suitable' for the purpose of achieving the desired objective. For example, in Case C-84/94 *United Kingdom v Council*[8] the United Kingdom unsuccessfully argued that a directive expressly adopted to improve health and safety at work was disproportionate on the basis that the link between the measures which it employed, ie a restriction on the amount of hours which individuals could work each week, and the desired objective was too tenuous. In Case C-331/88 *R v MAFF, ex p Fedesa*[9] the applicants unsuccessfully argued that a ban on the use of certain hormones in livestock farming was an inappropriate measure to adopt as it was impossible to apply in practice and would lead to the creation of a dangerous black market in those substances.

---

[5] Case C-331/88 *R v MAFF, ex p Fedesa* [1990] ECR I-4023 para 13; Joined Cases T-466/93 and others *O'Dwyer v Council* [1995] ECR II-2071 para 107; Joined Cases C-254/94 and others *Fattoria Autonoma Tabacchi* [1996] ECR I-4235 para 55.

[6] See in particular para 35 of the Opinion of Advocate-General van Gerven in Case C-159/90 *SPUC v Grogan* [1991] ECR I-4685.

[7] For example, see article 36 of the EC Treaty [new art 30] in relation to the free movement of goods.

[8] [1996] ECR I-5755 paras 31, 36–38 and 57–59.

[9] [1990] ECR I-4023 paras 12–15.

(ii) Are the means employed limited to what is necessary for the attainment of the legitimate objective?

Less restrictive measures The means employed will not be necessary for the attainment of the legitimate objective, and will therefore be disproportionate, where the administration could have adopted less restrictive measures to obtain the same objective. This is often described as the use of 'a steam hammer to crack a nut'.[10] The lawfulness of the measure and the determination whether the means employed were necessary to obtain the desired objective must be assessed in the light of the information available to the administration at the time of the adoption of the rule in question.[11]

In Case 261/81 *Rau v de Smedt*[12] the Court of Justice held that a Belgian law, which prohibited the sale of margarine unless it was sold in cubes, was contrary to the principle of proportionality. The Belgian Government argued that the law was necessary to protect the consumer by preventing any confusion between butter and margarine as the sale of margarine in cubes was rooted in the habits of Belgian consumers. The Court held that although protection of the consumer was a legitimate objective, the law was not necessary to achieve that aim, stating:

> Consumers may in fact be protected just as effectively by other measures, for example, by labelling, which hinder the free movement of goods less.

In Case 124/81 *Commission v United Kingdom*[13] the United Kingdom argued that a system of import licences for milk was necessary because it ensured that milk could be traced and then destroyed when it appeared that the milk had come from cattle infected with foot and mouth disease. The Court of Justice held that the licensing system pursued a legitimate objective, but that it was disproportionate. Obtaining certificates from importers would be less restrictive, but would still enable the relevant authorities to centralise and utilise the information necessary for the protection of animal and human health.

The principle of proportionality is not satisfied simply because the administration refrains from using the most drastic weapon in its arsenal. The administration must select, from the measures available that are capable of achieving the aim in question, the one that is least burdensome to the individual concerned. As Advocate-General Jacobs stated in Case C-24/90 *Faust*:[14]

> The use of a cannonball to kill a fly cannot be defended on the ground that a nuclear missile might have been used instead.

---

[10] As Lord Diplock stated in *R v Goldstein* [1983] 1 WLR 151 at 155B.
[11] Case C-280/93 *Germany v Council* [1994] ECR I-4973 para 90.
[12] [1982] ECR 3961 para 17. See also Case 178/84 *Commission v Germany* (the 'Beer case') [1987] ECR 1227.
[13] [1983] ECR 203 para 18.
[14] [1991] ECR I-4905 para 46.

Practicable alternatives Although there may be other, less restrictive methods of achieving the same objective, it is important to examine whether these are practicable alternatives. Relevant considerations are the costs and the administrative inconvenience of the suggested alternatives.[15]

Importance of the objective The importance of the objective is also relevant in determining whether the option chosen is necessary. As the Court of Justice stated in Case C-69/94 *France v Commission*:[16]

> ... it is necessary to ascertain whether the means which the provision applies in order to achieve its aim correspond to the importance of that aim and whether they are necessary in order to achieve it.

A breach of a secondary obligation, particularly of an administrative nature, should not generally be punished as severely as a breach of a primary obligation the observance of which is of fundamental importance to the proper functioning of the Community system. In Case 181/84 *R, ex p ED & F Man (Sugar) v IBAP*[17] the Court of Justice summarised this principle in the following way:

> Where Community legislation makes a distinction between a primary obligation, compliance with which is necessary in order to attain the objective sought, and a secondary obligation, essentially of an administrative nature, it cannot, without breaching the principle of proportionality, penalize failure to comply with the secondary obligation as severely as failure to comply with the primary obligation.

In such cases a lesser penalty for breach of the secondary obligation should be imposed. For example, in Case 122/78 *Buitoni v FORMA*[18] Community legislation provided that the grant of import licences for certain goods from outside the Community was conditional on the importer providing security as a guarantee that the goods would, in fact, be imported within the period specified in the licence. The whole of the security was forfeited if the goods were not imported within the specified period or if proof of importation had not been provided within six months after the expiry of the licence. The Court of Justice held that forfeiture of the security for failure to import the goods complied with the principle of proportionality. However, in contrast, it was contrary to the principle of proportionality to impose the same sanction for failure to provide proof within the required period merely to ensure administrative efficiency.

The importance of preventing fraud, particularly in the agricultural sector where large sums of money are paid by way of aid, will often justify severe penalties. In Case 272/81 *RU-MI v FORMA*[19] a Commission regulation

---

[15] See Case 272/81 *RU-MI v FORMA* [1982] ECR 4167 para 10.
[16] [1997] ECR I-2599 para 38; Case C-354/95 *R v MAFF, ex p National Farmers' Union* [1997] ECR I-4559 para 52.
[17] [1985] ECR 2889 para 20.
[18] [1979] ECR 677. See also Case 240/78 *Atalanta v Produktschap voor Vee en Vlees* [1979] ECR 2137 paras 13–16; Case 21/85 *Maas v BALM* [1986] ECR 3537 para 15. Contrast Case 272/81 *RU-MI v FORMA* [1982] ECR 4167 para 14, where this principle was held to be inapplicable.
[19] [1982] ECR 4167 paras 8–14. See also Case C-326/94 *Maas v BDBL* [1996] ECR I-2643; Case C-354/95 *R v MAFF, ex p National Farmers' Union* [1997] ECR I-4559 para 51.

provided for the payment of aid in respect of certain feedstuff if it had been prepared in accordance with certain formulae. The plaintiffs' process had varied very slightly from the given formulae and consequently they had not been paid any aid at all. The Court of Justice held that, in these circumstances, total non-payment of the aid was proportionate. The aid for this sort of feedstuff was considerably higher than for other feedstuffs and, in order to deter fraudulent use of the aid, the Commission was entitled to demand strict compliance with the formulae. The principle of proportionality did not dictate that the Commission should vary the severity of the sanction according to the gravity of the plaintiffs' failure to comply with the principal obligation (ie manufacturing the feeding stuff according to the correct formulae).

(iii) Are the disadvantages caused or restrictions imposed unacceptable given the objective pursued?

Disproportionate effects Even where the option chosen is the only option which is available to achieve the desired objective or it has been shown that the option chosen is necessary to achieve that objective, the disadvantages caused or restrictions imposed must not be wholly out of proportion to the objective pursued. This involves balancing competing interests. In practice this is a difficult hurdle for the affected persons to overcome. In Case 5/88 *Wachauf v Germany*[20] the Court of Justice described the nature of the task as follows:

> The fundamental rights recognised by the Court are not absolute, however, but must be considered in relation to their social function. Consequently, restrictions may be imposed on the exercise of those rights, in particular in the context of a common organisation of market, provided that those restrictions in fact correspond to objectives of general interest pursued by the Community and do not constitute, with regard to the aim pursued, a disproportionate and intolerable interference, impairing the very substance of those rights.

In Case C-331/88 *R v MAFF, ex p Fedesa*[21] Advocate-General Mischo stated, in relation to the banning of certain hormones in livestock feed on public safety grounds:

> As regards proportionality in the narrow sense, that is to say the weighing of damage caused to individual rights against the benefits accruing to the general interest, it should be stated that the maintenance of public health must take precedence over any other consideration. Once the Council had taken the view, in the context of its discretionary power, that it could not ignore the doubts felt by many Member States, and a large proportion of public opinion, as to the harmlessness of these substances, it was entitled to impose financial sacrifices on the persons concerned.

The Court echoed similar sentiments:[22]

> it must be stated that the importance of the objectives pursued is such as to justify even substantial negative financial consequences for certain traders.

---

[20] [1989] ECR 2609 para 18.
[21] [1990] ECR I-4023, para 42 of the Opinion.
[22] Ibid para 17. See also Case C-183/95 *Affish v Rijksdienst voor de Keuring van Vee en Vlees* [1997] ECR I-4315 para 42.

(b) Margin of appreciation

Misplaced criticism The Community law principle of proportionality requires courts to judge the necessity of an action. This will involve an examination of the alternative methods available for achieving the stated objective, the practicalities of those methods, the importance of the objective and the effect on persons concerned. There is unquestionably a balancing exercise to be carried out by the courts, and more is demanded of them than merely deciding whether the option chosen was within the range of options that could reasonably have been adopted.[23]

The principle is often criticised on the basis that it requires a court to substitute its own policies or values for those of the administration, rather than merely reviewing the legality of the acts of the administration. These criticisms are, to a large extent, misplaced since the Court of Justice has consistently held that in areas involving choices of discretionary policy relating to economic, political or social considerations the courts must defer, to a large extent, to the decision-maker.

Degree of intrusion Where the Community or the Member States possess a wide margin of appreciation in adopting the contested measure, the EC courts will not interfere with the measure unless they consider that there has been a manifest error.[24] In the context of the common agricultural policy, the Court of Justice stated in Case C-331/88 *R v MAFF, ex p Fedesa*:[25]

> However, with regard to judicial review of compliance with those conditions it must be stated that in matters concerning the common agricultural policy the Community legislature has a discretionary power which corresponds to the political responsibilities given to it by Articles 40 and 43 of the Treaty. Consequentially the legality of a measure adopted in that sphere can be effected only if the measure is manifestly inappropriate having regard to the objective which the competent institution is seeking to pursue . . .

In such cases, the national or Community authorities have to reconcile divergent interests and select options within the context of the policy choices which are their own responsibility. The Court of Justice has consistently held that while other means for achieving the desired result may be conceivable, the Court will not substitute its assessment of the appropriateness or otherwise of the measures adopted if those measures have not been proved to be manifestly inappropriate for achieving the objective pursued.[26]

The Court has applied this principle in the context of the following areas: legislation involving social policy choices,[27] the exercise of complex economic

---

[23] See the observations of Kennedy LJ in *R v Chief Constable of Sussex, ex p International Traders Ferry* [1997] 2 CMLR 164 at 182. See also Ch 9.

[24] Case T-162/94 *NMB v Commission* [1996] ECR II-427 paras 69–70. See also Ch 13, p 320.

[25] [1990] ECR I-4023 para 14.

[26] Case C-280/93 *Germany v Council* [1994] ECR I-4973 paras 90–94.

[27] Case C-84/94 *United Kingdom v Council* [1996] ECR I-5755 para 58 (the 'Working Time Directive case').

discretion,[28] consumer protection legislation,[29] and legislation under the common agricultural policy.[30]

Similarly, the Court of Justice has recognised that Member States have a wide margin of discretion in health and safety matters,[31] public morality issues,[32] and socio-cultural legislation such as the Sunday trading laws.[33]

2. LEGITIMATE EXPECTATIONS[34]

Definition The principle of legitimate expectations must be observed by the Community institutions and all national authorities responsible for applying Community law.[35] Despite slight variations in terminology, the principle of legitimate expectations applies where a representation by the administration has induced any person to entertain reasonable expectations.[36] This principle is the corollary of the principle of legal certainty, which gives a clue as to its scope. Both the principle of legal certainty and the principle of legitimate expectations stem from a requirement that individuals should have a clear understanding of their rights and obligations.[37]

---

[28] Case T-162/94 *NMB v Commission* [1996] ECR II-427 paras 69–73 (imposition of anti-dumping duties); Case C-103/96 *Directeur Générale Douanes v Eridania* [1997] ECR I-1453 para 30 (implementation of customs legislation).

[29] Case C-233/94 *Germany v Parliament* [1997] ECR I-2405 para 55 (adoption of directive on deposit guarantee schemes).

[30] Joined Cases C-254/94 and others *Fattoria Autonoma Tabacchi* [1996] ECR I-4235 para 56; Joined Cases T-466/93 and others *O'Dwyer v Council* [1995] ECR II-2071 para 107. See also Joined Cases 279/84 and others *Rau v Commission* [1987] ECR 1069 para 37.

[31] Joined Cases C-1/90 and C-176/90 *Aragonesa de Publicidad Exterior and Publivéa* [1991] ECR I-4151 para 17, where the Court of Justice held that a Spanish law which restricted the advertisement of alcohol did not appear to be manifestly unreasonable as part of a campaign against alcoholism. See also Case 174/82 *Sandoz* [1983] ECR 2445 para 15 (restriction of food additives on the grounds of public health).

[32] Paragraph 38 of the Opinion of Advocate-General van Gerven in Case C-159/90 *SPUC v Grogan* [1991] ECR I-4685.

[33] Case C-312/89 *Conforama* [1991] ECR I-997 paras 7–12. See also the judgment of Hoffmann J in *Stoke on Trent City Council v B&Q* [1991] Ch 48.

[34] See Eleanor Sharpston, 'Legitimate Expectations and Economic Reality' (1990) 15 ELRev 103.

[35] Case 316/86 *Hauptzollamt Hamburg v Krücken* [1988] ECR 2213 para 22. See also Ch 105, p 192.

[36] Case 289/81 *Mavridis v Parliament* [1983] ECR 1731 para 21; Case T-123/89 *Chomel v Commission* [1990] ECR II-131 para 25; Case T-571/93 *Lefebvre v Commission* [1995] ECR II-2379 para 72; Joined Cases T-481/93 and T-484/93 *Exporteurs in Levende Varkens v Commission* [1995] ECR II-2941 para 148; Case T-115/94 *Opel Austria v Council* [1997] ECR II-39 para 93.

[37] Case C-63/93 *Duff v Minister for Agriculture* [1996] ECR I-569 para 20, and para 25 of the Opinion of Advocate-General Cosmas; Case C-119/92 *Commission v Italy* [1994] ECR I-393 para 17.

Inducing an expectation The expectation must be induced by the administration. Unequivocal wording[38] or precise assurances[39] have been required by the EC courts. Furthermore, an inducement of a general nature cannot give rise to a legitimate expectation on the part of an individual. As the Court of First Instance stated in Case T-571/93 *Lefebvre v Commission*:[40]

> There is an important difference between a statement made by the Commission in general terms which cannot engender any valid expectations, and an assurance in precise terms, on which expectations may legitimately be based. The statements made by the Commission in the letters relied on by the applicants fall within the first category, since those letters were worded in very general terms. It follows that those statements are not such as to have been capable of engendering any valid expectations on the part of the applicants.

An expectation may arise implicitly from the administration's conduct.[41] In Case 120/86 *Mulder v Minister van Landbouw en Visserij*[42] Mr Mulder, a dairy farmer, had entered into a Community system under which he received payments in return for undertaking not to produce dairy products for a period of five years. After the expiry of the five-year period, he applied for a milk quota in order to recommence production. However, because he had not been producing milk in the year prior to his application, the application was rejected. The Court of Justice held that the regulation under which he was refused a quota infringed Mr Mulder's legitimate expectations. The producers had been encouraged to suspend milk production, not to terminate it. There was nothing in the regulation to suggest that if the non-marketing premium was accepted, they would, at the end of the period, be out of business. In short, the regulation left the producers with the clear understanding that they would not be excluded from milk production merely because they had taken advantage of the scheme. The Court of Justice stated:

> where such a producer, as in the present case, has been encouraged by a Community measure to suspend marketing for a limited period in the general interest and against payment of a premium he may legitimately expect not to be subject, upon the expiry of his undertaking, to restrictions which specifically affect him precisely because he availed himself of the possibilities offered by the Community provisions.

Legitimate expectations may be engendered by conduct, for example by delay. In Case 223/85 *RSV v Commission*[43] the Court of Justice annulled a decision of the Commission requiring the Netherlands to recover monies paid to

---

[38] Case C-119/92 *Commission v Italy* [1994] ECR I-393 para 17.

[39] Case T-123/89 *Chomel v Commission* [1990] ECR II-131 para 26.

[40] [1995] ECR II-2379 para 74.

[41] Case T-115/94 *OPel Austria v Council* [1997] ECR II-39 para 94 (deposit of Treaty instruments gives rise to a representation that the Community would not act inconsistently in the meantime); Case T-81/95 *Interhotel v Commission* [1997] ECR II-1265 para 55.

[42] [1988] ECR 2321 paras 21–28 and the Opinion of Advocate-General Slynn at p 2341. See also Case 170/86 *Von Deetzen* [1988] ECR 2355; Case C-189/89 *Spagl* [1990] ECR I-4539 para 22; Case C-217/89 *Pastlätter* [1990] ECR I-4585 para 13.

[43] [1987] ECR 4617 paras 12–19. *Cf* Case C-301/87 *France v Commission* [1990] ECR I-307

RSV as state aid, on the ground that the Commission had delayed 26 months before adopting the decision. This delay had established a legitimate expectation on the part of RSV that it would be entitled to retain the monies.

Expectation The expectation may be procedural in the sense that the person expects to be listened to or considered before the decision-maker takes a particular step.[44] Equally, the expectation may be substantive in the sense that the person expects a particular outcome, for example that the law will not be changed[45] or that a benefit will not be taken away.[46]

Reasonable expectation Whether an expectation is reasonable involves an examination of what an informed, 'prudent and discriminating' person could have foreseen.[47] For example, in areas where the Community institutions enjoy a wide discretionary power and where frequent adjustments to the legislative framework are necessary, such as in relation to the common agricultural policy, the prudent and discriminating trader would not usually expect that an existing situation will be maintained.[48]

There may be a breach of the principle of legitimate expectations if a Community institution abolishes with immediate effect and without warning a specific advantage without adopting appropriate transitional measures. In Case 127/80 *Grogan v Commission*[49] the Court of Justice annulled a Commission decision which reduced the monthly pension payable to the applicant. The Commission decision was adopted pursuant to a Council regulation adjusting

---

paras 25–28, where delay by the Commission in reaching a decision was justified due to the time required to obtain all necessary information. See also Case 5/82 *Hauptzollamt Krefeld v Maizena* [1982] ECR 4601 para 22, where the Court of Justice held that the fact that a Member State had followed a certain practice for several years, in breach of Community law, did not give rise to legitimate expectations, even where the Commission had failed to take action to put an end to the breach (see below at p 36).

[44] Case T-571/93 *Lefebvre v Commission* [1995] ECR II-2379 para 70, where the applicants contended, albeit unsuccessfully, that the Commission had failed to honour a promise that their interests would be taken into account when the Commission formulated its proposal for the common organisation of the market in bananas.

[45] Case T-115/94 *Opel Austria v Council* [1997] ECR II-39.

[46] Case 120/86 *Mulder v Minister van Landbouw en Visserij* [1988] ECR 2321 (resumption of milk production business); Case 223/85 *RSV Maschinefabrieken en Scheepswerven v Commission* [1987] ECR 4617 paras 12–19 (retention of State aid).

[47] Case 78/77 *Lührs v Hauptzollamt Hamburg-Jonas* [1978] ECR 169 paras 1–10; Case T-489/93 *Unifruit Hellas v Commission* [1994] ECR II-1201 para 51; Joined Cases T-481/93 and T-484/93 *Exporteurs in Levende Varkens v Commission* [1995] ECR II-2941 para 148; Case C-22/94 *Irish Farmers Association v MAFF* [1997] ECR I-1809 para 25 ('informed'). See also *R v Ministry of Agriculture Fisheries and Food, ex p Hamble (Offshore) Fisheries Ltd* [1995] 2 All ER 714, where Sedley J considered that the legitimacy of an expectation is based on fairness.

[48] Case 230/78 *Eridania v Minister of Agriculture and Forestry* [1979] ECR 2749 paras 20–22; Case C-350/88 *Delacre v Commission* [1990] ECR I-395 paras 31–38; Joined Cases C-258/90 and C-259/90 *Pesquerias De Bermeo v Commission* [1992] ECR I-2901 para 34; Case T-472/93 *Campo Ebro Industrial v Council* [1995] ECR II-421 para 52.

[49] [1982] ECR 869 para 34; Case 74/74 *CNTA v Commission* [1975] ECR 533 paras 42–43; Case 84/78 *Tomadini v Amministrazione delle Finanze* [1979] ECR 1801 para 20; Case 152/88 *Sofrimport v Commission* [1990] ECR I-2477 para 16.

the rates of exchange upon which pensions were calculated. The Court of Justice found that the Council had neglected to rectify exchange rates over a period of about seven years. This had given rise to legitimate expectations among pensioners as to the level of pension they would receive. The Court held that these legitimate expectations were not adequately protected by the new regulation which sought to regularise the position within ten months. The transition period should have been twice as long.

In contrast, a prudent and discriminating trader in the agricultural sector should expect that rules will change with immediate effect and without transitional measures. For example, in Case T-489/93 *Unifruit Hellas v Commission*[50] the applicants entered into contracts for the purchase and shipment of Chilean apples before the adoption of a Commission regulation imposing a charge on apples from Chile. The Court of First Instance held that the imposition of the charge was not contrary to any legitimate expectation. The charge was a contingency which should have been taken into consideration by the applicant, particularly given the fact that this was a complex area involving constant legislative change, and the fact that similar charges had been levied before.

Community institutions cannot be forced by virtue of the principle of the protection of legitimate expectations to apply Community rules *contra legem*. A promise not to enforce Community law does not engender any reasonable expectation,[51] nor does a practice of not enforcing Community law.[52] A reasonable expectation may be engendered that Community rules be applied in good faith. For example, in Case T-115/94 *Opel Austria v Council*[53] the Council adopted a regulation on 20 December 1993 imposing a customs duty on gearboxes originating in Austria knowing that the European Economic Area ('EEA') Agreement would enter into force on 1 January 1994 (which would prohibit customs duties). Opel Austria successfully contended that the regulation infringed its legitimate expectations. The Court of First Instance stated:

> In a situation where the Communities have deposited their instruments of approval of an international agreement and the date of entry into force of that agreement is known, traders may rely on the principle of protection of legitimate expectations in order to challenge the adoption by the institutions, during the period preceding the entry into force of that agreement, of any measure contrary to the provisions of that agreement which will have direct effect on them after it has entered into force.

Where a party has committed a manifest infringement of a Community measure he is not entitled to rely on that measure as giving rise to a legitimate expectation. This may be the case, for example, where an individual has not

---

[50] [1994] ECR II-1201 para 67; Case T-267/94 *Oleifici Italiani v Commission* [1997] ECR II-1239 paras 32–41.

[51] Case T-2/93 *Air France v Commission* [1994] ECR II-323 para 102.

[52] Case 316/86 *Hauptzollamt Hamburg v Krücken* [1988] ECR 2213 para 23; Case C-84/94 *United Kingdom v Council* [1996] ECR I-5755 para 19 (the 'Working Time Directive case').

[53] [1997] ECR II-39 para 94.

complied with all the conditions which would entitle him to receive a payment pursuant to that measure.[54]

Reliance The extent to which reliance is a prerequisite of the principle of legitimate expectations is not clear. There have been isolated cases in which the EC courts have noted that the applicant did 'not allege that it was led to take any decisions which caused it to suffer damage on the basis of the information given to it ...'.[55] In contrast, no detrimental reliance existed in Case T-115/94 *Opel Austria v Council*[56] since the car manufacturer was not 'led' into taking any decisions to its detriment; it was already importing gearboxes when the instruments of approval of the EEA Agreement were deposited. Moreover, detrimental reliance does not appear to function as a condition in the application of procedural legitimate expectations since the individual is awaiting a substantive decision. The position is probably that reliance constitutes evidence of inducement or the reasonableness of the expectation, but is not a precondition for the application of the principle.

What is clear is that the knowledge of the decision-maker that the individual has relied on the decision-maker's assurances is irrelevant to the application of the principle. In *R v Ministry of Agriculture Fisheries and Food, ex p Hamble Fisheries*[57] Sedley J summarised the position as follows:

> It is precisely because public authorities have public duties to perform that they can no more be estopped from performing them than they can contract out of them. This is why the decision-maker's knowledge or ignorance of the extent of reliance placed by the applicant upon the factors upon which the expectation is founded has no bearing upon the existence or legitimacy of the expectation. It is upon the practices or promises of the public authority that any such expectation will be built: whether it stands up depends not at all on how much the decision-maker knew of the applicant's reliance on the practice or promise. I do not think that any decision of the European Court of Justice or any English case which has been put before me suggests otherwise.

3. LEGAL CERTAINTY

Definition Community legislation must be certain and its application foreseeable by individuals. The principle of legal certainty requires that every measure of the institutions which has legal effect must be clear and precise and must be brought to the attention of the person concerned, so that he can ascertain, with certainty, the time at which the measure begins to produce legal effects.[58]

---

[54] Case C-96/89 *Commission v Netherlands* [1991] ECR I-2461 para 30; Case T-73/95 *Oliveira v Commission* [1997] ECR II-381 paras 27–28.

[55] For example, see Case T-493/93 *Hansa-Fisch v Commission* [1995] ECR II-575 para 50.

[56] [1997] ECR II-39 (discussed above).

[57] [1995] 2 All ER 714 at 725 h–j.

[58] Joined Cases T-18/89 and T-24/89 *Tagaras v Court of Justice* [1991] ECR II-53 para 40; Case T-14/91 *Weyrich v Commission* [1991] ECR II-235 para 48; Case T-115/94 *Opel Austria v Council* [1997] ECR II-39 para 124.

Legislation should not, therefore, be such as to cause confusion as to the nature of a person's rights and obligations. This includes the adoption of legislation which is ambiguous and the adoption of contradictory rules.[59] As Advocate-General Cosmas stated in Case C-63/93 *Duff v Minister for Agriculture*:[60]

> Particularly for the individual the principle of legality would in many ways lose its significance as a guarantee of a sphere of freedom, if the temporal succession of legal provisions concerning him was not governed by an elementary consistency and coherence sufficient to enable him to discern the consequences (legal and financial) of his activities.

The requirement of legal certainty is an objective test.[61] The principle is not necessarily infringed merely because the legislation presents some difficulties of interpretation. In Case C-354/95 *R v MAFF, ex p National Farmers Union*[62] the Court of Justice held that a regulation did not infringe the principle of legal certainty where the difficulties in interpretation it presented were due to the complexity of the matters involved and, if read carefully, its meaning could be understood by those involved professionally in the area at which it was aimed.

Member States The Member States must respect the principle of legal certainty when acting in areas covered by Community law. They must implement Community law in a way that gives persons a clear and precise understanding of their rights and obligations and does not cause confusion.[63]

Imposition of financial charges or sanctions The principle of legal certainty must be strictly observed in relation to Community measures which may entail financial consequences. The Court of Justice has stated:[64]

> rules imposing charges on the taxpayer must be clear and precise so that he may know without ambiguity what are his rights and obligations and may take steps accordingly.

Presumption of legality In the interests of legal certainty, parties are under an obligation to comply with a Community measure until it has been annulled or suspended by the EC courts, or withdrawn by the institution which adopted it, even though it may contain irregularities or contravene general principles of Community law.[65]

---

[59] Case T-115/94 *Opel Austria v Council* [1997] ECR II-39 para 125.

[60] [1996] ECR I-569, at para 24 of the Opinion.

[61] Paragraph 42 of the Opinion of Advocate-General Jacobs in Case C-177/96 *Belgium v Banque Indosuez* [1997] ECR I-000 (judgment of 16 October 1997).

[62] [1997] ECR I-4559 para 58.

[63] Case C-119/92 *Commission v Italy* [1994] ECR I-393 para 17.

[64] Case 169/80 *Administration des Douanes v Gondrand Frères* [1981] ECR 1931 para 17; Case 325/85 *Ireland v Commission* [1987] ECR 5041 para 18; Case 326/85 *Netherlands v Commission* [1987] ECR 5091 para 24; Joined Cases 92/87 and 93/87 *Commission v France and United Kingdom* [1989] ECR 405 para 22; Case C-30/89 *Commission v France* [1990] ECR I-691 para 23; Case C-143/93 *Van Es Douane Agenten v Inspecteur der Invoerrechten eb Accijnzen* [1996] ECR I-431 para 32.

[65] Joined Cases 7/56 and 3 to 7/57 *Algera v Common Assembly* [1957–58] ECR 39 at 60 and 61 (ECSC); Case 101/78 *Granaria v Hoofdproduktschap voor Akkerbouwprodukten* [1979] ECR 623 paras 4–5; Joined Cases 46/87 and 227/88 *Hoechst v Commission* [1989] ECR 2859 paras

4. NON-RETROACTIVITY

Definition It is necessary to distinguish between actual retroactivity and apparent retroactivity.[66] Actual retroactivity means that a measure takes effect prior to the date of its publication, or affects transactions which have already been concluded prior to that date. Apparent retroactivity means that a measure takes effect on the date of its publication and affects transactions which originated before that date but have not yet been completed.

Actual retroactivity Actual retroactivity is usually prohibited. Thus, as a general rule, Community measures may not take effect from a date prior to their publication or notification to the person(s) concerned. In Case 98/78 *Racke v Hauptzollamt Mainz*[67] the Court of Justice stated:

> A fundamental principle in the Community legal order requires that a measure adopted by the public authorities shall not be applicable to those concerned before they have the opportunity to make themselves acquainted with it.

Substantive rules will not be interpreted as applying to situations existing before their entry into force.[68] Thus, it is contrary to the principle of non-retroactivity for a regulation, which specifies the conditions for classification in a tariff heading, to apply to past transactions.[69] Furthermore, the protection of vested or acquired rights requires a case to be decided on the basis of the substantive law as it was when the relevant acts or events took place.[70]

The principle of actual retroactivity is not, however, without exception. A measure may have retroactive effect where two conditions are fulfilled: (a) the purpose to be achieved so demands; and (b) the legitimate expectations of those concerned by it are duly respected. The cases where actual retroactive effect has been permitted have concerned, for example, the accession of new Member States[71] and the need for the smooth functioning of the Common Agricultural Market.[72]

62–64. The presumption of validity does not apply to non-existent acts, see Ch 13, pp 323-324.

[66] See the Opinion of Advocate-General Roemer in Case 1/73 *Westzucker* [1973] ECR 723 at 739 where the terminology used is 'real' and 'quasi' retroactive. The terminology 'actual' and 'apparent' was used by Sedley J in *R v Ministry of Agriculture Fisheries and Food, ex p Hamble Fisheries* [1995] 2 All ER 714 at 726A-D.

[67] [1979] ECR 69 para 15; Case T-115/94 *Opel Austria v Council* [1997] ECR II-39 para 13 (backdating the issue of the *Official Journal*).

[68] Joined Cases C-121/91 and C-122/91 *CT Control (Rotterdam) v Commission* [1993] ECR I-3873 para 22.

[69] Case 158/78 *Biegi v Hauptzollamt Bochum* [1979] ECR 1103 para 11; Case 58/85 *Ethicon v Hauptzollamt Itzehoe* [1986] ECR 1131 para 13.

[70] Case 12/71 *Henck v Hauptzollamt Emmerich* [1971] ECR 743 para 5; Joined Cases 212 to 217/80 *Amministrazione delle Finanze v Salumi* [1981] ECR 2735 paras 9–10; Joined Cases C-121/91 and C-122/91 *CT Control (Rotterdam) v Commission* [1993] ECR I-3873 para 22.

[71] Case 337/88 *SAFA v Amministrazione delle Finanze* [1990] ECR 1 paras 13–18.

[72] Case 98/78 *Racke v Hauptzollamt Mainz* [1979] ECR 69 para 20; Case 99/78 *Decker v Hauptzollamt Landau* [1979] ECR 101 para 8.

In Case C-331/88 *R v MAFF, ex p Fedesa*[73] the Council adopted a directive banning the use of hormones in livestock farming. The directive was adopted on 7 March 1988 but stipulated that it should be implemented from 1 January 1988. The Court of Justice held that the directive did not infringe the principle of non-retroactivity. The first condition was satisfied because the directive was identical to an earlier directive adopted in 1985, but which had been annulled by the Court because of a procedural defect. The need for the retroactive application was necessary to avoid a legal vacuum. The second condition was satisfied because the applicants could not reasonably have expected the replacement directive to differ in substance from the first directive.

In Case C-368/89 *Crispoltoni*[74] the Court of Justice considered that neither condition was fulfilled. Mr Crispoltoni received an advance payment from the Community in respect of a quantity of tobacco which had been harvested in 1988. In 1989 the Commission adopted a regulation determining the maximum quantities of tobacco for which producers would be paid. This included the 1988 harvest. The purpose of the regulation was to curb an increase in the Community's tobacco production. The competent authorities then sought repayment from Mr Crispoltoni on the basis of the regulation. The Court of Justice ruled that the regulation, which produced actual retroactive effect, was invalid. The first condition was not fulfilled because the regulation could not curb production for 1988, the tobacco producers having already decided on the area to be cultivated for the 1988 harvest. The second condition was not fulfilled because the producers were entitled to expect that they would be notified in good time of any measure having effects on their investments.

Acts adopted by the Community institutions are presumed not to have actual retroactive effect.[75] In order for a Community measure to be interpreted as having retroactive effect, it must be clear from its 'terms, objective or general scheme'.[76] In addition, the statement of reasons contained in the measure must give particulars which justify the desired retroactive effect.[77]

In the context of criminal law, the prohibition of actual retroactive laws is absolute. In Case 63/83 *R v Kirk*[78] Kent Kirk, the master of a Danish fishing vessel, was fishing on 6 January 1983 in prohibited coastal waters contrary to the United Kingdom Sea Fish Order 1982. He was accordingly fined. Although the Order discriminated on the grounds of nationality, it had been authorised retroactively by a Community regulation adopted on 25 January 1983. The Court of Justice ruled that the Community regulation could not validate, *ex post*

---

[73] [1990] ECR I-4023 paras 41–49.

[74] [1991] ECR I-3695.

[75] Advocate-General Warner in Case 7/76 *IRCA v Amministrazione delle Finanze* [1976] ECR 1213 at 1238.

[76] Joined Cases 212/80 and 217/80 *Amministrazione delle Finanze v Salumi* [1981] ECR 2735 paras 9–10.

[77] Case 1/84R *Ilford v Commission* [1984] ECR 423 para 19.

[78] [1984] ECR 2689 paras 20–23; Case C-331/88 *R v MAFF, ex p Fedesa* [1990] ECR I-4023 para 42.

facto, a national measure which imposed criminal penalties and which, at the relevant time, was contrary to Community law. The Court stated:

> The principle that penal provisions may not have retroactive effect is one which is common to all the legal orders of the Member States and is enshrined in Article 7 of the European Convention for the Protection of Human Rights and Fundamental Freedoms as a fundamental right; it takes its place among the general principles of law whose observance is ensured by the Court of Justice.

Apparent retroactivity In general, apparent retroactivity is not prohibited. In Case 1/73 *Westzucker*[79] the Court of Justice stated:

> According to a generally accepted principle, the laws amending a legislative provision apply, unless otherwise provided, to the future consequences of situations which arose under the former law.

Changes in procedural rules will generally affect all proceedings pending at the time when they enter into force. Thus, where a time period within which the Commission had to decide on a customs appeal from a decision of the national customs authority was increased from four months to six months, the six-month period applied to the Commission even though the proceedings before the national authorities had already started before the increase.[80]

Apparent retroactivity has been described by the Court of Justice as not having 'retroactive effect in the proper sense of the expression'.[81] Apparent retroactivity is, in essence, concerned with the application of the principle of protection of a person's legitimate expectations. The main difference between actual and apparent retroactivity, in this respect, is that there is no presumption against apparent retroactivity, so that the burden of proving a breach of legitimate expectations rests with the person affected.

Judgments of EC courts Judgments of the EC courts are retrospective, unless the court itself limits the retroactive effect of its judgment under article 174 of the EEC Treaty [new art 231][82] or under the doctrine of temporal effects.[83]

Withdrawal of Community measures A Community institution may withdraw an unlawful measure, even retroactively, provided that the withdrawal occurs within a reasonable time and the institution gives proper consideration to the legitimate expectations of those affected by the measure.[84] The relevant

---

[79] [1973] ECR 723 para 5.
[80] Joined Cases 212/80 and 217/80 *Amministrazione delle Finanze v Salumi* [1981] ECR 2735 para 9; Joined Cases C-121/91 and C-122/91 *CT Control (Rotterdam) v Commission* [1993] ECR I-3873 paras 22–28.
[81] Case 74/74 *CNTA v Commission* [1975] ECR 533 para 32.
[82] Discussed further at Ch 13, pp 329–330.
[83] For example, see Case 43/75 *Defrenne v Sabena* [1976] ECR 455 at 480. (Temporal limitations are discussed at Ch 11, pp 240–241.)
[84] Joined Cases 7/56 and 3–7/57 *Algera v Common Assembly* [1957–58] ECR 39 at 55 and 56 (ECSC); Joined Cases 42/59 and 49/59 *SNUPAT v High Authority* [1961] ECR 53 at 86–88 (ECSC); Case 14/61 *Hoogovens v High Authority* [1962] ECR 253 (ECSC); Case 111/63 *Lemmerz-Werke v High Authority* [1965] ECR 677 at 690 (ECSC); Case 14/81 *Alpha Steel v Commission* [1982] ECR 749 paras 9–12 (ECSC); Case C-248/89 *Cargill v Commission* [1991]

time for determining whether the addressee of an administrative act has acquired legitimate expectations is the date when the act was notified, not the date when it was adopted or withdrawn.[85]

However, the retroactive withdrawal of a measure which has conferred individual rights or similar benefits is not permitted[86] unless the measure was based on false or incomplete information provided by the party concerned.[87]

5. EQUAL TREATMENT

Definition The principle of equal treatment (non-discrimination) requires that comparable situations must not be treated differently, and different situations must not be treated comparably, unless such treatment is objectively justified.[88] This principle features in specific provisions of Community law: notably: article 6 of the EC Treaty [new art 12] (which prohibits discrimination on the grounds of nationality); article 40(3) [new art 34] (which prohibits discrimination between Community producers or consumers within the context of the Common Agricultural Policy); and article 119 [new art 141], as supplemented by the Equal Pay Directive[89] (which provides that men and women should receive equal pay for equal work) and the Equal Treatment Directive (which provides that men and women should be treated equally as regards access to employment, conditions of employment and dismissal).[90] However, the Court of Justice has emphasised that these provisions are simply examples of the general principle of equality, which is one of the fundamental principles of Community law.[91]

(a) Unequal treatment

Comparable situations In the absence of objective justification, discrimination occurs when comparable situations are treated differently. The existence of a comparable situation is a question of fact, which must be proved, not merely alleged.[92]

ECR I-2987 para 20; Case T-73/95 *Oliveira v Commission* [1997] ECR II-381 para 42.
[85] Case C-90/95P *De Compte v Parliament* [1997] ECR I-1999 para 36.
[86] Case 159/82 *Verli-Wallace v Commission* [1983] ECR 2711 paras 8–11.
[87] Joined Cases 42/59 and 49/59 *SNUPAT v High Authority* [1961] ECR 53 (ECSC).
[88] Case 164/80 *De Pascale v Commission* [1982] ECR 909 para 20; Case 283/83 *Racke v Hauptzollamt Mainz* [1984] ECR 3791 para 7; Case 106/83 *Sermide v Cassa Conguaglio Zucchero* [1984] ECR 4209 para 28; Case C-217/91 *Spain v Commission* [1993] ECR 3923 paras 36–39; Case C-56/94 *SCAC* [1995] ECR I-1769 para 27; Case C-15/95 *EARL de Kerlast v Unicopia* [1997] ECR I-1961 para 35.
[89] Directive 75/711/EEC (OJ 1975 L45 p 19).
[90] Directive 76/207/EEC (OJ 1976 L39 p 40).
[91] Joined Cases 103/77 and 145/77 *Royal Scholten-Honig v IBAP* [1978] ECR 2037 paras 25–27; Case 147/79 *Hochstrass v Court of Justice* [1980] ECR 3005 para 7; Case C-280/93 *Germany v Council* [1994] ECR I-4973 para 67.
[92] Case T-571/93 *Lefebvre v Commission* [1995] ECR II-2379 para 80.

It is contrary to the principle of equal treatment to treat competitors differently.[93] This will involve an examination of the relevant market in which they compete[94] and whether products or services are regarded as competing will depend on their substitutability in terms of use[95] and price.[96] Even where there is competition between undertakings, other objective factors, such as the overall market structure, may prevent them from being in a comparable situation. In Joined Cases C-248/95 and C-249/95 *SAM Schiffahrt v Germany*[97] a Council regulation set up a fund to reduce overcapacity in the inland waterway transport sector. The owners of certain vessels, who were required to contribute to the fund, unsuccessfully contended that the regulation discriminated against them in favour of road and rail carriers. The Court held that:

> ...the owners of other means of transport, such as road and rail, are in an objectively different situation, since they are not experiencing overcapacity comparable to that in the inland waterways sector.

Occasionally, Community law presumes the existence of comparable situations, for example, in the case of persons of different nationalities or of different sex. If, therefore, a woman is treated differently because of her sex (eg because she is pregnant) this will constitute discrimination (in the absence of any objective justification).[98]

Direct and indirect discrimination The principle of equal treatment prohibits not only overt forms of discrimination but also all covert forms of discrimination, which, by application of other criteria of differentiation, lead in fact to the same discriminatory result. Thus, in Case 96/80 *Jenkins v Kingsgate (Clothing Productions)*[99] the Court of Justice ruled that a difference in pay between full-time and part-time workers could amount to discrimination on the ground of sex where the group of part-time workers was composed exclusively or predominantly of women. In Case C-398/92 *Mund & Fester v Hatrex International Transport*[100] the Court held that a German provision of civil law which allowed seizure of the Dutch defendant's goods in Germany simply on

---

[93] Case T-9/93 *Schöller v Commission* [1995] ECR 1611 para 163.
[94] *R v Ministry of Agriculture Fisheries and Food, ex p First City Trading* [1997] 1 CMLR 250 para 57; [1997] EuLR 193 at 214G.
[95] Joined Cases 117/76 and 16/77 *Ruckdeschel v Hauptzollamt Hamburg-St Annen* [1977] ECR 1753 para 8.
[96] Joined Cases 124/76 and 20/77 *Moulins Pont-à-Moussin* [1977] ECR 1795 para 18.
[97] [1997] ECR I-4475 para 55. Advocate-General Jacobs considered that road and rail transport were not interchangeable with inland waterway transport (para 41 of the Opinion). See also Case C-280/93 *Germany v Council* [1994] ECR I-4973 paras 70–72.
[98] Case C-177/88 *Dekker v VJV-Centrum* [1990] ECR I-3941 paras 10–12; Case C-32/93 *Webb v EMO Air Cargo* [1994] ECR I-3567 para 19.
[99] [1981] ECR 911. See also *R v Secretary of State for Employment, ex p Equal Opportunities Commission* [1995] 1 AC 1. As to covert discrimination regarding the freedom of movement of workers, see Case 152/73 *Sotgiu v Deutsche Bundespost* [1974] ECR 153 para 11; Case 71/76 *Thieffry* [1977] ECR 765; Case 107/83 *Ordre des avocats au Barreau de Paris v Klopp* [1984] ECR 2971.
[100] [1994] ECR I-467. See also Ch 6 at p 111 on the discriminatory residence requirement for security for costs imposed by RSC Ord 23.

the ground that enforcement of the judgment against the defendant would otherwise have to take place abroad was discriminatory. The rule was not directly discriminatory on the grounds of nationality since it applied even in the case of a German national living abroad. However, the rule was indirectly discriminatory as the great majority of cases in which enforcement would have to take place abroad would be against persons who were not German.

Positive discrimination In Case C-450/93 *Kalanke v Bremen*[101] the Court of Justice held that a German rule which guaranteed women absolute and unconditional priority for appointment and promotion went beyond promoting equal opportunities and infringed the principle of equal treatment for men and women.

Reverse discrimination Member States are entitled to treat their own nationals less favourably in areas which are not subject to Community rules or which have not been harmonised at Community level. They are, for example, entitled to tax national products more heavily than imported products,[102] impose more onerous administrative formalities on their own nationals,[103] and impose stricter conditions on the retailing of domestic goods.[104] To the extent, therefore, that the difference in treatment falls outside the scope of the EC Treaty, the principle of equal treatment guaranteed by Community law has no application.[105]

(b) Objective justification

Legitimate aim Unequal treatment will not be discriminatory where it is objectively justified.[106] For example, measures designed to avoid distortions of competition or to promote the effective functioning of the common agricultural markets constitute legitimate aims in the general interest justifying unequal treatment. In Case 8/82 *Wagner v BALM*[107] a Council regulation granted storage aid for sugar which remained in warehouses situated in one Member State, but refused aid for sugar in transit between two Member States. The difference in treatment was objectively justified on the grounds of the disproportionate cost of supervising the payment of aid for sugar which travelled from one Member State to another. In contrast, financial loss to an employer is not a legitimate ground to justify direct discrimination on the grounds of sex.[108]

---

[101] [1995] ECR I-3051.

[102] Case 86/78 *Peureux v Services Fiscaux* [1979] ECR 897 para 32.

[103] Case C-217/94 *Adige* [1996] ECR I-5287.

[104] Case 355/85 *Driancourt v Cognet* [1986] ECR 3231; Case 98/86 *Ministère public v Mathot* [1987] ECR 809.

[105] *R v Ministry of Agriculture Fisheries and Food, ex p First City Trading* [1997] 1 CMLR 250 paras 39–43; [1997] EuLR 195 at 210A-211F.

[106] Case 106/81 *Kind v EEC* [1982] ECR 2885 para 22; Joined Cases T-481/93 and T-484/93 *Exporteurs in Levende Varkens v Commission* [1995] ECR II-2941 para 142.

[107] [1983] ECR 371. See also Case 230/78 *Eridania v Minister of Agriculture and Forestry* [1979] ECR 2749 paras 17–19; Joined Cases 117/76 and 16/77 *Ruckdeschel v Hauptzollamt Hamburg-St Annen* [1977] ECR 1753 paras 7–10; Case 8/82 *Wagner v BALM* [1983] ECR 371 paras 18–21; Case C-56/94 *SCAC* [1995] ECR I-1769 para 27.

[108] Case C-177/88 *Dekker v VJV-Centrum* [1990] ECR I-3941 para 12.

In Case C-132/92 *Birds Eye Walls v Roberts*[109] Advocate-General van Gerven expressed the view that objective justification is not limited to situations involving indirect discrimination and, therefore, both direct and indirect discrimination are capable of being justified.

The legitimacy of any particular objective will differ on the nature of the discrimination. For example, although public safety constitutes a legitimate reason for justifying restrictions on the free movement of persons under article 56 of the EC Treaty [new art 46], there is no provision of Community law which provides that public safety considerations may be relied on to justify discrimination on the grounds of sex.[110]

Justification The justification must be proportionate. This means that the discriminatory measure must be appropriate and necessary in order to achieve the legitimate aim. Where there is a choice between several appropriate measures recourse must be had to the one which is not discriminatory, and the disadvantages caused by the discrimination must not be disproportionate to the aims pursued.[111] As Laws J stated in *R v Ministry of Agriculture Fisheries and Food, ex p First City Trading*:[112]

> ... the court will test the solution arrived at, and pass it only if substantial factual considerations are put forward in its justification: considerations which are relevant, reasonable and proportionate to the aim in view.

Differences in treatment are inherent in the creation of a common market in a particular product[113] or in the adoption of harmonising measures[114] and are, therefore, appropriate and necessary.

Margin of appreciation In *R v Ministry of Agriculture Fisheries and Food, ex p First City Trading*[115] Laws J, while requiring a substantive justification for a discriminatory decision, recognised that 'there is a nice question how far a 'margin of appreciation' is allowed to the decision-maker'. The Court of Justice allows a considerable margin of appreciation in circumstances where the decision-maker exercises a broad discretion in matters involving choices of economic, political or social policy.[116] In such cases, the Court of Justice is not concerned to agree or disagree with the decision-maker, or substitute its own policies or values. The Court will defer to the decision-maker unless it is shown that the decision-maker has committed a manifest error as to the appropriateness or necessity of the measure and as to the effects of the unequal

---

[109] [1993] ECR I-5579, at paras 12–14 of the Opinion.
[110] Case 222/84 *Johnston v Chief Constable of the Royal Ulster Constabulary* [1986] ECR 1651 para 27.
[111] Case 170/84 *Bilka v Weber von Hartz* [1986] ECR 1607 para 36.
[112] [1997] 1 CMLR 250 para 69; [1997] EuLR 193 at 219E.
[113] Case C-280/93 *Germany v Council* [1994] ECR I-4973 paras 73–75.
[114] Case C-331/88 *R v MAFF, ex p Fedesa* [1990] ECR I-4023 paras 19–21.
[115] [1997] 1 CMLR 250 para 67; [1997] EuLR 193 at 218G.
[116] This is clear from the consistent case-law of the EC courts concerning proportionality, which is an integral part of the principle of equal treatment. See above at pp 32-33. See also Ch 13, p 320.

treatment. As the Court of First Instance stated in Case T-267/94 *Oleifici Italiani v Commission*:[117]

> It is settled case-law that the principle of non-discrimination is one of the fundamental principles of Community law...That principle requires that comparable situations should not be treated in a different manner unless the difference is objectively justified.
>
> In addition, it should be borne in mind that in matters concerning the common agricultural policy, the Community legislature has a wide discretion which corresponds to the political responsibilities imposed on it by Articles 40 and 43 of the Treaty ... Consequently, the legality of a measure adopted in this sphere can be affected only if it is manifestly inappropriate having regard to the objective which the competent institution is seeking to pursue.

6. SUBSIDIARITY

Definition   The principle of subsidiarity was expressly introduced as a general principle of Community law by the insertion of article 3b into the EC Treaty [new art 5] by the Treaty on European Union. The second paragraph of article 3b provides that:

> In areas which do not fall within its exclusive competence, the Community shall take action, in accordance with the principle of subsidiarity, only if and in so far as the objectives of the proposed action cannot be sufficiently achieved by the Member States and can therefore, by reason of the scale or effects of the proposed action, be better achieved by the Community.

In Case T-29/92 *SPO v Commission*[118] the Court of First Instance held that the principle of subsidiarity did not, before the entry into force of the Treaty on European Union, constitute a general principle of law by reference to which the legality of Community acts could be reviewed.

The nature and scope of subsidiarity is still uncertain. As the wording of article 3b indicates, the principle of subsidiarity does not apply to areas in which the Community has exclusive competence (for example, free movement of goods, freedom of establishment and freedom to provide services).[119]

In Case C-84/94 *United Kingdom v Council*[120] the United Kingdom sought the annulment of a Council directive under article 173 of the EC Treaty [new art 230]. The United Kingdom invoked the principle of subsidiarity without expressly relying on it as a ground of annulment, and seemed to equate it with the principle of proportionality. However, Advocate-General Léger indicated that these two principles should be carefully distinguished. Subsidiarity

---

[117] [1997] ECR II-1239 paras 45–47. See also Case T-162/94 *NMB v Commission* [1996] ECR II-427 paras 116–120.

[118] [1995] ECR II-289 para 331.

[119] See para 130 of the Opinion of Advocate-General Lenz in Case C-415/93 *Bosman* [1995] ECR I-4921; and para 60 of his Opinion in Case C-11/95 *Commission v Belgium* [1996] ECR I-4115.

[120] [1996] ECR I-5755.

determines whether the Community is competent to act, while proportionality imposes limits on the scope of the acts which are adopted.[121]

7. FUNDAMENTAL RIGHTS

Definition Fundamental rights form an integral part of the general principles of Community law. Therefore, Community institutions must have regard to fundamental rights in applying and interpreting Community law.[122] In *Opinion 2/94*[123] the Court of Justice held that respect for human rights is a condition of the lawfulness of Community acts. In addition, Member States must, as far as possible, apply and implement Community rules in accordance with the fundamental rights recognised by Community law.[124] However, the EC courts do not have power to examine whether national legislation, which falls outside the scope of Community law, is compatible with fundamental rights.[125]

The concept of fundamental rights was not contained in the original EC Treaty, but has been developed by the case-law of the Court of Justice, drawing on two sources: first, the constitutional traditions common to the Member States; and, secondly, international treaties for the protection of human rights on which the Member States have collaborated or of which they are signatories.[126] The case-law of the Court of Justice is now reflected in article F(2) of the EU Treaty [new art 7] ('Maastricht Treaty')[127] which provides that:

> The Union shall respect fundamental rights, as guaranteed by the European Convention for the Protection of Human Rights and Fundamental Freedoms signed in Rome on 4 November 1950 and as they result from the constitutional traditions common to the Member States, as general principles of Community law.

A party cannot invoke a specific right present in the constitution of a single Member State unless that right is recognised generally by the constitutions of

---

[121] Paragraphs 122–126 of the Opinion. In its judgment (at paras 54–57), the Court of Justice did not draw such a sharply defined dividing line between the two principles. See also the Protocol on the application of the principles of subsidiarity and proportionality in the Amsterdam Treaty.

[122] Case 265/87 *Schräder v Hauptzollamt Gronau* [1989] ECR 2237 paras 13–14; Case C-260/89 *ERT* [1991] ECR I-2925 para 41; *Opinion 2/94* [1996] ECR I-1759 para 33.

[123] [1996] ECR I-1759 para 34.

[124] Case 5/88 *Wachauf v Germany* [1989] ECR 2609 paras 17–19; Case C-260/89 *ERT* [1991] ECR I-2925 paras 41–45; Case C-2/92 *Bostock* [1994] ECR I-955 para 16; Case C-351/92 *Graff v Hauptzollamt Köln-Rheinau* [1994] ECR I-3361 para 17.

[125] Joined Cases 60/84 and 61/84 *Cinéthèque v Fédération nationale des cinémas français* [1985] ECR 2065 paras 25–26; Case 12/86 *Demirel v Stadt Schwäbisch Gmünd* [1987] ECR 3719 para 28.

[126] Case 4/73 *Nold v Commission* [1974] ECR 491 paras 12–14 (ECSC); Case C-260/89 *ERT* [1991] ECR I-2925 paras 41–45. See also Case 29/69 *Stauder v Ulm* [1969] ECR 419 para 7; Case 11/70 *Internationale Handelsgesellschaft v Einfuhr- und Vorratsstelle Getreide* [1970] ECR 1125 paras 3–4.

[127] See also articles J.1(2) [new art 11] (fifth indent) (common foreign and security policy) and K.2(1) [new art 30] (cooperation in the fields of justice and home affairs) of the EU Treaty; article 130u(2) of the EC Treaty [new art 177] and Case C-268/94 *Portugal v Council* [1996] ECR I-6177 paras 14–29 (overseas development policy).

the Member States, so that it can be said to be a fundamental right present in Community law.[128]

The Court of Justice has recognised the right to enjoy property and the freedom to pursue a trade or business,[129] the right to privacy and the protection of medical confidentiality,[130] and the right not to be discriminated against on grounds of sex[131] as fundamental rights. These rights are not absolute but may be limited in order to facilitate the pursuit of the objectives of the EC Treaty. However, any restrictions must not constitute 'a disproportionate and intolerable interference, impairing the very substance of those rights'.[132] In Case C-183/95 *Affish v Rijksdienst voor de Keuring van Vee en Vlees*[133] the Court of Justice held that the importance of the objectives pursued by a Community measure may justify restrictions which have adverse consequences, and even substantial adverse consequences, for certain traders.

European Convention on Human Rights[134] The most important source of fundamental rights in the Community legal order is the European Convention on Human Rights.[135] The Community is not itself a signatory to the Convention;[136] however, it has committed itself to respect fundamental rights by means of political declarations[137] and various Treaty articles, notably article F(2) of the EU Treaty.[138] The Court of Justice has consistently held that 'the

---

[128] Case 11/70 *Internationale Handelsgesellschaft v Einfuhr- und Vorratsstelle Getreide* [1970] ECR 1125 paras 3–4; Case 4/73 *Nold v Commission* [1974] ECR 491 para 14 (ECSC); Case 44/79 *Hauer v Land Rheinland-Pfalz* [1979] ECR 3727; Case 63/83 *R v Kirk* [1984] ECR 2689 para 22; Case 374/87 *Orkem v Commission* [1989] ECR 3283 paras 28–30.

[129] Case 265/87 *Schräder v Hauptzollamt Gronau* [1989] ECR 2237 paras 13–19; Case 5/88 *Wachauf v Germany* [1989] ECR 2609 paras 17–18; Case T-521/93 *Atlanta v Communities* [1996] ECR II-1707 para 62; Joined Cases C-248/95 and C-249/95 *SAM Schiffart v Germany* [1997] ECR I-4475 para 72.

[130] Case C-62/90 *Commission v Germany* [1992] ECR I-2575 para 23.

[131] Case C-13/94 *P v S and Cornwall County Council* [1996] ECR I-2143 para 19.

[132] Case C-177/90 *Kühn v Landwirtschaftskammer Weser-Ems* [1992] ECR I-35 paras 16–17 (milk quotas); Case C-306/93 *SMW Winzersekt v Land Rheinland-Pfalz* [1994] ECR I-5555 paras 20–29 (prohibition of use of product designation 'méthode champenoise'); Joined Cases T-466/93 and others *O'Dwyer v Council* [1995] ECR II-2071 paras 98–99 (milk quotas); Case C-84/95 *Bosphorus v Minister for Transport, Energy and Communications* [1996] ECR I-3953 paras 19–27, and paras 58–68 of the Opinion of Advocate-General Jacobs (effect of international sanctions); Case T-390/94 *Schröder v Commission* [1997] ECR II-501 paras 125–131 (imposition of protective measures in relation to agriculture).

[133] [1997] ECR I-4315 para 42.

[134] Convention for the Protection of Human Rights and Fundamental Freedoms, signed on 4 November 1950.

[135] Case C-260/89 *ERT* [1991] ECR I-2925 para 41; Case C-219/91 *Ter Voort* [1992] ECR I-5485 para 34.

[136] *Opinion 2/94* [1996] ECR I-1759.

[137] See the Joint Declaration of the European Parliament, the Council and the Commission on fundamental rights of 5 April 1977 (OJ 1977 C103,p1); Preamble to the Single European Act (which refers to the European Convention on Human Rights and the European Social Charter); Declaration of fundamental rights and freedoms by the European Parliament of 12 April 1989. For further political declarations by the Member States and Community institutions, see point III.5 of the first part of *Opinion 2/94* [1996] ECR I-1759.

[138] See also articles J.1(2) (fifth indent) [new art 11] and article K.2(1) [new art 30] of the EU Treaty.

principles on which that Convention is based must be taken into consideration in Community law'.[139] As with other fundamental rights, the Court of Justice has held that rights arising under the European Convention on Human Rights are not absolute but may be limited in order to facilitate the pursuit of the objectives of the EC Treaty. However, any restrictions must not constitute a disproportionate and intolerable interference, impairing the very substance of those rights.[140]

The Court of Justice has expressly referred to a number of provisions of the European Convention on Human Rights in its case-law.[141] For example, in Case 63/83 *R v Kirk*[142] the Court of Justice held that a regulation could not have retroactive effect as, on the facts of the case, this would have contravened the general principle that penal provisions may not have retroactive effect. This principle is a fundamental right common to the legal systems of all the Member States and enshrined in article 7 of the European Convention on Human Rights and, thus, forms part of the general principles of Community law.

Case-law of the European Court of Human Rights The EC courts have referred to the case-law of the European Court of Human Rights as an aid to the interpretation and application of EC law.[143]

---

[139] Case 222/84 *Johnston v Chief Constable of the Royal Ulster Constabulary* [1986] ECR 1651 para 18; Case C-260/89 *ERT* [1991] ECR I-2925 para 41. See also paras 51–53 of the Opinion of Advocate-General Jacobs in Case C-84/95 *Bosphorus v Minister for Transport, Energy and Communications* [1996] ECR I-3953 for an analysis of the relationship between Community law and the European Convention on Human Rights.

[140] Case C-404/92P *X v Commission* [1994] ECR I-4737 paras 17–18; Case T-176/94 *K v Commission* [1995] ECR I–A–203 and II-621 paras 31 and 33.

[141] For example, see Case 130/75 *Prais v Council* [1976] ECR 1589 paras 8 and 16 (article 9); Case 136/79 *National Panasonic (UK) v Commission* [1980] ECR 2033 paras 17–20 (article 8); Case 44/79 *Hauer v Land Rheinland-Pfalz* [1979] ECR 3727 paras 17–19 (First Protocol); Case 222/84 *Johnston v Chief Constable of the Royal Ulster Constabulary* [1986] ECR 1651 para 18 (articles 6 and 13); Case 85/87 *Dow Benelux v Commission* [1989] ECR 3137 paras 28–30 (article 8); Case C-260/89 *ERT* [1991] ECR I-2925 paras 41–45 (article 10); Case C-219/91 *Ter Voort* [1992] ECR I-5485 paras 33–39 (article 10); Case C-97/91 *Borelli v Commission* [1992] ECR I-6313 para 14 (articles 6 and 13); Case C-404/92P *X v Commission* [1994] ECR I-4737 para 17 (article 8); Case T-107/94 *Kik v Council and Commission* [1995] ECR II-1717 para 39 (article 6); Case C-415/93 *Union Royale Belge des Sociétés de Football Association v Bosman* [1995] ECR I-4921 para 79 (article 11); para 55 of the Opinion of Advocate-General Jacobs in Case C-120/94 *Commission v Greece* [1996] ECR I-1513; Case C-368/95 *Vereinigte Familiapress Zeitungsverlags- und vertriebs v Bauer Verlag* [1997] ECR I-3689 paras 18 and 24–26 (article 10).

[142] [1984] ECR 2689 paras 20–23.

[143] Case C-13/94 *P v S and Cornwall County Council* [1996] ECR I-2143 para 16; Joined Cases C-74/95 and C-129/95 *X* [1996] ECR I-6609 para 25; Case C-368/95 *Vereinigte Familiapress Zeitungsverlags- und vertriebs v Bauer Verlag* [1997] ECR I-3689 paras 24–26.

Other sources The Court of Justice has also referred to the European Social Charter of 18 November 1961 and Convention No 111 of the International Labour Organisation[144] as sources of fundamental rights.[145] Article K.2 of the Maastricht Treaty [new art 30] provides that cooperation in the fields of justice and home affairs must be carried out in compliance with the Convention relating to the Status of Refugees of 28 July 1951.

Preliminary rulings The Court of Justice will provide a national court with an interpretation of fundamental rights, as laid down in particular in the European Convention on Human Rights, where the issue before the national court falls within the scope of Community law. However, the Court of Justice has no power to provide an interpretation of fundamental rights in cases which fall outside the scope of Community law.[146]

8. FORCE MAJEURE

Definition The concept of *force majeure* is not limited to absolute impossibility.[147] In the absence of a specific legislative definition, circumstances will only be considered to constitute *force majeure* where an external cause produces consequences which are inexorable and inevitable to the point of making it objectively impossible for the persons concerned to comply with their obligations.[148] Put another way, the concept of *force majeure* must be understood as meaning abnormal and unforeseeable circumstances beyond the control of the person concerned, whose consequences could not have been avoided despite the exercise of all due care.[149]

Excusable error Community law recognises a concept of excusable error, which has the effect of relieving a party from failure to comply with time-limits. The concept applies only in exceptional circumstances, in particular where the conduct of a Community institution has, either alone or to a decisive extent, given rise to understandable confusion on the part of the party concerned.[150] However, this concept applies only to areas of Community law where

---

[144] Case 149/77 *Defrenne v Sabena* [1978] ECR 1365 paras 25–28. The preamble to the Single European Act expressly refers to the European Social Charter.

[145] See also Case 374/87 *Orkem v Commission* [1989] ECR 3283 paras 18 and 31, where the Court of Justice referred to the International Covenant on Civil and Political Rights of 19 December 1966 *'United Nations Treaty Series'*, vol 999, p 171.

[146] Case C-260/89 *ERT* [1991] ECR I-2925 para 42; Case C-177/94 *Perfili* [1996] ECR I-161 para 20; Case C-144/95 *Maurin* [1996] ECR I-2909; Case C-299/95 *Kremzow v Austria* [1997] ECR I-2629 paras 14–19.

[147] Case C-124/92 *An Bord Bainne and Inter-Agra v IBAP* [1993] ECR I-5061 para 11; Case C-391/93 *Perrotta v Allgemeine Ortskrankenkasse München* [1995] ECR I-2079 paras 25–27.

[148] Joined Cases 154/78 and others *Valsabbia v Commission* [1980] ECR 907 para 140; Case C-12/92 *Huygen* [1993] ECR I-6381 paras 30–31.

[149] Case C-50/92 *Molkerei-Zentrale Süd* [1993] ECR I-1035 para 11; Case C-12/92 *Huygen* [1993] ECR I-6381 paras 30–31; Case C-97/95 *Pascoal & Filhos v Fazenda Pública* [1997] ECR I-4209 para 63.

[150] See further Ch 18, p 396.

implementation of Community rules is a matter for the Community institutions alone. Where the Member States are responsible for the implementation of Community rules, and no specific provisions dealing with excusable error are laid down in those rules, it is for the national authorities to decide, according to their own rules, questions concerning failure to comply with the applicable time-limits.[151]

9. PROCEDURAL RIGHTS

Definition The Community institutions must abide by general principles governing the protection of procedural rights, for example, the right to be heard,[152] the right of legal privilege,[153] confidentiality of business secrets[154] and the presumption of innocence.[155] These principles are particularly important in the context of proceedings by the Commission under the competition rules.[156]

10. LEGAL PRINCIPLES

Definition Community law recognises the principle *lex specialis derogat generali.*[157] In Case C-480/93P *Zunis Holding v Commission*[158] Advocate-General Lenz referred to the general legal principle that rights may not be exercised if to do so would constitute an abuse. In Case C-144/94 *Ufficio IVA di Trapani v Italittica*[159] Advocate-General Jacobs referred to the principle *nullum crimen, nulla poena sine lege.*

---

[151] Case C-285/93 *Dominikanerinnen-Kloster Altenhohenau v Hauptzollamt Rosenheim* [1995] ECR I-4069 paras 26–28.
[152] Discussed at Ch 13, pp 316–318.
[153] For example, see Case 155/79 *AM & S Europe v Commission* [1982] ECR 1575.
[154] For example, see Case T-30/91 *Solvay v Commission* [1995] ECR II-1775 para 88; Case T-353/94 *Postbank v Commission* [1996] ECR II-921 para 87. See also article 214 of the EC Treaty [new art 287].
[155] For example, see Case T-30/91 *Solvay v Commission* [1995] ECR II-1775 para 73.
[156] See Bellamy and Child, *Common Market Law of Competition*, 4th edn (Sweet & Maxwell, 1993), Ch 12; Kerse, *E.C. Antitrust Procedure*, 3rd edn (Sweet & Maxwell, 1994), Ch 8; Ortiz Blanco, *EC Competition Procedure* (Oxford, 1996).
[157] Case C-469/93 *Amministrazione delle Finanze v Chiquita Italia* [1995] ECR I-4533 para 61.
[158] [1996] ECR I-1, at para 23 of the Opinion. See also Ch 3, p 54.
[159] [1995] ECR I-3653, at para 46 of the Opinion.

Chapter 3

Supremacy of EC Law

1. DOCTRINE OF SUPREMACY

Definition The concept of supremacy[1] deals with the inter-relation of Community law and national law and provides that, where there is a conflict between a directly applicable or directly effective Community provision and national law, it is the Community provision which must be applied. The supremacy of Community law is not expressly provided for in the EC Treaty; it was established by the case-law of the Court of Justice.

Approach of the Court of Justice The Court of Justice views the EC Treaty as being a unique source of law, in terms of both international law and national law. In Case 6/64 *Flaminio Costa v ENEL*[2] it stated:

> By contrast with ordinary international treaties, the EEC Treaty has created its own legal system which, on the entry into force of the Treaty, became an integral part of the legal systems of the Member States and which their courts are bound to apply.

Having recognised that the Member States have limited their sovereign rights by virtue of the EC Treaty, the Court concluded:

> It follows from all these observations that the law stemming from the Treaty, an independent source of law, could not, because of its special and original nature, be overridden by domestic legal provisions, however framed, without being deprived of its character as Community law and without the legal basis of the Community itself being called into question.

The Court clearly viewed the principle of supremacy of Community law as being the necessary corollary of the Community's unique status as a supranational organisation, exercising sovereign powers ceded by the Member States.

Effect in national legal systems The effect of the principle of supremacy on the national legal systems of the Member States was examined in Case 106/77 *Amministrazione delle Finanze v Simmenthal*[3] which concerned a

---

[1] This is sometimes also referred to as the concept of 'primacy', from the French 'la primauté'.
[2] [1964] ECR 585 at 593–594.
[3] [1978] ECR 629.

preliminary reference made by an Italian court (the *Pretore di Susa*). Under Italian law, only the Italian Constitutional Court could declare that a national law was unconstitutional. The *Pretore*, having found that a subsequent national law conflicted with EC law, asked the European Court of Justice, *inter alia*, whether it was under a duty to disregard the conflicting national law without being obliged to refer the matter to the Constitutional Court. The Court of Justice held that every national court has a duty to apply Community law in its entirety, and to protect the rights conferred on individuals by Community law. National courts are, therefore, under an obligation to disregard any conflicting provision of national law, without waiting for the national law to be set aside by legislative or constitutional means. The judgment of the Court of Justice sets out the following important implications of the principle of supremacy.

(1) The entry into force of a Community measure which is directly applicable or directly effective:

(*a*) renders any conflicting provision of national law automatically inapplicable;[4]

(*b*) precludes the valid adoption of new national legislative measures to the extent to which they would be incompatible with the Community measure;[5]

(*c*) imposes an obligation on national courts, of their own motion if necessary, to refuse to apply any national legislative measure, even a subsequent one, which is incompatible with the Community measure.[6]

(2) Any provision of a national legal system and any legislative, administrative or judicial practice which might prevent a national court from having the power to do everything necessary to set aside national legislative provisions which conflict with directly applicable or directly effective Community law is itself incompatible with Community law.[7]

Validity of Community law cannot be challenged by reference to national law A further aspect of the principle of supremacy is that the validity of a Community legislative measure cannot be challenged by reference to national legal or constitutional principles. This is established by the judgment of the Court of Justice in Case 11/70 *Internationale Handelsgesellschaft v Einfuhr-*

---

[4] Ibid para 17.

[5] Ibid para 17. See also Case 43/71 *Politi v Italy* [1971] ECR 1039 para 9; Case C-343/92 *De Weerd v Bestuur van de Bedrijfsvereniging voor de Gezondheid* [1994] ECR I-571 paras 17–21.

[6] Case 106/77 *Amministrazione delle Finanze v Simmenthal* [1978] ECR 629 para 21. See also Case 6/64 *Costa v ENEL* [1964] ECR 585 at 593–594; Case 34/67 *Lück v Hauptzollamt Köln* [1968] ECR 245 at 251; Case 84/71 *Marimex v Italian Ministry for Finance* [1972] ECR 89 para 5; Case C-184/89 *Nimz v Freie und Hansestadt Hamburg* [1991] ECR I-297 paras 16–21; Joined Cases C-87 to 89/90 *Verholen v Sociale Verzekeringsbank* [1991] ECR I-3757 paras 11–16; Joined Cases C-13/91 and C-113/91 *Debus* [1992] ECR I-3617 paras 31–33; Case C-358/95 *Morellato v USL No 11, Pordenone* [1997] ECR I-1431 para 18.

[7] Case 106/77 *Amministrazione delle Finanze v Simmenthal* [1978] ECR 629 para 22. See also Case C-213/89 *Factortame* [1990] ECR I-2433.

und Vorratsstelle Getreide.[8] This case involved a preliminary reference from a German court which considered that a Community regulation was contrary to the German Basic Law. The Court of Justice held that the validity of the regulation had to be assessed in the light of Community law, not national law. The Court of Justice has consistently held that provisions contained in national constitutions cannot override the requirements of Community law.[9]

Exception to supremacy: abuse or fraud The Court of Justice has consistently held that Community law cannot be relied on for the purposes of abuse or fraud.[10] For example, in Case C-23/93 *TV10 v Commissariaat voor de Media*[11] the Court of Justice held that a broadcaster could not rely on article 59 of the EC Treaty [new art 49] (freedom to provide services) where it had established itself in one Member State solely to avoid having to comply with the domestic legislation of another Member State to which it was actually broadcasting.

Exception to supremacy: international agreements Pursuant to article 234 of the EC Treaty [new art 307], where a number of Member States and third countries are parties to an agreement entered into prior to the EEC Treaty, as between the Member States and the third countries the prior agreement will prevail over the requirements of Community law.[12]

Arbitrations In Case C-393/92 *Almelo*,[13] a preliminary reference was made by a national court which had been called upon to determine an appeal against an arbitration award. The arbitration agreement between the parties required the national court to give judgment on the basis of what was fair and reasonable. The Court of Justice held that, even in such a situation, the national court was bound to give effect to rules of Community law, in particular those relating to competition.

---

[8] [1970] ECR 1125 paras 3–4. See also Joined Cases 97 to 99/87 *Dow Chemical Ibérica v Commission* [1989] ECR 3165 paras 37–39.

[9] Case 149/79 *Commission v Belgium* [1980] ECR 3881 para 19; Case C-473/93 *Commission v Luxembourg* [1996] ECR I-3207 paras 37–38; Case C-290/94 *Commission v Greece* [1996] ECR I-3285.

[10] Case C-206/94 *Brennet v Paletta* [1996] ECR I-2357 para 24. See also Case 33/74 *Van Binsbergen v Bedrijfsvereniging Metaalnijverhied* [1974] ECR 1299 para 13 (freedom to provide services); Case 229/83 *Leclerc v 'Au Blé Vert'* [1985] ECR 1 para 27 (free movement of goods); Case 39/86 *Lair v Universität Hannover* [1988] ECR 3161 para 43 (free movement of workers); Case C-8/92 *General Milk Products v Hauptzollamt Hamburg-Jonas* [1993] ECR I-779 para 21 (Common Agricultural Policy). See also the eighth recital in the Preamble to the Second Banking Directive (Directive 89/646 of 15 December 1989 on the co-ordination of laws, regulations and administrative provisions relating to the taking up and pursuit of the business of credit institutions and amending Directive 77/780 (OJ 1989 L386 p 1).

[11] [1994] ECR I-4795 paras 20–21.

[12] Article 234 is discussed further at Ch 1, pp 22-23.

[13] [1994] ECR I-1477 para 23. See also Frank-Bernd Weigand, 'Evading EC Competition Law by Resorting to Arbitration?' [1993] 9 *Arbitration International* 249.

Criminal proceedings Community law has supremacy over national criminal legislation.[14] Thus, where a conviction is obtained on the basis of a national legislative measure which is contrary to Community law, that conviction is also incompatible with Community law.[15]

Administrative authorities/Government ministers The concept of supremacy is not restricted to proceedings before national courts; it applies equally to all state administrative authorities.[16] In *R v Secretary of State for the Home Department, ex p the Mayor of Burgess of the London Borough of Harrow*[17] the English High Court held that the Secretary of State was under an obligation to exercise the discretion accorded to him by an Act of Parliament in accordance with binding provisions of Community law.

2. APPLICATION IN ENGLISH COURTS

Effect on English courts The practical effect of the case-law of the Court of Justice concerning the principle of supremacy is that, if an English court is confronted with a conflict between a national law (whether case-law or statute law) and a directly applicable or directly effective Community measure, the judge is obliged to apply the Community measure in preference to the national law. This is the case regardless of whether the English law was passed before or after the Community measure. Furthermore, the judge is not entitled to wait for the conflicting English provision to be set aside by legislative or administrative intervention.

European Communities Act 1972 Section 2(1) of the European Communities Act 1972 provides that:

> All such rights, powers, liabilities, obligations and restrictions from time to time created or arising by or under the Treaties, and all such remedies and procedures from time to time provided for by or under the Treaties, as in accordance with the Treaties are without further enactment to be given legal effect or used in the United Kingdom shall be recognised and available in law, and be enforced, allowed and followed accordingly; and the expression 'enforceable Community right' and similar expressions shall be read as referring to one to which this subsection applies.

Section 2(4) of the European Communities Act 1972 provides:

---

14 Case 82/71 *Pubblico Ministero v SAIL* [1972] ECR 119 para 5.
15 Case 88/77 *Minister for Fisheries v Schonenberg* [1978] ECR 473 para 16; Case 269/80 *R v Tymen* [1981] ECR 3079 paras 15–17. The relationship between Community law and national criminal proceedings is discussed further at Ch 4, p 72 and Ch 5, p 95.
16 Case 103/88 *Costanzo v Comune di Milano* [1989] ECR 1839 paras 28–31. Note that the Court did not follow the conclusions adopted by Advocate-General Lenz at paras 28–36 of his Opinion. See also paras 12–13 of the Opinion of Advocate-General Elmer in Case C-431/92 *Commission v Germany* [1995] ECR I-2189; para 35 of the Opinion of Advocate-General Ruiz-Jarabo Colomer in Case C-358/95 *Morellato v USL No 11, Pordenone* [1997] ECR I-1431.
17 [1996] 2 CMLR 524 para 5.

... any such provision ... as might be made by Act of Parliament, and any enactment passed or to be passed ... shall be construed and have effect subject to the foregoing provisions of this section;....

Approach of English courts The English courts have recognised and given effect to the principle of supremacy in the national legal system.[18] In *Stoke-on-Trent City Council v B&Q plc*[19] Hoffmann J stated that 'The EEC Treaty is the supreme law of this country, taking precedence over Acts of Parliament'. However, rather than analysing the principle of supremacy as stemming from the unique character of the Community legal order, the English courts have tended to base their reasoning on s 2 of the European Communities Act 1972.[20]

An example of the approach of the English courts is illustrated by the decision in *Macarthys Ltd v Smith*[21] which concerned the interpretation of the Equal Pay Act 1970 and its relationship with article 119 of the EEC Treaty [new art 141], which establishes the principle that men and women should receive equal pay for equal work. Lord Denning MR held that:

> In construing our statute, we are entitled to look to the Treaty as an aid to its construction: and even more, not only as an aid but as an overriding force. If on close investigation it should appear that our legislation is deficient—or is inconsistent with Community law—by some oversight of our draftsmen—then it is our bounden duty to give priority to Community law. Such is the result of section 2(1) and (4) of the European Communities Act 1972.

The House of Lords considered the effect of the principle of supremacy in *R v Secretary of State for Transport, ex p Factortame Ltd (No 2)*.[22] In that case, owners of Spanish fishing boats sought an interim injunction suspending the application of Part II of the Merchant Shipping Act 1988 pending final judgment in their application for judicial review, on the basis that the Act was contrary to Community law. The House of Lords, when the case first came before it, held, *inter alia*, that the English courts could not grant such an injunction because of the rule in English law that an injunction cannot be granted against the Crown.[23] A preliminary reference on this issue was made to the Court of Justice, which held that, where an application was made for interim

---

[18] See the judgments of Lord Denning MR in *Application des Gaz SA v Falks Veritas Ltd* [1974] 1 Ch 381 and *HP Bulmer Ltd v J Bollinger SA* [1974] 1 Ch 401, for an early recognition of the principle of supremacy in English law.

[19] [1991] Ch 48 at 56D.

[20] An exception is the decision of Oliver LJ in *Bourgoin SA v Ministry of Agriculture, Fisheries and Food* [1986] QB 716 at 774D–775A, where he relied directly on Case 106/77 *Amministrazione delle Finanze v Simmenthal* [1978] ECR 629 as providing authority for the supremacy of Community law. See above pp 52-53.

[21] [1979] ICR 785 at 788C–789F. See also the further judgment as to costs reported at [1981] 1 QB 180 at 200E–G, where Lord Denning MR reiterated the effect of the principle of supremacy in English law. See also *Shields v E Coomes (Holdings) Ltd* [1978] 1 WLR 1408 at 1414B–1416B, per Lord Denning MR; *Aero Zipp Fasteners v YKK Fasteners (UK) Ltd* [1974] RPC 624 at 625; *WH Smith Do-It-All Ltd v Peterborough City Council* [1991] 1 QB 304 at 317C–F.

[22] [1991] 1 AC 603.

[23] *R v Secretary of State for Transport, ex p Factortame Ltd* [1990] 2 AC 85.

relief in a case concerning Community law, and a national court considered that the only obstacle which precluded such relief was a rule of national law, that court must set the rule aside.[24] When the House of Lords reconsidered the matter in light of the Court of Justice's ruling, it decided to grant the injunction sought. Lord Bridge made the following observations concerning the principle of supremacy:[25]

> Under the terms of the Act of 1972 it has always been clear that it was the duty of a United Kingdom court, when delivering final judgment, to override any rule of national law found to be in conflict with any directly enforceable rule of Community law. Similarly, when decisions of the European Court of Justice have exposed areas of United Kingdom statute law which failed to implement Council directives, Parliament has always loyally accepted the obligation to make appropriate and prompt amendments. Thus there is nothing in any way novel in according supremacy to rules of Community law in those areas to which they apply and to insist that, in the protection of rights under Community law, national courts must not be inhibited by rules of national law from granting interim relief in appropriate cases is no more than a logical recognition of that supremacy.

The decision of the House of Lords in *Factortame* is particularly important as it recognises the full extent of the principle of supremacy. The law that an injunction could not be obtained against the Crown was, in effect, a constitutional rule, based on the principle that the courts are merely an extension of the Sovereign's right to rule. In granting an interim injunction, the House of Lords recognised the supremacy of Community law over national constitutional principles.

Potential limitation A practical difference between the general approach of the English courts to the principle of supremacy and the approach of the Court of Justice might arise if the UK Parliament deliberately chose to pass an Act with the intention of repudiating its Community obligations. In *Macarthys Ltd v Smith*[26] Lord Denning MR observed that in such a case the English courts would probably be under a duty to follow the UK statute rather than the EEC Treaty. However, unless there is an intentional and express repudiation of the EC Treaty, the English courts are under a duty to give priority to the Treaty.

---

[24] Case C-213/89 *Factortame* [1990] ECR I-2433, [1991] 1 AC 603 at 640.

[25] [1991] 1 AC 603 at 659A–C.

[26] [1979] ICR 785 at 789E–F, per Lord Denning MR (see also the judgment of Lawton LJ at 796C–D); *Blackburn v Attorney General* [1971] 1 WLR 1037 at 1040–1041, per Lord Denning MR.

Chapter 4

Direct Effect

1. INTRODUCTION

Definition The principle of direct effect means that private parties are entitled to rely on a Community measure in the national courts even if that measure has not been implemented by national legislation.[1]

English law Section 2(1) of the European Communities Act 1972 provides that:

> All such rights, powers, liabilities, obligations and restrictions from time to time created or arising by or under the Treaties, and all such remedies and procedures from time to time provided for by or under the Treaties, as in accordance with the Treaties are without further enactment to be given legal effect or used in the United Kingdom shall be recognised and available in law, and be enforced, allowed and followed accordingly; and the expression 'enforceable Community right' and similar expressions shall be read as referring to one to which this subsection applies.

Directly effective Community provisions fall within this section and, therefore, are recognised and enforced by English courts even if they have not been enacted in national legislation.[2]

Relationship between direct effect and supremacy[3] The principle of supremacy obliges national courts to give precedence to directly effective Community provisions over conflicting national law, whether that law was passed prior or subsequently to the Community provision.[4] In addition, the Member States are under an obligation not to pass any new laws which conflict with directly effective Community provisions and to repeal pre-existing national laws which conflict.[5]

---

[1] Case 26/62 *Van Gend en Loos v Nederlandse administratie der belastingen* [1963] ECR 1. For early recognition of the principle of direct effect in English law, see *Shields v E Coomes (Holdings) Ltd* [1978] 1 WLR 1408 at 1414B–1416B, per Lord Denning MR.
[2] For example, see *Garden Cottage Foods Ltd v Milk Marketing Board* [1984] 1 AC 130 at 141C–D, per Lord Diplock; *MH Marshall v Southampton and South-West Hampshire Area Health Authority* [1990] 3 CMLR 425, [1991] ICR 136, per Staughton LJ.
[3] See Ch 3 in relation to the principle of supremacy.
[4] Case 148/78 *Pubblico Ministero v Ratti* [1979] ECR 1629 para 23.
[5] For example, see Case 167/73 *Commission v France* [1974] ECR 359 paras 34–48.

Recognition of the principle of direct effect The principle of direct effect is not expressly provided for in the EC Treaty. It was established by the Court of Justice in Case 26/62 *Van Gend en Loos v Nederlandse administratie der belastingen.*[6] In that case, a Dutch company, Van Gend en Loos, imported goods into the Netherlands from West Germany. The Dutch revenue authorities levied an import duty of 8 per cent on the goods. Van Gend en Loos challenged its liability to pay this duty before the Dutch courts, relying on article 12 of the EEC Treaty [new art 25], which requires Member States to refrain from introducing new customs duties on intra-Community trade or increasing existing duties. Van Gend en Loos argued that the Dutch Government was in breach of article 12 as it had raised the import duty on this classification of goods from 3 to 8 per cent. The Dutch court made a preliminary reference to the Court of Justice and one of the questions which it asked was whether article 12 creates rights for individuals which the national courts are obliged to protect. The Court of Justice held that article 12, which is clear and unconditional in its terms, does have direct effect.[7] The Court justified this finding on the basis that:

> ... the Community constitutes a new legal order of international law for the benefit of which the states have limited their sovereign rights, albeit within limited fields, and the subjects of which comprise not only Member States but also their nationals. Independently of the legislation of Member States, Community law therefore not only imposes obligations on individuals but is also intended to confer upon them rights which become part of their legal heritage. These rights arise not only where they are expressly granted by the Treaty, but also by reason of obligations which the Treaty imposes in a clearly defined way upon individuals as well as upon the Member States and upon the institutions of the Community.

In addition, the Court of Justice rejected the argument that breaches of Community law by Member States could be adequately sanctioned by proceedings under articles 169 and 170 of the EEC Treaty [new arts 226 and 227]. Proceedings under these articles can only be brought by the Commission or the Member States and, therefore, cannot provide individuals with a means of obtaining direct legal protection of their rights. The Court recognised that the binding effect of Community measures would be more likely to be enforced if individuals could rely directly on those rights in the national courts.

The importance of this judgment cannot be underestimated.[8] Instead of being simply an international treaty which imposes obligations on the signatory states alone, the EC Treaty has become a new and independent source of law which is integrated into the national legal systems of all the Member States, thus creating rights for individuals in the same way as national legislation. Furthermore, national courts have become, in essence, Community courts at a national level,

---

[6] [1963] ECR 1.
[7] Ibid at 11–13.
[8] Case 57/65 *Lütticke v Hauptzollamt Saarlouis* [1966] ECR 205 is another important example of an early Court judgment finding that an EEC Treaty article has direct effect (article 95) [new art 90].

as they are obliged to provide effective protection for directly effective Community law rights.

2. TEST TO ESTABLISH DIRECT EFFECT

Test for direct effect In order to have direct effect, the Community provision in question must be unconditional and sufficiently precise.[9]

Meaning of 'sufficiently precise' In order to have direct effect, a Community provision must be *sufficiently* precise to give rise to legal rights.[10] In Case 131/79 *R v Secretary of State for Home Affairs, ex p Santillo*[11] Advocate-General Warner rejected the submission of the UK Government that 'clear' in this context meant 'unambiguous' on the basis that:

> Ambiguity in legislative provisions is one of the things that courts exist to resolve. It is not the same as lack of precision. We are only too familiar in this Court with ambiguities in regulations. No-one has ever suggested however, and quite rightly, that an ambiguity in a regulation meant that it could not have direct effect. The same is true of directives, as the Court held in the *Van Duyn* case.

Meaning of 'unconditional' A provision will be 'unconditional' wherever it imposes an obligation which is not dependent on the adoption of any further measure either by the Community institutions or by the Member States.[12] For example, in Case 203/80 *Casati*[13] the Court of Justice held that article 67 of the EEC Treaty [repealed by the Amsterdam Treaty], which provided for the progressive abolition of restrictions on the movement of capital, did not have direct effect. The Court reached this conclusion on the basis that the obligation to liberalise capital movements in article 67 was not absolute, but was limited, to the extent that liberalisation 'was necessary to ensure the proper functioning of the Common Market'. This limitation recognised the fact that capital movements are closely connected with the economic and monetary policies of the Member States and, therefore, to avoid creating imbalances, liberalisation was subject to the assessment of the Council on what was necessary and appropriate, at any given time, in light of the degree of integration achieved between the Member States. The fact that the need for liberalisation was subject to the continuing assessment of the Council prevented article 67 from having direct effect.

---

[9] See Case 9/70 *Grad v Finanzamt Traunstein* [1970] ECR 825 para 9; Case 8/81 *Becker v Finanzamt Münster-Innenstadt* [1982] ECR 53 para 25; Joined Cases C-6/90 and C-9/90 *Francovich and Bonifaci v Italy* [1991] ECR I-5357 para 11.

[10] Discussed further in the context of directives at pp 65.

[11] [1980] ECR 1585 at 1611.

[12] See further below at pp 65-70.

[13] [1981] ECR 2595 paras 8–13. See also *R v Secretary of State for Trade and Industry, ex p Duddridge* [1996] 2 CMLR 361 paras 20–25, where the Court of Appeal held that article 130r of the EC Treaty [new art 174] was confined to defining the general environmental objectives of the Community and did not in itself impose any obligations on the Member States without further action by the Community institutions.

Vertical and horizontal direct effect There is an important distinction to be made between 'vertical' and 'horizontal' direct effect. A Community measure with vertical direct effect may be relied on as between individuals and the State. A Community measure with horizontal direct effect can be relied on by a private party against other private parties. The distinction is particularly important in relation to directives, as the Court of Justice has held that these are not capable of having horizontal direct effect.[14]

3. DIRECT EFFECT OF TREATY ARTICLES

Treaty articles Many treaty articles have been recognised as being sufficiently precise and unconditional to have direct effect. In 1983, the Commission produced a list of the treaty provisions which the Court of Justice had established as having direct effect, as well as those provisions which had been held not to have direct effect.[15]

Capable of creating rights for individuals Even though an EC Treaty article is directly effective in the sense of imposing an obligation which is sufficiently precise and unconditional to be relied on in the national courts, it will not necessarily be capable of creating substantive rights for individuals.[16] For example, in Case 6/64 *Costa v ENEL*[17] the Court of Justice held that article 102 of the EC Treaty [new art 97] imposes obligations on the Member States as States, but is not capable of creating rights for individuals. Article 102 imposes an obligation on Member States to consult with the Commission where they fear that a proposed national measure might distort competition within the Common Market.

Vertical and horizontal direct effect Directly effective treaty articles may have both vertical and horizontal direct effect. An example of horizontal direct effect is provided by the competition rules of articles 85 and 86 of the EC Treaty [new arts 81 and 82], which can be invoked by economic undertakings against each other in the national courts.[18] Further, in Case 36/74 *Walrave v Union Cycliste Internationale*[19] the Court of Justice held that article 7 [new art 12] (general prohibition of discrimination), article 48 [new art 39] (free movement of workers) and article 59 [new art 49] (freedom to provide services), all have horizontal direct effect and can be invoked in the national courts by private parties against other private parties (in that case, an international sporting federation). In Case 43/75 *Defrenne v Sabena*[20] the Court of Justice held,

---

[14] Discussed below at pp 70-72.

[15] OJ 1983 C177 p 13. Reproduced in Appendix A.

[16] See further below at pp 66-67.

[17] [1964] ECR 585 at 595. Confirmed in Case C-134/94 *Esso Española v Comunidad Autónoma de Canarias* [1995] ECR I-4223 para 22 (article 102 of the EC Treaty) [new art 97].

[18] Case 127/73 *BRT v SABAM* [1974] ECR 51 para 16; *Garden Cottage Foods v Milk Marketing Board* [1984] AC 130.

[19] [1974] ECR 1405.

[20] [1976] ECR 455 para 39.

Justice held, similarly, that article 119 [new art 141], which establishes the principle of equal pay for men and women, has horizontal direct effect.

4. DIRECT EFFECT OF REGULATIONS

Regulations Article 189 of the EC Treaty [new art 249] expressly provides that regulations are 'directly applicable' in all Member States.[21] The Court of Justice has often used the terms 'directly applicable' and 'directly effective' interchangeably, but has never expressly considered whether there is, in fact, a difference between the two concepts.[22] Logically, it must be the case that while all regulations are directly applicable, in the sense that they automatically become integrated into the national legal systems of the Member States without requiring national implementing legislation, they will not all necessarily have direct effect, in the sense of being sufficiently precise or unconditional to be relied on in the national courts, or be capable of creating rights for individuals.[23] Support for this is found in Case 87/82 *Rogers v Darthenay*,[24] where a regulation provided that, 'No device shall be used by means of which the mesh in any part of a fishing net is obstructed or otherwise effectively diminished. This provision does not exclude the use of the devices referred to in the detailed implementing rules to be adopted in accordance with the procedure laid down in Article 20'. The Court of Justice did not assume that because a regulation is directly applicable it must necessarily have direct effect. Rather, the Court applied the normal test for direct effect in holding that this was an 'independent and perfectly clear provision' which could, therefore, be relied on in the national proceedings. Indeed, if a regulation is not unconditional and sufficiently precise and is not capable of creating individual rights, it is not clear how a national court could protect such a 'right'.[25] For example, further national or Community legislation may be necessary to define individual rights under a

---

[21] See Ch 1, p 7.

[22] In Case 34/73 *Variola v Amministrazione Italiana delle Finanze* [1973] ECR 981 and Case 83/78 *Pigs Marketing Board v Redmond* [1978] ECR 2347 paras 66–67, the Court of Justice seemed to suggest that a directly applicable regulation would automatically have direct effect. See also Case C-83/94 *Leifer* [1995] ECR I-3231 paras 43–46.

[23] See Case 31/74 *Galli* [1975] ECR 47 at 70, Opinion of Advocate-General Warner; Case 74/76 *Ianelli & Volpi v Meroni* [1977] ECR 557 at 583, Opinion of Advocate-General Warner; and Case 131/79 *R v Secretary of State for Home Affairs, ex p Santillo* [1980] ECR 1585 at 1608–1609, Opinion of Advocate-General Warner. See also the legal submissions referred to in the judgment of Lloyd LJ in *An Bord Bainne Co-operative Ltd v Milk Marketing Board* [1988] 1 CMLR 605 paras 12–17.

[24] [1983] ECR 1579 para 11.

[25] See Case 43/71 *Politi v Italy* [1971] ECR 1039 paras 8–9; Case 84/71 *Marimex v Italian Ministry for Finance* [1972] ECR 89 paras 4–5; Case 93/71 *Leonesio v Italian Ministry for Agriculture and Forestry* [1972] ECR 287; Case 65/75 *Tasca* [1976] ECR 291 paras 15–16; and Case 148/78 *Pubblico Ministero v Ratti* [1979] ECR 1629 para 19; *Scotch Whisky Association and Others v Glen Kella Distillers Ltd* [1997] EULR 455 (Ch). All of these cases appear to suggest that a regulation can have direct effect only if it is 'capable of creating individual rights'.

regulation. Alternatively, the content of a regulation may not be suitable for creating individual rights. It may impose obligations on the Member States as between themselves which are irrelevant when considered in terms of individual rights (for example, obligations concerning economic or monetary policy).[26]

5. DIRECT EFFECT OF DECISIONS

Decisions Decisions addressed to Member States are capable of having direct effect.[27] This was established in Case 9/70 *Grad v Finanzamt Traunstein*,[28] where the Court of Justice was concerned with the combined effect of provisions contained in a decision and a directive. The Court emphasised that under article 189 of the EEC Treaty [new art 249] a decision is binding in its entirety upon those to whom it is addressed. Thus, where the Community authorities have imposed an obligation on a Member State to act in a certain way by means of a decision, the effectiveness (*l'effet utile*) of such a measure would be weakened if private parties could not invoke it in the national courts and the national courts could not take it into consideration as part of Community law.[29]

The fact that a decision permits a Member State to exercise certain derogations from clear and precise provisions does not prevent those provisions from having direct effect. However, where a decision sets down a time-limit for compliance with its provisions, it cannot have direct effect until that time-limit has expired.[30] Furthermore, in Case 30/75 *Unit-It v Amministrazione Finanzaria*[31] the Court of Justice held that a Member State could not rely on the provisions of a decision addressed to the Member States as against individual traders where the Member State concerned had failed to take the steps necessary to give effect to the decision in the national legal order.

Capable of creating rights for individuals Not all decisions are capable of creating rights for individuals. In Case 174/84 *Bulk Oil (Zug) v Sun International*[32] the Court of Justice held that a private party could not attack a measure adopted by a Member State on the basis that the Member State had failed to notify the other Member States and the Commission of the measure beforehand as required by a series of Council decisions. The Court held that the

---

[26] For a discussion of whether a Community measure may only have direct effect where it is capable of creating rights for individuals, see further below at pp 66–67.

[27] For a discussion of the direct effect of decisions, see Rosa Greaves, 'The Nature and Binding Effect of Decisions under Article 189 EC' (1996) 21 ELRev 3 at 11–13. See also Ch 1, pp 15–18 for a discussion of the legal status of decisions.

[28] [1970] ECR 825 paras 3–5.

[29] Case C-156/91 *Hansa Fleisch v Landrat des Kreises Schleswig-Flensburg* [1992] ECR I-5567 paras 11–17.

[30] Ibid paras 18–20.

[31] [1975] ECR 1419.

[32] [1986] ECR 559 paras 61–62. The issues as to whether a Community measure must be capable of creating rights for individuals in order to have direct effect is discussed in the context of directives below at pp 66–67.

obligation to notify contained in the decisions only concerned the institutional relationship between the Member State and the Community and the other Member States and therefore did not create individual rights which the national courts were obliged to protect.

6. DIRECT EFFECT OF DIRECTIVES[33]

(a) Recognition of direct effect of directives

Direct effect of directives Case 41/74 *Van Duyn v Home Office*[34] concerned a Dutch woman who was refused leave to enter the United Kingdom to take up employment as a secretary with the Church of Scientology. Leave to enter was refused as the Government considered that the activities of the Church were socially harmful. On a preliminary reference from the High Court, the Court of Justice held that article 3(1) of Council Directive 64/221,[35] which provides that measures taken to restrict entry to a Member State on grounds of public policy or public security should be based exclusively on the personal conduct of the individual concerned, had direct effect. The Court of Justice held that it would be incompatible with the binding effect attributed to directives by article 189 of the EEC Treaty [new art 249] to exclude, in principle, the possibility that they could be relied on by private parties before the national courts. The Court further held that where the Community authorities have imposed on Member States, by means of a directive, the obligation to pursue a particular course of conduct, the effectiveness (*l'effet utile*) of such an act would be weakened if individuals were prevented from relying on it before their national courts and if the courts themselves were prevented from taking it into consideration as an element of Community law. By allowing private parties to rely on directives in the national courts, the proper application of binding Community law would be more likely to be achieved throughout the Community.[36]

Direct effect of individual provisions Particular provisions which are capable of having direct effect will not necessarily be prevented from doing so by virtue of the fact that other provisions in the same directive are not capable of having direct effect. Thus, in Case 8/81 *Becker v Finanzamt Münster-Innenstadt*[37] the

---

[33] See, generally, Sacha Prechal, *Directives in European Community Law* (Oxford, 1995), Ch 11.

[34] [1974] ECR 1337 paras 9–15. See also Case 33/70 *SACE v Italian Ministry for Finance* [1970] ECR 1213 para 15, where it was held that a directive addressed to the Italian Government, which was intended to implement directly effective Treaty articles, had direct effect itself.

[35] Council Directive 64/221 of 25 February 1964 on the co-ordination of special measures concerning the movement and residence of foreign nationals, which are justified on grounds of public policy, public security or public health (OJ Special Edition, 1963–1964 at 117).

[36] See also Case 190/87 *Oberkreisdirektor des Kreises Borken v Moormann* [1988] ECR 4689 paras 21–24, where the Court of Justice stated that the direct effect of directives is based on the combined effect of articles 189 and 5 [new art 10] of the EEC Treaty.

[37] [1982] ECR 53 paras 29–30. Contrast Joined Cases C-6/90 and C-9/90 *Francovich and Bonifaci v Italy* [1991] ECR I-5357 paras 10–27.

Court of Justice held that, while certain provisions of the Sixth VAT Directive[38] could not have direct effect, other provisions, which were capable of having direct effect standing on their own and which could be severed from the general body of provisions and applied separately, could be relied on by private parties in the national courts. It follows from this approach that the relevant question is not necessarily whether a directive as a whole has direct effect, although this may indeed be the case, but whether particular provisions sought to be relied on within the directive can have direct effect when standing on their own.

(b) Test for direct effect of directives

Test In order for a provision of a directive to have direct effect it must be unconditional and sufficiently precise.[39] In addition, a provision of a directive cannot have direct effect until the implementation date for the directive has expired.[40]

Sufficiently precise Article 189 of the EC Treaty [new art 249] expressly provides that a Member State has a discretion as to the choice of form and methods by which to implement a directive into national law. However, this discretion as to form and method of implementation does not prevent a directive from having direct effect, as long as the *result* required to be achieved is defined in unequivocal terms.[41]

Unconditional A directive will be unconditional wherever it imposes an obligation which is not dependent on the adoption of any further measure either by the Community institutions or by the Member States.[42] In Joined Cases C-246 to 249/94 *Cooperativa Agricola Zootecnica S Antonio*[43] the Court of Justice held that a provision which provided that a customs debt was to be incurred wherever an importer failed to fulfil certain obligations 'unless the competent authorities are satisfied that these failures have no significant effect on the correct operation of the ... customs regime in question' had direct effect, as the obligation laid down was clear and the assessment of the national authorities was subject to review by the national courts.

Direct effect cannot arise until the implementation date has expired As directives must be implemented by Member States into their national law, a directive will usually set out a final date by which it must be implemented ('the implementation date'). After the implementation date has passed, if the

[38] Council Directive 77/388 (OJ 1977 L145 p 1).
[39] Case 8/81 *Becker v Finanzamt Münster-Innenstadt* [1982] ECR 53 paras 17–25; Joined Cases C-6/90 and C-9/90 *Francovich and Bonifaci v Italy* [1991] ECR I-5357 para 11; Case C-236/92 *Comitato di Coordinamento per la Difesa della Cava v Regione Lombardia* [1994] ECR I-483 paras 8–10.
[40] Case 148/78 *Pubblico Ministero v Ratti* [1979] ECR 1629 paras 24 and 39–46.
[41] Case C-389/95 *Klattner v Greece* [1997] ECR I-2719 para 33.
[42] Joined Cases C-246 to 249/94 *Cooperativa Agricola Zootecnica S Antonio* [1996] ECR I-4373 para 18; Case C-389/95 *Klattner v Greece* [1997] ECR I-2719 para 33.
[43] [1996] ECR I-4373 paras 9 and 16–26.

Member State has not adopted the necessary implementing legislation, a private party can rely on the direct effect of the directive in an action against the Member State and the directive will prevail over national law inconsistent with the directive. However, a directive cannot have direct effect until the implementation period specified has expired.[44] Until that date a Member State is free to rely on existing national law, even if it conflicts with the provisions required to be implemented by the directive.[45]

In Case C-316/93 *Vaneetveld v Le Foyer*[46] an insurance directive required the Member States to amend their national laws so as to comply with the directive by not later than 31 December 1987 and to inform the Commission thereof. However, the provisions thus amended were not required to be applicable until 31 December 1988. The Court of Justice held that, in these circumstances, the provisions of the directive could not have direct effect until 31 December 1988.

Capable of creating rights for individuals In Case 8/81 *Becker v Finanzamt Münster-Innenstadt*[47] the Court of Justice held that:

> ...wherever the provisions of a directive appear, as far as their subject-matter is concerned, to be unconditional and sufficiently precise, those provisions may, in the absence of implementing measures adopted within the prescribed period, *be relied upon as against any national provision which is incompatible with the directive OR in so far as the provisions define rights which individuals are able to assert against the State.* (emphasis added)

The *Becker* judgment was relied upon by the Scottish Court of Session (Outer House) in *Kincardine and Deeside District Council v Forestry Commissioners*[48] in rejecting an argument that a directive could only be relied on by a private party in national proceedings where it conferred rights on that private party. However, in *Twyford Parish Council v Secretary of State for the Environment*[49] the English High Court ruled that *Becker* should not be interpreted in that way, and held that a private party could only rely on a directive in national proceedings where rights conferred on that party by the directive had been infringed, thereby causing him to suffer in some way as a result of the failure to accord him his rights.[50]

---

[44] Case 148/78 *Pubblico Ministero v Ratti* [1979] ECR 1629 paras 24 and 39–46. See also paras 17–22 of the Opinion of Advocate-General Jacobs in Case C-156/91 *Hansa Fleisch v Landrat des Kreises Schleswig-Flensburg* [1992] ECR I-5567, where he rejected an argument that a directive could have direct effect against a Member State even before the deadline for implementation has passed where the State has attempted to implement the directive before the end of the prescribed period, but has done so incorrectly.

[45] Case 244/78 *Union Laitière Normande v French Dairy Farmers* [1979] ECR 2663 paras 13–15. Cf paras 11–53 of the Opinion of Advocate-General Jacobs in Case C-129/96 *Inter-Environnement Wallonie v Région Wallonne* [1997] ECR I-00 (Opinion of 24 April 1997).

[46] [1994] ECR I-763 paras 15–19.

[47] [1982] ECR 53 para 25. See also paras 67–68 of the Opinion of Advocate-General Elmer in Case C-72/95 *Kraaijeveld* [1996] ECR I-5403.

[48] [1994] 2 CMLR 869 para 28.

[49] [1992] 1 CMLR 276 paras 54–68.

[50] It must now be doubted whether the *Twyford Parish Council* judgment is still good law in light of

The issue of whether a directive must be capable of creating rights for individuals in order to have direct effect is a difficult one which cannot be definitively resolved by reference to the existing case-law of the Court of Justice.[51] It is also, to a certain extent, a misleading question to ask in the context of English law given the distinction between public and private law. Whilst it is natural to talk of private law 'rights', it is clear that applicants may seek public law remedies if they can establish a sufficient 'interest' in doing so, regardless of whether the decision which they seek to challenge has affected any legally recognised rights which they claim to possess or not.[52] Indeed, the House of Lords has expressly recognised that a representative organisation, acting in the general interest, may seek a declaration that a particular Act of Parliament is in breach of Community law.[53]

In many cases the concepts of direct effect and individual rights will be closely interlinked, as a private party will seek to invoke a directive in national proceedings as a source of positive rights. However, in light of the judgment of the Court of Justice in *Becker* it appears appropriate to recognise that the two concepts are, in reality, logically distinct. Thus, it should not be necessary for a directive to be capable of creating rights for individuals in order for it to have direct effect, that is, to be capable of being invoked against the State in the national courts. It should be sufficient to show that it is sufficiently precise and unconditional. Thus, for example, if a private party or representative organisation has 'sufficient interest' to bring judicial review proceedings as a matter of domestic law, there is no reason in principle why it should not be entitled to rely on a directive against an incompatible national measure, provided the State is in breach of a precise and unconditional provision of a directive. However, if a party before a national court wishes to rely on a directive as an independent source of substantive law rights, *a fortiori* it must be required to show in addition that the directive, given its nature and content, is capable of giving rise to such rights. Where a directive is found to create such directly effective rights, the national courts are bound to ensure that they are effectively protected.[54]

Discretion as to means of implementation Where the result required to be achieved pursuant to a directive is clear, the fact that a Member State has a discretion as to how to achieve that result does not prevent the directive from having direct effect.[55] For example, in Case 71/85 *Netherlands v Federatie*

---

the speeches of the House of Lords in *R v Secretary of State for Employment, ex p Equal Opportunities Commission* [1995] 1 AC 1 and *R v Secretary of State for Employment, ex p Seymour-Smith* [1997] 1 WLR 473. See further at Ch 10, pp 193-194.

[51] The issue is discussed in some detail by Prechal, *Directives in European Community Law* (Oxford, 1995) at pp 124–129, who takes the view that 'It is ... incorrect to maintain that only Community law provisions which (are intended to) grant rights to individuals are able to produce direct effect'.

[52] See Ch 10, pp 179-180.

[53] *R v Secretary of State for Employment, ex p Equal Opportunities Commission* [1995] 1 AC 1.

[54] See Ch 6.

[55] Case 8/81 *Becker v Finanzamt Münster-Innenstadt* [1982] ECR 53 paras 28–30; Case 286/85

Nederlandse Vakbeweging[56] the Court of Justice considered article 4(1) of Council Directive 79/7[57] which precludes all discrimination on grounds of sex with regard to social security. Article 5 of the directive obliges Member States to take 'the measures necessary to ensure that any laws, regulations and administrative provisions contrary to the principle of equal treatment are abolished'. The Court held that the result to be achieved by virtue of article 4(1) was sufficiently precise to have direct effect, and the fact that the Member States had a discretion as to the measures to be adopted under article 5 did not prevent article 4(1) from having direct effect.

In Case 222/84 *Johnston v Chief Constable of the Royal Ulster Constabulary*[58] the Court of Justice held that the following provision had direct effect:

> Member States shall introduce into their national legal systems such measures as are necessary to enable all persons who consider themselves wronged by failure to apply to them the principle of equal treatment ... to pursue their claims by judicial process after possible recourse to other competent authorities.

In contrast, in Joined Cases C-6/90 and C-9/90 *Francovich and Bonifaci v Italy*[59] the Court of Justice held that Council Directive 80/987 on the protection of employees in the event of their employers' insolvency[60] did not have direct effect. The directive required the Member States to set up a guarantee system to meet employees' outstanding claims against insolvent employers. The Court found that the provisions of the directive defining those entitled to the guarantee and the content of the guarantee were precise and unconditional. However, the directive could not have direct effect as it gave the Member States a wide discretion as to the organisation, operation and financing of the institutions which were to be responsible for providing the guarantee.

Discretion as to result to be achieved Where a Member State has a choice as to the result to be achieved under a directive, an individual may enforce the directive against the Member State on the basis of the option which places the least onerous burden on the State. For example, in Joined Cases C-6/90 and C-9/90 *Francovich and Bonifaci v Italy*[61] Council Directive 80/987 permitted Member States to choose between three methods of calculation as to the period to which the guarantee of payment in the event of an employer's insolvency was to relate. Thus, Member States could provide that employees should be entitled

---

McDermott and Cotter v Minister for Social Welfare [1987] ECR 1453 para 15; Case C-271/91 *Marshall v Southampton and South-West Hampshire AHA* [1993] ECR I-4367 paras 33–38.

[56] [1986] ECR 3855 paras 12–23.

[57] Council Directive 79/7 of 19 December 1978 on the progressive implementation of the principle of equal treatment for men and women in matters of social security (OJ 1979 L6 p 24).

[58] [1986] ECR 1651 paras 13–21 (see also the Opinion of Advocate-General Darmon at para 4). See also paras 8–13 of the Opinion of Advocate-General Lenz in Case C-192/94 *El Corte Inglés v Bláquez Rivero* [1996] ECR I-1281.

[59] [1991] ECR I-5357 paras 10–27.

[60] Council Directive 80/987 of 20 October 1980 on the approximation of the laws of the Member States relating to the protection of employees in the event of the insolvency of their employer (OJ 1980 L283 p 23).

[61] [1991] ECR I-5357 paras 15–20.

to back-pay: (1) up to the date of the onset of their employer's insolvency; (2) up to the date that a notice of dismissal was issued on account of the insolvency; or (3) up to the date of the onset of insolvency, alternatively of the discontinuance of the employment relationship. This particular provision was clear and unconditional as it was possible to determine the minimum guarantee provided for by the Directive by taking the date which entailed the least liability for the guarantee institution, namely the onset of the employer's insolvency. This choice was the least onerous as it would provide for the shortest duration of the guarantee period.

In Case C-91/92 *Faccini Dori v Recreb*[62] a directive provided that a consumer was to have the right to renounce a contract which he had entered into by sending notice within a period of *not less* than seven days from the time when the trader informed him of this right. The Court of Justice held that this provision was capable of having direct effect as it was possible to determine the minimum protection which would have to be provided in order to comply with the directive.

Discretion as to derogations Where a directive imposes an obligation on a Member State which is unconditional and sufficiently precise, the fact that the directive permits derogations from that primary obligation will not prevent it from having direct effect, provided that the derogations are themselves sufficiently clearly defined. In Joined Cases C-358/93 and C-416/93 *Bordessa*[63] the Court of Justice held that a provision in a directive which required Member States to abolish certain restrictions on movements of capital had direct effect, even though the directive permitted Member States to 'take all requisite measures to prevent infringements of their laws and regulations, *inter alia* in the field of taxation and prudential supervision of financial institutions, or to lay down procedures for the declaration of capital movements for purposes of administrative or statistical information'. The Court held that the possible derogations were amenable to review by the national courts and therefore were not an obstacle to direct effect.

Notification provisions In Case 380/87 *Enichem Base v Comune di Cinisello Balsamo*[64] manufacturers of plastic bags sought the annulment of a municipal decision which restricted the supply, sale and distribution of plastic bags. The manufacturers argued that the decision was contrary to the provisions of a directive on waste[65] which required the Member States to inform the Commission of all draft rules intended to encourage the prevention, recycling and processing of waste. The Court of Justice held that although the municipal decision in issue should have been notified to the Commission, the failure to do

---

[62] [1994] ECR I-3325 paras 12–18.
[63] [1995] ECR I-361 paras 17–18 and 32–35. See also Joined Cases C-19/90 and C-20/90 *Karella v Minister of Industry, Energy and Technology* [1991] ECR I-2691 paras 17–23 and, by analogy, Case 41/74 *Van Duyn v Home Office* [1974] ECR 1337 paras 4–8 (concerning article 48 of the EC Treaty) [new art 39].
[64] [1989] ECR 2491 paras 2 and 12–24.
[65] Council Directive 75/442 on waste (OJ 1975 L194 p 39).

so could not be relied upon by the manufacturers in the national courts as the relevant provision of the directive only concerned relations between the Member States and the Commission, and did not give rise to any rights for individuals. However, in a later case, Case C-194/94 *CIA Security International v Signalson*,[66] the Court of Justice held that a provision in a directive requiring Member States to communicate draft technical regulations to the Commission did create rights for individuals which could be relied upon in the national courts. The Court distinguished *Enichem Base* on the basis that the purpose of the notification provision in that case was simply to inform the Commission, whereas in *CIA Security International* the notification provisions formed part of a specific procedure of Community control for national technical regulations.

(c) Vertical/horizontal direct effect

Vertical/horizontal direct effect The Court of Justice has consistently held[67] that where a directive has direct effect:

(1) It may be relied on by a private party against the State or an emanation of the State ('vertical direct effect').

(2) It may not be relied on:

    (*a*) by a private party against another private party ('horizontal direct effect'); or

    (*b*) by the State or an emanation of the State against a private party.

No horizontal direct effect The Court of Justice has consistently held that the basis for the vertical direct effect of directives is that article 189 of the EC Treaty [new art 249] provides that a directive is binding 'upon each Member State to which it is addressed'. It would therefore be unacceptable to allow a Member State (or an emanation of the State), which has failed to adopt the implementing measures required by a directive within the prescribed period, to be able to rely on that failure so as to deprive individuals of the rights which they should have had under the directive.[68]

Despite the views of certain Advocates-General,[69] the Court has refused to recognise directives as having horizontal direct effect. This refusal is based on the fact that while article 189 provides that directives impose obligations on Member States, it does not expressly provide that they should impose

---

[66] [1996] ECR I-2201 paras 42–50.

[67] [1986] ECR 723 paras 48–49; Case C-221/88 *ECSC v Acciaierie e Ferriere Busseni* [1990] ECR I-495 paras 22–23 (ECSC); Case C-91/92 *Faccini Dori v Recreb* [1994] ECR I-3325 paras 19–25; Case C-192/94 *El Corte Inglés v Blázquez Rivero* [1996] ECR I-1281 paras 15–21.

[68] For example, see Case 148/78 *Pubblico Ministero v Ratti* [1979] ECR 1629 para 22; Case 8/81 *Becker v Finanzamt Münster-Innenstadt* [1982] ECR 53 para 24; Case 152/84 *Marshall v Southampton and South-West Hampshire AHA* [1986] ECR 723 paras 47–48.

[69] Paragraph 12 of the Opinion of Advocate-General van Gerven in Case C-271/91 *Marshall v Southampton and South-West Hampshire AHA* [1993] ECR I-4367; paras 18–36 of the Opinion of Advocate-General Jacobs in Case C-316/93 *Vaneetveld v Le Foyer* [1994] ECR I-763; paras 43–73 of the Opinion of Advocate-General Lenz in Case C-91/92 *Faccini Dori v Recreb* [1994] ECR I-3325.

obligations on private parties. Under article 189, regulations and decisions are the only measures which the Community institutions may adopt which directly impose obligations on private parties. It follows that directives may not impose obligations on private parties by means of direct effect.[70]

The Court has also emphasised[71] that the lack of horizontal direct effect of directives does not mean that parties cannot protect their rights as:

(1) the national courts are under an obligation to interpret national law, so far as is possible, in conformity with directives;[72] and

(2) where a Member State has failed to implement a directive into its national legal system, a private party who suffers loss as a result may have a claim in damages against the State.[73]

The repeated refusal of the Court to recognise that directives may have horizontal direct effect has been the subject of criticism by academic commentators.[74]

Logical basis for direct effect It is sometimes said that the vertical direct effect of directives can be seen as a form of 'estoppel' operating against a Member State[75] or as an application of the principle that the State should not be permitted to rely on its own wrong.[76] However it is analysed, it is clear that a private party can rely on directly effective rights as a 'sword or a shield' in an action involving a Member State;[77] in other words, a private party can rely on directly effective rights to found an action against a Member State and can also rely on such rights as a defence to an action brought by a Member State.[78]

---

[70] Case C-91/92 *Faccini Dori v Recreb* [1994] ECR I-3325 paras 22–24; Case C-192/94 *El Corte Inglés v Blázquez Rivero* [1996] ECR I-1281 paras 15–17.

[71] Case C-91/92 *Faccini Dori v Recreb* [1994] ECR I-3325 paras 26–27; Case C-192/94 *El Corte Inglés v Blázquez Rivero* [1996] ECR I-1281 para 22.

[72] See at Ch 5, pp 86-96.

[73] See at Ch 7, pp 128-148.

[74] For example, see Walter van Gerven, 'The Horizontal Effect of Directive Provisions Revisited: The Reality of Catchwords', in *Institutional Dynamics of European Integration, Essays in Honour of Henry G Schermers* (Kluwer, 1994) at p 353; Takis Tridimas, 'Horizontal effect of directives: a missed opportunity?' (1994) 19 ELRev 619; William Robinson, case-note on Case C-91/92 *Faccini Dori v Recreb* [1995] CML Rev 629; Emmert and Pereira de Azevedo, '*Les jeux sont faits: rien ne va plus ou une nouvelle occasion perdue par la CJCE*' [1995] RTD eur 11.

[75] In Case 80/86 *Kolpinghuis Nijmegen* [1987] ECR 3969 Advocate-General Mischo explicitly referred, in para 7 of his Opinion, to the concept of estoppel in this context.

[76] This is supported by the judgment in Case 152/84 *Marshall v Southampton and South-West Hampshire AHA* [1986] ECR 723 paras 46–47. In Case C-188/89 *Foster v British Gas* [1990] ECR I-3313 Advocate-General van Gerven identified the basis of the judgment in *Marshall* as deriving from the principle *nemo auditur propriam turpitudinem allegans* or 'the State cannot plead its own wrong' (para 5 of the Advocate-General's Opinion).

[77] See the Opinion of Advocate-General Sir Gordon Slynn in Case 152/84 *Marshall* [1986] ECR 723 at 734.

[78] Case 152/84 *Marshall* itself is an example of an individual relying on the principle of direct effect as a 'sword'; see also Case 188/89 *Foster v British Gas* [1990] ECR I-3313. Case 148/78 *Pubblico Ministero v Ratti* [1979] ECR 1629 is an example of direct effect being used as a 'shield'.

Member States cannot rely on directives against individuals This is the logical result of the analysis of the direct effect of directives set out in Case 152/84 *Marshall v Southampton and South West Hampshire AHA*[79] where the Court of Justice held that:

> ... a directive may not of itself impose obligations on an individual and ... a provision of a directive may not be relied upon as such against such a person.

On the basis of this passage, the Court of Justice concluded in Case 14/86 *Pretore di Salò v Persons Unknown*[80] that a directive which has not been implemented by national legislation cannot impose obligations on individuals, either in regard to other individuals or, *a fortiori*, in relation to the State itself.[81]

It follows that a Member State cannot rely on an unimplemented directive in order to establish or aggravate the criminal liability of private parties who are alleged to have breached the directive.[82] This principle was applied in Case 80/86 *Kolpinghuis Nijmegen*[83] in which a company running a café was prosecuted under Dutch law for selling water called 'mineral water' which was, in fact, tap-water and carbon dioxide. The prosecution sought to rely upon a Council directive concerning mineral waters in support of its case. However, the directive had not been implemented into Dutch law at the time of the alleged offence. The Court of Justice, relying on its judgment in *Marshall*, reiterated that an unimplemented directive could not be relied upon against a private party in proceedings before a national court.

Emanations of the State may rely on directives against the State In Joined Cases 231/87 and 129/88 *Ufficio distrettuale delle imposte dirette di Fiorenzuola d'Arda v Comune di Carpaneto Piacentino*[84] the Court of Justice held that a local authority was entitled to rely on the directly effective provisions of a directive in an action brought against it by the district tax office.

(d) Emanation of 'the State'

Test for emanation of the State As directives only have vertical direct effect, the definition of what constitutes 'the State' is very important. The approach of

---

[79] [1986] ECR 723 para 48.

[80] [1987] ECR 2545 paras 19–20. See also Joined Cases 372 to 374/85 *Ministère Public v Traen* [1987] ECR 2141 paras 23–26.

[81] See *Organon Laboratories Ltd v Department of Health and Social Security* [1990] 2 CMLR 49 paras 51–52, per Mustill LJ, for a recognition of this principle by the English courts.

[82] Case 14/86 *Pretore di Salò v Persons Unknown* [1987] ECR 2545 paras 19–20; Case C-168/95 *Arcaro* [1996] ECR I-4705 paras 36–38; para 37 of the Opinion of Advocate-General Jacobs in Joined Cases C-304/94, C-330/94, C-342/94 and C-224/95 *Tombesi* [1997] ECR I-3561.

[83] [1987] ECR 3969 paras 6–10.

[84] [1989] ECR 3235 paras 29–33.

the Court of Justice is very broad.[85] In Case 188/89 *Foster v British Gas*[86] the Court held that:[87]

> ... a body, whatever its legal form, which has been made responsible, pursuant to a measure adopted by the State, for providing a public service under the control of the State and has for that purpose special powers beyond those which result from the normal rules applicable in relations between individuals is included in any event among the bodies against which the provisions of a directive capable of having direct effect may be relied upon.

Thus, the Court emphasised three factors as indicating that a body constitutes an emanation of the State:

(1) the obligation to provide a public service;

(2) control by the State;

(3) special powers.

However, the use of the words 'is included ... among' suggest that this was not intended to be an exhaustive test.[88] This conclusion is supported by Case 222/84 *Johnston v Chief Constable of the Royal Ulster Constabulary*[89] in which the Court of Justice held that the Chief Constable, as an official responsible for the direction of the police service, constituted a public authority, whatever his relations with other organs of the State, because he was charged with a public duty, ie the maintenance of public order and safety. In that case, it appeared, therefore, that the fact that the Chief Constable was under an obligation to fulfil a public duty was sufficient to qualify him as an emanation of the State.

As a general rule, it is for the national courts to decide whether a particular body constitutes an emanation of the State, applying the guidelines laid down by the Court of Justice.[90] However, the Court of Justice has previously made findings that particular bodies should be considered as emanations of the State: in particular, national tax authorities,[91] public health authorities,[92] police forces[93] and local or regional authorities.[94]

---

[85] At para 34 of his Opinion in Case C-2/94 *Denkavit International v Kamer van Koophandel en Fabrieken* [1996] ECR I-2827, Advocate-General Jacobs stated that 'the principle according to which an unimplemented directive can impose obligations only on the State is a principle which has to be understood broadly, if it is not to have arbitrary consequences'.

[86] [1990] ECR I-3313 paras 16–22.

[87] Ibid para 20.

[88] This is the view taken by the English courts; see, for example, *Rolls-Royce plc v Doughty* [1992] ICR 538 at 552B, per Mustill LJ and *National Union of Teachers v Governing Body of St Mary's Church of England (Aided) Junior School* [1997] 3 CMLR 630 para 17; [1997] EuLR 221 at 226B–F, per Schieman LJ.

[89] [1986] ECR 1651 para 56.

[90] Case 152/84 *Marshall v Southampton and South-West Hampshire AHA* [1986] ECR 723 paras 49–50; Case 188/89 *Foster v British Gas* [1990] ECR I-3313 paras 13–15.

[91] Case 8/81 *Becker v Finanzamt Münster-Innenstadt* [1982] ECR 53.

[92] Case 152/84 *Marshall v Southampton and South-West Hampshire AHA* [1986] ECR 723 para 50.

[93] Case 222/84 *Johnston v Chief Constable of the Royal Ulster Constabulary* [1986] ECR 1651 para 56. See also *R v Chief Constable of Sussex, ex p International Traders Ferry Ltd*, [1997] 2 CMLR 164 para 29 (CA), in which it was common ground that, for the purposes of article 34 of the EC Treaty [new art 29], the Chief Constable of Sussex could be regarded as an emanation of the UK Government.

[94] Case 103/88 *Costanzo v Comune di Milano* [1989] ECR 1839 para 31, in which the Court of Justice held that 'all organs of the administration, including decentralized authorities such as

In Case 31/87 *Beentjes v Netherlands*[95] the Court of Justice held that a body (in this case a local land consolidation committee responsible for the grant of public works contracts) was an emanation of the State in light of the following characteristics:

(1) its composition and functions were laid down by legislation;
(2) its members were appointed by a public body;
(3) its acts were subject to supervision by the State; and
(4) its activities were financed by the State.

Capacity in which body acts is irrelevant Where a body is an emanation of the State, an individual can rely on a directly effective directive against that body or organisation, regardless of the capacity in which the latter is acting, whether in the realm of public law, as a public authority, or in the realm of private law, for example as an employer.[96]

General approach of the English courts When the House of Lords considered the *Foster* case in light of the Court of Justice's ruling[97] Lord Templeman (with whom the rest of the House agreed) stated that he could see no justification for adopting 'a narrow or strained construction' of the ruling of the Court of Justice which was 'couched in terms of broad principle and purposive language'.[98] Similarly, in *National Union of Teachers v Governing Body of St Mary's Church of England (Aided) Junior School*[99] the Court of Appeal held that it was wrong to treat the tripartite test relied on by the Court of Justice in *Foster* as if it were a statutory definition.

In *Rolls-Royce plc v Doughty*[100] the Court of Appeal recognised that the test established by the Court of Justice in *Foster* is neither exhaustive nor conclusive. However, the court held that if a body satisfies all the factors of the *Foster* test it will only be in exceptional circumstances that the body will not be classified as an emanation of the State. Conversely, the absence of a factor will not necessarily preclude a body from being identified with the State, provided the applicant can point to an additional factor, not contemplated by the Court of Justice in *Foster*.[101]

The fact that a body is engaged in commercial activities does not prevent it from being an emanation of the State.[102] Similarly, a body may qualify as an

---

municipalities' are bound by directly effective provisions of directives.

[95] [1988] ECR 4635 paras 7–12.

[96] Case 152/84 *Marshall v Southampton and South-West Hampshire AHA* [1986] ECR 723 para 49; Case 222/84 *Johnston v Chief Constable of the Royal Ulster Constabulary* [1986] ECR 1651 para 56; Case 188/89 *Foster v British Gas* [1990] ECR I-3313 para 17.

[97] *Foster v British Gas* [1991] 2 AC 306.

[98] Ibid at 315E–H.

[99] [1997] 3 CMLR 630, para 44; [1997] EuLR 221 at 235D–E.

[100] [1992] ICR 538 at 552B–C.

[101] See also the position in *National Union of Teachers v Governing Body of St Mary's Church of England (Aided) Junior School* [1997] 3 CMLR 630; [1997] EuLR 221, where the Court of Appeal found that the governing body of a voluntary aided school constituted an emanation of the State, without expressly considering whether it had any 'special powers'. Discussed below at pp 76-77.

[102] *Foster v British Gas* [1991] 2 AC 306 at 314F–G; *Griffin v South West Water Services Ltd* [1995] IRLR 15 at para 94. See also fn 3 to para 5 of the Opinion of Advocate-General La Pergola in

emanation of the State even though it is not under the control of central government.[103]

In practice, the English courts have approached each case on its own facts, and have relied on individual factors as indicating that a body is an emanation of the State.[104]

Regulatory bodies In *R v London Boroughs Transport Committee, ex p Freight Transport Association Ltd*[105] the Court of Appeal held that the London Boroughs Transport Committee was an emanation of the State as it exercised delegated regulatory powers over the use of roads and vehicles in its area.

Commercial bodies In *Foster v British Gas*[106] Lord Templeman held that the British Gas Corporation (the 'BGC', which at that time was still a nationalised industry) was an emanation of the State on the basis of the following factors. BGC was subject to the control of the State as, pursuant to the Gas Act 1972:

(1) It was established as a body corporate pursuant to statute.

(2) It was under a duty to provide a public service.

(3) It was responsible to the minister acting on behalf of the State and was subject to directions given by the Secretary of State. In this respect, it was irrelevant that the State did not have day-to-day control over its affairs.

(4) It was not independent and its members were appointed by the State.

(5) The State was entitled to retain the surplus revenue of the BGC. Therefore, the State would benefit if the Directive could not be relied on against the BGC.

Further, BGC had 'special powers beyond those which result from the normal rules applicable in relations between individuals' as, pursuant to the 1972 Act, it had a statutory monopoly for the supply of gas.

In *Griffin v South West Water Services Ltd*[107] Blackburne J found that South West Water Services Ltd ('SWW'), a subsidiary of one of the privatised water companies, was an emanation of the State. It was common ground that SWW was under a duty to provide a public service, ie to supply water, and also that it had 'special powers'.[108] As to the question of whether SWW was subject to the control of the State, the judge made the following points:[109]

Case C-16/94 *Dubois and Général Cargo Services v Garonor Exploitation* [1995] ECR I-2421 for an indication of the circumstances in which a company governed by private law may be classified as an emanation of the State.

[103] *National Union of Teachers v Governing Body of St Mary's Church of England (Aided) Junior School* [1997] 3 CMLR 630; [1997] EuLR 221.

[104] This approach is similar to that adopted by the Court of Justice in Case 31/87 *Beentjes v Netherlands* [1988] ECR 4635 paras 7–12.

[105] [1990] 3 CMLR 495 at paras 30–31, per Neill LJ and at para 57 per Sir Roger Ormrod. This issue was not discussed by the House of Lords on appeal.

[106] [1991] 2 AC 306 at 313D–316A.

[107] [1995] IRLR 15 at paras 82–120.

[108] The court (at para 93) referred to a number of powers conferred by statute, eg the power to impose temporary hosepipe bans, the power (with the approval of the Secretary of State) compulsorily to purchase land, the power to make by-laws, and the power to lay pipes in streets.

[109] At para 94.

(1) The question is not whether the *body* in question is under the control of the State but whether the *public service* in question is under the control of the State.

(2) The legal form of the body is irrelevant.

(3) The fact that a body is a commercial concern is irrelevant.

(4) It is irrelevant that the body does not carry out any traditional functions of the State and is not an agent of the State.

(5) It is irrelevant that the State does not possess any day-to-day control over the activities of the body.

The court held that on an analysis of the Water Act 1991 and the terms of SWW's licence as a water company, it was apparent that it performed its public service subject to the control of the State as, *inter alia*, SWW's appointment as a water company was made by the Secretary of State pursuant to statute, and that appointment could be terminated or varied by the Secretary of State. In addition, the Secretary of State was given wide powers of control, by means of the conditions attached to SWW's licence, over the manner in which SWW was to carry out its functions.

In contrast, in *Rolls-Royce plc v Doughty*[110] the Court of Appeal held that Rolls-Royce was not an emanation of the State in spite of the fact that it was a public limited company in which all the shares were held by nominees on behalf of the Crown, and it had a particularly close trading relationship with the State in respect of its military production. The Court of Appeal held that, despite these factors, Rolls-Royce was in reality 'a commercial undertaking which as part of its business traded with the state on terms which were negotiated at arm's length'. Mustill LJ held[111] that even if it could be assumed that Rolls-Royce was subject to the control of the State, its services (in relation to military production) 'were provided to the state, and not to the public for purposes which were of benefit to the state'. Furthermore, there was no basis on which Rolls-Royce could be said to have any 'special powers'.

Education bodies In *National Union of Teachers v Governing Body of St Mary's Church of England (Aided) Junior School*[112] the Court of Appeal held that the governing body of a voluntary aided school qualified as an emanation of the State as:

(1) the school provided a public service, ie education;

(2) duties were imposed on the governors by general legislation and by a statutory instrument adopted by the local education authority ('LEA') which was itself accepted to be an emanation of the State;

(3) the Governors were subject to control by the LEA or the Secretary of State; and

(4) the LEA would derive direct financial benefit if the directive could not be relied on against the school.

---

[110] [1992] ICR 538, [1992] IRLR 126.
[111] [1992] ICR 538 at 552D–F.
[112] [1997] 3 CMLR 630 paras 41-43; [1997] EuLR 221 at 234F–235D.

There was no discussion as to whether the governing body had any 'special powers' within the meaning of the *Foster* approach established by the Court of Justice. This judgment therefore provides some authority for the proposition that a body may constitute an emanation of the State even where it does not satisfy all of the 'conditions' mentioned in *Foster* by the Court of Justice.

7. DIRECT EFFECT OF RECOMMENDATIONS AND OPINIONS

No direct effect Recommendations and opinions do not have direct effect. This follows from the wording of article 189 of the EC Treaty [new art 249] which states that 'Recommendations and opinions shall have no binding force'. Therefore, recommendations and opinions cannot impose obligations on, or create rights for the benefit of, individuals.

Legal effects This does not mean that recommendations can never produce any legal effects in the national legal systems of Member States. National courts are under an obligation to take recommendations into account in interpreting national legislation.[113]

8. DIRECT EFFECT OF INTERNATIONAL AGREEMENTS

International agreements If an agreement between the Community and third countries expressly provides that its terms are or are not to have direct effect, that will be determinative of the matter. If the agreement does not contain such an express provision, it is for Community law to decide whether or not an agreement has direct effect within the Community legal order.[114] As a matter of Community law, a provision of an international agreement will have direct effect when, having regard to the wording, purpose and nature of the agreement,[115] the provision contains a clear and precise obligation which is not dependent on the adoption of any subsequent measure.[116] The fact that the other contracting party does not give direct effect to the provisions of an international agreement in its own national legal system does not in itself prevent the agreement from having direct effect as a matter of Community law.[117]

The Court of Justice has found that provisions contained in Community association and co-operation agreements (particularly those which resemble

---

[113] Case 322/88 *Grimaldi v Fonds des Maladies* [1989] ECR 4407 paras 16–19.

[114] Case 104/81 *Hauptzollamt Mainz v Kupferberg* [1982] ECR 3641 para 17.

[115] The Court consistently held that the GATT could not have direct effect due to the 'great flexibility' of its provisions. See below.

[116] Case 12/86 *Demirel v Stadt Schwäbisch Gmünd* [1987] ECR 3719 para 14; Case C-18/90 *ONEM v Kziber* [1991] ECR I-199 para 15; Case C-277/94 *Taflan-Met* [1996] ECR I-4085 para 24. The Court of Justice has not yet ruled on whether provisions of international agreements can have horizontal as well as vertical direct effect. For a discussion of this issue, see I MacLeod, ID Henry and Stephen Hyett, *The External Relations of the European Communities* (Clarendon Press, 1996), at pp 135–138.

[117] Case 104/81 *Hauptzollamt Mainz v Kupferberg* [1982] ECR 3641 para 18.

provisions contained in the EC Treaty) are capable of having direct effect.[118] Furthermore, in Case C-192/89 *Sevince v Staatssecretaris*[119] the Court held that decisions adopted by a Council of Association, established pursuant to the EEC–Turkey Association Agreement, had direct effect.[120]

Provisions of free trade agreements between the Community and third countries have been held to have direct effect.[121]

Provisions of the Lomé (formerly Yaoundé) Conventions are capable of having direct effect.[122]

In Case T-115/94 *Opel Austria v Council*[123] the Court of First Instance held that the provisions of the EEA Agreement may have direct effect.

GATT In Joined Cases 21 to 24/72 *International Fruit Co v Produktschap voor Groenten en Fruit*[124] the Court of Justice held that the General Agreement on Tariffs and Trade ('GATT') could not have direct effect due to the 'great flexibility' of its provisions, in particular those concerning the possibility for derogations, measures to be taken when confronted with exceptional difficulties and the settlement of conflicts between the contracting parties. However, the Court has held that a GATT provision which was, in itself, sufficiently precise and unconditional could have direct effect where it had been incorporated into a Community regulation.[125]

The GATT has now been subsumed by the Agreement Establishing the World Trade Organisation ('WTO'). The WTO Agreement is broader in scope

---

[118] Case 17/81 *Pabst & Richarz v Hauptzollamt Oldenburg* [1982] ECR 1331 paras 25–27 (EEC–Greece Association Agreement); Case C-18/90 *ONEM v Kziber* [1991] ECR I-199 paras 15–23 (EEC–Morocco Co-operation Agreement); Case C-432/92 *R v MAFF, ex p Anastasiou* [1994] ECR I-3087 paras 21–27 (EEC–Cyprus Association Agreement); Case C-58/93 *Yousfi v Belgium* [1994] ECR I-1353 paras 16–19 (EEC–Morocco Co-operation Agreement); C-103/94 *Krid v CNAVTS* [1995] ECR I-719 paras 21–24 (EEC–Algeria Co-operation Agreement). See also *R v Secretary of State for the Home Department, ex p Narin* [1990] 1 CMLR 682, where the QBD considered whether the EEC–Turkey Association Agreement had direct effect.

[119] [1990] ECR I-3461 paras 13–26. See also Case C-277/94 *Taflan-Met* [1996] ECR I-4085 paras 23–38, where the Court held that a decision of the EC–Turkey Association Council did not have direct effect as it required the adoption of supplementary implementing measures before it could be applied.

[120] Applied in Case C-355/93 *Ergoglu v Land Baden-Württemberg* [1994] ECR I-5113 para 11. See also Case C-188/91 *Deutsche Shell v Hauptzollamt Hamburg-Harburg* [1993] ECR I-363 paras 16–17, where the Court of Justice held that measures adopted by the Joint Committee of the EC–EFTA Convention on a Common Transit Procedure formed part of Community law, but did not expressly consider the question of direct effect.

[121] Case 104/81 *Hauptzollamt Mainz v Kupferberg* [1982] ECR 3641 paras 9–27 (EEC–Portugal Free Trade Agreement).

[122] Case 87/75 *Bresciani v Amministrazione delle Finanze* [1976] ECR 129 paras 16–26 (Yaoundé Convention); Case C-469/93 *Amministrazione delle Finanze v Chiquita Italia* [1995] ECR I-4533 paras 34–35.

[123] [1997] ECR II-39 paras 100–102.

[124] [1972] ECR 1219. See also Case 9/73 *Schlüter v Hauptzollamt Lörrach* [1973] ECR 1135 paras 28–30; Case 266/81 *SIOT v Ministero delle Finanze* [1983] ECR 731 paras 26–31; Joined Cases 267 to 269/81 *Amministrazione delle Finanze v SPI and SAMI* [1983] ECR 801 paras 21–26; Case C-280/93 *Germany v Council* [1994] ECR I-4973 paras 105–112; Case C-469/93 *Amministrazione delle Finanze v Chiquita Italia* [1995] ECR I-4533 paras 24–29.

[125] Case 9/73 *Schlüter v Hauptzollamt Lörrach* [1973] ECR 1135 paras 24–34.

than the original GATT (which dealt essentially with trade in goods), as it also contains separate agreements concerning services (the General Agreement on Trade in Services or 'GATS') and intellectual property rights (the Agreement on Trade-Related Aspects of Intellectual Property Rights or 'TRIPs'). In addition, the WTO Agreement contains more formal rules for dispute resolution[126] than applied under the original GATT. The Court of Justice has yet to consider whether the WTO Agreement is capable of having direct effect. However, in *Lenzing AG v Courtaulds Fibres Ltd*[127] the English High Court held that neither the WTO Agreement nor the TRIPs Agreement was capable of having direct effect as a matter of Community law.[128]

---

[126] These rules are contained in the Understanding on Rules and Procedures Governing the Settlement of Disputes.

[127] [1997] EuLR 237.

[128] See also Philip Lee and Brian Kennedy, 'The Potential Direct Effect of GATT 1994 in European Community Law' (1996) *Journal of World Trade* 67.

Chapter 5

Interpretation

1. INTERPRETATION OF COMMUNITY LAW

English courts Section 3(1) of the European Communities Act 1972[1] obliges the English courts to follow the same principles of interpretation as the EC courts in relation to Community law provisions.[2]

Uniform interpretation Terms used in Community law must be interpreted and implemented uniformly throughout the Community, except when an express or implied reference is made to national law.[3] Thus, unless a Community measure makes express reference to the laws of the Member States[4] or of third countries[5] it must normally be given an independent and uniform interpretation applying the principles of interpretation applicable under Community law.

Courts of the other Member States In *Wagamama Ltd v City Centre Restaurants plc*[6] Laddie J held that, in interpreting the provisions of a directive intended to harmonise the laws of the Member States:

> ... it is right that British courts should pay regard to decisions in the courts of other member states on equivalent provisions in their law. However ... [i]t would not be right for an English court to follow the route adopted by the courts of another Member State if it is firmly of a different view simply because the other court expressed a view first. The scope of European legislation is too important to be decided on a first-past-the-post basis.

---

[1] Reproduced at Ch 1, pp 19–20.
[2] See *HP Bulmer Ltd v J Bollinger SA* [1974] 1 Ch 401 at 419C–G and 425C–426E, per Lord Denning.
[3] Case 29/69 *Stauder v Ulm* [1969] ECR 419 paras 3–4; Case 49/71 *Hagen v Einfuhr- und Vorratsstelle Getreide* [1972] ECR 23 para 6; Case 327/82 *Ekro Vee en Vleeshandel v Produktschap voor Vee en Vlees* [1984] ECR 107 para 11; Case C-273/90 *Meico-Fell v Hauptzollamt Darmstadt* [1991] ECR I-5569 paras 8–12; Case C-468/93 *Gemeente Emmen v Belastingdienst Grote Ondernemingen* [1996] ECR I-1721 para 22.
[4] Case T-260/94 *Air Inter v Commission* [1997] ECR II-997 para 115.
[5] Case 12/73 *Muras v Hauptzollamt Hamburg-Jonas* [1973] ECR 963 paras 5–8.
[6] [1997] EuLR 313 at 325C–D.

Language versions The official language versions of a Community measure are all equally authentic and must be given a uniform interpretation.[7] Where there is doubt as to the meaning of a provision of Community law in one language version, the Court may refer to the wording of the provision as it appears in the other official language versions.[8] Furthermore, the fact that one language version is clear and unambiguous does not prevent a court from referring to other language versions to establish whether they are consistent.[9] In the case of divergence between different language versions,[10] the provision in question should be interpreted by reference to the purpose and general scheme of the rules of which it forms a part.[11]

In Case C-338/95 *Wiener v Hauptzollamt Emmerich*[12] Advocate-General Jacobs indicated that national courts should not be required:

> ... to examine any Community measure in every one of the official Community languages (now numbering eleven – or twelve, if the Treaties and certain other basic texts are in issue). That would involve in many cases a disproportionate effort on the part of the national courts; moreover reference to all the language versions of Community provisions is a method which appears rarely to be applied by the Court of Justice itself, although it is far better placed to do so than the national courts. In fact the very existence of many language versions is a further reason for not adopting an excessively literal approach to the interpretation of Community provisions, and for putting greater weight on the context and general scheme of the provisions and on their object and purpose.

The fact that the Court of Justice is generally in a better position than a national court to give a purposive interpretation of a Community provision in the light of all its different language versions is an important factor for an

---

[7] Case 19/67 *Sociale Verzekeringsbank v Van der Vecht* [1967] ECR 345 at 354; Case 283/81 *CILFIT v Ministry of Health* [1982] ECR 3415 para 18; Case C-219/95P *Ferriere Nord v Commission* [1997] ECR I-4411 para 15.

[8] Case 19/67 *Sociale Verzekeringsbank v Van der Vecht* [1967] ECR 345 at 354; Case 9/79 *Wörsdorfer v Raad van Arbeid* [1979] ECR 2717 paras 5–9; Case C-327/91 *France v Commission* [1994] ECR I-3641 paras 30–35; Case C-177/95 *Ebony Maritime v Prefetto della Provincia* [1997] ECR I-1111 paras 30–31.

[9] Case C-219/95P *Ferriere Nord v Commission* [1997] ECR I-4411 paras 13–15.

[10] See Case C-64/95 *Lubella v Hauptzollamt Cottbus* [1996] ECR I-5105 paras 17–18, where the Court of Justice resolved a divergence in one language version, the German, solely by reference to the other language versions. See also Joined Cases C-283, 291 and 292/94 *Denkavit International v Bundesamt für Finanzen* [1996] ECR I-5063 paras 24–25. *Cf* Case 80/76 *North Kerry Milk Products v Minister for Agriculture and Fisheries* [1977] ECR 425 para 11.

[11] Case 6/74 *Moulijn v Commission* [1974] ECR 1287 paras 10–11; Case 30/77 *R v Bouchereau* [1977] ECR 1999 paras 13–14; Case C-449/93 *Rockfon A/S v Specialarbejderforbundet i Danmark* [1995] ECR I-4291 paras 26–28, and paras 33, 36 and 39 of the Opinion of Advocate-General Cosmas. See also Case 80/76 *Kerry Milk v Minister for Agriculture and Fisheries* [1977] ECR 425 para 11; Case 803/79 *Roudolff* [1980] ECR 2015 para 7; Case C-372/88 *Milk Marketing Board v Cricket St Thomas Estate* [1990] ECR I-1345 paras 15–18.

[12] Opinion of 10 July 1997, para 65.

English court to consider in deciding whether to make a preliminary reference to the Court of Justice under article 177 of the EC Treaty [new art 234].[13]

In *R v Commissioners of Customs and Excise, ex p EMU Tabac*[14] the Court of Appeal laid down the following guidelines for the use of different language versions of Community texts in the English courts:

> It seems to us that an appropriate way of approaching the problems posed by differing authentic versions is for any party which proposes to rely on a version in a foreign tongue to alert the other side to this fact and to seek to agree a translation of that version. If there is agreement it is improbable that the court will wish to disagree. Certainly, if it does then it should indicate its views so that the parties can comment on them. If there is no agreement between the parties then the appropriate course is for the parties' legal advisers first to consider whether it is really likely to be productive in the national court to pursue submissions based on disputed translations of text expressed in foreign languages. That will seldom be the case. If, however, the conclusion of one or more parties is that it is likely to be productive then evidence by translators should be filed on each side. That will usually suffice for the judge to be prepared to come to a decision on the point. Cross-examination is an option, but not one which we would generally wish to encourage. In a case where the difference in meaning attributed to the authentic versions is crucial to the decision and the point is irresolvable on the affidavits then the appropriate course may well be to refer the matter to the ECJ which is linguistically better placed than any national court to resolve the matter.

Purposive or teleological approach In interpreting provisions of Community law, it is necessary to adopt a 'teleological' or 'purposive' approach. This means that as well as considering the wording of a provision, the context in which that wording appears and the purpose of the specific legislative framework of which it forms a part should also be considered.[15]

In Case 67/79 *Fellinger v Bundesanstalt für Arbeit*[16] Advocate-General Mayras stated:

> ... this Court may not substitute its discretion for that of the Community legislature; when the meaning of the legislation is clear it has to be applied with that meaning,

---

[13] *Customs and Excise v ApS Samex* [1983] 1 All ER 1042 at 1055G–1056B; *R v Commissioners of Customs and Excise, ex p EMU Tabac Sarl* ([1997] EuLR 153 at 160O). See also Case 283/81 *CILFIT v Ministry of Health* [1982] ECR 3415 paras 16–21. See further at Ch 11, p 221.

[14] [1997] EuLR 153 at 160B–D. See also *National Smokeless Fuels Ltd v Commissioners of Inland Revenue* [1986] 3 CMLR 227 para 25; and *R v Ministry of Agriculture, Fisheries and Food, ex p Portman Agrochemicals Ltd* [1994] 3 CMLR 18 para 31.

[15] Case C-30/93 *AC–ATEL Electronics Vertriebs* [1994] ECR I-2305 para 21; Case C-70/94 *Werner v Germany* [1995] ECR I-3189 para 21; Case C-221/95 *Inasti v Hervein and Hervillier* [1997] ECR I-609 para 15. See Case T-493/93 *Hansa-Fisch v Commission* [1995] ECR II-575 paras 32–34 for an example of an approach based on wording and context; and Case C-412/93 *Leclerc-Siplec v TF1 Publicité* [1995] ECR I-179 paras 28–48 for an example of an approach based on purpose.

[16] [1980] ECR 535 at 550. See also Case C-116/92 *Charlton v CPS* [1993] ECR I-6755 para 14, where the Court of Justice stated that, *where a provision is insufficiently clear and explicit*, its scope should be determined by examining its objectives and the legal context in which it is situated.

even if the solution prescribed may be thought to be unsatisfactory. That is not to say, however, that the literal construction of a provision must always be accepted. If such a construction were to lead to a nonsensical result in regard to a situation which the Court believed the provision was intended to cover, certain doubts might properly be entertained in regard to it. In other words, the clear meaning and the literal meaning are not synonymous.

There have been many cases in which the Court has rejected a literal interpretation in favour of another which it found more compatible with the objective and the whole scheme of the legislation in question.

For example, in Case C-406/92 *The Tatry*[17] the Court of Justice, applying a purposive approach, held that the term 'irreconcilable' in article 22 of the Brussels Convention on Jurisdiction and the Enforcement of Judgments in Civil and Commercial Matters had a different meaning from the same term used in article 27(3) of the Convention.[18]

Reference to the preamble is particularly important when a court is required to interpret a measure in accordance with its purpose as the preamble will usually set out the specific aims of the measure.[19]

The House of Lords has recognised that English courts must adopt a purposive approach when interpreting Community law.[20]

Preambles Courts may refer to the preamble to a Community measure as an aid to its interpretation.[21] Where there is a discrepancy between the preamble and the text of the measure, the latter will prevail.[22] Whilst a recital in a preamble may constitute an aid to the interpretation of a legal rule, it cannot, in itself, constitute such a rule.[23]

---

[17] [1994] ECR I-5439 paras 54–57.

[18] In relation to the Brussels Convention, see also Case 133/81 *Ivenel v Schwab* [1982] ECR 1891 paras 10–20; Case 201/82 *Gerling v Amministrazione dello Stato* [1983] ECR 2503 para 11. See also *Re Harrods (Buenos Aires) Ltd* [1992] Ch 72 at 98G–99C, per Bingham LJ.

[19] For example, see Case C-83/96 *Provincia Autonoma di Trento v Dega* [1997] ECR I-5001 paras 15–19, in which the Court also referred to a Commission reply to a Parliamentary question as a means to establish the purpose of the measure in issue.

[20] *Pickstone v Freemans plc* [1989] 1 AC 66; *Litster v Forth Dry Dock & Engineering Co Ltd* [1990] 1 AC 546 at 558E and 559E; *Foster v British Gas* [1991] 2 AC 306 at 315C–316A. See also *Thomas v Chief Adjudication Officer* [1991] 2 QB 164 at 179–182, per Slade LJ; *Adams v Lancashire County Council* (1996) *The Times*, 25 January.

[21] For example: Case 63/75 *Fonderies Roubaix v Fonderies Roux* [1976] ECR 111 paras 17–19; Case 50/76 *Amsterdam Bulb v Produktschap voor Siergewassen* [1977] ECR 137 paras 9–11; Case C-346/88 *Lactina Panchaud v Germany* [1989] ECR 4579 para 10; Joined Cases C-71/91 and C-178/91 *Ponente Carni and Cispanda Costruzioni* [1993] I-1915 paras 19–20. For English authorities concerning the use of a preamble in interpreting a Community provision, see *R v Robert Tymen* [1980] 3 CMLR 101 paras 28–29; *National Smokeless Fuels Ltd v Commissioners of Inland Revenue* [1986] 3 CMLR 227 para 24.

[22] Joined Cases 154/83 and 155/83 *Hoche v BALM* [1985] ECR 1215 para 13.

[23] Case 215/88 *Casa Fleischhandels v BALM* [1989] ECR 2789 para 31. See also para 53 of the Opinion of Advocate-General Lenz in Case C-112/89 *Upjohn v Farzoo* [1991] ECR I-1703, where he stated that 'A preamble ... may not and cannot replace a Community legislative text; its role is merely to clarify an existing text'.

Consistent with the Treaty When the wording of secondary legislation is open to more than one interpretation, preference should be given to the interpretation which renders it consistent with the EC Treaty.[24]

Implementing measures Where a measure has been adopted pursuant to secondary legislation, it must, if possible, be given an interpretation which is consistent with the measure which it is intended to implement.[25]

General principles of Community law When the wording of secondary legislation is open to more than one interpretation, preference should be given to the interpretation which renders it consistent with the general principles of Community law[26] and/or the European Convention for the Protection of Human Rights.[27]

Preparatory measures/legislative proposals Courts are entitled to refer to preparatory documents (*travaux préparatoires*)[28] and legislative proposals[29] as aids to interpretation.[30] For example, in *R v London Boroughs Transport Committee ex p Freight Transport Association Ltd*[31] the House of Lords referred to a Commission Green Paper as an aid to interpretation. In *R v Stock Exchange, ex p Else (1982) Ltd*[32] the Court of Appeal, when called upon to construe a directive, was referred (at its own request) to the proposal from the Commission, the Opinion of the European Parliament and the Opinion of the Economic and Social Committee. In Case C-83/96 *Provincia Autonoma di Trento v Dega*[33] the Court of Justice referred to an Opinion of the Economic and Social Committee.

---

[24] Case 218/82 *Commission v Council* [1983] ECR 4063 para 15; Joined Cases 201/85 and 202/85 *Klensch v Secrétaire d'Etat* [1986] ECR 3477 para 21; Case 220/83 *Commission v France* [1986] ECR 3663 para 15; Case C-135/93 *Spain v Commission* [1995] ECR I-1651 para 37; Case C-105/94 *Celestini v Saar-Sektkellerei Faber* [1997] ECR I-2971 para 32.

[25] Case C-90/92 *Tretter v Hauptzollamt Stuggart-Ost* [1993] ECR I-3569 para 11; Case C-61/94 *Commission v Germany* [1996] ECR I-3989 para 52.

[26] Case C-314/89 *Rauh v Hauptzollamt Nürnberg-Fürth* [1991] ECR I-1647 paras 17–24 (protection of legitimate expectations); Joined Cases C-90/90 and C-91/90 *Neu v Secrétaire d'Etat* [1991] ECR I-3617 paras 11–15 (freedom to pursue a trade or profession); Case C-98/91 *Herbrink v Minister van Landbouw, Natuurbeheer en Visserij* [1994] ECR I-223 para 9 (protection of legitimate expectations); Case C-105/94 *Celestini v Saar-Sektkellerei Faber* [1997] ECR I-2971 paras 32–37 (non-discrimination and proportionality).

[27] Paragraph 9 of the Opinion of Advocate-General van Gerven in Case C-273/90 *Meico-Fell v Hauptzollamt Darmstadt* [1991] ECR I-5569.

[28] Case 130/87 *Retter v Caisse de pension des employés privés* [1989] ECR 865 para 16.

[29] Case C-449/93 *Rockfon v Specialarbejderforbundet i Danmark* [1995] ECR I-4291 para 33 (Commission proposal for a directive); paras 42–43 of the Opinion of Advocate-General Léger in Case C-84/94 *United Kingdom v Council* [1996] ECR I-5755 (proposal made by Denmark at the Inter-Governmental Conference on the Single Act).

[30] The position in relation to the use of UK parliamentary materials is discussed below at pp 95-96.

[31] [1991] 1 WLR 828 at 839A–841B.

[32] [1993] QB 534 at 548, [1993] 1 All ER 420 at 429b–c. See also *Scotch Whisky Association v Glen Kella Distillers Ltd* [1997] EuLR 455 at 464E–466D, (reference to Opinion of Economic and Social Committee).

[33] [1997] ECR I-00 para 14 (judgment of 17 September 1997).

Council minutes/declarations As a general rule, a declaration contained in the minutes of meetings concerning the preparation or adoption of an act cannot be relied upon as an aid to the interpretation of that act[34] unless the declaration is expressly referred to in the provisions of the act.[35]

Equally, the Court has refused to have regard to expressions of intent made by Member States in the context of Council meetings at which a particular act was adopted.[36] In *R v Secretary of State for the Home Department, ex p Flynn*[37] the English High Court proceeded (without deciding the issue) on the basis that the General Declaration adopted by the Member States at the time when they signed the Single European Act could not be relied on as an aid to the interpretation of that Act.

Derogations Any derogations from rights arising under the EC Treaty must be narrowly construed.[38] A party who wishes to rely on a derogation bears the burden of proof in showing that it is applicable.[39]

---

[34] Case 429/85 *Commission v Italy* [1988] ECR 843 paras 8–9; Case C-292/89 *R v Immigration Appeal Tribunal, ex p Antonissen* [1991] ECR I-745 paras 17–18; Case C-306/89 *Commission v Greece* [1991] ECR I-5863 paras 6–8; Joined Cases C-197/94 and C-252/94 *Bautiaa and Société Française Maritime* [1996] ECR I-505 para 51; Case C-25/94 *Commission v Council* [1996] ECR I-1469, para 38. Contrast Case C-310/90 *Nationale Raad van de Orde van Architecten v Egle* [1992] ECR I-177 para 12, where the Court of Justice referred to a joint declaration of the Commission and the Council contained in the minutes of the session at which a directive was adopted, but only in order to confirm the interpretation the Court had given to that directive. This issue was discussed by Laddie J in *Wagamama Ltd v City Centre Restaurants plc* [1997] EuLR 313 at 322D–F, who came to the conclusion that minutes of Council meetings cannot be used in order to construe a directive, as such minutes are confidential and citizens of the European Union should be able to determine the scope of the laws which affect them on the basis of publicly available material.

[35] Case C-329/95 *VAG Sverige* [1997] ECR I-2675 para 23.

[36] Joined Cases C-283, 291 and 292/94 *Denkavit Internationaal v Bundesamt für Finanzen* [1996] ECR I-5063 paras 28–29. See also Case 278/84 *Germany v Commission* [1987] ECR 1 paras 17–18, where the Court of Justice held that it was not possible to take account of negotiations between a Member State and one of the Community institutions in interpreting a provision of a Community regulation which was of general scope.

[37] [1995] 3 CMLR 397 paras 19–36.

[38] Case C-40/93 *Commission v Italy* [1995] ECR I-1319 para 23; Case T-105/95 *WWF UK v Commission* [1997] ECR II-313 para 56. See also, for example, Case 2/74 *Reyners v Belgium* [1974] ECR 631 para 43 (freedom of establishment, article 55 of the EC Treaty [new art 45]); Case 41/74 *Van Duyn v Home Office* [1974] ECR 1337 (free movement of workers, article 48(3) of the EC Treaty [new art 39(3)]); Case C-70/93 *BMW v ALD* [1995] ECR I-3439 para 28 (block exemption, article 85 of the EC Treaty [new art 81]); Case C-450/93 *Kalanke v Bremen* [1995] ECR I-3051 para 21 (Equal Treatment Directive); Case T-60/96 *Merck v Commission* [1997] ECR II-849 para 47 (free movement of goods); Case T-260/94 *Air Inter v Commission* [1997] ECR II-997 para 135 (article 90(2) of the EC Treaty [new art 86(2)]).

[39] For example, see Case 251/78 *Denkavit Futtermittel v Minister für Ernährung, Lanwirtschaft und Forsten* [1979] ECR 3369 para 24 (free movement of goods, article 36 of the EC Treaty [new art 30]); Joined Cases 43 and 63/82 *VBVB and VBBB v Commission* [1984] ECR 19 para 52 (article 85(3) of the EC Treaty [new art 81(3)]); Case C-328/92 *Commission v Spain* [1994] ECR I-1569 paras 15–16 (public procurement); Case C-57/94 *Commission v Italy* [1995] ECR I-1249 para 23 (public procurement).

Application by analogy Where a measure contains an omission which is incompatible with a general principle of Community law, a court may remedy that omission by applying the rules contained in a different measure which is very similar to the one applicable in the case before it.[40] For example, where a regulation regulating imports from one third country contains provisions intended to protect the legitimate expectations of traders, whilst a similar regulation dealing with imports from a different third country fails to do so, the Court may apply the rules contained in the first regulation by analogy when interpreting the second regulation in order to fill the gap.[41]

International agreements Community secondary legislation must be interpreted, so far as possible, in a manner that is consistent with international agreements concluded by the Community.[42] Agreements to which all the Member States are parties have also been relied on by the Court of Justice as an aid to interpretation.[43] However, where some but not all the Member States are parties to an international agreement, it will not constitute a basis for the interpretation of Community law.[44]

In Case C-70/94 *Werner v Germany*[45] the Court of Justice referred to the General Agreement on Tariffs and Trade ('GATT') as an aid to the interpretation of a Community regulation governing international trade.

In Case C-84/95 *Bosphorous v Minister for Transport, Energy and Communications*[46] the Court of Justice referred to a UN Resolution in order to interpret a Community sanctions regulation which had been adopted in order to implement in the Community certain resolutions adopted by the UN Security Council.

Comparative law techniques Certain Advocates-General have made reference to the law of the United States as a potential aid to the interpretation of Community law.[47]

---

[40] Case T-489/93 *Unifruit Hellas v Commission* [1994] ECR II-1201 para 57.

[41] Case 165/84 *Krohn v BALM* [1985] ECR 3997 para 14.

[42] C–61/94 *Commission v Germany* [1996] ECR I-3989 para 52. See also Case C-316/95 *Generics v Smith Kline & French Laboratories* [1997] ECR I-3929 para 20, where the Court relied on the TRIPs Agreement (the Agreement on Trade-Related Aspects of Intellectual Property Rights, concluded as part of the World Trade Organization ('WTO') Agreement) as an aid to interpretation.

[43] Case 289/86 *Happy Family v Inspecteur der Omzetbelasting* [1988] ECR 3655 para 25.

[44] Case 269/86 *Mol v Inspecteur der Invoerrechten en Accijnzen* [1988] ECR 3627 para 24. Cf Case C-343/89 *Witzemann v Hauptzollamt München-Mitte* [1990] ECR I-4477 para 14, and para 23 of the Opinion of Advocate-General Jacobs, where the Court relied on a Convention to which all of the Member States were signatories and which had been ratified by all the Member States except Luxembourg.

[45] [1995] ECR I-3189 para 23. See also paras 51–52 of the Opinion of Advocate-General Jacobs in Case C-124/95 *R v HM Treasury, ex p Centro-com* [1997] ECR I-81, where he referred to the GATT as an aid to the interpretation of the concept of common commercial policy established under article 113 of the EC Treaty [new art 133].

[46] [1996] ECR I-3953 paras 13–14; see also paras 35 and 40 of the Opinion of Advocate-General Jacobs.

[47] See, for example, pp 688–691 of the Opinion of Advocate-General Mayras in Case 48/69 *ICI v Commission* ('Dyestuffs') [1972] ECR 619 (competition law); pp 936–937 of the Opinion of

Judgments of the EC courts Judgments of the EC courts contain two main parts: (a) the 'grounds', which contain the detailed reasoning of the court and which are presented in the form of numbered paragraphs; and (b) the 'operative part' or 'dispositif', which appears at the end of the judgment and contains the ruling of the court. The EC courts have consistently held that the operative part of a judgment must be interpreted in light of what is stated in the grounds.[48]

Commission decisions The operative part of a Commission decision must be interpreted in light of the reasoning upon which it is based.[49]

2. INTERPRETATION OF INTERNATIONAL AGREEMENTS CONCLUDED BY THE COMMUNITY

International agreements The fact that an international agreement contains a provision which has comparable, similar or even identical wording to a provision of the EC Treaty does not necessarily mean that it should be interpreted in the same manner as the equivalent EC provision. The provisions of an international agreement must be interpreted in the context of the agreement itself and with reference to its own specific terms and objectives.[50] Generally, the greater the degree of economic integration provided for by the international agreement, the more likely it is that it will be interpreted in the same manner as the EC Treaty.[51]

Uniform interpretation International agreements which are binding on the Community must be interpreted and applied uniformly in all the Member States. The Court of Justice therefore has jurisdiction to rule on the interpretation of international agreements under article 177 of the EC Treaty [new art 234].[52]

Advocate-General Warner in Case 96/80 *Jenkins v Kingsgate (Clothing Productions)* [1981] ECR 911 (sex discrimination); p 1616 of the Opinion of Advocate-General Darmon in Case 170/84 *Bilka v Weber von Hartz* [1986] ECR 1607 (sex discrimination); pp 5220–5224 of the Opinion of Advocate-General Darmon in Joined Cases 89 and others/85 *Ahlström v Commission* [1988] ECR 5193 (competition law); paras 39–40 of the Opinion of Advocate-General Lenz in Case C-480/93P *Zunis Holding v Commission* [1996] ECR I-1 (competition law).

[48] Joined Cases 97, 193, 99 and 215/86 *Asteris v Commission* [1988] ECR 2181 para 27; Case T-275/94 *CB v Commission* [1995] ECR II-2169 para 62.

[49] Joined Cases T-244/93 and T-486/93 *TWD v Commission* [1995] ECR II-2265 para 46.

[50] Case C-163/90 *Administration des Douanes v Legros* [1992] ECR I-4625 para 23 (EEC–Sweden Free Trade Agreement); Case C-312/91 *Metalsa* [1993] ECR I-3751 paras 10–11 (EEC–Austria Free Trade Agreement); Case C-469/93 *Amministrazione delle Finanze v Chiquita Italia* [1995] ECR I-4533 para 52 (Fourth Lomé Convention). See also Case 270/80 *Polydor v Harlequin Record Shops* [1982] ECR 329 (EEC–Portugal Free Trade Agreement); Case 104/81 *Hauptzollamt Mainz v Kupferberg* [1982] ECR 3641 paras 28–31 (EEC–Portugal Free Trade Agreement).

[51] See Case T-115/94 *Opel Austria v Council* [1997] ECR II-39 paras 103–118, where the Court of First Instance held that the term 'charge having equivalent effect' should have the same meaning under the EEA Agreement as it does under the EC Treaty.

[52] Joined Cases 267 to 269/81 *Amministrazione delle Finanze v SPI and SAMI* [1983] ECR 801 paras 14–15.

Vienna Conventions The Court of Justice has referred to the Vienna Convention of 23 May 1969 on the Law of Treaties and the Vienna Convention of 21 March 1986 on the Law of Treaties between States and International Organizations or between International Organizations as an aid to the interpretation of international agreements concluded by the Community.[53]

In *R v Secretary of State for the Home Department, ex p Flynn*[54] the English High Court held that the Vienna Convention could be relied on as an aid to interpretation of the Treaties establishing the European Community, including the Single European Act.

3. INTERPRETATION OF NATIONAL LAW

Rules of interpretation The normal approach to statutory interpretation under English law is that the intention of Parliament must be ascertained from the words used in the legislation, and those words are to be construed according to their plain and ordinary meaning. However, as a result of the case-law of the Court of Justice, special rules of construction apply in relation to national legislation which falls within an area of Community competence.[55] In particular, the national courts are under an obligation to interpret national law in conformity with Community law[56] whenever possible.[57] However, national courts are not obliged to distort the meaning of national legislation.[58]

The obligation of interpretation is of particular importance in relation to directives, and applies to all national legislation, whether or not it was specifically adopted to implement a directive, and whether it was adopted before or after the implementation date of a directive.[59]

Where it is not possible to interpret a national measure in accordance with a directive, the Court should then consider whether the national measure should be disapplied on the basis of the doctrine of direct effect.[60] Where a private party

---

[53] Case C-312/91 *Metalsa* [1993] ECR I-3751 paras 12–13; *Opinion 1/91* [1991] ECR I-6079 para 14; Case C-327/91 *France v Commission* [1994] ECR I-3641 para 25; Case C-432/92 *R v MAFF, ex p Anastasiou* [1994] ECR I-3087 paras 43, 46 and 50.

[54] [1995] 3 CMLR 397 paras 23–30 (QBD).

[55] See *Bulmer Ltd v Bollinger SA* [1974] 1 Ch 401 at 425C–426E, per Lord Denning MR.

[56] Note the judgment of the English High Court (QBD) in *R v Secretary of State for Trade and Industry, ex p Duddridge* [1995] 3 CMLR 231 paras 59–60, where Smith J held that, in relation to article 130r of the EC Treaty [new art 174], there was no obligation to interpret national law in accordance with Community policy as opposed to a Community obligation.

[57] Case 157/86 *Murphy v Bord Telecom Eireann* [1988] ECR 673 para 11 and Case C-165/91 *Van Munster v Rijksdienst voor pensioenen* [1994] ECR I-4661 paras 32–34 (treaty articles); Case C-106/89 *Marleasing v La Comercial Internacional de Alimentación* [1990] ECR I-4135 (directives). See also Case C-322/88 *Grimaldi v Fonds des maladies* [1989] ECR 4407 paras 18–19 (recommendations).

[58] See below at pp 90–93.

[59] Case C-106/89 *Marleasing v La Comercial Internacional de Alimentación* [1990] ECR I-4135 para 8; Case C-334/92 *Wagner Miret* [1993] ECR I-6911 para 20; Case C-421/92 *Habermann-Beltermann* [1994] ECR I-1657 para 10; Case C-91/92 *Faccini Dori v Recreb* [1994] ECR I-3325 para 26.

[60] See Case C-118/94 *Associazione Italiana per il WWF v Regione Veneto* [1996] ECR I-1223

cannot rely on his rights under a directive by reliance either on the obligation of interpretation or on the doctrine of direct effect, he may have a claim in damages against the State for failure to implement the directive properly or at all.[61]

Relationship with direct effect The obligation to interpret national law in conformity with Community law is of particular importance where a directive does not have direct effect or in cases between private parties. Directives do not have horizontal direct effect; a private party cannot rely on an unimplemented directive against another private party in the national courts.[62] However, where the national legislation is capable of being interpreted in accordance with a directive, the practical result of the obligation of interpretation is that a private party may be able to rely indirectly on the directive as against another private party (sometimes referred to as 'indirect effect')[63].

Obligation of interpretation The obligation of interpretation was recognised by the Court of Justice in Case 14/83 *Von Colson and Kamann v Land Nordrhein-Westfalen.*[64] The Court held that:

> ... the Member States' obligation arising from a directive to achieve the result envisaged by the directive and their duty under Article 5 of the Treaty[65] to take all appropriate measures, whether general or particular, to ensure the fulfilment of that obligation, is binding on all the authorities of Member States including, for matters within their jurisdiction, the courts. It follows that, in applying the national law and in particular the provisions of national law specifically introduced in order to implement [a directive], national courts are required to interpret their national law in the light of the wording and the purpose of the directive in order to achieve the result referred to in the third paragraph of Article 189.

National legislation predates Community provisions Following the decision in *Von Colson*, the obligation of interpretation was applied in subsequent cases in respect of national legislation which had been passed specifically to implement a directive.[66] However, it was only in Case C-106/89 *Marleasing v La Comercial Internacional de Alimentación*[67] that the Court of Justice clarified the general scope of the obligation to interpret all national legislation in conformity with a directive where possible and not just national legislation which had been passed specifically to implement a directive or

---

paras 18–19.
[61] See Ch 7, pp 128–148.
[62] See Ch 4, pp 70–72.
[63] However, see below at p 94.
[64] [1984] ECR 1891 para 26.
[65] Article 5 of the EC Treaty [new art 10] provides, *inter alia*:
    Member States shall take all appropriate measures, whether general or particular, to ensure fulfilment of the obligations arising out of this Treaty or resulting from action taken by the institutions of the Community.
[66] Case 79/83 *Harz v Deutsche Tradax* [1984] ECR 1921 para 26; Case 222/84 *Johnston v Chief Constable of the Royal Ulster Constabulary* [1986] ECR 1651 para 53; Case 80/86 *Kolpinghuis Nijmegen* [1987] ECR 3969 para 12; *Apple and Pear Development Council v Commissioners of Customs and Excise* [1987] 2 CMLR 634 at 654, para 27, per Lord Brightman (HL); Case 125/88 *Nijman* [1989] ECR 3533 para 6; *J Rothschild Holdings plc v Commissioners of Inland Revenue* [1989] 2 CMLR 621 paras 53–54 (CA).
[67] [1990] ECR I-4135.

legislation passed after the implementation date of the directive had expired. In this case, Marleasing SA brought an action in the Spanish courts seeking, *inter alia*, the annulment of the contract of association of La Comercial on the basis that its establishment was a sham transaction designed to defraud the creditors of one of the founders of La Comercial. Marleasing relied on certain articles of the Spanish Civil Code which provided that contracts without 'cause', or of which the 'cause' was unlawful, had no legal effect. However, article 11 of Directive 68/151,[68] which post-dates the Spanish Civil Code, contains an exhaustive list of the grounds upon which the nullity of a company may be ordered. These grounds do not include lack of 'cause'. At the time of the case, the Spanish Government had not yet implemented Directive 68/151. The Court of Justice held that:[69]

> ... in applying national law, whether the provisions in question were adopted before or after the directive, the national court called upon to interpret it is required to do so, as far as possible, in the light of the wording and the purpose of the directive in order to achieve the result pursued by the latter... .

In *Webb v Emo Air Cargo (UK) Ltd*[70] Lord Keith recognised that the decision in *Marleasing* imposes an obligation on the English courts to interpret national law in accordance with Community law as far as possible, regardless of whether the national legislation was adopted before or after the Community legislation.[71]

National legislation must be open to interpretation Following the decision in *Marleasing*, there was considerable academic debate[72] as to whether the Court of Justice in effect had introduced the principle of horizontal direct effect for directives by means of the obligation of interpretation. This argument rests on an analysis of the judgment which states that the national courts are under an absolute duty to interpret national law in conformity with a directive, even where, on its face, the national law conflicts with the directive. This 'absolutist' view of *Marleasing* is not borne out by a careful analysis of the decision. The Court of Justice specifically emphasised[73] that directives cannot have horizontal direct effect, as established in Case 152/84 *Marshall v Southampton and South*

---

[68] Council Directive 68/151 on co-ordination of safeguards which, for the protection of the interests of Member States and others, are required by Member States of companies within article 58 of the EEC Treaty, with a view to making such safeguards equivalent throughout the Community (OJ 1968 L65 p 8, Special Edition 1968(I) p 41).

[69] [1990] ECR I-4135 para 8.

[70] [1993] 1 WLR 49 at 59G, per Lord Keith.

[71] To the extent that the judgments in *Duke v GEC Reliance Ltd* [1988] 1 AC 618 and *Finnegan v Clowney Youth Training Programme Ltd* [1990] 2 AC 407 suggest otherwise, they should be treated as incorrect following the decision of the Court of Justice in *Marleasing*, and the House of Lords' decision in *Webb v Emo Air Cargo (UK) Ltd*.

[72] For example, see Mead, 'The Obligation to Apply European Law: Is Duke Dead?' (1991) 16 EL Rev 490; de Búrca, 'Giving Effect to European Community Directives' (1992) 55 MLR 215; Greenwood, 'Effect of EEC Directives in National Law' (1992) CLJ 3; Maltby, 'Marleasing: What is All the Fuss About?' (1993) 109 LQR 301.

[73] [1990] ECR I-4135 para 6.

West Hampshire AHA.[74] Furthermore, the Court of Justice held that the obligation to interpret national law in light of a Community directive applies only 'as far as possible'.[75]

Admittedly, the decision of the Court of Justice in *Marleasing* lacks depth of argument. However, the Opinion of Advocate-General van Gerven is more fully argued and dispels the view that *Marleasing* imposes an absolute obligation of interpretation on national courts. The Advocate-General described the obligation of interpretation in the following terms:[76]

> The obligation to interpret a provision of national law in conformity with a directive arises whenever the provision in question is to any extent open to interpretation. In those circumstances the national court must, having regard to the usual methods of interpretation in its legal system, give precedence to the method which enables it to construe the national provision concerned in a manner consistent with the directive.

On the particular facts of the case, Advocate-General van Gerven considered that the Spanish law was open to interpretation in order to conform with the directive.[77] This view is borne out by the decision in *Von Colson* itself, where the Court of Justice stated that the obligation on a national court to interpret national law in conformity with Community law applies only 'insofar as it is given discretion to do so under national law'.[78]

In Case C-468/93 *Gemeente Emmen v Belastingdienst Grote Ondernemingen*[79] Advocate-General Fennelly stated that the obligation of interpretation 'cannot go so far as to require a national court to do violence to or expressly contradict the terms of national law'.

Thus, according to the case-law of the Court of Justice, national courts are obliged to interpret national legislation in conformity with a directive only where the legislation is open to such an interpretation. They are not obliged to interpret the national legislation *contra legem*, in a way which is clearly contradictory to the words used.[80] This approach is consistent with the view of the English courts that they are not obliged to 'distort' the meaning of national

---

[74] [1986] ECR 723. See Ch 4, pp 70–72.

[75] [1990] ECR I-4135 para 8. This formulation has been consistently adopted by the Court of Justice in subsequent cases: see Case C-334/92 *Wagner Miret* [1993] ECR I-6911 para 20; Case C-421/92 *Habermann-Beltermann* [1994] ECR I-1657 para 10; Case C-91/92 *Faccini Dori v Recreb* [1994] ECR I-3325 para 26.

[76] Paragraph 8 of the Opinion.

[77] Paragraph 20 of the Opinion.

[78] [1984] ECR 1891 para 28.

[79] [1996] ECR I-1721, paras 33–34 of the Opinion. See also paras 38–42 of the Opinion of Advocate-General Elmer in Case C-168/95 *Arcaro* [1996] ECR I-4705 for useful guidance as to how the obligation of interpretation is to be applied in practice. In particular, he stated that the obligation of interpretation cannot be applied 'so as to undertake an actual redrafting of the provisions of national law'.

[80] See also para 10 of the Opinion of Advocate-General van Gerven in Case C-271/91 *Marshall v Southampton and South West Hampshire AHA* [1993] ECR I-4367.

legislation.[81] In *Duke v GEC Reliance Ltd*,[82] a case which predated *Marleasing*, the House of Lords was required to consider whether the UK Equal Pay Act 1970 and Sex Discrimination Act 1975 should be interpreted in a manner which gave effect to the Equal Treatment Directive[83] which was adopted in 1976. Lord Templeman held:[84]

> Of course a British court will always be willing and anxious to conclude that United Kingdom law is consistent with Community law. Where an Act is passed for the purpose of giving effect to an obligation imposed by a directive or other instrument a British court will seldom encounter difficulty in concluding that the language of the Act is effective for the intended purpose. But the construction of a British Act of Parliament is a matter of judgment to be determined by British courts and to be derived from the language of the legislation considered in the light of the circumstances prevailing at the date of enactment.

Lord Templeman concluded that the British courts were not entitled to distort the meaning of a British statute in order to give effect to Community legislation, and held that, in the particular case, the relevant words of the British statute were not 'reasonably capable' of bearing a meaning which conformed with Community law.[85]

Lord Keith considered this issue in *Webb v Emo Air Cargo (UK) Ltd*[86] where he held:[87]

> ... it is for a United Kingdom court to construe domestic legislation in any field covered by a Community Directive so as to accord with the interpretation of the Directive as laid down by the European Court of Justice, if that can be done without distorting the meaning of the domestic legislation: *Duke v GEC Reliance Systems Ltd* [1988] AC 618, 639-640, *per* Lord Templeman.[88]

Lord Keith analysed the *Marleasing* decision as imposing an obligation in these terms:[89]

---

[81] In relation to Scots law, see *Stirling District Council v Allan* (1995) *The Times*, 9 May, where the Court of Session (Inner House) held that a directive could not affect the construction of a national measure 'except to the extent that there might be an ambiguity' in the meaning of that measure.

[82] [1988] 1 AC 618. Applied in *Organon Laboratories Ltd v Department of Health and Social Security* [1990] 2 CMLR 49 at paras 48–50, per Mustill LJ. See also *Garland v British Rail Engineering Ltd* [1983] 2 AC 751.

[83] Council Directive 76/207 on the implementation of the principle of equal treatment for men and women as regards access to employment, vocational training and promotion, and working conditions (OJ 1976 L39 p 40).

[84] [1988] 1 AC 618 at 638F–G.

[85] Ibid at 639A–639H.

[86] [1993] 1 WLR 49.

[87] Ibid at 59F.

[88] This was the approach adopted by the Employment Appeal Tribunal in *J Bhudi v IMI Refiners Ltd* [1994] 2 CMLR 296 para 31, where it found that it was not possible to construe national legislation so as to conform with Community law. See also *Re Hartlebury Printers Ltd* [1994] 2 CMLR 704 para 22, where Morritt J held that the obligation of interpretation obliged the courts to attempt to reach an interpretation in conformity with a directive 'by proper processes of construction, not so far as the court is concerned by the equivalent of legislation'.

[89] [1993] 1 WLR 49 at 60F.

... a national court must construe a domestic law to accord with the terms of a Directive in the same field only if it is possible to do so. That means that the domestic law must be open to an interpretation consistent with the Directive whether or not it is also open to an interpretation inconsistent with it.

Where the national law will not support a construction which conforms with EC law, it is for Parliament to make the necessary amendments to the national law in order to prevent the United Kingdom from being in breach of its Treaty obligations. Where Community law is unclear, a reference to the Court of Justice will usually be appropriate.[90]

Purposive approach—implying words into national legislation The House of Lords adopted a broad approach to the question of interpretation of UK legislation in the context of Community law in both *Pickstone v Freemans*[91] and *Lister v Forth Dry Dock and Engineering Co Ltd (In Receivership)*.[92] The speeches in these cases recognised that the English courts are under an obligation to adopt a purposive approach to the interpretation of UK primary and subordinate legislation enacted to give effect to the UK's obligations under the EC Treaty. Thus, where legislation can be reasonably construed so as to conform with the UK's Community obligations, the English courts must do so, even if this involves a departure from the strict and literal application of the words used in the legislation.[93] Indeed, in both cases[94] the House of Lords held that, as a matter of language, the UK legislation at issue was 'unequivocal' and 'unambiguous' on its face. However, adopting a purposive approach, the House in both cases implied words into the legislation in order to comply with the UK's Treaty obligations.

Implementation period of directive has not expired A directive cannot have direct effect before the expiry of the time-limit laid down for its implementation.[95] It could be argued, by analogy, that no obligation to interpret national legislation in conformity with a directive should arise until the implementation period of the directive has expired. However, in Case C-156/91 *Hansa Fleisch v Landrat des Kreises Schleswig-Flensburg*[96] Advocate-General Jacobs suggested that the obligation of interpretation should arise prior to the expiry of the implementation date of a directive where a Member State has chosen to introduce national implementing legislation at an earlier date. In all other cases he considered that the obligation of interpretation could not arise until the implementation date for the directive had expired.

---

[90] As in *Webb v Emo Air Cargo Ltd* [1993] 1 WLR 49.

[91] [1989] 1 AC 66.

[92] [1990] 1 AC 546.

[93] *Pickstone v Freemans* [1989] 1 AC 66 at 112C–D, per Lord Keith, and at 125F–H and 127H–128A, per Lord Oliver: *Lister v Forth Dry Dock and Engineering Co Ltd (In Receivership)* [1990] 1 AC 546 at 558E and 559E–F, per Lord Templeman.

[94] *Pickstone v Freemans* [1989] 1 AC 66 at 125F–H, 126A–D, 126H–127C and 127H–128D, per Lord Oliver; *Lister v Forth Dry Dock and Engineering Co Ltd (In Receivership)* [1990] 1 AC 546 at 554G–H, per Lord Keith, and at 576D–577D, per Lord Oliver.

[95] Case 148/78 *Pubblico Ministero v Ratti* [1979] ECR 1629 paras 24 and 39–46. See Ch 4, pp 65–66.

[96] [1992] ECR I-5567, paras 23–27 of the Opinion.

The judgment in Case 80/86 *Kolpinghuis Nijmegen*[97] has been relied on as authority for the principle that the obligation of interpretation applies even before the expiry of the implementation date.[98] However, on close analysis it appears that the judgment does not provide support for this argument. In this case, the Court of Justice answered the third question of a preliminary reference from the *Arrondissementsrechtbank*, Arnhem, by reaffirming that national courts are required to interpret their national law in light of a relevant directive. However, the Court then stated that this general obligation of interpretation is limited, in that a directive which has not been implemented by national law cannot determine or aggravate the criminal liability of persons who act in contravention of the directive. The fourth question asked by the Dutch court was, *inter alia*, whether it made a difference to the answer to the third question if the implementation date for the relevant directive had not yet expired. The Court of Justice replied as follows:[99]

> As regards the third question concerning the limits which Community law might impose on the obligation or power of the national court to interpret the rules of its national law in the light of the directive, it makes no difference whether or not the period prescribed for implementation has expired.

It appears from this passage that the Court was emphasising that the fact that the implementation date for a directive has not yet expired does not affect the principle that a directive which has not been implemented by a national law cannot create or aggravate criminal liability. The Court did not address the question of whether or not the general obligation of interpretation is affected by the fact that the implementation date for a directive has expired.[100]

Directive not implemented into national law In Case C-168/95 *Arcaro*[101] the Court of Justice held that the obligation of interpretation cannot be applied so as to impose an obligation contained in a directive on an individual where the directive has not yet been transposed into national law.

Directive not unconditional and sufficiently precise The obligation of interpretation applies to a directive even if it is not 'unconditional and sufficiently precise'. This is a further difference between the obligation of interpretation and the doctrine of direct effect, as was recognised by Advocate-General Darmon in Case 177/88 *Dekker v VJV-Centrum*:[102]

---

[97] [1987] ECR 3969.

[98] See the Opinion of Advocate-General van Gerven in Case C-106/89 *Marleasing v La Comercial Internacional de Alimentación* [1990] ECR I-4135 at 4147, fn 16; and Schermers and Waelbroeck, *Judicial Protection in the European Communities*, 5th edn (Kluwer, 1991), at para 255.

[99] [1987] ECR 3969 paras 15–16.

[100] This analysis of Case 80/86 *Kolpinghuis Nijmegen* [1987] ECR 3969 is supported by para 26 of the Opinion of Advocate-General Jacobs in Case C-156/91 *Hansa Fleisch v Landrat des Kreises Schleswig-Flensburg* [1992] ECR I-5567.

[101] [1996] ECR I-4705 paras 41–42.

[102] [1990] ECR I-3941, para 15 of the Opinion. See also Opinion of Advocate-General van Gerven in Case C-106/89 *Marleasing v La Comercial Internacional de Alimentación* [1990] ECR I-4135 at 4146, fn 11.

It should be noted that my approach leads—as indeed previous judgments of the Court have done—to a distinction which has not often been stressed, between the possibility of relying on a directive, in cases where there are no national rules giving effect to its aims, so as to have its provisions applied directly (doctrine of 'direct effect') and reliance on a directive for the sole purpose of the interpretation of national law, including an interpretation of national provisions intended to implement the Community instrument (the doctrine of *interprétation conforme*). Whereas the former is confined to those provisions in directives which are sufficiently precise and unconditional, and cannot, according to the case-law, govern relations between individuals, the latter is very broad in scope, regardless of whether or not the directive has direct effect and regardless of the parties involved.

Criminal liability A directive which has not been implemented by national law cannot determine or aggravate the criminal liability of persons who act in contravention of the directive.[103] Thus, for example, national courts are not obliged to interpret national law in accordance with a directive where that would lead to the imposition of criminal liability which would not otherwise arise under national law.[104]

Recommendations Although article 189 of the EEC Treaty [new art 249] states that 'Recommendations and opinions shall have no binding force', so that they cannot have direct effect, they do have some legal effect in the national legal systems. In Case 322/88 *Grimaldi v Fonds des maladies*[105] the Court of Justice held that national courts are bound to take recommendations into consideration in deciding disputes submitted to them, in particular where they cast light on the interpretation of national measures adopted in order to implement them or where they are designed to supplement binding Community provisions.[106]

Reference to national parliamentary materials In *Pepper v Hart*[107] the House of Lords held that in construing a purely domestic statute reference could be made to parliamentary materials (for example *Hansard*) where: (a) the legislation was ambiguous or obscure or the literal meaning led to an absurdity; (b) the material relied on consisted of statements by a minister or promoter of the Bill which led to the enactment of the legislation together, if necessary, with such other parliamentary material as was necessary to understand such statements and their effects; and (c) the statements relied on were clear. A

---

[103] Case 80/86 *Kolpinghuis Nijmegen* [1987] ECR 3969 paras 11–14; Case C-168/95 *Arcaro* [1996] ECR I-4705 paras 41–42; Joined Cases C-74/95 and C-129/95 *X* [1996] ECR I-6609 paras 23–25, and paras 43–64 of the Opinion of Advocate-General Ruiz-Jarabo Colomer.

[104] See paras 24–26 of the Opinion of Advocate-General Jacobs in Joined Cases C-206/88 and C-207/88 *Vessoso and Zanetti* [1990] ECR I-1461.

[105] [1989] ECR 4407 paras 16–19.

[106] In *L Wadman v Carpenter Farrer Partnership* [1993] 3 CMLR 93 para 8 the Employment Appeal Tribunal indicated that the Code of Practice on measures to combat sexual harassment attached to the Commission Recommendation on the protection of the dignity of women and men at work (OJ 1992 L49 p 1) could be of assistance to industrial tribunals in considering what constitutes sexual harassment under British law.

[107] [1993] AC 593, [1993] 1 All ER 42. See also *Melluish (Inspector of Taxes) v BMI (No 3) Ltd* [1995] 3 WLR 630, [1995] 4 All ER 453.

Practice Direction has been issued which lays down the procedure to be followed by parties who wish to refer to any extract from *Hansard*.[108]

In *Three Rivers District Council v Bank of England (No 2)*[109] Clarke J, in granting leave to refer to two speeches made by ministers in Parliament, stated that where a court is seeking to construe a statute in conformity with Community law it was entitled to adopt a 'somewhat more flexible approach' than that laid down in *Pepper v Hart*. In reaching this conclusion, Clarke J relied, *inter alia*, on the speeches of the House of Lords in *Pickstone v Freemans plc*[110] which referred to draft regulations and parliamentary debate concerning those regulations,[111] as well as to the explanatory note which accompanied the regulations when they were adopted.[112] Clarke J also indicated that he would be likely to follow the same approach in relation to the admissibility of White Papers.

The approach adopted by Clarke J in *Three Rivers* was cited with approval by Wilson J in *Miss U v Mr W and the Attorney-General (No 1)*.[113]

---

[108] *Practice Direction (Hansard Extracts)* [1995] 1 WLR 192, [1995] 1 All ER 234.
[109] [1996] 2 All ER 363 at 366c–f (QBD).
[110] [1989] 1 AC 66.
[111] Ibid at 121H–122D, per Lord Templeman and at 112A–E, per Lord Keith.
[112] Ibid at 126H–128E, per Lord Oliver.
[113] [1997] EuLR 342 at 349B–D.

Part II

Remedies in English Courts for Breach of EC Law

Chapter 6

Effective Protection of EC Law Rights

1. PRINCIPLE OF EFFECTIVE PROTECTION

Duty on national courts Pursuant to article 5 of the EC Treaty [new art 10], it is the duty of national courts to ensure the legal protection of rights which individuals derive from Community law.[1] The underlying assumption of the Treaty is that Community law rights can be protected by national remedies enforced through the national courts in accordance with national procedural rules.[2] However, the legal autonomy of the national courts is subject to two overriding considerations of Community law. First, the national rules applicable to Community law cases cannot be discriminatory or less favourable than those relating to similar actions of a domestic nature (the principle of equivalence). Secondly, the national rules must not make it impossible in practice to exercise Community law rights (the principle of effective protection).

In defining the duty of 'sincere co-operation' between national courts and the Community, and the need to ensure effective protection of Community law rights, the Court of Justice stated in Joined Cases C-6/90 and C-9/90 *Francovich and Bonifaci v Italy:*[3]

> ... it has been consistently held that national courts whose task it is to apply the provisions of Community law in areas within their jurisdiction must ensure that those rules take full effect and must protect the rights which they confer on individuals (see in particular the judgments in Case 106/77 *Amministrazione delle Finanze v Simmenthal* [1978] ECR 629, paragraph 16, and Case C-213/89 *Factortame* [1990] ECR I-2433, paragraph 19).
>
> The full effectiveness of Community rules would be impaired and the protection of the rights which they grant would be weakened if individuals were unable to obtain

---

[1] Case 33/76 *Rewe v Landwirtschaftskammer Saarland* [1976] ECR 1989 para 5; Case C-213/89 *Factortame* [1990] ECR I-2433 para 19; Case C-2/88 *Imm Zwartveld* [1990] ECR I-3365 para 18; Case C-312/93 *Peterbroeck v Belgium* [1995] ECR I-4599 para 12.

[2] Para 29 of the Opinion of Advocate-General Jacobs in Joined Cases C-430/93 and C-431/93 *Van Schijndel v SPF* [1995] ECR I-4705.

[3] [1991] ECR I-5337 paras 32–33. One of the earlier references to effective protection is Case 179/84 *Bozzetti v Invernizzi* [1985] ECR 2301 para 17, where the Court of Justice stated that rights conferred on individuals by Community law 'must be effectively protected in each case'.

redress when their rights are infringed by a breach of Community law for which a Member State can be held responsible.

The principle of effective protection was recognised by Lord Bingham CJ in *R v Secretary of State for the Home Department, ex p Gallagher*[4] where he stated that:

> It is a cardinal principle of Community law that the laws of Member States should provide effective and adequate redress for violations of Community law by Member States where these result in infringement of specific individual rights conferred by the law of the Community.

Effective enforcement of Community law Article 5 of the EC Treaty imposes on Member States an obligation to enforce Community law. In the absence of any penalty imposed by Community law, the choice of penalties remains within the Member States' discretion. However, the Member States' discretion is also subject to the principles of equivalence and effectiveness. They must ensure that infringements of Community law are penalised under similar conditions, both procedural and substantive, to infringements of national law and that the penalty chosen must be 'effective, proportionate and dissuasive'.[5] Effective enforcement ensures the proper application of Community law and the effective protection of Community law rights.

Extent of protection The extent of the duty to ensure effective protection and effective enforcement will differ depending on the objective of the Community law provision breached and on the damage suffered. For example, in Case C-180/95 *Draehmpaehl v Urania Immobilienservice*[6] Mr Draehmpaehl claimed sex discrimination, contrary to Council Directive 76/207,[7] when he was not considered for a job vacancy which was only open to women. The Court of Justice considered that a compensation ceiling of three months' salary was legitimate in the case of those applicants who would not have been employed, even if the selection process had been free of discrimination. This penalty constituted effective enforcement of the sex discrimination legislation and thereby effectively protected Mr Draehmpaehl's Community law rights. The position is different when a victim of sex discrimination has actually lost employment as a result of sex discrimination. In *Marshall v Southampton and South West Hampshire Health Authority Teaching (No 2)*[8] Miss Marshall was forced to retire because of her sex contrary to Council Directive 76/207. The industrial tribunal assessed her financial loss at £18,405, although there was a statutory limit on any compensation of £6,250. The Court of Justice considered

---

[4] [1996] 2 CMLR 951 para 10.

[5] Case C-177/95 *Ebony Maritime v Preffetto Della Provincia* [1997] ECR I-1111 para 35. See also Ch 1, pp 9 and 13.

[6] [1997] ECR I-2195.

[7] Council Directive 76/207 of 9 February 1976 (OJ 1976 L39 p 40) on the implementation of the principle of equal treatment for men and women as regards access to employment, vocational training and promotion and working conditions.

[8] [1990] ICR 6 (EAT), [1991] ICR 136 (CA), Case C-271/91 [1993] ECR I-4367 (ECJ). See also Case 14/83 *Von Colson and Kamann v Land Nordrhein-Westfalen* [1984] ECR 1891 para 18.

that the objective of the Directive was to arrive at real equality of opportunity. This meant that there should be full compensation for the damage sustained as a result of the discrimination. Consequently, the industrial tribunal was required to set aside the statutory limit on the amount of compensation which could be awarded to Miss Marshall.

Enforcement of national law The principle of effective protection requires that national penalties should not be such as to constitute an obstacle to the effective exercise of Community law rights. In Case C-193/94 *Skanavi*[9] the Court of Justice ruled that Community law permitted Germany to require the holder of a driving licence issued by another Member State to exchange that licence for a German licence within one year of taking up normal residence there. Nevertheless, the sanction of imprisonment for breach of the German law was considered to be so disproportionate to the seriousness of the breach that it became an obstacle to the free movement of persons guaranteed by articles 48 [new art 39] and 52 [new art 43] of the EC Treaty.[10]

2. RIGHT TO JUDICIAL CONTROL

Access to the courts The existence of a judicial remedy is essential if an individual is to be able to seek effective protection of his Community law rights. In short, there must be a right to judicial control. This requirement was laid down by the Court of Justice in Case 222/84 *Johnston v Chief Constable of the Royal Ulster Constabulary.*[11] Mrs Johnston had been in the full-time reserve of the Royal Ulster Constabulary and, as a result of the decision not to arm women police officers, did not have her contract of employment renewed. On her application, under the Sex Discrimination (Northern Ireland) Order 1976 to the industrial tribunal, the Secretary of State signed a certificate under article 53(2) of the Order, which was conclusive evidence that the applicant had been refused full-time employment on the grounds of national security, public safety and public order. The Court of Justice held that this denial of access to the courts was a clear and unconditional breach of article 6 of Directive 76/207 on equal treatment for men and women,[12] which enables all persons who consider themselves wronged by discrimination 'to pursue their claims by judicial process'. The Court of Justice held that this requirement reflected a general principle of Community law which underlies the constitutional traditions

---

[9] [1996] ECR I-929 para 36.

[10] As to the principle of proportionality in Community law, see Ch 2, pp 27–33.

[11] [1986] ECR 1651 paras 13–21: applied generally in Case 222/86 *UNECTEF v Heylens* [1987] ECR 4097 para 14; Case C-340/89 *Vlassopoulou* [1991] ECR I-2357 para 22; Case C-97/91 *Borelli v Commission* [1992] ECR I-6313 para 14; and Case C-19/92 *Kraus v Land Baden-Württemberg* [1993] ECR I-1663 para 40.

[12] Council Directive 76/207 of 9 February 1976 (OJ 1976 L39 p 40) on the implementation of the principle of equal treatment for men and women as regards access to employment, vocational training and promotion and working conditions.

common to the Member States and which has been enshrined in articles 6 and 13 of the European Convention on Human Rights.

Similarly, in Case 178/84 *Commission v Germany* (the 'Beer case')[13] the Court of Justice stated that article 30 of the EEC Treaty [new art 28] did not prevent Member States from subjecting the use of certain food additives to prior authorisation. However, the principle of proportionality underlying article 36 of the EEC Treaty [new art 30] dictated that importers should have access to a system of authorisation and should be able to challenge any refusal to grant authorisation before the national courts.

Duty to give reasons In Case 222/86 *UNECTEF v Heylens*[14] the Court of Justice held that national authorities must give reasons for decisions which impinge upon directly effective rights, so as to enable individuals properly to exercise their right to judicial control. In this case, Mr Heylens, a Belgian national, was employed as a football trainer for a French football club. Under French law, a person had to possess either a French diploma or a recognised foreign diploma in order to practise as a football trainer. The French Minister for Sport refused to recognise Mr Heylens' Belgian diploma. There was no requirement under French law for the Minister to provide reasons for the refusal and no provision was made for any specific legal remedy against the decision. The Court held that the inability to appeal against the decision and the failure to give reasons infringed the right to judicial control. The Court stated:[15]

> Effective judicial review, which must be able to cover the legality of the reasons for the contested decision, presupposes in general that the court to which the matter is referred may require the competent authority to notify its reasons. But where, as in this case, it is more particularly a question of securing the effective protection of a fundamental right conferred by the Treaty on Community workers, the latter must also be able to defend that right under the best possible conditions and have the possibility of deciding, with a full knowledge of the relevant facts, whether there is any point in their applying to the courts. Consequently, in such circumstances the competent national authority is under a duty to inform them of the reasons on which its refusal is based, either in the decision itself or in a subsequent communication made at their request.

This duty to give reasons is consistent with article 190 of the Treaty [new art 253] which imposes a general duty on Community institutions to state the reasons on which administrative and legislative acts are based.[16] However, the duty on national authorities to give reasons is imposed by the Community law principle of effective protection; it does not arise from any extension of article 190. The principle of effective protection does not require that national legislative acts should state the reasons on which they are based even though they may impinge on Community law rights. As Advocate-General Fennelly stated in Case C-70/95 *Sodemare v Regione Lombardia*:[17]

---

[13] [1987] ECR 1227 paras 44–46.
[14] [1987] ECR 4097.
[15] Ibid para 15.
[16] See Ch 13, pp 310-315.
[17] [1997] ECR I-3395, at para 18 of the Opinion, upheld by the Court of Justice at paras 17–20 of

It is important to draw a distinction between legislative measures of general application and executive decisions affecting individuals. A requirement that reasons be given, at the time of enactment, for any national legislative measures even potentially capable of affecting the exercise of Community-law rights would, in my view, constitute an unwarranted and unnecessary intrusion into Member State competence. The breach of Community law by national legislation is determined in accordance with objective criteria. There is no evidence that the effectiveness of judicial protection is undermined by this approach.

Review of the merits The right to judicial control probably encompasses a review by the national court of the merits of an administrative decision. Such a right would be the logical consequence of the duty to give reasons since a reasoned decision should indicate to a court the substantive merit of the decision. Such a right would also be consistent with the duty on the courts to provide effective judicial protection to individuals. In Joined Cases C-65/95 and C-111/95 *Singh Shingara*[18] Advocate-General Ruiz-Jarabo de Colomer considered that article 9 of Directive 64/221,[19] which allows for deportation orders to be reviewed only on strict legal grounds (eg lack of competence), was itself unlawful. The Advocate-General stated:[20]

> ... there can only be 'effective protection' to the extent to which the legal remedy allows full review of the administrative act at issue.

In certain cases a review of the administrative act will involve a full review of the merits, rather than a mere examination of perversity, particularly where the individual has been fined. In *Hodgson v Commissioners of Customs and Excise*[21] Mr Hodgson arrived at Luton airport with a quantity of hand-rolling tobacco in his possession. The Commissioners found that the quantity of tobacco was above the prescribed limit for personal use and by virtue of article 5(3) of the Excise Duties (Personal Reliefs) Order 1992 (SI No 3155) an irrebuttable presumption arose that the tobacco was for commercial purposes.[22] He was thus liable to pay duty and a penalty was imposed. The Value Added Tax and Duties Tribunal held that this irrebuttable presumption was contrary to the principle of effective protection under Community law.[23] The irrebuttable presumption prevented a court from determining whether an offence had been committed, subject only to a possible challenge that the decision was perverse. The tribunal considered that this was not sufficient to protect Mr Hodgson's right to import tobacco for personal use.

---

the judgment.

[18] [1997] ECR I-3343.

[19] Directive 64/221 on measures concerning the movement and residence of foreign nationals which are justified on grounds of public policy, public security or public health (OJ English Special Edition 1963-1964 p 117). The Court did not address this question, holding that, in the circumstances of the case, the Directive provided for a remedy of judicial review.

[20] [1997] ECR I-3343 at para 88 of the opinion.

[21] [1997] EuLR 117 (VAT Tribunal).

[22] Article 5(3), as interpreted in *Customs and Excise Commissioners v Carrier* [1995] 4 All ER 38.

[23] And contrary to article 6 of the European Convention on Human Rights.

Preparatory measures The right to judicial control and the duty to state reasons concern final decisions only, and do not extend to opinions and other measures occurring in preparatory or investigative stages leading to a final decision.[24]

Directives Directives sometimes specifically require that there should be access to the courts or that there should be a duty to state reasons on the part of national authorities. For example, Directive 79/279[25] on official stock exchange listing requires Member States to ensure that decisions of the stock exchange refusing or discontinuing the listing of a company's shares are subject to review by the courts. Article 6 of Directive 76/207 on equal treatment for men and women enables all persons who consider themselves wronged by discrimination 'to pursue their claims by judicial process'.[26] Similarly, Directive 89/665,[27] on public procurement remedies, provides that decisions concerning public procurement should be reviewed effectively and as rapidly as possible, and that courts or separate review bodies should have the power to grant interim relief, quash any unlawful decisions and award damages. Article 2(8) of the Directive provides that where the bodies responsible for review procedures are not judicial in character, written reasons for their decisions should always be given and their decisions should be subject to review by a court or tribunal within the meaning of article 177 of the EC Treaty [new art 234].

3. REMEDIES

(a) Availability of remedies

Direct effect is a minimum guarantee The right of individuals to rely on directly effective provisions of Community law before national courts is only a minimum guarantee and cannot always constitute sufficient protection of Community law rights.[28] The national legal system must also ensure that individuals have access to effective remedies to protect their rights.

---

[24] Case 222/86 *UNECTEF v Heylens* [1987] ECR 4097 para 16.

[25] Council Directive 79/279 of 5 March 1979 co-ordinating the admission of securities to official stock exchange listing (OJ 1979 L66 p 21). Access to the courts does not extend to shareholders in a company. See the Court of Appeal in *R v International Stock Exchange of the United Kingdom and the Republic of Ireland Ltd, ex p Else (1982) Ltd* [1993] QB 534.

[26] Council Directive 76/207 of 19 February 1976 on the implementation of the principle of equal treatment for men and women as regards access to employment, vocational training and promotion and working conditions (OJ 1976 L39 p 40).

[27] Council Directive 89/665 of 21 December 1989 on the co-ordination of the laws, regulations and administrative provisions relating to the application of review procedures to the award of public supply and works contracts (OJ 1989 L395 p 33). See also Council Directive 92/13 of 25 February 1992 co-ordinating the laws, regulations and administrative provisions relating to the application of Community rules on the procurement procedures of entities operating in the water, energy, transport and telecommunications sectors (OJ 1992 L76 p 14).

[28] Joined Cases C-46/93 and C-48/93 *Brasserie du Pêcheur and Factortame* [1996] ECR I-1029 para 20.

In determining whether the national legal systems comply with the principle of effective protection, the Court of Justice has ruled that individuals have a right to claim damages from the State,[29] have a right to claim interim relief against the State[30] and have a right to claim restitution of charges unlawfully levied by the State.[31]

All domestic remedies Regard should be had to all available national remedies and the conditions under which they can be granted, in order to determine whether Community law is being effectively protected. For example, in *Bourgoin SA v Ministry of Agriculture, Fisheries and Food*[32] the majority of the Court of Appeal considered that the remedy of judicial review for an innocent, yet unlawful, breach of article 30 of the EEC Treaty by the Ministry provided adequate protection to individuals affected and that an award of damages (in the absence of an abusive breach) was not necessary.[33] Although subsequent case-law of the Court of Justice has established that there is a Community law right to damages where a Member State has committed a sufficiently serious breach of Community law,[34] the majority decision in *Bourgoin* remains good law in so far as it establishes that in other cases an individual would be effectively protected by the remedies available under RSC Ord 53.[35]

(b) Obligation to create a remedy

No obligation to create new remedies The duty of national courts to ensure the legal protection which individuals derive from Community law is unlikely to involve the invention of new remedies. On this basis, French courts could not be obliged to recognise the concept of equitable remedies known in English law in order to protect Community law rights. The Court of Justice has stated, *obiter*, that:[36]

> ... although the Treaty has made it possible in a number of instances for private persons to bring a direct action, where appropriate, before the Court of Justice, it was not intended to create new remedies in the national courts to ensure the observance of Community law other than those already laid down by national law.

---

[29] Joined Cases C-6/90 and C-9/90 *Francovich and Bonifaci v Italy* [1991] ECR I-5357. Joined Cases C-46/93 and C-48/93 *Brasserie du Pêcheur and Factortame* [1996] ECR I-1029. See Ch 7 on damages.

[30] Case C-221/89 *Factortame* [1991] ECR I-3905. See Ch 8 on injunctions.

[31] Case 33/76 *Rewe v Landwirtschaftskammer Saarland* [1976] ECR 1989; Case 199/82 *Amministrazione delle Finanze v San Giorgio* [1983] ECR 3595. See Ch 9 on restitution.

[32] [1986] 1 QB 716 at 785D–E, per Parker LJ, with whom Nourse LJ agreed. In contrast, Oliver LJ considered that judicial review in itself was not an effective remedy for such a breach. A denial of a remedy in damages for past loss caused by the act complained of would, he considered, infringe the principle of effective protection (at pp 769E–771G).

[33] As to the need for an adequate remedy, see below at pp 111-114.

[34] Joined Cases C-46/93 and C-48/93 *Brasserie du Pêcheur and Factortame* [1996] ECR I-1029.

[35] See Ch 7, p 129.

[36] Case 158/80 *Rewe v Hauptzollamt Kiel* [1981] ECR 1805 para 44.

Obligation to create jurisdiction It is unclear whether national courts must establish jurisdiction to grant a remedy where no such jurisdiction existed before, in order to protect Community law rights. However, two judgments of the House of Lords suggest that the principle of effective protection does require national courts and tribunals to create jurisdiction where none existed before.

In *Marshall v Southampton and South West Hampshire Health Authority (Teaching) (No 2)* the industrial tribunal, in assessing compensation in accordance with ss 65 and 66 of the Sex Discrimination Act 1975, awarded Miss Marshall compensation for loss of earnings and a sum representing interest on the ground that s 35A of the Supreme Court Act 1981 provided for an award of interest on damages. The Employment Appeal Tribunal[37] held that an industrial tribunal was not a court of record and had no inherent power to award interest on any monetary award. On appeal, Dillon LJ, in relation to the lack of jurisdiction to award interest, stated:[38]

> It is one thing, however, to write out of a national statute, by a form of estoppel..., a limitation in the statute on the power conferred by the statute on the national court to award compensation. It is not necessarily the same thing to write into the statute a power that is not there so as to enable the national court to make an award which the terms of the national statute give it no discretion to make.

On a reference made by the House of Lords, the Court of Justice held[39] that someone who had been dismissed as a result of sex discrimination was entitled to claim interest on the damages awarded. The Court of Justice did not deal with the issue whether Community law bestowed jurisdiction on the industrial tribunal to grant interest. Nevertheless, in the light of the preliminary ruling, the House of Lords restored the decision of the industrial tribunal, including the award of interest.[40]

In *R v Secretary of State for Transport, ex p Factortame Ltd (No 2)*[41] the House of Lords considered that, as a matter of English law, it could not grant an interim injunction in judicial review proceedings which sought to disapply an Act of Parliament in order to protect putative Community law rights because: (1) the Supreme Court Act 1981, s 31 did not give the courts the power; and (2) an Act of Parliament was presumed valid until declared invalid. However, on a reference for a preliminary ruling the Court of Justice ruled that the House of

---

[37] [1990] ICR 6.

[38] [1991] ICR 136 at 143E. Dillon LJ was, however, prepared to give the tribunal the power. The Court of Appeal held by majority that, whether or not the industrial tribunal had power to award interest, the statutory limit on the amount of compensation that could be awarded provided a complete defence to her claim for full compensation. This limitation was ruled unlawful by the Court of Justice in Case C-271/91 [1993] ECR I-4367.

[39] Case C-271/91 [1993] ECR I-4367. See also Case 14/83 *Von Colson and Kamann v Land Nordrhein-Westfalen* [1984] ECR 1891. Compare the approach of Lord Templeman in *Duke v Reliance Systems Ltd* [1988] 1 AC 618 at 641.

[40] [1994] 1 AC 530. This has now been put on a legislative footing; see the Sex Discrimination and Equal Pay (Remedies) Regulations 1993 (SI 1993 No 2798).

[41] [1990] 1 AC 603.

Lords should disapply these rules in so far as they precluded it from granting such interim relief.[42] Lord Bridge said of the ruling:[43]

> My Lords, when this appeal first came before the House last year your Lordships held that, as a matter of English law, the courts had no jurisdiction to grant interim relief in terms which would involve either overturning an English statute in advance of any decision by the European Court of Justice that the statute infringed Community law or granting an injunction against the Crown. It then became necessary to seek a preliminary ruling from the European Court of Justice as to whether Community law itself invested us with such jurisdiction. ...
>
> In June of this year we received the judgment of the European Court of Justice... affirming that we had jurisdiction, in the circumstances postulated, to grant interim relief for the protection of directly enforceable rights under Community law and that no limitation on our jurisdiction imposed by any rule of national law could stand as the sole obstacle to preclude the grant of such relief.

It would appear that the House of Lords considered that Community law vested the courts with the jurisdiction to grant an injunction where none existed before. On a closer analysis, however, the ruling is premised on the basis that the English courts had such jurisdiction, but were prevented from exercising it 'by the old common law rule that an interim injunction may not be granted against the Crown, that is to say against the Government, in conjunction with the presumption that an Act of Parliament is in conformity with Community law until such time as a decision on its compatibility with that law has been given'.[44]

4. PROCEDURAL, EVIDENTIAL AND SUBSTANTIVE RULES

(a) Application of national rules

Legal autonomy of the national courts   In the absence of Community rules on the subject, it is for the national courts, in order to determine how Community law rights should be protected, to apply their own rules on:

(1) procedure, for example:
   (a) which court has jurisdiction to hear the claim;[45]

---

[42] Case C-213/89 *Factortame* [1990] ECR I-2433, [1991] 1 AC 603.

[43] [1991] 1 AC 603 at 658A–E.

[44] The Court of Justice has been criticised for misinterpreting the questions referred to it by the House of Lords: see Lord Donaldson (1991) 25 *The Law Teacher* 4; case note by Toth in (1990) 27 CMLR 573; Barav, 'The effectiveness of judicial protection and the role of the national courts' in *Judicial Protection of Rights in the Community Legal Order* (Bruylant Bruxelles, 1997).

[45] Case 179/84 *Bozetti v Invernizzi* [1985] ECR 2301 para 17; Case C-446/93 *SEIM* [1996] ECR I-73 para 32; Case C-394/93 *Alonso-Pérez v Bundesanstalt für Arbeit* [1995] ECR I-4101 para 28.

    (*b*) security for costs;[46] and

    (*c*) limitation periods,[47] time-limits[48] and the related issue of whether courts can raise points of Community law of their own motion;[49]

  (2) evidence, for example:

    (*a*) evidential presumptions relating to the passing on of unlawful charges,[50] the failure to give discovery[51] or the quantity of excise goods that may be imported for personal use;[52]

    (*b*) the standard and burden of proof;[53]

    (*c*) privilege against self-incrimination and discovery of documents in EC competition cases;[54] and

    (*d*) the evidential weight of EC competition decisions;[55]

  (3) substantive issues, for example:

    (*a*) issues of causation,[56] mitigation and contributory negligence[57] in damages claims;

    (*b*) heads of damages;[58]

    (*c*) rates of interest;[59]

    (*d*) defence of set-off;[60]

    (*e*) defence of unjust enrichment;[61] and

    (*f*) severance of clauses in contracts which infringe the EC competition rules.[62]

---

[46] Case C-20/92 *Hubbard v Hamburger* [1993] ECR I-3777. See below at pp 110-111.

[47] Case 33/76 *Rewe v Landwirtschaftskammer Saarland* [1976] ECR 1989; Case 45/76 *Comet v Produktschap voor Siergewassen* [1976] ECR 2043 (reasonable time-limits). See pp 114-117.

[48] Case C-312/93 *Peterbroeck v Belgium* [1994] ECR I-4599.

[49] Joined Cases C-430/93 and C-431/93 *Van Schijndel v SPF* [1995] ECR I-4705.

[50] Case 199/82 *Amministrazione delle Finanze v San Giorgio* [1983] ECR 3593.

[51] Paragraph 116 of the Opinion of Advocate-General Jacobs in Case C-90/94 *Haahr Petroleum v Havn* [1997] ECR I-4085.

[52] *Hodgson v Commissioners of Customs and Excise* [1997] EuLR 116.

[53] Case C-242/95 *GT-Link v DSB* [1997] ECR I-4449 (judgment of 17 July 1997) (proving a breach of the EC competition rules); also Opinion of Advocate-General Jacobs in Joined Cases C-427/93 and others *Bristol Myers Squibb v Paranova* [1996] ECR I-3457 para 100 (trade mark infringement).

[54] *Re Westinghouse* [1978] AC 547.

[55] *Iberian UK Ltd v BPB Industries and British Gypsum Ltd* [1996] 2 CMLR 601; [1997] EuLR 1. See further at Ch 1, pp 17-18.

[56] Joined Cases C-6/90 and C-9/90 *Francovich and Bonifaci v Italy* [1991] ECR I-5357 para 43; Joined Cases C-46/93 and C-48/93 *Brasserie du Pêcheur and Factortame* [1996] ECR I-1029 para 65.

[57] Joined Cases C-46/93 and C-48/93 *Brasserie du Pêcheur and Factortame* [1996] ECR I-1029 paras 83–84.

[58] Ibid para 88.

[59] Case 130/79 *Express Dairy Foods v IBAP* [1980] ECR 1887; but note Case C-271/91 *Marshall v Southampton and South-West Hampshire AHA (Teaching) (No 2)* [1993] ECR I 4367. See also the Opinion of Advocate-General van Gerven in Case C-128/92 *Banks v British Coal Corporation* [1994] ECR I-1209.

[60] Case 177/78 *Pigs and Bacon Commission v McCarren* [1979] ECR 2161.

[61] Case 68/79 *Just v Danish Ministry for Fiscal Affairs* [1980] ECR 501.

[62] Case 56/65 *Société Technique Minière v Ulm* [1966] ECR 235; applied in *Chemidus Wavin Ltd* [1978] 3 CMLR 514; *Inntrepreneur v Mason* [1993] 2 CMLR 293; *Inntrepreneur v Boyes* [1993] 68 P&CR 77 (CA).

Limitation on national autonomy The right of national courts to apply their own rules when remedying a breach of Community law is subject to two limitations imposed by Community law. First, the national rules applicable to Community law cases cannot be discriminatory or less favourable than those relating to similar actions of a domestic nature (the principle of equivalence). Secondly, the national rules must not make it impossible in practice to exercise Community law rights (the principle of effective protection).[63]

(b) Equivalent protection

General rule Any national procedural, evidential or substantive rule is unenforceable if it treats Community claims less favourably than similar national claims[64] or treats litigants from other Member States less favourably than domestic litigants (without objective justification).[65]

Comparing similar claims In ascertaining whether claims based on Community law are treated less favourably than claims based on national law, a comparison needs to be made between the rule applicable to the Community claim and the rule which would be applicable if a similar domestic claim were being made. In Case C-261/95 *Palmisani*[66] Italy failed to implement Directive 80/987, which provided that a guarantee fund should be established to compensate employees in the event of their insolvent employers not paying their salaries. As a result of this failure, Italy was held liable to pay damages to employees who had suffered loss due to the absence of any guarantee fund.[67] Subsequently, Italy implemented the directive by a Legislative Decree. Article 2(7) of the Decree also provided for compensation to be paid to employees who had suffered loss, and laid down a one-year time-limit in which to bring an action for damages. This period was shorter than the normal five-year time-limit for bringing an action for damages under article 2043 of the Italian Civil Code. The Court of Justice considered that article 2(7) of the Decree and article 2043 of the Code pursued similar objectives, and that the one-year time-limit would breach the principle of equivalence if the referring court were satisfied that

---

[63] For example, see Case 33/76 *Zentralfinanz v Landwirtschaftskammer Saarland* [1976] ECR 1989 para 5; Case 199/82 *Amministrazione delle Finanze v San Giorgio* [1983] ECR 3595; Joined Cases C-6/90, C-9/90 *Francovich and Bonifaci v Italy* [1991] ECR I-5357 para 42; Joined Cases C-430/93 and C-431/93 *Van Schijndel v SFP* [1995] ECR I-4705 para 19; Case C-312/93 *Peterbroeck v Belgium* [1995] ECR I-4599 para 14; Case C-72/95 *Kraaijeveld* [1996] ECR I-5403; Case C-261/95 *Palmisani* [1997] ECR I-4025 para 27.

[64] See Joined Cases 66/79, 127/79 and 128/79 *Amministrazione delle Finanze v Salumi* [1980] ECR 1237 paras 17–21; and Joined Cases C-31 to C-44/91 *Lageder v Amministrazione delle Finanze* [1993] ECR I-1761 paras 22–29. See also para 58 of the Opinion of Advocate-General Jacobs in Case C-62/93 *BP Supergas v Greece* [1995] ECR I-1883; and para 28 of his Opinion of 15 June 1995 in Joined Cases C-430/93 and C-431/93 *Van Schijndel v SPF* [1995] ECR I-4705.

[65] See below at pp 110-111.

[66] [1997] ECR I-4025.

[67] Joined Cases C-6/90 and C-9/90 *Francovich and Bonifaci v Italy* [1991] ECR I-5357.

article 2043 could be relied on to bring damages claims against the State. The Court stated:[68]

> ... in order to establish the comparability of the two systems in question, the essential characteristics of the domestic system of reference must be examined ...
>
> If the ordinary Italian system on non-contractual liability were to prove incapable of serving as a basis for an action against public authorities for unlawful conduct for which they can be held responsible in the exercise of their powers and the national court were unable to undertake any other relevant comparison between the time-limit at issue and the conditions relating to similar claims of a domestic nature, the conclusion would have to be drawn, in view of the foregoing, that Community law does not preclude a Member State from requiring any action for reparation of the loss or damage sustained as a result of the belated transposition of the Directive to be brought within a limitation period of one year from the date of its transposition into national law.

The examination of the two systems to establish their comparability will not always be easy, particularly where Community legislation constitutes the basis for domestic legislation in the field in question. In Case C-180/95 *Draehmpaehl v Urania Immobilienservice*,[69] for example, the Court of Justice had regard to German 'civil law' and 'labour law' when examining whether an upper limit of three months' salary as compensation for sex discrimination infringed the principle of equivalence. It has been suggested that the UK public procurement regulations infringe the principle of equivalence on the basis that the claim for damages arising as a result of the authority's breach of statutory duty must be brought within three months from the date when the grounds for bringing the proceedings first arose.[70] Ultimately, the lawfulness of this time-limit, which is equivalent to the time period applicable in judicial review proceedings, will depend on the identification of a similar claim of a domestic nature.

Direct discrimination Article 6 of the EC Treaty [new art 12] expressly prohibits discrimination on the grounds of nationality. In Case C-20/90 *Hubbard v Hamburger*[71] Mr Hubbard, an English solicitor acting in his capacity as executor of a will in England, applied to the German courts for the transfer to his name of assets located in Germany which were part of the estate. Under German law he was obliged, as a foreign national, to provide security for costs. The Court of Justice held that this requirement was unenforceable on the basis that German nationals were not required to provide such security in a similar situation.

---

[68] Case C-261/95 *Palmisani* [1997] ECR I-4025 paras 38–39.

[69] [1997] ECR I-2195.

[70] Professor Sue Arrowsmith, *The Law of Public and Utilities Procurement* (Sweet & Maxwell, 1996), p 913. These regulations impose a statutory duty on contracting authorities not to infringe the provisions of the regulations, which is owed to suppliers of services, works or goods: see eg reg 32(4)(b) of the Public Services Contracts Regulations 1993 (SI 1993 No 3228).

[71] [1993] ECR I-3777; Case C-43/95 *Data Delecta* [1996] ECR I-4661; Case C-323/95 *Hayes v Kronenberger* [1997] ECR I-1711.

Indirect discrimination Indirect discrimination on the grounds of nationality is prohibited. Residence requirements, although not overtly discriminatory, may lead to indirect discrimination. An example is provided by RSC Order 23 which grants the English courts a discretion to order a plaintiff to give security for costs if the plaintiff is ordinarily resident out of the jurisdiction. In *Fitzgerald v Williams*[72] the Court of Appeal held that this residence condition covertly discriminated against nationals of other Member States because most plaintiffs in English proceedings who were ordinarily resident outside the jurisdiction would not be British. On this basis, the Court of Appeal set aside an order for security for costs made against 81 Irish citizens resident in Ireland who were seeking a worldwide *Mareva* injunction in the English courts. This difference in treatment was not objectively justified in the case of a Member State, such as Ireland, since it was a party to the Brussels Convention on Jurisdiction and the Enforcement of Judgments in Civil and Commercial Matters which facilitated the enforcement of judgments between Member States.

By contrast, a court does not infringe the principle of equivalence by making a security for costs order against an impecunious company resident in another Member State. No discrimination arises since the court has jurisdiction to make such an order against an impecunious English company under s 726 of the Companies Act 1985.[73]

(c) Effectiveness of national rules

Excessively difficult Any national condition concerning procedure, evidence or substance is unenforceable in so far as it makes it impossible in practice, or excessively difficult, for individuals to exercise their Community law rights.[74] In Case 199/82 *Amministrazione delle Finanze v San Giorgio*[75] an Italian trader had paid charges to the Italian authorities, which had been levied in breach of Community law. Italian law recognised the right to restitution where charges had been levied contrary to national law and Community law. However, the law presumed that the person who had paid the charges would pass them on to the consumer. To recover the charges from the Italian authorities the trader had to prove, by documentary evidence, that they had not been passed on. The Court of Justice considered that the requirement to prove a negative by documentary evidence, although not discriminatory, made it impossible, in practice, to

---

[72] [1996] 2 QB 657, disapproving of *Berkeley Administration Inc v McClelland* [1990] 2 QB 407 which was no longer good authority in the light of ruling of the Court of Justice in Case C-398/92 *Mund & Fester v Hatrex International Transport* [1994] ECR I-467. See also *Porzeleck KG v Porzeleck (UK) Ltd* [1987] 1 WLR 420.

[73] *Chequepoint SARL v McClelland* [1997] QB 51.

[74] Joined Cases C-430/93 and C-431/93 *Van Schijndel v SPF* [1995] ECR I-4705 para 17. The Court has also used the terms 'virtually impossible' and 'excessively difficult', for example; see Case 199/82 *Amministrazione delle Finanze v San Giorgio* [1983] ECR 3595 para 14. Advocate-General Jacobs has suggested that the formulation is 'unduly difficult'; see para 75 of his Opinion in Case C-2/94 *Denkavit International* [1996] ECR I-2827.

[75] [1983] ECR 3595; applied in Case 331/85 *Bianco v Directeur général des douanes* [1988] ECR 1099. Compare Case 68/79 *Just v Danish Ministry for Fiscal Affairs* [1980] ECR 501.

exercise the right to restitution guaranteed by Community law. As a result, the Court held that the requirement was unlawful.

The Court of Justice has considered that the following substantive English rules are contrary to the principle of effective protection: the requirement to prove misfeasance in public office when suing the United Kingdom for loss suffered as a result of the adoption of an Act of Parliament;[76] total exclusion of loss of profit as a head of damage;[77] and the requirement that, in order to be recoverable, money paid to a public authority under a mistake of law must have been paid under protest.[78]

The principle of effective protection precludes the adoption and application of national laws which are passed to limit the right to reimbursement of charges which have been declared contrary to Community law. In Case 309/85 *Barra v Belgium*[79] Mr Barra sought reimbursement of enrolment fees which he had paid before 13 February 1985, the date on which the Court of Justice gave judgment in Case 293/83 *Gravier v City of Liège*[80] in which the Court had held that the enrolment fee was unlawful. Approximately four months after the date of the Court's judgment, the Belgian state passed a law which provided that there would be no reimbursement except to those students who had brought court proceedings before the date of the *Gravier* judgment. This excluded Mr Barra, who had brought his action in March 1985. The Court of Justice ruled that such a law made it impossible to exercise the right to reimbursement of the fee which was guaranteed by Community law and should, therefore, be disapplied.[81]

National rules must be viewed in context Just as all available remedies must be considered in determining whether the domestic system of remedies complies with the principle of effective protection,[82] national procedural, evidential and substantial rules must be viewed in the light of the domestic judicial system as a whole when determining whether they make it impossible in practice to exercise Community law rights. In relation to procedural rules, the Court of Justice has stated:[83]

> ... each case which raises the question whether a national procedural provision renders application of Community law impossible or excessively difficult must be analysed by reference to the role of that provision in the procedure, its progress and its special features, viewed as a whole, before the various national instances. In the light of that analysis the basic principles of the domestic judicial system, such as

---

[76] Joined Cases C-46/93 and C-48/93 *Brasserie du Pêcheur and Factortame* [1996] ECR I-1029 para 73.

[77] Ibid para 87.

[78] Case C-212/94 *FMC v IBAP* [1996] ECR I-389 para 72.

[79] [1988] ECR 355. See also Case 240/87 *Deville v Administration des Impôts* [1988] ECR 3513.

[80] [1985] ECR 593.

[81] Only the EC courts have power to impose temporal limitations on the effect of their judgments; national courts may not do so. Temporal limitations are discussed at Ch 11, pp 240-241 and Ch 13, pp 329-330.

[82] See above at p 105.

[83] Joined Cases C-430/93 and C-431/93 *Van Schijndel v SPF* [1995] ECR I-4705 para 19; Case C-312/93 *Peterbroeck v Belgium* [1994] ECR I-4599 para 14. See also Hoskins, 'Tilting the Balance: Supremacy and National Procedural Rules' (1996) 21 ELRev 365.

protection of the rights of the defence, the principle of legal certainty and the proper conduct of procedure, must, where appropriate, be taken into consideration.

A comparison of the judgments in Joined Cases C-430/93 and C-431/93 *Van Schijndel v SPF*[84] and Case C-312/93 *Peterbroeck v Belgium*[85] illustrates this balancing exercise between the need to ensure the effectiveness of Community law and the respect for the legal autonomy of the national legal systems.

In *Van Schijndel* the Dutch authorities passed a decree making it compulsory for physiotherapists to belong to a particular pension fund. The fund could exempt those physiotherapists whose pensions were covered by a similar pension scheme, but refused to exempt Mr Van Schijndel. As a result, he was forced to make pension contributions to the fund. He successfully challenged the fund's refusal in the local court, arguing that the refusal was contrary to Dutch law. This decision was overturned by a higher court. He appealed to the Hoge Raad (Supreme Court), contending for the first time that the compulsory membership scheme infringed the EC competition rules. Under Dutch civil procedure, an appeal (cassation) to the Hoge Raad could only concern matters of law. The new pleas of competition law involved complex factual matters; he was therefore precluded from raising them and the court was precluded from raising them of its own motion. The Court of Justice held that this national procedural rule did not inhibit the effectiveness of Community law as its purpose was to ensure that litigants defined the factual scope of the dispute before the courts and to avoid undue delay inherent in the examination of new pleas before appellate courts.

By contrast, in *Peterbroeck* the balance between the autonomy of the national legal system and the effectiveness of Community law tilted the other way. Peterbroeck, a Belgian company, was charged tax on monies drawn from it by an associated Dutch company. Peterbroeck challenged this before the Tax Commissioner on the basis that it was contrary to a double taxation treaty between Belgium and the Netherlands. The Commissioner rejected the complaint. Peterbroeck appealed directly to the Court of Appeal, contending for the first time that the tax was contrary to article 52 of the EC Treaty[new art 43]. Under the Belgian Tax Code, new pleas could only be raised within 60 days from the lodging by the Commissioner with the Court of Appeal of a certified copy of the contested decision. The Court of Justice, emphasising the special nature of the rule, considered that it could not be reasonably justified on grounds of legal certainty or the proper administration of justice.[86] When the Belgian legal system as a whole was considered, the effect of the rule in *Peterbroeck*, unlike the rule in *Van Schijndel*, meant that it was impossible in practice for *any* court which was capable of making a reference to the Court of Justice under article 177 of the EC Treaty [new art 234] to raise of its own motion an issue of Community law in the tax field. This followed as the Commissioner was not a

[84] [1995] ECR I-4705.
[85] [1995] ECR I-4599.
[86] The Court of Justice did not follow the Opinion of Advocate-General Jacobs on this point.

court or tribunal within the meaning of article 177, and the 60-day period would usually have expired by the time the Court of Appeal heard the appeal.

Creation of new procedural rules Courts will have to create new procedural rules to deal with claims arising under Community law if none already exist. In *Cannon v Barnsley Metropolitan Borough Council*,[87] which concerned a claim of sex discrimination contrary to Council Directive 76/207,[88] Knox J, in the Employment Appeal Tribunal, remarked that there was no relevant provision in national law setting out a particular time period in which to bring a claim under Community law. He held that, in principle, English law was perfectly capable of creating such a time-limit, if necessary by analogy to statutory or common law time-limits. Similarly, in *Livingstone v Hepworth Refractories plc*[89] the plaintiff had retired and, at the same time, had signed an agreement whereby, in exchange for payment to him of £20,400, he waived all claims against his employer. Thereafter, he claimed that his pension fund had been operated contrary to Community law. The industrial tribunal dismissed the action for want of jurisdiction on the basis that the agreement waived all claims. Wood J, in the Employment Appeal Tribunal, held that the absence of specific procedural rules to deal with Community law claims relating to the plaintiff's pension should be filled by applying the procedures contained in the Sex Discrimination Act 1975. This Act included a code to protect employees against bad bargains. Consequently, the agreement was no bar to the action under Community law.

5. TIME-LIMITS

Public policy considerations Considerations of public policy and, in particular, legal certainty dictate that time-limits may be applied to bar proceedings. In Case 33/76 *Rewe v Landwirtschaftskammer Saarland*[90] the Court of Justice stated that:

> The laying down of such time-limits with regard to actions of a fiscal nature is an application of the fundamental principle of legal certainty protecting both the tax payer and the administration concerned.

Application of national time-limits In the absence of any time-limits laid down by Community law, it is for each national legal system to set down its own time-limits even where expiry of those limits necessarily entails the dismissal of an action founded on Community law. National time-limits are subject to the

---

[87] [1992] ICR 698.
[88] Council Directive 76/207 of 9 February 1976 on the implementation of the principle of equal treatment for men and women as regards access to employment, vocational training and promotion and working conditions (OJ 1976 L39 p 40).
[89] [1992] 3 CMLR 601.
[90] [1976] ECR 1989 para 5. See also Case 45/76 *Comet v Produktschap* [1976] ECR 2043 para 5.

overriding principles of equivalence and effectiveness. In the context of national time-limits, the Court of Justice in Case C-261/95 *Palmisani* stated:[91]

> ... it is on the basis of the rules of national law on liability that the State must make reparation for the consequences of the loss or damage caused; further, the conditions, in particular time-limits, for reparation of loss or damage laid down by national law must not be less favourable than those relating to similar domestic claims (principle of equivalence) and must not be so framed as to make it virtually impossible or excessively difficult to obtain reparation (principle of effectiveness).

Reasonable time-limits The Court of Justice has indicated that a five-year limitation period in restitution claims,[92] a one-year limitation period in damages claims[93] and a 60-day period in which to appeal to a Court of Appeal[94] are reasonable and cannot be regarded as rendering excessively difficult the exercise of rights conferred by Community law.

When time starts to run In Case C-208/90 *Emmott v Minister for Social Welfare*[95] the Court of Justice held that, where an applicant relies on rights arising under a directive against the State, the relevant national limitation period may only begin to run as from the date when the directive has been properly implemented into national law. The case concerned Directive 79/7 concerning equal treatment for men and women in matters of social security[96] for which the implementation date was 23 December 1984. In the Irish implementing legislation, which came into force in 1986, certain uniform rates and conditions were established for men and women. However, the relevant Act was not given retroactive effect as from 23 December 1984. In 1987 a judgment of the Court of Justice[97] established that the Directive entitled women in Mrs Emmott's position to equal treatment as from 23 December 1984. Mrs Emmott therefore wrote to the Irish authorities claiming that she was entitled to back-payments as from that date. The Minister for Social Welfare replied that since the Directive was still the subject of litigation before the High Court, no decision could be taken in relation to her claim at that stage, but that it would be considered once the High Court had given judgment. However, when the authorities failed to contact her as they had indicated, Mrs Emmott began judicial review proceedings before the Irish courts in January 1988. The Irish authorities sought to argue that Mrs Emmott's application was time-barred as it had not been made within the time period laid down by the relevant national rules.[98] The Court of

---

[91] [1997] ECR I-4025 para 27. The principles of equivalence and effectiveness are discussed above at pp 109–114.

[92] Case C-90/94 *Haahr Petroleum v Havn* [1997] ECR I-4085.

[93] Case C-261/95 *Palmisani* [1997] ECR I-4025 para 29.

[94] Case C-312/93 *Peterbroeck v Belgium* [1994] ECR I-4599 para 16.

[95] [1991] ECR I-4269.

[96] Council Directive 79/7 of 19 December 1978 on the progressive implementation of the principle of equal treatment for men and women in matters of social security (OJ 1979 L6 p 24).

[97] Case 286/85 *McDermott and Cotter v Minister for Social Welfare* [1987] ECR 1453.

[98] Ord 84, r 21(1) of the Rules of Superior Courts provides that an application for leave to apply for judicial review should be made promptly and in any event within three months from the date

Justice found that it would be contrary to Community law to allow the Irish authorities to rely on such a defence and held that:[99]

> ... until such time as a directive has been properly transposed, a defaulting Member State may not rely on an individual's delay in initiating proceedings against it in order to protect rights conferred upon him by the provisions of the directive and ... a period laid down by national law within which proceedings must be initiated cannot begin to run before that time.

The Court justified this finding on the basis that, until a directive has been properly implemented in national law, individuals are unable to ascertain the full extent of their rights. It would therefore be unjust to allow a Member State to rely on a national limitation period and so benefit from the uncertainty which it has caused by failing to implement the directive in the first place.

The judgment in *Emmott* may be criticised on the basis that it undermines the public policy consideration underlying time-limits. Although the judgment has not been expressly overruled it has been distinguished by the Court of Justice and the national courts to such an extent that its authority is of little value.

It is clear that *Emmott* is limited to the incorrect implementation of a directive and does not preclude Member States from relying on national time-limits where a breach of the Treaty is claimed.[100] Further, *Emmott* has no application where the directive confers no new substantive rights but has been adopted merely to give effect to or supplement a Treaty provision.[101] The judgment does not apply where the applicant is a pressure group which cannot assert any personal right conferred by the directive.[102] It has also been restricted to judicial review applications[103] and has not been applied where the incorrect implementation was made in good faith.[104]

More fundamentally, the judgment has been confined to its own facts.[105] Notwithstanding the more general language in *Emmott*, the judgment has been read by Advocate-General Jacobs and the English Court of Appeal as establishing the principle that a Member State may not rely on a limitation period where it is in default both in failing to implement a directive and has in some way contributed to the delay. In *Emmott* the Irish authorities had indicated that Mrs Emmott's claim would be dealt with at a later date but failed to do so, and subsequently, when she commenced legal proceedings, sought to rely on the relevant national limitation period. Thus, the mere fact that a directive has

---

when grounds for the application first arose.

[99] [1991] ECR I-4269 paras 21–23.

[100] Case C-90/94 *Haahr Petroleum v Havn* [1997] ECR I-4085 para 53; Joined Cases C-114/95 and C-115/95 *Texaco* [1997] ECR I-4263 para 49.

[101] *Biggs v Somerset County Council* [1996] 2 CMLR 292 paras 36–44; *Preston v Wolverhampton Healthcare Trust* [1997] EuLR 386 at 399D.

[102] Laws J in *R v Secretary of State for Trade and Industry, ex p Greenpeace* (judgment of 14 October 1997) (unreported).

[103] *Tate v Minister for Social Welfare* [1995] 1 CMLR 825 paras 65–86 (Irish High Court).

[104] *Downer v Onyx UK Ltd* [1995] 1 CMLR 559 para 11 (English industrial tribunal).

[105] Case C-90/94 *Haahr Petroleum v Havn* [1997] ECR I-4085 para 52; Joined Cases C-114/95 and C-115/95 *Texaco* [1997] ECR I-4263 para 48.

not been properly implemented does not, in the absence of other circumstances, preclude a Member State from relying upon a limitation period.[106]

Backdating Where a national rule imposes a limitation on the backdating of financial claims this will not come within the *Emmott* principle. This was established by the Court of Justice in Case C-338/91 *Steenhorst-Neerings*.[107] Mrs Steenhorst-Neerings claimed benefits pursuant to Directive 79/7 concerning equal treatment for men and women in matters of social security[108] (the same Directive as in *Emmott*). Her claim was backdated to 23 December 1984 (the date by which the Directive should have been implemented by the Member States). However, the relevant Dutch law only permitted an applicant to claim benefits backdated to one year before the date of her claim. Mrs Steenhorst-Neerings argued that, applying *Emmott*, Member States which had failed to implement a directive properly could not rely on an applicant's delay in initiating proceedings to deny rights claimed under the directive. This was rejected by the Court of Justice on the basis that a backdating rule did not prevent a private party from relying on a directive in the national court, but merely limited the quantum which she could claim. In other words, although the *extent* of Mrs Steenhorst-Neerings' claim was limited, it was not completely blocked by a national limitation rule.

The ruling in *Steenhorst-Neerings* was applied subsequently in Case C-410/92 *Johnson v Chief Adjudication Officer*[109] which concerned a UK rule that also imposed a one-year limit on the backdating of claims for social security benefits, and in Case C-394/93 *Alonso-Pérez v Bundesanstalt für Arbeit*[110] which concerned a German rule imposing a six-month limit on the backdating of claims for family benefits.

---

[106] *Preston v Wolverhampton Healthcare Trust* [1997] 2 CMLR 754, paras 47-51; [1997] EuLR 386 at 396G-399D applying Advocate-General Jacobs in Case C-2/94 *Denkavit International* [1996] ECR I-2827, paras 62-81 of the Opinion. See also paras 50-57 of Advocate-General Jacobs' Opinion in Case C-62/93 *BP Supergas v Greece* [1995] ECR I-1883; and paras 64-89 of his Opinion in Case C-188/95 *Fantask* [1997] ECR I-000 (judgment of 2 December 1997).

[107] [1993] ECR I-5475.

[108] Council Directive 79/7 of 19 December 1978 on the progressive implementation of the principle of equal treatment for men and women in matters of social security (OJ 1979 L6 p 24).

[109] [1994] ECR I-5483 paras 25-30.

[110] [1995] ECR I-4101 paras 7 and 30.

Chapter 7

Damages

1. ACTIONS AGAINST PRIVATE PARTIES

Need for an actionable wrong Before damages can be recovered, an actionable wrong must have been committed. As Lord Wright stated in *Bourhill v Young*,[1] a case which concerned the tort of negligence:

> Damage due to the legitimate exercise of a right is not actionable, even if the actor contemplates the damage. It is *damnum absque injuria*. The damage must be attributable to the breach by the defendant of some duty owing to the plaintiff.

On the same basis, not all breaches of Community law can give rise to an action for damages against private parties, since not all provisions of Community law impose duties or obligations on individuals. For example, a directive does not have horizontal direct effect and cannot, by itself, impose obligations on individuals. A breach of a directive is not, therefore, a wrong actionable at the suit of another.[2] Similarly, the system for reviewing State aids established by article 93 of the EC Treaty [new art 88] imposes no specific obligation on the recipient of aid. Consequently, the recipient is not liable to pay damages to a competitor for failing to verify that the aid was duly notified to the Commission.[3]

Available remedies The basic forms of private law remedies available in English law are damages, restitution, injunctive relief and declaratory relief. Although it is for the national legal systems to decide on the form of protection available in respect of directly effective Community law rights, the protection granted cannot make it impossible in practice to exercise those rights.[4] Injunctive or declaratory remedies can provide only future protection for Community law rights; they do not have any retrospective effect. Past loss or damage caused by a breach of Community law can only be effectively protected by the award of damages or restitution. It follows, therefore, that as a matter of

---

[1] [1943] AC 92 at 106.
[2] See further at Ch 4, pp 70–72 for a discussion on the lack of horizontal direct effect of directives.
[3] Case C-39/94 *SFEI v La Poste* [1996] ECR I-3547 paras 72–76.
[4] Case 33/76 *Rewe v Landwirtschaftskammer Saarland* [1976] ECR 1989; Case 45/76 *Comet v Produktschap* [1976] ECR 2043. See Ch 6, pp 107–114

Community law, where damages constitute the only effective remedy in a particular case, there is an obligation on the courts to ensure that such a remedy is available to the parties affected.[5]

Interest Where there is a right to damages as a result of a breach of Community law, the plaintiff is entitled to recover interest on any damages awarded to reflect the effluxion of time prior to judgment being obtained. The rate of interest remains within the discretion of the national court, provided that it satisfies the plaintiff's right to obtain effective compensation.[6]

Causes of action The English courts have accepted that an actionable wrong is committed where an individual breaches a duty imposed on him by a directly effective provision of Community law. However, some uncertainty remains as to how to categorise the nature of the breach and how to determine the relevant cause of action. Although the weight of authority favours breach of statutory duty as the relevant cause of action, a private action for damages for breach of a directly effective provision of Community law could, potentially, be brought on the grounds of an economic tort or an innominate tort.[7]

(a) Breach of statutory duty

(i) Breach of Community law categorised as breach of statutory duty
Garden Cottage Foods In *Garden Cottage Foods Ltd v Milk Marketing Board*[8] a majority of the House of Lords gave a very strong indication that damages are available to compensate loss suffered due to a breach of article 86 of the EC Treaty [new art 82]. In this case, the Milk Marketing Board allegedly held a dominant position in the supply of bulk butter in England and Wales. When it refused to supply Garden Cottage Foods Ltd, the company brought an action in the English courts for, *inter alia*, an injunction, restraining the Milk Marketing Board from withholding supplies of butter. This refusal, it was argued, constituted an abuse of a dominant position contrary to article 86. Parker J, at first instance, refused to grant the injunction on the basis that damages would be an adequate remedy. When the case reached the House of Lords, their Lordships had to consider the issue of whether damages could be awarded for a breach of article 86.

Lord Diplock, with whom three other members of the House agreed, categorised a breach of article 86 as a breach of a statutory duty. He stated:[9]

---

[5] Joined Cases C-6/90 and C-9/90 *Francovich and Bonifaci v Italy* [1991] ECR I-5357 paras 31–35; Opinion of Advocate-General van Gerven in Case C-128/92 *Banks v British Coal Corporation* [1994] ECR I-1209 para 45. Similar reasoning was adopted by Lord Diplock in *Garden Cottage Foods Ltd v Milk Marketing Board* [1984] 1 AC 130 at 144A–145G. See also *Bourgoin v Ministry of Agriculture, Fisheries and Food* [1986] 1 QB 716 at 770C–773E, per Lord Oliver (dissenting).

[6] Case C-271/91 *Marshall v Southampton and South-West Hampshire AHA* [1993] ECR I-4367 paras 27–32; Case 130/79 *Express Dairy Foods v IBAP* [1980] ECR 1887.

[7] See Precedent A.

[8] [1984] 1 AC 130.

[9] Ibid at 141C–E.

This article of the Treaty of Rome (the E.E.C. Treaty) was held by the European Court of Justice in *BRT v SABAM* (case 127/73) [1974] ECR 51, 62 to produce direct effects in relations between individuals and to create direct rights in respect of the individuals concerned which the national courts must protect. This decision of the European Court of Justice as to the effect of article 86 is one which section 3(1) of the European Communities Act 1972 requires your Lordships to follow. The rights which the article confers upon citizens in the United Kingdom accordingly fall within section 2(1) of the Act. They are without further enactment to be given legal effect in the United Kingdom and enforced accordingly.

A breach of the duty imposed by article 86 not to abuse a dominant position in the common market or in a substantial part of it, can thus be categorised in English law as a breach of statutory duty that is imposed not only for the purpose of promoting the general economic prosperity of the common market but also for the benefit of private individuals to whom loss or damage is caused by a breach of that duty.

It was, in his Lordship's view, unnecessary to invent new causes of action to deal with breaches of articles of the EEC Treaty. Furthermore, he could see no other categorisation which could give rise to a civil cause of action in English private law on the part of a private individual who sustained loss or damage by reason of a breach of a directly effective provision of the EEC Treaty. Although his Lordship conceded that his categorisation was not beyond argument, he considered that if a breach of article 86 gives rise to a civil cause of action at all, it must be a cause of action for which damages are available. His Lordship stated:[10]

> I, for my own part, find it difficult to see how it can ultimately be successfully argued ... that a contravention of article 86 which causes damage to an individual citizen does not give rise to a cause of action in English law of the nature of a cause of action for breach of statutory duty; but since it cannot be regarded as unarguable that is not a matter for final decision by your Lordships at the interlocutory stage that the instant case has reached. What, with great respect to those who think otherwise, I *do* regard as quite unarguable is the proposition ... that if such a contravention of article 86 gives rise to any cause of action at all, it gives rise to a cause of action for which there is no remedy in damages to compensate for loss already caused by that contravention but only a remedy by way of injunction to prevent future loss being caused.

Lord Wilberforce dissented. He considered that the question of whether damages were available for breach of article 86 was open to argument and he was not prepared to decide what he considered to be a difficult question of law during interlocutory proceedings. His Lordship stated:[11]

> So far as the Community is concerned, article 86 is enforced under Regulation No 17 by orders to desist (article 3), and if necessary by fines (article 15), and the Court of Justice has similar powers on review. Fines are not payable to persons injured by the prohibited conduct, and there is no way under Community law by which such persons can get damages. So the question is, whether the situation is changed, and the remedy extended, by the incorporation of article 86 into our law by section 2 of the European Communities Act 1972. To say that thereby what is prohibited action becomes a tort or a 'breach of statutory duty' is, in my opinion, a conclusionary

---

[10] Ibid at 144B–D.
[11] Ibid at 151G–152D.

statement concealing a vital and unexpressed step. All that section 2 says (relevantly) is that rights arising under the Treaty are to be available in law in the United Kingdom, but this does not suggest any transformation or enlargement in their character.

Subsequent cases Subsequent cases have adopted the approach of the majority of the House of Lords in *Garden Cottage Foods*. Thus, in *An Bord Bainne Co-operative v Milk Marketing Board*[12] Neill J stated that although the House of Lords in *Garden Cottage Foods* did not decide definitively that a breach of article 86 gives rise to a cause of action in English law:

> ... the speeches provide compelling support for the proposition that contraventions of EEC regulations which have 'direct effects' create direct rights in private law which the national courts must protect.

Similarly, in *Bourgoin v Ministry of Agriculture, Fisheries and Food*,[13] a case concerning article 30 of the EC Treaty [new art 28], Parker LJ considered that *Garden Cottage Foods* was 'clear authority that a private law action for breach of article 86 against an undertaking sounds in damages'. In *Plessey Co plc v General Electric Co plc and Siemens*[14] Morritt J stated:

> ... a breach of Article 85 is, in English law, the equivalent to the breach of a statutory duty imposed for the benefit of private individuals to whom loss or damage is caused by a breach of that duty.
> As *Garden Cottage Foods* makes plain, the rights so created in favour of individuals are ones which the national courts must protect by the normal remedies of damages or injunctions.

Breach of a directly effective provision of Community law which constitutes a breach of statutory duty has been described as a 'Eurotort'.[15]

(ii) Analysis of the tort

Definition In order to establish a cause of action based on breach of statutory duty, a plaintiff must show that:[16]

(1) the loss suffered is within the scope of the statute;
(2) the statute gives rise to a civil cause of action;
(3) there has been a breach of statutory duty; and
(4) the breach has caused the loss complained of.

(1) Loss suffered is within the scope of the statute

Imposition of a duty Whether the loss suffered is within the scope of the

---

[12] [1984] 1 CMLR 519 at para 24.

[13] [1986] 1 QB 716 at 787D. Nourse LJ, at p 790DE, stated that he was in 'entire agreement' with this view.

[14] [1990] ECC 384 paras 37-38. See also *Cutsforth v Mansfield Inns Ltd* [1986] 1 WLR 558 at 563G, per Sir Neil Lawson; *Argyll Group v The Distillers Co* [1986] 1 CMLR 764 at 767 and 769, per Lord Jauncey; *Merson v Rover Group* (unreported) 22 May 1992; *Leyland DAF v Automotive Products* [1994] 1 BCLC 245; Cf *R v Secretary of State for Transport, ex p Factortame Ltd* [1997] EuLR 475 on State liability (see below at pp 128–148).

[15] Henry J in *Barretts & Baird (Wholesale) v IPCS* [1987] IRLR 3 at 5.

[16] See, generally, *Clerk and Lindsell on Torts*, 17th edn (Sweet & Maxwell, 1995), Ch 11.

statute depends upon whether the statute imposes a duty for the benefit of the particular individual harmed. Where a duty is imposed for the benefit of individuals, a correlative right arises in those persons who may be injured by its contravention.[17]

The concept of direct effect appears neatly to satisfy this first condition to establish a cause of action.[18] A directly effective provision of Community law imposes, upon one person, a clear and unconditional obligation, which, in most cases, creates rights in others to whom that duty is owed. As the Court of Justice has stated, a directly effective provision of Community law is:[19]

> ... a direct source of rights and duties for all those affected thereby, whether Member States or individuals, who are parties to legal relationships under Community law.

These rights are fundamental rights, since Community law:[20]

> ... not only imposes obligations on individuals but is also intended to confer upon them rights which become part of their legal heritage.

Since s 2(1) of the European Communities Act 1972 provides the statutory basis for the recognition of directly effective rights and duties in the English legal system, any breach of a directly effective Community provision by a private party can be said to constitute a breach of the statutory duty imposed by the European Communities Act 1972. Therefore, Lord Diplock's analysis in this respect appears to be sound.[21]

The preamble to a Community measure and the preparatory material leading to its adoption may be of assistance in determining whether the provision imposes a duty for the benefit of particular individuals. Thus, in *Scotch Whisky Association and others v Glen Kella Distillers Ltd*[22] two whisky manufacturers sought to prevent Glen Kella from selling as whisky a white spirit which had not undergone the manufacturing process required by Regulation 1576/89.[23] Rattee J, construing the Regulation in the light of its recitals and of the Opinion of the Economic and Social Committee, concluded that the duty imposed by the Regulation on whisky manufacturers was imposed, *inter alios*, for the benefit of their competitors. Accordingly, a breach of the Regulation by Glen Kella was actionable at the suit of the two whisky manufacturers.

---

[17] *Butler v Fife Coal Co Ltd* [1912] AC 149 at 165, per Lord Kinnear.

[18] For an analysis of direct effect, see Ch 4.

[19] Case 106/77 *Amministrazione delle Finanze v Simmenthal* [1978] ECR 629 para 15.

[20] Case 26/62 *Van Gend en Loos v Nederlandse administratie der belastinge* [1963] ECR 1 at 12.

[21] This is the basis upon which the Divisional Court held that the Secretary of State for Transport was liable for breach of article 52 of the EC Treaty [new art 43] in *R v Secretary of State for Transport, ex p Factortame Ltd* [1997] EuLR 475 (see below at p 130).

[22] [1997] EuLR 445 at 464E–466D. See also *The Scotch Whisky Association v JD Vintners Ltd* [1997] EuLR 446 at 448F–451H; *Tattinger SA v Allbe Ltd* [1993] FSR 641. Compare the judgment of Clarke J in *Three Rivers v Bank of England* [1996] 3 All ER 558 at 603–622.

[23] Laying down general rules for the definition, description and presentation of spirit drinks (OJ 1989 L160 p 1).

(2) Statute gives rise to a civil cause of action

Duty to protect Since national courts are bound to protect directly effective rights which are conferred on individuals, any breach of a directly effective provision of Community law should *prima facie* give rise to a civil cause of action.

Other means of protection In English law, a civil cause of action may be denied where the right conferred by the statute is protected in some other way, for example by a criminal sanction.[24] Community law rights may also be protected by other means. The Commission or Member States may bring proceedings before the Court of Justice, respectively, under article 169 [new art 226] or 170 [new art 227] of the EC Treaty for a declaration that a Member State is in breach of its Treaty obligations. In relation to competition law, the Commission may act pursuant to Regulation 17, ordering the termination of a restrictive practice or imposing fines for breach of the competition rules.[25] However, these other means of protecting directly effective rights cannot prevent individuals from invoking their rights before the national courts. As the Court of Justice stated in Case 26/62 *Van Gend En Loos v Nederlandse administratie der belastungen:*[26]

> ... the argument based on Article 169 and 170 of the Treaty put forward by the three Governments which have submitted observations to the Court in their statements of case is misconceived. The fact that these Articles of the Treaty enable the Commission and the Member States to bring before the Court a State which has not fulfilled its obligations does not mean that individuals cannot plead these obligations, should the occasion arise, before a national court, any more than the fact that the Treaty places at the disposal of the Commission ways of ensuring that obligations imposed upon those subject to the Treaty are observed, precludes the possibility, in actions between individuals before a national court, of pleading infringements of these obligations.
>
> A restriction of the guarantees against an infringement of Article 12 by Member States to the procedures under Article 169 and 170 would remove all direct legal protection of the individual rights of their nationals. There is the risk that recourse to the procedure under these Articles would be ineffective if it were to occur after the implementation of a national decision taken contrary to the provisions of the Treaty.

(3) Breach of the statutory duty

Strict liability Under domestic law, liability for breach of statutory duty is usually strict or absolute. However, the courts have occasionally rejected a plaintiff's claim on the basis that the defendant took all reasonable steps to comply with the duty or on the basis that the breach was unavoidable. Whether or not liability depends on fault is determined by the proper construction of the

---

[24] *Monk v Warbey* [1935] 1 KB 75; *Lonrho Ltd v Shell Petroleum Co Ltd (No 2)* [1982] AC 173.

[25] Council Regulation No 17/62 of 6 February 1962 (OJ 1962 13 p 204), First Regulation implementing articles 85 and 86 of the EEC Treaty (Special Edition 1959–1962, p 87) as amended.

[26] [1963] ECR 1 at 13. See also Case 28/67 *Molkerei-Zentrale Westfalen v Hauptzollamt Paderborn* [1968] ECR 143. In respect of competition matters, see Case 127/73 *BRT v SABAM* [1974] ECR 51 at 63; and Lord Diplock in *Garden Cottage Foods Ltd v Milk Marketing Board* [1984] 1 AC 130 at 146H.

statute.[27] By contrast, since directly effective provisions of Community law, by definition, impose clear and unconditional duties, liability for breach of statutory duty in respect of Community law is likely to be strict or absolute. A breach of Community law is examined objectively and requires no examination of reasonableness.[28] For example, there is no scope for an English court to hold that, on the true construction of article 86, an undertaking is not in breach because it has acted reasonably.[29]

Sufficiently serious breach? The liability of Member States to pay damages for breach of Community law is dependent on the existence of a sufficiently serious breach. The relevant cause of action in respect of State liability is a breach of statutory duty, albeit of a *sui generis* nature.[30] The need to prove a serious breach is dictated by policy considerations, namely that the legislative and administrative functions of Member States should not be hindered by the prospect of damages claims.

Policy considerations relating to good administration do not apply to actions against private individuals. Nevertheless, the wide class of individuals to whom a statutory duty may be owed, and the absolute nature of the definition of a breach, potentially expose a defendant—particularly an undertaking in a dominant position—to an indeterminate amount of damages payable to an indeterminate number of plaintiffs. Despite this risk, it appears that there is no scope for the sufficiently serious breach condition to be imposed in actions against private parties. In Case C-128/92 *Banks v British Coal Corporation*[31] Advocate-General van Gerven stated that in the context of breach of the Community competition laws:

> ... it is sufficient if an undertaking infringes the directly effective provisions of Community competition law. In that regard there is no question of applying any criterion that is more favourable to those who engage in such conduct, such as that applied by the Court in Article 215 cases with a view to appraising the exercise by the authorities of a broad discretionary power, namely that a 'sufficiently serious breach of a superior rule of law for the protection of the individual has occurred': the relevant rules of competition impose on undertakings precise, directly effective obligations which are reflected in rights conferred on individuals ... Once a breach of such a provision, viewed in objective terms, is established, an action for damages can be brought on the basis of Community law ...[32]

---

[27] *Read v Croydon Corporation* [1938] 4 All ER 631 at 651 (where a statutory duty to supply pure water was construed as a duty to take all reasonable care). See also *Atkinson v Newcastle and Gateshead Waterworks Co* (1877) LR 2 Ex D 441.

[28] See Ch 12, pp 257-261 for a discussion of the objective nature of Member States' failure to fulfil EC Treaty obligations in the context of article 169.

[29] For example, Case T-65/89 *BPB Industries v Commission* [1993] ECR II-389 para 70.

[30] See below at p 130.

[31] [1994] ECR I-1209, at para 53 of the Opinion.

[32] The Court of Justice did not address this issue since it ruled that the competition rules of the ECSC Treaty, unlike those of the EC Treaty, do not have direct effect.

(4) Breach has caused the loss

Causation The plaintiff must show that on a balance of probabilities the breach of duty caused or materially contributed to his loss. This is a simple, factual 'but for' test of causation: would the damage have occurred but for the breach? However, even where the plaintiff can show causation in fact, the Court may still reject the defendant's breach of statutory duty as the legal cause of the damage in favour of some other more important factual cause.[33]

Co-extensive duties on defendant and plaintiff The situation may arise where both the plaintiff and the defendant are under a statutory duty not to breach a directly effective provision of Community law. For example, an agreement between a supplier and a distributor may contain an export ban prohibiting the distributor from selling outside the contract territory. If the export ban is subsequently invalidated as being contrary to article 85 of the EC Treaty [new art 81], which prohibits agreements that distort competition in the Common Market, can the distributor sue the supplier in damages for lost sales? The High Court has held that a contracting party cannot recover damages from his co-contractor on the grounds that article 85 does not afford such a plaintiff any Community law rights and that a cause of action cannot be founded on an illegal act (*ex turpi causa non oritur actio*).[34]

Whether this uncompromising approach is compatible with the principle of effective protection is likely, ultimately, to be determined by the Court of Justice. It is not one which has been adopted by the Supreme Court in the United States where a contracting party is not barred from bringing an action for damages where he is not *in pari delicto* (eg where the plaintiff was in a weaker bargaining position than his co-contractor).[35] A similar approach is adopted by the English courts when both the plaintiff and defendant are in breach of the same statutory duty. In such circumstances, the courts determine who was primarily at fault and do not regard the principle of *ex turpi causa non oritur actio* as affording a complete defence.[36] Consequently, it is arguable that, in the above example, the distributor may recover some of the loss caused by the export ban, especially where the distributor contracted on the basis of the supplier's standard terms and conditions. Clearly, different considerations may apply where one member of a price fixing cartel sues the other members for loss suffered as a result of its operation.

---

[33] *Clerk and Lindsell on Torts*, 17th edn (Sweet & Maxwell 1995), para 11–27.

[34] *Scottish and Newcastle Plc v Bond* (unreported judgment of HHJ Peter Crawford QC, 25 March 1997, (QBD); *Garry Parkes v Esso Petroleum Company Ltd* (unreported judgment of Sir Richard Scott VC, 11 February 1998, (Ch); *Trent Taverns Ltd v Sykes* (unreported judgment of David Steel J, 18 February 1998, (QBD). See also *Tinsley v Milligan* [1994] 1 AC 340 (HL).

[35] *Perma Life Mufflers v International Parts* [1968] 392 US 134 (Supreme Court); see also para 44 of the Opinion of Advocate-General van Gerven in Case-128/92 *Banks v British Coal Corporation* [1994] ECR I-1209.

[36] *National Coal Board v England* [1954] AC 403; *Boyle v Kodak* [1969] 1 WLR 661.

(b) Economic torts

(i) Unlawful interference with trade or business

Nature of the tort The tort of unlawful interference with trade or business is a relatively recent judicial development.[37] Although the precise limits of the tort have still to be defined, it appears that in order to establish a right to damages for unlawful interference, it is necessary to show that;

(1) there was an unlawful act;

(2) which foreseeably caused injury to the interests of another or which was done with the intention of harming another.

Unlawful act In *Lonrho plc v Fayed*[38] Dillon LJ indicated that the mere fact that an act is in breach of a statutory prohibition does not render it 'unlawful' for the purposes of the tort of unlawful interference. The complainant must show that on its true construction the statute which imposes the prohibition gives rise to a civil remedy. In *Barretts & Baird (Wholesale) v IPCS*[39] Henry J considered that a breach of statutory duty was, itself, unlawful. Breaches of the Restrictive Trade Practices Act 1976 are considered unlawful for the purposes of this tort,[40] and so, by analogy, would breaches of articles 85 and 86 of the EC Treaty [new arts 81 and 82]. Since directly effective Community provisions create rights for individuals which the English courts are bound to protect, breach of a directly effective provision should be considered 'unlawful' for the purposes of this tort.

Intention/foreseeability It is not necessary to prove that the predominant purpose of the tortfeasor was to injure the victim. In *Lonrho plc v Fayed*[41] Dillon LJ held that 'It has to be proved by a plaintiff who seeks to rely on this tort that the unlawful act was in some sense directed against the plaintiff or intended to harm the plaintiff'. Woolf LJ stated that 'If a defendant has deliberately embarked upon a course of conduct, the probable consequences of which to the plaintiff he appreciated, I do not see why the plaintiff should not be compensated'. The requirement that there be some degree of intention or foreseeability distinguishes this tort from the tort of breach of statutory duty.

Examples The tort of unlawful interference could form the basis of a cause of action where a company in a dominant position is engaged in a campaign of predatory pricing, with the specific intention of driving a competitor out of the market or of dissuading a potential competitor from entering that market. The tort could also arise where a supplier gave instructions to his distributors not to

---

[37] See *JT Stratford & Son Ltd v Lindley* [1965] AC 269 at 324, per Lord Reid, and at 328, per Viscount Radcliffe; *Merkur Island Shipping Corp v Laughton* [1983] 2 AC 570 at 609–610, per Lord Diplock; *Lonrho plc v Fayed* [1990] 2 QB 479 (CA) (the House of Lords affirmed the decision on other grounds at [1991] 3 WLR 188). See also *Clerk and Lindsell on Torts*, 17th edn (Sweet & Maxwell, 1995), para 23–56.

[38] [1990] 2 QB 479 at 488E–G.

[39] [1987] IRLR 3 at 6.

[40] For example see *Daily Mirror v Gardner* [1968] 2 QB 762; applied in *Brekkes Ltd v Cattel* [1972] 1 Ch 105, and considered good law in *Associated British Ports v TGWU* [1989] 1 WLR 939.

[41] [1990] 2 QB 479 at 489E and 494D.

supply a particular company which wished to undertake parallel imports of the goods concerned.

(ii) Conspiracy

Nature of the tort Liability for civil conspiracy may take two forms:[42]

(1) where two or more parties combine, with the predominant intention of causing injury to another, even though the means used are lawful; or

(2) where two or more parties intentionally injure another by use of unlawful means, even if their primary purpose is to further or protect their own interests.[43]

Example The tort of conspiracy may be applicable to the operation of a cartel. A claim based on the second type of civil conspiracy might be appropriate where there has been a breach of article 85, for example where a group of companies enter into a price-fixing agreement in an attempt to gain an advantage over other competitors. Although the primary purpose of the participants in the cartel may be to retain market share and protect their own interests, their conduct may be tortious if there is also an intent to injure a competitor. Consequently, any competitor which suffers loss as a result of the cartel may seek to rely on the tort of conspiracy. Breach of statutory duty should be pleaded in the alternative, as the necessary conditions are easier to satisfy.

(c) Innominate torts

Rejection of the concept In *Application des Gaz SA v Falks Veritas Ltd*[44] Lord Denning MR stated, *obiter*, that as articles 85 and 86 of the EC Treaty [new arts 81 and 82] have direct effect, they are part of English law and create new torts or wrongs called 'undue restriction of competition within the common market' and 'abuse of dominant position within the common market'. However, this approach of creating new torts to compensate for breaches of Community law was firmly rejected by Lord Diplock in *Garden Cottage Foods Ltd v Milk Marketing Board*[45] who stated that there was no reason to invent a wholly novel cause of action in order to deal with breaches of articles of the EC Treaty which have the same effect in the United Kingdom as statutes. Furthermore, in *Bourgoin SA v Ministry of Agriculture, Fisheries and Food*[46] Mann J, at first instance, described the formulation of a claim based on an innominate tort as 'obsolete'.

---

[42] *Lonrho plc v Fayed* [1992] 1 AC 448 contains a thorough analysis of the relevant case law.

[43] The arguments relating to the definition of 'unlawful means' in the context of the tort of unlawful interference should also apply to the tort of conspiracy. See above at p 126.

[44] [1974] 1 Ch 381 at 395H–396C. See also the judgment of Lord Denning MR in *Garden Cottage Foods Ltd v Milk Marketing Board* [1982] 3 WLR 514 at 516B–G.

[45] [1984] 1 AC 130 at 144F–G. See also the doubts expressed by Roskill LJ in *Valor International Ltd v Application des Gaz SA* [1978] 3 CMLR 87 at 99–100.

[46] [1986] 1 QB 716 at 734B–F, following a concession by counsel; see the comments of Oliver LJ at 775C–G.

2. ACTIONS AGAINST THE STATE

(a) General principles of liability

Principle of State liability The principle of State liability was established by the Court of Justice in Joined Cases C-6/90 and C-9/90 *Francovich and Bonifaci v Italy*[47] where it was held that:

> ... it is a principle of Community law that the Member States are obliged to make good loss and damage caused to individuals by breaches of Community law for which they can be held responsible.[48]

The principle of State liability is not expressly provided for in the Treaty. However, the Court of Justice has held that it is inherent in the Treaty, and particularly article 5 [new art 10], that Member States should take all appropriate measures to comply with their Treaty obligations, which includes rectifying any unlawful consequences due to their breach of Community law.[49] The principle of State liability also follows from the principle of effective protection of Community law rights. As the Court of Justice stated in Joined Cases C-6/90 and C-9/90 *Francovich and Bonifaci v Italy:*[50]

> ... it has been consistently held that the national courts whose task it is to apply the provisions of Community law in areas within their jurisdiction must ensure that those rules take full effect and must protect the rights which they confer on individuals.
>
> The full effectiveness of Community rules would be impaired and the protection of the rights which they grant would be weakened if individuals were unable to obtain redress when their rights are infringed by a breach of Community law for which a Member State can be held responsible.

---

[47] [1991] ECR I-5357 paras 31–37. See also Case 60/75 *Russo v AIMA* [1976] ECR 45 para 9; and Case 6/60 *Humblet v Belgium* [1960] ECR 559 for early judgments on State liability under the ECSC Treaty.

[48] Confirmed by the Court of Justice in Case C-334/92 *Wagner Miret* [1993] ECR I-6911; Case C-91/92 *Faccini Dori v Recreb* [1994] ECR I-3325; Joined Cases C-46/93 and C-48/93 *Brasserie du Pêcheur and Factortame* [1996] ECR I-1029; Case C-192/94 *El Corte Inglés v Blázquez Rivero* [1996] ECR I-1281; Case C-392/93 *R v HM Treasury, ex p British Telecommunications* [1996] ECR I-1631; Case C-5/94 *R v MAFF, ex p Hedley Lomas* [1996] ECR I-2553; Joined Cases C-178/94 and others *Dillenkofer v Germany* [1996] ECR I-4845; Joined Cases C-283/94, C-291/94 and C-292/94 *Denkavit International v Bundesamt für Finanzen* [1996] ECR I-5063; Case C-66/95 *R v Secretary of State for Social Security, ex p Sutton* [1997] ECR I-2163; Joined Cases C-94/95 and C-95/95 *Bonifaci v INPS ('Bonifaci II')* [1997] ECR I-3969; Case C-373/95 *Maso v INPS* [1997] ECR I-4051; Case C-261/95 *Palmisani v INPS* [1997] ECR I-4025. Applied by the Court of Appeal in *R v Secretary of State for the Home Department, ex p Gallagher* [1996] 2 CMLR 951; by the Commercial Court in *Coal Authority v HJ Banks and Co* [1997] EuLR 610; by the Divisional Court in *R v Secretary of State for Transport, ex p Factortame* [1997] EuLR 475, upheld by Court of Appeal, 8 April 1998; and by the German Federal Supreme Court in *Brasserie du Pêcheur v Germany* [1997] 1 CMLR 971.

[49] Joined Cases C-6/90 and C-9/90 *Francovich and Bonifaci v Italy* [1991] ECR I-5357 para 36. In Joined Cases C-46/93 and C-48/93 *Brasserie du Pêcheur and Factortame* [1996] ECR I-1029 para 24 the Court of Justice rejected an argument that State liability to pay damages could only be created by legislation, not by judicial interpretation of the EC Treaty.

[50] [1991] ECR I-5357 paras 32–33. For the principle of effective protection, see Ch 6.

Conditions of liability A Member State will incur liability for breach of Community law where:[51]

(1) the rule of Community law infringed is intended to confer rights on individuals;

(2) the breach is sufficiently serious; and

(3) there is a direct causal link between the breach of the obligation resting on the State and the damage sustained by the injured parties.

Need for a sufficiently serious breach The scope of the principle of State liability is, potentially, very far-reaching. Breaches of Community law by Member States are ascertained objectively; there is no element of fault involved in determining a breach.[52] If State liability in damages were to be based purely on breach, Member States might be faced with liability 'in an indeterminate amount for an indeterminate time to an indeterminate class'.[53] Governments would thereby be hindered by the prospect of actions for damages whenever the general interest required Member States to adopt measures which could adversely affect individual interests. It was in order to meet these concerns that the Court of Justice, in Joined Cases C-46/93 and C-48/93 *Brasserie du Pêcheur and Factortame*,[54] ruled that there must be a sufficiently serious breach of Community law before a Member State can incur liability; a breach *simpliciter* is not sufficient. In adopting this restrictive approach to State liability, the Court expressly applied by analogy the similar test for establishing the non-contractual liability of the Community institutions under the second paragraph of article 215 of the EC Treaty [new art 288].[55]

No requirement of fault The obligation to make reparation for damage caused to individuals cannot depend upon any fault going beyond that of a sufficiently serious breach of Community law. 'Imposition of such a supplementary condition would be tantamount to calling in question the right to reparation founded on the Community legal order.'[56] Thus, intentional or negligent conduct on the part of the State cannot be a condition of liability, although it is relevant in determining whether or not a given breach of Community law is sufficiently serious. This means that misfeasance in public office, which

---

[51] Joined Cases C-46/93 and C-48/93 *Brasserie du Pêcheur and Factortame* [1996] ECR I-1029 para 51. The substantive conditions of liability are analysed below at pp 133–142.

[52] Case 415/85 *Commission v Ireland* [1988] ECR 3097 para 9; Case 416/85 *Commission v United Kingdom* [1988] ECR 3127 para 9; Case C-209/89 *Commission v Italy* [1991] ECR I-1575 para 6.

[53] *Ultramares Corporation v Touche* [1931] 174 NE 441 at 444, per Cardozo J; *Three Rivers DC v Bank of England (No 3)* [1996] 3 All ER 558 at 632, per Clarke J.

[54] [1996] ECR I-1029.

[55] As to article 215, see Ch 16.

[56] Joined Cases C-46/93 and C-48/93 *Brasserie du Pêcheur and Factortame* [1996] ECR I-1029 para 79; Joined Cases C-178/94 and others *Dillenkofer v Germany* [1996] ECR I-4845 at para 28; *R v Secretary of State for Transport, ex p Factortame and others* [1997] EuLR 475 at 508E (Div Ct), upheld by Court of Appeal, 8 April 1998.

depends on malice or knowledge of the breach, is no longer an appropriate cause of action to determine State liability for breach of Community law.[57]

Cause of action The necessary corollary of applying the sufficiently serious test to the principle of State liability is that the nature of the claim is new to English law.[58] In *R v Secretary of State for Transport, ex p Factortame*[59] the Divisional Court considered that 'whilst it can be said that the cause of action is *sui generis*, it is of the character of a breach of statutory duty. The United Kingdom and its organs and agencies have not performed a duty which they were statutorily required to perform'. The statutory duty is one imposed by the European Communities Act 1972 not to act contrary to Community law.[60] The cause of action is *sui generis* because the conditions of substantive liability are primarily determined by Community law, not by domestic law.

Application of national rules Reparation must be made in accordance with domestic rules on liability, provided they are not less favourable than those relating to similar domestic claims (principle of equivalence) and do not make it excessively difficult to obtain reparation (principle of effectiveness).[61] The right to obtain compensation under Community law is therefore subject to national procedural rules (for example time-limits, limitation periods, competent courts[62]), and to national evidential rules.[63] National substantive conditions continue to apply insofar as they provide 'the framework within which the State must make reparation'.[64]

Thus, the meaning of principles such as causation, mitigation and contributory negligence are governed by national law. Nevertheless, since the Court of Justice has in terms equated the approach which a national court should adopt to that which the Court of Justice would adopt in dealing with an application for damages against the Community under article 215 of the EC Treaty [new art 288], a consideration of the case-law on article 215 will help to identify the

---

[57] On this basis, the actual decision in *Bourgoin v MAFF* [1986] 1 QB 716 can no longer be regarded as good law insofar as it decides that misfeasance in public office is the appropriate cause of action in claims involving Community law. However, the observations of Parker and Nourse LJJ concerning the policy considerations of not unduly hindering effective government and their reliance on article 215 of the EC Treaty remain valid.

[58] For the domestic law position, see *X (Minors) v Bedfordshire CC* [1995] 2 AC 633 at 730–740. Private law claims for damages may lie for breach of statutory duty *simpliciter*. See above at pp 123–124.

[59] [1997] EuLR 475 at 530G–531D. The *sui generis* nature of the cause of action was also recognised by Clarke J in *Three Rivers DC v Bank of England* [1996] 3 All ER 558 at 624d.

[60] See Ch 3.

[61] Joined Cases C-46/93 and C-48/93 *Brasserie du Pêcheur and Factortame* [1996] ECR I-1029 para 67. See Ch 6, pp 107–114.

[62] Case C-261/95 *Palmisani* [1997] ECR I-4025 para 27.

[63] Joined Cases C-6/90 and C-9/90 *Francovich and Bonifaci v Italy* [1991] ECR I-5357. See also Case 199/82 *Amministrazione delle Finanze v San Giorgio* [1983] ECR 3595 paras 11–18.

[64] Case C-66/95 *R v Secretary of State for Social Security, ex p Sutton* [1997] ECR I-2163 para 33. See also para 105 of the Opinion of Advocate-General Tesauro in Joined Cases C-46/93 and C-48/93 *Brasserie du Pêcheur and Factortame* [1996] ECR I-1029, where he stated that, 'It is therefore the detailed rules for effectuating the individual's right to reparation which are governed by national law ...'.

manner in which the principle of State liability is intended to apply.[65]

Nature of breach The principle of State liability applies regardless of whether the breach stems from primary legislation,[66] secondary legislation[67] or an administrative decision.[68] Furthermore, the test is the same irrespective of the type of breach, for example, the adoption of an act contrary to the Treaty,[69] the failure to abolish an act contrary to the Treaty,[70] misimplementation of a directive,[71] or non-implementation of a directive.[72] It follows that, unless less strict national rules apply to a particular type of breach,[73] there is a single test for liability in respect of all breaches by the State of Community law.[74]

In Joined Cases C-178/94 and others *Dillenkofer v Germany*[75] the Court of Justice confirmed that the sufficiently serious test applies equally to the non-implementation of a directive. This had not been apparent from the earlier judgment in Joined Cases C-6/90 and C-9/90 *Francovich and Bonifaci v Italy*.[76] A failure to implement a directive within the required time-limit will inevitably mean that the Member State has committed a sufficiently serious breach.

Less strict conditions Although a Member State may incur liability on the basis of conditions laid down by national law which are less strict than those established by Community law,[77] English law, subject to a few specific statutory exceptions, does not provide for State liability under less strict conditions, and so the Community law principles apply.[78] An area where less strict conditions have been laid down is public procurement. A breach of the domestic public procurement regulations, which implement the Remedies

---

[65] *R v Secretary of State for Transport, ex p Factortame* [1997] EuLR 475 at 511E (Div Ct); see also judgment of Court of Appeal, 8 April 1998.

[66] Joined Cases C-46/93 and C-48/93 *Brasserie du Pêcheur and Factortame* [1996] ECR I-1029.

[67] Case C-392/93 *R v HM Treasury, ex p British Telecommunications* [1996] ECR I-1631.

[68] Case C-5/94 *R v MAFF ex p Hedley Lomas* [1996] ECR I-2553. See below at p 146. In this respect, the principle of State liability differs from the non-contractual liability of the Community under article 215 of the EC Treaty. Where the Community institutions act in a purely administrative capacity, they may incur liability under article 215 even if the breach is not sufficiently serious. See Ch 16, pp 360–364.

[69] Joined Cases C-46/93 and C-48/93 *Brasserie du Pêcheur and Factortame* [1996] ECR I-1029. See below at p 143.

[70] Ibid. See below at p 145.

[71] Case C-392/93 *R v HM Treasury, ex p British Telecommunications* [1996] ECR I-1631. See below at p 147.

[72] Joined Cases C-178/94 and others *Dillenkofer v Germany* [1996] ECR I-4845. See below at p 145.

[73] See below under 'Less strict conditions'.

[74] Joined Cases C-178/94 and others *Dillenkofer v Germany* [1996] ECR I-4845 paras 20–27; Joined Cases C-94/95 and C-95/95 *Bonifaci v INPS* [1997] ECR I-3969 para 47. See also *R v Secretary of State for Transport, ex p Factortame* [1997] EuLR 475 at 507G–508D (Div Ct).

[75] [1996] ECR I-4845.

[76] [1991] ECR I-5357.

[77] Joined Cases C-46/93 and C-48/93 *Brasserie du Pêcheur and Factortame* [1996] ECR I-1029 para 66.

[78] *R v Secretary of State for Transport, ex p Factortame* [1997] EuLR 475 at 506F (Div Ct).

Directive[79] and the Utilities Remedies Directive,[80] amounts to a breach of a statutory duty owed to any aggrieved supplier or contractor. The action is for breach of statutory duty *simpliciter* (ie irrespective of any sufficiently serious breach).[81]

Definition of the State A Member State is liable to make reparation whichever organ of the State is responsible for the breach. In view of the fundamental requirement of the Community legal order that Community law be uniformly applied, the obligation to make good damage caused to individuals by breaches of Community law cannot depend on domestic rules as to the division of powers between the constitutional authorities. In international law, a State is viewed as a single entity irrespective of whether the breach is attributable to the legislature, the judiciary or the executive. This principle applies *a fortiori* in the Community legal order since all State authorities, including the legislature, are bound to comply with Community law.[82]

Community law defines the State in broad terms, going beyond merely the legislature and the executive.[83] For the purposes of the vertical direct effect of directives, the definition of 'organ of the State' has been extended to cover local authorities,[84] health authorities,[85] the police[86] and nationalised industries.[87] If these bodies are viewed as organs of the State when considering direct effect, it seems logical also to apply the principle of State liability to them. There are two probable exceptions. First, the principle should apply only where the State organ is acting in some administrative or public capacity (eg police refusing to protect livestock exporters allegedly in breach of article 30 of the EC Treaty [new art 28]), as opposed to a private capacity (eg discrimination between employees on grounds of sex). Secondly, where the State organ is merely applying a domestic law which is found to infringe Community law, the State organ (as opposed to the State itself) is not the proper defendant. In *Kirklees Metropolitan Borough Council v Wickes Building Supplies*[88] the House of Lords considered that the local authority could not be liable in damages for enforcing, allegedly contrary to article 30 of the EC Treaty, the Sunday trading ban provided for by s 47 of the Shops Act 1950. Lord Goff stated:[89]

---

[79] Directive 89/665 (OJ 1989 L395 p 33).

[80] Directive 92/13 (OJ 1992 L76 p 14).

[81] See reg 31 of the Public Works Contracts Regulations 1991 (SI No 2680); reg 30 of the Utilities Supply and Works Contracts Regulations 1992 (SI No 3279); reg 32 of the Public Services Contracts Regulations 1993 (SI No 3228); reg 29 of the Public Supply Contracts Regulations 1995 (SI No 201). See, generally, Professor Sue Arrowsmith, *The Law of Public and Utilities Procurement* (Sweet & Maxwell, 1996), Ch 18.

[82] Joined Cases C-46/93 and C-48/93 *Brasserie du Pêcheur and Factortame* [1996] ECR I-1029 paras 33–35.

[83] See Ch 4, pp 72–77.

[84] Case C-103/88 *Costanzo v Comune di Milano* [1989] ECR 1839.

[85] Case 152/84 *Marshall* [1986] ECR 723.

[86] Case 222/84 *Johnston* [1986] ECR 1651.

[87] Case C-188/89 *Foster v British Gas* [1990] ECR I-3313.

[88] [1993] AC 227.

[89] Ibid at 282G.

This is no doubt because it is the Government which would, on the hypothesis that section 47 was invalid because inconsistent with article 30, have failed to take the necessary steps to ensure that section 47 was amended or repealed as necessary. If so it would be wrong that the council, because it has performed its statutory duty under the national law to enforce section 47, was to find itself under a liability in damages as a result of performing that duty.

State acting *qua* State Different considerations will apply depending on whether the State is acting in a public or private capacity. For example, where a State has incorrectly implemented a directive on sex discrimination, the claims by its own employees for damages for sex discrimination would be based on the vertical direct effect of the directive. The nature of the dispute is that of employer and employee, and the employer's breach of Community law is the act of discrimination.[90] The action will be different to any damages claims brought against the State by other employees of private parties in respect of the failure correctly to implement the directive. (These employees would not be entitled to rely on the directive against their employer as directives do not have horizontal direct effect.[91]) These claims would involve the principle of State liability and the need to prove a sufficiently serious breach.

(b) Substantive conditions of liability

Three conditions Community law confers a right to reparation where three conditions are met:
  (1) the rule of law breached must be intended to confer identifiable rights on individuals;
  (2) the breach must be sufficiently serious; and
  (3) there must be a direct causal link between the breach and the damage sustained by the individual.
These conditions are, and are intended to be, difficult to meet.[92]

(i) The rule of law breached is intended to confer identifiable rights

Directly effective rights Most directly effective provisions of Community law by their very nature create rights for individuals.[93] For example, in Joined Cases C-46 and C-48/93 *Brasserie du Pêcheur and Factortame* the Court of Justice considered that the 'first condition is manifestly satisfied in the case of Article 30 of the Treaty, the relevant provision in Case C-46/93, and in the case of Article 52, the relevant provision in Case C-48/93'. Both these provisions impose clear and unconditional obligations on Member States and grant correlative rights to individuals.[94]

---

[90] For example, see Case C-177/88 *Dekker v VJV-Centrum* [1990] ECR I-3941.
[91] See Ch 4, p 70.
[92] *R v Secretary of State for Transport, ex p Factortame* [1997] EuLR 475 at 513A–B (Div Ct).
[93] See Ch 4, pp 66–67.
[94] Joined Cases C-46/93 and C-48/93 *Brasserie du Pêcheur and Factortame* [1996] ECR I-1029 para 54.

Non-directly effective rights A failure by a Member State to implement a directive may give rise to State liability, even where the provisions of the directive are not capable of having direct effect. Individuals may be unable to rely directly on the provisions of a directive in the national courts because they are insufficiently precise and unconditional. They may, however, be able to point to a right which would have been granted to them by the national legal order if the directive had been implemented. In these circumstances, breach of the obligation to implement the directive may give rise to an action for damages. The full effectiveness of Community law would be impaired if individuals were unable to obtain redress for the State's failure to provide them with the rights which they were intended to have under Community law.[95]

In Joined Cases C-6/90 and C-9/90 *Francovich and Bonifaci v Italy*[96] the Italian Republic had failed to implement Directive 80/987,[97] which provides that Member States should establish institutions to guarantee employees' salaries in the event of the employer's insolvency. Mr Francovich was employed by CDN Ellectronica and only received periodic payments of his salary. He successfully instituted proceedings before the Italian courts, which ordered CDN to pay 6,000,000 lira. When he was unable to satisfy his claim against the company because of its insolvency, he brought proceedings against the Italian Republic claiming either the guaranteed payment envisaged by Directive 80/987 or damages for non-implementation of the Directive. Two questions arose for determination by the Court of Justice: first, whether employees could rely on the Directive against the State in order to claim the guaranteed sum; and, secondly, whether the employees could sue the State in damages for the loss which they had suffered as a result of the non-implementation of the Directive.

The Court of Justice held that the Directive as a whole was not sufficiently precise and unconditional for employees to rely on it against the State in order to claim payment. This was because the Member States had a broad discretion to determine the organisation, operation and financing of the guarantee institution. Thus, there was no directly effective right to payment which could be relied on in the national courts.[98] However, the Court held that the Directive entailed the grant of rights to employees, namely a guaranteed payment of outstanding salary payments. Denial of this right could give rise to an action in damages against the defaulting Member State.[99]

Harmonising measures The first substantive condition of liability (*viz* the creation of individual rights) will not always be satisfied, since many directives do not involve the creation of rights for individuals, albeit that they impose

---

[95] Joined Cases C-46/93 and C-48/93 *Brasserie du Pêcheur and Factortame* [1996] ECR I-1029 para 21.

[96] [1991] ECR I-5357.

[97] Council Directive 80/987 on the approximation of the laws of the Member State relating to the protection of employees in the event of the insolvency of their employer (OJ 1980 L283 p 23).

[98] See Ch 4, p 68.

[99] Unfortunately for Mr Francovich, a subsequent ruling of the Court of Justice, in Case C-479/93 *Francovich v Italian Republic* [1995] ECR I-3843 ('*Francovich II*'), held that the Directive did not grant any rights to him because his former employer fell outside the ambit of the Directive.

obligations on Member States.[100] This is particularly the case in relation to harmonisation directives. In *Three Rivers v Bank of England*[101] the plaintiffs were depositors with the BCCI bank, which was licensed by the Bank of England. They lost the amounts deposited when BCCI went into liquidation. The plaintiffs claimed damages against the Bank of England for failing in its supervisory duties as required by Council Directive 77/780,[102] which harmonised national laws relating to the authorisation and supervision of banks. Although one of the purposes of the Directive was to protect savers, as was apparent from the preamble, Clarke J held that the Directive conferred no enforceable right on depositors that the Bank of England should properly supervise BCCI. The imposition of a supervisory duty on the regulator did not, in itself, confer a right on individuals to effective supervision.[103]

Sufficient precision The content of the right must be identifiable with sufficient precision on the basis of the Community provision alone and not in conjunction with other provisions adopted.[104] A right may be sufficiently precise even though the Member State is given a wide discretion to determine how the right is to be granted. Thus, in Joined Cases C-6/90 and C-9/90 *Francovich and Bonifaci v Italy*,[105] although Member States had a broad discretion to determine the nature of the appropriate guarantee institution, the content of the right to payment could be determined with sufficient precision.

A purposive interpretation may be necessary to clarify the nature of the alleged right. In Case C-178/94 and others *Dillenkofer v Germany*[106] Erich Dillenkofer paid for a holiday with a package tour operator. He cancelled the holiday on health grounds and could not get reimbursed because the tour operator had gone into liquidation. Mr Dillenkofer sued Germany for damages on the ground that he would have been protected against the insolvency of the operator if Germany had implemented Council Directive 90/314 on package holidays.[107] Article 7 provided that the tour operator was obliged to 'provide sufficient evidence of security for the refund of money paid over'. The Court, interpreting article 7 by reference to the preamble to the Directive, ruled that it actually granted a package traveller a right to a refund. The obligation to provide evidence of security would be meaningless if a tour operator were not, in fact, obliged to take steps to ensure that the traveller would be reimbursed.

---

[100] See Ch 4, pp 66–67.
[101] [1996] 3 All ER 558.
[102] Directive 77/780 on the coordination of laws, regulations and administrative provisions relating to the taking up and pursuit of the business of credit institutions (OJ 1977 L322 p 30).
[103] [1996] 3 All ER 558 at 603–622. See also *R v International Stock Exchange, ex p Else* [1993] QB 534; Case 380/87 *Enichem Base v Comune di Cinisello Balsamo* [1989] ECR 2491.
[104] Joined Cases C-178/94 and others *Dillenkofer v Germany* [1996] ECR I-4845 paras 43–45.
[105] [1991] ECR I-5357. See above at p 134 under 'non-directly effective rights'.
[106] [1996] ECR I-4845 paras 30–46.
[107] OJ 1990 L158 p 59.

(ii) Sufficiently serious breach

Sufficiently serious In Joined Cases C-46/93 and C-48/93 *Brasserie du Pêcheur and Factortame*[108] the Court of Justice held that:

> ... the decisive test for finding that a breach of Community law is sufficiently serious is whether the Member State or the Community institution concerned manifestly and gravely disregarded the limits on its discretion.
>
> The factors which the competent court may take into consideration include the clarity and precision of the rule breached, the measure of discretion left by that rule to the national or Community authorities, whether the infringement and the damage caused was intentional or involuntary, whether any error of law was excusable or inexcusable, the fact that the position taken by a Community institution may have contributed towards the omission, and the adoption or retention of national measures or practices contrary to Community law.
>
> On any view, a breach of Community law will clearly be sufficiently serious if it has persisted despite a judgment finding the infringement in question to be established, or a preliminary ruling or settled case-law of the Court on the matter from which it is clear that the conduct in question constituted an infringement.

Manifest and grave disregard A breach is sufficiently serious where the Member State has manifestly and gravely disregarded the limits of its powers.[109] It is not always easy to distinguish between manifest and grave. One view is that 'manifest' refers to the circumstances of the breach and 'grave' to its consequences. In *R v Secretary of State for Transport, ex p Factortame*[110] the Divisional Court declined to adopt this view, stating:

> We see no reason in principle to limit 'grave' to consequences. It may be that a breach is effected deliberately and with knowledge that what is being done is unlawful. Such a breach can properly be described as manifest and grave. If someone can show that he has suffered loss as a result, it does not seem to us that he should necessarily be deprived of compensation because, looked at overall, the consequence of the breach could not be described as grave.

(1) Manifest breach

Relevant considerations A manifest breach will be determined by objective considerations relating to the obviousness of the breach. Consideration should be given, in particular, to whether the error of law was excusable and to the margin of discretion left to the State in making its decision.

Excusable error A breach is excusable where the State acts with legitimate justification. An important factor is the clarity and precision of the rule breached so that, for example, a Member State will not commit a manifest breach by mis-implementing a directive which is imprecisely worded and which is reasonably capable of bearing the meaning ascribed to it by the State.[111] The fact

---

[108] [1996] ECR I-1029 paras 55–57.

[109] Joined Cases C-46/93 and C-48/93 *Brasserie du Pêcheur and Factortame* [1996] ECR I-1029 para 55.

[110] [1997] EuLR 475 at 512G–513A.

[111] Case C-392/93 *R v HM Treasury, ex p British Telecommunications* [1996] ECR I-1631 paras 43–45; Joined Cases C-283/94, C-291/94 and C-292/94 *Denkavit International v Bundesamt für Finanzen* [1996] ECR I-5063 paras 50–51.

that the State acted on legal advice does not, in itself, make the breach excusable.[112]

A breach will be inexcusable where the national rule is clearly contrary to earlier decisions of the Court of Justice.[113] On any view, a breach of Community law will be manifest if it has persisted despite a ruling from the Court of Justice or an order for interim measures made by the President of the Court pursuant to article 186 of the EC Treaty [new art 243].[114] The fact that other Member States have wrongly interpreted a Community rule is a mitigating factor,[115] as is the fact that a Community institution has sanctioned[116] or made no objection to a national rule[117] which is subsequently found to be in breach of Community law. By contrast, a Member State which continues to apply a national rule in the knowledge that the Commission considers the rule to be contrary to Community law is likely to act without legitimate justification.[118] As the Divisional Court stated in *R v Secretary of State for Transport, ex p Factortame*:[119]

> Where there is a doubt about the legality of any proposal, a failure by a member state to seek the views of the Commission or, if it receives them, to follow them is likely to lead to any breach being regarded as inexcusable and so manifest.

Discretion Where a Member State enjoys a measure of discretion, the choice made, although wrong, may not be an obvious disregard of the limits on its powers.[120] In contrast, where the State enjoys little or no discretion, a wrong decision is more likely to lead to a manifest breach of Community law. As the Court of Justice stated in Case C-5/94 *R v MAFF, ex p Hedley Lomas*:[121]

> ... where, at the time when it committed the infringement, the Member State in question was not called upon to make any legislative choices and had only considerably reduced, or even no, discretion, the mere infringement of Community law may be sufficient to establish the existence of a sufficiently serious breach.

A State will be found to have manifestly disregarded the limits on its powers when it fails to adopt any measures to implement a directive within the required time period as required by article 189 of the EC Treaty [new art 249]

---

[112] *R v Secretary of State for Transport, ex p Factortame* [1997] EuLR 475 at 515B–F, upheld by Court of Appeal, 8 April 1998.

[113] Joined Cases C-46/93 and C-48/93 *Brasserie du Pêcheur and Factortame* [1996] ECR I-1029 para 59.

[114] Ibid paras 57 and 64; *R v Secretary of State, ex p Factortame* [1997] EuLR 475 at 522D–524F (Div Ct), upheld by Court of Appeal, 8 April 1998.

[115] Case C-392/93 *R v HM Treasury, ex p British Telecommunications* [1996] ECR I-1631 paras 42–45.

[116] Joined Cases C-283/94, C-291/94 and C-292/94 *Denkavit International v Bundesamt für Finanzen* [1996] ECR I-5063 para 51.

[117] Case C-392/93 *R v HM Treasury, ex p British Telecommunications* [1996] ECR I-1631 paras 43–45.

[118] Joined Cases C-46/93 and C-48/93 *Brasserie du Pêcheur and Factortame* [1996] ECR I-1029 para 63.

[119] [1997] EuLR 475 at 519D.

[120] *R v Secretary of State for the Home Department, ex p Gallagher* [1996] 2 CMLR 951.

[121] [1996] ECR I-2553 para 28.

(non-implementation).[122] However, a Member State retains a margin of discretion when implementing a directive, for example in interpreting its provisions and giving effect to them through the adoption of national implementing measures. Thus, where a Member State has, in good faith, attempted to implement a directive within the required time period, but is subsequently held to have failed to implement it properly (mis-implementation), this will not necessarily be a manifest breach of Community law.[123]

A failure to amend domestic legislation to conform with a subsequent directive has been treated as a failure to implement.[124] However, where a Member State believed in good faith (but mistakenly) that its existing domestic law fully complied with the directive, logically such a failure should be treated as a mis-implementation. Whether the mistaken belief is sufficiently serious will depend on whether it constituted a manifest and grave disregard of the limits on its powers.

(2) Grave breach

Relevant considerations A grave breach will be viewed by reference to the seriousness of the breach. Consideration should be given, in particular, to the importance of the rule infringed, the effect on the applicant, and the intentions or knowledge of the State.

Importance of the rule infringed Where the Community is being sued for damages caused by a legislative act involving economic policy under article 215 of the EC Treaty [new art 288], it is necessary to prove a breach of a superior rule of law for the protection of the individual.[125] However, in the case of State liability, the importance of the rule infringed is merely a factor to be taken into account in assessing the gravity of the breach. In *R v Secretary of State for Transport, ex p Factortame*[126] the Divisional Court stated:

> But some principles are more important than others and, when consideration is given to a breach by a member state, it is obvious that a breach of a directive may not involve as important a principle as a breach of an article of the Treaty. We see no reason why the importance of the principle infringed should not be a factor to be taken into account. It can affect the seriousness of the breach. It is common ground that the prohibition against discrimination on the ground of nationality is one of the fundamental principles of the Treaty—indeed, one of the pillars upon which the whole edifice is constructed—and the same can be said of freedom of establishment ...

Effect on the applicant Where the breach affects a limited and clearly defined group of people, it is more likely to be considered grave. However, individuals are required to accept, within reasonable limits, certain harmful

---

[122] Joined Cases C-6/90 and C-9/90 *Francovich and Bonifaci v Italy* [1991] ECR I-5357; as explained in Joined Cases C-178/94 and others *Dillenkofer v Germany* [1996] ECR I-4845 paras 20–27.

[123] Case C-392/93 *R v HM Treasury, ex p British Telecommunications* [1996] ECR I-1631.

[124] Case C-334/92 *Wagner Miret* [1993] ECR I-6911.

[125] See Ch 16, pp 364–365.

[126] [1997] EuLR 475 at 514B–C.

effects on their economic activities so that where, for example, the breach causes them to suffer only a small percentage drop in profitability, it is less likely to be considered grave.[127] Where the applicant is considered no worse off, because, for example, the State has not complied with a procedural requirement, the courts are unlikely to categorise the breach as grave.[128]

Knowledge Clearly, an intentional breach of Community law will be treated with the utmost gravity. An intention to injure or an awareness that the national rule will necessarily injure certain individuals will also be an important factor. As Oliver LJ stated in *Bourgoin v MAFF*:[129]

> If an act is done deliberately and with knowledge of its consequences, I do not think that the actor can sensibly say that he did not 'intend' the consequences or that the act was not 'aimed' at the person who, it is known, will suffer them.

(iii) Causation

Direct link The plaintiff must show that, on the balance of probabilities, the injury for which he seeks compensation was caused, both in fact and in law, by the unlawful conduct of which he complains.[130]

The factual test is a 'but for' test; but for the breach, would the damage have occurred? In *R v Secretary of State for the Home Department, ex p Gallagher*[131] Mr Gallagher failed to prove a factual link between the breach of Community law (making an exclusion order before the procedural requirements of Directive 64/221[132] had been complied with) and the damage alleged to be suffered (loss of a chance of not being deported). He could not prove that the breach probably caused him to be excluded from the United Kingdom when he would not otherwise have been excluded. On the evidence, there was nothing to suggest that the Home Secretary's decision would have been any different had he complied with the Directive.

The plaintiff must also satisfy a legal test and show that the breach was the 'direct' cause of the loss.[133] Even if the breach was probably causative of the loss, the State will escape liability if the damage was also caused by another factor of some importance. The requirement of a sufficiently direct link means that in practice the chain of causation will often be broken either by the injured party or by the acts of third parties.[134]

---

[127] *R v Secretary of State for Transport, ex p Factortame* [1997] EuLR 475 at 513D–514A and 515G–516A. See also Ch 16, pp 367–368.

[128] *R v Secretary of State for the Home Department, ex p Gallagher* [1996] 2 CMLR 951.

[129] [1986] 1 QB 716 at 777H; applied by the Divisional Court in *R v Secretary of State for Transport, ex p Factortame* [1997] EuLR 475 at 517G–H.

[130] See *Clerk and Lindsell on Torts*, 17th edn (Sweet & Maxwell, 1995), para 11–28.

[131] [1996] 2 CMLR 951.

[132] Council Directive 64/221 on the co-ordination of special measures concerning the movement and residence of foreign nationals, which are justified on grounds of public policy, public security or public health (OJ Special Edition 1963–1964 p 117).

[133] Joined Cases C-46/93 and C-48/93 *Brasserie du Pêcheur and Factortame* [1996] ECR I-1029 para 51.

[134] For an application of this principle in the context of actions under article 215 of the EC Treaty [new art 288], see Joined Cases 64/76, 113/76 and others *Dumortier Frères v Council* [1979]

Contributory negligence and mitigation Although these issues remain a matter for domestic law, national courts are entitled, as a matter of Community law, to 'inquire whether the injured person showed reasonable care so as to avoid the loss or damage or to mitigate it'.[135] It is important to distinguish between contributory negligence and mitigation. The duty to mitigate involves taking reasonable steps to limit the damage caused by the State's breach of Community law, for example by seeking alternative sources of income.[136] Contributory negligence, on the other hand, falls squarely in the chain of causation. Since the plaintiff must prove a direct link between the damage and the breach, a relatively low degree of lack of care in preventing the loss occurring is likely to break the chain of causation. Even a delay in seeking injunctive relief to prevent the damage occurring could result in the chain being broken.[137]

Where the purpose of a directive is to protect individuals from certain adverse consequences, a plaintiff is unlikely to be held to have been contributorily negligent if he suffers those consequences as a result of the State's failure to implement the directive. In Case C-178/94 and others *Dillenkofer v Germany*[138] Mr Dillenkofer sued Germany for failing to afford him the protection he would have had against insolvent tour operators if Germany had implemented the Package Tour Directive. He had paid the full price of his holiday before obtaining the travel documents. Under German law, the consumer had the possibility of only paying 10 per cent of the total travel price before obtaining the relevant documents. The Court of Justice held that a package traveller who had paid the whole travel price could not be regarded as having acted negligently simply because he had not taken advantage of this possibility.

Causation and horizontal direct effect The principle of State liability will be particularly significant to an individual who is precluded from relying on a directly effective provision of a directive against another individual, by virtue of the fact that directives do not have horizontal direct effect.[139] In Case C-91/92 *Faccini Dori v Recreb*[140] Ms Dori purchased an English language correspondence course at Milan railway station. She sought to cancel the contract during the cooling-off period provided by Directive 85/577 on doorstep selling,[141] which, at the time, had not been implemented by the Italian Republic. The Court of Justice held that Ms Dori could not rely on the Directive as against the trader, but that she would have a cause of action for damages

---

ECR 3091 para 21. Discussed further at Ch 16, pp 368–370.

[135] Case C-178/94 and others *Dillenkofer v Germany* [1996] ECR I-4845 para 72.
[136] Joined Cases C-104/89 and C-37/90 *Mulder v Council* [1992] ECR I-3061 para 33.
[137] Joined Cases C-46/93 and C-48/93 *Brasserie du Pêcheur and Factortame* [1996] ECR I-1029 para 84, and particularly the Opinion of Advocate-General Tesauro at para 100.
[138] [1996] ECR I-4845 para 72.
[139] See Ch 4, pp 70–71.
[140] [1994] ECR I-3325. See also Case C-192/94 *El Corte Inglés v Blázquez Rivero* [1996] ECR I-1281.
[141] OJ 1985 L372 p 31.

against Italy for its failure to afford her the right of cancellation envisaged by the Directive.

In these circumstances a causal link may be established even though the purpose of the directive, once implemented, is to impose obligations on private parties, not on the State. As Advocate-General Mischo stated in Joined Cases C-6/90 and C-9/90 *Francovich and Bonifaci v Italy*:[142]

> One might nevertheless ask whether, within the category of directives which do not give rise to direct effect, a distinction should be made between those whose purpose it is to impose obligations on the State and those whose purpose is to impose obligations on private undertakings, there being no liability on the part of the State in the latter case. After all, in that case the State is responsible only for the failure to implement the directive and not for the circumstances which are the direct cause of the harm suffered by the citizen, such as the non-payment of wages, the insufficient remuneration of a woman, or the defective nature of a product.
>
> Conversely, where the directive imposes obligations on the State itself (or on an organization which must necessarily be identified with the State), its offence is two-fold: failure to implement the directive and failure to comply with the obligations which the directive imposes.
>
> I do not, however, think it is possible to make such a distinction, for the whole of the reasoning set out above is based on the principle that any failure to implement a directive *ipso facto* constitutes an infringement of Articles 5 and 189 of the Treaty, that is to say an unlawful act which must be made good by the State where it has caused harm to an individual.

(iv) Damage

Effective protection The level of damages awarded to compensate a plaintiff for a breach of Community law must be commensurate with the loss or damage actually sustained so as to ensure effective protection of his rights.[143] Although the issue of damages was not before the Divisional Court in *R v Secretary of State for Transport, ex p Factortame*,[144] the Court considered that the applicants would 'receive a full indemnity in respect of the losses which they have suffered as a result of the breaches by the United Kingdom of Community law'.

Where a Member State is liable to pay damages for non-implementation of a directive, it is compatible with the principle of effective protection to compensate the individual on the basis that the directive would have been implemented in the manner least onerous to the State.[145]

---

[142] [1991] ECR I-5357, at paras 67–68 of the Opinion. Note also the comments of Kennedy LJ in *R v Secretary of State for Employment, ex p Equal Opportunities Commission* [1993] 1 WLR 872 at 896D–E.

[143] Joined Cases C-46/93 and C-48/93 *Brasserie du Pêcheur and Factortame* [1996] ECR I-1029 para 82; Joined Cases C-94/95 and C-95/95 *Bonifaci v INPS* [1997] ECR I-3969 para 48.

[144] [1997] EuLR 475 at 529B–C.

[145] Joined Cases C-94/95 and C-95/95 *Bonifaci v INPS* [1997] ECR I-3969 paras 51–54; Case C-373/95 *Maso v INPS* [1997] ECR I-4051 paras 33–42.

Heads of damage Domestic law governs the particular heads of damage that are recoverable. However, loss of profit as a head of damage cannot be excluded in the context of economic or commercial litigation, as such an exclusion would make reparation of damage practically impossible.[146]

Exemplary damages An award of exemplary damages pursuant to a claim founded on a breach of Community law cannot be ruled out if such damages could be awarded pursuant to a similar claim founded on domestic law.[147] As a matter of English law, such damages may be awarded in respect of 'oppressive, arbitrary or unconstitutional action by the servants of the government'.[148] As regards breach of statutory duty (which is the relevant cause of action in State liability[149]), domestic law provides that exemplary damages can be awarded only if the relevant statute so provides. Since the European Communities Act 1972 makes no provision for such an award, exemplary damages are not available for breaches of Community law by the State.[150]

Interest Where an individual obtains damages against the State for breach of Community law, the individual is entitled to recover interest on any damages awarded to reflect the effluxion of time prior to judgment being obtained. The rate of interest remains within the discretion of the national court, provided it reflects the individual's right to obtain effective compensation.[151]

(c) Procedure

Writ action Even where the duty imposed on the public authority by Community law requires the exercise of discretion by the authority, the proper procedure is likely to be by way of writ rather than by way of judicial review. An injured party should not be required to bring judicial review proceedings in order to establish that the State has acted unlawfully as a precondition to claiming damages.[152] If this approach is correct, it means that an aggrieved party

---

[146] Joined Cases C-46/93 and C-48/93 *Brasserie du Pêcheur and Factortame* [1996] ECR I-1029 paras 81–90.

[147] Ibid, paras 88–89.

[148] Lord Devlin in *Rookes v Barnard* [1964] AC 1129 at 1126. However, exemplary damages are available only in respect of those causes of action for which such damages had been awarded prior to 1964 (*AB v South West Water Services Ltd* [1993] QB 507).

[149] See above at p 130.

[150] *R v Secretary of State, ex p Factortame* [1997] EuLR 475 at 524G–532G.

[151] Case C-271/91 *Marshall v Southampton and South West Hampshire AHA* [1993] ECR I-4367; Case C-66/95 *R v Secretary of State for Social Security, ex p Sutton* [1997] ECR I-2163.

[152] *X (Minors) v Bedfordshire CC* [1995] 2 AC 633 at 736G, per Lord Browne-Wilkinson, '... it leads in my judgment, mistakenly, to the contention that claims for damages for negligence in the exercise of statutory powers should for procedural purposes be classified as public law claims and therefore, under *O'Reilly v Mackman* [1983] 2 AC 237 should be brought in judicial review proceedings'. See also *An Bord Bainne Co-Operative (Irish Dairy Board) v Milk Marketing Board* [1984] 2 CMLR 584. The issue is not entirely clear, however: see *Cocks v Thanet District Council* [1983] 2 AC 286; *Clerk and Lindsell on Torts*, 17th edn (Sweet & Maxwell, 1995), para 11–15; para 101 of the Opinion of Advocate-General Tesauro in Joined Cases C-46/93 and C-48/93 *Brasserie du Pêcheur and Factortame* [1996] ECR I-1029.

will not be constrained by the three-month time-limit imposed in judicial review proceedings, but will have six years in which to bring an action.[153] This longer period in which to bring a damages claim is justified by the fact that, if successful, the individual will have proved a serious violation of its rights by the State.[154] Furthermore, this is analogous to the approach of the Court of Justice in dealing with actions for damages against the Community institutions. An action for damages brought under article 215 of the EC Treaty [new art 288] is regarded as an independent remedy, so that it is not necessary first to bring an action for annulment under article 173 of the EC Treaty [new art 230] (which is subject to a two-month limit) in order to establish the unlawfulness of the Community's conduct.[155]

Private law actions involving the Crown Special rules governing private law proceedings by and against the Crown are set out in the Crown Proceedings Act 1947 and RSC Ord 77.[156] Section 17 of the Crown Proceedings Act 1947 establishes the appropriate parties in actions involving the Crown. Civil proceedings against the Crown should be brought against the appropriate authorised government department.[157] Where no government department appears to be appropriate, or where there is doubt as to the appropriate department, the action should be brought against the Attorney-General.[158] Thus, actions for damages for non-implementation of a directive would normally be enforced by writ against the Attorney-General.[159]

(d) Examples of breach

(i) Adoption of legislative acts

Factortame Under the Common Market Fishing Policy, the Community fixes quotas limiting the amount of fish that each fishing fleet may catch. A practice known as 'quota hopping' arose whereby, according to the United Kingdom, its fishing quotas were plundered by vessels which, although flying the British flag, lacked any genuine link with the United Kingdom. To combat this, the Government introduced a new register for fishing vessels under the Merchant

---

[153] This is the limitation period applicable to the tort of breach of statutory duty under s 2 of the Limitation Act 1980. However, undue delay in commencing legal action, for example, to obtain an interim injunction to prevent damage occurring, may cause the chain of causation to be broken (see above at p 140).

[154] See paras 78–84 of the Opinion of Advocate-General Jacobs in Case C-188/95 *Fantask* [1997] ECR I-000 (judgment of 2 December 1997).

[155] Although the Court of Justice will declare as inadmissible an action for damages brought outside the time-limit required by article 173 where the true purpose of the damages action is to seek to annul the effects of the contested decision. See Ch 16, p 360.

[156] These rules govern, for example, service of proceedings, discovery, summary judgments, default judgments and execution of orders.

[157] Section 17(1) of the Crown Proceedings Act 1947 requires the Minister for the Civil Service to publish a list of the 'authorised' departments for the purposes of the Act.

[158] Section 17(3) of the Crown Proceedings Act 1947.

[159] *R v Secretary of State for Employment, ex p Equal Opportunities Commission* [1993] 1 WLR 872 at 882E–F, per Dillon LJ; and [1995] 1 AC 1 at 32D, per Lord Keith; *R v Secretary of State for Employment, ex p Seymour-Smith* [1997] 1 WLR 473 at 480E–F, per Lord Hoffmann.

Shipping Act 1988 and subordinate regulations. To be registered, owners and operators had to be British nationals (or, in the case of companies, at least 75 per cent of the shares had to be owned by British nationals) and the owners and operators (and a percentage of the directors and shareholders) had to be resident and domiciled in the United Kingdom. The new register came into effect on 31 March 1989. The applicants owned or operated fishing vessels which had previously flown the British flag, but which no longer met the nationality, residence or domicile conditions laid down in the 1988 Act. They sought judicial review of the Act on the grounds that it breached their right of establishment guaranteed by article 52 of the EC Treaty [new art 43], and they also claimed damages for loss caused by the breach.

Before the adoption of the Act, the Government received legal advice that the proposed legislation was compatible with Community law. The Commission took a different view and, on 28 March 1988, informed the Government that the three criteria were '*prima facie* contrary to the provisions of the right of establishment'. On 29 May 1989 the Commission issued a reasoned opinion that the nationality condition was unlawful, and on 7 August 1989 commenced infraction proceedings under article 169 of the EC Treaty [new art 226] against the United Kingdom. On 10 October 1989 the President of the Court of Justice made an interim order requiring the United Kingdom to suspend the application of the nationality condition pending judgment.[160] The next day, one applicant, who had failed to qualify for the register solely because of the nationality condition, applied to be registered, but was refused pending the adoption of amending legislation. The United Kingdom finally complied with the President's Order on 2 November 1989 by adopting an Order in Council pursuant to s 2(2) of the European Communities Act 1972.

In Case C-213/89 *Factortame*[161] ('*Factortame I*') the Court of Justice ruled that the English courts must have the power to grant interim relief suspending the effect of an Act of Parliament. In Case C-221/89 *Factortame*[162] ('*Factortame II*') the Court of Justice ruled that the nationality, residence and domicile requirements infringed article 52 of the EC Treaty. In Joined Cases C-46/93 and C-48/93 *Brasserie du Pêcheur and Factortame*[163] ('*Factortame III*') the Court of Justice ruled that the United Kingdom would be liable to compensate the applicants for losses suffered as a result of the adoption of the 1988 Act if it could be shown that the United Kingdom had committed a sufficiently serious breach of Community law.

Subsequently, the Divisional Court held that the imposition of the nationality, residence and domicile conditions were sufficiently serious to give rise to a liability to pay damages despite the fact that, at the time when the 1988 Act was

---

[160] Case C-246/89R *Commission v United Kingdom* [1989] ECR 3125.
[161] [1990] ECR I-2433. Discussed at Ch 8, pp 154–156.
[162] [1991] ECR I-3905.
[163] [1996] ECR I-1029.

implemented, the Government, as a result of legal advice obtained, believed that what was being done did not infringe Community law.[164] The Court had regard to the following factors:[165]

(1) The conditions introduced by the 1988 Act were intended to discriminate on the grounds of nationality.

(2) The United Kingdom was aware that the imposition of the conditions would necessarily injure the applicants as they were intended to ensure that the applicants would no longer fish against British quota.

(3) The United Kingdom had sought to achieve its object through primary legislation in order to ensure that its implementation would not be delayed by challenges in court (as, prior to the ruling of the Court of Justice in *Factortame I*, domestic law precluded the grant of any interim relief).

(4) The Commission's attitude to the proposed legislation was consistently hostile.

The Divisional Court also held that the failure to comply with the President's interim Order for a period of approximately three weeks in itself amounted to a sufficiently serious breach of Community law.[166] By refusing to register one of the applicants the day after the President's Order, on the basis that it was necessary to await the adoption of national implementing legislation, the United Kingdom had failed to comply with its obligation, under article 5 of the EC Treaty [new art 10], to comply with Community law.

(ii) Failure to abolish legislative acts

Brasserie du Pêcheur Brasserie du Pêcheur, a French brewer in Alsace, claimed that it was forced to discontinue exports of beer to Germany between 1981 and 1987 because the competent German authorities considered that the beer it produced did not comply with the *Reinheitsgebot* (the German beer purity law). The *Reinheitsgebot* contained two prohibitions: first, it prohibited beer being called 'bier' if it did not conform to certain purity requirements; secondly, it prohibited the marketing of beer which contained additives. In 1987 the Court of Justice ruled that both aspects of the *Reinheitsgebot* infringed article 30 of the EC Treaty [new art 28], as they constituted restrictions on the free movement of goods.[167]

Brasserie du Pêcheur consequently brought an action against Germany for damage suffered as a result of the import restrictions between 1981 and 1987. Following a preliminary reference the German Federal Supreme Court, applying the Court of Justice's ruling in Joined Cases C-46/93 and 48/93 *Brasserie du Pêcheur and Factortame*,[168] dismissed the claim.[169] The Supreme Court found that the designation prohibition was a sufficiently serious breach of Community law since the incompatibility of such rules had been clear from

---

[164] *R v Secretary of State for Transport, ex p Factortame* [1997] EuLR 475, upheld by Court of Appeal, 8 April 1998.

[165] Ibid at 517F–518F.

[166] Ibid at 522D–524F.

[167] Case 178/84 *Commission v Germany* [1987] ECR 1227.

[168] [1996] ECR I-1029.

[169] German Federal Supreme Court in *Brasserie du Pêcheur v Germany* [1997] 1 CMLR 971.

earlier judgments of the Court of Justice. However, applying German rules on causation, the Supreme Court held that this breach was not a necessary and sufficient cause of the loss. The loss in fact had been caused by preventative action adopted by the national authorities to ensure that beer containing additives was not put on the German market. Although the restriction on additives had therefore caused the loss, it did not constitute a sufficiently serious breach of Community law, as it was not until 1987 that it had become clear that such a prohibition was unjustifiable under EC law.

(iii) Adoption of administrative acts

Hedley Lomas The United Kingdom received complaints that Spanish slaughterhouses were not complying with the rules of Directive 74/577 on stunning of animals before slaughter.[170] As a result, the United Kingdom refused to issue licences for the export of live animals to Spain for slaughter between 1990 and 1993.

In 1992 Hedley Lomas applied for a licence for the export of live sheep which was refused. The Court of Justice held that the refusal to issue the licence was contrary to article 34 of the EC Treaty [new art 29] as it amounted to an export ban, and could not be justified under article 36 [new art 30] as the Directive had harmonised the relevant rules at a Community level. The United Kingdom was not entitled to adopt unilateral measures to obviate alleged breaches by another Member State.

The Court of Justice held that the breach was sufficiently serious primarily on the basis that, at the time when it committed the infringement in question, the United Kingdom, due to the existence of the harmonising Directive, was not called upon to exercise any legislative choices and it had considerably reduced, if any, discretion as to the acts which it could adopt.[171]

Moreover, the Government had been unable to provide any proof of non-compliance with the Directive by the particular slaughterhouse to which the animals were destined.

(iv) Non-implementation of directives

Dillenkofer v Germany Article 7 of Council Directive 90/314 on package travel, package holidays and package tours[172] provides that:

> The organizer and/or retailer party to the contract shall provide sufficient evidence of security for the refund of money paid over and for the repatriation of the consumer in the event of insolvency.

The Member States were required to implement the Directive before 31 December 1992. Germany did not adopt implementing measures until June 1994, which did not enter into force until 1 July 1994.

The plaintiffs were purchasers of package holidays, who, following the insolvency in 1993 of the two operators from whom they had bought their

---

[170] OJ 1974 L316 p 10.
[171] Case C-5/94 R v MAFF, ex p Hedley Lomas [1996] ECR I-2553.
[172] OJ 1990 L158 p 59.

packages, either never left for their destination or had to return from their holidays at their own expense. They had been unable to obtain reimbursement of the sums they had paid to the operators, nor of the expenses which they had incurred in returning home. They brought proceedings against the German State on the basis that if article 7 of the Directive had been transposed into German law within the prescribed period, they would have been protected against the insolvency of the operators from whom they had purchased their package holidays.

The Court of Justice held that article 7 of the Directive creates rights for individuals to be reimbursed or repatriated in the event of the insolvency of the organiser from whom they purchased their package holiday.[173]The Court further held that, in order for a Member State to incur liability for non-implementation of a directive, it must be shown to have committed a sufficiently serious breach of Community law. However, where a Member State has failed to adopt any implementation measures within the prescribed limitation period, that Member State will be considered to have manifestly and gravely disregarded the limits on its discretion.

(v) Mis-implementation of directives

R v HM Treasury, ex p British Telecommunications Council Directive 90/531[174] provides that telecommunications companies must follow certain public procurement procedures relating to the tendering of contracts. Article 8(1) contains an important proviso that such procedures need not be followed by the telecommunications companies where the telecommunication service is subject to effective competition. When implementing article 8 of the Directive the United Kingdom made an *a priori* decision that BT was not subject to effective competition in relation to certain services (eg basic voice telephony services). BT brought judicial review proceedings claiming that the United Kingdom had incorrectly implemented the Directive, and seeking damages for the loss suffered due to the additional expenses borne in complying with the procurement procedures.

The Court of Justice upheld BT's interpretation that it was for the contracting authority, namely BT, and not the State, to determine which services were subject to effective competition.[175] The Court, which had sufficient material before it to decide the question of liability, held that Community law did not require the United Kingdom to compensate BT for any loss suffered by the incorrect implementation. The Court, rejecting the Commission's argument that a failure properly to implement should be equated with a total failure to implement, considered that the breach was not sufficiently serious. Article 8(1) was imprecisely worded and was reasonably capable of bearing both BT's and

---

[173] Joined Cases C-178/94 and others *Dillenkofer v Germany* [1996] ECR I-4845.
[174] Council Directive 90/531 on the procurement procedures of entities operating in the water, energy, transport and telecommunications sectors (OJ 1990 L297 p 1).
[175] Case C-392/93 *R v HM Treasury, ex p British Telecommunications* [1996] ECR I-1631.

the United Kingdom's interpretation. The United Kingdom's interpretation was also shared by other Member States. Moreover, no guidance was available from the case-law of the Court as to the interpretation of article 8, nor had the Commission objected at the time when the domestic regulations had been adopted.

Chapter 8

Injunctions

1. ACTIONS AGAINST PRIVATE PARTIES

(a) Availability of injunctions

Effective protection As a matter of Community law it must be possible for national courts to award a final or interim injunction to protect a private party's directly effective Community law rights. In the context of preventing a breach of article 85 of the EC Treaty [new art 81] Peter Gibson J, in *Holleran v Daniel Thwaites*[1] stated that:

> ... the Court has power to prevent a person from abusing his rights, whether conferred on him by statute or contract, in order to create a breach of Community law.

Similarly, in *Garden Cottage Foods Ltd v Milk Marketing Board*[2] the House of Lords was unanimous in stating that the English courts have jurisdiction to grant an injunction to prevent an undertaking abusing its dominant position contrary to article 86 of the EC Treaty [new art 82]. Lord Wilberforce stated:[3]

> It can I think be accepted that a private person can sue in this country to prevent an infraction of article 86. This follows from the fact, which is indisputable, that this article is directly applicable in member states ... Since article 86 says that abuses of a dominant position are prohibited, and since prohibited conduct in England is sanctioned by an injunction, it would seem to follow that an action lies, at the instance of a private person, for an injunction to restrain the prohibited conduct.

(b) Principles applicable to interim injunctions

American Cyanamid principles The power of the English courts to grant interim injunctions is contained in s 37 of the Supreme Court Act 1981, under which the court may grant an injunction where it appears to be just and convenient to do so. Guidelines for the exercise of the court's discretion were

---

[1] [1989] 2 CMLR 917 para 51. See also *Cutsforth v Mansfield Inns Ltd* [1986] 1 WLR 558.
[2] [1984] 1 AC 130. The majority (Lord Wilberforce dissenting) considered that the relevant cause of action was a breach of statutory duty.
[3] Ibid at 151E–F.

laid down by the House of Lords in *American Cyanamid Co v Ethicon Ltd*[4] in the speech of Lord Diplock. Pursuant to these guidelines the grant of an interim injunction is usually examined in three stages:

(1) Is there a serious question to be tried?
(2) Would damages be an adequate remedy for either party?
(3) Where does the balance of convenience lie?

Serious question to be tried No serious question arises where the court is satisfied that the claim is frivolous or vexatious or where the material before the court discloses that the plaintiff has no real prospect of succeeding in his claim for a permanent injunction. However, it is not necessary for the plaintiff to show a *prima facie* case for substantive relief. It is not part of the court's function at this threshold stage to try to resolve conflicts of evidence on affidavit or to decide difficult questions of law which call for detailed consideration. If the plaintiff can show that there is a serious question to be tried the court can address the next question, ie whether it is just and convenient to grant an injunction.[5]

Adequacy of damages If damages to the plaintiff would be an adequate remedy, an interim injunction will not normally be granted. However, where payment of damages by the defendant would not adequately compensate the plaintiff, the court will consider whether, if an injunction were granted against the defendant, the plaintiff's cross-undertaking to pay damages would adequately compensate the defendant if the defendant were ultimately successful at trial. If the court considers that such a cross-undertaking would provide an adequate remedy, the plaintiff will usually be granted an interim injunction.

These principles were applied by the House of Lords in a Community law context in *Garden Cottage Foods Ltd v Milk Marketing Board*.[6] In this case the Milk Marketing Board (MMB), which was the major producer of bulk butter in England, rationalised its sales policy by selling directly to only four distributors. As a result, supplies of butter to the plaintiff ceased. The plaintiff's business consisted of buying butter from the MMB and reselling it to other traders. The plaintiff applied for an interim injunction to restrain the MMB from withholding direct supplies to it, arguing that the MMB's refusal to sell constituted an abuse of a dominant position contrary to article 86 of the EC Treaty. At first instance, Parker J declined to grant the injunction, on the ground that damages would constitute an adequate remedy. The majority of the House of Lords agreed. The purchase of butter from one of the four distributors, instead of directly from the MMB, would merely reduce the plaintiff's margin. This loss could be quantified; indeed, Lord Diplock considered that there could hardly be a clearer case of damages being an adequate remedy.

---

4 [1975] AC 396.
5 Ibid, at 407–408, per Lord Diplock.
6 [1984] 1 AC 130. See also *Cutsforth v Mansfield Inns Ltd* [1986] 1 WLR 558 at 567E–H (damages were not an adequate remedy to the plaintiffs); *Holleran v Daniel Thwaites* [1989] 2 CMLR 917 para 51; *Argyll Group plc v The Distillers Company plc* [1986] 1 CMLR 764.

Balance of convenience If there is doubt as to the adequacy of damages to both parties, the court will consider 'the balance of convenience', which entails balancing the risk of injustice to either party of granting or refusing an injunction. As Lord Bridge stated in *R v Secretary of State for Transport, ex p Factortame Ltd*:[7]

> A decision to grant or withhold interim relief in the protection of disputed rights at a time when the merits of the dispute cannot be finally resolved must always involve an element of risk. If, in the end, the claimant succeeds in a case where interim relief has been refused, he will have suffered an injustice. If, in the end, he fails in a case where interim relief has been granted, injustice will have been done to the other party. The objective which underlies the principles by which the discretion is to be guided must always be to ensure that the court shall choose the course which, in all the circumstances, appears to offer the best prospect that eventual injustice will be avoided or minimised.

For the purpose of deciding where the balance of convenience lies, the court will consider all the circumstances of the case. An important factor in deciding where the balance of convenience lies is whether one person will suffer irreparable damage to a greater extent than the other. If the extent of irreparable damage to each party would not differ widely, the courts may take into account the strength of each party's case in tipping the balance. An examination of the merits of the case is, however, an exceptional course. Where factors appear to be evenly balanced, the court is likely to seek to preserve the *status quo*. The court will look at the state of affairs existing during the period immediately preceding the writ, not at the period prior to the defendant's conduct which is complained of. However, the duration of the period prior to the writ must be more than minimal; otherwise the state of affairs prior to the commencement of the conduct complained of will be the *status quo*.[8]

Special cases The courts will not apply the *American Cyanamid* principles where the grant or refusal of the interlocutory injunction will have the practical effect of putting an end to the action by giving the plaintiff summary judgment.[9] In such a case the application for an injunction is no longer a holding operation pending a contemplated trial. In endeavouring to avoid injustice to either party the courts are reluctant to deprive a defendant of the opportunity of having his rights determined at trial. This was the approach adopted by Morritt J in *Plessey Co plc v General Electric Co plc*[10] where the plaintiff target company sought an interlocutory injunction to prevent the defendant company from making a takeover bid, on the basis that the takeover would be contrary to article 85 of the EC Treaty. Morritt J refused to grant an interim injunction preventing the defendant from making any offer for the shares, because to have done so

---

[7] [1991] 1 AC 603 at 659D–F. See also May LJ in *Cayne v Global Natural Resources plc* [1984] 1 All ER 225 at 237H; *Francome v Mirror Group Newspapers Ltd* [1984] 1 WLR 892.

[8] *American Cyanamid v Ethicon* [1975] AC 396 at 408G, per Lord Diplock. See also *Garden Cottage Foods v Milk Marketing Board* [1985] 1 AC 130 at 140C, per Lord Diplock.

[9] *NWL Ltd v Woods* [1979] 1 WLR 1294 at 1306; *Cayne v Global Natural Resources plc* [1984] 1 All ER 225.

[10] [1990] ECC 384.

would have prevented the defendant from complying with the Takeover Panel's rules and timetables, thus preventing the defendant from making any bid at all. It was only by refusing the injunction that final judgment in favour of the plaintiff could be avoided.

Further, the *American Cyanamid* principles are often not applied in the case of a mandatory interlocutory injunction. The effects of a mandatory injunction (eg an order that a patent licence be granted) can be more drastic than a prohibitory injunction. Normally, therefore, the plaintiff's case must be strong and clear before an interlocutory mandatory injunction will be granted. However, where the practical reality of the situation is such that it is necessary for some form of mandatory order to be made in the interim, the court may make the order, whether or not the high standard of probability of success at trial is made out.[11]

2. INTERIM RELIEF IN ACTIONS INVOLVING THE STATE

Two different types of application Applications for interim relief may arise where an applicant is seeking: (a) to disapply national law which is allegedly contrary to Community law or (b) to disapply national law which gives effect to a Community measure which is alleged to be unlawful. An example of the latter would be where national law implements a directive which is considered unlawful or where a national authority has collected charges pursuant to a regulation which is considered unlawful.

Different considerations apply to these two types of application. In the first type of application, the courts apply their own rules on interim relief and, in particular, the *American Cyanamid* principles; in the second type of application the courts are required to examine more fully the strength of the applicant's case, since the power of national courts to suspend Community law corresponds with the Court of Justice's power to grant interim relief under articles 185 and 186 of the EC Treaty [new arts 242 and 243].

(a) Interim orders disapplying national law alleged to be incompatible with EC law

(i) Jurisdiction
Stay of proceedings in judicial review proceedings Applicants seeking interim relief in judicial review proceedings may seek a stay of proceedings under RSC Ord 53, r 3(10)(*a*). An application for a 'stay of proceedings' embraces not only judicial proceedings, but also decisions of ministers and the decision-making process (if it has not been completed).[12] Although a stay and an

---

[11] *Leisure Data v Bell* [1988] FSR 367. See also *Redland Bricks v Morris* [1970] AC 652, per Lord Upjohn; *Films Rover International Ltd v Cannon Films Sales Ltd* [1987] 1 WLR 671.

[12] *R v Secretary of State for Education and Science, ex p Avon County Council* [1991] 1 QB 558. See also Lord Woolf in *M v Home Office* [1994] 1 AC 377; De Smith, Woolf and Jowell, *Judicial*

interim injunction may, on occasions, lead to the same result, it is clear that a stay is of more limited application. A stay is not coercive in the sense that it cannot direct a minister to act in a particular way. Moreover, it is doubtful whether the power granted under RSC Ord 53, r 3(10)(*a*) could be used to suspend the operation of an Act of Parliament, as an Act is not a 'proceeding'.

Interim injunctions against the Crown in civil proceedings The ability to obtain injunctive relief against the Crown in civil (ie private law) proceedings is restricted by s 21 of the Crown Proceedings Act 1947. Where a statute places a duty on a specified minister or other official, an action can be brought for breach of statutory duty claiming damages, or for an injunction. However, if the duty is placed on the Crown in general, s 21(2) prevents injunctive relief being granted against the minister. In many cases involving Community law the duty is more likely to be imposed on the Crown in general rather than a named minister. If this is correct, the aggrieved plaintiff may be forced to bring public law proceedings within the three-month time-limit provided by RSC Ord 53 if he wishes to seek injunctive relief to protect his Community law rights. Whether this restriction is compatible with Community law is open to doubt. In principle Community law leaves it to the domestic courts to determine the relevant courts in which proceedings are to be brought (eg in the Crown Office). This is subject to two overriding requirements: (1) the domestic rules must not treat cases involving Community law differently from purely domestic cases (principle of equivalence); and (2) the rules must afford adequate protection to the individual concerned (principle of effective protection).[13] It is against the principle of effective protection that s 21 will ultimately be tested.

Interim injunctions against the Crown in judicial review proceedings RSC Ord 53, r 3(10)(*b*), which is given statutory force by s 31 of the Supreme Court Act 1981, provides that applicants may seek an interlocutory injunction in judicial review proceedings. Initially, however, the English courts proved reluctant to grant interim relief against the Crown where the effect would be to disapply national law in order to protect putative Community law rights (ie rights which are only alleged, not established). In *R v Secretary of State for Transport, ex p Factortame Ltd*[14] the House of Lords considered that, as a matter of English law, there were two barriers to the grant of an interim injunction in judicial review proceedings to disapply an Act of Parliament or subordinate legislation which allegedly infringed Community law rights: (1) s 31 of the Supreme Court Act 1981 did not give the courts the power; and (2) the presumption that an Act of Parliament is valid until proved invalid prevented

---

Review of Administrative Action, 5th edn (Sweet & Maxwell), para 17-016.

13 See Ch 6, pp 109–114.

14 [1990] 2 AC 85. This was effectively overruled in *M v Home Office* [1994] 1 AC 377 where the House of Lords considered that the unqualified language of s 31 of the Supreme Court Act 1981 gave the courts jurisdiction to make coercive orders, such as injunctions, against ministers of the Crown acting in their official capacity. Therefore, under RSC Ord 53, r 3(10)(*b*) the court can grant interim injunctions against ministers where it is just and convenient to do so in all cases, not just those involving Community law.

the grant of such an injunction. On a preliminary reference from the House of Lords as to whether these barriers were compatible with Community law, the Court of Justice held that the principle of effective protection of Community law dictated that national courts must at least have jurisdiction to grant interim relief to disapply a national law to protect putative rights in Community law.[15]

Factortame **litigation** *Factortame* concerned the common market fishing policy under which the Community fixes quotas for the amount of fish each national fishing fleet may catch. A practice known as 'quota hopping' arose whereby, according to the United Kingdom, its fishing quotas were plundered by vessels flying a British flag but lacking any genuine link with the United Kingdom. In December 1985 the Government made it a condition for the grant of a fishing licence that 75 per cent of the crew should be resident in the United Kingdom. The Government also introduced a new register for fishing vessels under the Merchant Shipping Act 1988 and subordinate regulations. To be registered, owners and operators of the vessels had to be British nationals (or, in the case of companies, at least 75 per cent of the shares had to be owned by British nationals) and the owners and operators (and shareholders and directors) had to be resident and domiciled in the United Kingdom. The applicants (companies incorporated under UK law and their directors and shareholders, most of whom were Spanish nationals) owned, between them, 95 sea-fishing vessels. They did not meet the new nationality and residence conditions laid down by the 1988 Act. On an application for judicial review of the 1988 Act, the applicants argued that the conditions were contrary to article 7 of the EEC Treaty [new art 12] (discrimination on the grounds of nationality), article 52 [new art 43] (principle of freedom of establishment) and article 221 [new art 294] (non-discrimination as regards participation in the capital of companies or firms).

The Divisional Court (Neill LJ and Hodgson J) requested a preliminary ruling from the Court of Justice as to the compatibility of the 1988 Act with Community law.[16] The reference to the Court of Justice on the substantive question raised the issue of interim relief in the meantime. On the applicants' motion, the Divisional Court granted interim relief, ordering that:[17]

---

[15] Case C-213/89 *Factortame* [1990] ECR I-2433, [1991] 1 AC 603.

[16] *R v Secretary of State for Transport, ex p Factortame Ltd* [1989] 2 CMLR 353 at 357. On the substantive issue, the Court of Justice subsequently held in Case C-221/89 *Factortame* [1991] ECR I-3905 that the nationality, domicile and residence requirements imposed by the UK legislation were contrary to EC law. The Commission also took parallel proceedings against the United Kingdom under article 169 of the Treaty [new art 226]. In the course of these proceedings the Court of Justice made an interim order pursuant to article 186 [new art 243] requiring the United Kingdom to suspend the application of the nationality requirements in Case 246/89R *Commission v United Kingdom* [1989] ECR 3125. A claim for damages was subsequently brought against the United Kingdom by the applicants: see Ch 7, pp 143–145.

[17] [1989] 2 CMLR 353 para 26.

... the operation of Part II of the Merchant Shipping Act 1988 and the Merchant Shipping (Registration of Shipping Vessels) Regulations 1988 be disapplied, and the Secretary of State be restrained from enforcing the same.

The Court of Appeal (Lord Donaldson MR, Bingham and Mann LJJ) allowed the Secretary of State's appeal on the issue of interim relief and held that there was no jurisdiction in the court to disapply an Act of Parliament unless and until incompatibility with Community law had been established. Lord Donaldson MR stated:[18]

> Looking at British national law without reference to the European Communities Act 1972, it is fundamental to our (unwritten) constitution that it is for Parliament to legislate and for the judiciary to interpret and apply the fruits of Parliament's labours. Any attempt to interfere with primary legislation would be wholly unconstitutional. That apart, there is a well settled principle of British national law that the validity of subordinate legislation and the legality of acts done pursuant to the law declared by it are presumed unless and until its validity has been challenged in the courts *and* the courts have fully determined its invalidity (see *Hoffman La Roche v Secretary of State for Trade* [1975] AC 295 at 365, *per* Lord Diplock). The position in relation to primary legislation must be the same.

The House of Lords affirmed the decision of the Court of Appeal with regard to the lack of jurisdiction. Lord Bridge said of the order for interim relief:[19]

> Any such order, unlike any form of order for interim relief known to the law, would irreversibly determine in the applicants' favour for a period of some two years rights which are necessarily uncertain until the preliminary ruling of the ECJ has been given. If the applicants fail to establish the rights they claim before the ECJ, the effect of the interim relief granted would be to have conferred upon them rights directly contrary to Parliament's sovereign will and correspondingly to have deprived British fishing vessels, as defined by Parliament, of the enjoyment of a substantial proportion of the United Kingdom quota of stocks of fish protected by the common fisheries policy. I am clearly of the opinion that, as a matter of English law, the court has no power to make an order which has these consequences.

However, the House of Lords made a further preliminary reference to the Court of Justice enquiring whether Community law empowered or obliged an English court, irrespective of the position under national law, to provide effective interim protection of the putative rights under Community law claimed by the applicants. The Court of Justice, following the Opinion of Advocate-General Tesauro, ruled that the national courts must disapply any rule or presumption which prevents the court from at least having jurisdiction to protect putative, as well as established, rights under Community law. Referring to its earlier judgment in Case 106/77 *Amministrazione delle Finanze v Simmenthal*[20] the Court of Justice stated that a national court must have the power to set aside national law which prevents Community rules from having full force and effect. The Court deduced from this that the full effectiveness of

[18] *R v Secretary of State for Transport, ex p Factortame Ltd* [1989] 2 CMLR 353 para 19.
[19] *R v Secretary of State for Transport, ex p Factortame Ltd* [1990] 2 AC 85 at 142 and 143.
[20] [1978] ECR 629. Discussed at Ch 3, pp 52–53.

Community law would be impaired if national courts could not act to protect rights alleged to exist under Community law. The Court stated:[21]

> ... the full effectiveness of Community law would be just as much impaired if a rule of national law could prevent a court seised of a dispute governed by Community law from granting interim relief in order to ensure the full effectiveness of the judgment to be given on the existence of the rights claimed under Community law. It follows that a court which in those circumstances would grant interim relief, if it were not for a rule of national law, is obliged to set aside that rule.

Applying the ruling of the Court of Justice, the House of Lords granted the interim injunction sought on the basis that the applicants had strong grounds for challenging the validity of the provisions in the Merchant Shipping Act 1988 relating to residence and domicile.[22] In the *Agegate* case[23] the Court of Justice had rejected, as invalid, a condition of a fishing licence that 75 per cent of the vessel's crew be resident in the United Kingdom. Consequently, if such a residence qualification were rejected in respect of the crew it was difficult to see how a similar condition could be upheld in respect of owners and operators. Moreover, the House of Lords was also persuaded that serious and irreparable damage would be suffered by the applicants if an interim injunction were not granted.

(ii) Conditions for the grant of interim relief

National law is applicable In its reference to the Court of Justice in *Factortame* the House of Lords asked, *inter alia*, what the criteria would be in determining whether to disapply national law on an interim basis in order to protect putative Community law rights. The Court of Justice did not answer this question. At present, therefore, in the absence of any Community law or judgment determining the conditions for the grant of interim relief where national law is allegedly inconsistent with Community law, it is for the English courts to apply their own national rules[24] based on the guidelines laid down by Lord Diplock in *American Cyanamid*. Thus, in applying the ruling of the Court of Justice in *Factortame*[25], the House of Lords exercised its new-found jurisdiction and granted an interim injunction restraining the Secretary of State from withholding or withdrawing registration of the applicant's vessels in the register maintained under the Merchant Shipping Act 1988. In so doing, the majority of the House of Lords applied the guidelines laid down by Lord Diplock in *American Cyanamid*, albeit with some modification to take account of the public interest in ensuring that the law was enforced.

The grant of an interim injunction to restrain a breach by the State of putative rights in Community law must be examined in three stages:

---

[21] Case C-213/89 *Factortame* [1990] ECR I-2433 para 21.

[22] *R v Secretary of State for Transport, ex p Factortame Ltd (No 2)* [1991] 1 AC 603. The nationality condition has already been suspended: See footnote 16 above.

[23] Case 3/87 *R v MAFF, ex p Agegate Ltd* [1989] ECR 4459. See also Case C-216/87 *R v MAFF, ex p Jaderow Ltd* [1989] ECR 4509.

[24] This was the view adopted by Advocate-General Tesauro at para 33 of his Opinion in Case C-213/89 *Factortame* [1990] ECR I-2433.

[25] *R v Secretary of State for Transport, ex p Factortame Ltd (No 2)* [1991] 1 AC 603.

(1) Is there a serious question to be tried?

(2) Would an award of damages be an adequate remedy to either party?

(3) Where does the balance of convenience lie?

Serious question to be tried The majority of the House of Lords in *Factortame*[26] considered that, at the threshold stage, it is sufficient for the applicant to show that the claim is not vexatious or frivolous, but that there is a serious question to be tried. The applicant will usually have to show something more than an arguable case, but whether more can be shown is considered at the balance of convenience stage.

Adequacy of damages In cases involving law enforcement and the public interest, the problem as to whether an injunction should be granted will not usually be resolved by considering whether damages would be an adequate remedy for either party.

An authority acting in the public interest cannot normally be protected by a remedy in damages because it itself will have suffered none. Its interest will usually go beyond economic loss.[27] An offer to the authority of a cross-undertaking is therefore likely to be meaningless.

The individual is unlikely to be adequately compensated in damages for two reasons. First, where an individual applicant is seeking to disapply national law, he is unlikely to be able to recover damages even if he succeeds in challenging the legality of that law, due to the restrictive approach to State liability under Community law.[28] Secondly, where the Crown or a public authority is the applicant seeking to enforce the law, it is unusual to impose upon the Crown or the public authority a cross-undertaking in damages.[29] Very good reason must be shown why the Crown or the public authority should give such an undertaking. In *Kirklees Metropolitan Borough Council v Wickes Building Supplies*[30] the plaintiff council applied for an interlocutory injunction to restrain the defendant from trading on Sunday contrary to the Shops Act 1950. The defendant argued that the Shops Act 1950 conflicted with article 30 of the EEC Treaty [new art 28]. The question arose whether the plaintiff council should give a cross-undertaking in damages as a condition of being granted interlocutory relief. The House of Lords held that Mervyn Davies J, at first instance, was fully entitled to hold, on ordinary principles of English law, that no cross-undertaking should be given. The effect of requiring an undertaking in damages from the Council would be to cause the collapse of the law

---

[26] Ibid. Lord Jauncey (at p 679B) disagreed with this approach, considering that the presumption of validity of national legislation made the *American Cyanamid* test, of a serious question to be tried, inappropriate.

[27] *R v Secretary of State for Transport, ex p Factortame Ltd (No 2)* [1991] 1 AC 603 per Lord Goff at 673A.

[28] For an analysis of State liability in damages and the need to prove a sufficiently serious breach, see Ch 7, pp 128–148.

[29] *Hoffmann-La Roche & Co AG v Secretary of State for Trade and Industry* [1975] AC 295 (in so far as the principle applies to the Crown); and *Kirklees MBC v Wickes Building Supplies* [1993] AC 227 (in so far as the principle applies to public authorities).

[30] [1993] AC 227.

enforcement process in this area of law, and it was arguable that small retailers might suffer if large retailers were able to continue to trade on Sundays. Moreover, if the law was subsequently held to be invalid, the proper party to pay damages would be the State which had enacted the Act, not the public authority which had enforced it.

When the application is, in reality, a dispute between two trade competitors (for example the applicant is challenging a decision to license its competitor), the court may require the applicant to offer a cross-undertaking to the competitor, rather than to the licensing authority, as it is the competitor which will suffer financial loss if the injunction is granted. Alternatively, the applicant may decide to offer a cross-undertaking voluntarily.[31]

Balance of convenience In weighing the balance of convenience the court will have regard to the nature of the law sought to be disapplied: whether it is firmly embedded in the domestic legal order; whether it is secondary or primary legislation; and the category or numbers of persons it affects. In determining where the risk of causing an injustice lies, the courts must have regard to the wider considerations of the public interest, particularly in cases involving the application of the criminal law. In this context, Lord Goff stated in *Factortame (No 2)*:[32]

> ... particular stress should be placed upon the importance of upholding the law of the land, in the public interest, bearing in mind the need for stability in our society, and the duty placed upon certain authorities to enforce the law in the public interest. This is of itself an important factor to be weighed in the balance when assessing the balance of convenience. So if a public authority seeks to enforce what is on its face the law of the land, and the person against whom such action is taken challenges the validity of that law, matters of considerable weight have to be put into the balance to outweigh the desirability of enforcing, in the public interest, what is on its face the law, and so to justify the refusal of an interim injunction in favour of the authority, or to render it just or convenient to restrain the authority for the time being from enforcing the law.

The public interest factor means that only in exceptional cases will an interim injunction be granted to disapply national law. The presumption in favour of legislative validity will usually, but not invariably, require a challenger to show

---

[31] *R v Medicines Control Agency, ex p Smith and Nephew Pharmaceuticals Ltd* [1997] EuLR 657; *R v Licensing Authority, ex p Rhone Poulenc Rorer Ltd* (unreported) 23 December 1997, Laws J.

[32] Per Lord Goff in *R v Secretary of State for Transport, ex p Factortame (No 2)* [1991] 1 AC 603 at 673; applying *Smith v Inner London Education Authority* [1978] 1 All ER 411 at 422, per Browne LJ and *Sierbein v Westminster City Council* (1987) 86 LGR 431; *South Pembroke District Council v Wendy Fair Markets* [1994] 1 CMLR 213 para 44. In *R v Secretary of State for National Heritage, ex p Continental Television BV (Red Hot Dutch)* [1993] 2 CMLR 333 at 348, Leggatt LJ, in refusing an interim injunction, stated 'when the moral welfare of minors is weighed against the applicants' profits there can only be one side upon which the scales come

a strong *prima facie* case. A chance of eventual success, which is no more than even, is unlikely to be sufficient.[33] As Lord Goff stated:[34]

> In the end, the matter is one for the discretion of the court, taking into account all the circumstances of the case. Even so, the court should not restrain a public authority by interim injunction from enforcing an apparently authentic law unless it is satisfied, having regard to all the circumstances, that the challenge to the validity of the law is, prima facie, so firmly based as to justify so exceptional a course being taken.

Even in law enforcement cases, however, the court's discretion to grant interim relief is not fettered by any rule which requires the individual to show, in all cases, a strong *prima facie* case that the law is invalid. As Lord Goff stated:[35]

> It is impossible to foresee what cases may yet come before the courts; I cannot dismiss from my mind the possibility (no doubt remote) that such a party may suffer such serious and irreparable harm in the event of the law being enforced against him that it may be just or convenient to restrain its enforcement by an interim injunction even though so heavy a burden has not been discharged by him.

Article 177 references Where the court requests a preliminary ruling from the Court of Justice under article 177 of the EC Treaty [new art 234] the grant of an interim injunction will, in practice, be unlikely by virtue of the fact that the referring court will not be satisfied sufficiently of the merits of the applicant's case. As Lord Bingham MR (as he then was) has stated:[36]

> But in most cases where the court decides to refer it will be able to conclude little more than that the plaintiff's case is arguable or strongly arguable. It is not in our view sensible for a national court to consider in depth a question which, by referring, it declares itself unable to resolve, which the Court of Justice is, for familiar reasons, better placed to resolve and which the national court will never have to resolve.

Effect of *Zuckerfabrik* In Joined Cases C-143/88 and C-92/89 *Zuckerfabrik*[37] the Court of Justice ruled that national courts are not precluded by Community law from suspending a national measure based on a Community regulation, even though this has the effect of indirectly suspending the regulation. Referring to its judgment in Case C-213/89 *Factortame* the Court stated that:[38]

---

down': upheld by the Court of Appeal [1993] 3 CMLR 387.

[33] See per Glidewell LJ in *R v Secretary of State for National Heritage, ex p Continental Television BV (Red Hot Dutch)* [1993] 3 CMLR 387 para 20: *R v Medicines Control Agency, ex p Generics, and ex p Squibb* [1997] 2 CMLR 201, upheld on appeal (unreported judgment of 20 February 1997).

[34] [1991] 1 AC 603 at 674C-D.

[35] *R v Secretary of State for Transport, ex p Factortame (No 2)* [1991] 1 AC 603 at 674C; judgment of Sir Thomas Bingham in *R v HM Treasury, ex p British Telecommunications plc* [1994] 1 CMLR 621 at 647. Cf Lord Diplock in *Hoffmann-La Roche & Co AG v Secretary of State for Trade and Industry* [1975] AC 295 at 367.

[36] *R v HM Treasury, ex p British Telecommunications* [1994] 1 CMLR 621 para 43; applied by Owen J in *R v Medicines Control Agency, ex p Generics, and ex p Squibb* [1997] 2 CMLR 201 paras 21–25, upheld on appeal (unreported judgment of 20 February 1997).

[37] [1991] ECR I-415. Discussed below at p 161.

[38] Ibid para 20. See also Case C-465/93 *Atlanta Fruchthandelsgesellschaft* [1995] ECR I-3761 para 24.

The interim legal protection which Community law ensures for individuals before national courts must remain the same, irrespective of whether they contest the compatibility of national legal provisions with Community law or the validity of secondary Community law, in view of the fact that the dispute in both cases is based on Community law itself.

The Court of Justice also set out the principles to be applied when national courts grant interim relief disapplying national legislation which gives effect to Community law. There must, *inter alia*, be serious doubts as to the validity of the Community measure, and a threat of serious and irreparable damage to the applicant.[39] These are difficult conditions to satisfy and are more strict than the conditions laid down for interim relief by Lord Diplock in *American Cyanamid Co v Ethicon Ltd*.[40] Although it has been suggested that these conditions apply equally to the grant of an injunction to disapply national law which is allegedly contrary to Community law, as well as one to disapply national law which gives effect to Community law,[41] it is unlikely that the Court of Justice intended to lay down uniform conditions to be applied in all cases where a national court grants interim relief in a case concerning Community law. First, the passage cited above appears in the part of the judgment which deals specifically with the jurisdiction of national courts to suspend the implementation of Community legislation, whereas the conditions on which such injunctions are granted fall under a completely separate heading. Secondly, the conditions laid down in *Zuckerfabrik* correspond with the principles followed by the Court of Justice in applying article 185 of the EC Treaty [new art 242], when the Court is itself suspending Community legislation. Moreover, Community law is unlikely to require the application of such strict conditions in a *Factortame*-type situation where there is no challenge to the validity of Community law.

Criminal cases In *Kirklees Metropolitan Borough Council v Wickes Building Supplies*[42] Lord Goff considered the basis upon which an interim injunction should be granted in order to ensure compliance with the criminal law. He emphasised that the right to invoke the assistance of the civil courts in aid of the criminal law is an exceptional power, which must be exercised with great caution. Generally, it is confined to cases where the offence is frequently repeated in disregard of a (usually inadequate) penalty or to cases of emergency. While accepting that, in most cases, it will be necessary to show that the defendant plainly has no defence to a criminal prosecution, this will not apply in all cases. As an example, Lord Goff stated that where a defendant invoked a Community law defence with sufficient substance (but no more) to merit a preliminary reference to the Court of Justice under article 177 of the EC Treaty [new art 234], this should not, in itself, prevent the grant of an interim

---

[39] Joined Cases C-143/88 and C-92/89 *Zuckerfabrik* [1991] ECR I-415 para 33.

[40] [1975] AC 396. See above at pp 156–159.

[41] Advocate-General Mischo in Joined Cases C-6/90 and C-9/90 *Francovich and Bonifaci v Italy* [1991] ECR I-5357, para 55 of the Opinion. See also Lord Goff in *Kirklees Metropolitan Borough Council v Wickes Building Supplies* [1993] AC 227 at 280G–281A.

[42] [1993] AC 227 at 269A–271C. See also *Portsmouth City Council v Brian James Richards and Quietlynn Ltd* [1989] 1 CMLR 673.

injunction. To hold otherwise would encourage those seeking to profit from law-breaking activities to adopt this method of prolonging what might prove to be a source of illicit profit. The existence of an alleged defence is merely a matter to be taken into account in the exercise of the court's discretion when deciding whether it is just and convenient that interlocutory relief should be granted.

(b) Interim injunction disapplying national law and thereby disapplying Community law

(i) Jurisdiction to grant interim relief

Suspension of national measures National courts must have jurisdiction to order the suspension of national measures which give effect to Community law. The power to stay national measures corresponds to the EC courts' power to suspend the application of Community measures under article 185 of the EC Treaty [new art 242]. In Joined Cases C-143/88 and C-92/89 *Zuckerfabrik*[43] Zuckerfabrik sought the suspension of a levy which had been imposed by the German authorities pursuant to a Community regulation. It argued that the regulation was invalid and that this vitiated the national decision to impose the levy. The Court of Justice held that, even though regulations are directly applicable in the national legal orders pursuant to article 189 of the EC Treaty [new art 249], this does not preclude national courts from suspending an administrative decision which has been adopted on the basis of a Community regulation, even if this has the effect of suspending the application of the regulation. Referring to its judgment in *Factortame*[44] the Court stated:[45]

> In cases where national authorities are responsible for the administrative implementation of Community regulations, the legal protection guaranteed by Community law includes the right of individuals to challenge, as a preliminary issue, the legality of such regulations before national courts and to induce those courts to refer questions to the Court of Justice for a preliminary ruling.
>
> That right would be compromised if, pending delivery of a judgment of the Court, which alone has jurisdiction to declare that a Community regulation is invalid (see judgment in Case 314/85 *Foto-Frost v Hauptzollamt Lübeck-Ost* [1987] ECR 4199, at paragraph 20), individuals were not in a position, where certain conditions are satisfied, to obtain a decision granting suspension of enforcement which would make it possible for the effects of the disputed regulation to be rendered for the time being inoperative as regards them . . .
>
> The interim legal protection which Community law ensures for individuals before national courts must remain the same, irrespective of whether they contest the compatibility of national legal provisions with Community law or the validity of secondary Community law, in view of the fact that the dispute in both cases is based on Community law itself.

Positive orders The interim legal protection that Community law ensures for individuals extends to the ability of national courts to adopt positive orders

---

[43] [1991] ECR I-415.
[44] Case C-213/89 *Factortame* [1990] ECR I-2433.
[45] Joined Cases C-143/88 and C-92/89 *Zuckerfabrik* [1991] ECR I-415 paras 16–17 and 20.

which conflict with Community law. In Case C-465/93 *Atlanta Fruchthandels-gesellschaft*[46] Atlanta challenged the validity of the Council regulation which established the Common Organization of the market in bananas. The regulation provided for a system of import quotas for bananas imported from outside the Community and, in accordance with the regulation, the applicant was granted a quota. Considering its quota to be insufficient, Atlanta sought an order that its quota be increased. The relief sought was not a stay of the regulation as such, but an order which conflicted with the terms of the regulation. The Court of Justice held that the German court, as a matter of Community law, had the power to make such an order. The power to adopt interim measures corresponds to the EC courts' power under article 186 of the EC Treaty [new art 243]. The Court stated:[47]

> In the context of an action for annulment, the Treaty not only, in Article 185, authorizes the Court to order application of the contested act to be suspended, but also, in Article 186, confers on it the power to prescribe any necessary interim measures.
>
> The interim legal protection which the national courts must afford to individuals under Community law must be the same whether they seek suspension of enforcement of a national administrative measure adopted on the basis of a Community regulation or the grant of interim measures settling or regulating the disputed legal positions or relationships for their benefit.

Protection where the Community has failed to act Where the Community has failed to act and would, therefore, be open to challenge under article 175 of the EC Treaty [new art 232], the national court does not have jurisdiction to grant interim relief which disapplies Community law pending the adoption of the relevant Community measure. In Case C-68/95 *T. Port*,[48] which concerned the Common Organization in the market for bananas, the Commission had failed to adopt measures to protect those importers of bananas who were suffering hardship due to their allocation of a small quota. T. Port applied to the German courts for an order that the German authorities increase its quota pending the adoption by the Commission of such protective measures. The Court of Justice held that the national court had no jurisdiction to make such an order, stating:[49]

> The present case is not about granting interim measures in the context of the implementation of a Community regulation whose validity is being contested, in order to ensure interim protection of rights which individuals derive from the Community legal system, but about granting traders interim judicial protection in a situation where, by virtue of a Community regulation, the existence and scope of traders' rights must be established by a Community measure which the Commission has not yet adopted.
>
> The Treaty makes no provision for a reference for a preliminary ruling by which a national court asks the Court of Justice to rule that an institution has failed to act.

---

[46] [1995] ECR I-3761.
[47] Ibid paras 27–28.
[48] [1996] ECR I-6065.
[49] Ibid paras 52–53.

Consequently, national courts have no jurisdiction to order interim measures pending action on the part of the institution. Judicial review of alleged failure to act can be exercised only by the Community judicature.

As a result, where the Community has failed to act, a person is limited to bringing a direct action before the EC courts under article 175 [new art 232], coupled with an application for interim measures under article 186 [new art 243].[50]

(ii) Conditions for the grant of interim relief
Community law principles are applicable The principles laid down by Lord Diplock in *American Cyanamid,* which guide the English courts in respect of the grant of interim relief, do not apply to the grant of interim injunctions disapplying Community law. Since the national courts' power corresponds to the power granted to the EC courts under articles 185 and 186 of the EC Treaty [new arts 242 and 243], the national courts can grant interim relief only in circumstances where, at least, the conditions for granting relief under articles 185 and 186 are satisfied.[51] On this basis, a national court should grant interim relief which disapplies Community law only if:[52]

(1) there are serious doubts about the validity of the Community measure;
(2) there is urgency and a threat of serious and irreparable damage to the applicant; and
(3) account is taken of the Community's interest.

In its assessment of these conditions, the national court must respect any decisions of the EC courts ruling on the lawfulness of the relevant Community act or on an application for interim measures seeking similar interim relief at Community level. If the national court decides to grant the interim relief sought, it must make a preliminary reference to the Court of Justice concerning the validity of the relevant Community measure (unless the same issue is already pending before the Court of Justice).

Serious doubts The factual and legal circumstances relied on by the applicant must persuade the national court that there are serious doubts as to the validity of the Community provision. Regard should be had, in particular, to the extent of the Community institution's discretion in the sector concerned.[53] In the context of the Common Agricultural Policy, for example, the Community institutions are allowed a wide discretion, which makes a finding of invalidity less likely. If the EC courts have already upheld the validity of the contested Community provision, the national court cannot suspend its application unless

---

[50] Ibid paras 60–61. See Chs 15 and 17 respectively.
[51] See Ch 17 for an analysis of the conditions applicable to the grant of interim measures under articles 185 and 186 of the EC Treaty.
[52] Joined Cases C-143/88 and C-92/89 *Zuckerfabrik* [1991] ECR I-415 paras 22–33; Case C-465/93 *Atlanta Fruchthandelsgesellschaft* [1995] ECR I-3761 para 32; Case C-68/95 *T. Port* [1996] ECR I-6065 para 48.
[53] Case C-465/93 *Atlanta Fruchthandelsgesellschaft v* [1995] ECR I-3761 para 36. In the order for reference the national court must set out the reasons why it considers the Community provision to be invalid.

the grounds of illegality put forward before it differ from those rejected by the EC courts.[54]

Urgency and irreparable damage Urgency exists where the damage is liable to materialise before the ruling of the Court of Justice on the validity of the contested Community measure. Although purely financial damage is not usually regarded as irreparable, interim relief can be granted where the immediate enforcement of the national measure will lead to irreversible damage to the applicant, which could not be made good by compensation if the Community measure was subsequently to be declared invalid.[55]

Community interest The national court should consider whether the Community measure challenged would be deprived of all effectiveness if it was not immediately enforced. In that respect, the national court must take into account on the one hand, the potential damage caused to the Community by a large number of similar applications for interim relief and on the other hand, any special facts which distinguish the applicant from other operators. Furthermore, if suspending enforcement would be likely to involve a financial risk for the Community, the applicant should be required to provide adequate guarantees, such as the deposit of money or other security.[56] In considering the Community interest, the national court may, but is not bound to, grant the Community institution which adopted the contested measure an opportunity to make its views known before the national court.[57]

---

[54] Ibid paras 46–50.

[55] Ibid para 41; Joined Cases C-143/88 and C-92/89 *Zuckerfabrik* [1991] ECR I-413 paras 28–29.

[56] Joined cases C-143/88 and C-92/89 *Zuckerfabrik* [1991] ECRI–413 paras 30–32; Case C-465/93 *Atlanta* [1995] ECR I-3761 paras 43–45.

[57] Case C-334/95 *Krüger v Hauptzollamt Hamburg-Jonas* [1997] ECR I-4517 para 46; Case C-183/95 *Affish v Rijksdienst voor de Keuring van Vee en Vlees* [1997] ECR I-4315 paras 23–26.

Chapter 9

Restitution

1. RESTITUTION CLAIMS INVOLVING PUBLIC LAW OBLIGATIONS

(a) Community law principles of restitution

Right to restitution The EC courts have recognised the right to restitution in a number of situations:

(1) where a Member State has collected national taxes, duties or levies which are contrary to Community law (eg because they are contrary to article 12 [new art 25] or article 95 [new art 90] of the EC Treaty);[1]

(2) where a Member State has collected monies on behalf of the Community under a Community measure which has subsequently been held to be invalid by the EC courts;[2] and

(3) where a Member State has paid out monies which it mistakenly believed were due under a Community measure.[3]

Basis of the right to restitution Where a Member State has collected monies in contravention of a directly effective provision of Community law, the right to restitution arises from the duty imposed on the national courts by article 5 of the EC Treaty [new art 10] to ensure the effective protection of directly effective Community rights. As Advocate-General Tesauro stated in Joined Cases C-192 to C-218/95 *Comateb v Directeur Général des Douanes*:[4]

> The right to reimbursement of sums unduly levied by the authorities is therefore rooted in the direct effect of the relevant provisions of Community law and the effectiveness of the protection of the legal positions created by those provisions. It is quite clear that that protection would not be effective if a judgment declaring a charge to be unlawful because it was levied in breach of a Community rule having direct effect were not accompanied by the possibility for individuals to obtain reimbursement.

---

[1] Case 33/76 *Rewe v Landwirtschaftskammer Saarland* [1976] ECR 1989 para 5; Case 45/76 *Comet v Produktschap* [1976] ECR 2043 paras 11–19; Case 61/79 *Amministrazione delle Finanze v Denkavit Italiana* [1980] ECR 1205 para 25.

[2] Case 130/79 *Express Dairy Foods v IBAP* [1980] ECR 1887.

[3] Case 265/78 *Ferwerda v Produktschap voor Vee en Vlees* [1980] ECR 617 para 10.

[4] [1997] ECR I-165 para 11.

Where a Member State has mistakenly paid out monies which it believed to be due to a person under Community law, a similar right to restitution arises on behalf of the State. The direct effect of a Community provision may create obligations for the individual as well as confer rights. It is for the national courts, in pursuance of the duty of cooperation embodied in article 5 of the Treaty, to ensure that individuals comply with their Community obligations. If individuals were exempt from repaying monies wrongly paid to them, the effect would be to modify the content of the Community provision.[5]

Application of national rules In the absence of Community rules harmonising national rules on restitution, it is for the national courts to apply their own substantive, procedural and evidential rules to determine how the right to restitution may be exercised. Thus, national rules will apply in so far as they relate to limitation periods,[6] interest,[7] set-off,[8] and defences of unjust enrichment[9] or legitimate expectation,[10] provided that they satisfy the principles of equivalence and effective protection.[11]

However, the application of national rules is subject to two limitations:

(1) they must not be discriminatory or less favourable than those relating to similar actions of a domestic nature (principle of equivalence); and

(2) they must not make it impossible in practice to exercise the right to restitution (principle of effective protection).

For example, the Court of Justice has held that the English rule whereby money paid to a public authority under a mistake of law may be recovered only if it was paid under protest clearly infringes the principle of effective protection. Therefore, this principle must be disapplied in restitutionary claims based on Community law.[12]

Community rules Where the Community has legislated on the extent of any right to restitution, national rules cease to apply, provided that the Community rules satisfy the general principles of Community law, such as the principles of legitimate expectation and proportionality.[13]

---

[5] Case 265/78 *Ferwerda v Produktschap voor Vee en Vlees* [1980] ECR 617 paras 10–13.

[6] Case 33/76 *Rewe v Landwirtschafskammer Saarland* [1976] ECR 1989 para 5; Case 45/76 *Comet v Produktschap* [1976] ECR 2043 paras 11–19; Joined Cases 119/79 and 126/79 *Lippische Hauptgenossenschaft v BALM* [1980] ECR 1863 paras 7–10; Case 386/87 *Bessin et Salson v Administration des douanes* [1989] ECR 3551 paras 15–18; Case C-90/94 *Haahr Petroleum v Havn* [1997] ECR I-4085.

[7] Case 26/74 *Roquette Frères v Commission* [1976] ECR 677 paras 9–14; Case 130/79 *Express Dairy Foods v IBAP* [1980] ECR 1887 paras 15–17; Case 54/81 *Fromme v BALM* [1982] ECR 1449 paras 4–10.

[8] Case 177/78 *Pigs & Bacon Commission v McCarren* [1979] ECR 2161 paras 24–26. See also Case 222/82 *Apple and Pear Development Council v Lewis* [1983] ECR 4083 paras 36–42.

[9] See below at pp 167–168.

[10] See below at p 168.

[11] See generally Ch 6.

[12] Case C-212/94 *FMC v IBAP* [1996] ECR I-389 para 72; paras 90–91 of the opinion of Advocate-General Jacobs in Case C-188/95 *Fantask* [1997] ECR I-000 paras 90–91 (judgment of 2 December 1997).

[13] Case T-455/93 *Hedley Lomas (Ireland) v Commission* [1997] ECR II-1095.

Dual protection Since Community law principles apply whenever a person exercises rights guaranteed under Community law[14], there will be instances where these general principles apply alongside similar domestic principles, thus giving the individual dual protection. For example, to the extent that domestic and Community rules on legitimate expectation differ, the individual may choose whichever best serves his defence to a claim by the state for reimbursement of monies paid in breach of Community law.

Defence of unjust enrichment It is permissible for a national law to refuse restitution where this would result in the unjust enrichment of the claimant, for example, where he has already passed on the cost of the charges unduly levied in the prices charged to customers.[15] As the Court of Justice stated in Joined Cases C-192 to C-218/95 *Comateb v Directeur Général des Douanes*:[16]

> In such circumstances, the burden of the charge levied but not due has been borne not by the trader, but by the purchaser to whom the cost has been passed on. Therefore, to repay the trader the amount of the charge already received from the purchaser would be tantamount to paying him twice over, which may be described as unjust enrichment, whilst in no way remedying the consequences for the purchaser of the illegality of the charge.

If the final consumer is able to obtain reimbursement of the charge from the trader, the trader should, in principle, be able to obtain reimbursement from the national authorities.[17] Even where the charge has been passed on to the purchaser, repayment to the trader of the amount passed on will not necessarily constitute unjust enrichment, since the trader may justifiably claim that the effect of passing on the charge has resulted in lost sales. Such a claim should probably be classified as a claim for damages rather than a claim for restitution, with the consequence that the trader would have to prove a sufficiently serious breach of Community law in order to obtain compensation from the State.[18]

It is for the national courts to determine, in the light of the facts in each case, whether the burden of the charge has been passed on. National law cannot impose a presumption that the charge has been passed on, and national rules on unjust enrichment must satisfy the principles of equivalence and effective protection. In Case 199/82 *Amministrazione delle Finanze v San Giorgio*[19] an

---

[14] *R v Ministry of Agriculture Fisheries and Food, ex p First City Trading* [1997] 1 CMLR 250; [1997] EuLR 195. Discussed at Ch 10, pp 185–186.

[15] Case 68/79 *Just v Danish Ministry for Fiscal Affairs* [1980] ECR 501 paras 25–26; Case 811/79 *Amministrazione delle Finanze v Ariete* [1980] ECR 2545 paras 12–14; Case 826/79 *Amministrazione delle Finanze v MIRECO* [1980] ECR 2559 paras 13–14; Lord Goff in *Woolwich Equitable Building Society v Inland Revenue Commissioners* [1993] AC 70 at 177.

[16] [1997] ECR I-165 para 22.

[17] Joined Cases C-192 to 218/95 *Comateb v Directeur Général des Douanes* [1997] ECR I-165 para 24.

[18] Ibid paras 29–34. Case C-242/95 *GT–Link v DSB* [1997] ECR I-4449 para 60. For an analysis of the principle of State liability, see Ch 7, pp 128–148.

[19] [1983] ECR 3595 paras 11–18. See also Case 331/85 *Bianco v Directeur Général des Douanes* [1988] ECR 1099 paras 8–13; Case 104/86 *Commission v Italy* [1988] ECR 1799 paras 6–13; Joined Cases C-192 to 218/95 *Comateb v Directeur Général des Douanes* [1997] ECR I-165 para 25.

Italian trader had paid charges to the Italian authorities which had been levied in breach of Community law. Italian law recognised a right to restitution where charges had been levied contrary to national law and Community law. However, the law presumed that the person who had paid the charges would pass them on to the consumer. In order to recover the charges from the Italian authorities, the trader had to prove, by documentary evidence alone, that they had not been passed on. The Court of Justice considered that such a law was unlawful as it required the trader to prove a negative by documentary evidence. Although it was not discriminatory, it made it impossible or excessively difficult in practice to exercise the right to restitution granted by Community law.

Legitimate expectation Community law does not preclude a defence of legitimate expectation or legal certainty, based on national law, whereby financial benefits wrongly conferred on a trader cannot be recovered provided the error committed was not due to incorrect information supplied by the recipient or that, although the information was incorrect, it was supplied by the trader in good faith. Since the principle of legitimate expectation forms part of the Community legal order, it cannot be contrary to Community law for domestic courts to apply similar principles.[20] In *Carberry Milk Products v Minister for Agriculture*[21] the Irish Minister classified the company's product as milk protein powder. Relying on this, the company applied for and obtained export refunds under the Common Agricultural Policy in respect of the powder. Subsequently, the Minister reclassified the product as whey powder, for which no export refunds could be obtained. The Irish High Court held that the company was not liable to reimburse the refunds wrongly paid to it by the Minister. The court found that the company had at all times acted correctly, that the fault was entirely that of the Minister, and that it would infringe the company's legitimate expectations (a principle recognised in Irish law) if it was obliged to repay the refunds to the Minister.[22]

Temporal limitations Where the State has levied charges on the basis of a Community provision which is subsequently declared to be invalid, this may give rise to a large number of claims for restitution which may have serious financial consequences for the public purse. Consequently, the Court of Justice has, on certain occasions, limited the temporal effects of judgments made by it concerning the invalidity of a provision of Community law. For example, the Court may exclude any claims for restitution arising prior to the judgment of the Court. Alternatively, it may also limit the right of recovery to the party who brought the proceedings which led to the annulment of the relevant Community measure or to those who had already commenced legal proceedings or made an

---

[20] Case 265/78 *Ferwerda v Produktschap voor Vee en Vlees* [1980] ECR 617 para 17; Joined Cases C-205 to 215/82 *Deutsche Milchkontor v Germany* [1983] ECR 2633 para 30. As to the application of the principle of legitimate expectation to the recovery of State aid, see below pp 175–176.

[21] [1994] 3 CMLR 914.

[22] As to the defence of estoppel in English law, see Wade and Forsyth, *Administrative Law*, 7th edn (Oxford, 1994), p 268.

equivalent claim prior to the judgment of the Court of Justice.[23] The power to impose temporal limitations on the effect of a judgment can only be exercised by the EC courts in the course of the judgment itself. National authorities or courts have no power to impose temporal limitations on the effect of a judgment of the EC courts. The Court of Justice has disapproved of national laws passed to limit reimbursement solely to claimants who had commenced proceedings prior to a judgment by the Court of Justice declaring a national tax to be unlawful.[24]

English law: substantive rules It is for the English courts to apply their own substantive laws to give effect to Community law rights to restitution. However, these laws must not treat Community rights less favourably than comparable national rights, nor render the Community rights impossible to exercise in practice.[25] The English law of restitution, although somewhat underdeveloped, contains some special rules in relation to claims against public bodies. Prior to the decision of the House of Lords in *Woolwich Equitable Building Society v Inland Revenue Commissioners*[26] it was very difficult to succeed in a restitutionary claim against a public body. The normal principles of restitution applied so that a plaintiff would need to establish that payment was made under a mistake of fact or under duress. In most cases, monies were paid under a mistake of law and were, therefore, irrecoverable.[27] However, in *Woolwich* a majority of the House of Lords established a principle that money paid by a citizen to a public authority in the form of taxes or other levies pursuant to an *ultra vires* demand by the authority is *prima facie* recoverable by the citizen as of right.[28]

Lord Goff and Lord Slynn indicated that a *prima facie* right to restitution would also arise where the authority had misconstrued the relevant provision, ie it had made a mistake of law.[29] Lord Goff based his reasoning partly on the fact that, under Community law, a person who pays charges levied by a Member State in breach of Community law is entitled to repayment of those charges.[30] This view was accepted by the Court of Appeal in *British Steel v Customs and Excise Commissioners*,[31] in which British Steel sought restitution of monies

---

[23] For example, see Case 145/79 *Roquette Frères v France* [1980] ECR 2917 paras 50–53; Case 112/83 *Produits de maïs v Administration des douanes* [1985] ECR 719 paras 17–18. Temporal limitations are discussed at Ch 11, pp 240–241 and Ch 13, pp 329–330.

[24] Case 309/85 *Barra v Belgium* [1988] ECR 355. See also Case 240/87 *Deville v Administration des Impôts* [1988] ECR 3513.

[25] See above at pp 166–167, and Ch 6 at pp 107–114.

[26] [1993] AC 70. See the comments of Burrows, *The Law of Restitution*, 1st edn (Butterworths, 1993), pp 345–361.

[27] As a result of the principle established in *Bilbie v Lumley* (1802) 2 East 469.

[28] See the speeches of Lord Goff, Lord Browne-Wilkinson, and Lord Slynn (Lord Keith and Lord Jauncey dissenting).

[29] [1993] AC 70 at 177F–178B, per Lord Goff; at 204F–205B, per Lord Slynn.

[30] Ibid at 177C–E.

[31] [1997] 2 All ER 366.

paid by way of excise duty, contending that the Commissioners had misapplied the relevant legislation by failing to grant it relief. Richard Scott V-C stated:

> An unlawful demand for duty must, in a sense, always be an ultra vires demand. Whether the demand is based on ultra vires regulations, or on a mistaken view of the legal effect of valid regulations, or on a mistaken view of the facts of the case, it will, as it seems to me, be bound to be a demand outside the taxing power conferred by the empowering legislation. If, for any of these reasons, a demand for tax is an unlawful demand, it seems to me to follow from the speeches of the majority in the *Woolwich* case that the taxpayer would, *prima facie*, become entitled, on making payment pursuant to the unlawful demand, to a common law restitutionary right to repayment.[32]

Where a Member State has paid out monies which it mistakenly believed were due to third parties under a Community measure, it may be able to rely on the principle that, if the Crown pays money out of the consolidated fund without authority, such money is *ipso facto* recoverable if it can be traced.[33] Alternatively, the Member State may be able to rely on the general grounds of restitution (eg payment under a mistake of fact) to found a claim.[34] However, where the State has paid out monies under a mistake of law,[35] and these monies were not paid out of the consolidated fund or can no longer be traced, it is doubtful whether English law would give a right to recovery as there is no general right to restitution in respect of monies paid under a mistake of law. In such a case, it would be open to the State to argue that the English courts would be obliged to set aside the rule preventing recovery for a mistake of law because its application renders the Community law right of restitution impossible to exercise in practice.

English law: procedure As RSC Ord 53 does not provide for restitutionary remedies in the context of the judicial review procedure, it appears that restitutionary claims against public bodies must be brought under private law procedures, for example by writ. This is supported by the speech of Lord Slynn in *Woolwich* (above), where he said:[36]

> If a claim lies for money had and received, judicial review adds nothing. If the money falls in law to be repaid, a direct order for its repayment is more appropriate than a declaration that it should [be repaid] or an order setting aside a refusal to repay.

---

[32] Ibid at 376C.

[33] *Auckland Harbour Board v R* [1924] AC 318; *Woolwich Equitable Building Society v Inland Revenue Commissioners* [1993] AC 70 at 177B–C, per Lord Goff. See the comments of Burrows, *The Law of Restitution*, 1st edn (Butterworths, 1993), pp 330–332.

[34] For example, see *Holt v Markham* [1923] 1 KB 504; *Avon County Council v Howlett* [1983] 1 WLR 605.

[35] *Bilbie v Lumley* (1802) 2 East 469. See also *Holt v Markham* [1923] 1 KB 504; *Avon County Council v Howlett* [1983] 1 WLR 605.

[36] *Woolwich Equitable Building Society v Inland Revenue Commissioners* [1993] AC 70 at 200F–G; applied in *British Steel plc v Customs and Excise Commissioners* [1997] 2 All ER 366.

(b) Repayment and remission of import and export duties

Council Regulation 2913/92 The Community has adopted specific legislation in relation to the restitution of import and export duties. Council Regulation 2913/92, which establishes the Community Customs Code,[37] sets out the framework rules for the repayment and remission of import and export duties. Council Regulation 2913/92 is supplemented by more detailed rules in Commission Regulation 2454/93.[38]

Scope of the Regulations The Regulations apply only to taxes, charges, levies and duties created by various Community provisions and collected by the Member States on behalf of the Community. The duties covered include customs duties and charges having equivalent effect to customs duties, as well as agricultural duties.[39] The Regulations do not apply to national taxes, charges and duties, even when they are levied in breach of Community law;[40] nor is the Community Customs Code applicable to demands for repayment of export refunds.[41]

The Regulations set out three circumstances where repayment[42] or remission[43] will be granted:

(1) where the duties demanded are not legally due;

(2) where the customs declaration is invalidated; and

(3) where the goods are rejected by the importer on the basis that they are defective or do not correspond with the terms of the contract on the basis of which they were imported.

Duties not legally due[44] Duties which are not legally due may be repaid or remitted where the debtor makes an application to the appropriate customs office within three years of the date on which the amount of those duties was communicated to the debtor, subject to excusable delay caused by unforeseeable circumstances or *force majeure*. In addition, where the customs authorities discover within this period that duties are not legally due, they are required to repay or remit them on their own initiative. No repayment or remission will be

---

[37] Council Regulation 2913/92 of 12 October 1992 (OJ 1992 L302 p 1) establishing the Community Customs Code. This Regulation repealed Council Regulation 1430/79 (OJ 1979 L175 p 1) on the repayment or remission of import or export duties.

[38] Commission Regulation 2454/93 of 2 July 1993 (OJ 1993 L253 p 1) laying down provisions for the implementation of Council Regulation 2913/92 establishing the Community Customs Code (articles 877–912), as amended by Commission Regulation 3665/93 of 21 December 1993 (OJ 1993 L335 p 1).

[39] Regulation 2913/92, article 4(10) and (11).

[40] Joined Cases C-192 to 218/95 *Société Comateb v Directeur Général des Douanes* [1997] ECR I-165 para 11.

[41] Case C-334/95 *Krüger v Hauptzollamt Hamburg-Jonas* [1997] ECR I-4517 paras 36–40.

[42] Regulation 2913/92, article 235(1): 'repayment' means the total or partial refund of import or export duties which have been paid.

[43] Ibid, article 235(2): 'remission' means the waiver of all or part of a customs debt not yet paid.

[44] Ibid, article 236.

granted where the facts which led to the demand of the relevant duty were the result of deliberate action by the person concerned.

Customs declaration invalidated[45] Where a customs declaration has been invalidated, for example because goods were placed under a particular type of customs procedure as a result of an error,[46] duties paid may be recovered. The application for repayment must be made within the periods laid down for submission of the application for invalidation of the customs declaration.[47]

Goods rejected by importer[48] Subject to certain conditions, duties may be repaid or remitted where goods are rejected by the importer on the basis that they are defective or do not correspond with the terms of the contract on the basis of which they were imported. An application must be made to the appropriate customs office within 12 months from the date on which the amount of the debt was communicated to the debtor. However, the customs authorities may permit this period to be exceeded in exceptional cases.

Minimum amount[49] Generally, repayment or remission will be granted only if the relevant amount exceeds a minimum sum to be fixed by the Customs Code Committee.[50] However, national customs authorities have discretion to grant repayment or remission in respect of lower amounts.

Interest[51] Interest need not be paid in respect of repayment of duties, unless either a decision to grant a repayment is not implemented within three months of the date of adoption of the decision or national provisions so stipulate.

Appeals[52] Regulation 2913/92 sets down specific rules for the suspension of decisions of national customs authorities and appeals therefrom. The decision by the customs authority demanding payment may be suspended where there is a risk of irreparable harm to the trader, although the authority may still require the provision of security in the event of any suspension.[53]

2. RESTITUTION CLAIMS INVOLVING PRIVATE LAW OBLIGATIONS

General principles Where a private party has paid money to another in breach of his directly effective Community law rights, that person should, in principle, be entitled to bring a restitutionary claim in order to protect those rights. The right to restitution is a consequence of, and an adjunct to, the direct effect of the

---

[45] Ibid, article 237.
[46] Ibid, article 66.
[47] Ibid, article 66(2).
[48] Ibid, article 238.
[49] Ibid, article 240.
[50] This Committee is established under the terms of Regulation 2913/93. See articles 247–249.
[51] Ibid, article 241.
[52] Ibid, articles 243–246.
[53] Case C-130/95 *Giloy v Hauptzollamt Frankfurt am Main-Ost* [1997] ECR I-4291.

Community law provision.[54] To that extent, the right to restitution afforded by Community law is probably consistent with the general principle of unjust enrichment now recognised in English law.[55]

As in the case of restitution claims involving public law obligations, it is for national courts to apply their own substantive, procedural and evidential rules to determine how the right to restitution may be exercised in cases involving private disputes. In the context of article 85 of the EC Treaty [new art 81], the Court of Justice stated in Case 319/82 *SVCB v Kerpen & Kerpen*:[56]

> ... the automatic nullity decreed by Article 85(2) of the Treaty applies only to those contractual provisions which are incompatible with Article 85(1). The consequences of such nullity for other parts of the agreement and for any orders and deliveries made on the basis of the agreement and the resulting financial obligations are not a matter for community law.

Thus, rules relating to total failure of consideration,[57] change of position,[58] *ex turpi causa*,[59] the effect of passing on the charge,[60] the difference between mistake of law and fact,[61] and the difference between illegal and merely void contracts[62] are matters for national law. However, the national rules applied cannot be discriminatory or less favourable than those relating to similar actions of a domestic nature and must not make it impossible in practice to exercise the relevant Community law rights.[63]

EC competition rules The extent to which a person can recover money paid or property transferred under a contract which is prohibited under articles 85 or 86 [new arts 81 and 82] [new art 82] is unclear. It would appear that contracts contrary to either provision are illegal and not merely void since both articles provide for express prohibitions, and fines can be imposed for their breach. Generally, a restitutionary claim arising out of an illegal contract will be barred by the principle *ex turpi causa non oritur actio* ('the court will not lend its aid to a man who founds his action upon an immoral or an illegal act'). However, the courts may permit a restitutionary claim where the parties are not in *pari delicto*. In *Browning v Morris*[64] Lord Mansfield held that:

---

[54] Joined Cases C-192 to 218/95 *Comateb v Directeur Général des Douanes* [1997] ECR I-165 para 20.

[55] *Lipkin Gorman v Karpnale Ltd* [1991] 2 AC 548; *Kleinwort Benson v Birmingham City Council* [1996] 3 WLR 1139.

[56] [1983] ECR 4173 para 12.

[57] *Westdeutsche Bank Girozentrale v Islington London Borough Council* [1996] AC 669.

[58] *Lipkin Gorman v Karpnale* [1991] 2 AC 548.

[59] *Tinsley v Milligan* [1994] 1 AC 340.

[60] *Kleinwort Benson v Birmingham City Council* [1996] 3 WLR 1139.

[61] *Holt v Markham* [1923] 1 KB 504; *Avon County Council v Howlett* [1983] 1 WLR 605.

[62] *Westdeutsche Bank Girozentrale v Islington London Borough Council* [1994] 4 All ER 890 at 915, per Hobhouse J.

[63] See above at p 166.

[64] [1778] 2 Cowp 790, 98 English Reports 1364. Applied in *Kiriri Cotton Co Ltd v Dewani* [1960] AC 192 at 204, by Lord Denning (PC); *Re Cavalier Insurance Co Ltd* [1989] 2 Lloyd's Rep 430 at 449–450; see also Treitel, *The Law of Contract*, 9th edn (Sweet & Maxwell 1995), pp 452–458.

... where contracts or transactions are prohibited by positive statutes, for the sake of protecting one set of men from another set of men; the one, from their situation and condition, being liable to be oppressed or imposed upon by the other; there, the parties are not in pari delicto; and in furtherance of these statutes, the person injured, after the transaction is finished and completed, may bring his action and defeat the contract.

Article 86, which prohibits an abuse by a company in a dominant position, clearly contemplates exploitative conduct by one person to a contract. Similarly, article 85, which prohibits restrictive agreements, may be breached in situations where the two parties to a contract are in unequal bargaining positions (eg agreement between franchisor and franchisee). On the assumption that both article 85 and article 86 aim at least in part to protect individuals from anti-competitive conduct—an assumption supported by the fact that both articles are of direct effect—the *ex turpi causa* defence is unlikely to preclude a restitutionary claim in all cases.[65]

3. REPAYMENT OF STATE AIDS

General principles Article 92 of the EC Treaty [new art 87] provides that State aid which distorts competition within the Community is unlawful, unless it falls within the categories of aid which are permissible under article 92(2) and (3). The Commission has the power to order the Member State to recover unlawful State aid. Under article 93(3) [new art 88], a Member State should inform the Commission if it plans to grant or alter aid and should not grant any aid before the Commission has adopted a final decision sanctioning the aid.[66] This procedural obligation is of direct effect, which means that a competitor of the recipient may challenge the grant of unnotified aid in the national courts and seek the freezing or return of the aid.[67] Furthermore, the Commission has the power to order Member States to recover unnotified State aid where it has already been granted in breach of article 93(3).[68] A decision requiring repayment of State aid will also require interest to be recovered on the sum granted so as to eliminate any financial advantage incidental to the aid.[69]

Failure to recover Where the Commission adopts a decision requiring recovery of State aids, this imposes an obligation on the Member State to which it is addressed to take the necessary steps. If a Member State does not challenge

---

[65] A Jones, 'Recovery of Benefits Conferred under Contractual Obligations prohibited by Article 85 or 86 of the Treaty of Rome', [1996] 112 LQR 606. But see *Garry Parkes v Esso Petroleum Company Ltd* (unreported judgment of Sir Richard Scott VC, 11 February 1998, Ch D).

[66] The consequences of a failure to notify are set out in Case C-301/87 *France v Commission* [1990] ECR I-307.

[67] Commission Notice on Co-operation in the State aid field (OJ 1995 C312/8 para 10); Case C-354/90 *FNCE v France* [1991] ECR I-5505; Case T-49/93 *SIDE v Commission* [1995] ECR II-2501; *R v Secretary of State for National Heritage, ex p J Paul Getty Trust* [1997] EuLR 407.

[68] Case 301/87 *France v Commission* [1990] ECR I-307 paras 19–22; Case 142/87 *Belgium v Commission* [1990] ECR I-959 paras 14–18 and 66; Case C-305/89 *Italy v Commission* [1991] ECR I-1603 paras 38–42. See also Case 310/85 *Deufil v Commission* [1987] ECR 901 para 24.

[69] Case T-459/93 *Siemens v Commission* [1995] ECR II-1675 paras 95–107.

the validity of the Commission's decision under article 173 of the EC Treaty [new art 230], and fails to recover the sums paid as aid, the Commission may commence infraction proceedings against the Member State under article 93(2).[70] A Member State may not challenge the validity of the original Commission decision in such proceedings, nor may it rely on internal administrative, legal, political, financial or practical difficulties as a defence. However, a Member State will not be found to be in breach of its Community obligations where it can prove that it was absolutely impossible for it to recover the State aid.[71] If a Member State encounters unforeseen difficulties in implementing the order for recovery, it should, pursuant to article 5 of the EC Treaty [new art 10], inform the Commission in order to seek a solution.[72] In Case 63/87 *Commission v Greece*[73] Advocate-General Slynn indicated that a further defence available to a Member State is to argue that the Commission decision is unclear or ambiguous. In these circumstances it may be that it is absolutely impossible for the Member State to comply with the Commission decision because it is not possible to ascertain the nature of the obligation which the decision seeks to impose.

Challenging the decision The lawfulness of a decision ordering repayment of State aid may be challenged by a Member State or by the recipient under article 173 of the EC Treaty.[74] A delay by the Commission in deciding whether the aid is lawful may give rise to a legitimate expectation that the beneficiary may keep the aid. For example, in Case 223/85 *RSV v Commission*[75] the Court of Justice annulled a decision of the Commission requiring the Netherlands to recover monies paid to RSV as State aid, on the ground that the Commission had delayed 26 months before adopting the decision. This delay had established a legitimate expectation on the part of RSV that it would be entitled to retain the aid.

Recovery takes place under national law In principle, the recovery of aid unlawfully paid must take place in accordance with the relevant procedural provisions of national law, subject, however, to the proviso that those

---

[70] Article 93(2) of the EC Treaty establishes a special procedure for infraction proceedings against a Member State in the context of State aids, whereby the Commission is not obliged to follow the procedure under article 169 of the EC Treaty [new art 226]. See, generally, Ch 12.

[71] Case 52/84 *Commission v Belgium* [1986] ECR 89 paras 13–16; Case 213/85 *Commission v Netherlands* [1988] ECR 281 paras 22–24; Case 63/87 *Commission v Greece* [1988] ECR 2875 paras 8 and 14; Case C-5/89 *Commission v Germany* [1990] ECR I-3437 para 18.

[72] Case 52/84 *Commission v Belgium* [1986] ECR 89 para 16; Case C-303/88 *Italy v Commission* [1991] ECR I-1433 paras 56–58; Case C-183/91 *Commission v Greece* [1993] ECR I-3131.

[73] [1988] ECR 2875, Opinion of Advocate-General Slynn at para 2884. The Advocate-General referred to Case 70/72 *Commission v Germany* [1973] ECR 813 in support of this argument. For further discussion of defences in infraction proceedings, see Ch 12, pp 257–262.

[74] See Ch 13, pp 303–305.

[75] [1987] ECR 4617 paras 12–19. *Cf* Case 301/87 *France v Commission* [1990] ECR I-307 paras 25–28, where delay by the Commission in reaching a decision was justified due to the time required to obtain all the necessary information. See also Case C-294/90 *British Aerospace v Commission* [1992] ECR I-493; Joined Case T-551/93 and others *Industrias Pesqueras Campos v Commission* [1996] ECR II-247 paras 75–119.

provisions are to be applied in such a way that the recovery required by Community law is not rendered practically impossible.[76]

National rules which provide for defences based on principles of legitimate expectations apply to the recovery of unlawful State aids. Such defences cannot be considered contrary to Community law since they are recognised by Community law itself. However, except in exceptional circumstances, recipients of State aid cannot entertain legitimate expectations that the aid is lawful where it has not been granted in compliance with article 93. The Commission has published a communication in the *Official Journal*[77] informing potential recipients of State aid that they risk having to refund the aid if it has been granted illegally. Since a diligent person should normally be able to determine whether the necessary procedures have been followed, that person cannot have an expectation of keeping the aid in the event that they have not been.[78]

A failure by the national authority to recover the unlawful aid within the domestic time-limit will not usually give rise to any legitimate expectation that the aid can be kept. If, under national law, time starts to run from the grant of the unnotified aid, the recipient, as a diligent trader, cannot have a legitimate expectation that the grant of the aid is lawful. If time starts to run from the date of the Commission's decision that the aid is unlawful, the recipient knows at that date that the grant is unlawful and cannot have a legitimate expectation of keeping the aid simply by the lapse of time. Moreover, if recovery were precluded by national time-limits in either case, articles 92 and 93 would be deprived of all practical effect.[79]

---

[76] Case C-142/87 *Belgium v Commission* [1990] ECR I-959 para 61. See also Case 94/87 *Commission v Germany* [1989] ECR 175 para 12. For an English case concerning the recovery of State aids, see *Department of Trade and Industry v British Aerospace plc and Rover Group Holdings plc* [1991] 1 CMLR 165. For an example of the Belgian authorities proving in the liquidation of the recipient undertaking in order to recover aid granted unlawfully, see *Belgium v Tubemeuse* [1994] 3 CMLR 93.

[77] Commission Communication (OJ 1983 C318 p 3).

[78] Case C-5/89 *Commission v Germany* [1990] ECR I-3437 paras 12–16. See also Opinion of Advocate-General Darmon in Case 94/87 *Commission v Germany* [1989] ECR 175 at 187–188; Case C-183/91 *Commission v Greece* [1993] ECR I-3131 para 19; Case C-24/95 *Land Rheinland-Pfalz v Alcan Deutschland* [1997] ECR I-1591 para 25.

[79] Case C-5/89 *Commission v Germany* [1990] ECR I-3437 para 19; Joined Cases T-244/93 and T-486/93 *TWD v Commission* [1995] ECR II-2265 para 73; Case C-24/95 *Land Rheinland-Pfalz v Alcan Deutschland* [1997] ECR I-1591 para 25.

Chapter 10

Judicial Review

1. AVAILABILITY OF JUDICIAL REVIEW

(a) Appropriate procedure

Public/private law distinction It is for national law to classify the nature of rights afforded under Community law within its own legal system and to specify the courts and the procedures whereby those rights are to be enforced. Thus, it is for domestic law to decide whether a Community law right should be described as a private or public law right and whether such rights should be protected by means of private law (eg writ) proceedings or by way of judicial review. However, the domestic rules applied must not be less favourable than those relating to similar claims under national law (principle of equivalence) and must not render it impossible in practice for the Community law right to be exercised (principle of effective protection).[1]

English rules RSC Ord 53 establishes a specific judicial review procedure. No substantive application for judicial review may be made without first obtaining the leave of the court,[2] and applications for leave must be made promptly and in any event within three months from the date when grounds for the application first arose.[3]

In deciding whether proceedings should be commenced by way of private law proceedings or by way of judicial review, the general rule is that it would be an abuse of process for an applicant who wishes to challenge an administrative or legislative act to evade the requirements of leave and promptness laid down in RSC Ord 53 by bringing private law proceedings.[4] However, in considering whether a person should proceed by way of judicial review, the courts must look at the practical consequences of the choice made rather than just technical questions concerning the distinction between private and public law rights. If private law proceedings would not cause a significant disadvantage to the

---

[1] Case 13/68 *Salgoil v Italy* [1968] ECR 453 at 463; Case C-446/93 *SEIM* [1996] ECR I-73 para 32; *D Potter v Secretary of State for Employment* (unreported) 30 September 1996 (CA). See Ch 6, pp 107–114.

[2] RSC Ord 53, r. 3.

[3] RSC Ord 53, r. 4.

[4] Lord Diplock in *O'Reilly v Mackman* [1983] 2 AC 237 at 285D–G.

parties, the public or the court, then they should not normally be regarded as an abuse.[5] This pragmatism is of even more relevance in the Community law field where the question whether a directly effective provision creates a public or private right borders on the 'metaphysical' since, by definition, it almost invariably creates personal rights for individuals.[6]

Direct challenge Where an applicant mounts a direct challenge against a legislative or administrative act, the appropriate procedure is to bring an application by way of judicial review. The public interest is protected by the requirement of leave and by the need to make the application promptly and in any event within three months from when the grounds for bringing the application first arose.[7] In so far as these procedural requirements apply to proceedings alleging infringements of Community law rights, they are compatible with the principle of effective protection. They are comparable with the nature of judicial review proceedings before the EC courts under article 173 of the EC Treaty [new art 230] where the applicant must be directly and individually concerned by the contested act and has only two months in which to commence proceedings.[8]

Collateral challenge It is not an abuse of process for an individual to challenge the validity of a legislative or an administrative act by way of defence, for example where a prosecution has been brought against him for infringement of the contested act or where private law proceedings have been brought for sums alleged to be due under the contested act. The 'arguments for protecting public authorities against unmeritorious or dilatory challenges to their decisions have to be set against the arguments for preserving the ordinary rights of private citizens to defend themselves against unfounded claims'.[9] The possibility for individuals to mount such indirect challenges to public acts is consistent with the principle of effective protection. It is comparable with article 184 of the EC Treaty [new art 241], pursuant to which an individual may raise a plea of illegality in the EC courts outside the two-month period for the bringing of an action for annulment.[10]

---

[5] *Trustees of the Dennis Rye Pension Fund v Sheffield City Council* (1997) *The Times*, 20 August, per Lord Woolf MR. The flexibility of such an approach is also apparent in *Mercury Communications v Director General of Telecommunications* [1996] 1 WLR 48.

[6] *Bourgoin v MAFF* [1986] 1 QB 716 at 767A, per Oliver LJ. Parker LJ at 788C considered that there was 'no particular merit in the terms and they are in any event imprecise'.

[7] See below at pp 182–184.

[8] See Ch 13.

[9] *Wandsworth London Borough Council v Winder* [1985] AC 461 at 509D, per Lord Fraser. See also *O'Reilly v Mackman* [1983] 2 AC 237 at 285F, per Lord Diplock; *Roy v Kensington and Chelsea and Westminster Family Practitioner Committee* [1992] 1 AC 624 at 628H–629A, per Lord Bridge, and at 654A–B, per Lord Lowry. See also Wade and Forsyth, *Administrative Law*, 7th edn (Oxford, 1994), pp 321–328; Emery, 'Collateral Attack—Attacking *Ultra Vires* Action Indirectly in Courts and Tribunals' [1993] MLR 643 at 660–662.

[10] See Ch 14.

Monetary claims Claims for payment,[11] redundancy pay,[12] restitution,[13] or damages[14] raise private issues and may generally be brought by way of private law proceedings.

Factual issues Although discovery, interrogatories and cross-examination are, in principle, available in judicial review proceedings,[15] a claim which involves disputed issues of fact should generally proceed by way of writ action.[16] On this basis, a claim that a public body has breached article 90 of the EC Treaty [new art 86] in conjunction with articles 85 [new art 81] or 86 [new art 82] (the EC competition rules) is best commenced by writ.

(b) Locus standi

Sufficient interest Pursuant to RSC Ord 53, r 3 an applicant must first apply *ex parte* for leave to bring judicial review proceedings. Pursuant to RSC Ord 53, r 3(7) no leave will be granted unless the applicant has a sufficient interest in the matter to which the application relates. The question of sufficient interest may be examined at two stages. First, the *ex parte* stage acts as a filter, weeding out hopeless or vexatious applications. If leave is granted, the question of sufficient interest may then be fully argued at the substantive hearing.[17]

A 'sufficient' interest is a question of degree, which is examined in the light of the legal and factual context of the application. This usually connotes some personal interest in the relief sought. In *R v Attorney General, ex p ICI*[18] the Court of Appeal, upholding Woolf J, held that ICI had sufficient interest to challenge, by way of judicial review, the grant of State aid, which was alleged to be in breach of article 92 of the EC Treaty [new art 87], to one of its competitors, Shell. Sufficient interest is not limited to direct personal interest, and it is not essential for the applicant to benefit financially from the application.[19] In *R v HM Treasury, ex p Smedley*[20] Woolf J and the Court of Appeal both indicated

---

[11] *Trustees of the Dennis Rye Pension Fund v Sheffield City Council* (1997) *The Times*, 20 August, 'Judicial review was not intended to be used for debt collecting', per Lord Woolf MR.

[12] See *R v Secretary of State for Employment, ex p Equal Opportunities Commission* [1995] 1 AC 1, where the House of Lords held that an applicant who was refused redundancy pay under the Employment Protection Act 1978, but contrary to article 119 of the EC Treaty [new art 141] on equal pay, should proceed in the industrial tribunal.

[13] See Ch 9, p 170.

[14] See Ch 7, pp 142–143.

[15] RSC Ord 53, r 8.

[16] *Inland Revenue Commissioners v Rossminster Ltd* [1980] AC 952 at 1025H–1026A, per Lord Scarman; *R v Derbyshire County Council, ex p Noble* [1990] ICR 808 at 813C–D, per Woolf LJ; *Roy v Kensington and Chelsea and Westminster Family Practitioner Committee* [1992] 1 AC 624 at 646F–647C, per Lord Lowry; *Trustees of the Dennis Rye Pension Fund v Sheffield City Council* (1997) *The Times*, 20 August.

[17] *R v Inland Revenue Commissioners, ex p National Federation of Self-Employed and Small Businesses Ltd* [1982] AC 617.

[18] [1987] 1 CMLR 72.

[19] *R v Inland Revenue Commissioners, ex p National Federation of Self-Employed and Small Businesses Ltd* [1982] AC 617 at 646, per Lord Fraser; *R v Legal Aid Board, ex p Bateman* [1992] 1 WLR 711 at 718.

[20] [1985] 1 QB 657; referred to by Lord Woolf in *M v Home Office* [1994] 1 AC 377 at 413 G.

that Mr Smedley would have *locus standi* to challenge the legality of payments made by the United Kingdom out of the Consolidated Fund to the European Community to finance the Community's supplementary budget. Similarly, in *R v Secretary of State for Foreign and Commonwealth Affairs, ex p Rees-Mogg*[21] the applicant had sufficient interest to challenge the ratification by the United Kingdom of the Maastricht Treaty.

It is not necessary for an applicant to allege that a personal right has been infringed in order for him to be recognised as having standing. Individuals who are affected by a failure to implement a directive may have a sufficient interest to commence judicial review proceedings even though no personal right of theirs has been infringed.[22] Furthermore, pressure groups are likely to have a sufficient interest to bring judicial review proceedings even though no personal right of the group is infringed. As Lord Diplock stated in *R v Inland Revenue Commissioners, ex p National Federation of Self-Employed and Small Businesses Ltd*:[23]

> It would, in my view, be a grave lacuna in our system of public law if a pressure group, like the federation, or even a single public-spirited taxpayer, were prevented by outdated technical rules of locus standi from bringing the matter to the attention of the court to vindicate the rule of law and get the unlawful conduct stopped.

Similarly, in the context of proceedings brought by the Equal Opportunities Commission (EOC) Lord Keith stated:[24]

> In my opinion it would be a very retrograde step now to hold that the EOC has no *locus standi* to agitate in judicial review proceedings questions related to sex discrimination which are of public importance and affect a large section of the population.

Reviewable acts Closely linked to the question of sufficient standing is the question of what constitutes a reviewable act. Where an application seeks an order of *certiorari* there needs to be a decision capable of being quashed, for example, a measure which alters a person's rights or obligations, deprives the person of some benefit or advantage[25] or promulgates advice comparable to a ministerial circular.[26]

---

21 [1993] 3 CMLR 101.
22 *R v Secretary of State for Employment, ex p Seymour-Smith* [1997] 1 WLR 473 at 479G, per Lord Hoffmann; *Kincardine and Deeside District Council v Forestry Commissioners* [1994] 2 CMLR 869 para 28 (Court of Session, Outer House), which is to be preferred to the decision of McCullough J in *Twyford Parish Council v Secretary of State for the Environment* [1992] 1 CMLR 276 para 69. See Ch 4, pp 66–67.
23 [1982] AC 617 at 644E.
24 *R v Secretary of State for Employment, ex p Equal Opportunities Commission* [1995] 1 AC 1 at 26D, reversing the Court of Appeal (Kennedy and Hirst LJJ, Dillon LJ dissenting) which had held that no enforceable right belonging to the EOC had been infringed ([1993] 1 WLR 872). See also *R v Secretary of State for the Environment, ex p Friends of the Earth* [1994] 2 CMLR 760 paras 2–5: *R v Secretary of State of Trade and Industry, ex p Greenpeace* (unreported) 14 October 1997, Laws J.
25 *Council of Civil Service Unions v Minister for Civil Service* [1985] AC 374 at 408E, per Lord Diplock.
26 *Gillick v West Norfolk and Wisbech Area Health Authority* [1986] 1 AC 112 at 193G–194B, per

Where an applicant seeks a declaration that primary legislation is contrary to Community law, no decision needs to be identified other than the legislative act itself. Therefore, where it is contended that an Act of Parliament infringes Community law, it is unnecessary to engineer a decision letter from the relevant minister confirming the validity of the Act (or refusing to amend it).[27]

Since the applicant should move against the substantive decision which is the real basis of the complaint, the implementation of that decision in practice is unlikely to constitute a reviewable act. In *R v Customs and Excise, ex p Eurotunnel*[28] government orders implementing EC directives allowed air and sea carriers to make duty-free sales on board. Eurotunnel considered that the system was discriminatory because it could not sell duty-free goods on its trains and that, consequently, customs should collect duty from the air and sea carriers. The application was made some 18 months after the main orders entered into force. Eurotunnel argued that the subject-matter of the judicial review was the continuing practice of customs not to collect duty from the air and sea carriers and that therefore the application was in time. This was rejected by the Divisional Court since the real object of the attack was the order upon which the continuing practice was based.

The fact that the authority for the act does not derive from the exercise of the prerogative is not fatal, provided the body in question is performing a public function. Thus, acts of self-regulatory bodies, such as the Panel on Take-overs and Mergers and The Stock Exchange, may be the subject of judicial review proceedings.[29]

Draft legislation In certain circumstances, draft legislation is susceptible to judicial review. In *R v HM Treasury, ex p Smedley*[30] the Member States agreed to make certain loans to the Community to finance the Community's supplementary budget. The United Kingdom proposed to make its loan out of the Consolidated Fund using the Order in Council process, as permitted by s 1 of the European Communities Act 1972. This process could only be used if the agreement between the Member States could be described as a 'treaty ancillary to any of the [Community] Treaties'. Although the Order was still in draft and had not been approved by both Houses of Parliament, it seems that Mr Smedley would still have had sufficient standing to challenge its legality. The Court of Appeal, upholding Woolf J, considered that it was clear that the agreement could be regarded as a treaty ancillary to the Community Treaties, and that no disadvantage was involved in clarifying the position at the earliest opportunity.

Lord Bridge.

[27] *R v Secretary of State for Employment, ex p Equal Opportunities Commission* [1995] 1 AC 1 at 26F. See De Smith, Woolf and Jowell, *Judicial Review and Administrative Action*, 5th edn (Sweet & Maxwell, 1995), paras 2-025 to 2-028.

[28] [1995] CLC 392; (1995) *The Independent*, 23 February.

[29] *R v Panel on Take-overs and Mergers, ex p Datafin* [1987] QB 815; *R v International Stock Exchange, ex p Else (1982) Ltd* [1993] QB 534.

[30] [1985] 1 QB 657.

Nevertheless, only in exceptional cases will the court review draft parliament-ary legislation, especially where the draft is to be subject to further debate by Parliament. The better course is to await the adoption of the relevant act.[31]

Time-limits Pursuant to RSC Ord 53, r 4 an application for judicial review must be made promptly and, in any event, within three months from the date when grounds for the application first arose. The three-month time period is the limit and not every application which is brought within three months is necessarily made promptly.[32] The duty to act promptly applies with particular force in proceedings brought by public interest applicants since they cannot invoke a direct personal right which the courts can counterbalance against other third party rights which may be affected by the application.[33]

Community law permits reasonable time-limits to be imposed which, if not observed, will be a bar to claims brought under Community law.[34] The three-month time-limit established by RSC Ord 53 appears reasonable, and in Case C-208/90 *Emmott v Minister for Social Welfare*[35] the Court of Justice referred, without adverse comment, to Ord 84, r 21, para 1 of the Irish Rules of the Superior Courts 1986, which also imposed a three-month limitation period for judicial review proceedings. Indeed, it would be difficult to argue that the three-month time-limit provided by RSC Ord 53 is unduly restrictive since article 173 of the EC Treaty [new art 230] lays down a two-month time-limit for actions for annulment in the EC courts.

Delay Time starts to run from the date when grounds for the application first arise. Usually the grounds will first arise when the impugned decision takes effect. In the case of adoption of legislation which is allegedly contrary to Community law, grounds will often first arise when the statutory provision enters into force, although the date when it was made may be taken into consideration in determining whether the applicant has acted promptly (within the three-month time-limit).

In some instances, the date when the grounds for the application first arise will be after the legislation enters into force. For example, a bare challenge that implementing regulations do not correctly transpose a directive may be premature or theoretical where there is no evidence as to the adverse consequences of the misimplementation. In *R v Secretary of State for Trade and Industry, ex p Greenpeace*[36] Greenpeace sought judicial review of various licences awarded for oil exploration in the waters of the Atlantic Frontier. It claimed that the Government's failure to carry out an environmental impact

---

[31] An application challenging the Merchant Shipping Bill in *R v Secretary of State for Transport, ex p Factortame* (unreported) was held to be premature.

[32] *R v Independent Television Commission, ex p TV NI Ltd* (1991) *The Times*, 30 December; *R v Customs and Excise, ex p Eurotunnel* [1995] CLC 392; (1995) *The Independent*, 23 February.

[33] *R v Secretary of State for Trade and Industry, ex p Greenpeace* (unreported) 14 October 1997, Laws J.

[34] Case 33/76 *Rewe v Landwirtschaftskammer Saarland* [1976] ECR 1989. See Ch 6, pp 114–117.

[35] [1991] ECR I-4269.

[36] (Unreported) 14 October 1997, Laws J.

assessment in respect of a type of coral was in breach of the EU Habitats Directive (92/43) which allegedly applied to that area. The Directive had been implemented by the Conservation (Natural Habitats, etc) Regulations 1994, which applied to UK territorial waters, but did not extend to the Atlantic Frontier. In late 1995 the Government had publicised the areas in the Atlantic Frontier which would be offered for licensing, and in late 1996 invited applications for licences. The licences were awarded in early 1997 and Greenpeace brought proceedings just within three months from the date of the award. The argument that the grounds for the application first arose when the 1994 Regulations came into force was rejected by Laws J, who stated:

> Something a good deal more specific in the way of a potential threat posed by the limited scope of the regulations must have arisen before the applicants' duty, not least as a public interest plaintiff, to come to court promptly would be engaged.

In some instances the date when grounds for the application first arise will be before the entry into force of the impugned decision. In *R v Secretary of State for Trade and Industry, ex p Greenpeace* the applicant argued that the award of the licences in 1997 constituted the reviewable act (being a distinct executive act as opposed to the continuing application of the law). Laws J held that, even on this basis, the applicant was out of time since the grounds for bringing the application had first arisen in 1995 or 1996, when the damage caused by the alleged misimplementation of the Directive was imminent. At this point it had become clear that the Government would not undertake an environmental impact assessment, allegedly in breach of the Directive, when granting licences to explore for oil in the Atlantic Frontier. Similarly, in *Keymed v Forest Healthcare NHS Trust*,[37] grounds for suing in respect of a procurement contract awarded in breach of Regulation 29(4)(*b*) of the Public Supply Contracts Regulations 1995 arose when the health trust had failed to publicise the contract, not when the contract was awarded or the aggrieved party had knowledge of the contract. As Langley J stated:[38]

> If it were otherwise and a supplier could select the last breach available to him ... it would mean that he could sit back and do nothing even in respect of breaches of which he was aware or which he apprehended.

Where there is a continuing application of the unlawful act, the issue of delay will often depend on the correct identification of the reviewable act. In *R v Customs and Excise, ex p Eurotunnel*[39] leave was set aside on the grounds of delay, the application being made some 18 months after the orders implementing the directive had come into force. The Court rejected an argument that the illegality was continuing by virtue of the day-to-day implementation of the orders. In contrast, in *R v Secretary of State for Employment, ex p EOC*[40] the

---

[37] (Unreported) 12 October 1997.

[38] The wording of regulation 29(4)(*b*) is similar to that of RSC Ord 53, r 4.

[39] [1995] CLC 392; (1995) *The Independent*, 23 February. See also *R v HM Treasury, ex p Smedley* [1985] 1 QB 657 at 667B; *R v Secretary of State for Employment, ex p Seymour-Smith* [1995] ICR 889 at 902G, per Balcombe LJ (Div Ct), see also at 941 (CA) and [1997] 1 WLR 473 (HL). See above at p 180.

[40] [1995] 1 AC 1.

House of Lords granted a declaration that certain provisions of the Employment Protection (Consolidation) Act 1978 were incompatible with Community law, even though leave to bring judicial review proceedings had not been sought until 1990. However, the question of delay was not specifically argued before, or considered by, the House of Lords.

Non-implementation of directives There is still some uncertainty as to when grounds first arise in the case of non-implementation of directives. In Case C-208/90 *Emmott v Minister for Social Welfare*[41] the Court of Justice ruled that, until such time as a directive had been properly implemented, a defaulting Member State could not rely on an individual's delay to bar proceedings brought against the State to protect rights conferred on the individual by the directive. On this basis, the three-month time-limit for judicial review proceedings would not begin to run until a directive has been properly implemented into national law. However, the scope of this judgment has been substantially limited by subsequent case-law.[42]

Extension of time Where there has been delay in bringing judicial review proceedings, the court has power to extend the time-limit where there is good reason to do so.[43] A subsequent judgment of the Court of Justice, which clarifies an individual's rights under EC law, will not constitute a good reason for extending the time-limit.[44] Even if the Court considers that there is good reason, it may refuse leave where the extension would cause substantial prejudice to the rights of any person or would be detrimental to good administration.[45] An extension is unlikely where the effect will be to reopen past transactions which could result, for example, in monetary claims being made,[46] or where third parties have invested substantial sums on the strength of the decision.[47]

2. GROUNDS OF REVIEW

(a) Scope of the application of Community law principles

EC Treaty and secondary legislation Domestic legislation or administrative acts may be challenged as being contrary to the obligations contained in the EC Treaty or Community secondary legislation. The legality of domestic acts is therefore constrained by the Treaty, even though they are not dependent for

---

[41] [1991] ECR I-4269.

[42] See Ch 6, pp 115–117.

[43] RSC Ord 53, r 4(1).

[44] *R v MAFF, ex p Bostock* [1991] 1 CMLR 681.

[45] Supreme Court Act 1981, s 31(6); the House of Lords reconciled RSC Ord 53, r 4(1) and s 31(6) in *R v Dairy Produce Quota Tribunal, ex p Caswell* [1990] 2 AC 738.

[46] *R v Customs and Excise, ex p Eurotunnel* [1995] CLC 392 (repayment of duty); *R v Secretary of State for Employment, ex p Seymour-Smith* [1995] ICR 889 (unfair dismissal); although an extension was made in *R v MAFF, ex p NFU* [1995] 3 CMLR 116 where there was a risk of a reallocation of quota as a result of the judicial review application.

[47] *R v Secretary of State for Trade and Industry, ex p Greenpeace* (unreported) 14 October 1997 (at pp 22 and 41 of the transcript).

their authority on the Treaty but have been adopted solely by virtue of domestic law.[48]

General principles of law The exercise of discretionary power by the Community institutions is constrained by various general principles of Community law, for example proportionality, legitimate expectations, legal certainty, non-retroactivity, equal treatment and fundamental human rights.[49] The legality of domestic acts is also constrained by the general principles of Community law where the adoption of the domestic act is required or permitted by Community law. However, where an act is adopted solely on the basis of domestic law it will not be subject to these general principles. The reason for this is that the fundamental principles are not expressly provided for in the EC Treaty as free-standing principles; they have been developed by the EC courts to determine the reasonableness of the exercise of discretionary powers pursuant to the Treaty. The EC courts cannot add to the Treaty, they may only interpret it.

This approach to the application of the general principles of Community law in the national legal order was formulated by Laws J in *R v MAFF, ex p First City Trading Ltd.*[50] In 1996 the European Commission banned the export of beef from the United Kingdom. As a result, many beef exporters in the United Kingdom faced huge losses. To assist them, an aid package was introduced by the Slaughtering Industry (Emergency Aid) Scheme 1996, which benefited only those exporters who were also slaughterers or cutters. The applicant, who was an exporter but not a slaughterer or cutter, applied for judicial review, claiming that its exclusion was contrary to the Community law principle of equal treatment. Laws J held that this principle did not apply because although the aid scheme was rendered necessary by the EC export ban, it was not brought into existence pursuant to any power or obligation arising under Community law. Laws J stated:[51]

> These fundamental principles, which also include proportionality and legitimate expectation, are not provided for on the face of the Treaty of Rome. They have been developed by the ECJ (as Mr. Parker correctly submitted) out of the administrative law of the Member States. They are part of what may perhaps be called the common law of the Community. That being so, it is to my mind by no means self-evident that their contextual scope must be the same as that of Treaty provisions relating to discrimination or equal treatment, which are statute law taking effect according to their express terms. There is a critical distinction to be drawn between these following situations. On the one hand, a member state may take measures solely by virtue of its domestic law. On the other, a Community institution or Member State may take measures which it is authorised or obliged to take by force of the law of the Community. In the former situation I contemplate a measure which is neither required of the member state nor permitted to it by virtue of Community Treaty provisions. It is purely a domestic measure. Even so, it may affect the operation of

---

[48] Laws J in *R v MAFF, ex p First City Trading* [1997] 1 CMLR 250, para 39; [1997] EuLR 195 at 210C.

[49] See Ch 2.

[50] [1997] 1 CMLR 250; [1997] EuLR 195. See also the cases cited in Ch 2, p 44, footnotes 102–104.

[51] [1997] 1 CMLR 250, para 39; [1997] EuLR 195 at 210 A-E.

the common market and, accordingly, be held to be 'within the scope of application' of the Treaty. This was the *Phil Collins* case. It is of the first importance to notice that its falling within the Treaty's scope is by no means the same thing as it being done under powers or duties conferred or imposed by Community law. The second situation primarily includes (so far as member states are concerned) measures which Community law requires, such as, for example, law which is made to give effect to a directive. It includes also an act or decision done or taken by a member state in reliance on a derogation or permission granted by Community law; as where, for instance, a restriction on imports or exports is sought to be justified by reference to Article 36 of the Treaty. In the first situation, the measure is in no sense a function of the law of Europe, although its legality may be constrained by it. In the second, the measure is necessarily a creature of the law of Europe. Community law alone either demands it, or permits it.

Implementation of Community law The Community law principle of legitimate expectations was applied by Sedley J in *R v MAFF, ex p Hamble Fisheries (Offshore) Ltd*[52] to the grant of fishing licences which were introduced to implement the Community quota system. The argument that the Community law principle did not apply because the issue was an entirely domestic one was rejected by Sedley J, who stated:

> This seems to me, with respect, to be unreal. It may no doubt be said that the immediate exercise is the formulation of policy within a discretion conferred entirely by domestic legislation. But the purpose of legislation and policy alike is to permit the respondent, under the principle of subsidiarity, to exercise its powers for the purposes of implementing the Common Agricultural Policy of the European Community. If each Member State were governed in carrying out its part of this joint exercise by no law but its own domestic law, a major objective of the Policy would be frustrated. The availability of eventual recourse to the European Court of Justice from and against all Member States in relation to the carrying out of the Common Agricultural Policy must require domestic courts to have full regard to the case law of the European Court of Justice.

Derogation from Community law The general principles of Community law apply whenever the Member State acts pursuant to powers granted to it by Community law, for example, to derogate from rights granted to individuals by a directive[53] or by the EC Treaty.[54] In *R v MAFF, ex p Bell Line*[55] Forbes J held that a restriction on the importation of milk contrary to article 30 of the EC Treaty [new art 28] was disproportionate and could not, therefore, be justified under article 36 [new art 30]. Similarly, in *R v Chief Constable of Sussex, ex p International Traders Ferry Ltd*[56] the Court of Appeal applied the Community

---

[52] [1995] 2 All ER 714 at 724j – 725b, which Laws J, in *R v MAFF, ex p First City Trading* [1997] 1 CMLR 250 at para 44, [1997] EuLR 195 at 211G, considered was a second situation case.

[53] *Thomas v Chief Adjudication Officer* [1991] 2 QB 164 (the option granted to Member States by Directive 79/7 to differentiate between men and women in relation to benefit payments is subject to the principle of proportionality).

[54] For example, article 36, which derogates from articles 30 and 34 on the free movement of goods; article 48(3), which derogates from article 48 [new art 39] on the free movement of persons; and article 56 [new art 46] which derogates from article 52 [new art 43] on the right of establishment.

[55] [1984] 2 CMLR 502. See also *R v MAFF, ex p Roberts* [1991] 1 CMLR 555.

[56] [1997] 2 CMLR 164.

law principle of proportionality when determining whether a measure having an equivalent effect to an export ban of live animals contrary to article 34 [new art 29] could be justified on public policy grounds under article 36.

(b) Illegality

Supremacy The entry into force of a directly effective provision of Community law renders any conflicting provision of national law automatically inapplicable and precludes the valid adoption of new national legislative measures to the extent that they are incompatible with the Community measure.[57]

Secondary legislation Section 2(2) of the European Communities Act 1972 provides for the implementation of Community law by Order in Council or by Ministerial or Departmental Regulation. Where such subordinate legislation is contrary to Community law, it may also be challenged on the basis that it is *ultra vires* as a matter of English law since it is outside the scope of s 2(2). Such subordinate legislation is also *ultra vires* where it implements a Community provision that is itself invalid. As Henry J has stated:[58]

> If the directive is invalid, it is incapable of creating a Community obligation. Without a Community obligation, a statutory instrument purporting to give effect to a Community obligation is void.

(c) Procedural impropriety

Application of Community law principles Administrative decisions may be challenged under domestic law on the grounds of procedural impropriety.[59] Community law has developed similar principles of essential procedural requirements and, in circumstances where they allow the courts a greater degree of intrusion, they should be applied. However, the Community principles apply only where Community law has required or permitted the adoption of the relevant act.[60]

Duty to give reasons As a matter of domestic law, it is still the case that there is no general duty to give reasons for a decision, although the instances where the courts impose a particular obligation to give reasons can no longer be regarded as exceptional.[61] By contrast, the principle of effective protection under

---

[57] See Ch 3, pp 52–53.
[58] *R v MAFF, ex p Fedesa* [1988] 3 CMLR 661 para 5.
[59] See De Smith, Woolf and Jowell, *Judicial Review of Administrative Action*, 5th edn (Sweet & Maxwell, 1995), Chs 7–10; Wade and Forsyth, *Administrative Law*, 7th edn (Oxford, 1994), Chs 13–15.
[60] See above at pp 184–187.
[61] See De Smith, Woolf and Jowell, *Judicial Review of Administrative Action*, 5th edn (Sweet & Maxwell, 1995), pp 457–473; *R v Secretary of State for the Home Department, ex p Doody* [1994] 1 AC 531; *R v Higher Education Funding Council, ex p Institute of Dental Surgery* [1994] 1 WLR 242; *R v Ministry of Defence, ex p Murray* (1997) *The Times*, 17 December.

Community law requires national authorities to give reasons for any administrative decision which infringes upon directly effective Community law rights, so as to enable individuals properly to decide whether to challenge such decisions.[62]

Right to be heard Domestic law will often impose a duty on the administrative body to consult the person affected by the decision prior to its adoption.[63] This is a fundamental principle in Community law which applies in all proceedings initiated against a person which are liable to culminate in a measure adversely affecting that person.[64]

(d) Unreasonable exercise of power

Degree of intrusion The difference between *Wednesbury* unreasonableness and the application of the fundamental principles of Community law lies in the need for the decision-maker substantively to justify the decision made. In the case of *Wednesbury* unreasonableness, it is often sufficient for the court to test the reasonableness of the decision by reference to the range of options that could reasonably have been followed. Community law requires more from the decision-maker. It requires the court to judge the necessity of the action. This does not require the court to usurp the function of the decision-maker and to determine whether the decision was right or wrong. It does, however, require the decision-maker to justify the course of action taken, rather than merely set out the range of courses of action that could have been followed.[65] The distinction is neatly illustrated by Laws J in *R v MAFF, ex p First City Trading Ltd*:[66]

> The difference between *Wednesbury* and European review is that in the former case the legal limits lie further back. I think there are two factors. First, the limits of domestic review are not, as the law presently stands, constrained by the doctrine of proportionality. Secondly, at least as regards a requirement such as that of objective justification in an equal treatment case, the European rule requires the decision-maker to provide a fully reasoned case. It is not enough merely to set out the problem, and assert that within his discretion the Minister choose this or that solution, constrained only by the requirement that his decision must have been one which a reasonable minister might make. Rather the court will test the solution arrived at, and pass it only if substantial factual considerations are put forward in its justification: considerations which are relevant, reasonable, and proportionate to the aim in view. But as I understand the jurisprudence the court is not concerned to agree or disagree with the decision: that would be to travel beyond the boundaries of proper judicial authority, and usurp the primary decision-maker's function. Thus *Wednesbury* and

---

[62] See Ch 6, pp 102–103.

[63] See De Smith, Woolf and Jowell, *Judicial Review of Administrative Action*, 5th edn (Sweet & Maxwell, 1995), pp 432–441; *R v Secretary of State for the Home Department, ex p Doody* [1994] 1 AC 531; *R v Devon County Council, ex p Baker* [1995] 1 All ER 73.

[64] See Ch 13, pp 316–318.

[65] Wade and Forsyth, *Administrative Law*, 7th edn (Oxford, 1994), p 403, cited by Kennedy LJ in *R v Chief Constable of Sussex, ex p International Traders Ferry Ltd* [1997] 2 CMLR 164 para 50. See also Advocate-General Jacobs in Case C-24/90 *Faust* [1991] ECR I-4905, at para 45 of his Opinion.

[66] [1997] 1 CMLR 250, para 69, [1997] EuLR 195 at 219 D–F.

European review are different models—one looser, one tighter—of the same juridical concept, which is the imposition of compulsory standards on decision-makers so as to secure the repudiation of arbitrary power.

The margin of appreciation The extent to which the Court of Justice will interfere with the exercise of administrative or legislative power depends on the margin of appreciation afforded to the Community decision-maker. The margin of appreciation is greater when the act complained of arises from the exercise of a discretionary power involving economic, political or social responsibilities. In such cases the Court of Justice considers that:[67]

> the legality of a measure adopted in that sphere can be affected only if the measure is manifestly inappropriate having regard to the objective which the competent institution is seeking to pursue.

Similarly, national courts, when reviewing the reasonableness of administrative or legislative acts in the light of Community law principles, are entitled to take into account the margin of appreciation afforded to the national decision-maker. In respect of decisions involving choices of economic, political or social policy, the margin of appreciation is greater, and thus the degree of intrusion by the courts is lower. Indeed, where there is a wide margin of appreciation, in practical terms the court's power of review borders on applying *Wednesbury* unreasonableness even where Community law principles are being applied. In *R v Chief Constable of Sussex, ex p International Traders Ferry Ltd*[68] where the Court of Appeal had to determine whether the decision by the Chief Constable to reduce police protection was proportionate and could be justified under article 36 of the EC Treaty [new art 30], Kennedy LJ, referring to the wide margin of discretion afforded to the Chief Constable, stated:

> I accept, that in the context of this case and allowing for differences in terminology, each test will in practice yield the same result. To borrow a phrase from Lord Hoffman's recent lecture 'A Sense of Proportion' (14th November 1996) it is not possible to see daylight between them.

The national courts' reluctance to interfere, even on the basis of Community law principles, when the national decision-maker is faced with choices of economic and social considerations is typified by the judgment of Hoffmann J in *Stoke-on-Trent City Council v B&Q*.[69] In proceedings brought by the Council under s 222 of the Local Government Act 1972, Hoffmann J held that the ban on Sunday trading under s 47 of the Shops Act 1950 did not infringe article 30 of the EC Treaty [new art 28]. Relying on Canadian, American and Australian case-law, he stated:[70]

> In my judgment it is not my function to carry out the balancing exercise or to form my own view on whether the legislative objective could be achieved by other means.

---

[67] For example, see Case C-331/88 *R v MAFF, ex p Fedesa* [1990] ECR I-4023 paras 12–18. See Ch 2, pp 32–33 and 45–46; Ch 13, p 320.
[68] [1997] 2 CMLR 164 para 50.
[69] [1991] Ch 48. Cf *WH Smith v Peterborough City Council* [1991] 1 QB 304 at 342G–343G, per Schiemann J.
[70] [1991] Ch 48 at 69D–E.

These questions involve compromises between competing interests which in a democratic society must be resolved by the legislature. The duty of the court is only to inquire whether the compromise adopted by the United Kingdom Parliament, so far as it affects community trade, is one which a reasonable legislature could have reached. The function of the court is to review the acts of the legislature but not to substitute its own policies or values.

The Court of Justice, on a preliminary reference by the House of Lords, subsequently ruled that the English Sunday trading rules were not disproportionate.[71] In applying this ruling, the House of Lords was asked by counsel to criticise the approach adopted by Hoffmann J with regard to the question of proportionality. The House declined.[72] Although the approach of Hoffmann J was criticised by Advocate-General van Gerven,[73] Hoffmann J's concerns about the division of powers between the courts and the legislature reflect legitimate public policy considerations which have also been recognised by the Court of Justice. In practical terms, although Hoffmann J expressly rejected the principle of proportionality as a ground for review, he was in fact doing no more than applying the principle of proportionality to national legislation in a situation where the United Kingdom had a wide margin of discretion in regulating Sunday trading.

Proportionality It is a general principle of Community law that an administrative or a legislative act can be reviewed on the ground of proportionality. The principle has two main advantages over the application of *Wednesbury* unreasonableness.

First, in order for a measure to comply with the principle of proportionality it must be appropriate and necessary to achieve a legitimate objective, and the disadvantages caused must not be out of proportion to the benefits of the objective.[74] As Kennedy LJ stated in *R v Chief Constable of Sussex, ex p International Traders Ferry Ltd*,[75] 'Proportionality requires the Court to judge the necessity of the action taken as well as whether it was within the range of courses of action that could reasonably be followed'. By contrast, in purely domestic cases, the principle of proportionality is not a separate ground for seeking judicial review on the basis that to interfere with the discretion of an administrative body at a level lower than unreasonableness would be an abuse of the judge's supervisory jurisdiction. Not every decision to adopt measures which are stricter than necessary can be classed as perverse: the two principles are not coterminous. The difference was recognised by Watkins LJ in the Divisional Court in *R v Home Secretary, ex p Brind*:[76]

---

[71] Case C-169/91 *Stoke-on-Trent City Council v B&Q plc* [1992] ECR I-6635.

[72] *Stoke-on-Trent City Council v B&Q plc* [1993] AC 900.

[73] Case C-169/91 *Stoke-on-Trent City Council v B&Q plc* [1992] ECR I-6635, para 27 of the Opinion.

[74] See Ch 2, pp 27–33.

[75] [1997] 2 CMLR 164, para 50. See also *R v MAFF, ex p Bell Lines* [1984] 2 CMLR 502; *R v MAFF, ex p Roberts* [1991] 1 CMLR 555.

[76] [1990] 2 WLR 787 at 801; cited with approval by Lord Donaldson MR [1991] 1 AC 696 at 721H–722B (CA); see also [1991] 1 AC 696 at 766C–767G, per Lord Lowry (HL).

... in our view, the law of the United Kingdom has not developed so that a decision, which is neither perverse nor absurd and which is one which a reasonable minister properly taking into account the relevant law could take, becomes unlawful simply because it can be shown that it was not in proportion to the benefit to be obtained or the mischief to be avoided by the taking of the decision. In our opinion the application of such a concept of proportionality would result in the courts substituting their own decisions for that of the minister, and that is something which the courts of this country have consistently declined to do.

The second difference lies in the scope of application of these grounds of review in relation to legislative acts. In purely domestic cases, legislative acts or acts involving political judgment cannot be reviewed on the grounds of irrationality. For example, the formulation and implementation of national economic policy are matters which depend on political judgment, and any act adopted in this sphere would only be open to challenge on the grounds of bad faith or illegality.[77] By contrast, it is clear that in cases involving Community rights and obligations the courts may review domestic legislation on the grounds of proportionality.[78]

Equal treatment Equal treatment is a fundamental principle of Community law and constitutes a separate ground of review of administrative and legislative acts.[79] Where similar situations are treated differently or different situations are treated similarly, discrimination will arise unless objective justification can be shown for the difference in treatment. It is here that the Community law principle and *Wednesbury* unreasonableness differ. Community law will require evidence from the decision-maker to show that the unequal treatment was necessary and thus objectively justifiable. As Laws J stated in *R v MAFF, ex p First City Trading*:[80]

> But *Wednesbury* is not the test. By our domestic law, if a public decision-maker were to treat apparently identical cases differently there would no doubt be a prima facie *Wednesbury* case against him, since on the face of it such an approach bears the hallmark of irrationality. To that extent the rule is akin to European principle. The court would look for an explanation of the difference; but the justification offered would in the ordinary way only be rejected on grounds of perversity. That I think, marks the divide. The Community rule requires the decision maker to demonstrate a substantive justification for a discriminatory decision, although there is a nice question how far a 'margin of appreciation' is allowed to the decision maker. In case after case concerned with its fundamental principles the ECJ has proceeded on the footing that the facts must be examined by the reviewing Court and a view reached as to whether the decision taken measures up to the *substantive* standards which it has set.

---

[77] *R v Secretary of State for the Environment, ex p Nottinghamshire County Council* [1986] AC 240 at 250–251. See also *R v Environment Secretary, ex p Hammersmith London Borough Council* [1990] 1 AC 521 at 594, per Lord Bridge.
[78] *Stoke-on-Trent City Council v B&Q plc* [1991] Ch 48.
[79] See Ch 2, pp 42–46.
[80] [1997] 1 CMLR 250, para 67, [1997] EuLR 195 at 218 F – H.

Legitimate expectations The protection of legitimate expectations is a fundamental principle of Community law and constitutes a separate ground for reviewing unreasonable exercise of administrative or legislative power.[81] Under Community law the legitimate expectation may be of a substantive benefit or advantage as well as a procedural one. The decision-maker should not frustrate a legitimate expectation that something will or will not be done by the decision-maker (substantive legitimate expectations). Nor should the decision-maker frustrate a legitimate expectation that the applicant would be listened to before the decision is made (procedural legitimate expectations).

In contrast, although domestic law recognises a principle of legitimate expectations, it is limited to procedural fairness. The attempt by Sedley J in *R v MAFF, ex p Hamble Fisheries*[82] to introduce into domestic law the principle of substantive legitimate expectations was regarded as 'heresy' by the Court of Appeal in *R v Secretary of State for the Home Department, ex p Hargreaves*,[83] Pill LJ stating:

> The court can quash the decision only if, in relation to the expectation and in all the circumstances, the decision to apply the new policy in the particular case was unreasonable in the *Wednesbury* sense; ... The claim to a broad power to judge the fairness of a decision of substance, which I understand Sedley J to be making in *R v Ministry of Agriculture Fisheries and Food, ex p Hamble (Offshore) Fisheries Ltd* is in my view wrong in principle.

3. AVAILABLE REMEDIES

Prerogative remedies Under RSC Ord 53, r 1(1) an individual seeking an order of *mandamus, prohibition or certiorari* must proceed by way of judicial review. *Mandamus* cannot lie to force the Government to introduce new legislation in Parliament, for example, to implement a directive (the Crown cannot force itself to do something).[84] However, it will be available in order to require the performance of administrative acts, for example, against officials who are refusing to permit the landing of goods in contravention of article 30.[85]

Certiorari is not available to quash primary legislation, which means that declaratory relief is the appropriate remedy.[86] The effect of any declaration is that the Act stays on the statute book until repealed.[87] In *R v Secretary of State for Employment, ex p Seymour-Smith*, the Divisional Court and Court of Appeal refused to grant *certiorari* in respect of secondary legislation where it was not contended that the relevant order was invalid at the time of its adoption, but

---

[81] See Ch 2, pp 33–37.

[82] [1995] 1 CMLR 533.

[83] [1997] 1 WLR 906 at 924.

[84] *R v Secretary of State for Employment, ex p Seymour-Smith* [1997] 1 WLR 473 at 478D–E, per Lord Hoffmann.

[85] *Bourgoin SA v MAFF* [1986] QB 716 at 785 B – C.

[86] See below at pp 193–194.

[87] *R v Secretary of State for Employment, ex p Seymour-Smith* [1995] ICR 889 at 901H–902B, per Balcombe LJ (Div Ct); also at 941D, per Neil LJ (CA); and [1997] 1 WLR 473 (HL).

rather that it had become unlawful as a matter of Community law due to a change of circumstances since its adoption.[88]

Injunctions/damages RSC Ord 53, r 1(2) provides that an injunction may be granted on an application for judicial review where the court considers it just and convenient to do so, having regard to all the circumstances of the case. The power to grant injunctions includes interim injunctions ordering a minister to disapply an Act of Parliament to protect putative rights derived from Community law.[89] A court may award damages on an application for judicial review under RSC Ord 53, r 7, although usually a claim for damages will be commenced by writ.[90]

Declarations RSC Ord 53, r 1(2) provides that a declaration may be granted on an application for judicial review where the court considers it just and convenient to do so, having regard to all the circumstances of the case. In *R v Secretary of State for Employment, ex p Equal Opportunities Commission*[91] the House of Lords held that a public interest body was entitled to seek a declaration that an Act of Parliament was incompatible with Community law. Individuals who assert that they are directly affected by a failure to implement a directive should also have sufficient standing to apply for a declaration that national law is incompatible with Community law.[92] The purpose of such a declaration is to inform the Government that the law needs to be changed.

The courts will not grant a declaration where to do so will serve no purpose. In *R v Secretary of State for Employment, ex p Seymour-Smith*[93] the applicants were female employees who had been dismissed in 1991. Under the domestic Order then in force they were not entitled to seek compensation for unfair dismissal, as they had not been employed for two years at the date of their dismissal. The applicants wished to argue that the Order was contrary to the Equal Treatment Directive on the basis that it was indirectly discriminatory because fewer women than men could comply with it. However, they could not bring an application against their former employers in the national courts on the basis of the Directive, as their employers were private parties and directives do not have horizontal direct effect (ie they cannot be relied on against private parties).[94] The applicants therefore commenced judicial review proceedings. The Divisional Court, after examining substantial statistical and other evidence, concluded that the order had not been shown to be discriminatory. The Court of Appeal found that the order was discriminatory and made a declaration that, as

---

[88] *R v Secretary of State for Employment, ex p Seymour-Smith* [1995] ICR 889 at 902C, per Balcombe LJ (Div Ct); also at 941B–C, per Neil LJ (CA). This point was not expressly considered by the House of Lords ([1997] 1 WLR 473 at 476E, per Lord Hoffmann).

[89] RSC Ord 53, r 3(10)(b). See *R v Secretary of State for Transport, ex p Factortame Ltd (No 2)* [1991] 1 AC 603. See also Ch 8, pp 152–164.

[90] See above at p 179 and Ch 7, pp 142–143.

[91] [1995] 1 AC 1, overruling the majority decision of the Court of Appeal ([1993] 1 WLR 872).

[92] *R v Secretary of State for Employment, ex p Seymour-Smith* [1997] 1 WLR 473 at 479G, per Lord Hoffmann. See also Ch 4, pp 66–67.

[93] [1997] 1 WLR 473.

[94] See Ch 4, pp 70–72.

at the date of the employees' dismissals, it was incompatible with the Directive. The House of Lords discharged the declaration on the basis that it would serve no purpose, for the following reasons.

(1) The employees wished to obtain a declaration that the Order was incompatible with the Directive so that they could require the industrial tribunal not to give effect to the order, thus enabling them to pursue claims for unfair dismissal. Lord Hoffmann noted that the effect of such a declaration 'would be to give the Directive, by an easy two-stage process, the very effect which the jurisprudence of the Court of Justice says it cannot have, namely to impose obligations upon an individual'.[95] He therefore held that the case-law of the Court of Justice on horizontal direct effect made it clear that a declaration such as that granted by the Court of Appeal would not, in fact, enable the applicants to pursue their proceedings in the industrial tribunal.

(2) No declaration could be granted which would indicate to the Government that national law had to be amended to conform with the Directive. A declaration that the order was incompatible with the Directive as at the date when it was considered by the House of Lords could not be granted as no evidence had been provided of alleged discrimination at that date. A declaration that the order had been discriminatory and therefore unlawful in the past would not indicate to the Government that current United Kingdom legislation required to be amended in order to conform with the Directive.[96]

(3) The applicants submitted that the declaration sought could form the basis for a claim for damages against the State for failure to implement the Directive. However, Lord Hoffmann held that the courts will not make a declaration in judicial review proceedings merely to found a damages claim against the State.[97]

---

[95] [1997] 1 WLR 473 at 478E–F.
[96] Ibid at 479F–480D, per Lord Hoffmann.
[97] Ibid at 480E–F. See also *R v Secretary of State for Employment, ex p Equal Opportunities Commission* [1995] 1 AC 1 at 32B–D, per Lord Keith.

Part III

Preliminary References

Chapter 11

References to the Court of Justice for a Preliminary Ruling

1. INTRODUCTION

(a) Nature and purpose of the preliminary ruling procedure

Article 177[1] Article 177 of the EC Treaty [new art 234] provides:

The Court of Justice shall have jurisdiction to give preliminary rulings concerning:

(a) the interpretation of this Treaty;

(b) the validity and interpretation of acts of the institutions of the Community and of the ECB;

(c) the interpretation of the statutes of bodies established by an act of the Council, where those statutes so provide.

Where such a question is raised before any court or tribunal of a Member State, that court or tribunal may, if it considers that a decision on the question is necessary to enable it to give judgment, request the Court of Justice to give a ruling thereon.

Where any such question is raised in a case pending before a court or tribunal of a Member State against whose decisions there is no judicial remedy under national law, that court or tribunal shall bring the matter before the Court of Justice.

This is the preliminary ruling procedure under which a national court can ask the Court of Justice to give a ruling on certain questions of Community law. The ruling is preliminary because it is made before the national court gives final judgment. References must be made to the Court of Justice, not to the Court of First Instance.[2]

Discretionary and mandatory references Article 177 [new art 234] makes a distinction between discretionary and mandatory references. The second paragraph uses the permissive word 'may' in contrast to the obligatory word 'shall' in the third paragraph. Thus, courts and tribunals which are not courts of last resort have a discretion whether to make a preliminary reference to the

---

[1] See, generally, David Anderson, *References to the European Court* (Sweet & Maxwell, 1995).
[2] EC Treaty, article 168a(1) [new art 225(1)].

197

Court of Justice on questions of *interpretation* of EC law.[3] In contrast, courts or tribunals from whose decision there is no judicial remedy must refer questions of interpretation of Community law to the Court of Justice.[4] In addition, the case-law of the Court of Justice establishes that all courts or tribunals (whether or not courts of last resort) are under an obligation to make a reference to the Court of Justice where they consider that a Community measure may be invalid.[5]

Purpose of the procedure The purpose of the preliminary ruling procedure is to ensure that Community law is applied uniformly by national courts.[6] The Court of Justice is best placed to ensure this uniformity. As Bingham J stated in *Customs & Excise Commissioners v ApS Samex*:[7]

> It has a panoramic view of the Community and its institutions, a detailed knowledge of the treaties and of much subordinate legislation made under them, and an intimate familiarity with the functioning of the Community market which no national judge denied the collective experience of the Court of Justice could hope to achieve.

The Court of Justice does not give a decision on the facts or merits of the particular case referred to it under article 177 [new art 234].[8] Its jurisdiction is limited to the interpretation of Community law and the validity of Community acts. Once the Court of Justice has given judgment, it is for the national court which made the reference to apply that judgment to the facts of the particular case in order to reach a decision.[9] It is for this reason that the procedure is known as a 'preliminary ruling'. The ruling of the Court of Justice is preliminary to the substantive judgment of the national court.

Obligation on referring court In the English courts, it is normal practice for the parties to draft the terms of reference to the Court of Justice for approval by the referring court. However, the national court is ultimately responsible for ensuring that a reference is necessary and that the order for reference and questions are properly drafted. As Kerr LJ stated in *Portsmouth City Council v Richards and Quietlynn*:[10]

> It is very important that the concept of so-called references by consent should not creep into our practice. All references are by the court. The court must itself be satisfied of the need for the reference; that the factual material accompanying the

---

[3] See below, pp 214–224.

[4] See below, pp 224–228.

[5] See below, pp 228–229.

[6] Case 166/73 *Rheinmühlen v Einfuhr- und Vorratsstelle Getreide und Futtermittel* [1974] ECR 33 para 2; Case 66/80 *International Chemical Corporation v Amministrazione delle Finanze* [1981] ECR 1191 para 11; Case 314/85 *Foto-Frost v Haupzollamt Lübeck-Ost* [1987] ECR 4199 para 15.

[7] [1983] 1 All ER 1042 at 1055h.

[8] Case 5/69 *Völk v Vervaecke* [1969] ECR 295 paras 1–2; *EMI Records Ltd v CBS United Kingdom Ltd* [1975] 1 CMLR 285 para 31; Case C-98/94 *Schmidt v Rijksdienst voor Pensioenen* [1995] ECR I-2559 para 22.

[9] Joined Cases C-297/88 and C-197/89 *Dzodzi v Belgium* [1990] ECR I-3763 para 33; Case C-181/95 *Biogen v Smithkline Beecham Biologicals* [1996] ECR I-717 para 5.

[10] [1989] 1 CMLR 673 at 708.

reference is sufficient to provide a proper foundation for it, and that it is of sufficient assistance to the European Court to enable it to reach a decision ...

Role of the parties The parties have no right to demand a reference to the Court of Justice; the right to make a reference is that of the national courts. As the Court of Justice stated in Case 5/72 *Fratelli Grassi fu Davide v Italian Finance Administration*:[11]

> According to Article 177 of the Treaty it is for the national court and not the parties to the main action to bring the matter before the Court of Justice. Since the power to formulate the questions to be referred is vested in the national court alone the parties cannot alter the wording of those questions.

Consequently, any attempt by the parties to bring a matter directly before the Court of Justice will be held to be inadmissible by the Court of Justice.[12] As Lord Denning MR stated in *Bulmer v Bollinger*:[13]

> None of the parties can go off to the European court and complain. The European court would not listen to any party who went moaning to them. The European court take the view that the trial judge has a complete discretion to refer or not to refer: ... If a party wishes to challenge the decision of the trial judge in England—to refer or not to refer—he must appeal to the Court of Appeal in England.

National court's power to make reference of own motion National courts generally have power to make references to the Court of Justice of their own motion.[14] This is reflected in Ord 114, r 2 of the Rules of the Supreme Court, which provides that an order for reference may be made by the court of its own motion at any stage in a cause or matter.

Matters outside the scope of the order for reference The parties may not require the Court of Justice to deal with issues which have not been raised in the questions referred by the national court.[15] However, the Court of Justice has held that it is under a duty to interpret all the provisions of Community law which a national court needs in order to decide the case pending before it, even if those provisions are not expressly indicated in the questions referred by the

---

[11] [1972] ECR 443 para 4. See also Joined Cases 31/62 and 33/62 *Wöhrmann v Commission* [1962] ECR 501 at 507.

[12] Case 29/68 *Milchkoutor v Hauptzollamt Saarbrucken* [1969] ECR 165; see, in particular, the Opinion of Advocate-General Gand at 186.

[13] [1974] Ch 401 at 420H.

[14] For a discussion of the national court's power to refer matters of its own motion, see Case 166/73 *Rheinmülen v Einfuhr- und Vorratsstelle Getreide* [1974] ECR 33 para 3; Joined Cases C-87 to C-89/90 *Verholen v Sociale Verzekeringsbank* [1991] ECR I-3757 para 12; paras 44–46 of the Opinion of Advocate-General Jacobs of 4 May 1994 in Case C-312/93 *Peterbroeck v Belgium* [1995] ECR I-4599. See also Joined Cases C-430/93 and C-431/93 *Van Schijndel v SPF* [1995] ECR I-4705 paras 16–22; and Case C-312/93 *Peterbroeck v Belgium* [1995] ECR I-4599 paras 12–21. See further below at pp 229–230.

[15] Case 44/65 *Hessische Knappschaft v Singer* [1965] ECR 965 at 970; Case 247/86 *Alsatel v Novasam* [1988] ECR 5987 paras 7–8; paras 27–28 of the Opinion of Advocate-General Léger in Case C-66/95 *R v Secretary of State for Social Security, ex p Sutton* [1997] ECR I-2163.

national court.[16] Furthermore, the Court may consider the validity of a Community measure of its own motion even where the questions referred by the national court relate solely to the interpretation of that measure.[17]

Composition of national court A national court may only make a preliminary reference where the ruling of the Court of Justice is necessary to enable *it* to give judgment.[18] However, the composition of the national court which deals with the case following the judgment of the Court of Justice need not be the same as the court which made the reference.[19]

(b) Courts or tribunals entitled to refer

Introduction Article 177 [new art 234] provides that any court or tribunal of a Member State is competent to make a reference to the Court of Justice.

'Of a Member State' The court or tribunal must be 'of a Member State'. The geographical scope of the EC Treaty is defined in article 227 [new art 299] of that Treaty.[20]

Community law concept Whether a body constitutes a 'court or tribunal' is to be decided by reference to Community law, not national law.[21] Thus, in Case 246/80 *Broekmeulen v Huisarts Registratie Commissie*[22] the Court of Justice held that a Medical Appeals Committee could make a reference under article 177 [new art 234], although the Committee did not constitute a court or tribunal under Dutch law. Conversely, in Case C-111/94 *Job Centre Coop*[23] the Court of Justice held that it did not have jurisdiction to respond to a preliminary reference made by the *Tribunale Civile e Penale di Milano* (Civil and Criminal District Court, Milan) as the national court was in fact exercising an administrative function in the matter before it.

'Court or tribunal' The Court of Justice has given a wide interpretation to the phrase 'court or tribunal' (*juridiction* in the French text) to ensure that it can assist most bodies which determine the exercise of Community rights. In

---

[16] Case C-280/91 *Viessmann* [1993] ECR I-971 para 17; Case C-130/92 *OTO v Ministero delle Finanze* [1994] ECR I-3281 para 14; Case C-131/95 *Huijbrechts* [1997] ECR I-1409 para 11. See also Case 145/79 *Roquette Frères v France* [1980] ECR 2917 para 7.

[17] See para 42 of the Opinion of Advocate-General Léger in Joined Cases C-153/94 and C-204/94 *Faroe Seafood Co* [1996] ECR I-2465; paras 70–72 of the Opinion of Advocate-General Ruiz-Jarabo Colomer in Case C-340/94 *De Jaeck v Staatssecretaris van Financiën* [1997] ECR I-461. See also Case 62/76 *Strehl v National Pensioenfonds voor Mijnwerkers* [1977] ECR 211 paras 1, 9–10 and 18; Case 145/79 *Roquette Frères v France* [1980] ECR 2917 para 7.

[18] Case 338/85 *Pardini v Ministero del commercio con l' estero* [1988] ECR 2041 paras 7–11.

[19] *R v Secretary of State for the Home Department, ex p Adams* [1995] 3 CMLR 476 para 3.

[20] For example, see Joined Cases C-100/89 and C-101/89 *Kaefer and Procacci v France* [1990] ECR I-4647 and Case C-260/90 *Leplat* [1992] ECR I-643, where references were made by courts in French Polynesia.

[21] Case C-24/92 *Corbiau v Administration des Contributions du Luxembourg* [1993] ECR I-1277 para 15.

[22] [1981] ECR 2311 paras 11 and 17.

[23] [1995] ECR I-3361.

general, the Court of Justice considers that a body may be classified as a 'court or tribunal' for the purposes of Community law where it:[24]

(1) is established by law;[25]
(2) has a permanent existence;
(3) exercises binding jurisdiction and is charged with the settlement of disputes;[26]
(4) is bound by rules of adversarial procedure;[27]
(5) applies the rule of law;[28] and
(6) is independent of the parties appearing before it.[29]

However, these criteria are not applied strictly as if they constituted an inflexible rule.

Applying these general criteria, the Court of Justice has accepted references from, *inter alia*, a Dutch Pension Funds Arbitration Tribunal,[30] the Dutch Appeals Committee for General Medicine[31] and the Italian National Council of the Bar.[32] It has rejected references made by the Bar Council of the Cour de Paris[33] and by the Luxembourg Director of Taxation and Excise Duties.[34]

Where a court or tribunal exercises some functions which are 'judicial' in nature and some which are not, the Court of Justice will reply to preliminary references made in the context of judicial proceedings,[35] but not those made in the context of non-judicial proceedings.[36]

---

[24] Case 61/65 *Vaassen v Beambtenfonds Mijnbedrijf* [1996] ECR 261 at 273; Case C-393/92 *Almelo* [1994] ECR I-1477 para 21; Case C-54/96 *Dorsch Consult v Bundesbaugesellschaft Berlin* [1997] ECR I-4961 paras 23–38.

[25] Case 246/80 *Broekmeulen v Huisarts Registratie Commissie* [1981] ECR 2311 para 9; Case C-54/96 *Dorsch Consult v Bundesbaugesellschaft Berlin* [1997] ECR I-4961 paras 24–25.

[26] Case 138/80 *Borker* [1980] ECR 1975 para 4; Case 318/85 *Unterweger* [1986] ECR 955; Case C-428/93 *Monin Automobiles—Maison du Deux-Roues* [1994] ECR I-1707; Case C-111/94 *Job Centre Coop* [1995] ECR I-3361 paras 9–11; Case C-54/96 *Dorsch Consult v Bundesbaugesellschaft Berlin* [1997] ECR I-4961 paras 27–29 and 37. Cf the Opinion of Advocate-General Mayras in Case 36/73 *Nederlandse Spoorwegen v Minister van Verkeer en Waterstaat* [1973] ECR 1299 at 1317–1320 concerning the advisory jurisdiction of the Dutch *Raad van State*.

[27] Case 246/80 *Broekmeulen v Huisarts Registratie Commissie* [1981] ECR 2311 para 10; Case 318/85 *Unterweger* [1986] ECR 955 para 2; Case C-54/96 *Dorsch Consult v Bundesbaugesellschaft Berlin* [1997] ECR I-4961 paras 30–33.

[28] Cf Case C-393/92 *Almelo* [1994] ECR I-1477 paras 22–24, where a court required to review an arbitration award on the basis of what appeared 'fair and reasonable' was permitted to make a reference to the Court of Justice.

[29] Case C-24/92 *Corbiau v Administration des Contributions du Luxembourg* [1993] ECR I-1277; Joined Cases C-74/95 and C-129/95 *X* [1996] ECR I-6609 paras 17–20; Case C-54/96 *Dorsch Consult v Bundesbaugesellschaft Berlin* [1997] ECR I-4961 paras 34–36.

[30] Case 61/65 *Vaassen v Beambtenfonds Mijnbedrijf* [1966] ECR 261.

[31] Case 246/80 *Broekmeulen v Huisarts Registratie Commissie* [1981] ECR 2311.

[32] Case C-55/94 *Gebhard v Consiglio dell'Ordine degli Avvocati e Procuratori di Milano* [1995] ECR I-4165; see also paras 12–17 of the Opinion of Advocate-General Léger.

[33] Case 138/80 *Borker* [1980] ECR 1975.

[34] Case C-24/92 *Corbiau v Administration des Contributions du Luxembourg* [1993] ECR I-1277.

Where a decision made by a body which is not a 'court or tribunal' for the purposes of article 177 [new art 234] is challenged by way of judicial review before a body which does qualify as a court or tribunal, the latter body is entitled to make a preliminary reference to the Court of Justice.[37]

English courts and tribunals In England and Wales, references may be made by, *inter alia*, the magistrates' court,[38] the Crown Court,[39] the High Court, the Court of Appeal, the House of Lords, and other specialist courts such as the Patents Court. Many tribunals have the power to make a reference, and the Social Security Commissioner,[40] income tax commissioners,[41] industrial tribunals,[42] the Employment Appeal Tribunal[43] and the VAT Tribunal[44] have all done so.

Ex parte **proceedings** A reference may be made in the course of *ex parte* proceedings before the national court. However, the Court of Justice has indicated that it is generally preferable for a national court to allow an *inter partes* hearing to take place before making a reference.[45]

Interlocutory applications A national court has power to order a reference at the interlocutory stage of proceedings.[46]

For example, it is possible for a national court to make a reference to the Court of Justice before deciding whether or not to grant an interlocutory injunction.[47] However, the circumstances in which this is likely to be appropriate will be rare, particularly in view of the delay involved in the preliminary reference procedure.[48]

Where the national court does not have to make any further, relevant, factual findings and the only issue to be determined is one of Community law, it may grant or refuse the interlocutory injunction and at the same time make a reference to the Court of Justice in order to enable it to give a final judgment.[49]

---

[35] Case 14/86 *Pretore di Salò v Persons Unknown* [1987] ECR 2545 paras 6–7.

[36] Case C-111/94 *Job Centre Coop* [1995] ECR I-3361.

[37] Ibid para 11.

[38] For example, Case C-145/88 *Torfaen Borough Council v B & Q plc* [1989] ECR 3851.

[39] For example, Case C-235/94 *Bird* [1995] ECR I-3933.

[40] For example, Case 150/85 *Drake v Chief Adjudication Officer* [1986] ECR 1995.

[41] For example, Case 44/84 *Hurd v Jones* [1986] ECR 29.

[42] For example, Case 222/84 *Johnston v Chief Constable of the Royal Ulster Constabulary* [1986] ECR 1651; Case C-152/91 *Neath v Steeper* [1993] ECR I-6935.

[43] For example, Case 19/81 *Burton v British Railways Board* [1982] ECR 555.

[44] For example, Case 5/84 *Direct Cosmetics v Customs & Excise Commissioners* [1985] ECR 617.

[45] Joined Cases C-277/91, C-318/91 and C-319/91 *Ligur Carni v Unità Sanitaria Locale No XV di Genova* [1993] ECR I-6621 paras 15–16; Joined Cases C-332/92, C-333/92 and C-335/92 *Eurico Italia v Ente Nazionale Risi* [1994] ECR I-711 paras 10–11; Case C-18/93 *Corsica Ferries* [1994] ECR I-1783 para 12.

[46] *South Pembrokeshire District Council v Wendy Fair Markets Ltd* [1994] 1 CMLR 213 at paras 32–36, per Jacob J.

[47] For example, see *R v Secretary of State for Transport, ex p Factortame Ltd* [1990] 2 AC 85 (HL); Case C-213/89, *Factortame* [1990] ECR I-2433 (ECJ).

[48] *Portsmouth City Council v Richards and Quietlynn* [1989] 1 CMLR 673 at para 98, per Kerr LJ.

[49] Case C-159/90 *SPUC v Grogan* [1991] ECR I-4685 paras 11–13; Graham J in *EMI*

This is consistent with the Rules of the Supreme Court Ord 114, r 2, which states that a reference may be made at any stage of the proceedings.

Arbitration The admissibility of a preliminary reference made in the course of an arbitration will depend on the nature of the arbitration in question.[50] References may be acceptable when they are made in the context of arbitrations in which there is a degree of State involvement.[51] In contrast, arbitrators appointed purely pursuant to a contract between private parties cannot make references to the Court of Justice.[52] This fact must be borne in mind by an English judge when he is considering whether to grant leave to appeal against an arbitrator's decision. Usually, leave on general points of law will only be granted when the judge considers that the decision of the arbitrator on the question is obviously wrong or the question of law is of general public importance and the decision of the tribunal is at least open to serious doubt.[53] However, where a point of Community law has been raised before the arbitrator, leave to appeal should normally be granted whenever the point is 'capable of serious argument'.[54]

Where a court is called upon to review an arbitrator's decision, it may make a reference to the Court of Justice under article 177 [new art 234] in the context of those review proceedings. This is so even if the court is only required to carry out the review on the basis of what is fair and reasonable.[55]

(c) Scope of the Court of Justice's jurisdiction

Interpretation of the EC Treaty The Court of Justice has jurisdiction to interpret the provisions of the EC Treaty pursuant to article 177(1)(a) [new art 234(1)(a)].[56] This jurisdiction extends to the Protocol on the Privileges and Immunities of the Community annexed to the EC Treaty.[57] The Court of Justice only has limited jurisdiction in respect of the EU Treaty (the Maastricht Treaty). In particular, it has no competence in relation to the provisions governing foreign/security policy and justice/home affairs.[58]

Records v CBS [1975] 1 CMLR 285; see also *Polydor v Harlequin Record Shops* [1980] 2 CMLR 413 (where an interlocutory injunction was refused, but a reference was made).

[50] Case 102/81 *Nordsee v Reederei Mond* [1982] ECR 1095 para 9.

[51] Case 61/65 *Vaassen v Beambtenfonds Mijnbedrijf* [1966] ECR 261.

[52] Case 102/81 *Nordsee v Reederei Mond* [1982] ECR 1095.

[53] Arbitration Act 1996, s 69(3)(c).

[54] *Bulk Oil (Zug) AG v Sun International Ltd* [1984] 1 WLR 147 at 154H–155F, per Ackner LJ, confirming the decision of Bingham J to grant leave in [1983] 1 Lloyd's Rep 655.

[55] Case C-393/92 *Almelo v* [1994] ECR I-1477 paras 22–24.

[56] The Court of Justice also has jurisdiction to give preliminary rulings concerning the interpretation of: (*a*) the Euratom Treaty pursuant to article 150(1)(a) of that Treaty; and (*b*) the ECSC Treaty pursuant to article 41 of that Treaty, as interpreted by the Court of Justice in Case C-221/88 *ECSC v Acciaierie e ferriere Busseni* [1990] ECR I-495 paras 9–17 (ECSC).

[57] Case 32/67 *Van Leeuwen v Rotterdam* [1968] ECR 43.

[58] Article L of the EU Treaty [new art 46]. See Case C-167/94 *Grau Gromis* [1995] ECR I-1023

General issues of Community law The Court of Justice's jurisdiction under article 177 [new art 234] is not limited solely to interpreting specific articles of the EC Treaty. Interpretation of the EC Treaty also includes interpretation of Community law generally, as the EC Treaty is the basis for all Community law. For example, in Case C-213/89 *Factortame*[59] the Court of Justice dealt with two questions referred by the House of Lords concerning the effective protection of individuals' Community law rights and, in particular, the obligation on national courts to grant interim relief where such rights are in issue.

Acts of Accession The terms of the Accession Treaties by which States become members of the Community give the Court of Justice jurisdiction under article 177 [new art 234] to interpret the provisions of those treaties.[60]

Acts of the Community institutions and of the ECB[61] The Court of Justice has jurisdiction to give rulings on the interpretation and the validity of the acts of the Council, the Commission, the European Parliament, the Court of Auditors and the European Central Bank.[62] Unlike article 173 [new art 230], which excludes review by the Court of Justice of recommendations, opinions and all other acts which do not produce legal effects, article 177(1)(b) of the EC Treaty [new art 234(1)(6)] confers jurisdiction on the Court to give preliminary rulings on the validity and interpretation of all acts of the institutions of the Community without exception.[63]

The Court of Justice does not have jurisdiction to give an interpretation of a measure which has not yet been adopted by the Community institutions.[64]

Validity of acts of the Community institutions National courts are not competent to declare that Community measures are invalid. Thus, where a national court has substantial doubts about the *validity* of a Community measure and a decision on its validity is necessary for resolution of the dispute, the court must refer the issue to the Court of Justice.[65] Although article 177 of

---

para 6. This will be subject to alteration by the Amsterdam Treaty (if ratified).

[59] [1990] ECR I-2433.

[60] Case 44/84 *Hurd v Jones* [1986] ECR 29 paras 14–15.

[61] Although the wording of article 41 of the ECSC Treaty only gives the Court of Justice jurisdiction to give preliminary rulings on the validity of acts of the High Authority and of the Council, the Court of Justice has held that it also has jurisdiction to give preliminary rulings on the interpretation of such acts: Case C-221/88 *ECSC v Acciaierie e ferriere Busseni* [1990] ECR I-495 paras 9–17 (ECSC).

[62] Judgments of the Court of Justice itself are not open to review in the context of article 177 proceedings: Case 69/85 *Wünsche Handelsgesellschaft v Germany* [1986] ECR 947 paras 10–16.

[63] Case 322/88 *Grimaldi v Fonds des maladies* [1989] ECR 4407 paras 7–9 (Commission recommendation); Case C-188/91 *Deutsche Shell v Hauptzollamt Hamburg-Harburg* [1993] ECR I-363 para 18 (resolution of a body established under an international treaty to which the Community was a party).

[64] Case C-343/90 *Dias v Director da Alfândega do Porto* [1992] ECR I-4673 para 18; *cf* Case C-306/93 *SMW Winzersekt v Land Rheinland-Pfalz* [1994] ECR I-5555 paras 12–18 (where the Court of Justice held that a question concerning the validity of a regulation which had been adopted but was not yet in force at the time when the reference was made was admissible).

[65] Case 314/85 *Foto-Frost v Hauptzollant Lübeck-Ost* [1987] ECR 4199 paras 11–20; discussed below at pp 228–229.

the EC Treaty [new art 234] does not specify the grounds on which the validity of a Community act may be declared invalid, in practice the grounds are the same under both articles 173 [new art 230] and 177.[66] The jurisdiction to rule on validity under article 177 is not subject to the restrictive *locus standi* requirements or the two-month time-limit prescribed under article 173; however, a private party may be barred from questioning the validity of a Community act before the national court where he could undoubtedly have challenged that measure under article 173 at an earlier date, but failed to do so.[67] For example, in Case C-178/95 *Wiljo v Belgium*[68] the Court declined to answer questions relating to the validity of a Commission decision because the party which sought to challenge the decision before the national court could have challenged it under article 173 but had failed to do so.

Failure to act The Court of Justice does not have jurisdiction under article 177 [new art 234] to rule on whether an institution has failed to act.[69]

Directives The Court of Justice has jurisdiction to respond to a request from a national court for a ruling on the interpretation of a directive which has been transposed into national law.[70] However, the Court is not entitled to give a ruling on the interpretation of the national law which implements the directive.[71]

International treaties A number of different situations arise in relation to international treaties:

(1) International treaties entered into by the Community form an integral part of the Community legal order and may be the subject of preliminary rulings under article 177 of the EC Treaty [new art 234].[72] In addition, measures adopted by bodies established pursuant to such treaties may also be the subject of preliminary references.[73] The Court of Justice has frequently been called upon to interpret the provisions of Association and Co-operation Agreements entered into between the European Community and third countries.[74]

---

[66] The grounds upon which a Community act will be declared invalid are discussed at Ch 13, pp 307–324.

[67] Case C-188/92 *TWD v Germanv* [1994] ECR I-833; discussed at Ch 1, pp 15–17.

[68] [1997] ECR I-585.

[69] Case C-68/95 *T. Port* [1996] ECR I-6065 para 53.

[70] Case C-331/92 *Gestión Hotelera Internacional v Comunidad Autónoma de Canarias* [1994] ECR I-1329 paras 11–14, and para 15 of the Opinion of Advocate-General Lenz.

[71] Case C-37/92 *Vanacker and Lesage* [1993] ECR I-4947 paras 6–7.

[72] Case 181/73 *Haegeman v Belgium* [1974] ECR 449 paras 1–6. The status of such agreements in Community law is discussed at Ch 1, pp 20–22.

[73] Case C-192/89 *Sevince v Staatssecretaris* [1990] ECR I-3461 paras 8–11 (decisions adopted by the Council of Association established pursuant to EEC–Turkey Association Agreement), affirmed by Case C-237/91 *Kazim Kus v Landeshauptstadt Wiesbaden* [1992] ECR I-6781 para 9; Case C-188/91 *Deutsche Shell v Hauptzollamt Hamburg–Harburg* [1993] ECR I-363 paras 16–19 (resolution of the Joint Committee established pursuant to EEC/EFTA Convention on a Common Transit Procedure).

[74] See, for example, Case C-432/92 *R v MAFF, ex p Anastasiou* [1994] ECR I-3087 paras 21–27 (EEC–Cyprus Association Agreement); Case C-58/93 *Yousfi v Belgium* [1994] ECR I-1353 paras 16–19 (EEC–Morocco Co-operation Agreement); C-103/94 *Krid v CNAVTS* [1995] ECR

(2) The Court of Justice also has jurisdiction under article 177 to interpret international agreements in relation to which the Community has assumed the Member States' commitments, such as the General Agreement on Tariffs and Trade ('GATT').[75]

(3) International treaties concluded by Member States outside the framework of Community law do not come within article 177, even though they may relate to the Community in some way.[76]

(4) International treaties concluded by Member States prior to their accession to the Community which concern areas covered by Community law may not be the subject of preliminary references under article 177. It is for the national court to interpret the provisions of such treaties.[77]

In Case C-364/92 *SAT Fluggesellschaft v Eurocontrol*[78] the Court of Justice rejected Eurocontrol's argument that, as it was an international organisation whose relations with the Community were governed by public international law, it was outside the jurisdiction of the Court under article 177. The Court held that its competence to answer the questions referred to it by the national court, which concerned the interpretation of certain articles of the EC Treaty, was not affected by arguments concerning the legal status of Eurocontrol.

Fundamental rights/European Convention on Human Rights Under article 177 [new art 234] the Court of Justice will provide a national court with an interpretation of fundamental rights, as laid down in particular in the European Convention of Human Rights, where the issue before the national court falls within the scope of Community law. However, the Court of Justice has no power to provide an interpretation of fundamental rights in cases which fall outside the scope of Community law.[79]

Agreements between private undertakings required by Community law An agreement concluded by private undertakings does not fall within

---

I-719 paras 21–24 (EEC–Algeria Co-operation Agreement).

[75] Joined Cases 267 to 269/81 *Amministrazione delle Finanze v SPI and SAMI* [1983] ECR 801 paras 12–20; Joined Cases 290/81 and 291/81 *Compagnia Singer and Geigy v Amministrazione delle Finanze* [1983] ECR 847 para 7. It is doubtful whether the Court of Justice could rule on the validity of such treaties.

[76] Case 44/84 *Hurd v Jones* [1986] ECR 29 para 20 (treaties concluded by the Member States setting up the European schools); see also Case 130/73 *Vandeweghe v Berufsgenossenenschaft für die chemische Industrie* [1973] ECR 1329 para 2 (1957 bilateral agreement between Belgium and Germany).

[77] Case C-13/93 *ONEM v Minne* [1994] ECR I-371 paras 17–18; Case C-324/93 *R v Secretary of State for the Home Department, ex p Evans Medical* [1995] ECR I-563 paras 27–29. The status of such agreements in Community law is governed by article 234 of the EC Treaty [new art 307] which is discussed at Ch 1, pp 22–23.

[78] [1994] ECR I-43 paras 8–11.

[79] Case C-260/89 ERT [1991] ECR I-2925 para 42; Case C-177/94 *Perfili* [1996] ECR I-161 para 20; Case C-144/95 *Maurin* [1996] ECR I-2909; Case C-299/95 *Kremzow v Austria* [1997] ECR I-2629 paras 14–19.

article 177 [new art 234], even though the act may be required or envisaged by Community law.[80]

Criminal law Preliminary references may be made in the context of criminal proceedings.[81]

National law Article 177 of the EC Treaty [new art 234] does not give the Court of Justice jurisdiction either to interpret national law[82] or to decide upon the compatibility of national law with Community law.[83] Questions concerning national law will, where possible, be reformulated by the Court of Justice in order to identify the issues of Community law which are relevant to the case before the national court and to enable the Court of Justice to provide a useful answer to the national court.[84]

In certain cases, the Court will give a preliminary ruling concerning Community law, even where the situation before the national court is a purely domestic matter which falls outside the scope of Community law.[85] In particular it will do so where:

(1) The relevant domestic law specifically refers to or incorporates a provision of Community law into domestic law. For example, in Case C-231/89 *Gmurzynska-Bscher v Oberfinanzdirektion Köln*[86] a German law on turnover tax expressly adopted classifications laid down by Community customs legislation. The German court sought a preliminary ruling from the Court of Justice as to certain provisions of the relevant Community legislation and the Court held that it had jurisdiction to deal with such a request; or

---

[80] Case 152/83 *Demouche v Fonds de garantie automobile* [1987] ECR 3833 paras 15–21, (concerning the agreement between the National Insurance Bureaux relating to the Green Card scheme, which constituted a precondition for the entry into force of Council Directive 72/166 on the approximation of laws of the Member States relating to insurance against civil liability in respect of the use of motor vehicles (OJ 1972 (ii) (English special edition) p 360)).

[81] Case 82/71 *Pubblico Ministero v SAIL* [1972] ECR 119 paras 4–5.

[82] Case C-172/95 *Société Sucrière Agricole de Maizy v Directeur Régional des Impôts* [1996] ECR I-5581 para 13; Case C-341/94 *Allain* [1996] ECR I-4631 para 11; Case 435/93 *Dietz v Stichting Thuiszorg Rotterdam* [1996] ECR I-5223 para 39.

[83] Case 6/64 *Costa v ENEL* [1964] ECR 585 at 592–593; Case C-337/91 *Van Gemert-Derks* [1993] ECR I-5435 para 18; Joined Cases C-304/94, C-330/94, C-342/94 and C-225/95 *Tombesi* [1997] ECR I-3561 para 36.

[84] Case C-105/96 *Codiesel* [1997] ECR I-3465 paras 12–13. See also Case 148/85 *Direction Générale des Impôts v Forest* [1986] ECR 3449 paras 5–7; Case 20/87 *Ministère public v Gauchard* [1987] ECR 4879 para 9; Case C-369/89 *Piageme v Peeters* [1991] ECR I-2971 paras 4 and 7–8. Contrast Case 14/86 *Pretore Di Salò v Persons Unknown* [1987] ECR 2545 paras 15–16. See below, p 232.

[85] See Case C-28/95 *Leur-Bloem v Inspecteur der Belastingdienst/Ondernemingen Amsterdam 2* [1997] ECR I-4161 paras 16–34 and Case C-130/95 *Giloy v Hauptzollamt Frankfurt am Main-Ost* [1997] ECR I-4291 paras 16–29 for a comprehensive analysis of this issue. See paras 24–39 and 47–81 of the joint Opinion of Advocate-General Jacobs in these cases (delivered on 17 September 1996) for a summary and critique of the approach adopted by the Court of Justice on this issue.

[86] [1990] ECR I-4003 paras 15–26. See also Joined Cases C-297/88 and C-197/89 *Dzodzi v Belgium* [1990] ECR I-3763 paras 29–43.

(2) Community legislation is applicable by virtue of a contractual provision agreed between the parties to the proceedings before the national court.[87]

However, in Case C-346/93 *Kleinwort Benson*[88] the Court of Justice held that it did not have jurisdiction to give a preliminary ruling on questions submitted by the Court of Appeal concerning the Convention of 27 September 1968 on jurisdiction and the enforcement of judgments in civil and commercial matters (the 'Brussels Convention'). The dispute before the Court of Appeal concerned the question of whether the English or Scottish courts had jurisdiction to deal with the substantive matter. The jurisdiction issue was governed by the Civil Jurisdiction and Judgments Act 1982, the effect of which was that, to a large degree, the jurisdiction rules established by the Brussels Convention were to be applied in order to allocate jurisdiction between different jurisdictions within the United Kingdom. However, the Court of Justice held that it did not have jurisdiction to provide an interpretation of the Brussels Convention following a preliminary reference by the Court of Appeal because:

(1) The Brussels Convention was not fully incorporated by the relevant domestic statute.[89] In particular, the terms of the 1982 Act were not identical to those of the Brussels Convention, and the 1982 Act contained an express provision permitting the rules established by the Act to be modified so as to bear a different meaning from the provisions of the Brussels Convention as interpreted by the Court of Justice.

(2) Under the terms of the 1982 Act, the national courts were not bound to apply the judgments of the Court of Justice relating to the Brussels Convention when dealing with domestic jurisdiction disputes. Any judgment by the Court of Justice would therefore be purely advisory in nature.[90]

Facts There is a separation of functions between national courts and the Court of Justice under article 177 of the EC Treaty [new art 234] in relation to issues of fact. First, it is for the national court to ascertain the facts which have given rise to the dispute.[91] The Court of Justice must answer the national court's questions on the basis of the facts as they are set out in the order for reference, and cannot alter the factual basis of the preliminary reference in light of the submissions of the parties.[92] However, the Court of Justice is entitled to take account of

---

[87] Case C-88/91 *Federconsorzi v AIMA* [1992] ECR I-4035 paras 6–10.

[88] [1995] ECR I-615. The Court of Justice held that the request for a reference was inadmissible even though the referring court, the Court of Appeal, had expressly considered the scope of the Court of Justice's jurisdiction and decided that it was appropriate to make a reference: *Barclays Bank plc v Glasgow City Council* [1994] 2 WLR 466 at 475E–F.

[89] Compare Case C-341/94 *Allain* [1996] ECR I-4631 paras 9–13, where the Court of Justice replied to a reference even though national law did not incorporate any specific provision of Community law.

[90] Contrast Case C-73/89 *Fournier v Van Werven* [1992] ECR I-5621 paras 20–24, where the Court of Justice replied to a reference, even where the national court would not be bound by the judgment.

[91] Case 17/81 *Pabst & Richarz v Hauptzollamt Oldenburg* [1982] ECR 1331 para 12; Case C-30/93 *AC–ATEL Electronics Vertriebs v Hauptzollamt München-Mitte* [1994] ECR I-2305 para 17.

[92] Case C-30/93 *AC–ATEL Electronics Vertriebs* [1994] ECR I-2305 para 16; Case C-352/95 *Phytheron International v Bourdon* [1997] ECR I-1729 paras 9–14, see also paras 10–12 of the

information provided by the parties to the preliminary ruling procedure in order to clarify or complete factual matters which are not fully dealt with in the order for reference.[93] Furthermore, the Court of Justice may require the parties to the preliminary ruling procedure to provide it with further information.[94] The most common means of doing so is for the Court to write to the parties indicating the matters with which it wishes them to deal.[95] In principle, the Court of Justice has power to order formal preparatory enquiries in the context of preliminary reference proceedings.[96]

Secondly, in general the Court of Justice has no jurisdiction to apply the relevant rules of Community law to the facts of a specific case.[97] However, occasionally the Court of Justice may make a specific finding as to the application of Community law to a particular case where it has sufficient factual evidence before it to do so. For example, in Case C-169/91 *Stoke-on-Trent v B&Q*[98] the Court considered that the UK's Sunday trading laws were not disproportionate and, therefore, not unlawful under Community law, even though the question of whether or not a particular national measure is proportionate is normally a matter for the national courts.

Interpretation of the statutes of bodies established by an act of the Council Article 177(1)(c) of the EC Treaty [new art 234] governs the interpretation of the statutes of bodies established by an act of the Council. This is necessary, as the statute of the relevant body may not constitute an act within the meaning of article 177(1)(b). However, the power to interpret statutes of bodies established by an act of the Council has little practical significance; moreover, the power exists only where the statute so provides.[99]

Brussels and Rome Conventions The Convention on Jurisdiction and the Enforcement of Judgments in Civil and Commercial Matters (the 'Brussels Convention') does not constitute an act of the institutions within the meaning of article 177(1)(b) of the EC Treaty [new art 234(1)(b)]. However, the Court of

---

Opinion of Advocate-General Jacobs; Case C-223/95 *Moksel v Hauptzollamt Hamburg-Jonas* [1997] ECR I-2379 paras 19–20.

[93] See the Opinion of Advocate-General Warner in Case 51/75 *EMI Records v CBS United Kingdom* [1976] ECR 811 at 853–855. For example, see Case 131/77 *Milac v Hauptzollamt Saarbrücken* [1978] ECR 1041 para 6; Case 47/82 *Vismans v Inspecteur de Invoerrechtenen en Accijnzen,* [1982] ECR 3983 para 8. Contrast Case 247/86 *Alsatel v Novasam* [1988] ECR 5987 paras 21–22.

[94] Measures of organisation of procedure and preparatory inquiries are discussed at Ch 18, pp 406–407.

[95] For example, see Case C-17/94 *Gervais* [1995] ECR I-4353 para 21, and the Opinion of Advocate-General Elmer at paras 7–10.

[96] See the Opinion of Advocate-General Warner in Case 51/75 *EMI Records v CBS United Kingdom* [1976] ECR 811 at 854, and Case C-415/93 *Union Royale Belge des Sociétés de Football Association v Bosman* [1995] ECR I-4921 paras 52–54.

[97] Case C-98/94 *Schmidt v Rijksdienst voor Pensionen* [1995] ECR I-2559 para 22.

[98] [1992] ECR I-6635 paras 8–17. Contrast Case 145/88 *Torfaen Borough Council v B&Q* [1989] ECR 3851 paras 10–17. See also Case C-384/93 *Alpine Investments v Minister van Financiën* [1995] ECR I-1141 paras 40–56.

[99] For example, article 14 of the rules of the Administration Commission on Social Security for Migrant Workers (OJ 1973 C68 p 15).

Justice has jurisdiction to give preliminary rulings on the Brussels Convention by virtue of the Protocol of 3 June 1971 on the interpretation by the Court of Justice of the Convention (which is set out in Schedule 2 to the Civil Jurisdiction and Judgments Act 1982). In contrast, the Lugano Convention provides no procedure for preliminary references to be made to the Court of Justice.

The Convention on the Law applicable to Contractual Relations (the 'Rome Convention') contains two Protocols (signed at Brussels on 19 December 1988) (set out in Schedule 3 to the Contracts (Applicable Law) Act 1990) which will allow national courts to make preliminary references to the Court of Justice. However, neither Protocol is yet in force.

European Economic Area Article 107 and Protocol 34 of the Treaty on the European Economic Area (EEA) provides the possibility for courts and tribunals in the EFTA States to request the Court of Justice to rule on the interpretation of EEA law. The Court of Justice, in *Opinion 1/92*,[100] has stated that such rulings would be binding on the EFTA Treaty courts and tribunals. However, none of the EFTA States has yet taken the steps necessary to grant its courts jurisdiction to make such references.

(d) Inadmissible references

General rule[101] The general rule is that it is solely for the national court to decide whether it is necessary to make a preliminary reference to the Court of Justice and what the questions referred should be.[102] However, it is common for the Court of Justice to reformulate the questions referred to it in order to provide an answer which is useful to the national court.[103] Furthermore, the Court of Justice may decline to give a ruling in exceptional cases[104] where:

(1) the national court has failed to provide sufficient factual or legal background information;

(2) the questions referred are obviously irrelevant to the dispute before the referring court;

(3) the referring court is in effect seeking an advisory opinion on general or hypothetical issues;

(4) the request for a reference amounts to an abuse of the preliminary ruling procedure; and/or

---

[100] [1992] 2 CMLR 217.

[101] See Case C-343/90 *Dias v Director da Alfândega do Porto* [1992] ECR I-4673 paras 13–20 for an overview of the principles applicable to the inadmissibility of preliminary references.

[102] Case C-62/93 *BP Supergas v Greece* [1995] ECR I-1883 para 10; Case C-415/93 *Union Royale Belge des Sociétés de Football Association v Bosman* [1995] ECR I-4921 paras 59–61; Case C-183/95 *Affish v Rijksdienst voor de Keuring van Vee en Vlees* [1997] ECR I-4315 para 24.

[103] Case C-168/95 *Arcaro* [1996] ECR I-4705 para 21; Case C-334/95 *Krüger v Hauptzollamt Hamburg-Jonas* [1997] ECR I-4517 paras 22–23.

[104] Advocate-General Fennelly has stated that the Court of Justice should refuse to answer questions referred only where it is very clear that no genuinely useful answer can reasonably be given; see para 29 of his Opinion in Case C-105/94 *Celestini v Saar-Sektkellerei Faber* [1997] ECR I-2971.

(5) there is no dispute pending before the referring court.

In recent years, there has been a marked increase in the number of requests for preliminary rulings which have been declared inadmissible by the Court of Justice. The Court has the power to declare that a request for a preliminary ruling is manifestly inadmissible by means of a reasoned order without calling for written observations or holding an oral hearing.[105]

The Court of Justice will not investigate allegations that the national court did not have jurisdiction to deal with the dispute under national law or made the reference in breach of national procedural rules.

Insufficient information The order for reference made by the national court should be succinct and should:[106]

(1) describe the factual and domestic legal context of the dispute (or, at the very least, explain the factual circumstances on which the questions are based);[107]

(2) indicate why the national court has considered it necessary to make a reference; and

(3) in appropriate cases, provide a summary of the arguments of the parties.

A preliminary reference from a national court may be declared to be inadmissible if the order for reference fails to provide sufficient details of the factual and legal context of the dispute and of the reasons for making the reference. The information provided in the order for reference must not only be such as to enable the Court of Justice to provide a useful reply to the national court, but be sufficient to enable the Member States and the Community institutions to decide whether they wish to submit observations in the course of the proceedings before the Court of Justice.[108]

The level of detail required will vary according to the nature of the case and the content of the questions submitted.[109] For example, the Court of Justice will generally require a greater degree of information in competition cases, which often require consideration of complex factual and legal situations.[110] In contrast, questions raising specific technical issues do not require a particularly detailed description of the factual and legal background.[111]

The Court of Justice does not adopt a strict, formalistic approach to the admissibility of preliminary references. Even in cases where the order for reference does not contain any information about the facts of the case, the Court will endeavour to ascertain the relevant factual background from the national

---

[105] ECJ Rules of Procedure, article 92(1).

[106] *Note for Guidance on References by National Courts for Preliminary Rulings* para 6. Reproduced at Appendix H.

[107] Case C-378/93 *La Pyramide* [1994] ECR I-3999 para 14.

[108] Case C-2/96 *Sunino and Data* [1996] ECR I-1543 paras 4–7; Case C-196/96 *Lahlou* [1996] ECR I-3945 paras 4–7.

[109] Paragraph 16 of the Opinion of Advocate-General Ruiz-Jarabo Colomer in Case C-125/94 *Aprile v Amministrazione delle Finanze* [1995] ECR I-2919.

[110] Joined Cases C-320/90, C-321/90 and C-322/90 *Telemarsicabruzzo* [1993] ECR I-393 paras 6–7; Case C-157/92 *Pretore di Genova v Banchero* [1993] ECR I-1085 paras 4–5; Case C-386/92 *Monin Automobiles—Maison du Deux-Roues* [1993] ECR I-2049 paras 6–7.

[111] Case C-316/93 *Vaneetveld v Le Foyer* [1994] ECR I-763 para 13.

court's case-file as supplied with the order and/or from the parties' written and oral observations.[112] In certain cases, the Court of Justice may require the parties to the preliminary ruling procedure to provide it with further information in order to ensure that it has sufficient information to deal with a preliminary reference.[113] In Joined Cases C-133/93, C-300/93 and C-362/93 *Crispoltoni v Fattoria Autonoma Tabacchi*[114] the Court of Justice held that a request for a preliminary ruling was admissible even though the order for reference did not contain any information on the factual background to the case; the Court was already aware of the legal and factual context of the dispute because there had been a previous preliminary reference made by the same court concerning the same plaintiff.

Obvious irrelevance A request from a national court for a preliminary ruling will be rejected if it is obvious[115] that the questions referred bear no relation to the actual facts or subject-matter of the main action.[116] Where the questions are partly relevant and partly irrelevant, the Court of Justice will confine itself to dealing with the relevant aspects of the questions posed.[117]

Advisory/hypothetical questions The Court of Justice will not deliver advisory opinions on general or hypothetical questions.[118] The fact that a reference is made on the basis of assumed facts (for example, because the national court decides that it is appropriate to settle a particular legal issue before embarking on a complex factual analysis) will not render the reference

---

[112] Case 251/83 *Haug-Adrion v Frankfurter Versicherungs* [1984] ECR 4277 para 9; Case C-316/93 *Vaneetveld v Le Foyer* [1994] ECR I-763 paras 12–14; Case C-18/93 *Corsica Ferries* [1994] ECR I-1783 para 13; para 34 of the Opinion of Advocate-General Jacobs in Case C-39/94 *SFEI v La Poste* [1996] ECR I-3547. Cf Case C-66/97 *Banco de Fomento e Exterior v Pechim* [1997] ECR I-3757; paras 26–27 of the Opinion of Advocate-General Jacobs in Case C-284/96 *Tabouillot v Directeur des Services Fiscaux* (Opinion of 17 July 1997).

[113] For example, see Case C-17/94 *Gervais* [1995] ECR I-4353 paras 18–22, and the Opinion of Advocate-General Elmer at paras 7–10.

[114] [1994] ECR I-4863 paras 15–20.

[115] See paras 76–80 of the Opinion of Advocate-General Lenz in Case C-415/93 *Union Royale Belge des Sociétés de Football Association v Bosman* [1995] ECR I-4921, where he indicates that the Court of Justice should examine the need for a preliminary ruling only in exceptional cases and, therefore, a request for a preliminary ruling should be declared inadmissible only where there is *manifestly* no connection between the main action and the questions submitted.

[116] Case 126/80 *Salonia v Poidomani and Baglieri* [1981] ECR 1563 para 6; Case C-343/90 *Dias v Director Da Alfândega do Porto* [1992] ECR I-4673 paras 11–20; Case C-18/93 *Corsica Ferries* [1994] ECR I-1783 paras 14–16; Case C-297/93 *Grau-Hupka v Stadtgemeinde Bremen* [1994] ECR I-5535 paras 18–19 (in which the Court concluded that the question referred was irrelevant only after studying the case-file supplied by the national court).

[117] Case C-412/93 *Leclerc-Siplec v TF1 Publicité* [1995] ECR I-179 paras 8–16.

[118] Case C-83/91 *Meilicke v ADV/ORGA* [1992] ECR I-4871 para 25; Case C-412/93 *Leclerc-Siplec v TF1 Publicité* [1995] ECR I-179 paras 8–16; Case C-458/93 *Saddik* [1995] ECR I-511.

inadmissible provided it is made in the context of a genuine dispute between the parties.[119]

Abuse of procedure In exceptional cases, the Court of Justice will not respond to a request for a preliminary ruling where it appears that there is no genuine dispute between the parties in the national proceedings. In Case 104/79 *Foglia v Novello I*[120] and Case 244/80 *Foglia v Novello II*[121] the Court of Justice held that it did not have jurisdiction to give a ruling on the questions asked by the national court where the parties to the main proceedings had jointly fabricated a dispute as a device for obtaining a preliminary ruling.[122] The fact that the parties to the main proceedings are in agreement as to the result to be achieved by the preliminary reference does not, of itself, mean that the Court of Justice will refuse to provide an answer.[123]

No pending dispute A national court or tribunal is not entitled to make a preliminary reference to the Court of Justice unless a dispute is pending before it in the context of which it is called upon to give a decision capable of taking into account the preliminary ruling.[124] Similarly, once an English court has given judgment and its order has been drawn up, it is *functus officio* and has no power to make a reference under article 177 [new art 234].[125]

Furthermore, the Court of Justice has no jurisdiction to hear a reference for a preliminary ruling when, at the time it is made, the procedure before the referring court has already been terminated.[126] A national court which has made

---

[119] Case C-127/92 *Enderby v Frenchay Health Authority* [1993] ECR I-5535 paras 7–12; para 16 of the Opinion of Advocate-General Fennelly in Case C-90/96 *Petrie v Università degli Studi di Verona*, delivered on 20 March 1997.

[120] [1980] ECR 745 paras 9–11.

[121] [1981] ECR 3045 para 18.

[122] This was the analysis of the *Foglia v Novello* judgments adopted by the Court of Justice in Case C-105/94 *Celestini v Saar-Sektkellerei Faber* [1997] ECR I-2971 paras 20–23; see also paras 22–25 of the Opinion of Advocate-General Fennelly where he stated that the *Foglia v Novello* principle 'should be applied most sparingly and with the utmost caution by the Court'. See also paras 81–85 of the Opinion of Advocate-General Lenz in Case C-415/93 *Union Royale Belge des Sociétés de Football Association v Bosman* [1995] ECR I-4921.

[123] Case C-412/93 *Leclerc-Siplec v TF1 Publicité* [1995] ECR I-179 para 14, and para 10 of the Opinion of Advocate-General Jacobs.

[124] Case 338/85 *Pardini v Ministero del commercio con l'estero* [1988] ECR 2041 para 10. See also para 15 of the Opinion of Advocate-General Ruiz-Jarabo Colomer in Case C-77/95 *Züchner v Handelskrankenkasse (Ersatzkasse) Bremen* [1996] ECR I-5689, where he indicated that the Court of Justice had jurisdiction to deal with a preliminary reference made in the context of an interlocutory application for legal aid. The Court accepted that it had jurisdiction in such a case without expressly considering the matter.

[125] *SA Magnavision v General Optical Council (No 2)* [1987] 2 CMLR 262 paras 14–16, per Watkins LJ; *Chiron Corp v Murex Diagnostics Ltd* [1995] All ER (EC) 88 at 92g–93a, per Balcombe LJ (contrast Staughton LJ at 96b–f, dissenting).

[126] Case 338/85 *Pardini v Ministero del commercio con l'estero* [1988] ECR 2041 para 10; Joined Cases C-422/93, C-423/93 and C-424/93 *Zabala Erasun v Instituto Nacional de Empleo* [1995] ECR I-1567. Contrast Case C-3/90 *Bernini v Minister van Onderwijs en Wetenschappen* [1992] ECR I-1071 paras 9–11 and Case C-134/94 *Esso Española v Comunidad Autónoma de Canarias* [1995] ECR I-4223 paras 4–10, where the article 177 proceedings were maintained despite the apparent resolution of the main proceedings before the national courts. See the general comments at paras 16–24 of the Opinion of Advocate-General Jacobs in Case C-314/96

a reference should generally inform the Court of Justice that it wishes to withdraw its request for a preliminary ruling whenever the proceedings before the referring court have been settled or discontinued prior to the Court of Justice's judgment in the matter.[127]

Jurisdiction of referring court/national procedural rules/national laws The Court of Justice will not refuse to respond to a preliminary reference on the basis that the national court was allegedly not competent to hear the case or made the reference in breach of national procedural rules.[128] However, the Court of Justice is competent to provide interpretations of procedural and substantive provisions of Community law which may affect the issue of the national court's jurisdiction to decide the case before it.[129]

Similarly, the Court of Justice will not consider allegations that a preliminary reference has been sought on the basis of a misinterpretation of national law.[130]

2. DISCRETIONARY REFERENCES

Discretion to refer Courts and tribunals which are not courts of last resort have a discretion whether to make a preliminary reference to the Court of Justice on questions of *interpretation* of EC law. (In contrast, they are under an obligation to refer questions concerning the *validity* of Community acts where they believe that a particular act may be invalid.) The wording of article 177 [new art 234] makes it clear that a national court or tribunal should consider two matters in deciding whether to make a reference to the Court of Justice. These are:

    (1) whether a decision on the question of Community law is necessary to enable it to give judgment; and

    (2) if so, whether the court should, in the exercise of its discretion, order that a reference be made.

(a) A decision on the question of Community law is necessary

The Community point is substantially determinative The word 'necessary' should not be construed too narrowly. The view of Lord Denning MR in *Bulmer Ltd v Bollinger SA*[131] that the judgment of the Court of Justice must be

---

Djabali v Caisse d'Allocations Familiales de l'Essonne, delivered on 15 May 1997.

[127] See RSC, 114/1–6/20; *R v Secretary of State for the Home Department, ex p Adams* [1995] 3 CMLR 476 para 24.

[128] Case C-10/92 *Balocchi v Ministero delle Finanze* [1993] ECR I-5105 paras 15–17; Case C-472/93 *Spano v Fiat Geotech* [1995] ECR I-4321 paras 14 and 16; Case C-105/94 *Celestini v Saar-Sektkellerei Faber* [1997] ECR I-2971 para 20 (Court of Justice would not consider whether national court had jurisdiction pursuant to the Brussels Convention); Case C-54/96 *Dorsch Consult v Bundesbaugesellschaft Berlin* [1997] ECR I-4961 para 40.

[129] Paragraph 26 of Advocate-General Fennelly's Opinion (and the cases cited therein) in Case C-246/95 *Coen v Belgium* [1997] ECR I-403.

[130] Case C-83/94 *Leifer* [1995] ECR I-3231 para 41.

[131] [1974] Ch 401 at 422D–E.

'conclusive' so that, whichever way the point is decided, nothing more will remain for the national court but to give judgment, is unduly restrictive and has generally not been followed. In *Polydor v Harlequin Record Shops*[132] Ormrod LJ said:

> I would not, for my part, be inhibited by any nice questions of necessity, and would regard the word 'necessary' as meaning 'reasonably necessary' in ordinary English and not 'unavoidable'.

On the other hand, the word 'necessary' is stronger than 'desirable' or 'convenient'[133] and is generally understood to mean that the Community law point should be substantially determinative of the case.[134] Thus, for example, the national court may refuse to make a reference where the case can be disposed of on a point of national law[135] or on the facts.

Previous ruling of the Court of Justice Where the Court of Justice has already dealt with a particular issue of Community law, the national court is bound to follow that ruling by virtue of s 3(1) of the European Communities Act 1972.[136] The national court should not refuse to apply a previous ruling of the Court of Justice without making a new request for a preliminary ruling. (National courts are entitled to make a new reference to the Court of Justice on any question, even where the relevant issue has already been the subject of a judgment by the Court of Justice.[137]) Where the Court of Justice has made a previous ruling on a substantially similar point, a reference will generally not be necessary.

In some cases, the Court of Justice, having received a reference, will write to the national court informing it of a judgment of the Court of Justice on the same or a substantially similar issue and asking whether the national court wishes to maintain its request for a preliminary ruling in light of that judgment. In such circumstances, the decision as to whether to maintain its request for a reference lies wholly with the national court, which is fully entitled to indicate that it still wishes the Court of Justice to deal with its questions.[138]

---

[132] [1980] 2 CMLR 413 at 428. See also *R v Plymouth Justices, ex p Rogers* [1982] QB 863 at 869, [1982] 3 CMLR 221 at 227.

[133] *An Bord Bainne Co-operative Ltd v Milk Marketing Board* [1985] 1 CMLR 6 at 10, per Neil J.

[134] See Bingham J in *Customs & Excise Commissioners v APS Samex* [1983] 1 All ER 1042; and Macpherson J in *R v HM Treasury, ex p Daily Mail* [1987] 2 CMLR 1.

[135] For example, see *Countrywide Insurance Marketing Ltd v Commissioners of Customs and Excise* [1994] 3 CMLR 125 para 81 (VAT Tribunal).

[136] For example, see *R v Secretary of State for Social Services, ex p Bomore Medical Supplies Ltd* [1986] 1 CMLR 228 para 41. The binding nature of judgments of the Court of Justice is discussed at Ch 1, pp 19–20.

[137] Case 66/80 *International Chemical Corporation v Amministrazione delle Finanze* [1981] ECR 1191 para 14; Case 283/81 *CILFIT v Ministry of Health* [1982] ECR 3415 paras 13–15; Joined Cases C-332/92 and others *Eurico Italia v Ente Nazionale Risi* [1994] ECR I-711 paras 14–15; para 1 of the Opinion of Advocate-General Jacobs in Case C-457/93 *Kuratorium für Dialyse und Nierentransplantation v Lewark* [1996] ECR I-243. The status of judgments of the Court of Justice delivered in preliminary reference proceedings is discussed below at p 239.

[138] For example, see *Johnson v Chief Adjudication Officer* [1994] 2 CMLR 829 (CA) and Case C-192/94 *El Corte Inglés v Blázquez Rivero* [1996] ECR I-1281 paras 10–13.

Decide the facts first As a general rule, the national court should establish the facts of the case first before making a preliminary reference to the Court of Justice, as, once the facts have been investigated, a decision on the point of Community law may be unnecessary.[139] Furthermore, it will generally be easier to identify the precise points of Community law which are in issue and to formulate appropriate questions once the facts have been found.[140] In consequence, a reference should not generally be made before the pleadings have closed[141] unless the facts necessary for the making of the reference can be agreed between the parties.[142] For example, in judicial review proceedings it is possible for a reference to be made at the leave stage on the basis of facts and questions agreed between the parties prior to the hearing.

Although it is desirable to settle questions of fact and national law before making a reference, the national court retains complete discretion to make a reference at whatever stage of the proceedings it considers is most appropriate.[143] For example, in *R v Pharmaceutical Society of Great Britain, ex p Association of Pharmaceutical Importers*[144] the Court of Appeal referred the question of whether a restriction on a chemist substituting a differently named, but therapeutically identical, imported drug for that prescribed by a doctor was contrary to article 30 of the EEC Treaty [new art 28] on the free movement of goods, even though there were unresolved conflicts on factual matters, such as the effects on health and the importance of the so-called anxiety factor which might be caused by generic drugs.

The national court is fully entitled to weigh up any 'considerations of procedural organisation and efficiency' in determining the appropriate time for making a reference.[145] Thus, procedural efficiency may best be served by an early reference where, for example, the purpose of the question is to ascertain whether a provision of Community law has direct effect and is capable of giving rise to a cause of action.

---

[139] This general principle has been established by the case-law of the Court of Justice; see Joined Cases 36/80 and 71/80 *Irish Creamery Milk Suppliers Association v Ireland* [1981] ECR 735 paras 6–9, and Case C-83/91 *Meilicke v ADV/ORGA* [1992] ECR I-4871 para 26; and see the case-law of the English courts, per Lord Denning MR in *Bulmer Ltd v Bollinger SA* [1974] Ch 401 at 423C–D, per Bingham J in *Customs & Excise Commissioners v APS Samex* [1983] 1 All ER 1042 at 1055c, and per Neil J in *An Bord Bainne Co-operative Ltd v Milk Marketing Board* [1985] 1 CMLR 6 para 15.

[140] *Bulmer Ltd v Bollinger SA* [1974] 1 Ch 401 at 424D–E, per Lord Denning MR.

[141] *Geraldine Patricia Prince v Rt Honourable George Younger* [1984] 1 CMLR 723 para 19 (Court of Session). See also *Church of Scientology of California v Commissioners of Customs & Excise* [1980] 3 CMLR 114 para 16 (appeal hearing).

[142] *Lord Bethell v Sabena* [1983] 3 CMLR 1 paras 32–35.

[143] Joined Cases 36/80 and 71/80 *Irish Creamery Milk Suppliers Association v Ireland* [1981] ECR 735 paras 6–9; Case 14/86 *Pretore di Salò v Persons Unknown* [1987] ECR 2545 paras 8–14; *R v Minister of Agriculture Fisheries & Food and the Secretary of State for Health, ex p Fedesa* [1988] 3 CMLR 661 paras 37–38, per Henry J.

[144] [1987] 3 CMLR 951.

[145] Case 72/83 *Campus Oil v Minister for Industry and Energy* [1984] ECR 2727 para 10; applied in Case 14/86 *Pretore di Salò v Persons Unknown* [1986] ECR 2545 para 11; and see, in particular, the comments on *Bulmer Ltd v Bollinger SA* (above) made by Advocate-General Mancini at p 2557.

Assumed facts A reference may be made on the basis of assumed facts, for example because the national court decides that it is appropriate to settle a particular legal issue before embarking on a complex factual analysis.[146]

Criminal cases In *Henn and Darby v Director of Public Prosecutions*[147] Lord Diplock stated that:

> ... in a criminal trial upon indictment it can seldom be a proper exercise of the presiding judge's discretion to seek a preliminary ruling before the facts of the alleged offence have been ascertained, with the result that the proceedings will be held up for nine months or more[148] in order that at the end of the trial he may give to the jury an accurate instruction as to the relevant law, if the evidence turns out in the event to be as was anticipated at the time the reference was made—which may not always be the case. It is generally better ... that the question be decided by [the judge] in the first instance and reviewed hereafter if necessary through the hierarchy of the national courts.

These observations apply with added force to trials before magistrates.[149] However, where the prosecution's case is based on provisions of Community law, which the defence argues are invalid, an early reference may be desirable. As His Honour Judge Balston stated in *R v Lomas*:[150]

> To subject the defendant to a trial and the possibility of conviction on the basis of EEC law which may well turn out to be defective and of no effect is not only a waste of time and money and unfair to the defendant but to some might appear so farcical as to bring the law into disrepute.

Furthermore, where the issues of fact are not substantially in dispute, the Crown Courts or magistrates' courts are fully entitled to refer questions of Community law to the Court of Justice if they consider that an answer to those questions is necessary.[151] The unfortunate consequences of not making a reference in cases of this kind can be seen from *R v Tymen*, where the defendant was prosecuted for using fishing nets with meshes which were too small to comply with the requirements of regulations in the Fishing Nets (North East Atlantic) Order 1977, as amended. The facts were undisputed, but the defendant argued that the regulations were contrary to Community law. The Crown Court refused a reference to the Court of Justice,[152] imposed a fine on the defendant and forfeited the offending nets. On appeal, the Court of Appeal referred questions to the Court of Justice to ascertain whether the regulations were

---

[146] Case C-127/92 *Enderby v Frenchay Health Authority* [1993] ECR I-5535 paras 7–12; para 16 of the Opinion of Advocate-General Fennelly in Case C-90/96 *Petrie v Università degli Studi di Verona*, delivered on 20 March 1997. See also para 7 of the *Notes for Guidance on References by National Courts for Preliminary Rulings* issued by the Court of Justice. Reproduced at Appendix H.

[147] [1981] AC 850 at 904E–F.

[148] In 1996 the average duration of preliminary ruling proceedings before the Court of Justice was 20.8 months.

[149] *R v Plymouth Justices, ex p Rogers* [1982] QB 863 at 871B–C, per Lord Lane CJ.

[150] [1990] 1 CMLR 513 at 517.

[151] See *R v Plymouth Justices, ex p Rogers* [1982] QB 863; *Portsmouth City Council v Richards and Quietlynn Ltd* [1989] 1 CMLR 673 at 704.

[152] *R v Tymen* [1980] 3 CMLR 101 (Crown Court).

contrary to Community law.[153] The ruling by the Court of Justice was to the effect that the regulations were invalid and the conviction contrary to Community law.[154] An early reference by the Crown Court would have avoided the need for an appeal to the Court of Appeal and the defendant would not have been fined and had his nets forfeited.

(b) Guidelines as to the exercise of discretion

General approach In *Bulmer Ltd v Bollinger SA*[155] Lord Denning MR stated that:

> Unless the point is really difficult and important, it would seem better for the English judge to decide it himself...

This encourages national courts to think of themselves as an integral part of the Community judicial system, capable of considering and deciding questions of Community law for themselves.

However, the approach proposed by Sir Thomas Bingham MR in *R v International Stock Exchange, ex p Else Ltd*[156] had a different emphasis. He stated that:

> ... I understand the correct approach in principle of a national court (other than a final court of appeal) to be quite clear: if the facts have been found and the Community law issue is critical to the court's final decision, the appropriate course is ordinarily to refer the issue to the Court of Justice unless the national court can with complete confidence resolve the issue itself. In considering whether it can with complete confidence resolve the issue itself the national court must be fully mindful of the differences between national and Community legislation, of the pitfalls which face a national court venturing into what may be an unfamiliar field, of the need for uniform interpretation throughout the Community and of the great advantages enjoyed by the Court of Justice in construing Community instruments. *If the national court has any real doubt, it should ordinarily refer.* (emphasis added)

This latter dictum is often relied on by both counsel and judges.[157] However, it appears unduly restrictive and is very close to the mandatory obligation to make references which is imposed on courts of last resort.[158] Indeed, Sir Thomas Bingham indicated that his analysis was based, *inter alia*, on Case

---

[153] *R v Tymen* [1981] 2 CMLR 544 (CA).

[154] Case 269/80 *R v Tymen* [1981] ECR 3079 (ECJ).

[155] [1974] Ch 401 at 424F.

[156] [1993] QB 534 at 545C–G. See also the judgment of Sir Thomas Bingham MR in *Society of Lloyd's v John Stewart Clementson* [1995] 1 CMLR 693 para 18.

[157] For example, see *R v Minister of Agriculture, Fisheries and Food, ex p National Federation of Fishermen's Organisations* [1994] 1 CMLR 907 paras 24–25; *Re Aktiebolaget Draco* (1996), *The Times*, 27 March. See also *R v Ministry of Agriculture, Fisheries and Food, ex p Portman Agrochemicals Ltd* [1994] 3 CMLR 18 paras 17–18 where, in the context of an application to the Court of Appeal for leave to appeal from the Divisional Court, the Court of Appeal stated that it should not refuse leave unless it could 'with complete confidence' resolve the issue of Community law itself.

[158] The mandatory obligation to make preliminary references placed on courts of last resort is discussed below at pp 224–228.

283/81 *CILFIT*,[159] the leading judgment of the Court of Justice on the obligation to refer imposed on courts of last resort. By placing such a heavy emphasis on how clear the interpretation of the relevant Community law issue is, national courts may fail to give proper weight to the large number of other factors which might be relevant when deciding whether to make a reference.[160] Certainly, the clarity of the Community law issue is an important factor for a national court to take into account in deciding whether to make a reference; however, it should always be remembered that the Court of Justice has held that national courts have the 'widest discretion' in deciding whether or not to refer questions to the Court of Justice.[161] National courts should not be afraid to decide points of Community law without the help of the Court of Justice. Indeed, if every question of Community law which is not absolutely clear were referred to the Court of Justice, that Court would very quickly become overloaded.[162]

Similarly, it is relatively common for courts which are not courts of last resort to consider whether an issue is *acte clair* when deciding whether or not to make a reference. However, strictly speaking, the doctrine of *acte clair* is only relevant to courts of last resort, as it is an exception to the obligation which lies on such courts to refer questions of Community law to the Court of Justice. As it is an exception to the obligation to refer, the principle of *acte clair* is formulated very narrowly.[163] Although courts which are not courts of last resort might find it useful to refer to the doctrine of *acte clair* as guidance, it is important that they should not treat it as a principle binding upon them. National courts have the widest discretion in deciding whether or not to make a reference and are entitled to decide even difficult issues of Community law if they consider that it is appropriate to do so in all the circumstances of the case.

In Case C-338/95 *Wiener v Hauptzollamt Emmerich*[164] Advocate-General Jacobs suggested that national courts should show a 'greater measure of self-restraint' in deciding whether or not to order a preliminary reference to the Court of Justice. He considered that:

> A reference will be most appropriate where the question is one of general importance and where the ruling is likely to promote the uniform application of the law throughout the European Union. A reference will be least appropriate where there is an established body of case-law which could readily be transposed to the facts of the instant case; or where the question turns on a narrow point considered in the light of a

---

[159] [1982] ECR 3415.

[160] For this reason the approach adopted by Bingham J (as he then was) in *Customs and Excise Commissioners v ApS Samex* [1983] 1 All ER 1042 at 1055g–1056h appears preferable. See also the judgment of Lord Denning MR in *Bulmer Ltd v Bollinger SA* [1974] 1 Ch 401 at 422D–426E for a non-exhaustive list of relevant considerations.

[161] Case 166/73 *Rheinmülen v Einfuhr- und Vorratsstelle Getreide* [1974] ECR 33 paras 2–4. This discretion cannot be fettered by any national rules or judicial authority: see *Lord Bethell v Sabena* [1983] CMLR 1 para 12; Case C-312/93 *Peterbroeck v Belgium* [1995] ECR I-4599 para 13; Joined Cases C-430/93 and C-431/93 *Van Schijndel v SPF* [1995] ECR I-4705 para 18.

[162] *Bulmer Ltd v Bollinger SA* [1974] 1 Ch 401 at 424B–C, per Lord Denning MR.

[163] See below at p 227.

[164] Paragraphs 12–20 of the Opinion of 10 July 1997.

very specific set of facts and the ruling is unlikely to have any application beyond the instant case. Between those two extremes there is of course a wide spectrum of possibilities; nevertheless national courts themselves could properly assess whether it is appropriate to make a reference...

Delay/costs In 1996 the average length of time between lodging a request for a reference with the Court of Justice and the judgment of the Court of Justice was 20.8 months.[165] In order to save time and costs, it may therefore be best for the national judge to decide the issue of Community law himself rather than seeking a preliminary ruling.[166] A reference is more likely to be made where the party who will suffer from any delay is the party asking for the reference.[167]

However, where a reference to the Court of Justice is inevitable at some stage, an early reference may actually save time and costs. As Bingham J stated in *Customs & Excise Commissioners v APS Samex*:[168]

> The reference to the Court of Justice would be unlikely to take longer than appeals have normally taken to reach the Court of Appeal, at least until recently, and unlikely to cost much more. If, at the Court of Appeal stage, a reference were held to be necessary, the delay and expense would be roughly doubled.

Parties' wishes If both parties want the point to be referred to the Court of Justice, the national court should have regard to their wishes but it should not give them undue weight. It will be rare for the national court to disagree with the parties.[169] However, in *Portsmouth City Council v Richards and Quietlynn*[170] Kerr LJ stated that:

> It is very important that the concept of so-called references by consent should not creep into our practice. All references are by the court. The court must itself be satisfied of the need for the reference, that the factual material accompanying the reference is sufficient to provide a proper foundation for it, and that it is of sufficient assistance to the European Court to enable it to reach a decision...

---

[165] This figure is taken from the Weekly Summaries of the Court of Justice, Number 36 of 1996.

[166] *Bulmer Ltd v Bollinger SA* [1974] 1 Ch 401 at 423G–424A, per Lord Denning MR; *R v Ministry of Agriculture, Fisheries and Food, ex p Portman Agrochemicals Ltd* [1994] 3 CMLR 18 paras 19–21; *Adams v Lancashire County Council* (1996) *The Times*, 25 January.

[167] Per Lloyd LJ in *Generics UK Ltd v Smith-Kline and French Laboratories Ltd* [1990] 1 CMLR 416 at 435.

[168] [1983] 1 All ER 1042 at 1056f–g. See also *R v The Pharmaceutical Society of Great Britain, ex p the Association of Pharmaceutical Importers* [1987] 3 CMLR 951 at 972, per Kerr LJ, who stated:
> On the view which I take I would respectfully expect the House of Lords to feel bound to make a reference under the last paragraph of Article 177 in any event. On that basis an immediate reference by this court will obviously save considerable time and costs.

See also MacPherson J in *R v Her Majesty's Treasury, ex p Daily Mail* [1987] 2 CMLR 1 at 4. For delays in the prosecution of a criminal trial, see *R v Manchester Crown Court, ex p Acting DPP* [1992] 3 CMLR 329 at 345, per Leggatt LJ.

[169] See also *R v Ministry of Agriculture, Fisheries and Food, ex p Portman Agrochemicals Ltd* [1994] 3 CMLR 18 paras 19–21, where the main parties did not want a reference to be made, but interveners did.

[170] [1989] 1 CMLR 673 at 708.

General importance of Community law issue Where the issue raised is important for the Community as a whole, this will militate in favour of making a reference to the Court of Justice. As Kerr LJ stated in *R v The Pharmaceutical Society of Great Britain, ex p Association of Pharmaceutical Importers:*[171]

> There can equally be no doubt that the case is one of great general importance, not only for this country but for the Community in general, and that the Court of Justice in Luxembourg is in a far better position to reach a decision which is *communautaire* than this Court.

Pursuant to article 20 of the Protocol of the Statute of the Court of Justice (EC), all the Member States, the Commission and, where the validity or interpretation of an act of the Council is in issue, the Council, are entitled to make written and oral observations to the Court of Justice in the context of preliminary ruling proceedings.[172] Consequently, it is a material consideration, in referring a question to the Court of Justice, that where the interests of other Member States and the Community institutions are affected they should be entitled to make their views known to the Court.[173]

Parallel proceedings If there are parallel actions in other Member States there is a risk that different decisions will be made, thus compromising the uniform interpretation of Community law. In such circumstances it may be best to refer the matter to the Court of Justice.[174]

Similarly, where proceedings under article 169 of the EC Treaty [new art 226] have been brought by the Commission concerning a point similar or identical to one before the English court, a reference under article 177 [new art 234] may be appropriate so that the direct action and the indirect action can be heard on the same or successive days.[175]

Languages The special position of the Court of Justice is relevant where there is a need to examine the relevant Community text in different languages. As Bingham J stated in *Customs and Excise Commissioners v APS Samex:*[176]

> Where comparison falls to be made between Community texts in different languages, all texts being equally authentic, the multinational Court of Justice is equipped to carry out the task in a way which no national judge, whatever his linguistic skills, could rival.

---

[171] [1987] 3 CMLR 951 at 972. See also Nolan LJ in *R v IRC, ex p Commerzbank* [1991] 3 CMLR 633 at 646; and Bingham J in *Customs and Excise Commissioners v APS Samex* [1983] 1 All ER 1042 at 1056.

[172] See below at p 234.

[173] See *Customs and Excise Commissioners v APS Samex* [1983] 1 All ER 1042 at 1055h–j, per Bingham J. See also *R v The Pharmaceutical Society of Great Britain, ex p the Association of Pharmaceutical Importers* [1987] 3 CMLR 951 at 971, per Kerr LJ.

[174] For example, see *EMI Records v CBS* [1975] 1 CMLR 285 para 33.

[175] See Neill J in *An Bord Bainne Co-operative Ltd v Milk Marketing Board* [1985] 1 CMLR 6 paras 9 and 11 (but here no reference was made since all the relevant issues of fact had not been resolved and the judge considered that he could not formulate precisely all the questions on which a ruling was sought).

[176] [1983] 1 All ER 1042 at 1055j–1056a. Approved by the Court of Appeal in *R v Commissioners of Customs and Excise, ex p EMU Tabac Sarl* [1997] EuLR 153 at 160F–162A.

Purposive/teleological approach The canons of interpretation applicable to Community law are different from the strict, literal approach normally followed by the English courts. The Court of Justice will generally be in a better position than the national court to apply a purposive approach to the interpretation of Community law measures.[177]

Temporal limitations Where a particular interpretation of a Community provision would have severe economic consequences for third parties or for Member States, overriding considerations of legal certainty may dictate that the interpretation should have an effect *ex nunc* (from the date of the judgment) rather than *ex tunc* (from the date of the adoption of the Community provision). Consequently, it is a material consideration, in deciding whether to refer, that the Court of Justice alone has power to impose limitations on the time its judgments are to take effect.[178]

Point is raised in good faith A reference to the Court of Justice is unlikely where the question is being raised mischievously in order to obstruct or delay an almost inevitable adverse judgment, thus denying the other party his remedy.[179]

Binding national precedent The fact that, under domestic law, a court or tribunal is bound on points of law by the rulings of a superior court cannot, as a matter of Community law, prevent the inferior court or tribunal from seeking a preliminary ruling from the Court of Justice.[180] Thus, the fact that the House of Lords has previously considered a particular issue of Community law cannot prevent an inferior English court or tribunal making a reference to the Court of Justice on the same issue.

Inferior courts or tribunals Although magistrates' courts or inferior tribunals have the same discretion to refer a case to the Court of Justice as the High Court or the Crown Court, they should exercise considerable caution before referring, even after they have heard all the evidence. As Lord Lane CJ stated in *R v Plymouth Justices, ex p Rogers*:[181]

> If they come to a wrong decision on Community law, a higher court can make the reference and frequently the higher court would be the more suitable forum to do so. The higher court is as a rule in a better position to assess whether any reference is desirable. On references the form of the question referred is of importance and the higher court will normally be in a better position to assess the appropriateness of the question and to assist in formulating it clearly.

---

[177] *Customs and Excise Commissioners v APS Samex* [1983] 1 All ER 1042 at 1056a–b, per Bingham J.

[178] See below at pp 240–241 in relation to temporal limitations of the Court of Justice's judgments.

[179] See, generally, MacPherson J in *R v HM Treasury, ex p Daily Mail* [1987] 2 CMLR 1 at 4; see also Bingham J in *Customs and Excise Commissioners v APS Samex* [1983] 1 All ER 1042 at 1056d.

[180] Case 166/73 *Rheinmülen v Einfuhr- und Vorratsstelle Getreide* [1974] ECR 33. See also *Feehan v Commissioners of Customs and Excise* [1995] 1 CMLR 193 para 13.

[181] [1982] 3 CMLR 221 para 28.

(c) Appeal against the decision to refer or not to refer

Existence of an appeal The Court of Justice has indicated that although the national court has the widest discretion whether or not to make a reference, article 177 of the EC Treaty [new art 234] does not preclude the exercise of the discretion being subject to an appeal.[182]

Procedural rules A decision by the High Court to make a reference is deemed to be a final decision, and an appeal against the order lies to the Court of Appeal without leave. The notice of appeal[183] must be served within 14 days and not the usual 28 days.[184] However, if the judge refuses to make a reference, his decision is interlocutory and leave to appeal is necessary from the judge or from the Court of Appeal.[185] The normal period of 28 days for service of the notice of appeal applies.[186]

No special rules apply in relation to appeals against decisions to refer or not to refer made by courts other than the High Court.[187]

Nature of review by appellate court On appeal from an order or refusal to refer, an appellate court may not exercise an independent discretion of its own. It must defer to the lower court's exercise of discretion and must not interfere with it merely upon the ground that the members of the appellate court would have exercised the discretion differently. Only after the appellate court has reached the conclusion that the lower court's exercise of discretion must be set aside is it entitled to exercise an original discretion of its own.[188] As Stevenson LJ stated in *Bulmer Ltd v Bollinger SA*[189] the Court of Appeal will interfere with the exercise of judicial discretion to refer or not to refer 'when and only when the judge's decision ... exceeds the generous ambit within which reasonable disagreement is possible and is, in fact, plainly wrong'. Similarly, Lord Lane CJ stated in *R v Plymouth Justices, ex p Rogers*[190] that the Divisional Court would only interfere with the decision of a magistrates' court to refer 'as long as they have not misdirected themselves in law or acted unreasonably'. The Court of Appeal will, it seems, interfere with a judge's discretion to make a reference where it considers that the answer to the question is obvious and it is, therefore,

---

[182] Case 146/73 *Rheinmülen v Einfuhr- und Vorratsstelle Getreide* [1974] ECR 139 para 3.

[183] See Precedent E.

[184] RSC Ord 114, r 6 and 114/1–6/17.

[185] Supreme Court Act 1981, s 18(1)(h).

[186] RSC Ord 59, r 4.

[187] See Anderson, *References to the European Court* (Sweet & Maxwell, 1995), at 7–089 to 7–106.

[188] *Hadmor Productions v Hamilton* [1983] 1 AC 191 at 220, per Lord Diplock. See the High Court of Justiciary on appeal from the Sheriff Court in *Procurator Fiscal Elgin v James Cowie* [1990] 3 CMLR 445 para 20:

> ... although this court might not have thought it appropriate at this stage to seek a preliminary ruling from the European Court of Justice if we had been sitting as a court of first instance, we are clearly of opinion that it cannot be held that the sheriff was not entitled to conclude that a preliminary ruling should be sought.

[189] [1974] Ch 401 at 431B.

[190] [1982] 3 CMLR 221 at 227.

unnecessary to seek a ruling from the Court of Justice to enable the judge to give judgment.[191]

3. MANDATORY REFERENCES

Obligation to refer A national court or tribunal is under an obligation to make a reference to the Court of Justice where:

(1) an issue of Community law (concerning interpretation or validity) is necessary for the resolution of a dispute and there is no judicial remedy against the decision of the court or tribunal on that issue; or

(2) a substantial doubt has been raised concerning the validity of a Community measure and a decision on the validity of the measure is necessary for the resolution of the dispute.

It should be noted that the obligation to refer arises only where a decision on a question of Community law is *necessary* to enable the court or tribunal to give judgment.[192]

(a) Courts of last resort

(i) Which courts are covered?

Court of last resort The third paragraph of article 177 of the EC Treaty [new art 234] states that where a question of Community law is raised before a national court or tribunal 'against whose decision there is no judicial remedy under national law' that court or tribunal must refer the issue to the Court of Justice. In Case 6/64 *Costa v ENEL*[193] the Italian National Electricity Board (ENEL) brought proceedings against Mr Costa in the Milan magistrates' court in respect of his failure to pay an electricity bill. Due to the small sum of money involved there was no possibility of appeal against the decision of the court. On a reference by the magistrates' court, the Court of Justice stated that the magistrates' court was under an obligation to refer the matter to the Court as there was no judicial remedy against its decision. This indicates that the final court or tribunal means the highest court or tribunal in the particular case, rather than the highest court or tribunal in the country.[194]

Therefore, in the context of the English legal system, it is not simply the House of Lords which is under an obligation to refer matters to the Court of Justice. Any court or tribunal from whose judgment there is no possibility of

---

[191] See *R v International Stock Exchange of the United Kingdom and the Republic of Ireland, ex p Else (1982) Ltd* [1993] QB 534.

[192] The circumstances in which resolution of an issue of Community law is 'necessary' to enable a national court to give judgment are discussed above at pp 214–218.

[193] [1964] ECR 585 at 592. See also Case 107/76 *Hoffmann-La Roche v Centrafarm* [1977] ECR 957 paras 3 and 6, and the judgment of Advocate-General Capotorti at 979–980.

[194] At paras 25–28 of his Opinion in Case C-337/95 *Parfums Christian Dior v Evora* (Opinion of 29 April 1997), Advocate-General Jacobs indicated that a court of last resort was not obliged to make a reference to the Court of Justice on the first occasion that a case came before it, provided it would have a further opportunity to do so prior to taking a final decision.

appeal or other form of review will be under an obligation to make a reference. Thus, where there is no possibility of an appeal to the House of Lords from a decision of the Court of Appeal, the Court of Appeal will be the court of last resort (for example, where it refuses to grant leave to apply for judicial review or refuses leave to appeal to the Court of Appeal itself from a decision of a lower court).[195]

Leave to appeal Where an appeal lies from a lower court to a higher court only where leave to appeal is granted by either court, it is the higher court which is the court of last resort within the meaning of the third paragraph of article 177 [new art 234]. In deciding whether or not to grant leave, the higher court should therefore consider whether an issue of Community law arises which is necessary for the resolution of the case. If such an issue does arise, the higher court should grant leave to appeal unless the case falls within one of the exceptions to the obligation to refer (for example, the matter is *acte clair*).[196]

Where an appeal lies from a lower court to a higher court and the lower court has the power to prevent absolutely an appeal from its decision[197] the lower court is the court of last resort and should be obliged to refer any necessary issue of Community law to the Court of Justice before exercising its power not to allow an appeal (unless, for example, the point of Community law is *acte clair*).[198] Where it permits an appeal to take place, it will not be the court of last resort.[199]

Judicial review Where the decision of a tribunal may be challenged by means of judicial review, it is not the court of last resort, even though it is necessary to obtain leave from the High Court before commencing judicial review proceedings.[200]

Interlocutory proceedings A court or tribunal is not required to make a reference when a question of Community law is raised in interlocutory proceedings, even where there is no judicial remedy against the interlocutory order, provided the parties are entitled to raise the question again in the context of substantive proceedings.[201]

---

[195] *Chiron Corp v Murex Diagnostics Ltd* [1995] All ER (EC) 88 at 93b–d, per Balcombe LJ and at 94d–e, per Staughton LJ (commented on by Marie Demetriou, 'When is the House of Lords not a judicial remedy?' (1995) 20 EL Rev 628). See also *R v The Pharmaceutical Society of Great Britain, ex p The Association of Pharmaceutical Importers* [1987] 3 CMLR 951 at 969, per Kerr LJ.

[196] *Chiron Corp v Murex Diagnostics Ltd* [1995] All ER (EC) 88 at 93d and 94a–b, per Lord Balcombe, and at 95h–j, per Staughton LJ. See also *R v The Pharmaceutical Society of Great Britain, ex p The Association of Pharmaceutical Importers* [1987] 3 CMLR 951 at 969, per Kerr LJ; *Generics (UK) Ltd v Smith-Kline & French Laboratories Ltd* [1990] 1 CMLR 416 at para 71, per Lloyd LJ.

[197] For example, where the Divisional Court declines to certify a question of law as fit for consideration by the House of Lords in a criminal case.

[198] See *SA Magnavision v General Optical Council (No 2)* [1987] 2 CMLR 262.

[199] *Chiron Corp v Murex Diagnostics Ltd* [1995] All ER (EC) 88 at 95j–96a, per Staughton LJ.

[200] *Re a Holiday in Italy* [1975] 1 CMLR 184 at 188 (Decision of the National Insurance Commissioner).

[201] Case 107/76 *Hoffmann-La Roche v Centrafarm* [1977] ECR 957 para 6; Joined Cases 35/82 and 36/182 *Morson and Jhanjan v Netherlands* [1982] ECR 3723 paras 6–10; paras 23–24 of the

(ii) Exceptions to the obligation to refer imposed on courts of last resort
CILFIT In Case 283/81 *CILFIT v Ministry of Health*[202] the Court of Justice referred to three exceptions to the obligation to refer imposed on courts or tribunals of last resort. These are:

(1) where the question is irrelevant;
(2) where there has been a previous judgment of the Court of Justice on the question; and
(3) where the answer is obvious (*acte clair*).

Question is irrelevant Final courts or tribunals are not obliged to refer a question raised before them concerning the interpretation of Community law if that question is not relevant, ie if the answer to that question, regardless of what it may be, can in no way affect the outcome of the case. Thus, in *R v Licensing Authority, ex p Smith-Kline*[203] the question before the House of Lords was whether licensing authorities under the Medicines Act 1968 were entitled to make use of information supplied to them by a pharmaceutical company when they were considering whether to grant licences to market generic versions of that pharmaceutical company's drug. Lord Templeman stated that the only relevant law was English law, which did not protect the pharmaceutical companies against the use, by the licensing authority, of their confidential information. His Lordship refused a request for a preliminary ruling, stating that, in his opinion, 'no question of Community law arises in connection with confidentiality or otherwise'.

Previous judgment of the Court of Justice A previous decision by the Court of Justice in other proceedings which deals with identical or materially identical issues may deprive the obligation to refer of its purpose, although the final court is entitled to refer the same question to the Court of Justice for reconsideration by it. In *Re Sandhu*[204] the question of Community law before the House of Lords was whether a non-EEC spouse of an EEC worker was dependent for his rights of entry and residence in a Member State upon the EEC worker exercising EEC Treaty rights or whether the non-EEC spouse had an independent right under Community law. The Appellate Committee of the House of Lords granted leave to appeal on the basis that a reference was necessary, since the answer to the question was not so obvious as to leave no room for reasonable doubt. However, after the hearing by the Appellate Committee, the Court of Justice delivered a judgment in Case 267/83 *Diatta v Land Berlin*,[205] which interpreted Commun-

---

Opinion of Advocate-General Jacobs in Case C-337/95 *Parfums Christian Dior v Evora* (Opinion of 29 April 1997).

[202] [1982] ECR 3415. At paras 51–65 of his Opinion of 10 July 1997 in Case C-338/95 *Wiener v Hauptzollamt Emmerich* Advocate-General Jacobs suggested that the principles established in *CILFIT* should not be applied too strictly and that even courts of last resort should only be required to make a reference where a Community law issue of general importance has been raised and there is a genuine need for uniform interpretation.

[203] [1990] 1 AC 64. See also *Wellcome Foundation v Secretary of State for Social Services* [1988] 1 WLR 635.

[204] Decision of the House of Lords, 9 May 1985 (unreported).

[205] [1985] ECR 567.

ity law in such a way that the non-EEC spouse did not have an independent claim under Community law to remain in a Member State. The House of Lords, therefore, dismissed Mr Sandhu's appeal and declined to make a reference on the basis that the second exception in *CILFIT* applied.

Answer is obvious (*acte clair*) Where the correct application of Community law is so obvious as to leave no scope for any reasonable doubt, no reference is required. This is known as the doctrine of *acte clair*. However, before the national court reaches that conclusion it must be convinced that the matter would be equally obvious to the courts of the other Member States and to the Court of Justice, taking into account the characteristic features of Community law and the particular difficulties to which its interpretation gives rise, as follows:[206]

(1) Community legislation is drafted in several languages and the different language versions are all equally authentic. An interpretation of a provision of Community law, therefore, involves a comparison of the different language versions.[207]

(2) Even when the different language versions are entirely in accord with one another, Community law uses terminology which is peculiar to it. Legal concepts do not necessarily have the same meaning in Community law and in the law of the various Member States.

(3) Every provision of Community law must be placed in its context and interpreted in the light of the provisions of Community law as a whole, having regard to the objectives of the Community and to its state of evolution at the date on which the provision in question is to be applied.

Approach of the House of Lords The House of Lords has, in general, been mindful of its duty to refer under article 177 of the EC Treaty [new art 234][208] although it has, on occasions, refused a reference despite a question of Community law being clearly arguable. For example, in *R v London Boroughs Transport Committee, ex p Freight Transport Association Ltd*[209] and *Kirklees Borough Council v Wickes Building Supplies Ltd*[210] the House of Lords decided not to make a reference, despite reversing the Court of Appeal on a question of Community law. In *Re Sandhu*[211] Lord Bridge and Lord Templeman would have refused a reference on the basis of *acte clair*, despite the fact that they

---

[206] Case 283/81 *CILFIT v Ministry of Health* [1982] ECR 3415 paras 16–20.

[207] At para 65 of his Opinion of 10 July 1997 in Case C-338/95 *Wiener v Hauptzollamt Emmerich* Advocate-General Jacobs indicated that national courts should not be required to examine a Community measure in every one of the official Community languages. It would generally be more appropriate to adopt a purposive approach to interpretation.

[208] See, in particular, Lord Diplock in *R v Henn and Darby* [1981] AC 850 at 906A–C warning English judges 'not to be too ready to hold that because the meaning of the English text seems plain to them no question of interpretation can be involved'.

[209] [1992] 1 CMLR 5 at para 45, per Lord Templeman.

[210] [1992] 3 WLR 170 at 190C–D, per Lord Goff.

[211] Decision of the House of Lords, 9 May 1985 (unreported). See also the comments of Advocate-General Fennelly at para 38 of his Opinion in Case C-44/95 *Royal Society for the Protection of Birds* [1996] ECR I-3805.

differed from the judge at first instance and from one member of the Court of Appeal on the correct answer to the question of Community law, and despite the fact that three members of the House of Lords had concluded that the answer was not obvious.

(b) Questions of invalidity

Invalidity In Case 314/85 *Foto-Frost v Hauptzollamt Lübeck-Ost*[212] the Court of Justice has established that although national courts have the power to declare that acts of the Community institutions are valid, they do not have the power to declare such acts invalid. Consequently, where a substantial doubt is raised in the national court as to the validity of a Community measure and where it is clear that a decision on the validity of the measure is necessary for the resolution of the dispute, the national court is bound to refer the question to the Court of Justice for a preliminary ruling as to the validity of the Community measure. This obligation to refer applies to all national courts, whether or not they are courts of last resort, despite the fact that the second paragraph of article 177 of the EC Treaty [new art 234] appears to confer a general discretion on courts which are not courts of last resort as to whether or not to make a reference.

Grounds of invalidity In assessing the validity of a Community act, the Court of Justice applies the same principles as under article 173 of the EC Treaty [new art 230] (direct actions for the annulment of Community acts).[213]

Interim suspension of Community obligations National courts are competent, subject to certain conditions, to grant negative and positive interim injunctions, which have the effect of suspending the application of a Community act which the national court believes to be invalid.[214] Such interim relief should only be granted where:[215]

(1) the national court entertains serious doubts as to the validity of the relevant Community act;
(2) there is urgency, in that the interim relief is necessary to avoid serious and irreparable damage;
(3) the national court takes account of the Community interest; and
(4) the national court respects relevant decisions of the EC courts, both interlocutory and final.

If the national court grants interim relief in such circumstances, it must make a reference to the Court of Justice in relation to the validity of the relevant Community act, unless that issue is already before the Court of Justice. In its order for reference, the national court must indicate the basis upon which it

---

[212] [1987] ECR 4199 paras 11–20; Case C-27/95 *Woodspring District Council v Bakers of Nailsea* [1997] ECR I-1847 paras 19–20. See also *R v Searle* [1995] 3 CMLR 196 para 35 (CA).
[213] Grounds of invalidity are discussed at Ch 13, pp 307–324.
[214] See Ch 8, pp 161–164.
[215] Joined Cases C-143/88 and C-92/89 *Zuckerfabrik* [1991] ECR I-415 para 33, Case C-465/93 *Atlanta Fruchthandelsgesellschaft* [1995] ECR I-3761 para 51.

considers that the Court of Justice should find the Community act to be invalid.[216]

4. PROCEDURE BEFORE ENGLISH COURTS AND TRIBUNALS

(a) Application for a reference

(i) High Court and Court of Appeal

RSC, Ord 114 Order 114 of the rules governs the procedure by which the High Court and the Court of Appeal seek preliminary rulings from the Court of Justice under article 177 of the EC Treaty. An order referring a question to the Court of Justice for a preliminary ruling under article 177 may be made by the High Court or by the Court of Appeal of its own motion at any stage in a cause or matter, or on application by a party before or at the trial or hearing thereof.[217] Where the application is made before the trial or hearing, it is made by motion.[218] It is not unusual for an application for a reference to be made after the commencement of the trial or hearing.

In the High Court no order can be made except by a judge in person. Consequently, masters and district judges are not entitled to order references to the Court of Justice.[219] The order to refer must set out, in a schedule, the request for the preliminary ruling of the Court of Justice.[220] The notice of motion issued by the party applying for a reference should usually be accompanied by a draft order and schedule. If the parties agree that a reference should be made, they will usually agree on the form and content of the draft order and schedule, and submit it to the judge for approval. However, as the responsibility for making the reference rests with the court and not the parties, a decision to refer cannot be agreed by consent and the order for reference should not be expressed as having been made 'by consent'.[221]

If a reference is ordered, the Senior Master will send the Order for Reference (ie the order, schedule, judgment where appropriate and any other accompanying documents) to the Registry of the Court of Justice. However, the Senior Master does not transmit the file, unless the court otherwise orders, until the time for appealing against the order has expired or, if an appeal is entered within that time, until the appeal has been determined or otherwise disposed of.[222] Where both parties consent to a reference being made, they may waive their rights of appeal and ask the court to order the reference without waiting for the time to appeal to expire. This has the advantage of speeding up the process.

---

[216] Joined Cases C-143/88 and C-92/89 *Zuckerfabrik* [1991] ECR I-415 paras 23–24; Case C-465/93 *Atlanta Fruchthandelsgesellschaft* [1995] ECR I-3761 paras 32–36.

[217] RSC Ord 114, r 2(1).

[218] RSC Ord 114, r 2(2). See Precedent C.

[219] RSC Ord 114, r 2(3).

[220] RSC Ord 114, r 3. See Precedent D.

[221] RSC, 114/1–6/13.

[222] RSC Ord 114, r 5, and 114/1–6/18.

The proceedings in which an order is made are, unless the court otherwise orders, stayed until the Court of Justice has given a preliminary ruling on the question referred to it,[223] although proceedings may continue in respect of interlocutory matters.[224] It is not uncommon for an application for a reference to be accompanied by an application for an interim injunction to hold the position pending judgment of the Court of Justice.[225] In the case of the Court of Appeal (Criminal Division), no appeal or application for leave to appeal will, unless the court otherwise orders, be determined until the Court of Justice has given a preliminary ruling on the question referred to it.[226]

When a reference is made, costs will normally be reserved.[227]

(ii) County courts

CCR, Ord 19, r 11 The procedure for a reference for a preliminary ruling in the county court is substantially the same as in the High Court. Order 19, r 11 of the County Court Rules provides that an order may be made by the judge before or at the trial or hearing of any action or matter and either of his own motion or on the application of any party. The order must set out, in a schedule, the request for the preliminary ruling. The proceedings in which an order is made shall, unless the judge otherwise orders, be stayed until the Court of Justice has given a preliminary ruling on the question referred to it. Where an order has been made by the county court judge, a copy of it is sent to the Senior Master of the High Court for transmission to the Registrar of the Court of Justice. However, unless the judge orders otherwise, the copy will not be sent to the Senior Master until the time for appealing to the Court of Appeal against the order has expired or, if an appeal is entered within that time, until the appeal has been determined or otherwise disposed of.

(iii) Crown Court

Crown Court Rules Proceedings in which an order for reference has been made by the Crown Court must, unless the court otherwise determines, be adjourned until the Court of Justice has given its preliminary ruling on the questions referred to it. The Crown Court may, however, decide any preliminary or incidental question which may arise in the proceedings after an order but made for reference has been before a preliminary ruling has been given.[228] The content and form of the order are broadly similar to those required by RSC Ord 114.

---

[223] RSC Ord 114, r 4.

[224] See also RSC, 114/1–6/19. For an example relating to interlocutory injunctions, see the form of order in *Portsmouth City Council v Richards and Quietlynn* [1989] 1 CMLR 673 at para 141, per Sir Denys Buckley.

[225] For the principles applicable to injunctions, see Ch 8.

[226] Criminal Appeal (References to the European Court) Rules 1972 (SI No 1786), r 5.

[227] RSC 114/1–6/21.

[228] Crown Court Rules 1982 (SI No 1109), r 29.

(iv) Magistrates' courts and tribunals

Absence of formal rules No formal rules have been made for references from magistrates' courts and tribunals in England and Wales. Nevertheless, they have a wide discretion to refer questions to the Court of Justice for a preliminary ruling. References from these courts or tribunals are transmitted directly to the Registrar of the Court of Justice.

(b) Drafting the order to refer

The Order for Reference The Rules of the Supreme Court contain a prescribed form for an Order for Reference to the European Court of Justice, including a suggested form of Schedule.[229] Usually, a reference should contain the following:[230]

(1) a description of the parties and the addresses of the parties and their legal representatives;
(2) the background to the matter and the facts of the case;
(3) a summary of any judgment of a lower court;
(4) the relevant provisions of English law;
(5) the relevant provisions of Community law;
(6) the arguments of the parties on the issues of Community law;
(7) the reasons why the answers to the questions are considered necessary;
(8) the views of the referring court as to the appropriate answers to questions (if the matter has already been argued before it); and
(9) the actual questions which the national court wishes to be answered.

Whilst the necessary information may all be contained in the Schedule which accompanies the Order for Reference, it is also permissible for that information to be set out in the form of an interim judgment delivered by the referring court.[231]

A reference which contains insufficient legal and factual background may be declared inadmissible by the Court of Justice.[232]

The Order for Reference (including the Schedule and judgment where applicable) will have to be translated by the Court's translators into the other official languages of the Community. It should therefore be as concise and clear as possible.

Documents which are necessary for a proper understanding of the case, particularly the text of applicable national laws, should be appended to the Order for Reference. However, it should be borne in mind that accompanying documents are not usually translated into the other Community languages and, therefore, any essential passages from documents should be set out in the Order for Reference itself.[233]

---

[229] Prescribed form App A, No 109 (RSC Vol 2, para 110).
[230] Paragraph 6 of the *Note for Guidance on References by National Courts for Preliminary Rulings* issued by the Court of Justice (reproduced at Appendix H).
[231] For an example of such a judgment, see *Barbara Hopkins v National Power plc* [1994] 1 CMLR 147.
[232] For inadmissible references, see above at pp 210–214.
[233] Paragraph 6 of the *Note for Guidance on References by National Courts for Preliminary Rulings* issued by the Court of Justice (reproduced at Appendix H); RSC 114/1–6/15.

The questions The questions referred should be drafted so as to raise a general issue of Community law. The questions should not ask the Court of Justice to rule directly on the compatibility of a particular national measure with Community law, nor should they ask the Court to apply Community law to the particular facts of the case. If necessary, the Court of Justice will reformulate the questions referred by the national court so as to identify the particular point of Community law which is in issue.[234]

5. PROCEDURE IN THE COURT OF JUSTICE

(a) Generally

Procedural rules The procedure before the Court of Justice is governed by the Protocol on the Statute of the Court of Justice[235] which is annexed to the EC Treaty, and by the Rules of Procedure of the Court of Justice.[236] The procedure before the Court of Justice for preliminary references is the same as under direct actions, subject to adaptations necessitated by the nature of the reference for a preliminary ruling.[237] The main differences are at the written procedure stage.

Guidance to parties The Court of Justice has issued a document entitled *Notes for the guidance of Counsel in written and oral proceedings before the Court of Justice of the European Communities*[238] and *Notes for Guidance on References by National Courts for Preliminary Rulings*.[239] In addition, parties may contact the Registry to seek advice as to the appropriate practice to be followed.

Jurisdiction The Court of Justice has exclusive jurisdiction over requests for preliminary rulings under article 177 of the EC Treaty [new art 234].[240]

Procedure in brief After the order of the referring court is transmitted to the Court of Justice, the case is registered and given a number; for example, Case C-275/92 means the 275th case of 1992. After the case has been registered, it is assigned by the President of the Court to one of the judges to act as judge-rapporteur (often referred to as the 'reporting judge'). The judge-rapporteur is responsible for the conduct of the case.

Once the order has been registered in the Court of Justice, it is translated into the official languages of the Community and published in the *Official Journal of the European Communities* 'C' Series. In all cases, the order is also notified to

---

[234] For examples of how questions should be formulated, see Case C-228/94 *Atkins v Wrekin District Council* [1996] ECR I-3633 paras 7–8; Case C-329/95 *VAG Sverige* [1997] ECR I-2675 paras 16 and 17.

[235] Protocol on the Statute of the Court of Justice of the European Economic Community, signed at Brussels on 17 April 1957, as amended. See, in particular, article 20 of the Statute (reproduced at Appendix B).

[236] See, in particular, ECJ Rules of Procedure, articles 103–104 (reproduced at Appendix C).

[237] ECJ Rules of Procedure, article 103. The Rules of Procedure are discussed in detail in Ch 18.

[238] Reproduced at Appendix E.

[239] Reproduced at Appendix H.

[240] Article 168a(1) of the EC Treaty [new art 225].

the parties in the main action, to all the Member States and to the Commission. All the persons notified may submit written observations within a period of two months from the notification of the order.

Once the two-month period has expired, the written observations are translated into French (the internal working language of the Court of Justice). The judge-rapporteur prepares the Report for the Hearing, a wholly neutral document which summarises the facts of the case and the arguments put forward by the parties in their written observations. A copy of the Report for the Hearing is sent to the parties, Member States and Community institutions shortly before the oral hearing.

At the end of the oral hearing, the Advocate-General will usually indicate the date on which he intends to deliver his Opinion. Once he has delivered it, the Court will proceed to draft its judgment.

Language In preliminary reference proceedings, the language of the case is the language of the national court or tribunal which referred the matter to the Court of Justice. Thus, on a reference from an English court the language of the case will be English. The use of another of the official Community languages may be authorised for the oral procedure following a request by one of the parties to national proceedings.[241] Member States which intervene in the proceedings may submit observations in their own official language.[242]

Intervention The parties to the dispute before the referring court are automatically entitled to participate in the proceedings before the Court of Justice. The Commission, the Member States and, where the reference concerns an act for which they are responsible, the European Parliament, the Council or the European Central Bank are entitled to intervene directly in proceedings before the Court of Justice under article 177 [new art 234]. In addition, States which are parties to the EEA Agreement and the EFTA Surveillance Authority may intervene where one of the fields of application of the EEA Agreement is concerned.[243] Other parties will be permitted to participate in the proceedings before the Court of Justice only where they have formally intervened in the proceedings before the referring court.[244]

Rights of audience Member States and institutions of the Community are represented by an agent appointed for each case.[245] The parties to the proceedings before the national court may be represented before the Court of Justice by any person who is entitled to represent them in the proceedings before the referring court. Furthermore, parties to the national proceedings may also act on their own behalf in the proceedings before the Court of Justice,

---

[241] ECJ Rules of Procedure, article 29(2).
[242] Ibid article 29(3).
[243] Statute of the Court of Justice (EC), article 20.
[244] Case 6/64 *Costa v ENEL* [1964] ECR 585 at 614–615; Case C-181/95 *Biogen v Smithkline Beecham Biologicals* [1996] ECR I-717.
[245] Statute of the Court of Justice, article 17.

without being represented by a lawyer, if they have rights of audience before the referring court.[246] It is usual, however, for all parties to be represented.

(b) The written procedure

Notification After the order of the referring court has been registered at the Court of Justice, the Registrar of the Court of Justice must notify the Order for Reference to the parties, the Member States, the Commission and the other parties to the EEA Agreement and to the EFTA Surveillance Authority. The Order will also be notified to the Council or to the European Central Bank where the reference concerns an act which originates from one of them. Where the reference relates to an act which was adopted jointly by the European Parliament and the Council, the order will, in addition, be notified to those two institutions.[247] The parties notified[248] are entitled to submit statements of case (for the parties to the national proceedings) or written observations (for the intervenors) to the Court of Justice within two months of this notification.[249] The written procedure in proceedings under article 177 of the EC Treaty [new art 234] is, therefore, different from the procedure in direct actions, as there is no sequential exchange of pleadings (ie application, defence, reply and rejoinder). Parties to the proceedings before the Court of Justice must submit their written observations without seeing the observations of the other parties.

Time-limits A slip is enclosed with the notification of the Order for Reference, which should be returned to the Court of Justice, setting out the date on which the notification was received. The two-month time-limit for the submission of written observations is automatically extended by ten days in the case of the United Kingdom, on account of the distance from Luxembourg.[250] The Court has no jurisdiction to grant extensions in respect of the time periods laid down in the Rules of Procedure.

Detailed rules for reckoning periods of time are set out in the Rules of Procedure.[251] Regardless of the time of day when the parties receive the notification, time does not begin to run until the end of the day of notification. The period expires at the end of the day which, in the second month indicated by the time-limit (plus the ten-day extension on account of distance for the United Kingdom), bears the same number as the day from which time was set running. Therefore, for example, where the parties are notified of the order on 5 May, the

---

[246] ECJ Rules of Procedure, article 104(2). See para A(2)(b) of the *Notes for the guidance of Counsel in written and oral proceedings before the Court of Justice of the European Communities* (reproduced at Appendix E); para 5 of the Opinion of Advocate-General La Pergola in Case C-299/95 *Kremzow v Austria* [1997] ECR I-2629.

[247] Statute of the Court of Justice (EC), article 20.

[248] The EFTA States and the EFTA Surveillance Authority may only submit observations where the reference concerns one of the fields of application of the EEA Agreement.

[249] Statute of the Court of Justice (EC), article 20. There is no difference in form between 'statements of case' and 'written observations'; it is purely a terminological difference.

[250] ECJ Rules of Procedure, article 81(2). The relevant periods for each Member State are listed in Annex II, article 1 of the ECJ Rules of Procedure.

[251] ECJ Rules of Procedure, article 80.

period for submitting observations *prima facie* expires at midnight on 15 July.[252] Time periods include official holidays, Sundays and Saturdays, and are not suspended during judicial vacations.[253] However, if a time period ends on a Saturday, Sunday or official holiday, it is automatically extended to the end of the first following working day.[254]

Drafting the written observations There is no obligation on any of the parties to submit written observations. The parties may submit written observations and not attend the oral hearing or, alternatively, they may attend only the oral hearing. However, the Court of Justice strongly recommends the submission of written observations, as the time allowed for oral argument at the hearing is strictly limited.[255]

Since the written observations must be translated, they should be clear and concise.[256] The observations should set out the relevant facts and the relevant provisions of national law, legal argument and proposals for the answers which the Court of Justice should give to the questions referred by the national court. If a party accepts the description of the facts of the case and the relevant national law as set out in the Order for Reference, he may simply say so. If necessary, the observations may clarify or supplement the factual and legal background of the case before the referring court. However, references to additional facts or national law should be kept to a minimum, since the Court of Justice is concerned merely with the interpretation or the validity of Community law.[257]

The observations should contain the name and address of the party making them and those of the lawyer(s) representing him. They should also be dated and signed by the legal representative who has drafted them.[258] The observations may be lodged with the Registry of the Court of Justice by post[259] or in person.[260] The parties are not required to provide an address for service in Luxembourg, unlike in direct actions. In proceedings under article 177 of the EC Treaty [new art 234], service on the parties by the Registrar is usually made at the address of the party's legal representative.[261]

---

[252] Case 152/85 *Misset v Council* [1987] ECR 223; Case T-125/89 *Filtrona v Commission* [1990] ECR II-393.

[253] ECJ Rules of Procedure, article 80(1)(d) and (e).

[254] Ibid article 80(2). The relevant official holidays are listed in Annex I of the ECJ Rules of Procedure.

[255] Paragraph B(9) of *Notes for the guidance of Counsel in written and oral proceedings before the Court of Justice* (reproduced at Appendix E).

[256] See paras 6–8 of the Opinion of Advocate-General Jacobs in Case C-316/93 *Vaneetveld v Le Foyer* [1994] ECR I-763 for some general guidance as to the form which an Order for Reference should take. A model form of written observations is set out at Precedent F.

[257] See paras B(9) and B(13)(a) of *Notes for the guidance of Counsel in written and oral proceedings before the Court of Justice*.

[258] ECJ Rules of Procedure, article 37.

[259] The address is: Registry of the Court of Justice of the European Communities, L-2925 Luxembourg.

[260] Documents may be lodged with the security officers at the entrance to the Court buildings at any time of the day or night.

[261] Rules on the Internal Organisation of the Court, article 37(4).

Judge-rapporteur's preliminary report After the two-month period has expired and all the written observations have been translated, the judge-rapporteur presents a preliminary report to the other members of the Court. This report contains recommendations as to the conduct of the case (eg whether it should be heard by a chamber or by the full court, and whether the parties should be asked to provide any further information). This is a purely internal administrative document and copies of it are not provided to the parties.

Preparatory inquiries Although the Court of Justice apparently has power to order preliminary inquiries in the context of proceedings under article 177 of the EC Treaty [new art 234] in order to obtain further evidence,[262] this power is rarely exercised. It is far more common for the Court to use the more informal method of sending letters to the parties asking them to clarify or supplement particular factual or legal matters.

(c) The oral procedure

Purpose of the oral hearing The oral hearing is of particular importance in proceedings under article 177 of the EC Treaty [new art 234] as it is the only means by which the parties can comment on each other's written observations.[263] However, there is no obligation to appear at the oral hearing. Indeed, the Court of Justice may decide to dispense with the oral hearing, provided none of the parties or interveners has asked to present an oral argument.[264] The Court's current practice is to ask all participants in the proceedings to state their views as to the need for a hearing.[265]

Report for the hearing The judge-rapporteur prepares a report for the hearing summarising the facts of the case and the arguments contained in the written observations. This is circulated to the judges, the parties, the Member States and the other relevant Community institutions, before the hearing. If the report does not adequately set out the facts or the arguments, the parties should make this point in writing to the Registrar, setting out their proposed amendments. (If necessary, points concerning the report for the hearing can be made at the oral hearing itself.) The oral hearing is conducted on the basis that all the judges and parties before the Court are aware of the contents of the report for the hearing. Parties should refrain from simply repeating matters which have already been set out in the report for the hearing.

---

[262] Opinion of Advocate-General Warner in Case 51/75 *EMI Records v CBS United Kingdom* [1976] ECR 811 at 854; Case C-415/93 *Union Royale Belge des Sociétés de Football Association v Bosman* [1995] ECR I-4921 paras 52–54.

[263] The written observations are notified to all the parties once the necessary translations have been made.

[264] ECJ Rules of Procedure article 104 (4).

[265] Paragraph C(7) of the *Notes for the guidance of Counsel in written and oral proceedings before the Court of Justice of the European Communities* (reproduced at Appendix E).

Conduct of the oral hearing The parties are normally given approximately three weeks' advance warning of the date of the oral hearing. The main purpose of the oral hearing is not to repeat the written observations already made, but to supplement the written procedure. The hearing should be used to highlight points of importance, clarify difficult issues and respond to arguments raised by other parties. This latter aspect is particularly important in the context of preliminary references, as there is no opportunity to comment in writing on other parties' written observations.

The Court encourages advocates to provide copies of the notes upon which their speech will be based to the interpreters prior to the hearing. This facilitates the simultaneous interpretation of the advocate's speech.[266] Because of the use of simultaneous translation, it is vital that advocates address the Court in short sentences, using simple terms and not speaking too quickly.

Lawyers and agents wear their national robes. Barristers usually address the Court as 'My Lords'. Before the oral hearing begins, the legal representatives are usually invited to a room behind the Court to deal with any particular arrangements for the hearing. The judge-rapporteur or the Advocate-General may indicate particular matters which he would like to be developed in the oral submissions.

As a general rule, the time allowed for the speeches is usually a maximum of 30 minutes for each main party, except in cases before chambers of three judges, where the time permitted is usually limited to 15 minutes. Interveners are limited to a maximum of 15 minutes. These time-limits are rigorously enforced by the President; however, an allowance is made for any time used to reply to questions put by the Court. A party may apply for a longer period by sending a request to the Registrar at least 15 days before the hearing. The request must detail the reasons on which it is based and should indicate the amount of time being sought.[267]

After submissions have been made on behalf of each party, the judges and Advocate-General may ask questions.[268] Each speaker will then be given the opportunity to make a short reply.

Advocate-General's Opinion At the end of the oral hearing, the Advocate-General will usually indicate the date on which he intends to deliver his Opinion. It is not necessary for the parties to attend when the Opinion is delivered orally in Court. Delivery of the Opinion brings the oral procedure to an end.

---

[266] In addition, the interpreters read the case papers and relevant authorities cited in the written submissions prior to the hearing.

[267] *Notes for the guidance of Counsel in written and oral proceedings before the Court of Justice,* reproduced at Appendix E.

[268] ECJ Rules of Procedure, article 57.

(d) Judgment

Judgment The Court of Justice will then proceed to deliberate its judgment. The judgment is delivered in open court, although it is not necessary for those who made written or oral submissions to attend.

Question identical to previous ruling Where a preliminary reference is identical to a question on which the Court of Justice has already ruled, the Court may, after hearing the parties and the interveners, give its decision in the form of a reasoned order, referring to its previous judgment.[269] This procedure obviates the need to follow the full procedure leading up to judgment.

Interpretation of judgments Where the meaning of a judgment is unclear, neither the parties nor the national court which made the reference can bring an application for interpretation of the judgment under article 102 of the ECJ Rules of Procedure.[270] In this situation, the court which made the original reference must make a new reference, with the attendant delay that that involves.[271]

Delay In 1996 the average length of proceedings (from lodging of the preliminary reference with the Court of Justice to judgment) was 20.8 months.[272]

(e) Costs and legal aid

Costs It is for the national court which made the reference to decide on the costs of the reference according to its own national rules.[273] In *R v Intervention Board for Agricultural Produce, ex p Fish Producers' Organisation Ltd*[274] the Court of Appeal indicated that the cost of making a reference to the Court of Justice falls within the normal English rule that costs follow the event. Member States and Community institutions which intervene before the Court of Justice must bear their own costs.[275]

Legal aid A reference for a preliminary ruling is a step in the proceedings before the national court and, in principle, a party who is legally aided is entitled to have the national legal aid order extended to cover the proceedings before the Court of Justice.[276] Where the national authorities refuse legal aid, the Court of Justice may itself grant legal aid to facilitate the legal representation or attendance of a party.[277]

---

[269] ECJ Rules of Procedure, article 104(3).
[270] Case 40/70 *Sirena v Eda* [1979] ECR 3169. See Ch 18, p 412 for the rules concerning the interpretation of judgments delivered in direct actions.
[271] For example, see Case C-132/93 *Steen v Deutsche Bundespost* [1994] ECR I-2715.
[272] This figure is taken from the *Weekly Summaries* of the Court of Justice, Number 36 of 1996.
[273] ECJ Rules of Procedure, article 104(5); Case 62/72 *Bollmann v Hauptzollamt Hamburg-Waltershof* [1973] ECR 269.
[274] [1993] 1 CMLR 707.
[275] ECJ Rules of Procedure, article 69(4).
[276] *R v Marlborough Street Stipendiary Magistrates, ex p Bouchereau* [1977] 1 WLR 414.
[277] ECJ Rules of Procedure, article 104(5).

6. EFFECT OF PRELIMINARY RULINGS

Binding nature A preliminary ruling is binding on the national court which made the reference to the Court of Justice.[278] The referring court is not entitled to refer further questions back to the Court of Justice simply as a means of contesting the validity of the original judgment given by the Court. However, the referring court is entitled to make a further reference to the Court of Justice on a fresh question of law, where it has difficulty in understanding or applying the original judgment or where it submits new considerations which might lead the Court to give a different answer to the original question.[279]

Since the main purpose of article 177 of the EC Treaty [new art 234] is to ensure that Community law is applied uniformly by national courts, a ruling by the Court of Justice under article 177 also binds national courts other than the court which made the reference.[280] This is given effect in the United Kingdom by s 3(1) of the European Communities Act 1972, which provides that questions of Community law shall, if not referred to the Court of Justice, be decided 'in accordance with the principles laid down by and any relevant decision of' that Court. Thus, preliminary rulings by the Court of Justice are binding upon all courts in England, including the House of Lords.[281]

However, national courts are entitled to make a new reference to the Court of Justice on any question, even where the relevant issue has already been the subject of a judgment by the Court of Justice in different proceedings.[282] The Court of Justice has, on limited occasions, reconsidered its previous case-law.[283]

Where the Court of Justice declares that a Community measure is void in the context of preliminary ruling proceedings, the judgment imposes an obligation on the relevant Community institution to take the action necessary to remedy the illegality.[284]

---

[278] Case 29/68 *Milchkontor v Hauptzollamt Saarbrücken* [1969] ECR 165 para 2; Case 52/76 *Benedetti v Munari* [1977] ECR 163 para 26.

[279] Case 69/85 *Wünsche Handelsgesellschaft v Germany* [1986] ECR 947 paras 12–15. For example, see Case C-132/93 *Steen v Deutsche Bundespost* [1994] ECR I-2715 (referring court made second reference as it had difficulty understanding the original judgment).

[280] Case 66/80 *International Chemical Corporation v Amministrazione delle Finanze* [1981] ECR 1191 paras 9–13. See also the Opinion of Advocate-General Warner in Case 112/76 *Manzoni v Finrom* [1977] ECR 1647 at 1661–1663.

[281] See, in particular, the judgment of Lord Diplock in *Garland v British Rail* [1983] 2 AC 751 at 771G.

[282] Case 66/80 *International Chemical Corporation v Amministrazione delle Finanze* [1981] ECR 1191 para 14; Case 283/81 *CILFIT v Ministry of Health* [1982] ECR 3415 paras 13–15; Joined Cases C-332/92 and others *Eurico Italia v Ente Nazionale Risi* [1994] ECR I-711 paras 14–15.

[283] For example, see Case C-10/89 *CNL-Sucal v Hag GF* [1990] ECR I-3711 para 10; Joined Cases C-267/91 and C-268/91 *Keck and Mithouard* [1993] ECR I-6097 paras 15–16. See also Anthony Arnull, 'Owning up to fallibility: Precedent and the Court of Justice' [1993] 30 CML Rev 247.

[284] Joined Cases 117/76 and 16/77 *Ruckdeschel v Hauptzollamt Hamburg-St Annen* [1977] ECR 1753 paras 12–13; Case 66/80 *International Chemical Corporation v Amministrazione delle Finanze* [1981] ECR 1191 para 16.

Temporal effect A judgment of the Court of Justice in the context of proceedings under article 177 of the EC Treaty [new art 234] has retrospective effect. Thus, a preliminary ruling on the interpretation of a Community provision defines the meaning and scope of that provision as from the date when it entered into force.[285] Similarly, a ruling that a Community act is invalid takes effect as from the entry into force of that act *(ab initio)*[286]

Temporal limitations In exceptional cases, the Court of Justice may limit the retrospective effect of its judgments (concerning interpretation or validity) in the interests of legal certainty.[287] Where the Court of Justice declares that a Community measure is invalid in the context of preliminary reference proceedings, it sometimes states that the imposition of a temporal limitation is justified by analogy with article 174 of the EC Treaty [new art 231] which expressly provides for the imposition of temporal limitations in judgments under article 173 of the EC Treaty [new art 230] (actions for annulment).[288]

In general, the Court will only impose a temporal limitation on the effect of a judgment where:[289]

(1) there is a risk of serious economic repercussions owing to the large number of legal relationships already entered into in good faith on the basis of a legal provision considered to have a particular meaning or to be validly in force;[290] and

(2) both individuals and national authorities had been prompted to adopt practices which did not comply with Community law by reason of objective, significant uncertainty regarding the implications of Community provisions, to which the conduct of other Member States or the Commission may even have contributed.[291]

---

[285] Case 61/79 *Amministrazione delle Finanze v Denkavit Italiana* [1980] ECR 1205 para 16; Joined Cases C-197/94 and C-252/94 *Bautiaa and Société Française Maritime* [1996] ECR I-505 para 47.

[286] Case C-212/94 *FMC v IBAP* [1996] ECR I-389 para 55.

[287] Case 43/75 *Defrenne v Sabena* [1976] ECR 455 paras 69–75; Case 24/86 *Blaizot v University of Liège* [1988] ECR 379 paras 27–28; Case C-262/88 *Barber v Guardian Royal Exchange Assurance Group* [1990] ECR I-1889 para 41; Joined Cases C-197/94 and C-252/94 *Société Bautiaa v Directeur des Services Fiscaux des Landes* [1996] ECR I-505 paras 47–48.

[288] For example, see Case 4/79 *Providence Agricole de la Champagne v ONIC* [1980] ECR 2823 paras 44–45; Case 145/79 *Roquette Frères v France* [1980] ECR 2917 paras 50–53. Temporal limitations in the context of actions for annulment are discussed at Ch 13, pp 329–330.

[289] Joined Cases C-367 to 377/93 *Roders v Inspecteur der Invoerrechten en Accijnzen* [1995] ECR I-2229 para 43; Joined Cases C-197/94 and C-252/94 *Bautiaa and Société Française Maritime* [1996] ECR I-505 paras 47–48.

[290] In Case C-308/93 *Bestuur van de Sociale Verzekeringsbank v Cabanis-Issarte* [1996] ECR I-2097 paras 46–48 the Court of Justice limited the retrospective effect of its judgment where the Member States had indicated that it would have serious consequences for the funding of social security schemes but had not assessed, even in approximate terms, the potential financial consequences of the Court's judgment. The limitation was said to be necessary as the judgment modified the Court's previous case-law which had been relied on by both Member States and private parties.

[291] See fn 30 to para 43 of the Opinion of Advocate-General Cosmas in Joined Cases C-197/94 and C-252/94 *Bautiaa and Société Française Maritime* [1996] ECR I-505 for a discussion of what constitutes 'objective, significant uncertainty'.

The fact that a government might suffer significant financial loss is not enough in itself to justify limiting the effects of a judgment of the Court.[292]

The Court of Justice may impose a temporal limitation on the effects of its judgment in a number of ways. It may decide that its judgment will only apply prospectively:[293]

(1) for all persons;
(2) for all persons except the parties to the main proceedings before the referring court; or
(3) for all persons except those who have brought court proceedings or raised an equivalent claim under the applicable national law before the date of the judgment.[294] It appears that the notion of an 'equivalent claim' is not necessarily limited to the commencement of court proceedings. In Case C-228/92 *Roquette Frères v Hauptzollamt Geldern*[295] all persons who had submitted administrative complaints prior to the date of the Court of Justice's judgment were entitled to rely on that judgment.

It is for the Court of Justice alone to decide whether any temporal limitation should be placed on its ruling.[296] A request for the Court to impose a temporal limitation on its judgment may be made in the course of submissions at the oral hearing. It is not necessary to make such a request in the written observations.[297] However, a temporal restriction on the effects of a judgment may only be imposed in that actual judgment. The Court cannot restrict the temporal effect of a judgment in a later judgment.[298]

---

[292] Joined Cases C-367/93 to C-377/93 *Roders v Inspecteur der Invoerrechten en Accijnzen* [1995] ECR I-2229 para 48; Joined Cases C-197/94 and C-252/94 *Société Bautiaa v Directeur des Services Fiscaux des Landes* [1996] ECR I-505 paras 54–55.

[293] Case 112/83 *Produits de maïs v Administration des Douanes* [1985] ECR 719 para 18; Case 41/84 *Pinna v Caisse d'allocations familiales de la Savoie* [1986] ECR 1 para 29.

[294] For example, see Case C-415/93 *Union Royale Belge des Sociétés de Football Association v Bosman* [1995] ECR I-4921 paras 139–146.

[295] [1994] ECR I-1445 paras 17–30.

[296] Case 309/85 *Barra v Belgium* [1988] ECR 355 para 13: Case C-110/91 *Moroni v Collo* [1993] ECR I-6591 para 32.

[297] Footnote 26 to para 40 of the Opinion of Advocate-General Cosmas in Joined Cases C-197/94 and C-252/94 *Bautiaa and Société Française Maritime* [1996] ECR I-505.

[298] Case C-163/90 *Administration des Douanes v Legros* [1992] ECR I-4625 para 30; Case C-57/93 *Vroege* [1994] ECR I-4541 para 31.

Part IV

Remedies in EC Courts for Breach of EC Law

Chapter 12

Proceedings Against Member States for Breach of EC Law

1. —INFRACTION PROCEEDINGS BY THE COMMISSION

(a) Introduction

Article 169 Article 169 of the EC Treaty [new art 226] provides:

> If the Commission considers that a Member State has failed to fulfil an obligation under this Treaty, it shall deliver a reasoned opinion on the matter after giving the State concerned the opportunity to submit its observations.
>
> If the State concerned does not comply with the opinion within the period laid down by the Commission, the latter may bring the matter before the Court of Justice.

Purpose of infraction proceedings One of the roles of the Commission, as defined by article 155 of the EC Treaty [new art 211], is to 'ensure that the provisions of this Treaty and the measures taken by the institutions pursuant thereto are applied'. One of the main ways in which the Commission fulfils this role as 'guardian' of the Treaty is by taking infraction proceedings under article 169 against Member States which it considers to be in breach of their Community law obligations. As the Commission is acting in the general interest of the Community, it does not need to show that it has a specific legal interest in the matter before commencing infraction proceedings.[1]

Importance to private parties Although the remedy established in article 169 [new art 226] is only available to the Commission, it is also of importance to private parties as the Commission may be alerted to the possibility that a Member State is in breach of its obligations following a complaint by a private party. The Commission has published a standard form for private parties to make complaints to it.[2]

---

[1] Case 167/73 *Commission v France* [1974] ECR 359 paras 13–16; Case C-182/94 *Commission v Italy* [1995] ECR I-1465 para 5; Case C-431/92 *Commission v Germany* [1995] ECR I-2189 para 21.

[2] OJ 1989 C26 p 6, [1989] 1 CMLR 617; reproduced in Precedent G.

The advantage to the private party is clear in terms of legal costs, as it is the Commission which brings the case. One disadvantage is that the private party has no say in the running of the case. If the Commission decides to take up the complaint and to bring infraction proceedings under article 169, the private party is not entitled to intervene in the proceedings before the Court of Justice.[3] Furthermore, the choice whether or not to bring infraction proceedings lies solely within the discretion of the Commission. An individual who has made a complaint cannot challenge a decision of the Commission not to bring infraction proceedings on the basis of that complaint, either under article 173 or 175 of the EC Treaty [new arts 230 and 232].[4]

(b) Procedural conditions of admissibility

Outline   In outline, the procedure followed in infraction proceedings under article 169 [new art 226] is as follows:

(1) the Commission considers that a Member State is in breach of its Community law obligations;

(2) the Commission writes a letter of formal notice to the Member State concerned inviting its observations;

(3) the Commission delivers a reasoned opinion; and

(4) the Commission makes an application to the Court of Justice under article 169.

Stage 1: Existence of breach

(i) Categories of breach

Categories of breach   It is not possible to give an exhaustive list of the ways in which a Member State may be found to have infringed Community law. However, it is possible to identify certain main categories of breach.[5]

Adoption of legislation   The adoption by a Member State of a national measure which is contrary to Community law will constitute a breach of the EC Treaty. For example, in Case C-246/89 *Commission v United Kingdom*[6] the United Kingdom was found to be in breach of its Treaty obligations by enacting the Merchant Shipping Act 1988, which contravened, *inter alia*, article 52 of the EC Treaty [new art 43].

---

[3] Statute of the Court of Justice, article 37. See also Case 154/85R *Commission v Italy* [1985] ECR 1753 para 3.

[4] Case 48/65 *Lütticke v Commission* [1966] ECR 19 (article 173); Case 247/87 *Star Fruit v Commission* [1989] ECR 291 paras 10–14 (article 175); C-29/92 *Asia Motor France v Commission* [1992] ECR I-3935 paras 20–21 (article 173); Case T-47/96 *SDDDA v Commission* [1996] ECR II-1559 paras 41–43 (article 175). Cf Case C-107/95P *Bilanzbuchhalter v Commission* [1997] ECR I-947 paras 23–25 (refusal by the Commission to adopt a decision pursuant to article 90(3) [new art 86(3)] may be open to challenge in certain circumstances).

[5] See Ch 1 for a discussion of the obligations imposed on Member States by the different kinds of Community legislation.

[6] [1991] ECR I-4585, part of the *Factortame* litigation.

Failure to abolish legislation The mere continued existence of conflicting national legislation will be a breach of the EC Treaty, even if the national courts would not apply it due to the existence of overriding directly applicable or directly effective Community provisions.[7] For example, in Case 167/73 *Commission v France*[8] the Court of Justice found that the French *Code du Travail Maritime* conflicted with article 48 of the EC Treaty [new art 39] and Regulation 1612/68. The Court of Justice held that:

> ... although the objective legal position is clear, namely, that Article 48 and Regulation No 1612/68 are directly applicable in the territory of the French Republic, nevertheless the maintenance in these circumstances of the wording of the Code du Travail Maritime gives rise to an ambiguous state of affairs by maintaining, as regards those subject to the law who are concerned, a state of uncertainty as to the possibilities available to them of relying on Community law.

Failure to implement Failure by a Member State to implement a directive within the implementation period will constitute a breach.[9] In Case 31/69 *Commission v Italy*[10] the Italian Government argued that a failure to implement directly applicable Community legislation constituted a pure omission, the sanction for which did not come within article 169 [new art 226]. The Court of Justice rejected this argument and held that:

> A failure to act, like a positive act, may constitute a failure on the part of a Member State to fulfil an obligation.

Failure to implement properly A breach of the EC Treaty will occur where a Member State introduces national legislation which fails fully to implement a directive.[11] In addition, Member States are under an obligation to implement Community rules in accordance with the general principles of Community law[12] and, as far as possible, in accordance with fundamental human rights.[13]

Failure to co-operate If a Member State fails to co-operate with the Commission in the course of investigations into a possible breach of Community law, that will in itself constitute a breach of the Member State's duty of co-operation which arises under article 5 of the EC Treaty [new art 10].[14]

---

[7] Case 168/85 *Commission v Italy* [1986] ECR 2945 para 11; paras 17–19 of the Opinion of Advocate-General Jacobs in Case C-151/94 *Commission v Luxembourg* [1995] ECR I-3685 paras 17–19.

[8] [1974] ECR 359 para 41.

[9] The implementation of directives is discussed at Ch 1, pp 10–14.

[10] [1970] ECR 25 paras 7–10.

[11] For example, see Case C-337/89 *Commission v United Kingdom* [1992] ECR I-6103 (the 'Drinking Water case'); Case C-392/93 *R v HM Treasury, ex p British Telecommunications* [1996] ECR I-1631. The implementation of directives is discussed at Ch 1, pp 10–14.

[12] Case 230/78 *Eridania v Ministry for Agriculture and Forestry* [1979] ECR 2749 paras 29–32; Joined Cases C-31 to 44/91 *Lageder v Amministrazione delle finanze* [1993] ECR I-1761 para 33.

[13] Case 5/88 *Wachauf v Germany* [1989] ECR 2609 paras 17–19.

[14] Case 272/86 *Commission v Greece* [1988] ECR 4875 paras 26–32; Case C-35/88 *Commission v Greece* [1990] ECR I-3125 paras 38–42; Case C-61/90 *Commission v Greece* [1992] ECR I-2407 paras 29–31; Case C-137/91 *Commission v Greece* [1992] ECR I-4023; Case C-375/92 *Commission v Spain* [1994] ECR I-923 paras 23–26.

Failure to notify Certain directives impose a specific obligation on the Member States to inform the Commission of the measures which they have adopted to implement the directive. A Member State will be in breach of that obligation if it fails to provide information which is sufficiently clear and precise to allow the Commission to ascertain whether the directive has been properly implemented.[15] Where a Member State has failed to adopt the measures necessary to implement a directive, the Court of Justice will not make a separate finding of failure to comply with the obligation to communicate such measures to the Commission. It will simply make the primary finding of failure to implement.[16]

Breach of international agreements The Court of Justice has jurisdiction under article 169 to declare that a Member State has failed to comply with an international agreement concluded by the Community.[17]

(ii) Breach must be by a Member State

Wide definition of 'the State' Article 169 [new art 226] deals with breaches of Community law by a Member State. In Case 77/69 *Commission v Belgium*[18] the Court of Justice held that:

> ... the liability of a Member State under Article 169 arises whatever the agency of the State whose action or inaction is the cause of the failure to fulfil its obligations, even in the case of a constitutionally independent institution.

National Parliament A Member State is liable for the failure of its national Parliament to adopt legislation required by Community law. In Case 77/69 *Commission v Belgium*[19] the Belgian Government had placed a draft law before the national Parliament to rectify the situation complained of by the Commission. However, practical difficulties, notably the dissolution of the Belgian Parliament, had prevented the draft law being adopted. The Belgian Government argued that the delay in enacting the law amounted to a case of *force majeure*. This argument was rejected by the Court of Justice in the terms quoted above.

Local or regional entities A Member State is responsible for breaches of Community law caused by local or regional authorities. For example, in Case C-211/91 *Commission v Belgium*[20] the Belgian Government was held liable for

---

[15] Case 96/81 *Commission v Netherlands* [1982] ECR 1791 paras 7–8.

[16] Case C-303/93 *Commission v Italy* [1994] ECR I-1901 para 6; Case C-255/93 *Commission v France* [1994] ECR I-4949 para 29; Case C-365/93 *Commission v Greece* [1995] ECR I-499 paras 11–12; Case C-147/94 *Commission v Spain* [1995] ECR I-1015 paras 6–7.

[17] Case C-61/94 *Commission v Germany* [1996] ECR I-3989 paras 15–16.

[18] [1970] ECR 237 para 15. See also Case 8/70 *Commission v Italy* [1970] ECR 961 paras 8–9; Case 52/75 *Commission v Italy* [1976] ECR 277 para 14.

[19] [1970] ECR 237 para 15. See also, for example, Case 8/70 *Commission v Italy* [1970] ECR 961; Case 52/75 *Commission v Italy* [1976] ECR 277.

[20] [1992] ECR I-6757. See also Case C-42/89 *Commission v Belgium* [1990] ECR I-2821; Case C-362/90 *Commission v Italy* [1992] ECR I-2353; Case C-33/90 *Commission v Italy* [1991] ECR I-5987 paras 22–27. Cf Case C-8/88 *Germany v Commission* [1990] ECR I-2321 paras 12–13.

a decree passed by the Flemish regional government which was contrary to the EC Treaty rules on the freedom to provide services.

In Case C-431/92 *Commission v Germany*[21] the Commission brought an application under article 169 [new art 226] on the basis that the *Regierungspräsidium* (District Office) Darmstadt had granted consent for the construction of a power station without following the procedures required by the Environmental Impact Assessment Directive, which had not been implemented into German law as required. Germany submitted that the action was inadmissible on the ground that proceedings could be initiated under article 169 only in respect of a general failure to implement a directive correctly or at all, and not simply in respect of a failure to apply the requirements of a directive which had not yet been implemented to the facts of a specific case. This argument was rejected by the Court of Justice. The Court also dismissed Germany's arguments that the application was inadmissible on the basis that the relevant provisions of the directive did not have direct effect.

The action under article 169 must always be brought against the government of the Member State in question, even if the breach of Community law is due to the action or omission of a local or regional body.[22]

National courts Advocate-General Warner, in Case 9/75 *Meyer-Burckhardt v Commission*,[23] stated:

> It is trite law in this Court that compliance with the provisions of Community law is required of all the organs of a Member State, be they executive, legislative or judicial.[24]

However, he recognised that proceedings against a Member State for failure by one of its courts to comply with Community law should not be undertaken lightly by the Commission. In that case, the Advocate-General considered the obligation imposed by article 177 of the EC Treaty [new art 234] on national courts of last resort to make preliminary references to the Court of Justice. He stated:

> The third paragraph of Article 177 imposes an obligation that is as binding on Member States as any other obligation undertaken by them under the Treaty, for aught that compliance with it is a matter for their judicial organs.

In Case 30/77 *R v Bouchereau*[25] Advocate-General Warner reiterated that Member States could be held liable for breaches of Community law by their national courts. However, he refined the notion of breach occasioned by a national court as follows:

> It is obvious on the other hand that a Member State cannot be held to have failed to fulfil an obligation under the Treaty simply because one of its Courts has reached a wrong decision. Judicial error, whether due to the misapprehension of facts or to

---

[21] [1995] ECR I-2189 paras 19–26.
[22] Case C-95/97 *Région Wallonne v Commission* [1997] ECR I-1787 para 7.
[23] [1975] ECR 1171 at 1187. See also Joined Cases C-46/93 and C-48/93 *Brasserie du Pêcheur and Factortame* [1996] ECR I-1029 para 34.
[24] See Ch 2, pp 52–55.
[25] [1977] ECR 1999, Opinion of Advocate-General Warner at 2020.

misapprehension of the law, is not a breach of the Treaty. In the judicial sphere, Article 169 could only come into play in the event of a court of a Member State deliberately ignoring or disregarding Community law.

In practice, given the importance of the independence of the judiciary within the national constitutions of each Member State, the Commission is very reluctant to commence proceedings against Member States for the actions of their courts.

Commercial undertakings The Court of Justice has considered the question of what constitutes the 'State' in the context of the vertical direct effect of directives.[26] In Case 188/89 *Foster v British Gas*[27] the Court of Justice indicated that 'organizations or bodies which were subject to the authority or control of the State or had special powers beyond those which result from the normal rules applicable to relations between individuals' should be very wide. For example, it appears that the United Kingdom could arguably be held responsible under article 169 for breaches of Community law committed by public utilities.[28]

In Case 249/81 *Commission v Ireland*[29] the Irish Government was held to be responsible for the acts of a private company, the Irish Goods Council, as the Government had appointed the members of the company's management committee, granted the company public subsidies and defined the general scope and nature of the company's activities.

Stage 2: Letter of formal notice

Purpose of letter of formal notice Before it may commence infraction proceedings in the Court of Justice under article 169 [new art 226], the Commission must first send the Member State concerned a letter of formal notice inviting it to make observations on the alleged breach of Community law. The purpose of this pre-litigation procedure is twofold: first, it gives the Member State concerned an opportunity to comply with its obligations under Community law; and, secondly, it allows the State to avail itself of its right of defence against the complaints made by the Commission.[30]

Contents of letter The letter of formal notice must clearly define the subject-matter of the dispute and indicate the factors necessary for the Member State to prepare its defence.[31] However, the letter need not be as detailed as the reasoned opinion which constitutes the next stage of infraction proceedings. Indeed, the Court of Justice has recognised that the initial letter 'of necessity will contain only an initial brief summary of the complaints'.[32]

---

[26] See Ch 4, pp 72–77.

[27] [1990] ECR I-3313 para 18.

[28] See *Foster v British Gas* [1991] 2 AC 306, in which the House of Lords held that British Gas was part of the State for the purposes of the vertical direct effect of a directive. See also Case C-173/94 *Commission v Belgium* [1996] ECR I-3265.

[29] [1982] ECR 4005.

[30] Case 293/85 *Commission v Belgium* [1988] ECR 305 para 13.

[31] Case 211/81 *Commission v Denmark* [1982] ECR 4547 para 8; Case 51/83 *Commission v Italy* [1984] ECR 2793 para 4; Case 274/83 *Commission v Italy* [1985] ECR 1077 para 19.

[32] Case 274/83 *Commission v Italy* [1985] ECR 1077 para 21; Case C-289/94 *Commission v Italy*

The Court of Justice has held that the opportunity for the Member State to submit its observations constitutes an essential guarantee required by the EC Treaty; observance of that guarantee is an essential formal requirement of the procedure under article 169 [new art 226], even if the Member State does not consider it necessary to avail itself of that opportunity.[33] If the Commission's letter of formal notice fails to identify in sufficient detail the nature and scope of the complaint, the matter will be held to be inadmissible when it comes before the Court of Justice.[34] Furthermore, the Commission cannot introduce new matters into the proceedings which were not raised in its letter of formal notice. Any attempt to do so will render consideration of the new matters inadmissible before the Court of Justice, even if the Member State has submitted observations on the basis of the 'extended' reasoned opinion.[35]

Reasonable time to respond In Case 293/85 *Commission v Belgium*[36] the Court of Justice stated:

> ... the Commission must allow Member States a reasonable period to reply to the letter of formal notice and to comply with a reasoned opinion, or, where appropriate, to prepare their defence. In order to determine whether the period allowed is reasonable, account must be taken of all the circumstances of the case. Thus, very short periods may be justified in particular circumstances, especially where there is an urgent need to remedy a breach or where the Member State concerned is fully aware of the Commission's views long before the procedure starts.

The Commission argued that the time-limits laid down in the initial letter (8 days) and the reasoned opinion (15 days) were not absolute and that it would have considered replies submitted by the Belgian Government after those time-limits. The Court of Justice rejected this argument as irrelevant because a Member State cannot know in advance whether, and to what extent, the Commission will grant an extension of the time-limits it has set down. Having considered all the circumstances, the Court of Justice held that the time-limits imposed were too short. In particular, the Court held that the Commission could not rely on urgency which it had itself created by failing to take action earlier. The Court, therefore, declared the action inadmissible, as the pre-litigation procedure had not been properly carried out.

Discussions In practice, once the Commission has issued its initial letter, discussions and/or exchange of correspondence will usually take place with the Member State in an attempt to resolve the dispute.

[1996] ECR I-4405 para 16.

[33] Case 31/69 *Commission v Italy* [1970] ECR 25 para 13; Case 211/81 *Commission v Denmark* [1982] ECR 4547 para 9; Case 51/83 *Commission v Italy* [1984] ECR 2793 para 5; Case 274/83 *Commission v Italy* [1985] ECR 1077 para 20.

[34] See Case C-272/91 *Commission v Italy* [1994] ECR I-1409 paras 14–17. Contrast Case C-135/94 *Commission v Italy* [1995] ECR I-1805 paras 3–12.

[35] Case 193/80 *Commission v Italy* [1981] ECR 3019 para 12; Case 51/83 *Commission v Italy* [1984] ECR 2793 paras 6–9.

[36] [1988] ECR 305 paras 10–20.

Termination of breach before reasoned opinion issued If a Member State puts an end to the breach before the Commission issues its reasoned opinion, the Commission is not entitled to bring infraction proceedings before the Court of Justice in respect of that breach. The Court will declare any such action inadmissible.[37] However, a mere promise or undertaking by the Member State to comply with the relevant Community law obligation does not prevent the Commission from bringing infraction proceedings before the Court of Justice.[38]

Stage 3: Reasoned opinion

Delivery of a reasoned opinion If the matter has not been satisfactorily resolved after the Commission has sent its initial letter and the Member State concerned has had the opportunity to submit its observations, the Commission may continue the infraction process by delivering a reasoned opinion.

Contents of reasoned opinion The reasoned opinion must contain a coherent statement of the reasons why the Commission believes that the Member State is in breach of its Community law obligations, so that the Member State is made fully aware of the complaint being made against it.[39] However, the reasoned opinion is not required to indicate the steps which the Commission considers are necessary to eliminate the breach,[40] nor is it required to address all the counter-arguments raised by the Member State in its observations.[41]

As the opportunity for the Member State to submit its observations is an essential guarantee provided for by article 169 [new art 226], the reasoned opinion and the initial letter must be founded on the same grounds and submissions.[42] However, the Commission is entitled to set out in detail in the reasoned opinion the complaints which it has already made more generally in its initial letter of formal notice.[43] Furthermore, in its reasoned opinion the Commission may reply to defences or arguments raised by the Member State in its response to the letter of formal notice.[44]

---

[37] Case 240/86 *Commission v Greece* [1988] ECR 1835.

[38] Case C-79/94 *Commission v Greece* [1995] ECR I-1071 paras 7 and 10, see also para 15 of the Opinion of Advocate-General Lenz.

[39] Case 325/82 *Commission v Germany* [1984] ECR 777 para 8; Case C-272/91 *Commission v Italy* [1994] ECR I-1409 para 16; Case C-223/96 *Commission v France* [1997] ECR I-3201 para 12. See also Case C-431/92 *Commission v Germany* [1995] ECR I-2189 paras 16–18.

[40] Case C-247/89 *Commission v Portugal* [1991] ECR I-3659 para 22.

[41] Case 7/61 *Commission v Italy* [1961] ECR 317 at 326–327. See also paras 13–27 of the Opinion of Advocate-General La Pergola in Case C-96/95 *Commission v Germany* [1997] ECR I-1653.

[42] Cf Case C-152/89 *Commission v Luxembourg* [1991] ECR I-3141 paras 8–11, where the Court of Justice held that the application was admissible even though it was not in exactly the same terms as the reasoned opinion. This was because the conduct of the whole pre-trial procedure was such that the Luxembourg Government had not been deprived of the opportunity to reply to the point raised in the application.

[43] Case C-289/94 *Commission v Italy* [1996] ECR I-4405 paras 15–17; Case C-279/94 *Commission v Italy* [1997] ECR I-4681 paras 14–15.

[44] Case 74/82 *Commission v Ireland* [1984] ECR 317 para 20. See also paras 13–23 of the Opinion of Advocate-General Lenz in Case C-337/89 *Commission v United Kingdom* [1992] ECR I-6103.

The proper conduct of the pre-litigation procedure is also necessary to ensure that if the matter is brought before the Court of Justice the dispute between the parties will be clearly defined. In Case C-266/94 *Commission v Spain*[45] the Court of Justice held that infraction proceedings brought by the Commission were inadmissible as the reasoned opinion did not take account of the Member State's response to the letter of formal notice. Indeed, the reasoned opinion wrongly stated that the Spanish Government had failed to respond to the letter of formal notice.

Reasonable time-limit for compliance The Commission must allow the Member State a reasonable time to comply with the reasoned opinion.[46] If it fails to do so, the application to the Court of Justice will be declared inadmissible. In Case 74/82 *Commission v Ireland*[47] the Court of Justice held that it was unreasonable for the Commission to allow Ireland only five days to amend legislation which had been applied for more than 40 years. However, in the circumstances of the case this defect did not render the Commission's application to the Court of Justice inadmissible, as the Commission had waited several months until the Irish Government actually replied to the reasoned opinion before bringing the case before the Court of Justice.

The question of whether or not the time-limit set down in the reasoned opinion is reasonable must be decided taking into account all relevant circumstances. The Commission may be entitled to impose a short time-limit where the Member State concerned has been aware of the Commission's point of view for some time.[48]

Effect of compliance with the reasoned opinion If the Member State complies with the reasoned opinion within the time-limit laid down, or if the breach of Community law ceases to exist for whatever reason, the Commission cannot bring the matter before the Court of Justice.[49]

However, where the breach ceases to exist after the time-limit set down in the reasoned opinion, the Commission may still bring the question before the Court as the proceedings still have a purpose, for example clarification of the legal position by a ruling of the Court or establishing the existence of a breach of Community law which may give rise to liability in damages on the part of the Member State concerned.[50] Thus, for example, amendments made to national legislation after the expiry of the period set by the reasoned opinion will not be

---

[45] [1995] ECR I-1975.

[46] Case 293/85 *Commission v Belgium* [1988] ECR 305 paras 10–20; Case C-473/93 *Commission v Luxembourg* [1996] ECR I-3207 paras 17–24.

[47] [1984] ECR 317 paras 8–14.

[48] Case 85/85 *Commission v Belgium* [1986] ECR 1149 paras 8–13; Case C-247/89 *Commission v Portugal* [1991] ECR I-3659 para 25; Case C-56/90 *Commission v United Kingdom* [1993] ECR I-4109 paras 16–19.

[49] Case C-362/90 *Commission v Italy* [1992] ECR I-2353 paras 9–13.

[50] For example, see Case 7/61 *Commission v Italy* [1961] ECR 317 at 326; Case 39/72 *Commission v Italy* [1973] ECR 101 paras 9–11; Case 154/85 *Commission v Italy* [1987] ECR 2717 para 6.

considered by the Court of Justice in determining whether there has been a breach.[51]

In practice, the Commission may be prepared to abandon proceedings where the breach is remedied before the hearing. However, in such circumstances it is usual for the Member State to be required to pay the Commission's costs.[52]

Stage 4: Hearing before the Court of Justice

(i) Application to the Court of Justice

Jurisdiction Proceedings under article 169 [new art 226] must be brought before the Court of Justice (not the Court of First Instance).

Commission's discretion The Commission has an absolute discretion whether or not to bring proceedings under article 169 [new art 226].[53] The Court of Justice will not question whether that discretion has been exercised wisely,[54] nor will it consider the motives behind the decision of the Commission to bring proceedings.[55]

Furthermore, the Commission has a discretion as to when it will bring an action under article 169. Thus, in Case C-317/92 *Commission v Germany*[56] the Court of Justice held that proceedings under article 169 were admissible even though the Commission had done nothing for two years after sending the reasoned opinion.[57] In addition, the Commission is generally not precluded from commencing proceedings by virtue of the fact that a lengthy period has passed since it first became aware of a Member State's breach.[58] However, in Case C-96/89 *Commission v Netherlands*[59] the Court of Justice indicated that excessive delay by the Commission may infringe the Member State's rights of defence where this makes it more difficult for the Member State to refute the Commission's arguments.

---

[51] Case C-280/89 *Commission v Ireland* [1992] ECR I-6185 para 7; Case C-123/94 *Commission v Greece* [1995] ECR I-1457 para 7; Case C-433/93 *Commission v Germany* [1995] ECR I-2303 paras 13–15; Case C-290/94 *Commission v Greece* [1996] ECR I-3285 para 27.

[52] For example, Case C-176/94 *Commission v Luxembourg*, Order of 1 March 1995 (unreported); Case C-270/94 *Commission v Italy*, Order of 18 May 1995 (unreported).

[53] Case 329/88 *Commission v Greece* [1989] ECR 4159; Case C-431/92 *Commission v Germany* [1995] ECR I-2189 para 22.

[54] Case 200/88 *Commission v Greece* [1990] ECR I-4299 paras 8–9; Case C-209/88 *Commission v Italy* [1990] ECR I-4313 paras 15–16; Case C-317/92 *Commission v Germany* [1994] ECR I-2039 paras 2 and 5.

[55] Case 415/85 *Commission v Ireland* [1988] ECR 3097 paras 8–9; Case 416/85 *Commission v United Kingdom* [1988] ECR 3127 paras 8–9.

[56] [1994] ECR I-2039 paras 2 and 4.

[57] See also Case C-56/90 *Commission v United Kingdom* [1993] ECR I-4109 paras 11–15, where the Commission delayed in issuing a reasoned opinion following receipt of the UK's response to the letter of formal notice.

[58] Case 7/68 *Commission v Italy* [1968] ECR 423 at 428; Case 7/71 *Commission v France* [1971] ECR 1003 paras 2–6; Case C-146/89 *Commission v United Kingdom* [1991] ECR I-3533 para 49; Case C-422/92 *Commission v Germany* [1995] ECR I-1097 paras 15–18.

[59] [1991] ECR I-2461 paras 14–18.

Grounds of application The Commission's initial letter of formal notice delimits the subject-matter of the Commission's complaint. Therefore, the reasoned opinion and the terms of the application to the Court of Justice must be founded on the same grounds as those specified in the initial letter. Matters raised by the Commission which were not put forward in the course of the pre-trial procedure will be declared inadmissible by the Court of Justice.[60] However, the grounds put forward in the application to the Court need not be identical with those contained in the reasoned opinion. The Commission may deal in the application with arguments and defences raised by the Member State in its response to the reasoned opinion.[61]

Where the Court of Justice has dismissed an action as being inadmissible on the basis that the Commission raised new matters which had not been contained in the reasoned opinion, the Commission is entitled to issue a new application to the Court based on the original reasoned opinion without having to recommence the whole pre-litigation procedure.[62]

Where a Member State replaces the law challenged in the Commission's reasoned opinion with a new law which substantially reproduces the original law, the Commission will be entitled to challenge the new law without commencing new proceedings.[63] Thus, in Case C-105/91 *Commission v Greece*[64] the Greek Government argued that the action was inadmissible as the application to the Court of Justice challenged a national law which was not attacked in the Commission's reasoned opinion. The Court of Justice rejected this argument on the basis that the new law mentioned in the application had been adopted after the delivery of the reasoned opinion and had maintained in place the whole system of taxation on cars which had originally been challenged in the reasoned opinion.

The Commission is entitled to amend the declaration which it sought from the Court of Justice in the reasoned opinion where the effect of the amendment is to narrow, but not to extend, its original claim, provided the amendment seeks a declaration which is only different in scope, but not in kind, from that sought

---

[60] Case 211/81 *Commission v Denmark* [1982] ECR 4547 paras 5–17; Case 298/86 *Commission v Belgium* [1988] ECR 4343 paras 9–11; Case C-52/90 *Commission v Denmark* [1992] ECR I-2187 paras 23–24; Case C-198/90 *Commission v Netherlands* [1991] ECR I-5799 paras 13–16; Case C-279/89 *Commission v United Kingdom* [1992] ECR I-5785 paras 12–17; Case C-210/91 *Commission v Greece* [1992] ECR I-6735 paras 8–12; Case C-296/92 *Commission v Italy* [1994] ECR I-1 paras 11–14; Case C-96/95 *Commission v Germany* [1997] ECR I-1653 paras 17–28.

[61] Case 211/81 *Commission v Denmark* [1982] ECR 4547 paras 5–17; Case C-243/89 *Commission v Denmark* [1992] ECR I-3353 paras 9–22.

[62] Case C-57/94 *Commission v Italy* [1995] ECR I-1249 paras 8–14.

[63] Case 45/64 *Commission v Italy* [1965] ECR 857 at 864–865; Case C-42/89 *Commission v Belgium* [1990] ECR I-2821 paras 8–11; Case C-11/95 *Commission v Belgium* [1996] ECR I-4115 paras 73–74.

[64] [1992] ECR I-5871 paras 11–15.

in the reasoned opinion.[65] For example, in Case C-274/93 *Commission v Luxembourg*[66] the Commission made an application to the Court of Justice under article 169 [new art 226] for a declaration that Luxembourg had failed to adopt any measures to implement a directive. Subsequently, the Luxembourg Government communicated the text of a pre-existing national law to the Commission. The Commission therefore sought to amend its application to seek a declaration that the transposition was incomplete. The Court of Justice declared the action to be inadmissible as, under the terms of the amended declaration, the Court would be required to carry out a detailed examination of the Luxembourg law without the Luxembourg Government having had the chance to put forward its arguments on that matter in the pre-litigation procedure. However, as the inadmissibility of the application was entirely due to the conduct of the Luxembourg Government, it was ordered to pay the Commission's costs. A similar situation arose in Case C-117/95 *Commission v Italy*;[67] however, there the Court found that the application based on the amended declaration was admissible, as brief consideration of the national law confirmed that it did not fully implement the relevant directives and this was accepted by the Italian Government.

Contents of application The application must set out, in sufficient detail, the grounds of fact and law relied upon.[68] It is not permissible simply to refer to the grounds of complaint set out in the initial letter and reasoned opinion.[69]

Interim relief The Commission may make an application to the Court of Justice under article 186 of the EC Treaty [new art 243] for an order granting interim measures.[70] If the conditions for the grant of interim relief are fulfilled, the Court may order the Member State to suspend enforcement of a contested measure,[71] including Acts of Parliament.[72]

Burden of proof It is for the Commission to prove that a Member State is in breach of its Community law obligations.[73] Failure to provide sufficient

---

[65] Case C-279/94 *Commission v Italy* [1997] ECR I-4681 paras 24–25. For example, see Case C-365/93 *Commission v Greece* [1995] ECR I-499; Case C-132/94 *Commission v Ireland* [1995] ECR I-4789; Case C-16/95 *Commission v Spain* [1995] ECR I-4883. See also paras 13–28 of the Opinion of Advocate-General Fennelly in Case C-117/95 *Commission v Italy* [1996] ECR I-4689. The views of the Advocate-General were not wholly followed by the Court of Justice in its judgment.

[66] [1996] ECR I-2019.

[67] [1996] ECR I-4689.

[68] Statute of the Court of Justice, article 19; ECJ Rules of Procedure, article 38(1) (c). Case C-52/90 *Commission v Denmark* [1992] ECR I-2187; Case C-431/92 *Commission v Germany* [1995] ECR I-2189 paras 41–45; Case C-223/96 *Commission v France* [1997] ECR I-3201 paras 14–15.

[69] Case C-347/88 *Commission v Greece* [1990] ECR I-4747 paras 26–30; Case C-43/90 *Commission v Germany* [1992] ECR I-1909 paras 5–9. See also Ch 18, p 398.

[70] For the law concerning interim measures, see Ch 17.

[71] For example, see Case 154/85R *Commission v Italy* [1985] ECR 1753; Case 293/85R *Commission v Belgium* [1985] ECR 3521; Case 45/87R *Commission v Ireland* [1987] ECR 1369.

[72] Case 246/89R *Commission v United Kingdom* [1989] ECR 3125.

[73] Case C-279/94 *Commission v Italy* [1997] ECR I-4681 para 33 (judgment of 16 September 1997).

evidence will cause the application to be dismissed.[74] During the course of the pleadings, the burden of proof may shift to the Member State, for example where a Member State seeks to rely on a derogation.[75]

Date of breach The Court of Justice will examine the question of whether there has been a breach of Community law as at the date of the expiry of the period laid down in the reasoned opinion and will not take account of any subsequent changes.[76]

(ii) Defences

(a) Strict approach

Objective nature of breach If the Commission brings an action before the Court, the Court will consider, as an objective fact, whether the Member State is in breach of its Community obligations.[77] The Court adopts a very strict, literal approach to the enforcement of Member States' Community law obligations and has considered (and rejected) a wide number of defences put forward by Member States.

Interpretation by national courts National laws, regulations or administrative provisions must be assessed in the light of the interpretation given to them by national courts.[78]

(b) Defences rejected by the Court of Justice

Undertaking/promise to comply A mere promise or undertaking by a Member State to comply with the relevant Community law obligation does not provide a defence. The breach must actually be remedied within the time-limit required by the reasoned opinion.[79]

---

[74] Case C-64/88 *Commission v France* [1991] ECR I-2727 paras 7–11 (Commission withheld confidential information); Case C-210/91 *Commission v Greece* [1992] ECR I-6735 paras 21–24 (failure to provide factual evidence); Case C-300/95 *Commission v United Kingdom* [1997] ECR I-2649 paras 31 and 37–38 (failure to provide evidence of approach of national courts); Case C-61/94 *Commission v Germany* [1996] ECR I-3989 para 61.

[75] Opinion of Advocate-General Warner in Case 12/74 *Commission v Germany* [1975] ECR 181 at 213–214; Case 199/85 *Commission v Italy* [1987] ECR 1039 paras 14–15 (Member State seeking to rely on a derogation); Case C-327/90 *Commission v Greece* [1992] ECR I-3033 para 20.

[76] Case 200/88 *Commission v Greece* [1990] ECR I-4299 para 13; Case C-61/94 *Commission v Germany* [1996] ECR I-3989 para 42; Case C-302/95 *Commission v Italy* [1996] ECR I-6765 para 13.

[77] Case 301/81 *Commission v Belgium* [1983] ECR 467 para 8; Case C-209/89 *Commission v Italy* [1991] ECR I-1575 para 6; Case C-73/92 *Commission v Spain* [1993] ECR I-5997 paras 18–19.

[78] Case C-382/92 *Commission v United Kingdom* [1994] ECR I-2435 paras 32–39; Case C-300/95 *Commission v United Kingdom* [1997] ECR I-2649 paras 37–38. Contrast Case C-240/95 *Schmidt* [1996] ECR I-3179 paras 14–16 and Case C-236/95 *Commission v Greece* [1996] ECR I-4459 paras 8 and 12–14, where the Court held that national case-law was not sufficient to prevent the Member State from being in breach of its Community law obligations.

[79] Case C-80/92 *Commission v Belgium* [1994] ECR I-1019 paras 18–19; Case C-79/94 *Commission v Greece* [1995] ECR I-1071 paras 7 and 10; see also para 15 of the Opinion of Advocate-General Lenz.

National law in process of amendment The fact that national law is in the course of being amended is not a defence. National law must comply with Community law at the time when the period allowed for compliance by the reasoned opinion expires.[80]

Administrative practice The fact that a Member State has issued circulars or administrative directions requiring compliance with Community law rather than conflicting national law does not constitute a defence to infraction proceedings.[81]

Amendment to Community legislation The fact that a proposal for a Community legislative measure has already been submitted to the Council which, if adopted, would terminate the Member State's breach, does not provide a defence.[82] Furthermore, in Case C-182/94 *Commission v Italy*[83], Italy was found to have failed to have implemented two directives even though the directives had been amended in the course of the infraction proceedings.

Failure to act by Community institution The Member States cannot seek to justify a breach of Community law on the basis that a Community institution has failed to carry out its obligations.[84]

Breach by other Member States A Member State may not justify its own breach of Community law by relying on the fact that another Member State is in breach of its obligations.[85] Thus, in Case 232/78 *Commission v France*[86] the Court of Justice held that:

> A Member State cannot under any circumstances unilaterally adopt, on its own authority, corrective measures or measures to protect trade designed to prevent any failure on the part of another Member State to comply with the rules laid down by the Treaty.

National interest A Member State cannot justify the failure to give effect to Community legislation on the basis that it had opposed certain aspects of the

[80] Case C-317/92 *Commission v Germany* [1994] ECR I-2039 paras 2–3.
[81] Case 168/85 *Commission v Italy* [1986] ECR 2945 paras 12–13; Case 169/87 *Commission v France* [1988] ECR 4093 paras 11–12; Case C-317/92 *Commission v Germany* [1994] ECR I-2039 para 3; Case C-151/94 *Commission v Luxembourg* [1995] ECR I-3685 para 18; Case C-334/94 *Commission v France* [1996] ECR I-1307 paras 27–30.
[82] Case 220/83 *Commission v France* [1986] ECR 3663 paras 6–7; Case C-236/88 *Commission v France* [1990] ECR I-3163 para 19; Case C-310/89 *Commission v Netherlands* [1991] ECR I-1381; Case C-317/92 *Commission v Germany* [1994] ECR I-2039 paras 2 and 5.
[83] [1995] ECR I-1465; see also paras 4–5 of the Opinion of Advocate-General Lenz.
[84] Joined Cases 90/63 and 91/63 *Commission v Luxembourg and Belgium* [1964] ECR 625 at 631.
[85] Case 52/75 *Commission v Italy* [1976] ECR 277 para 11; Case C-146/89 *Commission v United Kingdom* [1991] ECR I-3533 para 47; Case C-101/94 *Commission v Italy* [1996] ECR I-2691 para 27; Case C-11/95 *Commission v Belgium* [1996] ECR I-4115 para 37; Case C-14/96 *Denuit* [1997] ECR I-2785 para 35. See also paras 27–30 of the Opinion of Advocate-General Léger in Case C-5/94 *R v MAFF, ex p Hedley Lomas* [1996] ECR I-2553.
[86] [1979] ECR 2729 para 9.

legislation during its adoption, nor on the basis that it considers the legislation to be contrary to its own national interests.[87]

Breach of directly applicable/directly effective measures Where a Member State is in breach of a directly applicable or directly effective Community measure, the Member State cannot rely on the fact that private parties are entitled to invoke the Community legislation in the national courts as a defence in infraction proceedings.[88]

National constitutional rules The fact that the offending national rule is contained in a national constitution is not a defence to infraction proceedings.[89]

Internal political or legal difficulties A Member State may not plead 'provisions, practices or circumstances in its internal legal system' in order to justify a failure to comply with Community directives.[90] For example, the fact that national implementing legislation could not be adopted because of the dissolution of Parliament and the calling of a general election did not provide a defence in Case C-107/96 *Commission v Spain*.[91]

Administrative, practical or financial difficulties A Member State cannot plead internal administrative or practical difficulties in order to justify a breach of Community law.[92] For example, in Case 39/72 *Commission v Italy*[93] the Italian Government sought to justify its failure to introduce a system of premiums for slaughtering on the basis of the special characteristics of Italian agriculture and the lack of adequate lower level administration. These arguments were rejected by the Court of Justice. In Case C-56/90 *Commission v United Kingdom*[94] and Case C-337/89 *Commission v United Kingdom*[95] the Court of Justice rejected the United Kingdom's arguments that certain water directives required Member States only to take all practicable steps to comply with the standards laid down.

Equally, financial difficulties do not provide a defence.[96]

---

[87] Case 39/72 *Commission v Italy* [1971] ECR 101 para 20; Case 128/78 *Commission v United Kingdom* [1979] ECR 419 para 9.

[88] Case C-253/95 *Commission v Germany* [1996] ECR I-2423 para 13; Case C-290/94 *Commission v Greece* [1996] ECR I-3285 para 29.

[89] Case C-473/93 *Commission v Luxembourg* [1996] ECR I-3207 paras 37–38. See also paras 129–133 of the Opinion of Advocate-General Léger in Case C-290/94 *Commission v Greece* [1996] ECR I-3285.

[90] Case 77/69 *Commission v Belgium* [1970] ECR 237; Case 8/70 *Commission v Italy* [1970] ECR 961 paras 8–9; Case 39/72 *Commission v Italy* [1973] ECR 101 paras 10–11; Case 254/83 *Commission v Italy* [1984] ECR 3395; Case C-205/96 *Commission v Belgium* [1997] ECR I-795 paras 8–10.

[91] [1997] ECR I-3193 paras 9–10. See also Case C-290/94 *Commission v Greece* [1996] ECR I-3285 paras 26 and 30.

[92] Case 58/83 *Commission v Greece* [1984] ECR 2027 para 11; Case C-337/89 *Commission v United Kingdom* [1992] ECR I-6103 paras 14–15.

[93] [1973] ECR 101 paras 19–23.

[94] [1993] ECR I-4109 paras 40–44.

[95] [1992] ECR I-6103 paras 17–25.

[96] Case C-42/89 *Commission v Belgium* [1990] ECR I-2821 para 24.

Social unrest The fact that compliance with Community law might lead to social unrest was not accepted as a defence in Case C-52/95 *Commission v France*.[97]

Equivalent national legislation A Member State cannot rely on the fact that national legislation already fulfils the aims of a directive by different means where the directive itself sets out particular measures to be adopted.[98]

More effective measures Where a regulation requires Member States to adopt particular measures, a Member State may not adopt different measures on the basis that it believes them to be more effective.[99]

No adverse effect on the Common Market An argument that a breach of Community obligations produces no adverse effects on the functioning of the Common Market does not provide a defence.[100]

De minimis Member States cannot argue that a breach of Community law should be excused because it is *de minimis*. In Case C-209/89 *Commission v Italy*[101] the Court held that:

> ... a Member State is guilty of a failure to fulfil its obligations under the Treaty regardless of the frequency or the scale of the circumstances complained of.

Implementation period of directive too short It is not a defence for a Member State to argue that the implementation period set down in a directive is too short given the complexity of its subject-matter. If the implementation period is too short, the Member State must seek an extension of time from the competent Community institution.[102]

Approval/inaction by the Commission In Case 288/83 *Commission v Ireland*[103] the Court of Justice held that:

> ... the Commission cannot, even by approving expressly or by implication a measure adopted unilaterally by a Member State, confer on that State the right to maintain provisions which are objectively contrary to Community law.

---

[97] [1995] ECR I-4443 paras 37–38.

[98] Case 128/78 *Commission v United Kingdom* [1979] ECR 419; Case 215/83 *Commission v Belgium* [1985] ECR 1039 para 25; Case C-313/89 *Commission v Spain* [1991] ECR I-5231 paras 11–12.

[99] Case C-28/89 *Germany v Commission* [1991] ECR I-581 para 17; Case C-54/91 *Germany v Commission* [1993] ECR I-3300 para 38.

[100] Case 95/77 *Commission v Netherlands* [1978] ECR 863 para 13; Case 209/88 *Commission v Italy* [1990] ECR I-4313 paras 12–14; Case C-209/89 *Commission v Italy* [1991] ECR I-1575 para 6.

[101] [1991] ECR I-1575 paras 18–19. See also Case C-209/88 *Commission v Italy* [1990] ECR I-4313 para 13; Case C-105/91 *Commission v Greece* [1992] ECR I-5871 paras 19–20; Case C-43/97 *Commission v Italy* [1997] ECR I-4671 paras 7–9.

[102] Case 52/75 *Commission v Italy* [1976] ECR 277 paras 7–13; Joined Cases C-178, 179 and 188–190/94 *Dillenkofer v Germany* [1996] ECR I-4845 para 54.

[103] [1985] ECR 1761 para 22. See also Joined Cases 142/80 and 143/80 *Amministrazione delle Finanze v Essevi and Salengo* [1981] ECR 1413 paras 13–18; Case C-56/90 *Commission v United Kingdom* [1993] ECR I-4109 paras 11–15; Case C-359/93 *Commission v Netherlands* [1995] ECR I-157 paras 10–15; and Case C-79/94 *Commission v Greece* [1995] ECR I-1071 paras 8 and 11 (concerning the Community public procurement rules).

In Case C-37/93 *Commission v Belgium*[104] the Court of Justice rejected the argument put forward by Belgium that it had submitted draft laws to the Commission and was awaiting its comments before submitting them to its national Parliament.

Legal uncertainty Where a Member State has acted in breach of Community law, the fact that the legal position was uncertain at the time when it acted does not provide a defence.[105]

(c) Possible defences

Procedural defects The procedure followed by the Commission prior to bringing an action before the Court of Justice is a purely administrative stage which is not reviewable under article 173 or 175 of the EC Treaty [new arts 230 and 232].[106] It follows that the validity of a letter of formal notice or a reasoned opinion cannot be challenged in separate proceedings.[107] Any defects in the pre-litigation procedure can, however, be relied on as a defence in the main action and may render the Commission's application inadmissible.[108] The Court of Justice has jurisdiction to examine, of its own motion, the question of whether the procedural preconditions required by article 169 [new art 226] have been complied with.[109]

Invalidity of Community measure In Case 226/87 *Commission v Greece*[110] the Court of Justice held that a Member State is not entitled to challenge the validity of a decision addressed to it as a defence in an action under article 169 alleging that it has failed to comply with that decision. Similarly, in Case C-74/91 *Commission v Germany*[111] the Court held that a Member State could not challenge the unlawfulness of a directive which it was alleged not to have implemented.

In contrast, in Case C-258/89 *Commission v Spain*[112] Advocate-General Darmon considered that Member States should be entitled to invoke article 184

---

[104] [1993] ECR I-6295.

[105] Case 7/71 *Commission v France* [1971] ECR 1003 para 47 (EURATOM); Case C-73/92 *Commission v Spain* [1993] ECR I-5997 paras 18–19.

[106] Case 48/65 *Lütticke v Commission* [1966] ECR 19.

[107] Joined Cases 6/69 and 11/69 *Commission v France* [1969] ECR 523 at 35–37.

[108] For example, Case C-296/92 *Commission v Italy* [1994] ECR I-1 paras 11–14; Case C-40/92 *Commission v United Kingdom* [1994] ECR I-989 paras 37–40; Case C-266/94 *Commission v Spain* [1995] ECR I-1975.

[109] Case C-362/90 *Commission v Italy* [1992] ECR I-2353 para 8.

[110] [1988] ECR 3611 para 14. See Case 156/77 *Commission v Belgium* [1978] ECR 1881 paras 21–22, where the Court of Justice held that a Member State was not entitled to rely on article 184 [new art 241] in order to challenge the validity of an individual decision which had been addressed to it. See also Case C-183/91 *Commission v Greece* [1993] ECR I-3131 paras 9–10 (concerning proceedings under article 93(2) of the EC Treaty [new art 88(2)] dealing with State aids).

[111] [1992] ECR I-5437 para 10.

[112] [1991] ECR I-3977, para 23 of the Opinion. See also Case 226/87 *Commission v Greece* [1988] ECR 3611, para 3617 of the Opinion of Advocate-General Mancini. This issue is discussed further Ch 14, p 333.

of the EC Treaty [new art 241] to challenge the validity of a regulation in the context of proceedings under article 169 [new art 226].

'Non-existent' Community measure In Case 226/87 *Commission v Greece*[113] the Court of Justice indicated that it would be a defence to proceedings under article 169 [new art 226] if the measure at issue contained such particularly serious and manifest defects that it could be deemed non-existent.

Absolute impossibility The Court of Justice has indicated that where a Member State can show that it was 'absolutely impossible' to comply with its EC Treaty obligations, this may provide a defence to proceedings under article 169 [new art 226].[114] However, where it appears that it is impossible for a Member State to fulfil its EC Treaty obligations, it is under an obligation to submit these problems to the Commission and to propose appropriate solutions. If the Member State fails to communicate with the Commission, it will be in breach of its duty of co-operation under article 5 of the EC Treaty [new art 10].[115]

Force majeure In Case C-52/95 *Commission v France*[116] Advocate-General Fennelly considered that, in wholly exceptional circumstances, a Member State might be able to rely on *force majeure* as a defence in infraction proceedings.

2. INFRACTION PROCEEDINGS BY A MEMBER STATE

Article 170 Article 170 of the EC Treaty [new art 227] provides that:

> A Member State which considers that another Member State has failed to fulfil an obligation under this Treaty may bring the matter before the Court of Justice.
>
> Before a Member State brings an action against another Member State for an alleged infringement of an obligation under this Treaty, it shall bring the matter before the Commission.
>
> The Commission shall deliver a reasoned opinion after each of the States concerned has been given the opportunity to submit its own case and its observations on the other party's case both orally and in writing.
>
> If the Commission has not delivered an opinion within three months of the date on which the matter was brought before it, the absence of such opinion shall not prevent the matter from being brought before the Court of Justice.

---

[113] [1988] ECR 3611 para 16. See also Joined Cases 6/69 and 11/69 *Commission v France* [1969] ECR 523 paras 10–13; Case C-74/91 *Commission v Germany* [1992] ECR I-5437 paras 10–11. Non-existent acts are discussed at Ch 13, pp 323–324.

[114] Case 52/84 *Commission v Belgium* [1986] ECR 89 paras 14–16; Case 213/85 *Commission v Netherlands* [1988] ECR 281 paras 22–24; Case C-183/91 *Commission v Greece* [1993] ECR I-3131 paras 10–21; Case C-348/93 *Commission v Italy* [1995] ECR I-673 para 17. These cases concerned infraction proceedings under the special infraction procedure for State aids (article 93(2) of the EC Treaty [new art 88(2)]). Case C-74/91 *Commission v Germany* [1992] ECR I-5437 para 12 recognises the availability of this defence in the context of proceedings under article 169. See also Case C-50/94 *Greece v Commission* [1996] ECR I-3331 para 39.

[115] Case C-217/88 *Commission v Germany* [1990] ECR I-2879 para 33.

[116] [1995] ECR I-4443, paras 31–32 of the Opinion. See also Case 101/84 *Commission v Italy* [1985] ECR 2629 paras 15–16. *Force majeure* is discussed at Ch 2, pp 50–51.

Article 170 provides the means for a Member State to bring infraction proceedings against another Member State which it considers is in breach of its EC Treaty obligations. However, the complaint must first be brought before the Commission. If the Commission issues a reasoned opinion, the procedure which follows is the same as that under article 169 [new art 226]. If the Commission does not adopt a reasoned opinion within three months of the complaint made to it, the Member State can take the matter directly before the Court of Justice. Perhaps because of the political implications of proceeding against a fellow Member State, there is only one example of a Member State pursuing an action under article 170 to judgment.[117]

3. SPECIAL INFRACTION PROCEDURES

Special procedures Some EC Treaty articles permit the Commission or a Member State to bring infraction proceedings directly before the Court of Justice, without satisfying the procedural preconditions of article 169 or 170 [new arts 226 and 227].[118] These are:

(1) article 93(2) [new art 88(2)] concerning State aids;[119]
(2) article 110a(4) [new art 95(9)] concerning derogations from harmonisation measures;
(3) article 225 [new art 298] concerning derogations on the grounds of national security.[120]

4. EFFECT OF JUDGMENT OF COURT OF JUSTICE

Article 171 Article 171 of the EC Treaty [new art 228] provides that:

1. If the Court of Justice finds that a Member State has failed to fulfil an obligation under this Treaty, the State shall be required to take the necessary measures to comply with the judgment of the Court of Justice.
2. If the Commission considers that the Member State concerned has not taken such measures it shall, after giving that State the opportunity to submit its observations, issue a reasoned opinion specifying the points on which the Member State concerned has not complied with the judgment of the Court of Justice.

If the Member State concerned fails to take the necessary measures to comply with the Court's judgment within the time-limit laid down by the Commission, the latter may bring the case before the Court of Justice. In doing so it shall specify the amount

---

[117] Case 141/78 *France v United Kingdom* [1979] ECR 2923.
[118] See also article 180(a) [new art 237(a)], which sets down a special procedure for the enforcement of Member States' obligations under the Statute of the European Investment Bank.
[119] For a discussion of the relationship between article 169 and article 93(2), see Case 156/77 *Commission v Belgium* [1978] ECR 1881 paras 5–13; Case C-35/88 *Commission v Greece* [1990] ECR I-3125 paras 8–13; Case C-294/90 *British Aerospace v Commission* [1992] ECR I-493; Case C-61/90 *Commission v Greece* [1992] ECR I-2407 paras 25–28; Case T-358/94 *Air France v Commission* [1996] ECR II-2109 para 60.
[120] For example, see Case C-120/94 *Commission v Greece* [1996] ECR I-1513.

of the lump sum or penalty payment to be paid by the Member State concerned which it considers appropriate in the circumstances.

If the Court of Justice finds that the Member State concerned has not complied with its judgment it may impose a lump sum or penalty payment on it.

This procedure shall be without prejudice to Article 170.

Effect of judgment A judgment by the Court of Justice under article 169 [new art 226] is declaratory in form and does not, in itself, cure any breach on the part of the Member State. However, it does impose an obligation on the Member State concerned to take all necessary measures to remedy its default. In particular, the judgment:[121]

(1) prohibits competent national authorities applying a national law adjudged to be incompatible with the Treaty;

(2) imposes an obligation on the national authorities to introduce, repeal or amend legislative acts so as to ensure compliance with Community law; and

(3) imposes an obligation on the courts of the Member State concerned to ensure, when performing their duties, that the Court's judgment is complied with.

Where the Commission brings proceedings on the basis that a Member State has failed to take specific measures, the judgment of the Court of Justice, although purely declaratory in form, will, in practice, impose an obligation on the Member State to adopt the relevant measures.[122]

Time for compliance Although article 171 [new art 228] does not specify the period within which a judgment must be complied with, the Court of Justice has held that the process of complying with a judgment must be initiated at once and must be completed as soon as possible.[123] The Court of Justice has no power to grant a Member State a specific 'period of grace' to allow it to comply with its Community obligations.[124]

Failure to comply with judgment If a Member State fails to comply with a judgment of the Court of Justice under article 169 [new art 226], it is in breach of its obligations under article 171(1) [new art 228(1)] and the Commission may bring new infraction proceedings under article 169 based on the breach of

---

[121] Case 48/71 *Commission v Italy* [1972] ECR 527 para 7; Joined Cases 24/80R and 97/80R *Commission v France* [1980] ECR 1319 para 16; Joined Cases 314 to 316/81 and 83/82 *Procureur de la République v Waterkeyn* [1982] ECR 4337 paras 14–15.

[122] Case 70/72 *Commission v Germany* [1973] ECR 813 paras 10–13.

[123] Case 169/87 *Commission v France* [1988] ECR 4093 paras 13–14; Case C-375/89 *Commission v Belgium* [1991] ECR I-383; Case C-328/90 *Commission v Greece* [1992] ECR I-425; Case C-75/91 *Commission v Netherlands* [1992] ECR I-549; Case C-334/94 *Commission v France* [1996] ECR I-1307 para 31. See also *R v Secretary of State for the Environment, ex p Friends of the Earth* [1994] 2 CMLR 760 (QBD) and [1996] 1 CMLR 117 (CA) where the English courts considered the nature of the obligation imposed on the United Kingdom to remedy its breach following a judgment of the Court of Justice under article 169.

[124] Case C-473/93 *Commission v Luxembourg* [1996] ECR I-3207 paras 51–52, and paras 211–223 of the Opinion of Advocate-General Léger.

article 171(1). It is not necessary to relitigate the original breach.[125]

The Court of Justice adopts the same strict approach to breaches of article 171(1) as it does in proceedings under article 169. For example, a Member State will not be permitted under article 171(1) to rely on political difficulties as a defence.[126]

Where the Court has already made a judgment against a Member State under article 169 and the Commission brings fresh proceedings for failure to comply with article 171(1), the Court of Justice will not grant interim measures where this would simply have the same effect as the original judgment, that is, requiring the Member State to take the necessary measures to put an end to the breach.[127]

Financial penalties Article 171(2) [new art 228(2)] was added by the Maastricht Treaty, and gives the Court of Justice jurisdiction, on an application by the Commission, to impose a lump sum or penalty payment on a Member State which has failed to comply with a judgment under article 169 [new art 226]. To date, no such financial penalty has been imposed.

Basis of civil liability In Case 39/72 *Commission v Italy*[128] the Court of Justice held that:

> ... a judgment by the Court under Articles 169 and 171 of the Treaty may be of substantive interest as establishing the basis of a responsibility that a Member State can incur as a result of its default, as regards other Member States, the Community or private parties.

Furthermore, in Joined Cases 314 to 316/81 and 83/82 *Procureur de la République v Waterkeyn*[129] the Court of Justice emphasised that where a judgment under article 169 [new art 226] establishes that a Member State is in breach of its Community law obligations, the national courts must take account of the relevant elements of law established by a judgment under article 169 in an action brought in the national courts. This demonstrates the practical importance of infraction proceedings to private parties. A judgment under article 169, which binds the English courts by virtue of the European Communities Act 1972,[130] can provide the basis for an action by private parties in their own

---

[125] For example, see Case 48/71 *Commission v Italy* [1972] ECR 527; Case C-266/89 *Commission v Italy* [1991] ECR I-2411. See also paras 8–30 of the Opinion of Advocate-General Fennelly in Case C-334/94 *Commission v France* [1996] ECR I-1307, where he took the view that in cases where the Commission issues its reasoned opinion after 1 November 1993 it is obliged to adopt the article 171(2) procedure for the enforcement of article 171(1). This issue was not considered by the Court of Justice in its judgment. However, in the *Report of the Court of Justice on Certain Aspects of the Application of the Treaty on European Union* (Luxembourg, May 1995) the Court stated that the new version of article 171 *enables* the Commission to bring an action seeking imposition of penalties on a Member State. This suggests that the Commission has a choice whether or not to pursue the article 171(2) procedure.

[126] Case 48/71 *Commission v Italy* [1972] ECR 527.

[127] Joined Cases 24/80R and 97/80R *Commission v France* [1980] ECR 1319.

[128] [1973] ECR 101 para 11. See also Case 309/84 *Commission v Italy* [1986] ECR 599 para 18; and Case 240/86 *Commission v Greece* [1988] ECR 1835 para 14.

[129] [1982] ECR 4337 paras 13–16.

[130] See Ch 1, pp 19–20.

national courts for restitution of monies paid[131] or for damages in respect of any loss which they have suffered as a result of the relevant breach.[132]

---

[131] See Ch 9.

[132] For example, see *R v Secretary of State for Transport, ex p Factortame Ltd* [1997] EuLR 475 (Div Ct) (discussed at Ch 7, pp 128–148). It is not necessary for the Court to have delivered a judgment under article 169 before a Member State can incur liability in damages for breach of Community law: see Joined Cases C-46/93 and C-48/93 *Brasserie du Pêcheur and Factortame Ltd* [1996] ECR I-1029 paras 91–96.

Chapter 13

Judicial Review of EC Acts

1. INTRODUCTION

Article 173 Article 173 of the EC Treaty [new art 230] provides:

> The Court of Justice shall review the legality of acts adopted jointly by the European Parliament and the Council, of acts of the Council, of the Commission and of the ECB, other than recommendations or opinions, and of acts of the European Parliament intended to produce legal effects *vis-à-vis* third parties.
>
> It shall for this purpose have jurisdiction in actions brought by a Member State, the Council or the Commission on grounds of lack of competence, infringement of an essential procedural requirement, infringement of this Treaty or of any rule of law relating to its application, or misuse of powers.
>
> The Court shall have jurisdiction under the same conditions in actions brought by the European Parliament and by the ECB for the purpose of protecting their prerogatives.
>
> Any natural or legal person may, under the same conditions, institute proceedings against a decision addressed to that person or against a decision which, although in the form of a regulation or a decision addressed to another person, is of direct and individual concern to the former.
>
> The proceedings provided for in this Article shall be instituted within two months of the publication of the measure, or of its notification to the plaintiff, or, in the absence thereof, of the day on which it came to the knowledge of the latter, as the case may be.

Purpose of article 173 Article 173 [new art 230] provides the basis for judicial review by the EC courts of acts of the Community institutions. If an action under article 173 is successful, the EC court declares the act concerned to be void.[1] For this reason, actions brought under article 173 are often referred to as 'actions for annulment'. The EC courts do not have competence under article 173 to rule on the compatibility of a national measure with Community law.[2]

***Locus standi*/nature of the applicant** Article 173 [new art 230] establishes different *locus standi* rules depending on the nature of the applicant. Applicants

---

[1] Article 174 of the EC Treaty [new art 231]: discussed below at pp 328–330. Applicants are not entitled to seek general declarations of fact or law: Case C-303/96P *Bernardi v Parliament* [1997] ECR I-1239 para 45.

[2] Case C-347/87 *Triveneta Zuccheri v Commission* [1990] ECR I-1083 para 16; Case T-575/93 *Koelman v Commission* [1996] ECR II-1 paras 29–30.

fall into three categories: (a) the Member States, the Council and the Commission ('privileged applicants'); (b) the European Parliament and the European Central Bank ('ECB') ('semi-privileged applicants'); and (c) other natural or legal persons ('non-privileged applicants'). In order to establish that it has *locus standi*, a privileged applicant must show that the measure which it wishes to challenge is a 'reviewable act'. A semi-privileged applicant must show that the relevant measure is a reviewable act which affects its prerogatives.[3] A non-privileged applicant must show that the relevant measure is a reviewable act which is of 'direct and individual concern' to it.

Jurisdiction Actions by privileged and semi-privileged applicants under article 173 [new art 230] must be made to the Court of Justice. Actions by non-privileged applicants under article 173 must be made to the Court of First Instance.[4]

Burden of proof The burden of proving the invalidity of a Community act rests on the applicant.[5]

Admissibility Where the defendant Community institution considers that an applicant does not have *locus standi* to challenge the act in question, it may ask the court to decide the question of admissibility as a preliminary issue.[6] The EC courts may consider the question of admissibility of their own motion, even where it has not been raised by the parties.[7]

2. REVIEWABLE ACTS

Test for reviewable acts For an act to be amenable to review under article 173 [new art 230]:

  (1) it must be an act of a Community institution;
  (2) it must be intended to produce legal effects;
  (3) in relation to non-privileged applicants, the applicant must have an interest in seeing the act annulled;
  (4) it must not be a purely preparatory measure;
  (5) it must not be a purely confirmatory measure;

---

[3] If ratified, the Amsterdam Treaty will amend article 173 of the EC Treaty to allow the Court of Auditors to bring applications for annulment in order to protect its prerogatives.

[4] Article 3 of Council Decision 88/591 of 24 October 1988 (OJ 1988 L319 p 1) (corrected text at OJ 1989 C215 p 1), as substituted by Council Decision 93/350 of 8 June 1993 (OJ 1993 L144 p 21), as amended by Council Decision 94/149 of 7 March 1994 (OJ 1994 L66 p 29).

[5] Case T-11/89 *Shell International Chemical Co v Commission* [1992] ECR II-757 para 374; paras 15–16 of the Opinion of Advocate-General Fennelly in Case C-50/94 *Greece v Commission* [1996] ECR I-3331.

[6] ECJ Rules of Procedure, article 91; CFI Rules of Procedure, article 114.

[7] ECJ Rules of Procedure, article 92(2); CFI Rules of Procedure, article 113. Case 92/78 *Simmenthal v Commission* [1979] ECR 777 para 22; Case 294/83 *Parti écologiste 'Les Verts' v Parliament* [1986] ECR 1339 para 19; Joined Cases C-305/86 and C-160/87 *Neotype Techmashexport v Commission and Council* [1990] ECR I-2945 para 18; Case C-313/90 *CIRFS v Commission* [1993] ECR I-1125 para 23; Case C-225/91 *Matra v Commission* [1993] ECR I-3203 para 13.

(6) a refusal to act will only be open to challenge if the act which the institution has refused to adopt would itself have been open to challenge by the applicant under article 173.

Furthermore, it is the substance of the measure under consideration which is decisive, not its form.

Acts of the institutions The first paragraph of article 173 [new art 230] defines the types of acts which may be reviewed. It provides that:

> The Court of Justice shall review the legality of acts adopted jointly by the European Parliament and the Council, of acts of the Council, of the Commission and of the ECB, other than recommendations or opinions, and of acts of the European Parliament intended to produce legal effects *vis-à-vis* third parties.

In essence, an action for annulment may be brought against all measures adopted by the institutions, whatever their nature or form, which are intended to have legal effects.[8] Although it is not clear whether an annulment action could be brought against an institution which is not specifically referred to in article 173[9] the Court of Justice has, in the past, allowed applications to be brought in such circumstances against the European Parliament[10] (before the adoption of the Maastricht Treaty) and the Court of Auditors.[11]

Measures adopted by a Community institution may be challenged under article 173 even if the measures were not adopted pursuant to Treaty provisions but rather pursuant to a power conferred by an agreement to which all the Member States were parties.[12]

Acts of the Member States Acts of the Member States are not capable of being the subject of an action for annulment under article 173 [new art 230]. Thus, in Case C-253/94P *Roujansky v Council*[13] the Court of Justice held that an action challenging the legality of the Maastricht Treaty was inadmissible. The Court also dismissed a claim challenging a declaration of the Member States meeting as the 'European Council'. (The European Council is distinct from the Council of the European Union. The latter is a Community institution, whereas the former term is used to connote the summit meetings of the Heads of State or Government of the Member States and the President of the Commission, which

---

[8] Joined Cases C-181/91 and C-248/91 *Parliament v Council and Commission* [1993] ECR I-3685 para 13; Case T-509/93 *Richco v Commission* [1996] ECR II-1181 para 25. See below at pp 270–274.

[9] See Case C-25/94 *Commission v Council* [1996] ECR I-1469 paras 22–28, and paras 46–48 of the Opinion of Advocate-General Jacobs for a discussion of the position of the Permanent Representatives Committee ('Coreper'); and Case T-460/93 *Etienne Tête v EIB* [1993] ECR II-1258 paras 16–21 in relation to the European Investment Bank.

[10] Case 294/83 *Parti Écologiste 'Les Verts' v Parliament* [1986] ECR 1339. Prior to the adoption of the Maastricht Treaty, article 173 of the EEC Treaty did not specifically provide for annulment actions against the Parliament.

[11] Joined Cases 193 and 194/87 *Maurissen v Court of Auditors* [1989] ECR 1045 paras 41–42, and paras 49–57 of the Opinion of Advocate-General Darmon.

[12] Case C-316/91 *Parliament v Council* [1994] ECR I-625 paras 6–9.

[13] [1995] ECR I-7; see also Case C-264/94P *Bonnamy v Council* [1995] ECR I-15. See also Case C-313/89 *Commission v Spain* [1991] ECR I-5231 paras 9–10 in relation to the Treaty of Accession for Spain and Portugal.

take place at least twice a year.[14]) In Joined Cases C-181/91 and C-248/91 *Parliament v Council and Commission*[15] the Court of Justice dismissed an application which sought to challenge an act adopted by the Member States, even though it had been adopted in the context of a meeting of the Council of the European Union. In Case T-271/94 *Branco v Commission*[16] the Court of First Instance held that national measures implementing Community acts were not capable of review under article 173.

Substance not form Article 189 of the EC Treaty [new art 249] sets out certain types of act which may be adopted by the Community institutions, namely regulations, directives, decisions, recommendations and opinions. Article 173 [new art 230] expressly provides that recommendations and opinions may not be the subject of an action for annulment. However, it is not necessary for an act to be formally categorised as a 'regulation', 'directive' or 'decision' in order for it to be reviewable. An action for annulment may be brought against all measures adopted by the institutions, whatever their nature or form, which are intended to have legal effects.[17] In deciding whether or not an act is reviewable, the EC courts will look at its substance, rather than its form.[18] This approach was established by the judgment of the Court of Justice in Case 22/70 *Commission v Council*[19] (the '*ERTA*' case), in which the Court held that 'conclusions' adopted by the Council establishing the course of action to be taken by the individual Member States in negotiating a European transport agreement with non-Member States amounted to reviewable acts.

In Case C-325/91 *France v Commission*[20] the Court of Justice examined a document which was entitled 'Communication from the Commission to the Member States' and which dealt with the application of the Community rules on State aids and, in particular, with article 5 of Directive 80/723.[21] The Directive required the Member States to keep certain records which the Commission could demand to inspect. The communication, while purporting simply to clarify the application of the Directive, set out a detailed list of information which was to be provided to the Commission on an annual basis. The Court held that this constituted an attempt to impose obligations on the Member States which went beyond those provided for by the original Directive. Therefore, the

---

[14] See article D of the Treaty on European Union [new art 4].

[15] [1993] ECR I-3685 paras 9–14.

[16] [1996] ECR II-749 para 53.

[17] Joined Cases C-181/91 and C-248/91 *Parliament v Council and Commission* [1993] ECR I-3685 para 13; Case T-509/93 *Richco v Commission* [1996] ECR I-1181 para 25.

[18] Opinion of Advocate-General Roemer in Joined Cases 8 to 11/66 *Cimenteries v Commission* [1967] ECR 75 at 100–101; Case 60/81 *IBM v Commission* [1981] ECR 2639 para 9; Case C-50/90 *Sunzest v Commission* [1991] ECR I-2917 para 12; Joined Cases C-213/88 and C-39/89 *Luxembourg v Parliament* [1991] ECR I-5643 para 15.

[19] [1971] ECR 263 paras 34–55.

[20] [1993] ECR I-3283 paras 1–23. See also Case C-303/90 *France v Commission* [1991] ECR I-5315 paras 7–25 (Code of Conduct adopted by Commission dealing with Structural Fund irregularities).

[21] Commission Directive 80/723 (OJ 1980 L195 p 35) on the transparency of financial relations between Member States and public undertakings.

'communication' was an act intended to produce legal effects and constituted a reviewable act subject to article 173 of the EEC Treaty. The Court went on to annul the act because it did not state the legal basis on which it was purported to be based.

In Case T-3/93 *Air France v Commission*[22] the Court of First Instance held that an oral statement by the spokesman for the Commissioner responsible for competition matters that the proposed merger between British Airways and Dan Air did not fall within the threshold of Community competence constituted an act which was amenable to review under article 173.

Legal effects The Court of Justice has consistently held that an action for annulment may be brought against all measures adopted by the institutions, whatever their nature or form, which produce binding legal effects.[23]

An example of the application of the 'legal effects' test is the judgment in Joined Cases 8 to 11/66 *Cimenteries v Commission*.[24] The issue in that case concerned Council Regulation 17/62,[25] which sets out the main procedural rules for competition matters. Article 15(5) of Regulation 17/62 provides that undertakings which notify their agreements to the Commission are exempt from the system of fines imposed for anti-competitive behaviour until the Commission reaches a final decision. However, article 15(6) provides that, after a preliminary examination, the Commission may withdraw this exemption, so that undertakings are at risk if they continue with their agreement and it is subsequently found to be contrary to article 85 of the EC Treaty [new art 81]. The act challenged in *Cimenteries v Commission* was a letter from the Commission withdrawing the exemption from fines under article 15(6). The Court of Justice held that, as the effect of the Commission's letter was that the undertakings ceased to benefit from the exemption from fines, this brought about a distinct change in their legal position and produced binding legal effects affecting the interests of the undertakings. The letter was therefore reviewable under article 173 [new art 230].

By way of further examples, the EC courts have held that acts are open to review in the following contexts:

(1) a Commission letter refusing to recognise a contract as being in conformity with Community financing conditions;[26]

---

[22] [1994] ECR II-121 paras 8 and 55–60.

[23] Case 22/70 *Commission v Council* [1971] ECR 263 para 42 (the '*ERTA*' case); Case 60/81 *IBM v Commission* [1981] ECR 2639 para 9; Joined Cases C-181/91 and C-248/91 *Parliament v Council and Commission* [1993] ECR I-3685 para 13; Case T-509/93 *Richco v Commission* [1996] ECR I-1181 para 25. At para 45 of his Opinion in Case C-25/94 *Commission v Council* [1995] ECR I-1469 Advocate-General Jacobs stated that, 'The *ERTA* case shows that it is necessary to take a broad view of admissibility'.

[24] [1967] ECR 75 at 90–93.

[25] Regulation 17/62 of 6 February 1962 (OJ 1962 L13 p 204), First Regulation implementing articles 85, 86 of the EEC Treaty (as amended) (English Special Edition, 1959–1962, p 87).

[26] Case T-509/93 *Richco v Commission* [1996] ECR II-1181 paras 25–28. See also Case C-395/95P *Geotronics v Commission* [1997] ECR I-2271 paras 1 and 8–16 (Commission letter rejecting tender under the PHARE Programme).

(2) a Commission letter refusing access to a non-confidential file in the context of anti-dumping proceedings;[27]

(3) the conclusion by the Commission of an international agreement which was itself intended to produce legal effects (EC–US Competition Law Agreement);[28]

(4) definitions of position by the Council which might affect the Community's external competence;[29]

(5) atypical acts of the Commission which create new rights and obligations,[30] for example:

> (a) 'internal instructions' adopted by the Commission empowering itself to take samples of products for the purposes of the management of the European Agricultural Guidance and Guarantee Fund;[31]

> (b) a 'Code of Conduct' on the financial control of structural funds adopted by the Commission establishing specific obligations on the Member States in relation to the content, frequency and means of communicating certain information to the Commission;[32]

> (c) a 'Communication' by the Commission to the Member States requiring them to provide certain information in the context of State aid;[33]

> (d) a 'Commission Communication on an Internal Market for Pension Funds', published in the 'C' series of the *Official Journal*, which was essentially identical to a proposal for a directive which had not been adopted by the Council.[34]

In contrast, acts have been held to be incapable of review in the following contexts:

(1) a Commission telex giving an interpretation of a Commission Regulation concerning export refunds;[35]

(2) a Commission letter concerning the interpretation of a directive;[36]

---

[27] Case C-170/89 *BEUC v Commission* [1991] ECR I-5709 paras 9–12.

[28] Case C-327/91 *France v Commission* [1994] ECR I-3641 paras 13–17.

[29] Case C-25/94 *Commission v Council* [1996] ECR I-1469 paras 21–37, see also para 45 of the Opinion of Advocate-General Jacobs.

[30] See the analysis in the Opinion of Advocate-General Tesauro in Case C-57/95 *France v Commission* [1997] ECR I-1627. Contrast Case C-58/94 *Netherlands v Council* [1996] ECR I-2169 paras 23–27, where a 'Code of Conduct concerning public access to Council and Commission documents' was held not to produce legal effects as it constituted an act of 'purely voluntary coordination'.

[31] Case C-366/88 *France v Commission* [1990] ECR I-3571.

[32] Case C-303/90 *France v Commission* [1991] ECR I-5315 paras 7–25.

[33] Case C-325/91 *France v Commission* [1993] ECR I-3283 paras 8–23.

[34] Case C-57/95 *France v Commission* [1997] ECR I-1627 paras 12–23, and paras 9–10 of the Opinion of Advocate-General Tesauro.

[35] Case 133/79 *Sucrimex v Commission* [1980] ECR 1299 paras 16–18. See also Case C-64/93 *Donatab v Commission* [1993] ECR I-3595 paras 13–16.

[36] Case C-50/90 *Sunzest v Commission* [1991] ECR I-2917 paras 12–14.

(3) a Commission letter indicating ineligibility to participate in contracts funded by the European Development Fund;[37]

(4) a Commission telex requesting Member States to supply certain information and announcing an intention to adopt certain measures.[38]

Legal effects/competition law In the context of competition procedures before the Commission, the following measures, *inter alia*, although not adopted in the form of decisions, will be open to challenge under article 173 of the EC Treaty [new art 230]:

(1) a decision to undertake an investigation pursuant to article 14 of Regulation 17/62;[39]

(2) a letter from the Commission withdrawing the exemption from fines pursuant to article 15(6) of Regulation 17/62;[40]

(3) a letter from the Commission rejecting a complaint on the basis that it does not display a sufficient Community interest to justify further investigation of the case;[41]

(4) a letter from the Commission rejecting a complaint following an investigation of the conduct complained of;[42]

(5) the communication of confidential documents to a complainant by the Commission.[43]

The following measures, *inter alia*, may not be challenged by a separate application under article 173 of the EC Treaty (although an individual will be able to raise such procedural breaches in the context of a challenge to the final decision of the Commission):

(1) a letter indicating that the Commission had initiated an investigation of an undertaking under article 3 of Regulation 17;[44]

(2) a statement of objections under article 2 of Regulation 99/63;[45]

---

[37] Case 182/80 *Gauff v Commission* [1982] ECR 799 paras 15–18.

[38] Joined Cases C-66/91 and C-66/91R *Emerald Meats v Commission* [1991] ECR I-1143 paras 26–29.

[39] Joined Cases 97 to 99/87 *Dow Chemical Ibérica v Commission* [1989] ECR 3165 (where the Court of Justice considered the substance of the application without questioning its admissibility). Contrast Case T-9/97 *Elf Atochem v Commission* [1997] ECR II-909 paras 18–27.

[40] Joined Cases 8 to 11/66 *Cimenteries v Commission* [1967] ECR 75 at 90–93.

[41] Case T-24/90 *Automec v Commission* [1992] ECR II-2223 paras 71–86; Case T-114/92 *BEMIM v Commission* [1995] ECR II-147; Case T-5/93 *Tremblay v Commission* [1995] ECR II-185; Case T-77/95 *SFEI v Commission* [1997] ECR II-1.

[42] Case 298/93 *CICCE v Commission* [1985] ECR 1105; Joined Cases 142/84 and 156/84 *BAT v Commission* [1987] ECR 4487 paras 11–12; Case T-64/89 *Automec v Commission* [1990] ECR II-367 para 47; Case C-39/93P *SFEI v Commission* [1994] ECR I-2681 paras 27–30; Case T-37/92 *BEUC and NCC v Commission* [1994] ECR II-285 para 30; Case C-19/93P *Rendo v Commission* [1995] ECR I-3319 paras 27–28; Case T-186/94 *Guérin Automobiles v Commission* [1995] ECR II-1753 para 24—upheld on appeal in Case C-282/95P *Guérin Automobiles v Commission* [1997] ECR I-1503.

[43] Case 53/85 *AKZO Chemie v Commission* [1986] ECR 1965 paras 16–18.

[44] Case 60/81 *IBM v Commission* [1981] ECR 2639 paras 2 and 21.

[45] Ibid.

(3) a letter to an undertaking under investigation by the Commission refusing to provide the full text of a statement of objections;[46]

(4) a letter to an undertaking under investigation refusing access to the complete file, with the exception of internal or confidential documents;[47]

(5) a letter from the Commissioner responsible for competition indicating changes which would have to be made to an agreement in order for the Commission to grant it an exemption under article 85(3) of the EC Treaty [new art 81(3)];[48]

(6) a letter to a complainant to inform it of the Commission's initial reaction to its complaint (forming part of the correspondence exchanged between the Commission and the complainant prior to the sending of a communication pursuant to article 6 of Regulation 99/63);[49]

(7) a letter sent to a complainant by the Commission pursuant to article 6 of Regulation 99/63 indicating that, on the information available to it, the Commission intends to reject the complaint and inviting the complainant to submit further comments;[50]

(8) comfort letters.[51]

Non-privileged applicants: interest in acting In cases involving private parties, a measure will be open to challenge only where it produces binding legal effects which affect the interests of the applicant by bringing about a distinct change in its legal position.[52] For example, in Case 60/81 *IBM v Commission*,[53] a competition case, the measure challenged was a letter from the Commission to IBM which stated that the Commission had initiated procedures under Regulation 17. The Commission also enclosed a 'statement of objections' in which it indicated its views as to why IBM's behaviour was *prima facie* anti-competitive, and invited IBM to submit a written reply. The Court of Justice, whilst recognising that the initiation of the formal procedure under Regulation 17 was capable of producing legal effects in so far as it put an end to the jurisdiction of the competition authorities in the Member States and crystallised the Commission's case against IBM, held that these effects did not

---

[46] Joined Cases T-10 to T-12/92 *Cimenteries v Commission* [1992] ECR II-2667 paras 28–50.

[47] Ibid.

[48] Case T-113/89 *Nefarma v Commission* [1990] ECR II-797 paras 66–96.

[49] Case T-64/89 *Automec v Commission* [1990] ECR II-367 paras 25–65; Case T-37/92 *BEUC and NCC v Commission* [1994] ECR II-285 para 30.

[50] Case T-64/89 *Automec v Commission* [1990] ECR II-367 para 46; Case T-37/92 *BEUC and NCC v Commission* [1994] ECR II-285 para 30.

[51] Case T-575/93 *Koelman v Commission* [1996] ECR II-1 paras 40–42. See also Joined Cases 253/78 and 1–3/79 *Procureur de la République v Giry and Guerlain* [1980] ECR 2327 paras 9–12.

[52] For example, see Case 60/81 *IBM v Commission* [1981] ECR 2639 para 9; Case T-154/94 *CSF and CSME v Commission* [1996] ECR II-1377 para 37; Case T-541/93 *Connaughton v Council* [1997] ECR II-549 para 30 . See also the Opinion of Advocate-General Roemer in Joined Cases 8 to 11/66 *Cimenteries v Commission* [1967] ECR 75 at 103, where he stated that 'not every kind of legal effect is sufficient ... one must take a narrower view and see whether the legal effects are capable of *adversely affecting substantial interests*'.

[53] [1981] ECR 2639.

'adversely affect the interests of the undertaking concerned'.

Furthermore, applications for annulment brought by non-privileged applicants are admissible only where the applicant has an interest in seeing the contested measure annulled.[54] For example, in Case T-443/93 *Casillo Grani v Commission*[55] the Court of First Instance declared that a company's interest in acting disappeared when it was declared to be insolvent. It then had no future interest to protect and it had not suffered any detriment in the past due to the contested act. In Case T-138/89 *NBV and NVB v Commission*[56] the Court of First Instance held that an applicant could not challenge the reasoning adopted by the Commission in reaching a decision where the applicant was not challenging the operative part of the decision (which was in its favour).

The fact that a measure has been revoked does not necessarily mean that an applicant will not have a legal interest in bringing or continuing an action under article 173 [new art 230], as an annulment judgment places a duty on the institution concerned to take the necessary measures to comply with the judgment.[57] The institution may thus be required to take adequate steps to restore the applicant to its original situation or to avoid the adoption of an identical measure in the future.[58]

Similarly, the fact that a contested act has become a *fait accompli*, for example because it has already been implemented or the applicant has already complied with its requirements, does not preclude the applicant from challenging that act under article 173. Annulment of the contested act may produce legal consequences in so far as it would prevent the relevant institution from repeating its actions in the future.[59]

Preparatory measures Measures which are merely part of the process by which a final decision is reached are not reviewable. The EC courts have consistently held that in the case of acts or decisions drawn up in the course of a procedure involving several stages, only measures which definitively determine the

---

[54] Joined Cases T-480/93 and T-483/93 *Antillean Rice Mills v Commission* [1995] ECR II-2305 para 59; Case T-117/95 *Corman v Commission* [1997] ECR II-95 paras 82–83.

[55] [1995] ECR II-1375.

[56] [1992] ECR II-2182 para 31. See also Joined Cases T-24/93 and others *Compagnie Maritime Belge Transports v Commission* [1996] ECR II-1201 para 150.

[57] Joined Cases T-480/93 and T-483/93 *Antillean Rice Mills v Commission* [1995] ECR II-2305 paras 59–60; Joined Cases T-481/93 and T-484/93 *Exporteurs in Levende Varkens v Commission* [1995] ECR II-2941 paras 45–48. *Cf* Case T-25/96 *Arbeitsgemeinschaft Deutscher Luftfahrt-Unternehmen* [1997] ECR II-363.

[58] Contrast Case T-22/96 *Langdon v Commission* [1996] ECR II-1009, where the Commission revoked the decision challenged on the basis that it had been adopted on the basis of a procedure which had been declared to be unlawful by the Court of First Instance in an unrelated case. In these circumstances, the Court declared that the application had become devoid of purpose as the revocation of the contested decision, before its implementation, 'had produced effects equivalent to those of a judgment by the Court annulling it'. See also Case C-123/92 *Lezzi Pietro v Commission* [1993] ECR I-809 paras 8–11; Case T-13/96 *TEAM v Commission* [1997] ECR II-983 paras 23–28.

[59] Case 53/85 *AKZO Chemie v Commission* [1986] ECR 1965 para 21; Case 207/86 *Apesco v Commission* [1988] ECR 2151 paras 15–16; Case T-46/92 *Scottish Football Association v Commission* [1994] ECR II-1039 paras 11–15. See also para 49 of the Opinion of Advocate-General Jacobs in Case C-25/94 *Commission v Council* [1996] ECR I-1469.

position of the institution following the completion of that procedure will be challengeable. Intermediate measures whose purpose is to prepare for the final decision will not be open to challenge.[60] However, it is not necessary for the measure to be the final step in the whole administrative process. A measure which is itself the culmination of a special procedure distinct from that intended to permit the relevant institution to take a decision on the substance of the case will be open to challenge.[61] Thus, in Joined Cases 8 to 11/66 *Cimenteries v Commission*[62] the Court of Justice found that a decision to withdraw the exemption from fines in the context of a competition investigation constituted the 'culmination of a special procedure' distinct from the procedure under which a decision on the substance of the matter as a whole is taken.[63] Furthermore, in Case C-47/91 *Italy v Commission*[64] the Court of Justice held that a Commission decision under article 93(3) of the EC Treaty [new art 88(3)] to investigate new State aid was not merely a preparatory step. The effect of such a decision was to require the Member State to delay paying the aid pending the resolution of the Commission's investigation, and this produced irreversible effects which could not be remedied by means of a challenge to the Commission's final substantive decision. In contrast, in Case 60/81 *IBM v Commission*[65] the Court of Justice held that both the initiation of the investigative procedure and the statement of objections in a competition matter were merely procedural measures adopted as part of the process leading to a final substantive decision.

Whilst measures of a purely preparatory character are not themselves reviewable under article 173 [new art 230], any legal defects in those preparatory acts may be relied on in challenging the definitive act to which they lead.[66]

Confirmatory measures A measure which merely confirms a previous measure is not reviewable.[67] This is important because of the strict

---

[60] Case 60/81 *IBM v Commission* [1981] ECR 2639 para 10; Case T-277/94 *AITEC v Commission* [1996] ECR II-351 para 51; Case T-75/96N *Söktas v Commission* [1996] ECR II-859 para 19; Case T-212/95 *Oficemen v Commission* [1997] ECR II-1161 para 53.

[61] Joined Cases 8 to 11/66 *Cimenteries v Commission* [1967] ECR 75 at 92; Case 60/81 *IBM v Commission* [1981] ECR 2639 paras 10–11; Case 53/85 *AKZO Chemie v Commission* [1986] ECR 1965 paras 19–20. In Case T-9/97 *Elf Atochem v Commission* [1997] ECR II-909 para 21 the Court of First Instance held that, 'Only in the case of measures immediately and irreversibly affecting the legal situation of the undertaking concerned could an action for annulment justifiably be held admissible before the administrative procedure is completed'.

[62] [1967] ECR 75 at 92.

[63] Ibid.

[64] [1992] ECR I-4145 paras 27–30.

[65] [1981] ECR 2639 para 21. See also Joined Cases T-10 to 12/92R and T-14/92R, 15/92R *Cimenteries v Commission* [1992] ECR II-1571 para 45.

[66] Case 60/81 *IBM v Commission* [1981] ECR 2639 para 12; Case C-156/87 *Gestetner Holdings v Council and Commission* [1990] ECR I-781 paras 7–10.

[67] Joined Cases 42/59 and 49/59 *SNUPAT v High Authority* [1961] ECR 53 at 74 (ECSC); Case 22/70 *Commission v Council* [1971] ECR 263 paras 65–66; Case 26/76 *Metro SB-Großmärkte v Commission* [1977] ECR 1875 paras 3–4; Case 44/81 *Germany v Commission* [1982] ECR 1855 paras 8–12; Case C-12/90 *Infortec v Commission* [1990] ECR I-4265 para 10; Case C-480/93P *Zunis Holding v Commission* [1996] ECR I-1 para 14.

two-month limitation period for actions under article 173 [new art 230].[68] A party who has failed to challenge an original measure within the two-month time-limit cannot circumvent that limitation rule by seeking to challenge a later measure which is purely confirmatory of the first measure or by seeking to challenge a subsequent letter refusing to reconsider the original measure.[69] In contrast, where the confirmed decision has not yet become final *vis-à-vis* the person concerned (a decision becomes final where the time for challenging it has expired without any legal challenge to its validity having been made), an applicant may contest either the confirmed or confirmatory decision, or both.[70] Furthermore, the rule precluding review of confirmatory measures does not apply where there has been a substantial change of circumstances since the adoption of the first measure,[71] nor where the second measure extends the temporal application of the first measure.[72]

The definition of a 'confirmatory measure' was examined in Case 44/81 *Germany v Commission*.[73] In this case the Commission had sent letters to the German Federal Ministry of Labour in July 1980 refusing to make certain payments allocated to Germany from the Social Fund. Further letters and dialogue ensued, which came to an end when the Commission wrote another letter in December 1980, again refusing to make the payments. The act challenged under article 173 was the letter of December 1980. The Commission argued that this letter did not constitute a reviewable act as it was purely confirmatory of the July letters. However, the Court of Justice held that it was clear from the context that the Commission only reached a final, unequivocal and definitive decision in December. The July letters were not expressed to be merely provisional but, because the Commission was subsequently prepared to discuss the matter, the July letters could not constitute definitive decisions.[74]

Refusals to act The EC courts have consistently held that the mere fact that a letter has been sent by a Community institution to a person in response to a prior request by that person is not sufficient for that letter to be reviewable under article 173 [new art 230]. It must be shown that the response produces legal effects.[75] Furthermore, an application to annul a refusal to act will be admissible

---

[68] Discussed below at pp 324–327.
[69] Case 2/71 *Germany v Commission* [1971] ECR 669 para 7.
[70] Joined Cases 193 and 194/87 *Maurissen v Court of Auditors* [1989] ECR 1045 para 26; Case T-64/92 *Chavane de Dalmassy v Commission* [1994] ECR-SC II-723 para 25.
[71] Joined Cases 42/59 and 49/59 *SNUPAT v High Authority* [1961] ECR 53 at 76 (ECSC).
[72] Case C-135/93 *Spain v Commission* [1995] ECR I-1651 paras 13 and 29–30.
[73] [1982] ECR 1855 paras 8–12.
[74] See also the judgment in Case 22/70 *Commission v Council* [1971] ECR 263 paras 65–66, where the Court of Justice looked at the factual background in deciding that a measure was not purely confirmatory.
[75] Case C-25/92 *Miethke v Parliament* [1993] ECR I-473 para 10; Case T-83/92 *Zunis Holding v Commission* [1993] ECR II-1169 para 30 (upheld on different grounds on appeal in Case C-480/93P *Zunis Holding v Commission* [1996] ECR I-1); Case T-5/96 *Sveriges Betodlares Centralförening v Commission* [1996] ECR II-1299 para 26; Case T-154/94 *CSF and CSME v Commission* [1996] ECR I-1377 para 51; Case T-277/94 *AITEC v Commission* [1996] ECR II-351 para 50.

only if the act which the institution has refused to adopt would itself have been open to challenge by the applicant under article 173 (for example, it would have produced legal effects and would have been of direct and individual concern to the applicant where he is a private party).[76]

Acts of the European Parliament Prior to the adoption of the Maastricht Treaty, article 173 [new art 230] did not expressly provide for any review of acts of the European Parliament. However, the case-law of the Court of Justice established that acts of the European Parliament which were intended to have legal effects *vis-à-vis* third parties were reviewable. In Case 294/83 *Parti Écologiste 'Les Verts' v Parliament*[77] the Court of Justice observed that, at the time of its drafting, the EEC Treaty merely granted powers of consultation and political control to the Parliament. It was only later that the Parliament acquired power to adopt measures intended to have legal effects *vis-à-vis* third parties and, therefore, it had become essential to interpret article 173 so as to permit the legality of such acts to be reviewable in order to uphold the rule of law in the Community.

Article 173 has been amended by the Maastricht Treaty so that it now expressly provides for review of acts adopted jointly by the European Parliament and the Council, and of acts of the European Parliament intended to produce legal effects *vis-à-vis* third parties.[78]

Delegated acts In Joined Cases 32/58 and 33/58 *SNUPAT v High Authority*[79] the High Authority, which was at that time the equivalent of the Commission under the ECSC Treaty, had set up two subordinate bodies to administer a subsidy system for steel scrap. A steel-making firm sought to challenge a decision of one of the subordinate bodies under article 33 of the ECSC Treaty (which is equivalent to article 173 of the EC Treaty [new art 230]). Although article 33 only provides for review of acts of the High Authority, the Court of Justice held that the decisions adopted by the subordinate body were *prima facie* reviewable as they were equivalent to decisions of the High Authority. The Court reached this conclusion on the basis that the subordinate body derived its powers from the High Authority, and its decisions, in fact, constituted the final administrative stage under the subsidy system.

---

[76] Case T-83/92 *Zunis Holding v Commission* [1993] ECR II-1169 para 31 (upheld on different grounds on appeal in Case C-480/93P *Zunis Holding v Commission* [1996] ECR I-1); Case T-330/94 *Salt Union v Commission* [1996] ECR II-1475 para 32; Case T-5/96 *Sveriges Betodlares Centralförening v Commission* [1996] ECR II-1299 para 28.

[77] [1986] ECR 1339 paras 20–25. See also Case 78/85 *Group of the European Right v Parliament* [1986] ECR 1753; Case 34/86 *Council v Parliament* [1986] ECR 2155; Case 190/84 *Parti écologiste 'Les Verts' v Parliament* [1988] ECR 1017; Joined Cases C-213/88 and C-39/89 *Luxembourg v Parliament* [1991] ECR I-5643 para 15; Case C-314/91 *Weber v Parliament* [1993] ECR I-1093 paras 7–12. See also Case 108/83 *Luxembourg v Parliament* [1984] ECR 1945.

[78] See, for example, Case C-41/95 *Council v Parliament* [1995] ECR I-4411, which was brought pursuant to article 173 of the EC Treaty, as amended.

[79] [1959] ECR 127 at 137–138 (ECSC).

3. PRIVILEGED APPLICANTS: LOCUS STANDI

Definition of privileged applicants The Member States, the Council and the Commission are all privileged applicants under article 173 [new art 230]. However, only the national government authorities of each Member State are considered to be privileged applicants. Governments of regions or autonomous communities, such as the Walloon Region of Belgium, must satisfy the *locus standi* requirements imposed on non-privileged applicants.[80]

Locus standi In order to bring an action under article 173 [new art 230] a privileged applicant need only show that the measure it wishes to challenge is a 'reviewable act'. It is not necessary for it to show that it has a specific interest to protect in bringing the action. It is sufficient that its application alleges 'some genuine illegality with some actual consequences'. However, privileged applicants are not entitled to ask the court for advisory opinions which might be relevant in other cases in the future.[81]

4. SEMI-PRIVILEGED APPLICANTS: LOCUS STANDI

Definition of semi-privileged applicants The European Parliament and the European Central Bank ('ECB') are semi-privileged applicants under article 173.[82]

Locus standi In order to bring an action under article 173 [new art 230] a semi-privileged applicant must show that the relevant measure is a reviewable act which affects its prerogatives.

European Parliament as applicant Prior to the adoption of the Maastricht Treaty, article 173 [new art 230] did not expressly provide that the European Parliament had a right to bring actions for annulment. Although the Court of Justice initially held that the Parliament did not have any right to seek judicial review under article 173[83], the Court departed from its previous decision in Case C-70/88 *Parliament v Council*.[84] In this case, the Court held that the Parliament could seek judicial review under article 173 on the same basis as the other Community institutions provided the action was brought solely to safeguard the Parliament's own prerogatives, and that the action was founded only on submissions alleging infringement of those prerogatives. On the facts of the case, the Parliament sought review of a Council regulation on the grounds that it

---

[80] Case C-95/97 *Région Wallonne v Commission* [1997] ECR I-1787 cf Case C-298/89 *Gibraltar v Council* [1993] ECR I-3605.

[81] See paras 53–54 of the Opinion of Advocate-General Jacobs in Case 25/94 *Commission v Council* [1996] ECR I-1469. See also Case 41/83 *Italy v Commission* [1985] ECR 873 paras 29–30; Case 45/86 *Commission v Council* [1987] ECR 1493 para 3, and paras 24–42 of the Opinion of Advocate-General Lenz.

[82] If ratified, the Amsterdam Treaty will amend article 173 of the EC Treaty to allow the Court of Auditors to bring applications for annulment in order to protect its prerogatives.

[83] Case 302/87 *Parliament v Council* [1988] ECR 5615 (the 'Comitology' case).

[84] [1990] ECR I-2041 paras 26–27 (the 'Chernobyl' case); followed in Case C-65/90 *Parliament v Council* [1992] ECR I-4593 paras 10–15.

had been adopted on the wrong legal basis. The regulation had been adopted on the basis of article 31 of the Euratom Treaty, which requires the Council simply to consult the Parliament. The Parliament argued that the regulation should have been based on article 100a of the EEC Treaty [new art 95], which would have required the Council to cooperate with the Parliament in relation to its adoption, and that the Council's choice of legal basis had, therefore, prevented the Parliament from playing its proper role in the adoption process. In view of these arguments, the Parliament's application was declared to be admissible.

The Maastricht Treaty amended article 173 so that it now expressly recognises that the European Parliament is entitled to bring actions for annulment in order to protect its prerogatives. This amendment reflects the prior case-law of the Court of Justice.[85] Thus, for example, the Parliament is entitled to bring an action under article 173 where it alleges that a measure was adopted on the wrong legal basis, with the result that the Parliament did not play the role in its adoption required by the Treaty (for example consultation, cooperation or co-decision).[86] In contrast, the European Parliament is not entitled to seek review of an act on the basis that it has been inadequately reasoned in breach of article 190 of the EC Treaty [new art 253].[87]

5. NON-PRIVILEGED APPLICANTS: LOCUS STANDI[88]

(a) Natural or legal persons

Legal personality An applicant will be recognised as a legal person if, at the latest by the expiry of the period prescribed for proceedings to be instituted, it has acquired legal personality in accordance with the law governing its constitution or if it has been treated as an independent legal entity by the Community institutions.[89]

---

[85] Case C-65/90 *Parliament v Council* [1992] ECR I-4593 paras 10–15; Case C-316/91 *Parliament v Council* [1994] ECR I-625 paras 10–13; Case C-156/93 *Parliament v Commission* [1995] ECR I-2019 para 10; C-303/94 *Parliament v Council* [1996] ECR I-2943 para 17.

[86] Case C-70/88 *Parliament v Council* [1990] ECR I-2041 paras 27–31; Case C-316/91 *Parliament v Council* [1994] ECR I-625 para 16; Case C-187/93 *Parliament v Council* [1994] ECR I-2857 paras 14–16; Case C-156/93 *Parliament v Commission* [1995] ECR I-2019 paras 12–13; Case C-360/93 *Parliament v Council* [1996] ECR I-1195 paras 17–19; C-303/94 *Parliament v Council* [1996] ECR I-2943 paras 19–20. Annulment of Community measures on the ground of incorrect legal basis is discussed further below at pp 320–322.

[87] Case C-156/93 *Parliament v Commission* [1995] ECR I-2019 paras 10–11; Case C-303/94 *Parliament v Council* [1996] ECR I-2943 paras 17–18.

[88] See also Albors-Llorens, *Private Parties in European Community Law (Challenging Community Measures)* (Oxford, 1996).

[89] Case T-161/94 *Sinochem Heilongjiang v Council* [1996] ECR II-695 paras 31–35. See also Case 135/81 *Groupement des Agences de Voyages v Commission* [1982] ECR 3799 paras 8–13; paras 23–47 of the Opinion of Advocate-General Lenz in Case C-298/89 *Gibraltar v Council* [1993] ECR I-3605.

Third country nationals Individuals or legal entities from countries which are not members of the European Union are entitled to bring actions for annulment under article 173 of the EC Treaty [new art 230].[90]

(b) Reviewable acts

Reviewable acts The rules governing the *locus standi* of private parties are set down in the fourth paragraph of article 173 of the EC Treaty [new art 230], which provides that:

> Any natural or legal person may ... institute proceedings against a decision addressed to that person or against a decision which, although in the form of a regulation or a decision addressed to another person, is of direct and individual concern to the former.

Read literally, article 173 only permits review of acts which are, in substance, decisions. This was indeed the approach adopted by the EC courts for a substantial period. However, recent case-law of the Court of Justice has now established that a private party has standing to seek review of a measure of general application (for example a regulation) wherever he can show that the relevant act is of direct and individual concern to him.

Decision addressed to the applicant The addressee of a decision may seek review of that decision without having to show that it is of direct and individual concern to him. The fact that a measure is not expressly adopted in the form of a decision does not prevent it from being classified as such. The EC courts will examine the substance of an act in order to establish whether it should, in fact, be classified as a decision within the meaning of article 189 of the EC Treaty [new art 249].[91] For example, letters sent by Community institutions may amount to decisions and, therefore, be subject to review under article 173 [new art 230].[92] The EC courts have recognised, *inter alia*, the following measures as constituting decisions capable of review under article 173:[93]

(1) an oral statement by the spokesman for the Commissioner responsible for competition matters that a proposed merger did not fall within the threshold of Community competence under the Merger Regulation;[94]

(2) the communication of confidential documents to a complainant by the Commission in the context of competition proceedings;[95]

---

[90] For example, see Case T-509/93 *Richco v Commission* [1996] ECR I-1181 (applicant was a Bermudan company); Case T-75/96R *Söktas v Commission* [1996] ECR II-859 (applicant was a Turkish company).

[91] See Rosa Greaves, 'The Nature and Binding Effect of Decisions under Article 189 EC' (1996) 21 ELRev 3 at 8–10.

[92] For example, see Joined Cases 8 to 11/66 *Cimenteries v Commission* [1967] ECR 75 at 90–93 (discussed above at p 271).

[93] See further above at pp 268–278.

[94] Case T-3/93 *Air France v Commission* [1994] ECR II-121 paras 8, 55–60.

[95] Case 53/85 *AKZO Chemie v Commission* [1986] ECR 1965 paras 14–22.

(3) a Commission letter indicating a decision to close the file on a competition complaint;[96]

(4) a letter refusing access to a non-confidential file in the context of an anti-dumping procedure.[97]

Decision addressed to another person A private party may seek review of a decision addressed to another person where the decision is of direct and individual concern to the person seeking review. The phrase 'decisions addressed to another person' includes decisions addressed to Member States.[98]

Decision in the form of a regulation The Court of Justice has held that the purpose of allowing private parties to seek review of decisions adopted in the form of regulations is to prevent Community institutions avoiding the possibility of review by the simple device of adopting an act which is, in substance, a decision in the form of a regulation.[99]

The test of what constitutes a regulation and what constitutes a decision is set out in article 189 of the EC Treaty [new art 249]. Article 189 states that regulations are of general application, whereas decisions are binding only on those to whom they are addressed.[100] Thus, the crucial difference lies in the general legislative nature of regulations, in contrast to decisions, which are directed at specific and identifiable legal persons.[101] In deciding whether an act constitutes a decision (or bundle of individual decisions[102]) or a regulation, the following factors must be borne in mind:

(1) a measure does not lose its character as a regulation simply because it may be factually possible to ascertain the number, or even the identity, of the persons to which it applies at any given time.[103]

---

[96] Case C-39/93P *SFEI v Commission* [1994] ECR I-2681 paras 27–30. For an analysis of the different stages in the investigation of a competition complaint by the Commission, see Case T-186/94 *Guérin Automobiles v Commission* [1995] ECR II-1753 para 24, upheld on appeal in Case C-282/95P *Guérin Automobiles v Commission* [1997] ECR I-1503.

[97] Case C-170/89 *BEUC v Commission* [1991] ECR I-5709 paras 9–12.

[98] Case 25/62 *Plaumann v Commission* [1963] ECR 95, and the Opinion of Advocate-General Roemer at 112–113.

[99] Case 101/76 *Koninklijke Scholten Honig v Council and Commission* [1977] ECR 797 para 6; Case 162/78 *Wagner v Commission* [1979] ECR 3467 para 16; Joined Cases 789/79 and 790/79 *Calpak v Commission* [1980] ECR 1949 para 7; Case T-298/94 *Roquette Frères v Council* [1996] ECR II-1531 para 35.

[100] See Ch 1, pp 7–8 and 14–15.

[101] *Producteurs de fruits v Council* [1962] ECR 471; Case C-298/89 *Gibraltar v Council* [1993] Joined cases 16 and 17/62 ECR I-3605 para 15.

[102] Joined Cases 41 to 44/70 *Fruit Company v Commission* [1971] ECR 411 paras 5–21; Joined Cases 87/77, 130/77, 22/83, 9/84 and 10/84 *Salerno v Commission and Council* [1985] ECR 2523 paras 29–30; Case C-354/87 *Weddel v Commission* [1990] ECR I-3847 paras 16–23; Case T-197/95 *Sveriges Betodlares Centralförening v Commission* [1996] ECR II-1283 para 24.

[103] Case 6/68 *Zuckerfabrik Watenstedt v Council* [1968] ECR 409; Case 101/76 *Koninklijke Scholten-Honig v Council and Commission* [1977] ECR 797; Joined Cases 789/79 and 790/79 *Calpak v Commission* [1980] ECR 1949 para 9; Case 64/80 *Giuffrida and Campogrande v Council* [1981] ECR 693; Case 307/81 *Alusuisse Italia v Council and Commission* [1982] ECR 3463 para 11; Case 147/83 *Binderer v Commission* [1985] ECR 257 para 13; Case 26/86 *Deutz und Geldermann v Council* [1987] ECR 941.

(2) the fact that a legal provision may have different practical effects for the different persons to whom it applies does not prevent it from being a regulation.[104]

(3) a measure does not cease to have general application by virtue of the fact that it contains temporal or geographical limitations or derogations.[105] For example, in Case 30/67 *Industria Molitaria Imolese v Council*[106] certain provisions in a regulation fixed intervention prices for common wheat at the Bologna and Ancona marketing centres. The Court of Justice held that an application for review by milling undertakings situated in Bologna and Ancona was inadmissible as the provisions challenged simply affected the interests of users and traders in the abstract, albeit within the ambit of each marketing centre.

The EC courts traditionally have adopted a very restrictive approach to the question of what constitutes a decision.[107] A striking example is provided by Case 242/81 *Roquette Frères v Council*.[108] In this case, the applicant, a producer of isoglucose, challenged the legality of a Council regulation which introduced production levies for isoglucose. The applicant argued that the regulation was in substance a decision as there were only nine isoglucose producers in the whole of the Community, the identities of which were known to the Council. The Court of Justice rejected this argument and held that the measure was of general application as it did not expressly fix the amount of the levy for each specific producer, but rather it established a system for the setting of the levies on an annual basis which depended on purely objective factors (such as the level of production of sugar and isoglucose in the Community in the relevant marketing year). The Court emphasised that:[109]

---

[104] Case 6/68 *Zuckerfabrik Watenstedt v Council* [1968] ECR 409 at 415; Case 63/69 *Compagnie Française Commerciale v Commission* [1970] ECR 205 paras 6–10; Case 65/69 *Compagnie d'Approvisionnement v Commission* [1970] ECR 229 paras 6–10; Case 101/76 *Koninklijke Scholten-Honig v Council and Commission* [1977] ECR 797; Case T-472/93 *Campo Ebro Industrial v Council* [1995] ECR II-421 paras 34–36; Case T-197/95 *Sveriges Betodlares Centralförening v Commission* [1996] ECR II-1283 para 29.

[105] Case 6/68 *Zuckerfabrik Watenstedt v Council* [1968] ECR 409 at 415; Joined Cases 103 to 109/78 *Société des Usines de Beauport v Council* [1979] ECR 17 paras 12–19; Case C-298/89 *Gibraltar v Council* [1993] ECR I-3605 para 18.

[106] [1968] ECR 115 at 121.

[107] See, for example, Joined Cases 16/62 and 17/62 *Producteurs de fruits v Council* [1962] ECR 471 paras 2–3; Case 25/62 *Plaumann v Commission* [1963] ECR 95 at 107; Case 101/76 *Koninklijke Scholten-Honig v Council and Commission* [1977] ECR 797 para 6; Case 162/78 *Wagner v Commission* [1979] ECR 3467 para 17; Joined Cases 789/79 and 790/79 *Calpak v Commission* [1980] ECR 1949 para 8; Case 242/81 *Roquette Frères v Council* [1982] ECR 3213 paras 5–6; Case 307/81 *Alusuisse Italia v Council and Commission* [1982] ECR 3463 para 8; Case 40/84 *Casteels v Commission* [1985] ECR 667 paras 9–12.

[108] [1982] ECR 3213. See also Case T-472/93 *Campo Ebro Industrial v Council* [1995] ECR II-421 paras 29–33, where the only producers of isoglucose in Spain were held not to have standing to challenge a regulation dealing with sugar sector prices in Spain.

[109] Case 242/81 *Roquette Frères v Council* [1982] ECR 3213 para 7.

... a measure does not cease to be a regulation because it is possible to determine more or less exactly the number or even the identity of the persons to whom it applies at any given time as long as it is established that such application takes effect by virtue of an objective legal or factual situation defined by the measure in question in relation to its purpose.

The crucial factor in deciding that the measure was of general application was that the measure challenged applied to producers of isoglucose as a general class and not to named producers. As Advocate-General Reischl stated in his Opinion:[110]

The determinant factor is whether it may be assumed that the number of parties concerned will remain unchanged. However, nobody can predict that with certainty. It is in fact impossible to rule out certain changes, either through the disappearance of an undertaking or by the founding of new undertakings, even if that does perhaps appear improbable.

Regulations/measures of general application On the strict wording of the fourth paragraph of article 173 [new art 230], a private party is not permitted to seek review of a regulation or indeed any other act which is of general application. However, the recent case-law of the EC courts has established that, in spite of the wording of article 173, an applicant may challenge such an act where he is directly and individually concerned by it.[111]

In Case C-358/89 *Extramet Industrie v Council*[112] an importer of calcium metal into the Community was held to have standing to challenge the legality of a regulation which imposed an anti-dumping duty on imports of calcium metal into the Community from China and the Soviet Union. The Court of Justice declared that the application was admissible despite the fact that it expressly recognised in its judgment that the regulation was legislative in character. In Case C-309/89 *Codorniu v Council*[113] a Spanish producer of sparkling wines successfully challenged the legality of a regulation which reserved the use of the term '*crémant*' for certain types of sparkling wine produced in France and Luxembourg. Again, the Court declared that the application was admissible even though the regulation was of a legislative nature.

It has now become settled case-law that an action under article 173 may be brought against a measure which is 'legislative' or 'normative' in nature or 'of general application' where it is of direct and individual concern to the applicant.[114]

---

[110] Case 242/81 *Roquette Frères v Council* [1982] ECR 3213 at 3233.

[111] See Anthony Arnull, 'Private Applicants and the Action for Annulment under Article 173 of the EC Treaty' [1995] CML Rev 7 at 34–40.

[112] [1991] ECR I-2501 paras 13–14.

[113] [1994] ECR I-1853 paras 17–19.

[114] Case C-358/89 *Extramet Industrie v Council* [1991] ECR I-2501 paras 13–14; Case C-309/89 *Codorniu v Council* [1994] ECR I-1853 paras 17–19; Joined Cases T-480/93 and T-483/93 *Antillean Rice Mills v Commission* [1995] ECR II-2305 para 66; Joined Cases T-481/93 and T-484/93 *Exporteurs in Levende Varkens v Commission* [1995] ECR II-2941 para 50; Case T-482/93 *Weber v Commission* [1996] ECR II-609 para 56; Case T-298/94 *Roquette Frères v Council* [1996] ECR II-1531 para 37; Case C-10/95P *Asocarne v Council* [1995] ECR I-4149 para 43; Case T-18/95 *Atlanta v Commission* [1996] ECR II-1669 para 47; case C-87/95P

Directives A directive is a form of indirect regulatory or legislative measure (as it requires the Member States to implement its requirements into their own national laws). It will therefore usually be a measure which is general in nature and effect.[115] In Case C-298/89 *Gibraltar v Council*[116] an annulment action against a directive was declared to be inadmissible on the basis of the traditional case-law of the Court of Justice that measures of general application were not open to review under article 173 [new art 230]. As discussed above, this is no longer the position following the judgments of the Court of Justice in Case C-358/89 *Extramet Industrie v Council*[117] and Case C-309/89 *Codorniu v Council*.[118] This was recognised in Case C-10/95P *Asocarne v Council*[119] in which the applicant sought annulment of a directive. The application was found to be inadmissible on the basis that the applicant was not individually concerned by the directive; however, the Court of Justice expressly reiterated that a normative provision (such as a directive) will be open to challenge under article 173 where it is of individual concern to the applicant. In principle, there is no reason why a private party should not be able to challenge a directive under article 173 provided he can show that he is directly and individually concerned by it.[120]

Current legal position Until the judgments of the Court of Justice in Case C-358/89 *Extramet Industrie v Council*[121] and Case C-309/89 *Codorniu v Council*,[122] whenever a party sought to challenge a measure of general application, it was formally necessary for him to show that the contested measure constituted a decision in substance if not in form, and was of direct and individual concern to him. Given the developments in the case-law it should now be sufficient for an applicant simply to show that the measure is of direct and individual concern to him.

However, the EC courts have not explicitly stated that it is now unnecessary for an applicant to show that a measure of general application is, in substance, a decision for the purposes of an annulment action. Indeed, the position is still not completely clear as it is common for the EC courts to refer to the previous case-law as to what constitutes a decision before reiterating that the fact that a measure is of general application is no longer a bar to review under article 173

CNPAAP [1996] ECR I-2003 para 36; Case T-168/95R *Eridania v Council* [1995] ECR II-2817 para 29; Case T-197/95 *Sveriges Betodlares Centralförening v Commission* [1996] ECR II-1283 para 31; Case T-60/96 *Merck v Commission* [1997] ECR II-849 paras 39–41.

[115] Case C-298/89 *Gibraltar v Council* [1993] ECR I-3605 para 16; Case C-10/95P *Asocarne* [1995] ECR I-4149 para 29.

[116] [1993] ECR I-3605.

[117] [1991] ECR I-2501.

[118] [1994] ECR I-1853.

[119] [1995] ECR I-4149 para 43.

[120] See Paul Nihoul, 'La recevabilité des recours en annulation introduits par un particulier à l'encontre d'un acte communautaire de portée générale' [1994] RTD eur 171 at 174–175; Anthony Arnull, 'Private Applicants and the Action for Annulment under Article 173 of the EC Treaty' [1995] CML Rev 7 at 46–47.

[121] [1991] ECR I-2501.

[122] [1994] ECR I-1853.

[new art 230] as long as the applicant is individually concerned by the measure challenged.[123]

Logically, it is difficult to see on what basis an applicant could be required to continue to show that a measure of general application is in substance a decision. In both *Extramet* and *Codorniu*, applications were declared to be admissible against general legislative measures on the basis that the applicant was directly and individually concerned by them. Furthermore, both Advocate-General Jacobs[124] and Advocate-General Lenz[125] have indicated that they consider that the requirement to show that a measure is in substance a decision has now been subsumed by the requirement of individual concern.

On this basis, private parties should have *locus standi* under article 173 in the following situations:

(1) where a decision has been addressed to the person bringing the proceedings;

(2) where a decision addressed to another person is of direct and individual concern to the person bringing the proceedings; and

(3) where a measure of general application (for example a regulation or directive) is of direct and individual concern to the person bringing the proceedings.

However, given the uncertain nature of the EC courts' case-law, where there are grounds for arguing that a general measure is in substance a decision or is of limited scope, an applicant would be well advised to put forward arguments to this effect in his application, as well as making submissions on direct and individual concern. This is because the more limited the scope of a measure, the more likely the EC courts are to find that the requirement of individual concern is satisfied. However, it must be emphasised that the EC courts will probably continue to adopt a very restrictive approach to the question of *locus standi* for private parties seeking review of measures of general application.

Severance The EC courts have power to annul particular provisions of a measure wherever the relevant provision can be removed from the measure without robbing it altogether of its substance and legal effects.[126] Thus, a private party may bring an action for annulment under article 173 [new art 230] against a particular provision of a measure; it is not necessary to challenge the measure as a whole.[127]

---

[123] For example, see Case C-10/95P *Asocarne* [1995] ECR I-4149 paras 28–33; Case T-482/93 *Weber v Commission* [1996] ECR II-609 paras 55–56; Case T-47/95 *Terres Rouges Consultant v Commission* [1997] ECR I-481 paras 39–44. Furthermore, in Case T-472/93 *Campo Ebro Industrial v Council* [1995] ECR II-421, decided after *Extramet* and *Codorniu*, the Court of First Instance did expressly declare an action to be inadmissible on the basis that it sought to challenge a measure of general application. However, this decision should now be regarded as an isolated case as it is clearly in conflict with the current state of the case-law.

[124] See paras 34–53 of his Opinion in Case C-358/89 *Extramet Industrie v Council* [1991] ECR I-2501.

[125] See paras 19–37 of his Opinion in Case C-309/89 *Codorniu v Council* [1994] ECR I-1853. See also para 97 of his Opinion in Case C-298/89 *Gibraltar v Council* [1993] ECR I-3605.

[126] Paragraph 17 of the Opinion of Advocate-General Lenz in Case C-309/89 *Codorniu v Council* [1994] ECR I-1853.

[127] Joined Cases 16/62 and 17/62 *Producteurs de fruits v Council* [1962] ECR 471 para 2; Case

(c) Direct concern

Definition of 'direct concern' In Case 100/74 *Société CAM v Commission*[128] Advocate-General Warner gave the following definition of 'direct concern':

> The answer to the question whether such a decision is of 'direct concern' to [the applicant] depends upon whether or not the decision is the direct cause of an effect on that person. This means that, in general, the answer depends upon whether the decision leaves a discretion to the Member State to which it is addressed. If the action to be taken by the Member State on the decision is automatic or is, at all events, a foregone conclusion, then the decision is of direct concern to any person affected by that action. If, on the other hand, the decision leaves it to the Member State whether to act or not to act, it is the action, or inaction, of the Member State that is of direct concern to the person affected, not the decision itself.

Thus, a measure adopted by a Community institution which simply creates a power in favour of the Member States concerned or which leaves a margin of discretion as to the manner of its implementation *prima facie* cannot be of direct concern within the meaning of article 173 of the EC Treaty [new art 230].[129] However, purely facultative Community measures may be of direct concern to an applicant where, in all the circumstances of the case, there is no doubt that the Member State will make use of the power.[130] For example, in Case 62/70 *Werner A Bock v Commission*[131] and Case 11/82 *Piraiki-Patraiki v Commission*[132] the Member States concerned had specifically requested that the Commission grant them the relevant facultative powers.[133]

C–309/89 *Codorniu v Council* [1994] ECR I-1853.

[128] [1975] ECR 1393 at 1410–1411. Approved by Advocate-General Jacobs at para 11 of his Opinion in Case C-358/89 *Extramet Industrie v Council* [1991] ECR I-2501.

[129] Joined Cases 10/68 and 18/68 *Eridania v Commission* [1969] ECR 459 paras 8–14; Case 69/69 *Alcan v Commission* [1970] ECR 385 paras 8–9; Joined Cases 41 to 44/70 *Fruit Company v Commission* [1971] ECR 411 paras 23–28; Case 123/77 *UNICME v Council* [1978] ECR 845; Joined Cases 103 to 109/78 *Usines de Beauport v Council* [1979] ECR 17 paras 20–22; Case 222/83 *Differdange v Commission* [1984] ECR 2889 para 12; Case 294/83 *Parti écologiste 'Les Verts' v Parliament* [1986] ECR 1339 para 31; Joined Cases 87/77, 130/77, 22/83, 9/84 and 10/84 *Salerno v Commission and Council* [1985] ECR 2523 para 31 (staff case); Joined Cases T-480/93 and T-483/93 *Antillean Rice Mills v Commission* [1995] ECR II-2305 para 63.

[130] Case 11/82 *Piraiki-Patraiki v Commission* [1985] ECR 207 paras 6–10; Case T-435/93 *ASPEC v Commission* [1995] ECR II-1281 paras 60–61; Case T-155/94 *Climax Paper Converters v Council* [1996] ECR II-873 para 53; Case T-266/94 *Skibsværftsforeningen v Commission* [1996] ECR II-1399 paras 49–50; Case T-380/94 *AIUFFASS v Commission* [1996] ECR II-2169 paras 46–47.

[131] [1971] ECR 897 paras 6–8.

[132] [1985] ECR 207 paras 8–10. See also Joined Cases 106/63 and 107/63 *Toepfer v Commission* [1965] ECR 405.

[133] In Case 11/82 *Piraiki-Patraiki v Commission* [1985] ECR 207, Advocate-General Verloren van Themaat (at p 216 of his Opinion) stated that:

> A measure taken by the Community is defined as being of direct material concern to an interested party if, even though it requires the adoption of a further national implementing measure, it is possible to foresee with certainty or with a high degree of probability that the implementing measure will affect the applicant and the manner in which it will do so.

(d) Individual concern

Test Since its decision in Case 25/62 *Plaumann v Commission*,[134] the Court of Justice has consistently held that:

> Persons other than those to whom a decision is addressed may only claim to be individually concerned if that decision affects them by reason of certain attributes which are peculiar to them or by reason of circumstances in which they are differentiated from all other persons and by virtue of these factors distinguishes them individually just as in the case of the person addressed.

In certain judgments the EC courts have stated that the provisions of the Treaty regarding the right of interested parties to bring an action must not be interpreted restrictively.[135] However, in practice the *locus standi* rules concerning non-privileged parties have been applied very narrowly.

The criteria to be applied in determining individual concern overlap substantially with the criteria which have been applied to distinguish between regulations and decisions.[136] In particular:

(1) An applicant will not be individually concerned where he belongs to a group or class which is affected by a measure drafted in abstract or objective terms. For example, in Case 25/62 *Plaumann v Commission*[137] the applicant, an importer of clementines into Germany, sought to challenge a decision of the Commission which refused an authorisation sought by the German Government to vary the customs duty levied on clementines imported into Germany from third countries. The Court of Justice held that the applicant, who was affected by the disputed decision simply by reason of its participation in a commercial activity which might be carried out at any time by any person, was not individually concerned by the decision. In other words, the fact that the applicant was a member of the class of persons who imported clementines into Germany was not sufficient to satisfy the requirement of individual concern.

(2) The fact that it is possible to determine, more or less precisely, the number, or even the identity, of the persons to whom a measure applies at any given time does not mean that the measure must be regarded as being of individual concern to them.[138] For example, in Case 307/81 *Alusuisse Italia v Council and Commission*[139] a regulation which imposed an anti-dumping duty

---

[134] [1963] ECR 95 at 107; Case C-309/89 *Codorniu v Council* [1994] ECR I-1853 para 20; Joined Cases T-480/93 and T-483/93 *Antillean Rice Mills v Commission* [1995] ECR II-2305 para 66.

[135] Case 25/62 *Plaumann v Commission* [1963] ECR 95 at 106–107; Joined Cases T-447 to 449/93 *AITEC v Commission* [1995] ECR II-1971 para 34; Joined Cases T-528/93 and others *Métropole Télévision v Commission* [1996] ECR II-649 para 60.

[136] Discussed above at pp 282–284.

[137] [1963] ECR 95; Joined Cases 10/68 and 18/68 *Eridania v Commission* [1969] ECR 459 paras 5–7; Case T-183/94 *Cantina cooperativa fra produttori vitivinicoli di Torre di Mosto v Commission* [1995] ECR II-1941 paras 47–52.

[138] Case 123/77 *UNICME v Council* [1978] ECR 845; Case 231/82 *Spijker v Commission* [1983] ECR 2559 paras 8–11; Case C-213/91 *Abertal v Commission* [1993] ECR I-3265 paras 16–24; Joined Cases T-481/93 and T-484/93 *Exporteurs in Levende Varkens* [1995] ECR II-2941 para 53; Case C-209/94P *Buralux v Council* [1996] ECR I-615 paras 24–28.

[139] [1982] ECR 3463 paras 9–12.

on importers of orthoxylene from Puerto Rico and the United States was held not to be of individual concern to the applicant, even though it might have been possible to identify the limited numbers of traders affected by the regulation at the time of its adoption. The regulation imposed the anti-dumping duty on persons solely by reference to the objective criterion that they were importers of that product; it did not expressly name the persons on whom the duties were to be imposed.

Although the current state of the case-law is far from clear, in general terms the EC courts will find that the requirements of individual concern are satisfied where:

(1) the applicant is a member of a closed class, the membership of which was absolutely fixed and incapable of alteration at the time of adoption of the measure challenged *and* there is a 'causal link' or 'special connection' between his position and the provision challenged; or

(2) the Commission is, by virtue of specific provisions, under a duty to take account of the consequences of a provision which it envisages adopting for the situation of certain individuals, and the applicant belongs to that group of individuals; or

(3) the applicant is affected by the provision challenged by reason of certain attributes which are peculiar to him or by reason of circumstances which differentiate him from all other persons; or

(4) the provision challenged adversely affects a specific right of the applicant; or

(5) the applicant is expressly named in the provision challenged.

An applicant will not be individually concerned by a measure solely on the basis that he has participated in the procedure leading to its adoption, or has made representations or a complaint to the Commission prior to the adoption of a particular measure.

Closed or fixed class Until recently, it appeared that the case-law of the Court of Justice established that a private party would be individually concerned by a measure where he belonged to a class of parties affected by the measure which was absolutely fixed and incapable of alteration at the time of adoption of that measure. The most common way in which a class may be absolutely fixed is where the measure has retrospective effect in respect of a specific group of people.[140] For example:

(1) In Joined Cases 106/63 and 107/63 *Toepfer v Commission*[141] the Court of Justice looked at all the factual circumstances of the case and decided that, when the contested measures were adopted, the only persons who could be affected by them were importers who had applied for an import licence during the

---

[140] See Case 62/70 *Bock v Commission* [1971] ECR 897 paras 9–10; Case 88/76 *exportation des sucres v Commission* [1977] ECR 709 paras 9–11; Joined Cases 87/77, 130/77, 22/83, 9/84 and 10/84 *Salerno v Commission and Council* [1985] ECR 2523 para 30 (staff case); Case 232/81 *Agricola Commerciale Olio v Commission* [1984] ECR 3881 paras 10–11; Case 92/78 *Simmenthal v Commission* [1979] ECR 777 paras 18–26.

[141] [1965] ECR 405 at 411–412; see also the Opinion of Advocate-General Roemer at 437–439.

course of the day of 1 October 1963. They were therefore individually concerned.

(2) In Joined Cases 41 to 44/70 *Fruit Company v Commission*[142] the measure challenged affected parties who had made applications for import licences prior to the adoption of the measure. Therefore, when the measure was adopted the number of applications which could be affected by it was fixed; no new applications could be added. It followed that the measure challenged, which was in the form of a regulation, was to be treated as a 'conglomeration of individual decisions', and the persons within the fixed class were individually concerned by those decisions.

(3) In Case 100/74 *CAM v Commission*[143] the regulation challenged concerned the import levies and export refunds for cereals and rice. Under Community legislation concerning the common organisation of the market in cereals, the exporters of certain cereals were authorised to request advance fixing of export refunds. The regulation affected a class of traders but, because it affected only those traders who had requested advance fixing, it applied only to a finite and known number of cereal exporters. The Court, therefore, held that an application under article 173 [new art 230] by an exporter thus affected was admissible.

However, the Court of First Instance has now interpreted the Court of Justice's case-law on the basis that the mere fact that a trader forms part of a closed group of traders, to which no individual could be added at the time when the regulation was adopted, is not in itself sufficient for the trader in question to be regarded as individually concerned.[144] This approach is supported by certain Advocate-Generals' Opinions. Advocate-General Tesauro has stated[145] that not only must there be a closed class of identifiable persons affected by the relevant measure, but there must also be a causal link between the institution's knowledge of the applicant's situation and the measure adopted. This view has been supported by Advocate-General Lenz,[146] who has stated that there must be 'a specific connection between the applicant's situation (in the broadest sense) and the contested measure'.

In view of the approach adopted by the Court of First Instance, an applicant should argue not only that he is a member of a fixed class, but also expressly indicate that there is a 'causal link' or 'special connection' between his position and the measure challenged. On the basis of the existing case-law, examples of such special connections would appear to include:

---

[142] [1971] ECR 411 paras 14–22.

[143] [1975] ECR 1393 paras 3–20.

[144] Case T-489/93 *Unifruit Hellas v Commission* [1994] ECR II-1201 paras 24–26; Case T-482/93 *Weber v Commission* [1996] ECR II-609 paras 63–66; Case T-298/94 *Roquette Frères v Council* [1996] ECR II-1531 paras 41–44.

[145] Case C-244/88 *Usines coopératives de déshydratation du Vexin v Commission* [1989] ECR 3811 at 3820–3822.

[146] Case C-309/89 *Codorniu v Council* [1994] ECR I-1853, paras 39–40 of the Opinion.

(1) where the Commission is under an obligation to take account of the position of certain parties before adopting a measure which might affect such parties;[147]

(2) where the Commission adopts a measure which affects individual applications for import licences which have already been lodged (as in Joined Cases 106/63 and 107/63 *Toepfer v Commission*[148] and Joined Cases 41 to 44/70 *International Fruit Company v Commission*[149]); and

(3) where the Commission adopts a measure which affects established categories of export licences with refunds fixed in advance which have already been granted (as in Case 100/74 *CAM v Commission*[150]).

It is unclear whether, in order to establish whether or not a fixed class exists, the EC courts will be prepared to 'sever' a provision which produces both retroactive and prospective effects. In Case 62/70 *Bock v Commission*[151] the applicant was permitted to challenge a Commission decision which authorised Germany to exclude from Community treatment certain products originating in China which were in free circulation in the Benelux countries. This authorisation applied to future imports as well as imports in relation to which applications for import licences were already pending before the German authorities. The Court of Justice held that as the applicant had only challenged the decision to the extent that it covered imports for which licence applications were already pending at the date of its entry into force, the number of importers concerned in this way was fixed and ascertainable. However, such cases are isolated, and in Case 45/81 *Moksel Import-Export v Commission*[152] the Court of Justice expressly refused to adopt such an approach.

Commission's duty to consider position of applicant Where the Commission, by virtue of specific provisions, is under a duty to take account of the effects of a measure which it envisages adopting on the situation of certain individuals, those individuals will be individually concerned by the measure adopted.[153] For example:

---

[147] Case T-489/93 *Unifruit Hellas v Commission* [1994] ECR II-1201 paras 23–26. See also the cases discussed below under the heading 'Commission's duty to consider position of applicant', at pp 291–293.

[148] [1965] ECR 405 at 411–412.

[149] [1971] ECR 411 paras 16–22. See also Case 62/70 *Bock v Commission* [1971] ECR 897 paras 9–10; Case 232/81 *Agricola Commerciale Olio v Commission* [1984] ECR 3881 paras 10–11; Case T-482/93 *Weber v Commission* [1996] ECR II-609 paras 63–66. See also Case T-70/94 *Comafrica v Commission* [1996] ECR II-1741 paras 38–43.

[150] [1975] ECR 1393 paras 14–19. See also Case 88/76 *Exportation des sucres v Commission* [1977] ECR 709 paras 9–11; Case T-482/93 *Weber v Commission* [1996] ECR II-609 paras 63–66.

[151] [1971] ECR 897 paras 9–11. See also the Opinion of Advocate-General Warner in Case 162/87 *Wagner v Commission* [1979] ECR 3467 at 3494.

[152] [1982] ECR 1129 paras 11–19. See also Case C-229/88 *Cargill v Commission* [1990] ECR I-1303.

[153] Joined Cases T-480/93 and T-483/93 *Antillean Rice Mills v Commission* [1995] ECR II-2305 para 67; Joined Cases T-481/93 and T-484/93 *Exporteurs in Levende Varkens v Commission* [1995] ECR II-2941 para 61; Case T-197/95 *Sveriges Betodlares Centralförening v Commission*

(1) In Case 152/88 *Sofrimport v Commission*[154] the Commission adopted a regulation suspending the issue of import licences for dessert apples originating in Chile. As a result of this regulation, Sofrimport was prevented from importing a specific cargo of dessert apples which had been *en route* to the Community before the regulation was adopted. The Court of Justice found that importers of Chilean apples which were in transit when the relevant regulation was adopted constituted a restricted group which could not be added to after the measures challenged came into effect. In addition, the Commission was under a specific obligation in adopting such a measure to take account of the special position of products in transit to the Community. In light of the existence of the closed class and the Commission's obligation to consider traders in its position, the applicant was held to be individually concerned by the regulation challenged.

(2) In Case 11/82 *Piraiki-Patraiki v Commission*[155] Greek cotton producers successfully challenged the validity of a Commission decision adopted in October 1981, which authorised France to impose a quota system on imports of cotton yarn from Greece during November 1981 to January 1982. Prior to the adoption of the decision, certain cotton producers had already entered into contracts to export cotton into France during the relevant period. Furthermore, article 130 of the Greek Act of Accession to the European Communities imposed an obligation on the Commission, when it was considering whether to allow a Member State to adopt protective measures, to take account of the negative effects which such measures might have on the undertakings concerned. The Court of Justice held that the producers who had already entered into contracts with French customers before the date of the contested decision were individually concerned by the decision, as the execution of their contracts was wholly or partly prevented by the adoption of the decision. In contrast, producers who had not entered into export contracts prior to the adoption of the decision were not individually concerned.

Judgments of the Court of First Instance in a number of cases support the view that the existence of a specific duty on the Commission to take account of the consequences of a measure it plans to adopt on the situation of certain private parties is sufficient to satisfy the requirements of individual concern.[156] This view appears correct as a matter of principle because wherever the Commission is under an obligation to take account of certain parties before

---

[1996] ECR II-1283 paras 31–32.

[154] [1990] ECR I-2477 paras 10–13. See the analysis of this judgment in Case T-489/93 *Unifruit Hellas v Commission* [1994] ECR II-1201 paras 24–26.

[155] [1985] ECR 207 paras 11–19. See the analysis of this judgment in Case C-209/94P *Buralux v Council* [1996] ECR I-615 paras 31–34.

[156] Joined Cases T-480/93 and T-483/93 *Antillean Rice Mills v Commission* [1995] ECR II-2305 para 67; Joined Cases T-481/93 and T-484/93 *Exporteurs in Levende Varkens v Commission* [1995] ECR II-2941 para 61; Case T-168/95R *Eridania v Council* [1995] ECR II-2817 para 29; Case T-197/95 *Sveriges Betodlares Centralförening v Commission* [1996] ECR II-1283 paras 31–32; Case T-60/96 *Merck v Commission* [1997] ECR II-849 paras 57–71.

adopting a measure, those parties should be able to bring legal proceedings in order to protect their 'right' to be so considered.[157]

However, the case-law of the Court of Justice has not yet recognised the existence of the general principle in such express terms as the Court of First Instance. In Case C-209/94P *Buralux v Council*[158] the Court of Justice stated that the judgment in *Piraiki-Patraiki* was based on a series of special circumstances which included not only the specific duty imposed on the Commission, but also the fact that the applicants were 'members of a limited class of traders identified or identifiable by the Commission' who were 'particularly affected by the decision at issue' by virtue of the contracts which they had already entered into at the time when the contested measure was adopted. In view of the current uncertainty as to the position of the Court of Justice, it would be advisable for any applicant to argue (wherever possible) not only that the Commission was under a specific obligation to take account of parties in his position prior to adopting the measure challenged, but also that he belonged to 'a limited class of traders identified or identifiable by the Commission' who were particularly affected by the decision at issue.

Differentiation from all other persons/effect on a specific right Where the impact of a measure is particularly severe on one party by reason of certain attributes which are peculiar to them or by reason of circumstances in which they are differentiated from all other persons, the Court of Justice may be prepared to recognise that that party is individually concerned by that measure. However, such cases are rare.

In Case C-358/89 *Extramet Industrie v Council*[159] Extramet was permitted to challenge a regulation imposing an anti-dumping duty on imports of calcium metal originating in China and the Soviet Union because it was the largest importer of calcium metal into the Community, essentially from China and the Soviet Union. It was also an end-user of the product. In addition, Extramet's business depended to a very large extent on such imports, as there was a limited number of manufacturers of the product concerned and it was difficult for Extramet to obtain supplies from the sole Community producer which was its main competitor for the processed product. The Court of Justice held that this specific set of circumstances differentiated the applicant from all other importers potentially affected by the regulation, so that the applicant was individually concerned by the measure.

In Case C-309/89 *Codorniu v Council*[160] Codorniu, a Spanish producer of

---

[157] *Cf* the position in relation to competition, anti-dumping and State aid cases considered below at pp 296–305.

[158] [1996] ECR I-615 paras 31–34.

[159] [1991] ECR I-2501 paras 13–18. See also Case T-435/93 *ASPEC v Commission* [1995] ECR II-1281 paras 62–71; and Case T-442/93 *AAC v Commission* [1995] ECR II-1329 paras 47–54, where a decision by the Commission approving the grant of State aid to an Italian undertaking was held to be of individual concern to competitors of that undertaking given the conditions prevailing on the relevant product market at that time (limited number of producers, significant increase in production capacity on the part of the Italian undertaking as a result of the aid).

[160] [1994] ECR I-1853 paras 14–23.

sparkling wines, successfully challenged the legality of a regulation which reserved the use of the term '*crémant*' for certain types of sparkling wine produced in France and Luxembourg. The contested provision prevented Codorniu from using the graphic trade mark 'Gran Cremant de Codorniu' which it had registered in Spain in 1924, and which it had used both before and after registration. The Court of Justice held that this situation differentiated Codorniu from all other traders. Although not expressly relied on, the fact that Codorniu was the main Community producer of the type of sparkling wines affected no doubt played a part in the Court's decision, particularly as other producers established in Spain also used the term 'Gran Cremant'.

These decisions indicate that the EC courts will be prepared to recognise that an applicant belonging to an objective class of traders affected by a measure will be individually concerned where, on the facts of the case, he is particularly severely affected by the measure. In *Extramet* the relevant consequences were economic. In *Codorniu* the Court focused on the fact that the regulation removed the applicant's right to use a graphic trade mark which it had enjoyed since 1924.[161]

The EC courts have, on several occasions, held that the principle established in *Codorniu* is inapplicable where the contested measure has not adversely affected any 'specific right' of the applicant.[162] Whilst the reference to rights is understandable in the factual context of *Codorniu*, it is difficult to understand in the context of *Extramet*. The applicant in that case was individually concerned by the measure challenged by virtue of the particularly severe effects the measure produced on its business, not because it affected any identifiable rights.[163] The reference to 'specific rights' in the subsequent case-law of the EC courts indicates that they will recognise individual concern on the basis of the applicant's particular factual situation only in exceptional cases.

In Case T-60/96 *Merck v Commission*[164] the Court of First Instance held that the fact that an applicant was also a party to proceedings before the national courts, in the course of which questions were raised which were linked to those concerning the validity of the measure in issue in the annulment proceedings before the EC courts, was not sufficient in itself to satisfy the requirement of individual concern.

In Case T-585/93 *Greenpeace v Commission*[165] the applicants argued that the EC courts should adopt a different approach in environmental cases since,

---

[161] The mere fact that an act adversely affects a person's economic or competitive position is insufficient to satisfy the requirement of individual concern. See Joined Cases 10 and 18/68 *Eridania v Commission* [1969] ECR 459 para 7; Case T-60/96 *Merck v Commission* [1997] ECR II-849 paras 50–52.

[162] Case C-10/95P *Asocarne* [1995] ECR I-4149 para 43; Case C-87/95P *CNPAAP v Commission* [1996] ECR I-2003 para 36; Case T-18/95 *Atlanta v Commission* [1996] ECR II-1669 para 49.

[163] See Case T-219/95R *Danielsson v Commission* [1995] ECR II-3051 para 72, where the Court of First Instance distinguished between a measure which produced effects peculiar to a particular party and a measure which affected a right specific to a particular party.

[164] [1997] ECR II-849 paras 53–55.

[165] [1995] ECR II-2205 paras 48–58. This judgment was appealed to the Court of Justice. *Cf* the position taken by Advocate-General Cosmas at paras 98–109 of his Opinion in Case C-321/95P

wherever a measure was alleged to produce environmental consequences, it would be impossible to show that any particular person was more affected than all others. By definition, harm to the environment impacts in similar ways on large numbers of people. However, the Court of First Instance declined to depart from the traditional approach, and the application was therefore dismissed as inadmissible.

Applicant named in the measure Where a person is named in a measure so that it is clear that the measure is aimed at a specific individual (or individuals), the person named will satisfy the requirements of individual concern. In Case 138/79 *Roquette Frères v Council*[166] the measure challenged was a regulation which fixed the production quota for isoglucose within the Community. An annex to the regulation set out the basic quotas for the year in question in relation to six specifically named undertakings. The Court of Justice held that these undertakings were directly and individually concerned by the measure. In Case C-135/92 *Fiskano v Commission*[167] the Commission sent a letter to the relevant Swedish authorities informing them of a penalty which had been imposed on the vessel *Lavön*. The Court of Justice held that Fiskano, as the owners of the vessel, were individually concerned by the decision contained in the letter.

Participation in adoption of the measure The fact that an applicant has participated in the procedure leading to the adoption of a legislative measure does not give the applicant *locus standi* to seek review of that measure.[168] For example, in Case 147/83 *Binderer v Commission*[169] the applicant, Binderer, imported wines into Germany. Following the adoption of a regulation laying down detailed rules for the description and presentation of wines, Binderer made a proposal to the Commission concerning the proper translation of certain Hungarian terms. The Commission approved the proposal in a letter, but, subsequently, in an amending regulation, the use of the translations proposed by Binderer was expressly prohibited on the labels of imported wines. Binderer sought to challenge this amendment claiming, *inter alia*, that the way in which the contested provision was adopted proved that it was directed solely at the applicant. This was rejected by the Court of Justice.

Similarly, the mere fact that an applicant has corresponded with the Commission or made a complaint to the Commission on a specific matter does not in itself mean that that person will be individually concerned by any measure adopted by the Commission dealing with that matter, unless the

---

Stichting Greenpeace Council (Greenpeace International) v Commission (Opinion of 23 September 1997).

[166] [1980] ECR 3333 paras 13–16; see also the Opinion of Advocate-General Reischl at 3368.

[167] [1994] ECR I-2885 paras 21–26.

[168] Case C-10/95P *Asocarne v Council* [1995] ECR I-4149 para 40.

[169] [1985] ECR 257 paras 1–15. See also Case 72/74 *Union syndicale v Council* [1975] ECR 401 para 19; Case 307/81 *Alusuisse Italia v Council and Commission* [1982] ECR 3463 paras 12–13.

relevant Community legislation lays down specific procedural guarantees for such a person, which give it a right to be heard.[170]

6. COMPETITION AND ANTI–DUMPING: *LOCUS STANDI*

(a) Introduction

Liberal approach The EC courts have adopted a more liberal approach to the question of *locus standi*, and particularly individual concern, in the context of competition law (articles 85 and 86 [new arts 81 and 82] of the EC Treaty and the Merger Regulation), anti-dumping and State aids. Presumably this is due to the fact that the measures adopted in these areas by the Commission are often individual in nature, involving responses to particular problems concerning identifiable parties. In addition, in the fields of competition law and anti-dumping, regulations have been adopted which grant specific procedural rights to private parties in the context of administrative procedures before the Commission.

In accordance with the express wording of article 173 [new art 230], any person to whom a decision is addressed will have standing to challenge that decision. However, in addition the EC courts have repeatedly held that where a Community regulation gives procedural guarantees to private parties, those parties must be entitled to institute proceedings before the EC courts under article 173 in order to protect their legitimate interests. Furthermore, the EC courts have been prepared to recognise private parties as being individually concerned by Community measures where their competitive position is particularly affected by that measure, even where they do not belong to a closed class.[171]

(b) Competition law: articles 85 and 86 of the EC Treaty

Procedural rights Detailed procedural rules have been adopted for the application of articles 85 and 86 of the EC Treaty [new arts 81 and 82], in particular by Regulation 17.[172] The EC courts have established that these rights may give rise to *locus standi* to challenge Commission decisions adopted pursuant to Regulation 17.

Complainants Article 3(2)(*b*) of Regulation 17 provides that natural or legal persons who claim a 'legitimate interest' may make complaints to the Commission in respect of articles 85 and 86 of the EC Treaty. The case-law of the EC courts establishes that a person who has made such a complaint must be

---

[170] Joined Cases T-481/93 and T-484/93 *Exporteurs in Levende Varkens v Commission* [1995] ECR II-2941 para 59; Case T-585/93 *Greenpeace v Commission* [1995] ECR II-2205 para 56; Case T-60/96 *Merck v Commission* [1997] ECR II-849 paras 72–74. See further below at pp 302–303.

[171] Contrast the restrictive position in other areas of EC law as set out in Joined Cases 10 and 18/68 *Eridania v Commission* [1969] ECR 459 para 7.

[172] Council Regulation No 17 of 6 February 1962, First Regulation implementing articles 85 and 86 of the EC Treaty (OJ, English Special Edition, 1959–1962, p 87) (as amended).

able, if its request is not complied with either wholly or in part, to institute proceedings in order to protect its legitimate interest.[173] Situations giving rise to a legitimate interest have included: a complaint about the legality of a distribution system by an individual refused access to that system;[174] a complaint by consumer groups about an agreement to restrict the imports of Japanese cars;[175] and a complaint by an association representing discothèque operators about the conduct of societies which manage copyright in musical works.[176]

Negative clearance/article 85(3) exemptions Article 19(3) of Regulation 17 provides that where the Commission intends to give negative clearance to an agreement, decision or practice in relation to articles 85 and/or 86 of the EC Treaty or to grant an exemption to an agreement pursuant to article 85(3) of the EC Treaty, it must first publish a notice in the *Official Journal* inviting 'all interested third parties' to submit their observations. A private party with a legitimate interest which has submitted observations pursuant to such a notice will have standing to challenge the Commission's final decision, even though it is not addressed to that party.[177] A private party will have a legitimate interest where, for example, it was refused access to a selective distribution system, which was then granted an exemption by the Commission under article 85(3).[178]

In Joined Cases T-528/93, and others *Métropole Télévision v Commission*[179] the Court of First Instance held that a party whose competitive position was affected by a Commission decision pursuant to article 85(3) of the EC Treaty must be classed as an 'interested party' within the meaning of article 19(3) of Regulation 17. Its status as an interested party was sufficient to regard it as being individually concerned by the Commission decision, even though it had not exercised its procedural rights in any way. This is clearly a very liberal approach to individual concern, as it would give 'all interested parties' the right to challenge Commission exemption decisions, regardless of whether they had played any part in the administrative proceedings before the Commission.

---

[173] Case 26/76 *Metro SB-Großmärkte v Commission* [1977] ECR 1875 para 13; Case 210/81 *Demo-Studio Schmidt v Commission* [1983] ECR 3045 paras 14–15; Case T-37/92 *BEUC and NCC v Commission* [1994] ECR II-285 para 36; Case T-114/92 *BEMIM v Commission* [1995] ECR II-147 paras 25–30. See also Ignace Maselis and Hans M Gilliams, 'Rights of Complainants in Community Law' (1997) 22 EL Rev 103 at 107–108; and C S Kerse, 'The Complainant in Competition Cases: A Progress Report' (1997) CML Rev 213 at 217–225.

[174] Case 26/76 *Metro SB-Großmärkte v Commission* [1977] ECR 1875 para 13; Case 210/81 *Demo-Studio Schmidt v Commission* [1983] ECR 3045 para 15.

[175] Case T-37/92 *BEUC and NCC v Commission* [1994] ECR II-285 paras 1–2 and 36.

[176] Case T-114/92 *BEMIM v Commission* [1995] ECR II-147 paras 25–30.

[177] Case 75/84 *Metro SB-Großmärkte v Commission* [1986] ECR 3021 paras 21–23. See also Case T-19/92 *Leclerc v Commission* [1996] ECR II-1851 paras 54–60.

[178] Case 75/84 *Metro SB-Großmärkte v Commission* [1986] ECR 3021 paras 21–22.

[179] [1996] ECR II-649 paras 60–62. The Court relied on the judgments in Case T-96/92 *CCE de la Société Générale des Grandes Sources v Commission* [1995] ECR II-1213 paras 35–36; and Case T-12/93 *CCE de Vittel v Commission* [1995] ECR II-1247 paras 46–47 (discussed below at pp 298–299).

A more restrictive view is apparent in Case T-87/92 *BVBA Kruidvat v Commission*,[180] which was decided by a different chamber of the Court of First Instance. In this case, the Court held that a competitor was not entitled to challenge a Commission decision pursuant to article 85(3) of the EC Treaty. The Court held that the applicant was not individually concerned by the decision as, *inter alia*, it had not lodged a complaint under article 3 of Regulation 17/62, nor had it participated in the administrative procedure under article 19(3) of that Regulation. The applicant, as a competitor, was clearly an interested party within the meaning of article 19(3) of the Regulation; however, the judgment makes no reference to the judgment in *Métropole*. The implicit refusal to apply *Métropole* suggests that that approach cannot be regarded as being firmly established at the level of the Court of First Instance.

Article 90 In Case T-32/93 *Ladbroke v Commission*[181] the Court of First Instance held that a complainant who had participated in an investigation under article 90 of the EC Treaty [new art 86] would not be individually concerned by the Commission's final decision, as mere participation in a Commission investigation was not sufficient to establish individual concern in the absence of a Community measure granting the applicant specific procedural guarantees. Neither Regulation 17 nor Regulation 99/63 apply in the context of article 90 of the EC Treaty; their scope is limited to articles 85 and 86.

(c) Competition law: Merger Regulation

Procedural rights The Merger Regulation[182] establishes specific procedural rules to be followed by the Commission in the exercise of its functions. Article 18(4) provides that while the Commission may hear any natural or legal persons, only natural or legal persons showing a sufficient interest, and especially members of the administrative or management bodies of the undertakings concerned or the recognised representatives of their employees, have a *right* to be heard.

In Case T-96/92 *CCE de la Société Générale des Grandes Sources v Commission*[183] the Court of First Instance held that as article 18(4) expressly identified recognised representatives of employees as third parties *with a sufficient interest* and, therefore, a right to make representations, this sufficed to make them individually concerned by a Commission decision approving a take-over. It was not necessary for the representatives to provide specific proof that their legitimate interests would be affected by the Commission decision.[184] Furthermore, the Court held that it was sufficient for the purposes of individual

---

[180] [1996] ECR II-1375 paras 61–70.

[181] [1994] ECR II-1015 para 43.

[182] Council Regulation 4064/89 of 21 December 1989 (OJ 1989 L395 p 1) on the control of concentrations between undertakings (corrected version at OJ 1990 L257 p 14).

[183] [1995] ECR II-1213 paras 25–47. See also Case T-12/93 *CCE de Vittel v Commission* [1995] ECR II-1247 paras 35–60, which is in similar terms.

[184] [1995] ECR II-1213 para 31.

concern that employees' representatives had an express right to make representations under the Merger Regulation; it was not necessary for them to have actually exercised those rights and taken part in the procedure.[185] However, the Court found that the employees' representatives were not directly concerned by the decision since, *inter alia*, job losses and changes in social benefits for employees would not be inevitable following the take-over, but would depend on decisions made by management.[186] As the employees' representatives were not directly concerned by the Commission's final decision, they were not entitled to challenge that decision on the basis that it was wrong as a matter of substantive law. However, they were entitled to challenge its lawfulness on the basis that the Commission had acted in breach of the procedural guarantees given to them by the Merger Regulation. The Court would annul the decision only if it found a *clear* breach of the relevant procedural guarantees, such as to prejudice the applicants' rights to make an effective statement of their position if they had applied to do so.[187]

In his Opinion in Case C-480/93P *Zunis Holding v Commission*[188] Advocate-General Lenz took the view that shareholders in an undertaking affected by a proposed concentration could not rely on the procedural guarantees established by article 18(4) of the Merger Regulation in order to establish that they were individually concerned by a Commission decision adopted pursuant to that Regulation. First, he doubted that shareholders had a 'sufficient interest' entitling them to be heard under article 18(4). In any event, he believed that even if they did have such a right, a Commission decision under the Merger Regulation would not affect their legitimate interests since the purpose of the Regulation is to protect competition, not the interests of shareholders *qua* shareholders.

Factual differentiation[189] In the context of mergers, the Court of First Instance has adopted a liberal approach to the question of individual concern and has been prepared to find that, in view of its factual position, a private party is sufficiently differentiated from all other persons as to be individually concerned, even where that party does not belong to a closed class. Case T-2/93 *Air France v Commission*[190] concerned a Commission decision under the Merger Regulation which found that a joint venture between British Airways and TAT was compatible with Community law. Air France was held to be individually concerned by that decision as: (a) it had participated in the administrative procedure leading to the adoption of the decision; (b) the decision, in assessing the effect of the joint venture on competition, had mainly been based on the position of Air France; and (c) Air France had been obliged,

---

[185] Ibid paras 35–37.

[186] Ibid paras 38–45.

[187] Ibid paras 46–47.

[188] [1996] ECR I-1, at paras 36–45 of the Opinion. The Court of Justice did not deal with this aspect of the case in its judgment.

[189] See Adrian Brown, 'Judicial Review of Commission Decisions under the Merger Regulation: The First Cases' [1994] 6 ECLR 296.

[190] [1994] ECR II-323 paras 40–47.

under the terms of an agreement between itself, the French Government and TAT, to give up the whole of its interest in TAT only four months before the British Airways joint venture was notified to the Commission.

In Case T-3/93 *Air France v Commission*[191] the Court of First Instance held that Air France was individually concerned by a Commission decision under the Merger Regulation which approved the take-over of Dan Air by British Airways. The Court held that the situation of Air France was clearly different from other international air carriers as the routes affected concerned connections between France and the United Kingdom, and Belgium and the United Kingdom. However it is difficult to see how it can be said that this factual situation differentiated Air France from all other air carriers, particularly other carriers which operated between the United Kingdom and France or Belgium. Presumably the Court of First Instance felt that Air France's application should be declared to be admissible due to the particularly severe effects which the decision had on its competitive position.

(d) Anti-dumping

Procedural rights[192] The basic anti-dumping Regulation[193] establishes a number of specific procedural rights for Community producers (as did its predecessors), including the right to make a complaint to the Commission. In Case 191/82 *Fediol v Commission*[194] the Court of Justice held that a complainant had *locus standi* to challenge a Commission decision rejecting its complaint by virtue of the specific rights granted to it by the basic Regulation.

Furthermore, a private party which has played an important part in the making of a complaint which leads to the adoption of a regulation imposing anti-dumping duties may also have *locus standi*. In Case 264/82 *Timex Corporation v Council and Commission*[195] Timex was permitted to challenge a regulation imposing an anti-dumping duty on mechanical wristwatches originating in the Soviet Union, even though the regulation had not been adopted specifically in response to a complaint by Timex. The Court of Justice based its decision on the fact that:

(1) the complaint which led to the opening of the investigation procedure, lodged by the British Clock and Watch Manufacturers' Association Ltd, owed its origin to a complaint previously lodged by Timex, which had been rejected by the Commission;

(2) Timex's views were heard during the investigation procedure and the conduct of that procedure was largely determined by Timex's observations;

---

[191] [1994] ECR II-121 para 82.

[192] See Anthony Arnull, 'Challenging EC Anti-dumping Regulations: The Problem of Admissibility' [1992] 2 ECLR 73 at 76–77.

[193] Currently Council Regulation 384/96 of 22 December 1995 (OJ 1996 L56 p 1) on protection against dumped imports from countries not members of the European Community.

[194] [1983] ECR 2913.

[195] [1985] ECR 849 paras 8–17.

(3) the preamble to the regulation expressly indicated that the anti-dumping duty imposed took account of 'the extent of the injury caused to Timex by the dumped imports';

(4) Timex was the leading manufacturer of mechanical watches and watch movements in the Community and the only manufacturer of those products in the United Kingdom.

The Court's decision in this case seemed to be based partly on the basis of procedural guarantees and partly on the basis that, on the facts of the case, Timex was particularly affected by the regulation adopted.

Where a private party is directly and individually concerned by a Commission regulation or decision in the field of anti-dumping, it is entitled to challenge the legality of that measure on both substantive grounds (manifest error in assessment of the facts, failure to take essential matters into consideration, misuse of powers) and procedural grounds (failure to observe the procedural guarantees granted to the applicant).[196]

Exporters/importers Anti-dumping duties are generally imposed on the basis of investigations concerning the production prices and export prices of producers and exporters who have been individually identified. In contrast, importers will not usually be named in regulations imposing anti-dumping duties, and will simply form part of the open class of actual or potential importers of the products concerned. However, although anti-dumping duties are imposed by regulations which are legislative in character, the EC courts have consistently held that they may be of individual concern to individual undertakings in the following circumstances:

(1) where a producer or exporter is identified in the measures adopted by the Commission or was concerned by the preliminary investigations;[197]

(2) where an importer is associated with an exporter and their resale prices have been taken into account in calculating export prices;[198]

(3) where a trader (exporter or importer) can establish the existence of certain attributes which are peculiar to it and which differentiate it from all other traders.[199] For example, in Case C-358/89 *Extramet Industrie v*

---

[196] Case 191/82 *Fediol v Commission* [1983] ECR 2913 para 30; Case 264/82 *Timex Corporation v Council and Commission* [1985] ECR 849 para 16.

[197] Joined Cases 239/82 and 275/82 *Allied Corporation v Commission* [1984] ECR 1005 paras 10–12; Case 53/83 *Allied Corporation v Council* [1985] ECR 1621 para 4; Case C-75/92 *Gao Yao (Hong Kong) Hua Fa Industrial Co v Council* [1994] ECR I-3141 paras 26–32; Case T-161/94 *Sinochem Heilongjiang v Council* [1996] ECR II-695 paras 45–49; Case T-155/94 *Climax Paper Converters v Council* [1996] ECR II-873 paras 45–52.

[198] Case 113/77 *NTN Toyo Bearing Co v Council* [1979] ECR 1185 paras 7–12; Case 118/77 *ISO v Council* [1979] ECR 1277 paras 8–16; Joined Cases 239/82 and 275/82 *Allied Corporation v Commission* [1984] ECR 1005 paras 10–15; Case 279/86 *Sermes v Commission* [1987] ECR 3109 paras 14–17; Joined Cases C-305/86 and C-160/87 *Neotype Techmashexport v Commission and Council* [1990] ECR I-2945 paras 17–22; Case C-358/89 *Extramet Industrie v Council* [1991] ECR I-2501 para 15; T-164/94 *Ferchimex v Council* [1995] ECR II-2681 paras 34–36.

[199] Case T-161/94 *Sinochem Heilongjiang v Council* [1996] ECR II-695 paras 45–49.

Council[200] the applicant was entitled to challenge a regulation imposing anti-dumping duties as it was the largest importer of the product concerned and an end-user of the product. In addition, its business depended heavily on imports, particularly as the sole Community producer was also its main competitor for the processed product.

Where a regulation imposes different anti-dumping duties on different undertakings, each undertaking may challenge only the provisions imposing the particular duty on it.[201]

(e) Summary of principles relating to standing arising from procedural guarantees

Although the case-law in this area is complex, the similarities between the regulatory systems applying to articles 85 and 86 [new arts 81 and 82], mergers and anti-dumping mean that it is possible to identify the following general principles as to when individual concern will arise from the existence of procedural guarantees.

(1) A private party will be individually concerned by a Commission decision (or anti-dumping regulation) where it participated in the administrative procedure before the Commission pursuant to specific procedural rights granted to it by a Community legislative act.[202]

(2) Where Community legislation gives procedural rights to private parties, they will be individually concerned by a Commission decision (or anti-dumping regulation) by virtue of the existence of those rights, even if they have not actually exercised them.[203]

(3) A private party will not be individually concerned by a Commission decision (or anti-dumping regulation) merely because it has participated in the administrative procedure leading to the adoption of that decision. It must show that it is entitled to claim procedural guarantees on the basis of the specific provisions of a Community legislative act.[204]

(4) Where the private party is both directly and individually concerned by the relevant measure, it will be entitled to challenge the legality of that measure on both substantive grounds (eg manifest error in assessment of the facts, failure to take essential matters into consideration or misuse of powers) and procedural grounds (failure to observe the procedural guarantees granted to the

---

[200] [1991] ECR I-2501 paras 13–18.

[201] Case 258/84 *Nippon Seiko KK v Council* [1987] ECR 1923 paras 5–7; Case C-156/87 *Gestetner Holdings v Council and Commission* [1990] ECR I-781 para 12.

[202] Case 169/84 *COFAZ v Commission* [1986] ECR 391 para 23; Case T-96/92 *CCE de la Société Générale des Grandes Sources v Commission* [1995] ECR II-1213 para 46; Joined Cases T-447/93, T-448/93 and T-449/93 *AITEC v Commission* [1995] ECR II-1971 para 35.

[203] Case T-96/92 *CCE de la Société Générale des Grandes Sources v Commission* [1995] ECR II-1213 paras 35–37; Joined Cases T-528/93, T-542/93, T-543/93 and T-546/93 *Métropole Télévision v Commission* [1996] ECR II-649 paras 60–62. *Cf* Case T-87/92 *Kruidvat v Commission* [1996] ECR II-1375 paras 61–70.

[204] Case T-32/93 *Ladbroke v Commission* [1994] ECR II-1015 para 43.

applicant).[205] Where the private party is not directly concerned by the relevant measure, it will be entitled to attack it on procedural grounds alone.[206]

7. STATE AID: *LOCUS STANDI*

Procedural background No regulation giving parties specific procedural guarantees has been adopted in the context of State aids. However, the EC courts have adopted a liberal approach to standing.

The basic rules for dealing with State aids are contained in the EC Treaty itself. Under article 93(3) [new art 88(3)], once the Commission has been notified of any plans to grant or alter aid, it must adopt a *prima facie* opinion of the legality of the aid in question. If it takes the view that the aid is not compatible with the EC Treaty, it must initiate the full investigative procedure provided for by article 93(2) [new art 88(2)]. This procedure requires, *inter alia*, that 'the parties concerned' should be entitled to submit their comments to the Commission.[207]

Procedural rights/article 93(2) In Case 169/84 *COFAZ v Commission*[208] the Court of Justice held that, in view of the right given to 'the parties concerned' to submit observations under article 93(2), a private party will be individually concerned by a decision taken by the Commission under that article where:

(1) it was at the origin of a complaint which led to the opening of the Commission's investigation;
(2) its views were heard during that procedure;
(3) the conduct of the procedure was largely determined by its observations; and
(4) its position on the market is significantly affected by the aid which is the subject of the contested decision (which indicates that it has a legitimate interest to protect).

For the purposes of deciding whether an applicant has standing to challenge a Commission decision, the EC courts will not make a definitive finding as to the effect the aid might have on their market position. It is sufficient for the applicant to adduce pertinent reasons to show that the Commission's decision may adversely affect its legitimate interests by significantly jeopardising its position on the market in question.[209]

---

[205] Case 191/82 *Fediol v Commission* [1983] ECR 2913 para 30; Case 264/82 *Timex Corporation v Council and Commission* [1985] ECR 849 para 16; Case T-96/92 *CCE de la Société Générale des Grandes Sources v Commission* [1995] ECR II-1213 para 46.

[206] Case T-96/92 *CCE de la Société Générale des Grandes Sources v Commission* [1995] ECR II-1213 para 46.

[207] See Ignace Maselis and Hans M Gilliams, 'Rights of Complainants in Community Law' (1997) 22 EL Rev 103 at 113–122.

[208] [1986] ECR 391 paras 22–28. Applied in Joined Cases T-447/93, T-448/93 and T-449/93 *AITEC v Commission* [1995] ECR II-1971 paras 34–40. See also Case T-49/93 *SIDE v Commission* [1995] ECR II-2501 paras 31–38.

[209] Case 169/84 *COFAZ v Commission* [1986] ECR 391 paras 27–28; Joined Cases T-447/93, T-448/93 and T-449/93 *AITEC v Commission* [1995] ECR II-1971 paras 39–40.

Procedural rights/article 93(3) In Case C-198/91 *Cook v Commission*[210] the Court of Justice held that 'parties concerned' within the meaning of article 93(2) have *locus standi* to challenge a Commission decision under article 93(3) finding that the grant of aid is compatible with the common market. 'Parties concerned' have been broadly defined as persons, undertakings or associations whose interests might be affected by the grant of aid, in particular competing undertakings and trade associations.[211] Although the Commission is not required to seek the views of third parties when it conducts a preliminary investigation under article 93(3), the Court found that concerned parties must have the right to challenge a decision by the Commission that aid is compatible with the EC Treaty, otherwise they would be deprived of the procedural guarantees they are intended to enjoy under article 93(2).

The approach adopted by the Court of Justice in *Cook* was distinguished by the Court of First Instance in Case T-398/94 *Kahn Scheepvaart v Commission*.[212] The Court of First Instance held that the approach outlined in *Cook* should apply only where the aid which the Commission had found to be compatible with the common market was an *individual* aid granted to a specific party. In contrast, where the Commission had declared that a *general* aid scheme was compatible with the common market, before the grant of any individual aids pursuant to that scheme, it was not possible to talk of 'competing undertakings' entitled to procedural guarantees under article 93(2) of the Treaty.

Recipients of State aid A recipient of individual aid which is the subject-matter of a Commission decision adopted on the basis of article 93 of the EC Treaty has *locus standi* to challenge that decision, even though it is addressed to a Member State.[213]

Factual differentiation Two cases involving a Commission decision under article 93(2) approving the grant of aid by Italy to Italgrani, an Italian manufacturer of starch products, provide good examples of the Court's liberal approach to factual differentiation as a ground of individual concern in the context of State aids. In Case T-442/93 *AAC v Commission*[214] the Court of First Instance held that SPAD was individually concerned by the contested decision as: (a) SPAD was one of the two largest Italian producers of the products affected and was a direct competitor of the recipient of the aid; (b) SPAD had played an important role in the participation of Assochimica, an Italian association, in the administrative procedure leading to the contested decision;

---

[210] [1993] ECR I-2487 paras 20–26. Applied in Case C-225/91 *Matra v Commission* [1993] ECR I-3203 paras 14–20.

[211] Case 323/82 *Intermills v Commission* [1984] ECR 3809 para 16. Contrast Case C-295/92 *Landbouwschap v Commission* [1992] ECR I-5003, where the applicant was held not to be in competition with the beneficiaries of the aid in question.

[212] [1996] ECR II-477 paras 47–50.

[213] Case 730/79 *Philip Morris v Commission* [1980] ECR 2671 para 5; Case C-188/92 *TWD v Germany* [1994] ECR I-833 para 14.

[214] [1995] ECR II-1329 paras 47–54.

and (c) the planned increase in production by the recipient of the aid would entail roughly a 50 per cent increase in annual Italian production. In Case T-435/93 *ASPEC v Commission*[215] the Court held that Dutch, French and German competitors of Italgrani were individually concerned by the contested decision in view of: (a) the limited number of existing producers of the products concerned; and (b) the serious effect the significant increase in capacity proposed by the recipient of the aid might have on those producers. This is a particularly liberal judgment, as the requirement of individual concern was satisfied solely on the basis of the effect of the aid on the market position of competitors to the recipient of the aid. There was no indication that the applicants had participated in the administrative proceedings before the Commission.

8. EUROPEAN STRUCTURAL FUNDS: *LOCUS STANDI*

A Commission decision reducing European Structural Fund assistance, although addressed to a Member State, is of direct and individual concern to the person benefiting from that assistance, as it deprives that person of the assistance which had initially been granted to it, and the Member State does not have any discretion of its own in that respect.[216]

9. REPRESENTATIVE ORGANISATIONS: *LOCUS STANDI*

Representative organisations/associations of undertakings A representative organisation, such as a trade association or trade union, will not satisfy the requirements of individual concern solely on the basis that it is acting in the collective interests of its members.[217] If the individual members do not have standing to challenge the relevant measure they cannot obtain the right to do so simply by acting collectively. However, a representative organisation will have *locus standi* to bring an action under article 173 [new art 230] in its own name whenever it falls within any one of the following categories:

(1) It is the addressee of the measure challenged;[218]

(2) It is acting on behalf of one or more of its members, who would themselves have standing to challenge the contested act, and is doing so in

---

215 [1995] ECR II-1281 paras 69–71. Followed in Case T-266/94 *Skibsværftsforeningen* [1996] ECR II-1399 paras 44–48.

216 Case T-450/93 *Lisrestal Organização Gestão de Restaurantes Colectivos v Commission* [1994] ECR II-1177 para 46; Case T-85/94 *Branco v Commission* [1995] ECR II-45 paras 25–26.

217 Joined Cases 16/62 and 17/62 *Producteurs de fruits v Council* [1962] ECR 471 at 479–480; Case 282/85 *DEFI v Commission* [1986] ECR 2469; Case 117/86 *UFADE v Council and Commission* [1986] ECR 3255 para 12; Case T-585/93 *Greenpeace Council v Commission* [1995] ECR II-2205 paras 59–63; Case T-197/95 *Sveriges Betodlares Centralförening v Commission* [1996] ECR II-1283 para 35.

218 Joined Cases T-481/93 and T-484/93 *Exporteurs in Levende Varkens v Commission* [1995] ECR II-2941 para 64.

accordance with the powers conferred on it by its statutes and without any objection from those members;[219]

(3) It falls within a class which is granted specific procedural rights by Community legislation. Regulation 17/62 and the basic anti-dumping Regulation establish the right for representative organisations or associations of undertakings to make complaints and to take part in the administrative procedures before the Commission. In these circumstances, the EC courts have consistently accepted that such bodies have standing to challenge a Commission decision taken in response to their complaint.[220] For example, in Case T-114/92 *BEMIM v Commission*[221] the Court of First Instance held that an association of undertakings will have a legitimate interest to challenge a Commission decision rejecting its complaint made pursuant to Regulation 17/62 where it is entitled to represent the interests of its members, and the conduct complained of is liable adversely to affect the interests of its members. Similarly, as the Merger Regulation specifically establishes that bodies such as the recognised representatives of the employees affected have a right to be heard, those representatives have been held to be individually concerned by Commission merger decisions.[222] However, the mere fact that a representative organisation has made representations to the institution prior to the adoption of the measure is not sufficient in itself to give it standing to challenge that measure, in the absence of specific procedural rights;[223]

(4) It has an interest to protect which is distinct from that of its members because it has an important role as a negotiator in the area affected by the contested measure. To date, this principle has been applied only in the context of State aid and competition law. In Joined Cases 67, 68 and 70/85 *Van der Kooy v Commission*[224] the *Landbouwschap* (a body established under public law to protect the common interests of agricultural undertakings) was held to be individually concerned by a Commission decision pursuant to article 93(2) of the EC Treaty [new art 88(2)], which found that the preferential tariff for natural gas applied in the Netherlands in respect of glasshouse growers constituted a State aid which was incompatible with the common market. The Court held that the *Landbouwschap* was individually concerned by the decision because it had

---

[219] Joined Cases T-447/93, T-448/93 and T-449/93 *AITEC v Commission* [1995] ECR II-1971 paras 53–62; Joined Cases T-481/93 and T-484/93 *Exporteurs in Levende Varkens v Commission* [1995] ECR II-2941 para 64; Case T-19/92 *Leclerc v Commission* [1996] ECR II-1851 para 62; Case T-380/94 *AIUFFASS v Commission* [1996] ECR II-2169 para 50.

[220] Case 191/82 *Fediol v Commission* [1983] ECR 2913 (anti-dumping); Case T-37/92 *BEUC and NCC v Commission* [1994] ECR II-285 para 36 (competition); Case T-19/92 *Leclerc v Commission* [1996] ECR II-1851 paras 54–60 (competition).

[221] [1995] ECR II-147 paras 25–30.

[222] Case T-96/92 *CCE de la Société Générale des Grandes Sources v* [1995] ECR II-1213 paras 30–32. See also Case T-12/93 *CCE de Vittel v Commission* [1995] ECR II-1247 paras 40–42, which is in similar terms.

[223] Case T-585/93 *Greenpeace v Commission* [1995] ECR II-2205 paras 59–63; Case C-10/95P *Asocarne v Council* [1995] ECR I-4149 paras 36–40.

[224] [1988] ECR 219 paras 17–25. Cited with approval in Joined Cases T-481/93 and T-484/93 *Exporteurs in Levende Varkens v Commission* [1995] ECR II-2941 para 64.

negotiated the gas tariff as the representative of the growers' organisations and was a party to the contract with the gas companies which fixed the level of the tariff. This role was specifically mentioned several times in the Commission decision. In addition, the *Landbouwschap* had taken an active part in the procedure before the Commission by submitting written comments to the Commission and by keeping in close contact with the responsible officials throughout the procedure. In Case C-313/90 *CIRFS v Commission*[225] the Court of Justice held that an association of undertakings, CIRFS, was individually concerned by a Commission decision not to initiate the procedure provided for by article 93(2) in respect of aid granted by the French Government to an undertaking which was a competitor to CIRFS' members. CIRFS represented the major undertakings in the economic sector in question, it had been in discussions with the Commission on the subject of the application of the State aid rules to that sector, and it had actively pursued negotiations with the Commission in the course of the administrative procedure leading to the adoption of the Commission's decision.[226] In Case T-19/92 *Leclerc v Commission*[227] the applicant, Galec, was a cooperative society whose members were retailers trading under the name 'E. Leclerc'. The Court of First Instance held that Galec was individually concerned by a Commission decision under article 85(3) of the EC Treaty, [new art 81(3)] which granted an exemption to the network of exclusive distribution contracts operated by Yves Saint Laurent. The Court held that the decision adversely affected Galec's own interests in its capacity as a negotiator, as its objects under its statutes included the negotiation of the Leclerc Centre's supply contracts.

10. GROUNDS OF REVIEW

(a) Introduction

Article 173 Article 173 of the EC Treaty [new art 230] sets out four grounds of review. These are:
(1) lack of competence;
(2) infringement of an essential procedural requirement;
(3) infringement of the EC Treaty or of any rule of law relating to its application; and
(4) misuse of powers.
In addition, the Court of Justice has recognised that certain acts may be so defective as to be 'non-existent'.

---

[225] [1993] ECR I-1125 paras 28–30. See the analysis of this judgment in Case C-10/95P *Asocarne v Council* [1995] ECR I-4149 paras 38–39.
[226] These judgments were followed by the Court of First Instance in Case T-380/94 *AIUFFASS v Commission* [1996] ECR II-2169 paras 27–52.
[227] [1996] ECR II-1851 para 61.

Pleadings The grounds of review under article 173 [new art 230] are the same for all applicants, whether privileged, semi-privileged or non-privileged. The Court of Justice does not adhere strictly to the four grounds of review and it is not uncommon for the Court to annul an act without expressly referring to the specific grounds set out in article 173. However, as a matter of pleading, an applicant should state the grounds in article 173 on which it relies as the judgment in Case 42/84 *Remia v Commission*,[228] establishes that submissions must be set out in the application with sufficient precision in order to ascertain whether they come within the grounds of action enumerated in article 173.

Date at which legality assessed The legality of the contested measure must be assessed on the basis of the facts and the law as they stood at the time when the measure was adopted (and not when it entered into force).[229]

(b) Lack of competence

Definition Lack of competence arises where a Community institution acts outside its powers in adopting a particular measure.[230] Community institutions can act only on the basis of powers granted by the EC Treaty[231] (or on the basis of powers granted by secondary legislation which, in turn, is based on a specific EC Treaty provision).[232] The Community institutions have no inherent powers.

Examples Examples of cases in which acts have been annulled on the ground of lack of competence include the following.

(1) Joined Cases 228/82 and 229/82 *Ford of Europe v Commission*,[233] where a Commission decision imposing interim measures was declared void by the Court of Justice. The Commission had exceeded the limits of its powers as the terms of the interim order went beyond what the Commission could adopt in a final order.

(2) Case 108/83 *Luxembourg v Parliament*,[234] where the European Parliament was held to have exceeded the limits of its powers by adopting a resolution which would have reduced the services carried out and the number of staff in Luxembourg.

(3) Case 9/56 *Meroni v High Authority*[235] (a case under the European Coal and Steel Treaty), where a decision taken by an agency to which the High

---

[228] [1985] ECR 2545 para 16. See also Joined Cases 19/60, 21/60, 2/61 and 3/61 *Fives Lille Cail v High Authority* [1961] ECR 281 at 294–295 (ECSC).

[229] Case T-115/94 *Opel Austria v Council* [1997] ECR II-39 paras 87–88. See also Joined Cases T-79/95 and T-80/95 *SNCF v Commission* [1996] ECR II-1491 para 48.

[230] Article 4(1) of the EC Treaty [new art 7(1)] provides that 'Each institution shall act within the limits of the powers conferred upon it by this Treaty'.

[231] Case C-57/95 *France v Commission* [1997] ECR I-1627 para 24.

[232] Case C-103/96 *Directeur Général des Douanes v Eridania* [1997] ECR I-1453 para 20.

[233] [1984] ECR 1129 paras 17–24.

[234] [1984] ECR 1945 paras 25–32.

[235] [1957–58] ECR 133.

Authority (the Commission) had delegated power was annulled because the act by which power was delegated to the agency was itself illegal. The delegating act was held to be illegal because the High Authority had acted outside the scope of its competence.[236]

(4) Joined Cases T-80/89 and others *BASF v Commission,*[237] where a decision establishing an infringement of article 85 of the EC Treaty [new art 81] was annulled, *inter alia*, on the ground that its adoption had been delegated to a single Member of the Commission contrary to the principle of collegiality referred to in the Commission's Rules of Procedure.

(5) There have been a number of cases where the Commission has adopted 'atypical acts' which have been annulled on the ground of lack of competence. For example, in Case C-57/95 *France v Commission*[238] the Court of Justice annulled an act entitled 'Commission Communication on an Internal Market for Pension Funds'. The Commission maintained that the Communication merely interpreted the obligations which Member States were already subject to by virtue of the provisions of the EC Treaty dealing with freedom of establishment, freedom to provide services and free movement of capital. However, the Court found that the Communication purported to impose obligations distinct from those provided for by the relevant Treaty articles. Only the Council was empowered to adopt such measures by the EC Treaty and therefore the Communication was annulled on the ground of lack of competence.

(c) Infringement of an essential procedural requirement

Sources In certain areas of Community law, legislation has been adopted which sets down detailed procedural rules to be followed.[239] However, the case-law of the EC courts is also an important source of procedural rights.

---

[236] See paras 46–50 of the Opinion of Advocate-General Jacobs in Case C-156/93 *Parliament v Commission* [1995] ECR I-2019 for an analysis of the competence of the Commission where it exercises powers delegated to it by the Council pursuant to article 145 of the EC Treaty [new art 202].

[237] [1995] ECR II-729 paras 96–102.

[238] [1997] ECR I-1627 paras 11–26; see also paras 14–15 and 20–22 of the Opinion of Advocate-General Tesauro for an analysis of the invalidity of atypical acts adopted by the Commission. Other cases involving atypical acts include Case C-366/88 *France v Commission* [1990] ECR I-3571 ('internal instructions' adopted by the Commission empowering itself to take samples of products for the purpose of the management of the European Agricultural Guidance and Guarantee Fund); Case C-303/90 *France v Commission* [1991] ECR I-5315 paras 7–25 ('Code of Conduct' on the financial control of structural funds adopted by the Commission establishing specific obligations on the Member States in relation to the content, frequency and means of communicating certain information to the Commission); Case C-325/91 *France v Commission* [1993] ECR I-3283 paras 8–23 ('Communication' by the Commission to the Member States requiring them to provide certain information in the context of State aid).

[239] For example, competition, merger control, anti-dumping, Community trade marks and customs. The principles relating to essential procedural requirements are of particular importance in competition law. The relevant issues are dealt with in detail in specialist works such as Bellamy and Child, *Common Market Law of Competition*, 4th edn (Sweet & Maxwell, 1993), Ch 12; Kerse, *EC Antitrust Procedure*, 3rd edn (Sweet & Maxwell, 1994), Chs 4 and 8; Ortiz-Blanco, *EC Competition Procedure* (Oxford, 1996).

EC courts' power to raise of own motion The EC courts may consider of their own motion issues concerning infringement of essential procedural requirements.[240]

Effect of infringement Where there have been procedural irregularities, a measure will be annulled only if, in the absence of those irregularities, there might have been a different substantive result.[241] Furthermore, where the breach relates only to matters of secondary importance, the validity of the whole measure will not be affected.[242]

Examples There is no exhaustive list of what constitutes an essential procedural requirement. However, the following main examples will be considered:

(1) requirement to give reasons;
(2) consultation/cooperation;
(3) right to be heard;
(4) compliance with internal rules of procedure;
(5) principle of good administration.

(i) Requirement to give reasons

Article 190 Article 190 of the EC Treaty [new art 253] provides:

> Regulations, directives and decisions adopted jointly by the European Parliament and the Council, and such acts adopted by the Council or the Commission, shall state the reasons on which they are based and shall refer to any proposals or opinions which were required to be obtained pursuant to this Treaty.

In Case 22/70 *Commission v Council*[243] the Court of Justice held that the requirements of article 190 cannot be extended to measures other than regulations, directives or decisions.

Sufficient reasons According to the settled case-law of the Court of Justice, the reasons given for a particular measure must show clearly and unequivocally

---

[240] Case C-291/89 *Interhotel v Commission* [1991] ECR I-2257 para 14; Case C-304/89 *Oliveira v Commission* [1991] ECR I-2283 para 18.

[241] Joined Cases 40 to 48/73 and others *'Suiker Unie' v Commission* [1975] ECR 1663 paras 89–92 (where premature public statements were held to be a breach of the right to a fair trial); Case 30/78 *Distillers Co v Commission* [1980] ECR 2229 para 26 (right to be heard), see also the Opinion of Advocate-General Warner at 2290–2291; Joined Cases 209 to 215/78 and 218/78 *Van Landewyck v Commission* [1980] ECR 3125 paras 45–47 (wrongful disclosure of trade secrets); Joined Cases 100 to 103/80 *Musique Diffusion Française v Commission* [1983] ECR 1825, Opinion of Advocate-General Sir Gordon Slynn at 1927 (right to be heard); Case T-266/94 *Skibsværftsforeningen v Commission* [1996] ECR II-1399 para 243 (failure to comply with procedure laid down by a directive).

[242] Joined Cases 40 to 48/73 and others *'Suiker Unie' UA v Commission* [1975] ECR 1663 paras 94–99 (unduly short time-limits for submission of observations); Joined Cases 100 to 103/80 *Musique Diffusion Française v Commission* [1983] ECR 1825 paras 24–30 (right to be heard/failure to disclose documents); Case 107/82 *AEG v Commission* [1983] ECR 3151 paras 21–30 (right to be heard/failure to disclose documents).

[243] [1971] ECR 263 paras 97–100 (the *ERTA* case).

the reasoning of the institution which enacted the measure so as to inform the persons concerned of the justification for the measure adopted and to enable the Court of Justice to exercise its powers of review.[244] 'Persons concerned' includes Member States and all interested private parties and is not limited to the addressees of the relevant measure.[245] It is not necessary for the reasons to deal with every relevant point of fact and law. The adequacy of the reasons will be assessed not only by reference to the wording used, but also taking into account the context and the whole body of legal rules governing the matter in question.[246]

Nature of the measure Whether or not the reasons given are sufficient will depend on the nature of the measure in question.[247] Regulations, which are measures of general application, will not usually require as detailed reasoning as decisions, which are addressed to particular parties.[248] In Case 5/67 *Beus v Hauptzollamt München*[249] the Court of Justice held that the reasoning behind a regulation may be confined to indicating the general situation which led to its adoption and the general objectives which it is intended to achieve. Furthermore, where a regulation forms part of a wider set of provisions, the reasoning must be judged in the context of the whole of the rules of which it forms a part.[250] Thus, the Court of Justice has consistently held that the statement of reasons on which regulations are based is not required to specify the often very numerous and complex matters of fact or law dealt with in regulations, provided the latter fall within the general scheme of the body of measures of which they form part.[251]

---

[244] Case C-122/94 *Commission v Council* [1996] ECR I-1881 para 29; Case T-57/91 *NALOO v Commission* [1996] ECR II-1019 paras 298–300 (ECSC); Case C-278/95P *Siemens v Commission* [1997] ECR I-2507 para 17; Case C-285/94 *Italy v Commission* [1997] ECR II-3519 para 48.

[245] Case 294/81 *Control Data Belgium v Commission* [1983] ECR 911 paras 12–15. See also Case 24/62 *Germany v Commission* [1963] ECR 63 at 69; Case C-41/93 *France v Commission* [1994] ECR I-1829 para 34; Case T-459/93 *Siemens v Commission* [1995] ECR II-1675 para 31; Case T-16/91RV *Rendo v Commission* [1996] ECR II-1827 para 43. However, it appears that third parties may not be entitled to such detailed reasoning as parties directly involved in the matters leading to the adoption of the contested act: see Case T-266/94 *Skibsværftsforeningen* [1996] ECR II-1399 paras 236–239.

[246] Case C-122/94 *Commission v Council* [1996] ECR I-1881 para 29; Case C-278/95P *Siemens v Commission* [1997] ECR I-2507 para 17; Case C-285/94 *Italy v Commission* [1997] ECR II-3519 para 48.

[247] Case C-181/90 *Consorgan v Commission* [1992] ECR I-3557 paras 13–18; Case C-466/93 *Atlanta Fruchthandelsgesellschaft* [1995] ECR I-3799 para 16.

[248] Case 18/62 *Barge v High Authority* [1963] ECR 259 at 280 (ECSC); Case 5/67 *Beus v Hauptzollamt München* [1968] ECR 83 at 95; paras 38–41 and 191 of the Opinion of Advocate-General Léger in Case C-150/94 *United Kingdom v Council* and Case C-284/94 *Spain v Council* (Opinion of 26 September 1996).

[249] [1968] ECR 83 at 95. See also Case 3/83 *Abrias v Commission* [1985] ECR 1995 para 30 (staff case).

[250] Case 92/77 *An Bord Bainne v Minister for Agriculture* [1978] ECR 497 para 36; Case 125/77 *Koninklijke Scholten-Honig v Hoofdproduktschap voor Akkerbouwprodukten* [1978] ECR 1991 paras 17–22; Joined Cases C-9/95, C-23/95 and C-156/95 *Belgium v Commission* [1997] ECR I-645 para 44.

[251] Case C-27/90 *SITPA v ONIFLHOR* [1991] ECR I-133 paras 10 and 15–16 (excusable factual error in reasoning); Case C-241/95 *R v IBAP, ex p Accrington Beef Co Ltd* [1996] ECR I-6699 para 39.

A decision must set out in a clear and unequivocal manner the principal issues of law and fact upon which it is based.[252] However, there is no requirement to discuss all the matters of fact and law which may have been discussed or raised prior to the adoption of the decision, provided the decisive facts and legal considerations are set out. This is of particular importance in competition cases.[253] A decision which fits into a well-established line of decisions may be reasoned in a summary manner, for example, by reference to the other decisions. However, if it goes appreciably further than the previous decisions, the Commission must give an account of its reasoning.[254] It is particularly important to provide clear reasons where a decision has adverse consequences for the addressee.[255]

Context/practical realities The adequacy of reasoning must be assessed practically in the light of the circumstances of the particular case.[256] The degree of precision of the statement of reasons for a decision must be weighed against practical realities and the time and technical facilities available for making the decision.[257] For example, in Case 16/65 *Schwarze v Einfuhr- Und Vorratsstelle Getreide*[258] the Commission published weekly decisions setting certain agricultural prices. The Court of Justice held that the degree of precision of the statement of reasons for such decisions must be weighed against the practical realities of making such regular, technical decisions. It would be impractical to require the Commission to provide detailed reasoning for such decisions and,

---

[252] Case 24/62 *Germany v Commission* [1963] ECR 63 at 69; Case C-350/88 *Delacre v Commission* [1990] ECR I-395 paras 15–16.

[253] Joined Cases 43/82 and 63/82 *VBVB and VBBB v Commission* [1984] ECR 19 paras 21–22; Case 42/84 *Remia v Commission* [1985] ECR 2545 para 26. Case T-3/89 *Atochem v Commission* [1991] ECR II-1177 para 222; Case T-114/92 *BEMIM v Commission* [1995] ECR II-147 para 41; Case T-387/94 *Asia Motor France v Commission* [1996] ECR II-961 paras 103–104. Contrast Case T-95/94 *Sytraval* [1995] ECR II-2651 para 62, where the Court of First Instance held that:

> Whilst it is clear from the case-law that the Commission is not required to discuss all the issues of fact and law raised by the parties concerned . . ., it is none the less obliged to give a reasoned answer to each of the objections raised in the complaint, if only by referring where appropriate to the *de minimis* rule where the point in question is so insignificant as not to warrant the Commission spending any time on it.

See also Case T-34/93 *Société Générale v Commission* [1995] ECR II-545 paras 62–63 for the degree of reasoning required to justify a request for information in the context of a competition investigation pursuant to article 11(3) of Regulation 17.

[254] Case 73/74 *Groupement des fabricants de papiers peints de Belgique v Commission* [1975] ECR 1491 para 31; Case C-350/88 *Delacre v Commission* [1990] ECR I-395 para 15.

[255] See Case T-85/94 *Branco v Commission* [1995] ECR II-45 paras 32–29 concerning a Commission decision reducing the amount of European Social Fund assistance originally granted to the applicant; and paras 42–43 of the Opinion of Advocate-General La Pergola in Case C-32/95P *Commission v Lisresal* [1996] ECR I-5373.

[256] Joined Cases C-329/93, C-62/95 and C-63/95 *Germany v Commission* [1996] ECR I-5151 paras 31–32; Case T-16/91RV *Rendo v Commission* [1996] ECR II-1827 para 44. See also Case C-56/93 *Belgium v Commission* [1996] ECR I-723 paras 85–89.

[257] Case C-350/88 *Delacre v Commission* [1990] ECR I-395 para 16.

[258] [1965] ECR 877 at 887–889.

therefore, the Court held that it was sufficient for the Commission to confine itself to setting out, in a general form, the essential factors and the procedure followed in taking each decision. Interested parties' rights to judicial review could be adequately protected by the Commission providing the technical data to any party who challenged such a decision before a court. In Case C-22/94 *Irish Farmers Association v MAFF*[259] the Court of Justice held that although the wording of a regulation did not clearly indicate the reasons for its adoption, those reasons were apparent once one took into account the factual background against which it was adopted.

In Case T-19/95 *Adia Interim v Commission*[260] the Court of First Instance held that the requirements of article 190 [new art 253] were fulfilled by a system whereby a Community institution informed unsuccessful tenderers for public contracts of their rejection by a simple unreasoned communication, and only provided a reasoned explanation subsequently if expressly requested to do so by a tenderer.

Applicant's involvement in adoption Where the applicant was involved in the process of adoption of the contested measure, the EC courts will generally require less detailed reasoning than might otherwise be the case.[261] This approach can be criticised on the grounds that it fails to recognise that the rights of third parties who are directly and individually concerned by a measure, but who played no part in its adoption, may be compromised if full and proper reasoning is not adopted for every measure.[262]

Individual clauses Where a measure is composed of several elements, it may be necessary for each element to be properly reasoned.[263] However, where the justification for a particular clause is inherently obvious from the measure as a whole, it does not require special reasoning.[264]

Legal basis The legal basis for a particular act must be readily identifiable. However, the measure need not expressly identify the precise legal basis if this is discernible from the other parts of the measure.[265] For example, in Case 203/86 *Spain v Council*[266] the Court of Justice held that an implementing

---

[259] [1997] ECR I-1809 para 41.

[260] [1996] ECR II-321 paras 30–33.

[261] Case 13/72 *Netherlands v Commission* [1973] ECR 27 paras 11–13; Case 819/79 *Germany v Commission* [1981] ECR 21 paras 19–21; Case 1251/79 *Italy v Commission* [1981] ECR 205 paras 20–21; Joined Cases T-480/93 and T-483/93 *Antillean Rice Mills v Commission* [1995] ECR II-2305 paras 170–172; Case C-478/93 *Netherlands v Commission* [1995] ECR I-3081 paras 47–53; Case T-266/94 *Skibsværftsforeningen* [1996] ECR II-1399 paras 236–239; Case T-504/93 *Ladbroke v Commission* [1997] ECR II-923 para 52.

[262] Case 294/81 *Control Data Belgium v Commission* [1983] ECR 911 paras 12–15.

[263] Joined Cases 4/78, 19/78 and 28/78 *Salerno v Commission* [1978] ECR 2403.

[264] Case 57/72 *Westzucker v Einfuhr- und Vorratsstelle Zucker* [1973] ECR 321 para 19; Case T-150/89 *Martinelli v Commission* [1995] ECR II-1165 para 66.

[265] Case 45/86 *Commission v Council* [1987] ECR 1493 para 9. See also Case C-325/91 *France v Commission* [1993] ECR I-3283 para 26, and paras 14–15 of the Opinion of Advocate-General Tesauro in Case C-57/95 *France v Commission* [1997] ECR I-1627 (concerning 'atypical acts' adopted by the Commission).

[266] [1988] ECR 4563 paras 36–38.

regulation adopted under the terms of a basic regulation need only identify the provision of the basic regulation on which it is based. It is not necessary for the implementing regulation to expressly state the Treaty article on which the basic regulation is itself based. In Case T-92/91 *Henrichs v Commission*[267] the Court of First Instance held that a decision which did not expressly state the legal basis on which it was adopted was not invalid because there could have been no doubt that the addressee of the decision, who held a doctorate in law, was aware of the correct legal basis. This approach, which bases the question of legality on the personal knowledge of the addressee of an act, is open to criticism, as it fails to account for the interests of third parties who may be unable to discern the legal basis of an act from its terms.

Commission proposal The proposal from the Commission must be referred to in acts which can be adopted only on a proposal from the Commission. However, it is not necessary to refer to any amendment which may subsequently have been made to that proposal, unless the Commission had withdrawn its proposal and replaced it with a fresh proposal.[268]

Factual errors/contradictions Factual errors or contradictions in the reasons provided for a measure will not necessarily lead to the annulment of that measure, provided they are minor in nature.[269]

Ambiguities Reasoning which is not immediately clear will not necessarily infringe article 190 [new art 253], provided that ambiguities may be resolved by a reasonable process of interpretation.[270]

Errors of assessment Arguments concerning alleged errors of assessment in the reasoning provided must be considered in relation to the substance of the case. They are not relevant to the issue of infringement of essential procedural requirements.[271]

Technical/scientific choices Where a contested measure clearly discloses the essential objective pursued by the institution, it is not necessary for it to provide a specific statement of reasons for each of the technical choices made.[272]

---

[267] [1993] ECR II-611 para 15.

[268] Case C-280/93 *Germany v Council* [1994] ECR I-4973 para 37.

[269] Case C-27/90 *SITPA v ONIFLHOR* [1991] ECR I-133 paras 15–16; Case T-77/95 *SFEI v Commission* [1997] ECR II-1 paras 84–87.

[270] Case T-16/91RV *Rendo v Commission* [1996] ECR II-1827 paras 46 and 55.

[271] Joined Cases C-296/93 and C-307/93 *France and Ireland v Commission* [1996] ECR I-795 para 76; Case C-84/94 *United Kingdom v Council* [1996] ECR I-5755 para 82.

[272] Case C-466/93 *Atlanta Fruchthandelsgesellschaft* [1995] ECR I-3799 para 16; Case C-122/94 *Commission v Council* [1996] ECR I-881 para 29; Case C-84/94 *United Kingdom v Council* [1996] ECR I-5755 para 79. Contrast Case C-269/90 *Technische Universität München* [1991] ECR I-5469 paras 26–27, where a Commission decision was annulled, *inter alia*, on the ground that it did not contain a sufficient statement of scientific reasons.

Ex post reasons Reasons for a decision have to appear in the actual body of the decision. The EC courts will not take account of further reasons given during the course of proceedings before those courts[273], save in exceptional circumstances.[274]

EC courts' power to raise of own motion The fact that a statement of reasons is lacking or inadequate constitutes a matter of public interest which may, and even must, be raised by the EC courts of their own motion.[275]

(ii) Consultation/cooperation/co-decision

European Parliament/consultation Where the Treaty provides that the European Parliament should be consulted before a measure is adopted[276] this constitutes an essential formal requirement. Breach of this requirement will render the measure concerned void.[277] In general, it is not sufficient for the Council simply to request the Parliament's opinion; the Parliament must actually have expressed an opinion before the relevant act can be adopted.[278] In an emergency (for example, where a matter is urgent), the Council must use all the methods available to it under the EC Treaty and the Parliament's Rules of Procedure to obtain the Parliament's opinion within the time required. Failure to do so will cause the act concerned to be annulled.[279] However, where the Council has taken all appropriate steps and the failure to adopt an opinion within the time required is the fault of the Parliament, the Council is entitled to adopt the act concerned without waiting to receive the Parliament's views.[280]

The Council is not required to refrain from considering a Commission proposal or from searching for a general approach or even a common position before the Parliament's opinion is delivered, provided it does not adopt its final position before it has been informed of that opinion.[281]

---

[273] Case 195/80 *Michel v Parliament* [1981] ECR 2861 para 22 (staff case); Case T-61/89 *Dansk Pelsdyravlerforening v Commission* [1992] ECR II-1931 para 131; Case T-230/94 *Farrugia v Commission* [1996] ECR II-195 para 36; paras 21–22 of the Opinion of Advocate-General Léger in Case C-310/93P *BPB Industries and British Gypsum v Commission* [1995] ECR I-865; T-16/91RV *Rendo v Commission* [1996] ECR II-1827 paras 45 and 55.

[274] For example, see Joined Cases 64, 71 to 73 and 78/86 *Sergio v Commission* [1988] ECR 1399 paras 51–53 (a staff case) where the Court of Justice held that, in exceptional circumstances, reasons given *ex post* may be taken into consideration.

[275] Case T-61/89 *Dansk Pelsdyravlerforening v Commission* [1992] ECR II-1931 para 129; Case C-166/95P *Commission v Daffix* [1997] ECR I-983 paras 23–25 (staff case); Case T-4/96 *S v Court of Justice* [1997] ECR II-1125 para 53 (staff case).

[276] For example, articles 43(2) [new art 37] and 100 [new art 94] of the EC Treaty.

[277] Case C-21/94 *Parliament v Council* [1995] ECR I-1827 para 17; Case C-392/95 *Parliament v Council* [1997] ECR I-3213 para 14.

[278] Case 138/79 *Roquette Frères v Council* [1980] ECR 3333 paras 32–37; Case 139/79 *Maizena v Council* [1980] ECR 3393 paras 33–38.

[279] Case 138/79 *Roquette Frères v Council* [1980] ECR 3333 para 36; Case 139/79 *Maizena v Council* [1980] ECR 3393 para 37.

[280] Case C-65/93 *Parliament v Council* [1995] ECR I-643 paras 21–28.

[281] Case C-417/93 *Parliament v Council* [1995] ECR I-1185 paras 10–11. See also Case 114/81 *Tunnel Refineries v Council* [1982] ECR 3189 para 18, where the Court of Justice held that the Council was entitled to adopt a regulation the day after the Parliament had given its (favourable) opinion.

The Parliament must be reconsulted whenever the text proposed to be adopted, viewed as a whole, departs substantially from the text on which the Parliament has already been consulted, except where the amendments essentially correspond to the wishes of the Parliament itself.[282] Once a basic regulation laying down the essential elements of a particular issue has been adopted, there is no requirement for the Council to consult the Parliament in relation to subsequent detailed implementing measures adopted on the basis of that regulation.[283]

European Parliament/cooperation/co-decision The cooperation[284] and co-decision[285] procedures introduced by the Single European Act and the Maastricht Treaty provided a strengthened basis for participation by the European Parliament in the legislative process. Failure to comply with either of these procedures when required to do so by the EC Treaty would certainly constitute an infringement of an essential procedural requirement.

Advisory committees/consultation Failure to consult an advisory committee may constitute a breach of an essential procedural requirement.[286]

(iii) Right to be heard/right to a fair hearing/audi alteram partem[287]
Definition Observance of the right to be heard is a fundamental principle of Community law which must be respected in all proceedings initiated against a person which are liable to culminate in a measure adversely affecting that person.[288] The principle applies both where the conduct of those proceedings is

---

[282] Case C-65/90 *Parliament v Council* [1992] ECR I-4593 para 16; Joined Cases C-13 to 16/92 *Driessen en Zonen v Minister van Verkeer en Waterstaat* [1993] ECR I-4751 paras 23–26; Case C-388/92 *Parliament v Council* [1994] ECR I-2067 paras 10 and 15–19; Case C-280/93 *Germany v Council* [1994] ECR I-4973 paras 38–42; Case C-21/94 *Parliament v Council* [1995] ECR I-1827 para 18, and paras 30–34 of the Opinion of Advocate-General Léger; Case C-392/95 *Parliament v Council* [1997] ECR I-3213 para 15.

[283] Case 46/86 *Romkes v Officier van Justitie* [1987] ECR 2671 para 16; Case C-417/93 *Parliament v Council* [1995] ECR I-1185 paras 30–33; Case C-156/93 *Parliament v Commission* [1995] ECR I-2019 paras 16 and 18.

[284] Article 189c of the EC Treaty [new art 252].

[285] Article 189b of the EC Treaty [new art 251].

[286] Case C-212/91 *Angelopharm v Freie und Hansestadt Hamburg* [1994] ECR I-171 paras 19–41 (Scientific Committee on Cosmetology). Contrast Case 35/78 *NGJ Schouten v Hoofdproduktschap voor Akkerbouwprodukten* [1978] ECR 2543 paras 41–46, and paras 72–76 of the Opinion of Advocate-General Léger in Case C-241/95 *R v IBAP, ex p Accrington Beef Co* [1996] ECR I-6699 (Management Committees for agricultural products), and para 20 of the Opinion of Advocate-General Jacobs in Case C-401/93 *Goldstar Europe v Hauptzollamt Ludwigshafen* [1994] ECR I-5587 (Combined Customs Tariff Nomenclature Committee).

[287] See Koen Lenaerts and Jan Vanhamme, 'Procedural Rights of Private Parties in the Community Administrative Process' (1997) 34 CML Rev 531.

[288] The right to be heard does not apply to the adoption of a generally applicable Community legislative measure, see Case T-521/93 *Atlanta v European Community* [1996] ECR II-1707 paras 70–73.

not subject to any specific procedural rules[289] and also where procedural rules do exist but fail to give express effect to the principle.[290] The right to be heard requires that the person concerned must have the opportunity to make known his views prior to the adoption of any decision which will significantly affect his interests including, where relevant, his views on the facts and documents in the possession of the decision-maker.[291]

The scope of the right to be heard will depend on the nature of the decision in question.[292] Thus, the procedure followed by an institution in respect of a provisional decision need not be as rigorous as that followed for a final decision.[293] However, the right to be heard must not be irremediably impaired during preliminary enquiry procedures which may be decisive in respect of the outcome of the final decision.[294] The EC courts have held that respect for the right to be heard is of particular importance in cases where the decision-maker is required to carry out complex technical evaluations or to exercise a power of discretion.[295]

The right to be heard applies not only to persons to whom a decision is to be addressed but also to parties who, although not addresses, will be affected by the decision.[296] Persons who will be directly affected by a decision are entitled to more stringent procedural guarantees than those who will be less affected.[297]

---

[289] Case C-301/87 *France v Commission* [1990] ECR I-307 paras 29–30; Joined Cases C-48/90 and C-66/90 *Netherlands v Commission* [1992] ECR I-565 para 44 (decision affecting a Member State); Case C-135/92 *Fiskano v Commission* [1994] ECR I-2885 paras 39–41 (imposition of a penalty); Case C-32/95P *Commission v Lisrestal* [1996] ECR I-5373 para 21, and paras 32–33 of the Opinion of Advocate-General La Pergola (demand for repayment of monies from the European Social Fund). Contrast Case T-109/94 *Windpark Groothusen v Commission* [1995] ECR II-3007 paras 46–51 (Case C-32/95P *Lisrestal* distinguished).

[290] Case T-260/94 *Air Inter v Commission* [1997] ECR II-997 para 60.

[291] Case 234/84 *Belgium v Commission* [1986] ECR 2263 paras 25–31 (business confidentiality); Case 40/85 *Belgium v Commission* [1986] ECR 2321 para 28; Case C-269/90 *Technische Universität München* [1991] ECR I-5469 para 25; Joined Cases C-48/90 and C-66/90 *Netherlands v Commission* [1992] ECR I-565 paras 44–46; Case T-30/91 *Solvay v Commission* [1995] ECR II-1775 paras 59–60 (access to the file in competition cases); Case T-36/91 *ICI v Commission* [1995] ECR II-1847 paras 69–70 (access to the file in competition cases); Case T-161/94 *Sinochem Heilongjiang v Council* [1996] ECR II-695 para 75.

[292] Case C-342/89 *Germany v Commission* [1991] ECR I-5031 para 17; Case C-346/89 *Italy v Commission* [1991] ECR I-5057 para 17.

[293] Case C-342/89 *Germany v Commission* [1991] ECR I-5031 paras 17–21.

[294] Case T-34/93 *Société Générale v Commission* [1995] ECR II-545 para 73.

[295] Case C-269/90 *Technische Universität München* [1991] ECR I-5469 paras 13–14; Case T-346/94 *France-Aviation v Commission* [1995] ECR II-2841 paras 32–34 (repayment of customs duty).

[296] Case T-260/94 *Air Inter v Commission* [1997] ECR II-997 paras 61–63. In this case, at para 80, the Court of First Instance also held that the applicant was entitled to argue that the Commission had failed to respect the right to be heard of the French Republic (the addressee of the decision), as this constituted an essential procedural requirement within the meaning of article 173[new art 230].

[297] Case T-96/92 *CCE de la Société Générale des Grandes Sources v Commission* [1995] ECR II-1213 para 56.

Effect of breach Where there has been a breach of the right to be heard, the relevant measure will only be annulled where it can be shown that a different substantive result might have been reached were it not for that breach.[298] Furthermore, where the breach relates only to matters of secondary importance, the validity of the whole decision will not be affected.[299] Where procedural irregularities relating to the right to be heard have occurred, they cannot be remedied during the proceedings before the EC courts.[300]

Competition cases The right to be heard is of particular importance in competition proceedings before the Commission, as they may lead to the undertakings involved being subject to fines.[301] The specific regulations which set out the procedure to be followed by the Commission in exercising its competition law powers contain express provisions giving effect to the right to be heard.[302]

(iv) Internal rules of procedure[303]

Effect of breach Where the purpose of the rules of procedure of a Community institution is to organise the internal functioning of its services in the interests of good administration, private parties will not be entitled to rely on any alleged breach of those rules which are not intended to ensure protection for individuals.[304] In contrast, internal rules of procedure which are intended to protect individuals will constitute a ground of annulment.[305] For example, in competition cases, the EC courts have held that breach of the Commission's

---

[298] Case 30/78 *Distillers Co v Commission* [1980] ECR 2229 para 26, and the Opinion of Advocate-General Warner at 2290–2291 and the cases cited therein; Case C-301/87 *France v Commission* [1990] ECR I-307 para 31; Case C-142/87 *Belgium v Commission* [1990] ECR I-959 para 48. Contrast Case T-32/91 *Solvay v Commission* [1995] ECR II-1825 para 52.

[299] Joined Cases 100 to 103/80 *Musique Diffusion Française v Commission* [1983] ECR 1825 paras 24–30; Case 107/82 *AEG v Commission* [1983] ECR 3151 paras 21–30.

[300] Case T-30/91 *Solvay v Commission* [1995] ECR II-1775 para 98. Contrast Case 85/76 *Hoffmann-La Roche v Commission* [1979] ECR 461 paras 12–19, where the Commission produced further information at the request of the Court during the written procedure. This aspect of the decision was criticised by Advocate-General Warner in his Opinion in Case 30/78 *Distillers Co v Commission* [1980] ECR 2229 at 2296–2298.

[301] Bellamy and Child, *Common Market Law of Competition*, 4th edn (Sweet & Maxwell, 1993), Ch 12; Kerse, *EC Antitrust Procedure*, 3rd edn (Sweet & Maxwell, 1994), Ch 4; Ortiz-Blanco, *EC Competition Procedure* (Oxford, 1996).

[302] See, in particular, article 19 of Council Regulation 17/62 of 6 February 1962 (OJ 1962 13 p 204) First Regulation implementing articles 85, 86 of the EEC Treaty (Special Edition 1959–1962 p 87) (as amended); and Commission Regulation 99/63 on the hearings provided for in article 19(1), (2) of Council Regulation 17/62 (OJ 1962 127 p 2263) (Special Edition 1963–1964 p 47). See also Case 17/74 *Transocean Marine Paint Association v Commission* [1974] ECR 1063 para 15; Case 85/76 *Hoffmann-La Roche v Commission* [1979] ECR 461 paras 8–11.

[303] The nature of 'measures of internal organisation' was analysed by the Court of Justice in Case C-58/94 *Netherlands v Council* [1996] ECR I-2169 paras 28–39.

[304] Case C-69/89 *Nakajima All Precision Co v Council* [1991] ECR I-2069 paras 48–51. See also Case C-280/93 *Germany v Council* [1994] ECR I-4973 paras 27–28 and 31–36.

[305] See para 20 of the Opinion of Advocate-General Tesauro in Case C-58/94 *Netherlands v Council* [1996] ECR I-2169. The Advocate-General also refers to case-law establishing that, whenever rules of procedure are laid down, the institutions may not subsequently depart from them without giving reasons for doing so.

Rules of Procedure concerning the authentication of decisions may constitute a ground of annulment.[306] In Case T-69/89 *RTE v Commission*[307] the Court of First Instance held that failure to comply with an internal procedural rule cannot render the final decision unlawful unless it is sufficiently substantial and has a harmful effect on the legal and factual situation of the party alleging a procedural irregularity.

(v) Principle of good administration

Definition The principle of good administration requires a decision-maker to:
(1) adopt a definitive decision within a reasonable time;[308] and
(2) apply due diligence in the decision-making process and adopt its decision on the basis of all information which might have a bearing on the result.[309]

The Community institutions are required to deal with matters 'with all the care that a large and well-equipped organization owes to those having dealings with it'.[310]

(d) Infringement of the EC Treaty or of any rule of law relating to its application

Infringement of the EC Treaty This ground of review is very broad in scope. As the EC Treaty is, in effect, the constitution of the Community, any breach of Community law can be said to be a breach of the EC Treaty.

Purely formal error The Court of First Instance has held that an error of law which is purely formal in nature and which does not have any decisive influence on the substance of the measure in question will not cause the annulment of that measure.[311]

---

[306] Case C-137/92P *Commission v BASF* [1994] ECR I-2555 paras 72–78; Joined Cases T-80/89 and others *BASF v Commission* [1995] ECR II-729 paras 114–121; Case T-435/93 *ASPEC v Commission* [1995] ECR II-1281 paras 122–126; Case T-32/91 *Solvay v Commission* [1995] ECR II-1825 paras 46–54. Contrast Case T-275/94 *CB v Commission* [1995] ECR II-2169 paras 69–72.

[307] [1991] ECR II-485 para 27. Contrast Case T-32/91 *Solvay v Commission* [1995] ECR II-1825 para 52.

[308] Case C-282/95P *Guérin Automobiles v Commission* [1997] ECR I-1503 para 37. See also Case T-83/91 *Tetra Pak v Commission* [1994] ECR II-755 para 30.

[309] Case T-73/95 *Oliveira v Commission* [1997] ECR II-381 para 32; Case T-81/95 *Interhotel v Commission* [1997] ECR II-1265 para 63. See also Case C-269/90 *Technische Universität München* [1991] ECR I-5469 paras 13–14.

[310] Case T-47/93 *C v Commission* [1994] ECR-SC I-A-233 at 236–237 and II-743 para 35 (staff case); and Joined Cases T-90/91 and T-62/92 *De Compte v Parliament* [1995] ECR-SC II-1 para 65.

[311] Case T-75/95 *Günzler Aluminium v Commission* [1996] ECR II-497 para 55; Case T-106/95 *FFSA v Commission* [1997] ECR II-229 para 199.

Review of exercise of discretion The EC courts will not simply substitute their assessment for that of the defendant institution.[312] In particular, where a Community institution has a wide degree of discretion, the Court will only interfere with the exercise of that discretion if the institution has committed a manifest error or has misused its powers.[313] This approach is particularly important in areas where the relevant institution has been required to analyse a complex economic situation.[314] In such cases, the discretion enjoyed by the institution may extend not only to the nature and scope of the measure to be adopted, but also to its assessment of the relevant factual situation.[315]

The legality of the measure must be assessed in the light of the information available to the institution when the measure was adopted.[316] Furthermore, where the Community institution is required to assess the future effects of a proposed measure and those effects cannot be accurately foreseen, its assessment will be open to challenge only if it appears manifestly incorrect in the light of the information available to it at the time of adoption of the measure.[317]

Correct legal basis[318] All measures of Community secondary legislation must be based, directly or indirectly, on specific provisions of the EC Treaty.[319] Failure to adopt a measure on the correct legal basis is a ground for

---

[312] Case C-225/91 *Matra v Commission* [1993] ECR I-3203 paras 23–25; Case T-266/94 *Skibsværftsforeningen* [1996] ECR II-1399 para 168.

[313] Case C-405/92 *Etablissements Armand Mondiet v Armement Islais* [1993] ECR I-6133 para 32 (scientific assessment); Case C-306/93 *SMW Winzersekt v Land Rheinland-Pfalz* [1994] ECR I-5555 para 21 (political choices); Joined Cases T-244/93 and T-486/93 *TWD v Commission* [1995] ECR II-2265 (economic and social assessments); Case T-155/94 *Climax Paper Converters v Council* [1996] ECR II-873 paras 98 and 135 (economic, political and legal (national law) assessments); Case T-266/94 *Foreningen af Jernskibs- og Maskinbyggerier i Danmark, Skibsværftsforeningen* [1996] ECR II-1399 para 170 (economic and technical assessment); Case C-84/94 *United Kingdom v Council* [1996] ECR I-5755 paras 57–58 (social policy legislation); Case C-169/95 *Spain v Commission* [1997] ECR I-135 para 34 (State aid); Joined Cases C-248/95 and C-249/95 *SAM Schiffahrt v Germany* [1997] ECR I-4475 paras 23–24 (legislative discretion).

[314] Case T-7/93 *Langnese-Iglo v Commission* [1995] ECR II-1533 para 178 (competition law—article 85(3)) [new art 81(3)]; Case C-56/93 *Belgium v Commission* [1996] ECR I-723 para 11 (State aid); Case T-387/94 *Asia Motor France v Commission* [1996] ECR II-961 para 46 (competition law—rejection of complaints); Case T-106/95 *FFSA v Commission* [1997] ECR II-229 paras 98–101 (competition); Case C-26/96 *Rotexchemie International v Hauptzollamt Hamburg-Waltershof* [1997] ECR I-2817 paras 10–11 (anti-dumping); Case C-285/94 *Italy v Commission* [1997] ECR I-3519 para 39 (common agricultural policy).

[315] Case 166/78 *Italy v Council* [1979] ECR 2575 para 14.

[316] Case 234/84 *Belgium v Commission* [1986] ECR 2263 para 16; Case C-241/94 *France v Commission* [1996] ECR I-4551 para 33.

[317] Joined Cases C-133/93, C-300/93 and C-362/93 *Crispoltoni v Fattoria Autonoma Tabacchi* [1994] ECR I-4863 para 43; Case C-280/93 *Germany v Council* [1994] ECR I-4973 paras 90–91.

[318] See Nicholas Emiliou, 'Opening Pandora's box: the Legal Basis of Community Measures before the Court of Justice' (1994) 19 EL Rev 488.

[319] Article 4(1) of the EC Treaty [new art 7(1)] provides that 'Each institution shall act within the limits of the powers conferred upon it by this Treaty'.

annulment.[320] The practical importance of the choice of legal basis is that it may affect the procedure to be followed for adoption of a measure, for example, whether the measure is to be adopted unanimously or by majority voting and whether the role of the European Parliament is to be one of consultation, cooperation or co-decision.

The Community institutions are not free to adopt whatever legal basis they wish. The choice of legal basis for a particular measure must be based on objective factors which are amenable to judicial review, including, in particular, the aim and content of the measure.[321] In practice, the Court will analyse the preamble and provisions of the measure concerned in order to establish its main objectives and effects. Objectives which are merely ancillary to the main object of the measure will not affect the choice of legal basis.[322] In particular, the mere fact that a measure may affect the establishment or functioning of the internal market is not sufficient to justify reliance on article 100a of the EC Treaty [new art 95] as the legal basis for that measure where those effects are merely ancillary to the main aim of the measure.[323]

Where a measure pursues a number of objectives so that the institution's power to adopt it is based on two distinct provisions of the Treaty, it must be adopted on the basis of both of those provisions[324] unless this will interfere with the proper role of the Parliament in the legislative process.[325] This would be the case where one of the provisions required the cooperation procedure to be followed, while the other merely required consultation of the European Parliament. In contrast, where the objective of a measure is covered by two provisions of the EC Treaty, one of which is merely a specific application of the other more general measure, the measure should be based on the specific provision alone.[326]

---

[320] However, where the illegality is a purely formal defect not capable of affecting the content of the contested measure, even the choice of an incorrect legal basis will not render that measure void. See Case 165/87 *Commission v Council* [1988] ECR 5545 paras 18–21; Case C-62/88 *Greece v Council* [1990] ECR I-1527 paras 10–12.

[321] Case 45/86 *Commission v Council* [1987] ECR 1493 para 11 (articles 113 and 235); Case C-70/88 *Parliament v Council* [1991] ECR I-4529 ('Chernobyl') (article 31 of the EAEC Treaty/article 100a of the EC Treaty); Case C-84/94 *United Kingdom v Council* [1996] ECR I-5755 para 25 (articles 100, 118a [new art 95] and 235).

[322] Case C-268/94 *Portugal v Council* [1996] ECR I-6177 paras 21, 37–39 (articles 113, 130y and 235).

[323] Case C-155/91 *Commission v Council* [1993] ECR I-939 paras 5–21 (articles 100a and 130s); contrast Case C-300/89 *Commission v Council* [1991] ECR I-2867 paras 10–25 ('Titanium dioxide') (articles 100a and 130s); Case C-426/93 *Germany v Council* [1995] ECR I-3723 paras 26–33 (articles 100a and 213); Case C-271/94 *Parliament v Council* [1996] ECR I-1689 para 32 (articles 100a and 129c).

[324] Case 165/87 *Commission v Council* [1988] ECR 5545 (articles 28 and 113).

[325] Case C-300/89 *Commission v Council* [1991] ECR I-2867 paras 10–25 (articles 100a and 130s).

[326] Case 68/86 *United Kingdom v Council* [1988] ECR 855 para 15 (articles 43 and 100); Case 131/86 *United Kingdom v Council* [1988] ECR 905 para 20 (articles 43 and 100); Case C-271/94 *Parliament v Council* [1996] ECR I-1689 para 33 (articles 100a and 129c).

A measure may only be based on article 235 of the EC Treaty [new art 308] where no other provision of the Treaty gives the Community institutions the necessary power to adopt that measure.[327]

The fact that the Council has adopted a previous measure on a particular legal basis is irrelevant. A mere Council practice cannot derogate from the rules laid down in the EC Treaty.[328] Ultimately, it is for the Court of Justice to determine what is the proper legal basis of any Community act. Furthermore, where a measure is adopted to replace a previous measure, the new measure is not required to have the same legal basis as the original measure.[329]

General principles/fundamental rights A Community measure may be annulled on the ground that it infringes a general principle of Community law or a fundamental right.[330] For example, in Case 223/85 *RSV Maschinefabrieken en Scheepswerven v Commission*[331] the Court of Justice annulled a Commission decision which violated the principle of legitimate expectations.[332] Furthermore, the principle of legal certainty requires that every measure of the institutions which has legal effects must be clear and precise and must be brought to the notice of the person concerned in such a way that he can ascertain exactly the time at which the measure comes into being and starts to have legal effects. The requirement of legal certainty is particularly important in relation to measures which are liable to entail financial consequences.[333] In Case T-115/94 *Opel Austria v Council*[334] the Court of First Instance annulled a regulation, *inter alia*, on the ground that the Council had deliberately backdated the issue of the *Official Journal* in which it was published.

General Agreement on Tariffs and Trade (GATT) The EC courts may review the lawfulness of a Community act from the point of view of the GATT rules if the act challenged was intended to implement a particular obligation

---

[327] Case 45/86 *Commission v Council* [1987] ECR 1493 (articles 113 and 235); Case 165/87 *Commission v Council* [1988] ECR 5545 (articles 28, 113 and 235); Case C-350/92 *Spain v Council* [1995] ECR I-1985 paras 25–40 (articles 100, 100a and 235); Case C-268/94 *Portugal v Council* [1996] ECR I-6177 para 21 (articles 113, 130y and 235).

[328] Case C-84/94 *United Kingdom v Council* [1996] ECR I-5755 para 19 (articles 100, 118a and 235).

[329] Case C-187/93 *Parliament v Council* [1994] ECR I-2857 para 28 (articles 100a, 113 and 130s).

[330] General principles and fundamental rights are discussed in Ch 2. If ratified, the Amsterdam Treaty will expressly recognise the power of the EC courts to review the acts of the Community institutions in light of fundamental rights by means of an amendment to article L of the EU Treaty [new art 46(d)].

[331] [1987] ECR 4617. See also Case 112/77 *Töpfer v Commission* [1978] ECR 1019 paras 18–19; Case T-115/94 *Opel Austria v Council* [1997] ECR II-39 para 123.

[332] At para 198 of his Opinion in Case C-150/94 *United Kingdom v Council* and Case C-284/94 *Spain v Council* (Opinion of 26 September 1996), Advocate-General LÈger stated that a Member State should be entitled to challenge the validity of a measure on the basis that it breached the legitimate expectations of certain traders affected by it. The Member State should not be required to show that it had a specific interest which had been affected by the relevant measure.

[333] Case T-115/94 *Opel Austria v Council* [1997] ECR II-39 para 124.

[334] Ibid paras 131–133.

entered into within the framework of GATT or if the act expressly refers to specific provisions of GATT.[335]

(e) Misuse of powers

Definition Misuse of powers will be established only where it appears, on the basis of objective, relevant and consistent factors, that a measure has been adopted with the exclusive or main purpose of achieving an end other than that stated, or of evading a procedure specifically prescribed by the EC Treaty for dealing with the circumstances of the case.[336] This ground of review is rarely successful because of the difficulties in proving that the purpose behind a measure is different from that stated in it.[337] Where more than one aim is pursued by a measure, including an improper aim, this will not render the measure invalid for misuse of powers as long as the improper aim does not prevent the proper aim being achieved.[338]

In Case T-489/93 *Unifruit Hellas v Commission*[339] the Court of First Instance held that a misuse of powers could arise only when the institution concerned enjoyed a wide discretion. In Case C-267/94 *France v Commission*[340] Advocate-General Ruiz-Jarabo Colomer considered that the ground of misuse of powers could apply to legislative acts as well as to mere administrative or implementing measures.[341]

(f) Non-existent acts

Definition In the interests of legal certainty a Community measure is presumed to be valid until it has been repealed by a court, or withdrawn by the institution which adopted it, even though it may contain irregularities. However, in exceptional circumstances a measure may be deemed to be non-existent if it exhibits serious and manifest defects. The gravity of the irregularity must be 'so obvious that it cannot be tolerated by the Community legal order'.[342] Where an act is non-existent, neither the addressee of the measure nor the enacting institution is bound to comply with it. There is no need for the prior intervention of the courts.

---

[335] Case C-280/93 *Germany v Council* [1994] ECR I-4973 paras 110–111.

[336] Case C-331/88 *R v MAFF, ex p Fedesa* [1990] ECR I-4023 para 24; Case C-84/94 *United Kingdom v Council* [1996] ECR I-5755 para 69; Case C-285/94 *Italy v Commission* [1997] ECR I-3519 para 52.

[337] The plea succeeded in Case T-106/92 *Frederiksen v Parliament* [1995] ECR-SC II-99 paras 47–60 (a staff case).

[338] Case 1/54 *France v High Authority* [1954–1956] ECR 1 at 16 (ECSC).

[339] [1994] ECR II-1201 para 84.

[340] [1995] ECR I-4845, at paras 76–79 of the Opinion.

[341] In Joined Cases 32, 52 and 57/87 *ISA v Commission* [1988] ECR 3305 para 19 the Court of Justice annulled an ECSC decision on the ground of misuse of powers.

[342] Case C-137/92P *Commission v BASF* [1994] ECR I-2555 paras 48–50. See also Case 15/85 *Consorzio Cooperative d'Abruzzo v Commission* [1987] ECR 1005 para 10; Case T-156/89 *Mordt v Court of Justice* [1991] ECR II-407 para 84 (a staff case); Case C-135/93 *Spain v Commission* [1995] ECR I-1651 para 18.

No time-limit Where an act is alleged to be non-existent, it may be challenged under the article 173 [new art 230] procedure, even where the two-month time-limit has expired.[343] Indeed, the Court is obliged to raise the question of non-existence of its own motion if necessary.[344]

Judgment/costs Technically, actions against a non-existent measure will be declared inadmissible, as there is no justiciable act to form the subject-matter of the action.[345] In practical terms, a judgment to this effect will serve as a declaration that the contested act is non-existent. Because the action is declared inadmissible, the applicant will *prima facie* have to bear his own costs. However, the Rules of Procedure permit the Court to order that the costs be shared or that the parties bear their own costs where the circumstances are exceptional, or that the successful party pays the costs which it has unreasonably or vexatiously caused the other party to incur.[346]

11. TIME-LIMIT FOR APPLICATIONS

Time-limits The fifth paragraph of article 173 of the EC Treaty [new art 230] provides that an application must be commenced within two months of the publication of the measure, or of its notification to the applicant or, failing that, within two months of the day on which it came to the knowledge of the applicant.[347]

The time-limits applied before the EC courts are governed exclusively by Community law. A party is not entitled to rely on provisions concerning time under national law.[348] Detailed rules for reckoning periods of time are set out in the Rules of Procedure.[349] Time periods include official holidays, Sundays and

---

[343] Joined Cases 6/69 and 11/69 *Commission v France* [1969] ECR 523 paras 10–13; Case 15/85 *Consorzio Cooperative d'Abruzzo v Commission* [1987] ECR 1005 para 10; Joined Cases T-79/89, T-84/89 and others *BASF v Commission* [1992] ECR II-315 para 101 (note that the substantive decision was overturned by the Court of Justice in Case C-137/92P *Commission v BASF* [1994] ECR I-2555 paras 44–55).

[344] Joined Cases T-79/89, T-84/89 and others *BASF v Commission* [1992] ECR II-315 para 101.

[345] Ibid. See also Joined Cases 1/57 and 14/57 *Usines à Tubes de la Sarre v High Authority* [1957] ECR 105 at 112–113 (ECSC).

[346] ECJ Rules of Procedure, article 69(3); CFI Rules of Procedure, article 87(3).

[347] At para 22 of his Opinion in Case C-143/95P *Commission v Socurte* [1997] ECR I-1 Advocate-General Lenz stated that 'notification' encompasses 'publication'. This suggests that, for all persons, the two-month time-limit will run from the date of publication of a measure even if it is later notified separately to any individual person. He also stated that the two-month period may run only from the date of knowledge of an applicant where the decision has been neither published nor formally notified to the person concerned. See also Joined Cases 172/83 and 226/83 *Hoogovens v Commission* [1985] ECR 2831 para 8 (ECSC); and the Opinion of Advocate-General Mancini in Joined Cases 358/85 and 51/86 *France v Parliament* [1988] ECR 4821 at 4838 as to the circumstances in which a measure may be challenged before publication and/or notification.

[348] Case 209/83 *Valsabbia v Commission* [1984] ECR 3089 (ECSC); Case C-12/90 *Infortec v Commission* [1990] ECR I-4265 para 10.

[349] ECJ Rules of Procedure, articles 80–82; CFI Rules of Procedure, articles 101–103.

Saturdays, and are not suspended during judicial vacations. However, if a time period ends on a Saturday, Sunday or official holiday[350] it is automatically extended to the end of the first following working day. The two-month time-limit begins to run the day after notification or from the end of the fourteenth day after the publication of the measure in the *Official Journal*.[351] In practice, this means that the two-month period will expire at the end of the day which bears the same number as the day from which time was set running, for example the day of notification.[352] An additional extension of 10 days exists for parties who are habitually resident in the United Kingdom[353] to take account of distance.[354]

The EC courts apply the relevant time-limits very strictly in order to preserve legal certainty.[355] They have no discretion to extend the mandatory time-limit set down by article 173.[356] A party who alleges that an application is out of time must prove the date on which the measure was notified.[357] In addition, the EC courts have power to examine the question of time-limits of their own motion.[358]

Where an applicant allows the two-month time-limit to expire he cannot start time running again by asking the institution to reconsider its decision and bringing an action against the refusal confirming the decision previously taken.[359]

---

[350] The relevant official holidays are listed in Annex I of the ECJ Rules of Procedure.

[351] ECJ Rules of Procedure, article 81(1); CFI Rules of Procedure, article 102(1). See Case T-125/89 *Filtrona v Commission* [1990] ECR II-393; Case C-59/91 *France v Commission* [1992] ECR I-525 paras 3–7 (meaning of 'calendar month').

[352] Case 152/85 *Misset v Council* [1987] ECR 223 para 8 (staff case); Joined Cases 281/85, 283 to 285/85 and 287/85 *Germany v Commission* [1987] ECR 3203 para 5; Case C-59/91 *France v Commission* [1992] ECR I-525 paras 3–7.

[353] The application of the extension of time depends on where the applicant is habitually resident. The place of residence of the applicant's lawyer is irrelevant; see Case 28/65 *Fonzi v Commission* [1966] ECR 477.

[354] ECJ Rules of Procedure, article 81(2); CFI Rules of Procedure, article 102(2). The relevant periods for each Member State are listed in Annex II, article 1 of the ECJ Rules of Procedure.

[355] Case 152/85 *Misset v Council* [1987] ECR 223 para 11 (staff case); Case 257/85 *Dufay v Parliament* [1987] ECR 1561 paras 9–10 (Court rejected an argument based on article 6 of the European Convention on Human Rights) (staff case).

[356] Case 4/67 *Muller v Commission* [1967] ECR 365 (ECSC staff case); Joined Cases T-80/89 and others *BASF v Commission* [1995] ECR II-729 para 58; Joined Cases T-121/96 and T-151/96 *MAAS v Commission* [1997] ECR II-000 para 38 (judgment of 18 September 1997).

[357] Joined Cases 32/58 and 33/58 *SNUPAT v High Authority* [1959] ECR 127 at 136 (ECSC); Case 42/58 *SAFE v High Authority* [1959] ECR 183 at 190 (ECSC); Joined Cases 193/87 and 194/87 *Maurissen v Court of Auditors* [1989] ECR 1045 (staff case); Case T-1/90 *Pérez-Mínguez Casariego v Commission* [1991] ECR II-143 para 37 (staff case); Joined Cases T-70/92 and T-71/92 *Florimex v Commission* [1997] ECR II-693 paras 71–76.

[358] Case 33/72 *Gunnella v Commission* [1973] ECR 475 para 4 (staff case); Joined Cases T-121/96 and T-151/96 *MAAS v Commission* [1997] ECR II-000 para 39 (judgment of 18 September 1997).

[359] Case T-514/93 *Cobrecaf v Commission* [1995] ECR II-621 para 40.

Publication A measure is presumed to be published on the date on the cover of the *Official Journal of the European Communities* in which it appears, unless there is evidence that the issue was not, in fact, available until a later date.[360] Publication in the *Official Journal* must enable interested parties to gain precise knowledge of the content and grounds of the act in dispute, enabling them to exercise their right of action.[361]

Notification A measure is duly notified once it has been communicated to the person to whom it is addressed and that person is in a position to take cognisance of it.[362] Notification will usually take place by a registered letter, accompanied by a form headed 'Acknowledgement of Receipt', to be completed by the recipient or delivered by hand against receipt. Regardless of the time of day when the measure in question is notified, time does not begin to run until the end of the day of notification.[363]

An irregularity in the procedure for notification of a decision cannot affect the validity of that decision, although it may prevent the two-month period within which an application must be lodged from starting to run.[364]

An applicant will not be deemed to have been notified of a Community measure until it has been communicated to him with sufficient detail to enable him to identify the measure adopted and to ascertain its precise content in such a way as to enable him to exercise his right to institute proceedings.[365] Those requirements will not be satisfied where the applicant receives only a brief summary of the contents of a decision in a letter.[366] Once a party is aware of the existence of a decision affecting him, there is an obligation on him to request the whole text of that decision within a reasonable period, should he wish to challenge it.[367]

---

[360] Case 99/78 *Decker v Hauptzollamt Landau* [1979] ECR 101 paras 2–5; Case –337/88 *SAFA v Amministrazione delle finanze* [1990] ECR I-1 paras 8–12.

[361] Case T-109/94 *Windpark Groothusen v Commission* [1995] ECR II-3007 paras 24–25.

[362] Case 48/69 *ICI v Commission* [1972] ECR 619 paras 34–44 (service on subsidiary company unacceptable); Case 6/72 *Europemballage and Continental Can v Commission* [1973] ECR 215 paras 9–10; Case 42/85 *Cockerill-Sambre v Commission* [1985] ECR 3749 para 10 (ECSC); Case T-12/90 *Bayer v Commission* [1991] ECR II-219 paras 17–21, upheld by the Court of Justice on appeal in Case C-195/91P *Bayer v Commission* [1994] ECR I-5619 paras 16–21; Joined Cases T-80/89 and others *BASF v Commission* [1995] ECR II-729 para; Case T-380/94 *AIUFFASS v Commission* [1996] ECR I-2169 paras 40–43.

[363] Case 152/85 *Misset v Council* [1987] ECR 223 (staff case).

[364] Case 48/69 *ICI v Commission* [1972] ECR 619 paras 39–40.

[365] Case 76/79 *Könecke v Commission* [1980] ECR 665 para 7; Case 59/84 *Tezi v Commission* [1986] ECR 887 paras 9–12; Case C-12/90 *Infortec v Commission* [1990] ECR I-4265 paras 8–9.

[366] Case C-143/95P *Commission v Socurte* [1997] ECR I-1 paras 31–33. *Cf* Joined Cases T-121/96 and T-151/96 *MAAS v Commission* [1997] ECR II-000 paras 40–45 (judgment of 18 September 1997), where a fax expressly referred to another document of which the applicant had a copy.

[367] Case 236/86 *Dillinger Hüttenwerke v Commission* [1988] ECR 3761 para 14 (ECSC); Case C-80/88 *Wirtschaftsvereinigung Eisen- und Stahlindustrie v Commission* [1990] ECR I-4413 para 22 (ECSC); Case C-102/92 *Ferriere Acciaierie Sarde v Commission* [1993] ECR I-801 para 18 (ECSC); Case T-109/94 *Windpark Groothusen v Commission* [1995] ECR II-3007 paras 26–29; Joined Cases T-432 to 434/93 *SOCURTE v Commission* [1995] ECR

Exceptions A party's failure to comply with time-limits may be excused if he proves the existence of an excusable error, unforeseeable circumstances[368] or *force majeure*.[369] The concept of excusable error must be interpreted narrowly and will apply only in exceptional circumstances, for example where the conduct of the institution concerned was, either alone or to a decisive extent, such as to give rise to understandable confusion in the mind of a person acting in good faith and exercising normal care and attention.[370]

The concept of *force majeure* covers unusual circumstances which make it impossible for the relevant act to be carried out. Even though it does not require absolute impossibility, it does require abnormal difficulties, which are independent of the will of the person concerned and which are apparently inevitable, even if all due care is taken.[371] In Case C-195/91P *Bayer v Commission*[372] the Court of Justice held that the concept of *force majeure* contains an objective element relating to abnormal circumstances unconnected with the applicant in question and a subjective element involving the obligation, on his part, to guard against the consequences of the abnormal event by taking appropriate steps without making unreasonable sacrifices. In particular, the applicant must pay close attention to the course of the procedure set in motion and demonstrate diligence in seeking to comply with the prescribed time-limits.

The two-month time-limit does not apply where the validity of an act is questioned under article 184[373] of the EC Treaty [new art 241]; nor does it apply in the context of a preliminary reference under article 177 of the EC Treaty [new art 234] unless the party who wishes to challenge the validity of the Community act before the national court was fully aware of the act and was undoubtedly able to challenge it under article 173 of the EC Treaty [new art 230] but failed to do so.[374] No time-limit applies in respect of non-existent acts.[375]

II-503 paras 49–51, upheld on appeal by the Court of Justice in Case C-143/95P *Commission v Socurte* [1997] ECR I-1 paras 30–33.

[368] See Joined Cases 25/65 and 26/65 *SIMET and FERAM v High Authority* [1967] ECR 33 (ECSC), where a postal delay was held to constitute an 'unforeseeable circumstance'. Contrast Case C-59/91 *France v Commission* [1992] ECR I-525 paras 8–12, where the applicants were not permitted to rely on a postal delay.

[369] Statute of the Court of Justice, article 42.

[370] Case T-12/90 *Bayer v Commission* [1991] ECR II-219 paras 28–29, upheld by the Court of Justice on appeal in Case C-195/91P *Bayer v Commission* [1994] ECR I-5619 paras 25–28; Case T-514/93 *Cobrecaf v Commission* [1995] ECR II-621 para 40. See also Case 25/68 *Schertzer v Parliament* [1977] ECR 1729 paras 10–21 (staff case); Case 117/78 *Orlandi v Commission* [1979] ECR 1613 paras 6–12 (staff case).

[371] Case 284/82 *Busseni v Commission* [1984] ECR 557 para 11 (ECSC); Case 224/83 *Vittoria v Commission* [1984] ECR 2349 (ECSC); Case 209/83 *Valsabbia v Commission* [1984] ECR 3089 (ECSC); Case 42/85 *Cockerill-Sambre v Commission* [1985] ECR 3749 (ECSC); Case T-12/90 *Bayer v Commission* [1991] ECR II-219 para 44, upheld by the Court of Justice on appeal in Case C-195/91P *Bayer v Commission* [1994] ECR I-5619 paras 30–33.

[372] [1994] ECR I-5619 para 32.

[373] See Ch 14.

[374] Case C-188/92 *TWD v Germany* [1994] ECR I-833. Discussed at Ch 1, pp 15–18.

[375] See above at p 324.

12. EFFECT OF JUDGMENT

Article 174 Article 174 of the EC Treaty [new art 231] provides:

> If the action is well founded, the Court of Justice shall declare the act concerned to be void.
>
> In the case of a regulation, however, the Court of Justice shall, if it considers this necessary, state which of the effects of the regulation which it has declared void shall be considered as definitive.

Article 176/effect of judgment Article 176 of the EC Treaty [new art 233] imposes an obligation on the institution concerned to take all necessary measures to comply with the judgment.[376] The institution may be required to take adequate steps to restore the applicant to its original situation or to avoid the adoption of an identical measure.[377] The institution is allowed a reasonable period within which to comply with the judgment.[378] However, the EC courts may only declare that the act challenged is void; they are not entitled to order an institution to adopt specific measures[379] nor are they entitled to impose a time-limit for compliance.[380]

A finding that an act is void is of general application; it does not bind only the particular parties. Therefore, it may be relied on in proceedings in both national and EC courts. In addition, a judgment under article 173 [new art 230] may provide the basis for a claim for damages against the institution concerned under article 215 of the EC Treaty [new art 288].[381]

Competition cases In Case T-227/95 *Assidomän Kraft Products v Commission*[382] the Court of First Instance considered the obligations on the Commission where it was requested to review a decision which it had adopted in light of a subsequent judgment of the Court of Justice. The Commission had adopted a decision (the 'Wood Pulp decision') which found that a number of undertakings were in breach of article 85 of the EC Treaty [new art 81].

---

[376] See Joined Cases 97/86, 99/86, 193/86 and 215/86 *Asteris and Greece v Commission* [1988] ECR 2181 paras 26–33 for an analysis of the obligations imposed by article 176. See also Case T-387/94 *Asia Motor France v Commission* [1996] ECR II-961 paras 38–40 for the remedies available where an institution fails to comply with a judgment under article 173 [new art 230].

[377] Joined Cases T-480/93 and T-483/93 *Antillean Rice Mills v Commission* [1995] ECR II-2305 para 60; Case T-25/96 *Arbeitsgemeinschaft Deutscher Luftfahrt-Unternehmen* [1997] ECR II-363 para 17.

[378] Case C-21/94 *Parliament v Council* [1995] ECR I-1827 para 33; Case T-73/95 *Oliveira v Commission* [1997] ECR II-381 paras 41, 45 and 47. Delay in the conduct of the procedure for compliance with a judgment will not of itself affect the validity of the act ultimately adopted: see Case T-81/95 *Interhotel v Commission* [1997] ECR II-1265 para 66.

[379] Case 53/85 *AKZO Chemie v Commission* [1986] ECR 1965 para 23; Case 15/85 *Consorzio Cooperative d'Abruzzo v Commission* [1987] ECR 1005 para 18; C-199/91 *Foyer culturel du Sart-Tilman v Commission* [1993] ECR I-2667 paras 15–18; Case T-548/93 *Ladbroke v Commission* [1995] ECR II-2565 paras 53–55.

[380] Case C-21/94 *Parliament v Council* [1995] ECR I-1827 para 33.

[381] See Ch 16, pp 359–360.

[382] [1997] ECR II-1185 paras 85 and 92.

Certain of the undertakings successfully challenged the decision before the Court of Justice. Undertakings which had not taken part in those legal proceedings then sent a letter to the Commission asking it to reconsider their legal position in the light of the judgment and to refund the fines they had paid. The Court of First Instance held that the Commission was required, in accordance with article 176 of the EC Treaty, [new art 233][383] to review the legality of its original decision and to determine whether it was appropriate to repay the fines.

Partial annulment The second paragraph of article 174 allows the EC courts to declare that certain provisions of a Community measure which it has declared to be void should nonetheless be treated as being valid.[384] Although article 174 refers expressly to regulations only, the Court of Justice has applied this principle to other types of Community acts. For example, in Case 17/74 *Transocean Marine Paint Association v Commission*[385] the Court of Justice annulled a particular provision of a Commission decision, leaving the remainder intact.

The Court will not exercise the power of partial annulment where the invalid parts of the measure are inseparable from the measure as a whole, so that without them the measure would no longer be capable of producing legal effects.[386] An application to the Court may expressly seek the annulment of a particular provision of a measure.[387] However, if the Court decides that it is not possible to sever that provision from the measure as a whole, it may declare the action inadmissible, unless the application seeks the annulment of the whole measure in the alternative.[388]

Temporal limitation[389] An act annulled under article 173 of the EC Treaty [new art 230] is void *ab initio*: it is treated as if it had never existed.[390] However, in certain cases, relying on the second paragraph of article 174 [new art 231], the EC courts have declared that the annulment of the measure should be effective only from the date of the judgment. For example, in Case 34/86 *Council v Parliament*[391] the Court of Justice found that the 1986 Community budget was illegal after a substantial part of the financial year had already elapsed, and held that the annulment should have effect only from the date of the

---

[383] Discussed above at p 328.

[384] For example, see Case 34/86 *Council v Parliament* [1986] ECR 2155 para 48.

[385] [1974] ECR 1063 paras 20–21. See also Case 92/78 *Simmenthal v Commission* [1979] ECR 777 paras 106–107 (Commission decision); Case C-360/93 *Parliament v Council* [1996] ECR I-1195 paras 32–36 (Council decisions).

[386] Joined Cases T-79/95 and T-80/95 *SNCF v Commission* [1996] ECR II-1491 paras 64–65.

[387] For example, see Case 17/74 *Transocean Marine Paint Association v Commission* [1974] ECR 1063 paras 1–3.

[388] Case 37/71 *Jamet v Commission* [1972] ECR 483 paras 9–11 (staff case).

[389] See Niamh Hyland, 'Temporal limitation of the effects of judgments of the Court of Justice—A review of recent case-law' (1995) *Irish Journal of European Law* 208. See also Ch 11, pp 240–241.

[390] Joined Cases 97/86, 99/86, 193/86 and 215/86 *Asteris and Greece v Commission* [1988] ECR 2181 para 30.

[391] [1986] ECR 2155 para 48.

judgment, so that the validity of payments made and commitments entered into under the illegal budget could not be called into question. Furthermore, in other cases the EC courts have held that the annulled measure should continue in force until it could be replaced by a new measure.[392]

[392] Case C-65/90 *Parliament v Council* [1992] ECR I-4593 paras 22–24; Case C-21/94 *Parliament v Council* [1995] ECR I-1827 paras 29–32 (Council directive); Case C-271/94 *Parliament v Council* [1996] ECR I-1689 paras 36–40 (Council decision).

Chapter 14

Plea of Illegality

1. NATURE OF ARTICLE 184

Article 184 Article 184 of the EC Treaty [new art 241] provides that:

> Notwithstanding the expiry of the period laid down in the fifth paragraph of Article 173, any party may, in proceedings in which a regulation adopted jointly by the European Parliament and the Council, or a regulation of the Council, of the Commission, or of the ECB is at issue, plead the grounds specified in the second paragraph of Article 173 in order to invoke before the Court of Justice the inapplicability of that regulation.

Purpose Article 184 allows applicants to challenge a Community measure after the two-month period for challenging it directly under article 173 [new art 230] has expired. Thus, in Joined Cases 87/77, 130/77, 22/83, 9/84 and 10/84 *Salerno v Commission and Council*[1] the Court of Justice held:

> ... the sole purpose of Article 184 is to protect parties against the application of an unlawful regulation where the regulation itself can no longer be challenged owing to the expiry of the period laid down in Article 173.

No independent right of action Parties cannot bring a direct action before the Court of Justice based solely on article 184.[2] The plea of illegality will normally arise where a specific implementing measure is being attacked under article 173 and the validity of the regulation on which the implementing measure is based is called into question. In Case 92/78 *Simmenthal v Commission*[3] the applicant had brought an action under article 173 against a decision of the Commission which was of direct and individual concern to it. The Court of Justice held that a plea of illegality aimed at the regulations on which that decision was based was also admissible under article 184.

Article 184 may be invoked only in the context of a separate, independently admissible cause of action. Thus, where the main action is itself inadmissible,

---

[1] [1985] ECR 2523 para 36. See also Joined Cases 31/62 and 33/62 *Wöhrmann v Commission* [1962] ECR 501 at 507.
[2] Ibid at 506–507; Case 44/65 *Hessische Knappschaft v Singer* [1965] ECR 965 at 970; Case 33/80 *Albini v Council and Commission* [1981] ECR 2141 para 17; Joined Cases 87/77, 130/77, 22/83, 9/84 and 10/84 *Salerno v Commission and Council* [1985] ECR 2523 para 36.
[3] [1979] ECR 777 paras 34–43.

an applicant will not be entitled to rely on article 184. In Joined Cases 89/86 and 91/86 *Étoile commerciale and CNTA v Commission*[4] the applicant's challenge to a regulation under article 184 was declared to be inadmissible, as the primary claim under article 173, in respect of an implementing measure, was itself inadmissible, the implementing measure not being of direct and individual concern to the applicant.

Particular importance for private parties Article 184 is of particular importance in relation to private parties. Where a Community institution adopts a regulation its legality cannot be challenged by private parties under article 173 unless it is of direct and individual concern to them.[5] However, subsequent measures adopted on the basis of a regulation may be of direct and individual concern to them or may, indeed, be addressed to them. Article 184 permits private parties to challenge not only the implementing measures but also, indirectly, the regulation upon which they are based.[6]

2. SCOPE OF ARTICLE 184

Private parties Natural or legal persons may not rely on article 184 [new art 241] against a measure which they could previously have challenged under article 173 [new art 230] but did not do so within the prescribed two-month time period.[7]

Member States Member States, as privileged applicants, have an automatic right to challenge acts of the Community institutions under article 173. Therefore, if the approach adopted in relation to private parties was applied to Member States, they would never be able to rely on article 184. However, a number of Advocates-General have supported the view that Member States are entitled to invoke article 184.[8] For example, in his Opinion in Case 181/85 *France v Commission*[9] Advocate-General Sir Gordon Slynn emphasised that the words 'any party' are used in article 184 and specifically rejected the Commission's submission that the rights of the Member States under article 184 should be limited because of their privileged status under article 173, and therefore should only be entitled to invoke article 184 where they had been

---

[4] [1987] ECR 3005 para 22. See also Case T-154/94 *CSF and CSME v Commission* [1997] ECR II-1377 paras 15–17; Case C-64/93 *Donatab v Commission* [1993] ECR I-3595 paras 19–20.
[5] See Ch 13, pp 287–307.
[6] Case 262/80 *Andersen v Parliament* [1984] ECR 195 paras 5–7.
[7] Case 92/78 *Simmenthal v Commission* [1979] ECR 777 para 39; Joined Cases T-244/93 and T-486/93 *TWD v Commission* [1995] ECR II-2265 para 103 (in which the Court of First Instance applied, by analogy, the reasoning adopted by the Court of Justice in Case C-188/92 *TWD v Germany* [1994] ECR I-833 (discussed at Ch 1, pp 15–17).
[8] Opinion of Advocate-General Roemer in Case 32/65 *Italy v Council and Commission* [1966] ECR 389 at 414; Opinion of Advocate-General Mancini in Case 204/86 *Greece v Council* [1988] ECR 5323 at 5343–5345; paras 12–32 of the Opinion of Advocate-General Darmon in Case C-258/89 *Commission v Spain* [1991] ECR I-3977.
[9] [1987] ECR 689 at 702–703.

'taken by surprise' by the way in which a regulation had been implemented. The issue was not addressed by the Court of Justice in its judgment.

In Case C-135/93 *Spain v Commission*[10] the Court of Justice held that:

> to accept that an applicant could, in an action for annulment of a decision, raise a plea of illegality against an earlier act of the same kind, annulment of which he could have sought directly, would make it possible indirectly to challenge earlier decisions which were not contested within the period for bringing proceedings prescribed in Article 173 of the Treaty, thereby circumventing that time-limit.

Although Spain did not expressly rely on article 184 in this case, the reasoning adopted by the Court does support an argument that Member States should never be entitled to rely on article 184 because of their status as privileged applicants under article 173.

Article 169 proceedings If Member States are entitled to rely on article 184, this would provide a potential defence to infraction proceedings brought by the Commission under article 169 of the EC Treaty [new art 226]. In Case C-258/89 *Commission v Spain*[11] Advocate-General Darmon considered that Member States should be entitled to invoke article 184 in respect of a regulation in the context of proceedings under article 169. However, in Case 156/77 *Commission v Belgium*[12] the Court of Justice held that a Member State could not rely on article 184 in the context of article 169 proceedings in order to challenge a Commission decision which had been specifically addressed to it.

Community institutions As indicated above, in Case 181/85 *France v Commission*[13] Advocate-General Sir Gordon Slynn stated that Member States should be permitted to rely on article 184 as it expressly states that it may be relied on by 'any party', and this view has been supported by a number of other Advocates-General.[14] In principle, Community institutions should also come within the express wording of article 184. However, Community institutions are, like Member States, privileged applicants under article 173. If Member States are precluded from relying on article 184 for this reason, the same should apply to Community institutions.

3. ACTS WHICH MAY BE CHALLENGED

Necessary connection The Court of Justice has consistently held that article 184 of the EC Treaty[new art 241] may be pleaded to challenge the legality of a

---

[10] [1995] ECR I-1651 paras 16–17.
[11] [1991] ECR I-3977, at para 23 of the Opinion. See also the Opinion of Advocate-General Mancini in Case 226/87 *Commission v Greece* [1988] ECR 3611 at 3617.
[12] [1978] ECR 1881 paras 18–25; see also pp 1908 and 1909 of the Opinion of Advocate-General Mayras.
[13] [1987] ECR 689 at 702 and 703, Opinion of Advocate-General Sir Gordon Slynn.
[14] Opinion of Advocate-General Roemer in Case 32/65 *Italy v Council and Commission* [1966] ECR 389 at 414; Opinion of Advocate-General Mancini in Case 204/86 *Greece v Council* [1988] ECR 5323 at 5343–5345; paras 12–32 of the Opinion of Advocate-General Darmon in Case C-258/89 *Commission v Spain* [1991] ECR I-3977.

regulation which provides the specific legal basis of a measure which is at issue in the action.[15] It is not clear whether this is the only basis on which article 184 may be invoked. In Case 32/65 *Italy v Council and Commission*[16] the Court of Justice adopted a more general approach when it indicated that an applicant can challenge the validity of a regulation which is applicable 'directly or indirectly' to the issue with which the main application is concerned. The Court of Justice held that the regulation in question in that case could not be attacked under article 184 as there was no 'necessary connection' between it and the measures which formed the primary subject-matter of the action, rather than simply relying on the argument that the regulation did not provide the specific legal basis for those measures.

Confirmatory regulations Under article 173 an applicant may not challenge a purely confirmatory measure as this would allow it, in effect, to challenge the original measure after the relevant two-month time-limit had expired.[17] In contrast, as the specific purpose of article 184 is to permit the legality of a measure to be questioned after the expiry of the two-month time-limit provided for by article 173, a party is entitled to rely on article 184 to challenge the applicability of a purely confirmatory regulation.[18]

Acts other than regulations The wording of article 184 appears to indicate that the plea of illegality can be raised only in respect of regulations. However, in Case 92/78 *Simmenthal v Commission*[19] the Court of Justice held that:

> The field of application of [article 184] must therefore include acts of the institutions which, although they are not in the form of a regulation, nevertheless produce similar effects and on those grounds may not be challenged under Article 173 by natural or legal persons other than Community institutions and Member States.

In that case the applicant was contesting a decision taken on the basis of an invitation to tender. The specific decision was of direct and individual concern to the applicant; however, the notice to tender was a measure of general application and, therefore, could not have been challenged by a private party under article 173 of the EC Treaty. The Court of Justice held that these constituted good grounds for permitting the applicant to challenge the validity of the notice to tender under article 184.[20]

---

[15] Case 92/78 *Simmenthal v Commission* [1979] ECR 777 para 39; Joined Cases 87/77, 130/77, 22/83, 9/84 and 10/84 *Salerno v Commission and Council* [1985] ECR 2523 para 36.

[16] [1966] ECR 389 at 409–410. See the Opinion of Advocate-General Sir Gordon Slynn in Case 181/85 *France v Commission* [1987] ECR 689 at 703; and the Opinion of Advocate-General Mischo in Joined Cases 181/86 and 184/86 *Del Plato v Commission* [1987] ECR 4991 at 5004. See also Case 21/64 *Macchiorlati v High Authority* [1965] ECR 175 at 187–188 (ECSC).

[17] See Ch 13, pp 276–277.

[18] Case T-64/92 *Chavane de Dalmassy v Commission* [1994] ECR-SC II-723 paras 41–46.

[19] [1979] ECR 777 paras 39–43.

[20] This is in line with the Court's general approach in considering the substance, not form, of Community measures. See also Case 216/82 *Universität Hamburg v Hauptzollamt Hamburg-Kehrwieder* [1983] ECR 2771 paras 5–12.

4. GROUNDS OF INAPPLICABILITY

Same grounds as under article 173 The grounds upon which a Community measure may be declared inapplicable under article 184 of the EC Treaty [new art 241] are the same as those under article 173 [new art 230],[21] namely:

(1) lack of competence;
(2) infringement of an essential procedural requirement;
(3) infringement of the EC Treaty or of any rule of law relating to its application; and
(4) misuse of powers.

5. EFFECT OF JUDGMENT

Inapplicable, not void In Joined Cases 31/62 and 33/62 *Wöhrmann v Commission*[22] the Court of Justice emphasised that the purpose of article 184 [new art 241] is limited to rendering a regulation inapplicable in a particular case 'without thereby in any way calling in issue the regulation itself'. This stems from the fact that a judgment based on article 184 has the effect of circumventing the two-month limitation period set down in article 173 [new art 230], which is imposed in the interests of legal certainty. However, as all other measures based on the same regulation will also be at risk of being held inapplicable under article 184, the Commission or Council will usually take steps to replace the illegal regulation with a legal one.

6. PROCEEDINGS IN NATIONAL COURTS

Comparable principle Although the plea of illegality under article 184 of the EC Treaty [new art 241] is restricted to proceedings before the EC courts, the Court of Justice has held that a party may rely on a comparable principle in proceedings brought in the national courts where the validity of a Community regulation is in issue in those proceedings. In Case 216/82 *Universität Hamburg v Hauptzollamt Hamburg-Kehrwieder*[23] the applicant brought proceedings in the German courts to challenge a decision taken by the German customs authorities. The Court of Justice held that the applicant was entitled to challenge the validity of the Commission decision on which the national decision was based because article 184 reflected a general principle of law applicable in all proceedings. However, a private party may not question the validity of a Community act in proceedings before a national court where he could undoubtedly have challenged that act directly under article 173 of the EC Treaty

---

[21] Case C-64/93 *Donatab v Commission* [1993] ECR I-3595 para 18. Grounds of invalidity are discussed at Ch 13, pp 307–324.
[22] [1962] ECR 501 at 507.
[23] [1983] ECR 2771 paras 5–12.

[new art 230] but failed to do so within the two-month period prescribed.[24]

Where the validity of a Community measure is challenged in the course of national proceedings, the national court must refer the question of validity to the Court of Justice under article 177 of the EC Treaty [new art 234].[25]

---

[24] Case C-188/92 *TWD v Germany* [1994] ECR I-833. Discussed at Ch 1, pp 15–17.
[25] Case 314/85 *Foto-Frost v Hauptzollamt Lübeck-Ost* [1987] ECR 4199 paras 11–20. See Ch 11, pp 228–229.

Chapter 15

Judicial Review of Failure to Act

1. INTRODUCTION

Article 175 Article 175 of the EC Treaty [new art 232] provides that:

> Should the European Parliament, the Council or the Commission, in infringement of this Treaty, fail to act, the Member States and the other institutions of the Community may bring an action before the Court of Justice to have the infringement established.
>
> The action shall be admissible only if the institution concerned has first been called upon to act. If, within two months of being so called upon, the institution concerned has not defined its position, the action may be brought within a further period of two months.
>
> Any natural or legal person may, under the conditions laid down in the preceding paragraphs, complain to the Court of Justice that an institution of the Community has failed to address to that person any act other than a recommendation or an opinion.
>
> The Court of Justice shall have jurisdiction, under the same conditions, in actions or proceedings brought by the ECB in the areas falling within the latter's field of competence and in actions or proceedings brought against the latter.

Nature of Article 175 Article 175 of the EC Treaty provides the legal basis for review by the EC courts of failure to act by the Community institutions. It is intended:[1]

> to prevent an institution, which has wrongly failed to adopt an act or take a given measure, from evading permanently its responsibilities and escaping any judicial sanction by resorting to silence or by giving a procrastinating, evasive or insufficiently binding reply when called upon to act.

If an institution is found to have contravened article 175, the Court of Justice will make a declaration indicating that the institution is in breach of its EC

---

[1] Case 377/87 *Parliament v Council* [1988] ECR 4017, paras 12–13 of the Opinion of Advocate-General Mischo.

Treaty obligations. Article 176 [new art 233] then requires the institution to take the necessary measures to comply with the judgment of the Court of Justice.[2]

Proceedings under article 175 are intended to establish an illegal omission. In Joined Cases 10/68 and 18/68 *Eridania v Commission*[3] the applicants had called upon the Commission to revoke certain acts. When the Commission failed to respond, the applicants began proceedings under article 175. The Court of Justice held that these proceedings were inadmissible. Their true purpose was the revocation of certain acts, rather than a declaration of failure to act by the Commission; therefore, the appropriate means of recourse was under article 173 of the EC Treaty [new art 230].

Jurisdiction Applications by the Member States and the Community institutions under article 175 must be made to the Court of Justice. Applications by natural or legal persons under article 175 must be made to the Court of First Instance.[4]

2. PARTIES

Defendants Article 175 of the EC Treaty [new art 232] provides that failure to act by the Council, Commission, European Parliament or European Central Bank ('ECB') may be subject to review by the EC courts.[5]

Privileged applicants Article 175 provides that the Member States and the Community institutions may bring an action before the Court of Justice in order to challenge a failure to act.[6] The Member States and the institutions are 'privileged applicants', as they are entitled to challenge the failure to adopt all types of measures, including measures which would not have been addressed to them, and measures of general application.

In Case 13/83 *Parliament v Council*[7] the Court of Justice rejected an argument that the Parliament was not entitled to bring an action against the Council under article 175, and held that article 175 gives the same right of action to all the Community institutions.[8] Advocate-General Lenz stated that the right of action of the Parliament does not require proof of a special interest

---

[2] See below at p 349.

[3] [1969] ECR 459 paras 15–18. See also Case T-117/96 *Intertronic Cornelis v Commission* [1997] ECR II-141 paras 23–25.

[4] Article 3 of Council Decision 8/591 of 24 October 1988 (OJ 1989 C215 p 1) as substituted by Council Directive 93/350 of 8 June 1993 (OJ 1993 L144 p 21) as amended by Council Decision 94/149 of 7 March 1994 (OJ 1994 L66 p 29).

[5] The Treaty on European Union ('Maastricht Treaty') amended article 175 so as to make failure to act by the European Parliament and the European Central Bank subject to review.

[6] However, in Case 13/83 *Parliament v Council* [1985] ECR 1513 Advocate-General Lenz (at p 1519 of his Opinion) stated that the Court of Justice would not be entitled to bring an action under article 175 'because it is responsible for legal protection and does not itself seek it'.

[7] [1985] ECR 1513 paras 13–19.

[8] In a subsequent case, Case 377/87 *Parliament v Council* [1988] ECR 4017, the right of the Parliament to bring an action under article 175 was not questioned.

requiring protection.[9] However, the right of the ECB to bring proceedings under article 175 is expressly limited to areas falling within its field of competence.

Non-privileged applicants Natural or legal persons are 'non-privileged applicants', as they are only entitled to challenge the failure to adopt limited types of measures, ie measures, other than recommendations or opinions, which are addressed to them or of direct and individual concern to them.[10]

3. CONDITIONS OF LIABILITY

(a) Relevant acts

(i) Obligation to act

Obligation to act An institution cannot be challenged for failure to adopt a measure which it has no obligation to adopt.[11] This applies whether the applicant is privileged or non-privileged. In particular, where the Council or Commission has a discretion whether or not to act, it will not be possible to challenge a failure to act by proceedings under article 175 [new art 232].[12] For example, where the Commission has decided, pursuant to its discretion, not to pursue an article 169 [new art 226] action against a Member State for infringement of the EC Treaty, its failure to do so cannot be challenged.[13]

Proceedings under article 175 may be declared inadmissible not only where the Council or Commission have a discretion whether or not to act, but also where they have a discretion as to how to act. In Case 13/83 *Parliament v Council*[14] the Parliament brought proceedings under article 175 alleging that the Council had failed to implement a common transport policy as required by the EEC Treaty. The Court held that although the EEC Treaty established specific time-limits for the adoption of a common transport policy, the Council had a discretion to determine the content and means for implementing such a policy. The Council's obligations in this regard were, therefore, not sufficiently

---

[9] Paragraph 2.2 of the Opinion. This is in contrast to the position under article 173 of the EC Treaty, [new art 230] which provides that the European Parliament may only bring annulment proceedings for the purpose of protecting its prerogatives (see Ch 13, pp 279–280).

[10] See below at pp 341–343.

[11] Case T-32/93 *Ladbroke v Commission* [1994] ECR II-1015 para 35; Case T-74/92 *Ladbroke v Commission* [1995] ECR II-115 para 39; Case T-277/94 *AITEC v Commission* [1996] ECR II-351 paras 65–73. See also Opinion of Advocate-General Gand in Case 48/65 *Lütticke v Commission* [1966] ECR 19 at 32; Opinion of Advocate-General Roemer in Joined Cases 10/68 and 18/68 *Eridania v Commission* [1969] ECR 459 at 494; Opinion of Advocate-General Gand in Case 6/70 *Borromeo v Commission* [1970] ECR 815 at 822; Opinion of Advocate-General Sir Gordon Slynn in Case 246/81 *Lord Bethell v Commission* [1982] ECR 2277 at 2296; para 22 of the Opinion of Advocate-General Darmon in Joined Cases 166/86 and 220/86 *Irish Cement v Commission* [1988] ECR 6473.

[12] Case T-167/95 *Kuchlenz-Winter v Council* [1996] ECR II-1607 paras 24–25 (staff case).

[13] Case 247/87 *Star Fruit v Commission* [1989] ECR 291 paras 10–14; Case T-126/95 *Dumez v Commission* [1995] ECR II-2863 para 44; Case T-575/93 *Koelman v Commission* [1996] ECR II-1 paras 71–72 (articles 169 and 90(3) [new art 86] of the EC Treaty); Case T-47/96 *SDDDA v Commission* [1996] ECR II-1559 paras 41–42.

[14] [1985] ECR 1513.

specific to be the subject of proceedings under article 175.[15] However, the Court held that the obligation to introduce a common transport policy included the obligation to ensure the freedom to provide transport services, and this specific obligation was sufficiently well-defined to be the subject of proceedings under article 175.[16]

Competition matters Private parties are entitled to lodge complaints concerning competition matters with the Commission.[17] If the Commission decides not to act on the complaint, it is under an obligation to inform the complainant of its reasons for not doing so and to invite the complainant to submit any further comments in writing, within a given time-limit.[18] If the Commission fails to comply with this obligation, the complainant is entitled to bring proceedings under article 175.[19]

(ii) Legal effects

Legal effects Some authorities suggest that the concept of a measure capable of giving rise to an action is identical under articles 173 and 175 [new arts 230 and 232].[20] This would mean that only a failure to adopt acts which produce legal effects would be open to challenge under article 175.[21] Thus, in Case 377/87 *Parliament v Council*[22] Advocate-General Mischo, equating proceedings under article 175 with proceedings under article 173, considered that a failure to act within article 175 arises wherever the Council or Commission fails to adopt a measure, of whatever nature, form or description, which is capable of producing legal effects *vis-à-vis* third parties.[23]

However, the Court of Justice in Case 302/87 *Parliament v Council*[24] appeared to suggest that, in certain circumstances, failure to adopt an act which

---

[15] Ibid paras 47–53 of the judgment.

[16] Ibid paras 64–68 of the judgment.

[17] Article 3(2)(b) of Council Regulation 17 of 6 February 1962, First Regulation implementing articles 85 and 86 of the Treaty (OJ, English Special Edition 1959–1962 p 87) (as amended).

[18] Article 6 of Commission Regulation 99 of 25 July 1963, on the hearings provided for in articles 19(1) and (2) of Council Regulation No 17 (OJ 1962 127 p 2263) (OJ, English Special Edition 1963–1964 p 47).

[19] Case T-28/90 *Asia Motor France v Commission* [1992] ECR II-2285 para 29. See also Case 125/78 *GEMA v Commission* [1979] ECR 3173 paras 14–23; Case T-24/90 *Automec v Commission* [1992] ECR II-2223 paras 71–80 (where the Court of First Instance held that the Commission was under an obligation to give proper consideration to the issues of fact and law raised by a complainant before deciding whether or not to act on the complaint).

[20] Case 15/70 *Chevalley v Commission* [1970] ECR 975 para 6. This was cited with approval by Advocate-General Darmon in Joined Cases 166/86 and 220/86 *Irish Cement v Commission* [1988] ECR 6473, at para 42 of his Opinion.

[21] See Ch 13, pp 271–274 in relation to the notion of binding legal effects in the context of article 173.

[22] [1988] ECR 4017, paras 28–30 of the Opinion of Advocate-General Mischo. This view was not expressly adopted by the Court of Justice in its judgment.

[23] See also Case 8/71 *Komponistenverband v Commission* [1971] ECR 705 at 715, in which Advocate-General Roemer considered that the concept of an 'act' for the purposes of article 175 includes 'any measure producing certain legal effects binding the institution in a certain way', including some procedural matters.

[24] [1988] ECR 5615 para 16.

would not produce legal effects might be reviewable under article 175. The Court based this observation on the judgment in Case 377/87 *Parliament v Council*,[25] which it interpreted as establishing that the Parliament would be entitled to obtain a judgment under article 175 where the Council had failed to adopt a draft budget, even though the draft budget itself, once adopted, could not be challenged under article 173 [new art 230] as it is a preparatory measure. Although the draft budget did not produce legal effects, the Council was under a legal obligation to adopt it. Therefore, it was necessary to permit the Parliament to bring proceedings under article 175 in order to ensure that the Council's failure to fulfil its Community law obligations did not go unchecked.[26] In Case C-41/92 *Liberal Democrats v European Parliament*[27] Advocate-General Darmon suggested that where an institution fails to adopt a preparatory measure which is a necessary precondition for the adoption by another institution of a definitive measure producing legal effects, that failure to act may itself be reviewable under article 175.

(iii) Recommendations and opinions

Recommendations and opinions The third limb of article 175 of the EC Treaty [new art 232] expressly excludes the rights of private parties to complain of the failure to adopt recommendations or opinions. In order to determine the nature of the complaint, the Court of Justice will look at the substance of an applicant's complaint, rather than its form. In both Case 6/70 *Borromeo Arese v Commission*[28] and Case 15/70 *Chevalley v Commission*[29] the applicants complained of a failure by the Commission to adopt decisions which they had called upon it to make. However, the Court of Justice held that, in substance, the applicants were not seeking decisions from the Commission, but rather advice as to their own particular situations, which was equivalent to seeking an opinion and, therefore, not subject to review under article 175.[30]

(iv) Party to whom the act is addressed

Distinction between privileged and non-privileged applicants Member States and Community institutions are entitled to challenge the failure to adopt an act which would have been addressed to third parties and acts of general application. In contrast, private parties may only challenge the failure to adopt an act which would have been addressed to them or which would have been of direct and individual concern to them.

---

[25] [1988] ECR 4017.

[26] On the actual facts of Case 377/87 *Parliament v Council* the Court of Justice dismissed the action under article 175 as the Council adopted a draft budget before judgment was given.

[27] [1993] ECR I-3153, paras 25–83 of the Opinion. The Advocate-General considered that the Parliament's failure to act produced legal effects *vis-à-vis* the Council in as much as it made it impossible for the Council to fulfil the task assigned to it. This issue did not arise for consideration by the Court in its judgment.

[28] [1970] ECR 815.

[29] [1970] ECR 975.

[30] See also Case C-257/90 *Italsolar v Commission* [1993] ECR I-9 paras 28–31.

Act addressed to complainant   Where a private party complains of a failure to adopt a decision which would have been specifically addressed to him, an action under article 175 [new art 232] is admissible.[31] In Case 15/71 *Mackprang v Commission*[32] the applicant complained of an alleged failure by the Commission to adopt a decision addressed to the Member States. The Court of Justice held that such a general provision could not be described as an act which could be addressed to the applicant. In Case 246/81 *Lord Bethell v Commission*[33] Lord Bethell brought an action under, *inter alia*, article 175, for a declaration that the Commission had failed to adopt measures to combat the alleged anti-competitive behaviour of European airlines. The Court of Justice held that this application was inadmissible as, in substance, Lord Bethell was not asking the Commission to adopt a decision in respect of him, but to open an inquiry with regard to third parties and to take decisions in respect of them.

Where the applicant complains of an institution's alleged failure to adopt a decision which would have been addressed to him, the Court of Justice will consider the substance rather than the form of the complaint, in order to establish whether the institution would have been capable of adopting such a decision.[34] Thus, in Case C-247/90 *Emrich v Commission*[35] the applicant complained of the Commission's failure to address a decision to her which would have the effect of allowing her to practise as a *Rechtsanwalt* (lawyer) before the German courts. The Court of Justice held that this action was inadmissible as, within the system of the EEC Treaty, the only measure which the Commission could have taken would have been to initiate proceedings under article 169 [new art 226] against the Federal Republic of Germany. Indeed, the same applicant had previously brought an action complaining of the Commission's failure to initiate article 169 proceedings against Germany, which had, likewise, been held to be inadmissible.[36]

Acts addressed to third parties but of direct and individual concern to applicants   Article 173 [new art 230] expressly provides that private parties may challenge decisions which, although not addressed to them, are of direct and individual concern to them.[37] In contrast, the wording of article 175 [new art 232] provides for review only where there has been a failure to *address* to the applicant an act other than a recommendation or opinion. However, the case-law of the Court of Justice has established that private parties may also bring proceedings under article 175 where an institution has failed to adopt an

---

[31] Case C-371/89R *Emrich v Commission* [1990] ECR I-1555; Case C-72/90 *Asia Motor France v Commission* [1990] ECR I-2182 paras 10–12; Case T-3/90 *Prodifarma v Commission* [1991] ECR II-1 para 35.

[32] [1971] ECR 797 para 4.

[33] [1982] ECR 2277 paras 15–17.

[34] See Case 90/78 *Granaria v Council and Commission* [1979] ECR 1081 paras 12–15, where the Court of Justice held that the only legal instrument which could have satisfied the applicant's complaint would have been a regulation; therefore, the application was rejected. See also Case 60/79 *Producteurs de Vins de Table et Vins de Pays v Commission* [1979] ECR 2429.

[35] [1990] ECR I-3913 paras 5–7.

[36] Case C-371/89R *Emrich v Commission* [1990] ECR I-1555.

[37] The concepts of direct and individual concern are discussed at Ch 13, pp 287–307.

act which would have been of direct and individual concern to them.[38] It would be highly unsatisfactory if private parties were not permitted to challenge the failure to adopt acts which would have been of direct and individual concern to them, as they would then be in a stronger position if an institution expressly refused to act, rather than simply ignoring a call to act. This arises because an express refusal to act can be challenged by private parties under article 173 where the act, if adopted, would itself have been reviewable under article 173. This includes circumstances where the relevant act would have been of direct and individual concern to the private party.[39]

(b) Institution must be called upon to act

Called upon to act An action under article 175 of the EC Treaty [new art 232] is admissible only if the institution concerned has first been 'called upon to act'.[40] The purpose of this condition of admissibility is to make the institution aware that its failure to act is regarded by the potential applicant as a breach of Community law and to give the institution the opportunity of avoiding legal proceedings under article 175 by adopting the act requested or suitably defining its position. In order to satisfy this precondition, the institution should be clearly informed of the nature of the measures called for, and it must be made plain that, if the institution fails to act, legal proceedings will be initiated.[41] If an applicant fails to address a request to act to the relevant institution within the meaning of article 175, any subsequent action brought on the basis of that article will be declared inadmissible.[42]

An action for failure to act may only be brought by an applicant who has himself called upon the institution to act. An applicant may not rely upon the fact that the institution has been called upon to act by a third party.[43]

---

[38] Case C-107/91 *ENU v Commission* [1993] ECR I-599 paras 14–19 (EAEC); Case C-68/95 *T Port* [1996] ECR I-6065 paras 58–59.

[39] See the Opinion of Advocate-General Dutheillet de Lamothe in Case 15/71 *Mackprang v Commission* [1971] ECR 797 at 807–808; para 19 of the Opinion of Advocate-General Gulmann in Joined Cases C-15/91 and C-108/91 *Buckl & Söhne v Commission* [1992] ECR I-6061. The review of express refusals to act under article 173 is discussed at Ch 13, pp 277–278.

[40] Where an action is brought under article 175, the application commencing the action must be accompanied by documentary evidence of the date on which the institution was called upon to act: article 19 of the Statute of the Court of Justice.

[41] Opinion of Advocate-General Roemer in Case 8/71 *Komponistenverband v Commission* [1971] ECR 705 at 716; Case 13/83 *Parliament v Council* [1985] ECR 1513 paras 35–36, and the Opinion of Advocate-General Lenz at 1526–1527; Case 25/85 *Nuovo Campsider v Commission* [1986] ECR 1531 (ECSC); Joined Cases 81/85 and 119/85 *Usinor v Commission* [1986] ECR 1777 paras 15–16 (ECSC); Case T-28/90 *Asia Motor France v Commission* [1992] ECR II-2285 paras 25–28. See also para 12 of the Opinion of Advocate-General Gulmann in Joined Cases C-15/91 and C-108/91 *Buckl & Söhne v Commission* [1992] ECR I-6061, where he suggested that the Court of Justice should not declare of its own motion that an action was inadmissible on the basis that the call to act was deficient where the defendant institution did not itself raise the point.

[42] Case T-64/96 *De Jorio v Council* [1997] ECR II-127 para 39.

[43] Ibid para 40. Contrast the Opinion of Advocate-General Darmon in Case 302/87 *Parliament v Council* [1988] ECR 5615 at 5613, fn 20, where he noted that article 175 does not

The document calling upon the institution to act determines the scope of the subject-matter of the action. Thus, if legal proceedings are subsequently commenced under article 175, they must be confined to the scope of the original call to act.[44]

No express limitation period for call to act Article 175 of the EC Treaty does not impose an express time-limit on the period which may elapse between an institution's failure to act and its being called upon to act. However, in Joined Cases 166/86 and 220/86 *Irish Cement v Commission*[45] Advocate-General Darmon indicated that there should not be an unreasonable period between the time when an applicant becomes aware of the institution's failure to act and the time when the applicant calls upon the institution to rectify that failure. Given the complexity of the issues in that case (which concerned State aid), Advocate-General Darmon considered that a delay of 11 months before calling upon the Commission to act was not unreasonable. In Case C-107/91 *ENU v Commission*[46] the Court of Justice held that a period of 16 months did not bar an action for failure to act as there had been frequent contact between the parties concerning the problem.[47] In contrast, in Case 59/70 *Netherlands v Commission*,[48] a case under article 35 of the ECSC Treaty, the Court of Justice held that a delay of 18 months before calling upon the High Authority (the Commission) to act was unreasonable and rendered the action inadmissible.

Sufficient time to act An applicant must allow the relevant institution a reasonable time to carry out its Community law obligations before calling upon it to act. In Case T-74/92 *Ladbroke v Commission*[49] the Court of First Instance held that the Commission could not be held to have failed to act within the meaning of article 175 when, at the time when it was called upon to act by the applicant, it (the Commission) had not had sufficient time to investigate fully and to adopt a position on the applicant's complaint under article 85(1) of the EC Treaty [new art 81(1)]. On the facts of that case, five months had elapsed between the adoption of a statement of objections and the formal request to act. The Court held that the application under article 175 should be dismissed as unfounded.

(c) No definition of position

Definition of position Having been called upon to act, an institution has two months within which to define its position. If the institution does not respond

---

expressly require that the applicant before the Court should necessarily be the one which initially called upon the institution to act.

[44] Opinion of Advocate-General Lenz in Case 13/83 *Parliament v Council* [1985] ECR 1513 at 1526–1527.

[45] [1988] ECR 6473, at paras 15–21 of the Opinion of Advocate-General Darmon.

[46] [1993] ECR I-599 paras 23–25 (EAEC).

[47] See also Case 13/83 *Parliament v Council* [1985] ECR 1513, where proceedings under article 175 were partially successful even though the Council had been called upon to act 13 years after its initial failure. Note, however, that the Court did not expressly consider the effect of this delay.

[48] [1971] ECR 639 (ECSC).

[49] [1995] ECR II-115 paras 44–46. *Cf* Case T-38/96 *Guérin Automobiles v Commission* [1997] ECR II-1223 paras 23–27.

within that period, proceedings under article 175 [new art 232] may be commenced within a further period of two months.

An institution will only be held to have defined its position where it has positively and unequivocally given notice of its intention to act or not to act as required.[50] In considering whether the relevant institution has defined its position, the Court of Justice will look at the nature and substance of any reply. In Case 13/83 *Parliament v Council*[51] the Parliament had included, in its letter to the Council calling upon it to act, a list of actions which, in its opinion, ought to be taken by the Council to remedy its failure to establish a common transport policy. In assessing the Council's reply, the Court of Justice held:[52]

> The Council's reply, on the other hand, was confined to setting out what action it had already taken in relation to transport without commenting 'on the legal aspects' of the correspondence initiated by the Parliament. The reply neither denied nor confirmed the alleged failure to act nor gave any indication of the Council's views as to the measures which, according to the Parliament, remained to be taken. Such a reply cannot be regarded as a definition of position within the meaning of the second paragraph of Article 175.

Failure to respond If the institution fails to give any response, having been called upon to act, it will not have defined its position.

Definition of position after commencement of proceedings Where the relevant institution defines its position after proceedings have been commenced under article 175 [new art 232], but before judgment, the Court of Justice has held that the proceedings become devoid of purpose so that there is no need to give a decision.[53] It has been questioned whether it is correct to say that proceedings under article 175 are truly devoid of purpose once the institution has acted, as the applicant may wish to bring an action for damages against the institution under article 215 [new art 288], based on its failure to act.[54] However,

---

[50] Paragraph 3.2.2.1 of the Opinion of Advocate-General Lenz in Case 13/83 *Parliament v Council* [1985] ECR 1513.

[51] Ibid paras 20–27 of the judgment. See also the Opinion of Advocate-General Gand at 821–822 in Case 6/70 *Borromeo v Commission* [1970] ECR 815, where he rejects the Commission's argument that an 'implied refusal' constituted a definition of position for the purposes of article 175. However, contrast the approach of Advocate-General Capotorti in Case 125/78 *GEMA v Commission* [1979] ECR 3173 at 3198–3199, where he indicated that a letter, which could be considered as 'information pure and simple' and which did not amount to a decision, could be described as a definition of position.

[52] Case 13/83 *Parliament v Council* [1985] ECR 1513 para 25.

[53] Case 103/63 *Rhenania v Commission* [1964] ECR 425; Case 377/87 *Parliament v Council* [1988] ECR 4017 paras 8–10; Case 383/87 *Commission v Council* [1988] ECR 4051 paras 8–10; Case T-28/90 *Asia Motor France v Commission* [1992] ECR II-2285 paras 30 and 34–38; Case C-41/92 *Liberal Democrats v Parliament* [1993] ECR I-3153; Joined Cases C-15/91 and C-108/91 *Buckl & Söhne v Commission* [1992] ECR I-6061 paras 1–18 (contrast para 16 of the Opinion of Advocate-General Gulmann), where an express refusal to act was only adopted after the commencement of proceedings. See also Case T-81/95 *Interhotel v Commission* [1997] ECR II-1265 para 67 where the Court of First Instance rejected an argument that a decision was invalid because it was adopted over two months after the Commission had been called upon to act under article 175 of the EC Treaty.

[54] For example, see Wyatt and Dashwood, *Substantive Law of the EEC*, 3rd edn (Sweet & Maxwell, 1993), pp 140–141.

an applicant is not required to obtain a judgment under article 175 prior to commencing proceedings under article 215. The failure to act may be established in proceedings under article 215.[55]

Different act adopted before judgment Proceedings under article 175 will be declared inadmissible where the institution called upon to act has adopted a measure different from that desired by the applicant, as this does not constitute a failure to act.[56] The act adopted may be open to challenge under article 173 of the EC Treaty [new art 230].

Express refusal: private parties In cases involving private parties, an express refusal to act constitutes a definition of position[57] even if no reasons are given for the refusal.[58] This means that no proceedings can be brought under article 175. However, the refusal itself may be challenged under article 173 if the positive act which the institution refuses to take could itself have been challenged under article 173.[59] In Case 42/71 *Nordgetreide v Commission*[60] the Court declared as inadmissible an action under article 173 seeking review of a refusal by the Commission to amend a regulation by an act which would itself have taken the form of a regulation and which would not have been of direct and individual concern to the applicant (a private party). Equally, where the individual calls upon an institution to adopt a measure which does not produce legal effects, a refusal to act will not be reviewable under article 173 because the measure itself would not have been reviewable under article 173 if it had been adopted.[61]

In Case C-19/93P *Rendo v Commission*[62] Advocate-General Tesauro suggested that, where a Commission decision concerning the competition rules

---

[55] Case 4/69 *Lütticke v Commission* [1971] ECR 325 at 336 (see Ch 16, pp 359–360). Compare the position under article 169 [new art 226] (see Ch 12, pp 253–254) where the Court of Justice has held that the proceedings still have an object even where the breach of Community law is remedied after the time-limit set down in the reasoned opinion. Advocate-General Mischo discusses this difference between articles 169 and 175 at paras 114–135 of his Opinion in Case 377/87 *Parliament v Council* [1988] ECR 4017.

[56] Case 8/71 *Komponistenverband v Commission* [1971] ECR 705 para 2; Joined Cases 166/86 and 220/86 *Irish Cement v Commission* [1988] ECR 6473 para 17; Joined Cases C-15/91 and C-108/91 *Buckl & Söhne v Commission* [1992] ECR I-6061 paras 16–17; Case T-38/96 *Guérin Automobiles v Commission* [1997] ECR II-1223 para 24.

[57] Case 48/65 *Lütticke v Commission* [1966] ECR 19; Case 42/71 *Nordgetreide v Commission* [1972] ECR 105; Case 125/78 *GEMA v Commission* [1979] ECR 3173 paras 14–23; Joined Cases C-15/91 and C-108/91 *Buckl & Söhne v Commission* [1992] ECR I-6061 paras 1–18; Case C-250/90 *Control Union v Commission* [1991] ECR I-3585.

[58] Opinion of Advocate-General Dutheillet de Lamothe in Case 15/70 *Chevalley v Commission* [1970] ECR 975 at 983.

[59] Case 48/65 *Lütticke v Commission* [1966] ECR 19, and the Opinion of Advocate-General Gand at 31; Opinion of Advocate-General Darmon in Case 302/87 *Parliament v Council* [1988] ECR 5615 at 5630; paras 37–41 of the Opinion of Advocate-General Darmon in Joined Cases 166/86 and 220/86 *Irish Cement v Commission* [1988] ECR 6473; Case C-87/89 *SONITO v Commission* [1990] ECR I-1981 paras 5–9; Joined Cases C-15/91 and C-108/91 *Buckl & Söhne v Commission* [1992] ECR I-6061 paras 21–22.

[60] [1972] ECR 105.

[61] For example, see Case 48/65 *Lütticke v Commission* [1966] ECR 19.

[62] [1995] ECR I-3319, at paras 25–27 of the Opinion.

fails to deal with certain aspects of a complaint, the complainant's remedy is to seek annulment of the decision under article 173 on the basis that there has been a partial or implied rejection of its complaint rather than to bring an action for failure to act under article 175.

Definition of position need not be reviewable under article 173 An act which is not open to an action for annulment under article 173 of the EC Treaty may, nevertheless, constitute a 'definition of position' within the meaning of article 175. In Case T-186/94 *Guérin Automobiles v Commission*[63] Guérin submitted a complaint to the Commission under article 85 of the EC Treaty [new art 81]. Having first called upon the Commission to act in respect of its complaint, Guérin then commenced proceedings under article 175. The Commission subsequently sent to Guérin a letter under article 6 of Regulation No 99/63[64] indicating that the Commission intended to reject the complaint on the information then available to it, and inviting Guérin to submit further comments. The Court of First Instance held that this letter constituted a definition of position for the purposes of article 175 even though it was not open to challenge under article 173. This judgment was upheld by the Court of Justice on appeal.[65]

Express refusal: privileged applicants It appears that in relation to privileged applicants an express refusal to act may not always constitute a definition of position. This contrasts with the case-law relating to non-privileged applicants.[66] In Case 302/87 *Parliament v Council*[67] the Court of Justice held that:

> A refusal to act, however explicit it may be, can be brought before the Court under Article 175 since it does not put an end to failure to act.

The Court based its observations on Case 377/87 *Parliament v Council*,[68] which concerned the Council's failure to adopt a draft budget, despite its legal obligation to do so. The Court of Justice recognised that if the Council's refusal to act in that case was considered to be a definition of position, that would have rendered article 175 proceedings inadmissible. Furthermore, the refusal to act would not have been reviewable under article 173 because the draft budget, being a preparatory measure, would not, in itself, have been open to review under article 173 if it had been adopted. This would have created a gap in the system of judicial review established by the EEC Treaty, as the Council's failure to fulfil its Community obligations would not have been open to challenge by any applicant, under article 173 or 175.[69] The Court of Justice

---

[63] [1995] ECR II-1753 paras 22–35.

[64] Commission Regulation No 99/63/EEC on the hearings provided for in article 19(1) and (2) of Council Regulation No 17 (OJ 1963 127 p 2268) (OJ, Special Edition 1963–64 p 47).

[65] Case C-282/95P *Guérin Automobiles v Commission* [1997] ECR I-1503 paras 33–40. See also Case T-38/96 *Guérin Automobiles v Commission* [1997] ECR II-1223 paras 25–34.

[66] See above at pp 346–347.

[67] [1988] ECR 5615 paras 14–17.

[68] [1988] ECR 4017.

[69] See paras 9 and 14–15 of the Opinion of Advocate-General Gulmann in Joined Cases C-15/91

ensured that the Council's failure to act was subject to judicial review by holding that a refusal to act does not constitute a definition of position in relation to privileged applicants and, therefore, can be challenged under article 175.

In Case T-226/95 *Kuchlenz-Winter v Commission*[70] the Court of First Instance suggested that the judgment in Case 302/87 *Parliament v Council* could be justified on the basis that the Parliament would have been deprived of all judicial protection if the Court of Justice had found that the Council's refusal to act constituted a definition of position under article 175. Alternatively, it is possible that the distinction created by the case-law between privileged and non-privileged applicants arises due to the special role played by privileged applicants in ensuring that the Community institutions fulfil their general Community law obligations.

Pleadings Where an applicant is uncertain whether or not the institution's response constitutes a definition of its position, it may be appropriate to bring proceedings under both articles 175 and 173 in the alternative.[71] An applicant will not be permitted to convert an action originally brought under article 175 to an action under article 173 during the course of proceedings.[72]

Limitation period for Court proceedings Pursuant to the second limb of article 175, an application to the EC courts for failure to act must be made within four months of the date on which the formal letter calling upon the institution to act was sent. Failure to comply with this requirement will cause the application to be dismissed as inadmissible.[73]

4. POSSIBLE DEFENCES

Objective difficulties The existence of objective difficulties for the institution required to act does not provide a defence. Under article 175 of the EC Treaty [new art 232] the Court of Justice must hold that there has been an infringement of the Treaty if it finds that the Council or Commission has failed to act when under an obligation to do so. Article 175 takes no account of how difficult it may be for the institution to comply with the obligation.[74]

---

and C-108/91 *Buckl & Söhne v Commission* [1992] ECR I-6061.
[70] [1996] ECR II-1619 para 32.
[71] For examples of this approach, see Case 48/65 *Lütticke v Commission* [1966] ECR 19; Case 15/70 *Chevalley v Commission* [1970] ECR 975. See also Joined Cases C-15/91 and C-108/91 *Buckl & Söhne v Commission* [1992] ECR I-6061 paras 32–34, which discusses the cost implications of such an approach.
[72] Case 125/78 *GEMA v Commission* [1979] ECR 3173 paras 24–26; Case T-28/90 *Asia Motor France v Commission* [1992] ECR II-2283 paras 43–44.
[73] Case T-195/95 *Guérin Automobiles v Commission* [1996] ECR II-171 paras 18–23.
[74] Case 13/83 *Parliament v Council* [1985] ECR 1513 para 48; see also the detailed discussion of this issue by Advocate-General Lenz in this case at 1546–1549.

Absolute impossibility In Case 377/87 *Parliament v Council*[75] Advocate-General Mischo considered that, where it was absolutely impossible for an institution to comply with its obligation to act, its failure to do so should not be regarded as an infringement of article 175.

Direct applicability Where an institution is under an obligation to adopt detailed implementing rules, the fact that the measure which imposes that obligation is itself directly applicable does not excuse the institution's failure to act.[76]

5. EFFECT OF JUDGMENT

Obligation to comply The EC courts do not have jurisdiction to order the Community institutions to adopt specific measures.[77] However, although the order pronounced by the EC courts under article 175 [new art 232] is in the form of a declaration, article 176 of the EC Treaty [new art 233] imposes an obligation on the part of the institution concerned to take the necessary measures to comply with the judgment of the Court.[78] Article 176 of the EC Treaty provides:

> The institution or institutions whose act has been declared void or whose failure to act has been declared contrary to this Treaty shall be required to take the necessary measures to comply with the judgment of the Court of Justice.
>
> This obligation shall not affect any obligation which may result from the application of the second paragraph of Article 215.
>
> This article shall also apply to the ECB.

Time-limit for compliance In Case 13/83 *Parliament v Council*[79] the Court of Justice held that since article 176 does not prescribe a time-limit for compliance, it must be inferred that the institution has a 'reasonable period' for that purpose. In addition, a judgment under article 176 can provide the basis for an action for damages against the relevant institution under article 215 [new art 288].[80] If the relevant institution fails to fulfil its obligations under article 176, a further application may be made under article 175.[81]

---

[75] [1988] ECR 4017, paras 100–111 of the Opinion.

[76] Case 13/83 *Parliament v Council* [1985] ECR 1513 paras 59–63. Articles 59 and 60 of the EC Treaty [new arts 49 and 50] (which are themselves directly applicable) required the Council to adopt detailed rules ensuring freedom to provide services in the transport sector.

[77] Case T-74/92 *Ladbroke v Commission* [1995] ECR II-115 paras 74–76.

[78] Case 377/87 *Parliament v Council* [1988] ECR 4017 para 9; Case 383/87 *Commission v Council* [1988] ECR 4051 para 9. In Case 8/71 *Komponistenverband v Commission* [1971] ECR 705 at 715, Advocate-General Roemer stated that, in practice, the result attained under article 176 could be equivalent to 'a direct order to the Commission to perform a specific action'.

[79] [1985] ECR 1513 para 69.

[80] Case 377/87 *Parliament v Council* [1988] ECR 4017 para 9; Case 383/87 *Commission v Council* [1988] ECR 4051 para 9. See Ch 16.

[81] Joined Cases 97/86, 193/86, 99/86 and 215/86 *Asteris and Greece v Commission* [1988] ECR 2181 para 32.

Chapter 16

Suing the Community in Damages

1. INTRODUCTION

(a) Contractual liability

Basis of liability Articles 181 [new art 238], 183 [new art 240] and 215, para 1 [new art 288] of the EC Treaty provide the basis of the contractual liability of the Community.

Article 181 provides:

> The Court of Justice shall have jurisdiction to give judgment pursuant to any arbitration clause contained in a contract concluded by or on behalf of the Community, whether that contract be governed by public or private law.

Article 183 provides:

> Save where jurisdiction is conferred on the Court of Justice by this Treaty, disputes to which the Community is a party shall not on that ground be excluded from the jurisdiction of the courts or tribunals of the Member States.

The first paragraph of article 215 provides:

> The contractual liability of the Community shall be governed by the law applicable to the contract in question.

Relevant court The Community may be sued for breach of contract (eg failing to pay a contractor for repairs done to a building occupied by the Commission) or sue for breach of contract (eg defective repairs on the part of the contractor) in the same way as any party to a contract. Article 183 provides that any action for breach of contract to which the Community is a party may be brought in the national courts of the Member States. Alternatively, article 181 allows the EC courts to hear any contractual dispute provided the contract gives the court jurisdiction. The reference to 'arbitration clause' in article 181 should be understood as a reference to 'jurisdiction clause'. For example, in Case 23/76 *Pellegrini v Commission*[1] a construction contract provided that 'the Court of

---

[1] [1976] ECR 1807. See also Case 109/81 *Pace v Commission* [1982] ECR 2469; Case 23/81 *Commission v Royale Belge* [1983] ECR 2685; Case C-142/91 *Cebag v Commission* [1993] ECR I-553 (arbitration clause provided for in EC regulation).

Justice of the European Communities shall have jurisdiction in any dispute between the Commission and the contractor relating to this agreement'. Under article 181 the EC courts may also hear and determine any counterclaim directly connected with the obligations arising from the contract with the Community.[2]

Acting pursuant to article 168a of the EC Treaty [new art 225], the Council has transferred to the Court of First Instance the jurisdiction of the Court of Justice in contractual disputes (subject to a right of appeal on points of law to the Court of Justice) where the action is brought by a natural or legal person. Where the action is brought by the Community, the Court of Justice alone has jurisdiction under article 181.[3]

Applicable law Where the EC courts are called on to determine a contractual dispute, they apply the national law applicable to the contract,[4] there being no Community law of contract. The applicable law is often determined in a choice of law clause in the contract.[5] Although the EC courts may apply national law, their jurisdiction to hear the dispute cannot be ousted by national procedural law.[6] However, a national rule which requires an application for conciliation to be submitted before any legal action is taken will be applied by the EC courts. Thus, any action brought before the Court of First Instance in disregard of this preliminary requirement is inadmissible.[7]

(b) Staff cases

Basis for liability Articles 179 [new art 236] and 215, para 4 [new art 288] of the EC Treaty provide the basis of the Community's liability in staff disputes.

Article 179 provides:

> The Court of Justice shall have jurisdiction in any dispute between the Community and its servants within the limits and under the conditions laid down in the Staff Regulations or the Conditions of Employment.

Article 215, para 4 provides:

> The personal liability of its servants towards the Community shall be governed by the provisions laid down in their Staff Regulations or in the Conditions of Employment applicable to them.

---

[2] Case C-114/94 *IDE v Commission* [1997] ECR I-803 para 82.

[3] Council Decision 88/591 (OJ 1988 L319 p 1) (corrected text at OJ 1989 C215 p 1), as amended by Council Decision 93/350 (OJ 1993 L144 p 21). The Court of First Instance has jurisdiction only in relation to actions brought under article 181 where the contract was concluded after 1 August 1993 (article 3 of Council Decision 93/350).

[4] Article 215, para 1 of the EC Treaty.

[5] For example, Case 318/81 *Commission v CODEMI* [1985] ECR 3693 (Belgian law applicable in a construction contract); Case 23/76 *Pellegrini v Commission* [1976] ECR 1807 (Italian law in a cleaning contract).

[6] Case C-209/90 *Commission v Feilhauser* [1992] ECR I-2613.

[7] Case C-299/93 *Bauer v Commission* [1995] ECR I-839.

Staff Regulations Disputes between the Community and its servants are governed by Regulation 31/61,[8] which contains the Staff Regulations of Community officials and the conditions of employment of other servants. Under article 91 of the Staff Regulations the Court of Justice has jurisdiction to award damages in disputes of a financial nature. In general, a Community employee should make a complaint to the Community institution and bring a claim for compensation within three months following rejection of the complaint. Disputes which originate in the relationship of employment between a Community institution and an employee should be brought under the Staff Regulations and not under article 215, para 1 or 2 of the EC Treaty.[9]

Relevant court Acting pursuant to article 168a of the EC Treaty [new art 225], the Council has transferred to the Court of First Instance the jurisdiction of the Court of Justice in staff cases (subject to a right of appeal on points of law to the Court of Justice).[10]

(c) Non-contractual liability

Basis for liability Articles 178 [new arts 235 and 288] and 215, para 2 of the EC Treaty provide the basis of the Community's non-contractual liability, which may loosely be described as tortious liability.

Article 178 provides:

> The Court of Justice shall have jurisdiction in disputes relating to compensation for damage provided for in the second paragraph of Article 215.

Article 215, para 2 provides:

> In the case of non-contractual liability, the Community shall, in accordance with the general principles common to the laws of the Member States, make good any damage caused by its institutions or by its servants in the performance of their duties.

Relevant court Acting pursuant to article 168a of the EC Treaty [new art 225], the Council has transferred to the Court of First Instance the jurisdiction of the Court of Justice in non-contractual disputes (subject to a right of appeal on points of law to the Court of Justice) where the action is brought by a natural or legal person.[11] Non-contractual liability of the Community is determined exclusively by the EC courts. Therefore, any action which is not of a contractual

---

[8] Regulation 259/68 (OJ 1968 L56 p 1) (Special Edition 1968 p 30) (as amended). For the conditions of employment of Community officials and other servants, see *Halsbury's Laws*, 4th edn (Butterworths), Vol 52, paras 1.105–1.117; for a commentary on staff disputes, see ibid paras 2.101–2.115.

[9] Case 9/75 *Meyer-Burckhardt v Commission* [1975] ECR 1171; Case 48/76 *Reinarz v Commission* [1977] ECR 291. Compare Case C-299/93 *Bauer v Commission* [1995] ECR I-839.

[10] Decision 88/591 (OJ 1988 L319 p 1) (corrected text at OJ 1989 C215 p 1), as amended by Council Decision 93/350 (OJ 1993 L144 p 21).

[11] Decision 88/591 (OJ 1988 L319 p 1) (corrected text at OJ 1989 C215 p 1), as amended by Council Decision 93/350 (OJ 1993 L144 p 21), as amended by Council Decision 94/149 of 7 March 1994 (OJ 1994 L66 p 29).

nature and which seeks to establish the liability of the Community in damages should not be brought in the national courts.[12]

Applicable law The applicable law is Community law, but, in applying Community law, the EC courts have regard to the general principles common to the laws of the Member States. For example, the courts have drawn on principles common to Member States when reaching conclusions on interest,[13] mitigation,[14] liability for legislative acts,[15] remoteness,[16] assessment of damage,[17] assignment of the cause of action[18] and time bars.[19]

2. ADMISSIBILITY OF ACTIONS IN NON-CONTRACTUAL MATTERS

(a) Parties

Applicant Any natural or legal person, including a Member State, who has suffered damage may bring an action under articles 178 and 215, para 2 [new arts 235 and 288]. The damage suffered must be personal to the applicant.[20] Where damage has been suffered by members of a trade union or trade association, only the members (and not the trade union or association) may bring the action for damages before the Court of Justice. Consequently, a co-operative cannot seek to enforce a collective right to compensation for damage to the financial interests of its members.[21] If a trade association wishes to acquire an interest so as to bring proceedings on behalf of its members, the members must first assign their cause of action to the association.[22]

Assignee A claim for damages may be assigned and then enforced by the assignee against the Community.[23] However, the assignment must be made in good faith. In Case 250/78 *DEKA v EEC*[24] the Court of Justice held that an assignment of a claim for damages by an insolvent assignor was abusive and invalid on the basis that it was intended to prevent the Community from setting

---

12 Case 101/78 *Granaria v Hoofdproduktschap voor Akkerbouwprodukten* [1979] ECR 623.
13 Case 152/88 *Sofrimport v Commission* [1990] ECR I-2477; Joined Cases 256/80 and 5/81 *Birra Wührer v Council and Commission* [1984] ECR 3693.
14 Joined Cases C-104/89 and C-37/90 *Mulder v Council* [1992] ECR I-3061.
15 Joined Cases 83/76, 94/76 and others *HNL v Council and Commission* [1978] ECR 1209.
16 Joined Cases 64/76, 113/76 and others *Dumortier Frères v Council* [1979] ECR 3091 para 21.
17 Case 261/78 *Interquell Stärke-Chemie v EEC* [1982] ECR 3271.
18 Case 250/78 *DEKA v EEC* [1983] ECR 421; Joined Cases 256/80 and 5/81 *Birra Wührer v Council and Commission* [1984] ECR 3693.
19 Case 20/88 *Roquette Frères v Commission* [1989] ECR 1553.
20 Case 353/88 *Briantex v Commission* [1989] ECR 3623 para 6.
21 Case 72/74 *Union syndicale v Council* [1975] ECR 401 at 411; Case 114/83 *Société d'Initiatives et de Coopération Agricoles v Commission* [1984] ECR 2589.
22 Case T-53/96 *Syndicat des Producteurs de Viande Bovine v Commission* [1996] ECR II-1579 para 28.
23 Case 238/78 *Ireks Arkady v Council* [1979] ECR 2955 para 5; Case 133/79 *Sucrimex v Commission* [1980] ECR 1299.
24 [1983] ECR 421.

off, against the damages claim, a claim for a refund of sums wrongly paid to the assignor. When an applicant assigns his rights, he ceases to be entitled to compensation and any claim for damages subsequently brought by him will be dismissed.[25]

Intervener Article 37, para 2 of the Statute of the Court of Justice provides that the right to intervene is open to any person 'establishing an interest in the result of any case submitted to the Court'.[26] The existence of such an interest must be assessed in the light of the purpose of the action which, in non-contractual disputes, is the payment of compensation. In Joined Cases 197/80 and others *Ludwigshafener Walzmühle v Council and Commission*[27] the Court rejected an application by a German trade union to intervene in an action for damages, since the purpose of the intervention was to ensure the economic well-being of the applicants and the continued employment of the employees. This did not constitute a specific interest in any payment of compensation.

Defendant Although the liability is that of the Community, the proper defendant is the Community institution which is alleged to have caused the damage.[28] If an action arises from a regulation adopted by the Council of Ministers on a proposal from the Commission, an action may be brought against both institutions.[29] The term 'institutions' employed in the second paragraph of article 215 has been held to apply not just to the Community institutions listed in article 4(1) of the EC Treaty [new art 7],[30] but also Community bodies such as the European Investment Bank.[31] Following the ratification of the Treaty of European Union ('Maastricht Treaty'), the European Central Bank has been expressly identified as a potential defendant in the third paragraph of article 215.

(b) Time-limit for bringing an action

Five-year limitation period Article 43 of the Statute of the Court of Justice (EC) provides for a limitation period of five years. This limitation period must be pleaded by the defendant before the Court will consider the issue.[32] Article 43 provides:

> Proceedings against the Community in matters arising from non-contractual liability shall be barred after a period of five years from the occurrence of the event giving rise thereto. The period of limitation shall be interrupted if proceedings are instituted

---

[25] Joined Cases 256/80 and 5/81 *Birra Wührer v Council and Commission* [1984] ECR 3693.

[26] Intervention is dealt with at Ch 18, pp 403–406.

[27] [1981] ECR 1041.

[28] Case 353/88 *Briantex v Commission* [1989] ECR 3623.

[29] Joined Cases 63/72 and 69/72 *Werhahn v Council* [1973] ECR 1229 at 1247.

[30] Ie the European Parliament, Council, Commission, Court of Justice and Court of Auditors.

[31] Case C-370/91 *SGEEM and Etroy v EIB* [1992] ECR I-6211.

[32] Case 20/88 *Roquette Frères v Commission* [1989] ECR 1553 para 13. Compare the position in relation to actions for annulment under article 173 of the EC Treaty [new art 230], discussed at para 38 of the Opinion of Advocate-General Jacobs in Case C-312/93 *Peterbroeck v Belgium* [1995] ECR I-4599. See further Ch 13 at pp 324–325.

before the Court or if prior to such proceedings an application is made by the aggrieved party to the relevant institution of the Community. In the latter event the proceedings must be instituted within the period of two months provided for in Article 173; the provisions of the second paragraph of Article 175 shall apply where appropriate.

Commencement of the limitation period The limitation period does not begin to run until all three conditions for liability are satisfied (ie unlawfulness, damage and causation).[33] Consequently, where the liability of the Community arises from a legislative measure, the limitation period begins only when the harmful effects are produced, not when the regulation is published.[34] Time does not start to run where the applicant is unaware of the unlawful event and therefore does not have a reasonable time to submit an application to the Court or to the relevant institution before the expiry of the limitation period.[35] It is important to note that it is knowledge of the event and not of its unlawfulness which is the critical factor.[36] The five-year period starts at the end of the day on which the conditions for liability are satisfied. Where an unlawful regulation is adopted and causes damage on a continuing basis, the limitation period does not merely run from the date of the adoption of the regulation, but runs afresh from each successive day on which the conditions for liability are satisfied.[37]

Expiry of the limitation period The limitation period expires at the end of the day which, in the month of the fifth year, bears the same number as the day on which time was set running. If the end of the period falls on a Saturday, Sunday or on an official holiday, the time is extended until the end of the first following working day.[38] The time-limit is extended by ten days in the case of the United Kingdom on account of distance.[39] The defendant institutions may themselves agree with the applicant to extend the limitation period and therefore waive the right to plead the time bar in respect of the extended period.[40]

Suspension of the limitation period The limitation period is suspended if the aggrieved party first submits a claim to the defendant institution; in other words, time does not run while the Community decides whether or not to compensate the applicant. For example, if an applicant submits a claim for compensation to the Commission on 23 June 1982, the applicant can claim compensation for

---

[33] See below at pp 360–372.

[34] Case 256/80 and 5/81 *Birra Wührer v Council and Commission* [1982] ECR 85; Case 51/81 *De Franceschi v Council and Commission* [1982] ECR 117.

[35] Case 145/83 *Adams v Commission* [1985] ECR 3539 para 50.

[36] Case T-554/93 *Saint and Murray v Council* [1997] ECR II-563 para 84; Case T-20/94 *Hartmann v Council* [1997] ECR II-595 para 111.

[37] Case T-554/93 *Saint and Murray v Council* [1997] ECR II-563 para 88.

[38] ECJ Rules of Procedure, article 80 (2) CFI Rules of Procedure, article 101(2); as interpreted in Case 152/85 *Misset v Council* [1987] ECR 223 and Case T-125/89 *Filtrona v Commission* [1990] ECR II-393.

[39] ECJ Rules of Procedure, article 81(2) and Annex II, article 1; CFI Rules of Procedure, article 102(2); Case T-571/93 *Lefebvre v Commission* [1995] ECR II-2379 para 26.

[40] Case T-554/93 *Saint and Murray v Council* [1997] ECR II-563 para 91; Case T-20/94 *Hartmann v Council* [1997] ECR II-595 para 135.

damage suffered as from 23 June 1977, even though court proceedings are subsequently commenced after 23 June 1982.[41]

Where an applicant does not commence court proceedings within two months after the rejection by the Community institution of its claim, the third sentence of article 43 of the Statute does not mean that he is then time-barred from bringing his claim. The consequence of not bringing proceedings within the two-month time-limit is that the limitation period is considered to have continued to run (without suspension) throughout the settlement process with the Community institution.[42]

(c) Lack of jurisdiction

Declining jurisdiction The EC courts may decline jurisdiction in three situations:

(1) where the true author of the decision alleged to have caused the damage is a Member State or a national authority;

(2) where the applicant has not exhausted the national remedies to obtain compensation;

(3) where the applicant is claiming the repayment of sums paid to a national authority.

Community not the author of the decision The EC courts have jurisdiction only to award compensation for damage caused by the Community institutions or by their servants in the performance of their duties. Damage caused by Member States or by national authorities cannot give rise to liability on the part of the Community, and national courts retain sole jurisdiction to order compensation for such damage. For example, in Case C-72/90 *Asia Motor France v Commission*[43] the Court of Justice held that it had no jurisdiction to hear a claim brought under articles 178 and 215 [new arts 235 and 288] in respect of attempts by France to prevent the importation into France of Japanese motor cars.

Where the decision adversely affecting the applicant was adopted by a national body acting so as to implement Community rules, the EC courts have jurisdiction under article 215 if the unlawful conduct can be attributed to a Community institution. This is so where the Commission dictates what action the national authority should take, so that the Commission is the true author of the national act. In contrast, where the national authority has a discretion to take action, the Community will not incur liability for the unlawfulness of the

---

[41] Joined Cases 256/80 and 5/81 *Birra Würher v Council and Commission* [1984] ECR 3693 paras 20–23.

[42] Joined Cases 5/66, 7/66 and others *Kampffmeyer v Commission* [1967] ECR 245; Case 11/72 *Giordano v Commission* [1973] ECR 417 paras 5–7; Case T-167/94 *Nölle v Council* [1995] ECR II-2589 para 30.

[43] [1990] ECR I-2181. See also Joined Cases 31/86 and 35/86 *LAISA v Council* [1988] ECR 2285; Case 169/73 *Compagnie Continentale v Council* [1975] ECR 117 (effects of the Act of

national act. Two judgments of the Court of Justice illustrate this distinction: Case 133/79 *Sucrimex v Commission*[44] and Case 175/84 *Krohn v Commission*.[45]

In the first case, Sucrimex sold a quantity of sugar pursuant to export licences which fixed the rate of export refund. The licences were lost. The relevant authorities issued replacement licences and the sugar was exported under those licences. Sucrimex sought export refunds at the rate fixed in the original licences. However, the French authorities paid only the refund applicable on the day when the customs formalities were completed, which was lower than the refund which would have been payable at the fixed rate. The French authorities relied on an opinion given in a telex by the Commission that replacement licences could not be used to obtain refunds at a rate fixed in advance. Sucrimex's claim for compensation against the Commission was dismissed by the Court of Justice as inadmissible, on the basis that Sucrimex should have proceeded against the French authorities for their refusal to grant the disputed refunds. The Commission's opinion was not binding on the French authorities; therefore, it was not the Commission but the national authorities who were the authors of the decision to refuse the refunds.

In the second case, Krohn requested import licences from the German authorities to import a quantity of manioc from Thailand. Under the provisions of Regulation 2029/82 it was the task of the national authorities to issue the licences, except where they were informed by the Commission that the conditions for importation were not fulfilled. The Commission informed the German authorities by telex that the conditions were not fulfilled and the German authorities duly refused the import licences. The Court of Justice held that the application for compensation under article 215 was admissible on the basis that the Regulation did not:

> merely confer upon the Commission the right to give an opinion on the decision to be adopted in the context of the cooperation between itself and the national bodies responsible for applying the Community rules, but actually empower it to insist that such national bodies refuse requests for import licences ...

It followed, therefore, that the unlawful conduct alleged by the applicant in order to establish its claim for compensation was to be attributed not to the German authorities, who were bound to comply with the Commission's instructions, but to the Commission itself.

Exhaustion of national remedies The action for damages under article 215 must be examined in the light of the whole system of legal protection for the individual, and the admissibility of such an action is dependent on the exhaustion of national remedies. This principle is particularly important within the framework of the Common Agricultural Policy, where national intervention

---

Accession not an act of the Council).

[44] [1980] ECR 1299. See also Case 217/81 *Interagra v Commission* [1982] ECR 2233; Joined Cases 89/86 and 91/86 *Étoile commerciale and CNTA v Commission* [1987] ECR 3005 (national body ordering the applicant to repay subsidies as a result of the Commission refusing to recognise the subsidies as chargeable to the EAGGF).

[45] [1986] ECR 753 paras 21, 23. See also Case 59/83 *Biovilac v EEC* [1984] ECR 4057.

agencies have an important role to play. In Case 12/79 *Wagner v Commission*,[46] where a national authority had refused a request for the cancellation of an export licence pursuant to a Commission regulation, an action for damages against the Commission was held to be inadmissible on the basis that the applicant should first have challenged the national authority's refusal in the domestic courts.

The national proceedings available must, however, provide an effective means of protection for the individual concerned so that, where the national action does not afford the possibility of obtaining compensation for the loss suffered, an action against the Community will be admissible.[47] In Case 281/82 *Unifrex v Commission*[48] Unifrex, an exporter of cereals to Italy, claimed compensation from the Community on the basis that the French authorities had not paid to it the correct level of monetary compensatory amounts (MCAs) due under the applicable Community regulations. The Commission argued that the claim was inadmissible because the applicant had not challenged the amount of the MCAs in the national courts. The Court of Justice rejected this argument on the ground that such a challenge would not have effectively protected the applicant. It stated that:

> Even if the disputed Community rules were declared invalid by a preliminary ruling of the Court given in the context of such proceedings and the national decision were annulled, that annulment could not have required the national authorities to pay higher monetary compensatory amounts to the applicant, without the prior intervention of the Community legislature.

Consequently, an applicant need not incur expense in bringing fruitless proceedings in the national courts to prove that there is no effective remedy. Instead, the applicant may explain the national legal position in its application under article 215.

Where a national authority merely implements a Community measure, it is not responsible for its unlawfulness.[49] If, in such a case, national law does not provide for compensation, prior exhaustion of domestic remedies will not ensure effective protection. Thus, in Case T-167/94 *Nölle v Council*[50] a Community regulation which imposed anti-dumping duties on paint originating from China was declared unlawful. The applicant importer claimed compensation from the Council in respect of bank interest incurred on sums which it had

---

[46] [1979] ECR 3657.

[47] Case 175/84 *Krohn v Commission* [1986] ECR 753 paras 27–28; Case 20/88 *Roquette Frères v Commission* [1989] ECR 1553 para 15.

[48] [1984] ECR 1969 para 12. Similarly, Case 126/76 *Dietz v Commission* [1977] ECR 2431. See also Case 81/86 *De Boer Buizen v Council and Commission* [1987] ECR 3677 para 10 (where the annulment, by a national court, of a refusal to grant a licence would not have had the effect of either giving the applicant the right to a licence or to compensation); Joined Cases 197 and 200/80 and others *Ludwigshafener Walzmühle v Council and Commission* [1981] ECR 3211 para 8 (recourse to the national courts was not open to the applicants, who were manufacturers, only to importers who had paid the levy which was alleged to be unlawful).

[49] Joined Cases 106 and 120/87 *Asteris v Greece* [1988] ECR 5515 para 18.

[50] [1995] ECR II-2589. See also Joined Cases T-481/93 and T-483/93 *Exporteurs in Levende Varkens v Commission* [1995] ECR II-2941 paras 69–72 (which seems to suggest that the possibility of domestic redress is irrelevant in this situation).

had to borrow in order to pay anti-dumping duties. The action was held to be admissible because the German customs authorities were bound to collect the duties and under German law the authority could incur liability to pay damage only if fault could be established.

The Community will not be liable under article 215 to pay damage for loss incurred by the applicant in commencing domestic litigation. In Case T-167/94 *Nölle v Council*, the importer, having successfully challenged the legality of the anti-dumping duties in the German courts (*via* a preliminary ruling), was unable to recover all of its legal costs under German law. The Court of First Instance ruled that the Community could not be liable to pay the balance as damages since the question of costs was a matter solely for domestic law.

Repayment of sums paid to a national authority A claim for the reimbursement of sums collected by national authorities on behalf of the Community must be brought in the national courts, even though the amount paid was fixed by the Community. As the Court stated in Case 99/74 *Grand Moulins v Commission*:[51]

> The refusal by a Community institution to pay a debt which may be owed by a Member State under Community law is not a matter involving the non-contractual liability of the Community.

The extent of reimbursement is, therefore, a matter for national law, provided that no provisions of Community law are relevant.[52] By contrast, a claim for compensation for the abolition, by the Community, of production refunds which should have been paid by national authorities should be brought under article 215, since this is not a claim for repayment but for payment (ie compensation).[53]

(d) Independent cause of action

Independent cause of action Claims for damages often arise after the Court of Justice has annulled a Community provision under article 173 of the EC Treaty [new art 230], or has ruled that the provision is invalid under article 177 [new art 234]. It is important to note, however, that the action for damages under article 215 [new art 288] is an independent remedy, ie it is not necessary first to bring an action under article 173 to determine the unlawfulness of the Community act[54] or an action under article 175 [new art 232] to determine the unlawfulness

---

[51] [1975] ECR 1531 para 16. See also Case 30/66 *Becher v Commission* [1967] ECR 285 at 298; Case 46/75 *IBC v Commission* [1976] ECR 65; Case 26/74 *Roquette Frères v Commission* [1976] ECR 677 para 11; Case 175/84 *Krohn v Commission* [1986] ECR 753 para 33.

[52] Limited rules have been laid down by the Community relating to the repayment of import and export duties. See Ch 9, pp 171–172.

[53] Joined Cases 64/76, 113/76 and others *Dumortier Frères v Council* [1979] ECR 3091 para 6; Joined Cases 261/78 and 262/78 *Interquell Stärke-Chemie v EEC* [1979] ECR 3045 para 6. See also Case 281/84 *Zuckerfabrik v Council and Commission* [1987] ECR 49 para 12; Case 281/82 *Unifrex v Commission* [1984] ECR 1969; Case C-282/90 *Vreugdenhil v Commission* [1992] ECR I-1937 paras 11–15.

[54] Case 5/71 *Schöppenstedt v Council* [1971] ECR 975, overruling Case 25/62 *Plaumann v Commission* [1963] ECR 95, in so far as the Court there stated that it could not 'by way of an action for compensation take steps which would nullify the legal effects of a decision which ...

of the Community's failure to act.[55] The action for damages differs, in particular, from an action for annulment, in that its purpose is not to set aside a specific measure but to repair the damage caused by an institution. The autonomous nature of an article 215 action enables a plaintiff to challenge the lawfulness of a Community directive or regulation, even though the directive or the regulation would not be of direct and individual concern to the plaintiff and could not, therefore, be challenged under article 173.[56]

Abuse of process Where the damages claim is aimed at securing the withdrawal of an individual decision, the claim will be declared inadmissible as an abuse of process. Thus, in Joined Cases C-199/94P and C-200/94P *Pevasa and Inspeca v Commission*[57] the Commission refused to grant the applicants financial aid to construct a fishing vessel. Although an action under article 173 to annul the refusal was time-barred, the applicant sought, in the alternative, damages for the same amount which had been claimed as aid. The damages claim was held to be inadmissible on the basis that it was indirectly seeking the annulment of the contested decision rejecting the applicant's request for financial aid.

3. SUBSTANTIVE CONDITIONS OF NON-CONTRACTUAL LIABILITY

(a) Distinction between administrative and legislative acts

Conditions of liability Different conditions of liability apply depending on whether the loss has been caused by an administrative act or a legislative act. In order to succeed in a claim for damages, the applicant must prove[58]: (a) that there has been unlawful conduct on the part of the Community, (b) which has caused damage, and (c) that there is a causal link between the unlawful conduct and the damage claimed.[59] In relation to administrative acts, the requirement of unlawful conduct will be satisfied by any infringement of law. In contrast, in

---

has not been annulled'; Case C-87/89 *SONITO v Commission* [1990] ECR I-1981; Case 175/84 *Krohn v Commission* [1986] ECR 753.

[55] Case 4/69 *Lütticke v Commission* [1971] ECR 325 para 6.

[56] Case T-489/93 *Unifruit Hellas v Commission* [1994] ECR II-1201 para 31; Case T-485/93 *Dreyfus v Commission* [1996] ECR II-1101 paras 65–70.

[57] [1995] ECR I-3709. See also Case T-514/93 *Cobrecaf v Commission* [1995] ECR II-621; Case T-485/93 *Dreyfus v Commission* [1996] ECR II-1101 paras 65–70. As to staff cases, see Case 106/80 *Fournier v Commission* [1981] ECR 2759 para 17 and, in particular, the Opinion of Advocate-General Sir Gordon Slynn at 2777–2780; Case T-27/92 *Camera-Lampitelli v Commission* [1993] ECR II-873 para 27.

[58] The burden of proof is on the applicant: Case T-451/93 *San Marco v Commission* [1994] ECR II-1061 para 77.

[59] Case 4/69 *Lütticke v Commission* [1971] ECR 325 para 10; Case 59/84 *Tezi v Commission* [1986] ECR 887 para 70; Joined Cases 326/86 and 66/88 *Francesconi v Commission* [1989] ECR 2087 para 8; Case C-55/90 *Cato v Commission* [1992] ECR I-2533; Case T-185/94 *Geotronics v Commission* [1995] ECR II-2795 para 39; Case T-485/93 *Dreyfus v Commission* [1996] ECR II-1101 para 69.

relation to legislative measures the unlawful conduct of the Community must amount to a breach of a superior rule of law for the protection of individuals. Furthermore, if the institution has adopted the legislative measure in the exercise of a wide discretion, particularly involving choices of economic policy, a sufficiently serious breach of Community law must be proved.[60]

Distinction between administrative and legislative acts The nature of a measure is not determined by its title or form, but rather whether or not it produces effects which are of general application.[61] In Joined Cases T-481/93 and T-484/93 *Exporteurs in Levende Varkens v Commission*[62], the Council had adopted Directive 90/425[63] on veterinary checks concerning intra-Community trade in live animals. In 1993 the Commission was informed that swine vesicular disease had been reported in Italy and the Netherlands. Acting pursuant to the Directive, the Commission adopted Decision 93/128, which prevented both countries from exporting live pigs to other Member States. The applicant sued the Commission for damages, claiming that the ban was disproportionate. The applicant claimed that it did not have to prove a sufficiently serious breach of a superior rule of law since the decision was not a legislative measure, but merely imposed specific obligations on the two countries. The Court of First Instance disagreed and, applying the stricter test for legislative measures, stated:[64]

> It is true that the decision produces, *vis-à-vis* those two Member States, the legal effects of an individual measure. In relation to the applicants, however, the decision produces the effects of a generally applicable measure, in the same way, for example, as a regulation prohibiting exporters established in the Netherlands and Italy from exporting live pigs to other Member States. Decision 93/128 is therefore a generally applicable measure *vis-à-vis* the abstract category to which the applicants belong and is, consequently, of a legislative nature in relation to them.

Individual concern A finding in an action for annulment that an applicant is individually concerned by the contested measure does not preclude the same measure from being considered legislative in the context of a claim for damages. In Joined Cases T-480/93 and T-483/93 *Antillean Rice Mills v Commission*[65] the Commission adopted a decision imposing a minimum selling price on rice imported from the Netherlands Antilles. The applicant exporters sought annulment of the decision and damages for loss suffered. The Court of

---

[60] Joined Cases T-481/93 and T-484/93 *Exporteurs in Levende Varkens v Commission* [1995] ECR II-2941 paras 79–81; Case T-390/94 *Schröder v Commission* [1997] ECR II-501 paras 49–52. See also Case 5/71 *Schöppenstedt v Council* [1971] ECR 975; Case 153/73 *Holtz and Willemsen v Council* [1974] ECR 675; Joined Cases 261/78 and 262/78 *Interquell Stärke-Chemie v EEC* [1979] ECR 3045; Case 50/86 *Grands Moulins v EEC* [1987] ECR 4833. The substantive conditions of liability for legislative acts are discussed further below at pp 364–368.

[61] See Ch 13 at pp 282–284.

[62] [1995] ECR II-2941 paras 86–88. See also Case T-390/94 *Schröder v Commission* [1997] ECR II-501.

[63] OJ 1990 L224 p 29.

[64] [1995] ECR II-2941 para 87.

[65] [1995] ECR II-2305. See further Ch 13 at pp 288–296.

First Instance held that although the decision was addressed to all of the Member States, it was of direct and individual concern to the applicants by virtue of the fact that they already had rice in transit when the decision was adopted. The Court annulled the decision on the grounds of proportionality, but dismissed the claim for damages on the basis that no sufficiently serious breach was shown. The Court of First Instance held that the stricter test for legislative measures was applicable since the decision applied to any trader importing Antillean rice into the Community. It stated:[66]

> Even though such a measure may be regarded as a decision with regard to the applicants in question when determining the admissibility of the action for annulment, its legislative nature does not thereby cease to exist, since its intrinsic nature and sphere of application are not modified by that assessment.

(b) Unlawful conduct by the Community

(i) Generally

Unlawful conduct The conduct must be unlawful or, as is sometimes stated, illegal or wrongful. Whether unlawful, illegal or wrongful, the conduct must be contrary to law, not merely unfair.[67] The most obvious way of proving unlawfulness is by challenging the Community provision under one of the heads of review listed in article 173 of the EC Treaty [new art 230], namely lack of competence, infringement of an essential procedural requirement, infringement of the EC Treaty or of any rule of law relating to its application or misuse of powers.[68] However, liability for wrongful acts is not limited to these grounds of review. Liability may also arise as a result of negligence. In Case C-330/88 *Grifoni v EAEC*[69] Mr Grifoni was contracted to carry out certain work on a meteorological station at the ISPRA research centre, run by the Commission. The Commission did not provide him with a safety harness, nor had it fitted a safety rail along the roof's edge, which was contrary to Italian law on industrial safety. Mr Grifoni fell and suffered serious injury. The Court of Justice held that the Commission was liable to him for the damage suffered, since it had failed to show due diligence with regard to the requisite safety measures.

---

[66] [1995] ECR II-2305 para 185.

[67] For example Case 4/69 *Lütticke v Commission* [1971] ECR 325 (illegal); Case 56/75Rev *Elz v Commission* [1976] ECR 1097 (wrongful); Case 59/84 *Tezi v Commission* [1986] ECR 887 (unlawful).

[68] See Ch 13 at pp 307–324.

[69] [1991] ECR I-1045; and Case C-308/87 *Grifoni v Commission* [1994] ECR I-341 (the claim was brought under the EURATOM Treaty, article 188, which is equivalent to article 215 of the EC Treaty). See also Joined Cases 169/83 and 136/84 *Leussink v Commission* [1986] ECR 2801 (failure to exercise due diligence with regard to the maintenance of an official car); Case T-514/93 *Cobrecaf v Commission* [1995] ECR II-621 (lack of care in not rectifying an error for 15 months); T-167/94 *Nölle v Council* [1995] ECR II-2589 (breach of the principle of good administration in failing properly to evaluate the reference country in an anti-dumping investigation).

No fault liability No fault liability exists in some Member States where an application for compensation may be brought with respect to a lawful act of the administration provided the applicant can show that he has suffered abnormal and severe loss as a result of the act. This is sometimes known under the German legal concept of *Sonderopfer* (special sacrifice) or under the French concept of *rupture de l'égalité devant les charges publiques* (unequal discharge of public burdens). The Court of Justice has not yet accepted the concept of the Community being liable without fault. On the other hand, the Court has not expressly rejected the concept, preferring to base its judgments on other grounds.[70]

Conduct by the Community Liability may arise by virtue of the adoption of any measure, whether by international treaty,[71] regulation,[72] directive,[73] decision[74] or resolution.[75] It is unnecessary for the act to have binding force, but it must have some legal effect.[76] The Community cannot be liable for acts which have not been adopted by its institutions. Consequently, the publication of a pamphlet by a political group of the European Parliament on its own initiative was not regarded as an act of the Parliament capable of giving rise to a cause of action in damages.[77]

Failure to act A failure to act may result in liability to pay damages, provided the relevant institution was under a legal obligation to act. In Case 145/83 *Adams v Commission*[78] Mr Adams provided the Commission with information concerning a breach of the competition rules by his employer, Hoffman-La Roche, in Switzerland. The Court held that the Commission was under a duty to warn him that he was under investigation by the Swiss authorities, and that a failure to fulfil that duty rendered the Community liable in damages.

Acts of servants Article 215, para 2 of the EC Treaty [new art 288] provides that the Community is liable to make good any damage caused by its servants in the performance of their duties. The Community is liable only for the acts of its

---

[70] Case 59/83 *Biovilac v EEC* [1984] ECR 4057 paras 27–29 (damage did not exceed the limits of the economic risks inherent in the sector concerned); Case 26/81 *Oleifici Mediterranei v EEC* [1982] ECR 3057 para 26 (no causation), see also the Opinion of Advocate-General Verloren van Themaat at 3089–3090; Joined Cases 9/71 and 11/71 *Cie d'Approvisionnement v Commission* [1972] ECR 391 para 45 (adoption of a measure of general economic interest).

[71] Case T-572/93 *Odigitria v Council and Commission* [1995] ECR II-2025.

[72] Joined Cases 64/76 and 113/76 and others *Dumortier Frères v Council* [1979] ECR 3091.

[73] For example, Case C-63/89 *Assurances du Crédit v Council and Commission* [1991] ECR I-1799.

[74] Case 30/66 *Becher v Commission* [1967] ECR 285.

[75] Case 169/73 *Compagnie Continentale v Council* [1975] ECR 117 (misleading information contained in a resolution).

[76] Case T-75/96R *Söktas v Commission* [1996] ECR II-859 para 31. Contrast Case C-146/91 *KYDEP v Council and Commission* [1994] ECR I-4199 paras 24–26. See Ch 13, pp 271–274.

[77] Case C-201/89 *Le Pen v Puhl* [1990] ECR I-1183.

[78] [1985] ECR 3539. See also Case 56/75Rev *Elz v Commission* [1976] ECR 1097; Case 289/83 *GAARM v Commission* [1984] ECR 4295; Case C-146/91 *KYDEP v Council and Commission* [1994] ECR I-4199 para 58; Case T-572/93 *Odigitria v Council and Commission* [1995] ECR II-2025 para 35; Case T-571/93 *Lefebvre v Commission* [1995] ECR II-2379 para 58.

servants which 'by virtue of an internal and direct relationship, are the necessary extension of the tasks entrusted to the institutions'.[79] For example, the Court of Justice has held that a traffic accident caused by a Community civil servant in a private car in the course of his employment could not render the Community liable in damages.[80]

(ii) Legislative measures

Restrictive approach It is only exceptionally that the Community incurs liability for the adoption of legislative measures. Mere unlawfulness is not sufficient to give rise to liability in respect of legislative acts. The Community can incur liability for loss caused by such acts only if there has been a breach of a superior rule of law for the protection of individuals. Further, if the institution has adopted the legislative measure in the exercise of a wide discretion, particularly involving choices of economic policy, a sufficiently serious breach of Community law must be proved. As the Court stated in Joined Cases 83/76, 94/76 and others *HNL v Council and Commission*:[81]

> This restrictive view is explained by the consideration that the legislative authority, even where the validity of its measures is subject to judicial review, cannot always be hindered in making its decisions by the prospect of applications for damages whenever it has occasion to adopt legislative measures in the public interest which may adversely affect the interests of individuals.

Superior rule of law for the protection of the individual The expression 'rule of law' means that it must be mandatory for the institutions to observe the provision in question. However, it is not every breach of a mandatory rule of law which gives rise to liability; the rule of law must serve to protect individuals. The principles of equal treatment,[82] legitimate expectation,[83] proportionality,[84] non-retroactivity,[85] misuse of powers,[86] the right to be heard,[87] the right to property and the right to pursue an occupation or trade,[88] and free trade between Member States[89] are all examples of superior rules of law for the protection of the individual.

---

[79] Case 9/69 *Sayag v Leduc* [1969] ECR 329 para 7.

[80] Ibid.

[81] [1978] ECR 1209 para 5. See also Case 5/71 *Schöppenstedt v Council* [1971] ECR 975; Case 153/73 *Holtz and Willemsen v Council* [1974] ECR 675; Joined Cases 261/78 and 262/78 *Interquell Stärke-Chemie v EEC* [1979] ECR 3045; Case 50/86 *Grands Moulins v EEC* [1987] ECR 4833.

[82] Joined Cases 64/76, 113/76 and others *Dumortier Frères v Council* [1979] ECR 3091 para 11.

[83] Joined Cases C-104/89 and C-37/90 *Mulder v Council*; Case 152/88 *Sofrimport v Commission* [1990] ECR I-2477; Case 74/74 *CNTA v Commission* [1975] ECR 533.

[84] Case 281/84 *Zuckerfabrik v Council and Commission* [1987] ECR 49 para 35.

[85] Case 74/74 *CNTA v Commission* [1975] ECR 533 paras 28–32 (dismissed on the facts).

[86] Case T-489/93 *Unifruit Hellas v Commission* [1994] ECR II-1201 para 40.

[87] Joined Cases T-481/93 and T-483/93 *Exporteurs in Levende Varkens v Commission* [1995] ECR II-2941 para 102.

[88] Case T-390/94 *Schröder v Commission* [1997] ECR II-501 paras 65–66.

[89] Case 30/66 *Becher v Commission* [1967] ECR 285 at 297.

A lack of reasoning is sufficient to vitiate a Community measure under article 190 of the EC Treaty [new art 253], but it does not constitute a superior rule of law for the protection of the individual.[90] Furthermore, the Court of Justice has held that the fact that an institution was not legally competent to adopt a particular measure did not constitute a breach of a rule of law for the protection of individuals.[91]

Discretion Legislation adopted within the framework of the Common Agricultural Policy will involve choices of economic and political policy, since the Community possesses a wide discretion to attain the objectives of the Common Agricultural Policy, particularly those listed in article 39 of the EC Treaty [new art 33].[92] Regulations imposing anti-dumping duties,[93] safeguard measures,[94] and harmonising legislation in the insurance sector[95] have also been held to involve choices of economic policy. The Community also has a broad discretion when adopting legislation involving choices of social policy.[96]

Sufficiently serious breach In order to show that there is a sufficiently serious breach, the applicant must prove that the Community has manifestly and gravely disregarded the limits on the exercise of its power.[97] Although the EC courts do not always distinguish between the concepts of manifest and grave breaches, it is possible to extract from the judgments relevant considerations to determine whether a particular breach is manifest or grave.

(1) Manifest breach
Excusable error A breach will be manifest when the defendant institution has made an obvious error of judgment. This depends primarily on whether it has made an excusable error: for example, whether the decision is clearly unreasonable, whether the institution has properly taken account of relevant facts, whether it was put on notice before committing the breach, or whether the error was merely technical.[98] These factors are each dealt with below.

---

[90] Case 106/81 *Kind v EEC* [1982] ECR 2885 para 14; Case C-119/88 *AERPO v Commission* [1990] ECR I-2189; Joined Cases T-481/93 and T-483/93 *Exporteurs in Levende Varkens v Commission* [1995] ECR II-2941 para 104.

[91] Case C-282/90 *Vreugdenhil v Commission* [1992] ECR I-1937 paras 16–24. The Court of First Instance took a different view in Case T-390/94 *Schröder v Commission* [1997] ECR II-501 paras 65–66, although Case C-282/90 was not referred to.

[92] Joined Cases 54 to 60/76 *Compagnie Industrielle du Comité de Loheac v Council and Commission* [1977] ECR 645 para 15; Joined Cases T-481/93 and T-483/93 *Exporteurs in Levende Varkens v Commission* [1995] ECR II-2941 paras 89–97.

[93] Case 122/86 *Epicheiriseon v Council and Commission (No 2)* [1989] ECR 3959; applied in Case T-167/94 *Nölle v Council* [1995] ECR II-2589.

[94] Joined Cases T-480/93 and T-483/93 *Antillean Rice Mills v Commission* [1995] ECR II-2305.

[95] Case C-63/89 *Assurances du Crédit v Council and Commission* [1991] ECR I-1799 (Directive 73/239 on non-life insurance).

[96] See generally, Ch 13 at p 320.

[97] Joined Cases C-104/89 and C-37/90 *Mulder v Council* [1992] ECR I-3061 para 12; Joined Cases T-480/93 and T-483/93 *Antillean Rice Mills v Commission* [1995] ECR II-2305 para 190.

[98] See para 15 of the Opinion of Advocate-General van Gerven in Joined Cases C-104/89 and C-37/90 *Mulder v Council and Commission* [1992] ECR I-3061, where he stated that, only

Reasonableness A decision made in the exercise of a wide discretion may still be reasonable although the choice made is wrong. This is illustrated by Joined Cases C-104/89 and C-37/90 *Mulder v Council*.[99] The applicants had taken advantage of the Council's system of paying premiums for the non-marketing of milk and had, accordingly, suspended production for a period of five years. After this period, the applicants were informed that they could not resume production since they had no reference year on which to base the quantity of milk they would be entitled to produce. In a preliminary ruling under article 177 of the EC Treaty [new art 234], the Court of Justice held that the Community system was unlawful on the ground that it was in breach of the principle of legitimate expectation, in so far as the system did not provide for the allocation of a reference quantity. Following that judgment, the Council adopted a regulation which provided for a special reference quantity for those dairy farmers who had been paid the premium for not producing milk. The special reference quantity was equal to 60 per cent of the quantity of milk delivered by them in the year prior to the start of the five-year period. This 60 per cent rule was also declared invalid by the Court in a subsequent preliminary ruling on the basis that it also infringed the principle of legitimate expectation. In the subsequent damages action, the Court held that the complete failure to set any reference quantity constituted a manifest and grave disregard of the limits of the Community's discretionary powers. However, the Community was not held liable in damages for the 60 per cent rule. Although that rule had infringed a superior rule of law, the breach was not regarded as sufficiently serious since there had been some attempt to take account of the returning farmers' interests, and the rule had sought to strike a balance between the producers concerned and the fragile state of the milk sector.

Failure to take into account relevant considerations A failure to take account of a limited and clearly defined group makes the breach all the more obvious and less excusable. For example, the Community was held liable in:

(1) Joined Cases 64/76 and 113/76 and others *Dumortier Frères v Council*,[100] where the Council was found to have discriminated against the applicants who comprised the entire maize grits industry of the Community;

(2) Case C-152/88 *Sofrimport v Commission*,[101] where the limited and clearly defined group were importers who had goods in transit;

(3) Joined Cases C-104/89 and C-37/90 *Mulder v Council*,[102] where the group were dairy producers who had been paid a premium to produce no milk;

---

where the public authority's error is inexcusable, that is to say where it could not reasonably have been committed, have powers been manifestly and gravely disregarded.

[99] [1992] ECR I-3061. See also Case T-571/93 *Lefebvre v Commission* [1995] ECR II-2379 at para 56 (adequate explanation given for decision to exclude products from Community treatment under article 115 of the EC Treaty [new art 134]); Case T-167/94 *Nölle v Council* [1995] ECR II-2589 at paras 88–91.

[100] [1979] ECR 3091.

[101] [1990] ECR I-2477.

[102] [1992] ECR I-3061.

(4) Case 74/74 *CNTA v Commission*,[103] where the category was traders who had irrevocably undertaken export transactions.

However, damages were not awarded in Joined Cases 83/76, 94/76 and others *HNL v Council and Commission*,[104] where the unlawful measure affected a very wide category of traders, namely all buyers of compound feeding-stuffs containing protein.

Notice of breach Where the defendant institution has been put on notice of a breach, but has not acted to rectify the situation, the Court is more likely to find that the institution has manifestly disregarded the limits upon its discretionary power. In Joined Cases 64/76, 113/76 and others *Dumortier Frères v Council*[105] the Council abolished production refunds for grits intended for the brewing of beer in March 1975. A factor which persuaded the Court to award damages to the applicants, who were grits producers, was that the Council had not acted upon a proposal made by the Commission in June 1975 to reintroduce the refunds.[106]

Mere technical errors Technical errors which lead to *de facto* discrimination between producers of similar products are unlikely to constitute a manifest breach.[107]

(2) Grave breach

Extent of damage The greater the damage the more likely it is that a grave breach will have occurred. In Joined Cases C-104/89 and C-37/90 *Mulder v Council*[108] the breach of the principle of legitimate expectations was grave, since the effect of the Community regulation adopted was to prevent the dairy producers affected from resuming any marketing of milk. By contrast, in Joined Cases 83/76, 94/76 and others *HNL v Council and Commission*[109] the adoption of a regulation, which discriminated between producers as to the price of feeding-stuffs, was held not to constitute a grave breach, since the effect on their production costs (which rose by about 2 per cent) was limited, rising by about 2 per cent. Thus, commercial undertakings must accept that a loss of competitiveness or a loss of profit may result from the adoption of Community legislation. These risks form part of the economic risks inherent in the activities of a commercial undertaking, as does, for example, an increase in energy costs. As the Court of Justice stated in *HNL v Council*:

> individuals may be required, in the sectors coming within the economic policy of the Community, to accept within reasonable limits certain harmful effects on their

---

[103] [1975] ECR 533.

[104] [1978] ECR 1209.

[105] [1979] ECR 3091.

[106] See also the Opinion of Advocate-General Tesauro in Case C-63/89 *Assurances du Crédit v Council and Commission* [1991] ECR I-1799 at 1839.

[107] Case 20/88 *Roquette Frères v Commission* [1989] ECR 1553 para 26; Joined Cases 194 to 206/83 *Asteris v Commission* [1985] ECR 2815 para 23.

[108] [1992] ECR I-3061.

[109] [1978] ECR 1209 paras 6–8. See also Case 50/86 *Grands Moulins v EEC* [1987] ECR 4833 para 21.

economic interests as a result of a legislative measure without being able to obtain compensation from public funds even if that measure has been declared null and void.

An abnormal or unforeseeable degree of loss is likely to fall outside the bounds of economic risks inherent in the sector concerned and is, therefore, likely to be considered grave. In Case 152/88 *Sofrimport v Commission*[110] a Commission regulation prevented the applicant from importing Chilean apples into the Community, even though the goods were already in transit. This was contrary to a Council regulation which required the Commission, when adopting protective measures, to take account of the special position of products in transit. The Court held that the damage suffered by the importer went beyond the limits of the economic risks inherent in the applicants' business, in that the very purpose of the Council regulation was precisely to limit damage to importers with goods in transit.

Conduct verging on the arbitrary An arbitrary abuse of power will almost inevitably lead to a grave breach being committed. However, arbitrary conduct is not a necessary condition of liability. Although in Case 143/77 *Koninklijke Scholten-Honig v Council and Commission*[111] the Court of Justice held that grave disregard implied conduct verging on the arbitrary, the Court subsequently stated in Case C-220/91P *Commission v Stahlwerke Peine-Salzgitter*[112] that a finding of arbitrary conduct was not 'a necessary condition or formulation for the Community to be held liable ...'.

(c) Causation

Direct link Article 215 of the EC Treaty [new art 288] does not impose an obligation on the Community to make good every harmful consequence of its unlawful conduct. The Court has held that the damage suffered must be a direct consequence of the unlawful conduct. In Joined Cases 64/76, 113/76 and others *Dumortier Frères v Council*[113] some applicants claimed that the unlawful abolition of production refunds had forced them to close their factories. The Council argued that the factories had closed because of the obsolescence of the

---

[110] [1990] ECR I-2477. See also Case 74/74 *CNTA v Commission* [1975] ECR 533; Joined Cases 64/76, 113/76 and others *Dumortier Frères v Council* [1979] ECR 3091; Case C-104/89 *Mulder v Council* [1992] ECR I-3061 para 17; Joined Cases T-480/93 and T-483/93 *Antillean Rice Mills v Commission* [1995] ECR II-2305 para 200.

[111] [1979] ECR 3583. See also Joined Cases 116/77 and 124/77 *Amylum v Council and Commission* [1979] ECR 3497.

[112] [1993] ECR I-2393 para 51. The matter is not entirely clear, however, since the Court of First Instance has continued to refer to the need to prove arbitrary conduct; see eg Case T-167/94 *Nölle v Council* [1995] ECR II-2589 para 87; Joined Cases T-481/93 and T-483/93 *Exporteurs in Levende Varkens v Commission* [1995] ECR II-2941 para 120.

[113] [1979] ECR 3091 para 21. See also Case 153/73 *Holtz and Willemsen v Council* [1974] ECR 675 para 7; Joined Cases 71/84 and 72/84 *Surcouf v Commission* [1985] ECR 2925 para 9; Case T-168/94 *Blackspur DIY v Council and Commission* [1995] ECR II-2627 para 52 (appeal dismissed in Case C-362/95P *Blackspur DIY v Council and Commission* [1997] ECR I-4775; Case T-175/94 *International Procurement Services v Commission* [1996] ECR II-729 para 55; Case T-7/96 *Perillo v Commission* [1997] ECR II-1061 paras 41–46.

plant and managerial and other financial problems. The Court rejected the claim for compensation for the closures, stating:

> The data supplied by the parties on that question in the course of the proceedings are not such as to establish the true causes of the further damage alleged. However, it is sufficient to state that even if it were assumed that the abolition of the refunds exacerbated the difficulties encountered by those applicants, those difficulties would not be a sufficiently direct consequence of the unlawful conduct of the Council to render the Community liable to make good the damage.

The requirement of a direct causal link means that the negligence of the applicant may break the chain of causation. Although the Court has on occasions reduced the amount recoverable by as much as 50 per cent on the grounds of contributory negligence,[114] it is clear that a relatively low degree of lack of care on the part of the applicant will break the chain of causation and that the direct link between the damage and the breach will generally be broken where the damage has been caused entirely or even partially[115] by the applicant's own conduct. In Joined Cases 241/78 and others *DGV v Council*[116] DGV and several other manufacturers of grits successfully claimed compensation for the abolition of production refunds for grits intended for the brewing of beer. However, the claim by one applicant was rejected on the basis that it had commenced production of maize grits only after the Council's decision to abolish the refunds for grits. The Court held that the loss suffered by the applicant was not caused by the Community, but by the applicant's own decision to enter that particular market.

In determining whether the applicant has been partially or exclusively responsible for the damage suffered, the Court applies a 'prudent person' test.[117] This introduces an element of foreseeability of loss, not on the part of the defendant institution but on the part of the applicant. In Case 74/74 *CNTA v Commission*[118] the Court ordered that the applicant be compensated for loss suffered due to the immediate withdrawal of monetary compensatory amounts, since it was not foreseeable that the Community would re-expose a trader to an exchange risk as regards transactions irrevocably undertaken by it. The Court considered that 'a trader, even a prudent one' might legitimately omit to cover himself against such a risk. By contrast, in Case 169/73 *Compagnie Continentale v Council*[119] the applicant claimed compensation for loss suffered

---

[114] Case 145/83 *Adams v Commission* [1985] ECR 3539; Case 308/87 *Grifoni v EAEC* [1990] ECR I-1203.

[115] Case T-514/93 *Cobrecaf v Commission* [1995] ECR II-621 para 67.

[116] [1979] ECR 3017 para 19.

[117] Case 30/66 *Becher v Commission* [1967] ECR 285 at 299; Case 74/74 *CNTA v Commission* [1975] ECR 533 para 41; Case 169/73 *Compagnie Continentale v Council* [1975] ECR 117 para 23; Case 97/76 *Merkur v Commission* [1977] ECR 1063 para 9; Case 26/81 *Oleifici Mediterranei v EEC* [1982] ECR 3057 paras 22–24; Case T-572/93 *Odigitria v Council and Commission* [1995] ECR II-2025 para 70; Joined Cases T-480/93 and T-483/93 *Antillean Rice Mills v Commission* [1995] ECR II-2305 para 207.

[118] [1975] ECR 533 paras 38–46. The applicant ultimately failed to prove that it had suffered any loss: [1976] ECR 797.

[119] [1975] ECR 117.

due to the Council abandoning a system of fixed compensatory amounts in favour of a flexible system. The Court held that the chain of causation had been broken since a 'prudent exporter fully informed of the conditions of the market' would not have concluded that the monetary compensatory amounts would remain fixed.

A defective statement of reasons under article 190 [new art 253] which results in the annulment of an administrative decision will give rise to liability in damages only if the applicant can show that the decision would otherwise have been favourable, so that a direct causal link exists between the alleged damage and the statement of reasons.[120] Further, the Court will not award damages where this will unjustly enrich the applicant, ie where the applicant has passed on the loss to his customers or has raised his prices when production refunds have been abolished.[121]

Mitigation The injured party must act to mitigate any loss caused by the Community by showing reasonable diligence in limiting the extent of his loss. This includes commencing proceedings[122] and obtaining alternative income. In Joined Cases C-104/89 and C-37/90 *Mulder v Council*[123] the applicants had taken advantage of the Council's system of paying premiums for the non-marketing of milk and had, accordingly, suspended production for a period of five years. After this period, the applicants were informed that they could not resume production as they had no reference year on which to base the calculation of the appropriate quota. The Court held that the Community had acted unlawfully and was liable to compensate the applicants for the loss suffered. The quantum of damages was based on the loss of earnings less any income from replacement activities. The Court stated that the replacement income included actual income and income which 'they could have obtained had they reasonably engaged in such activities'. Perversely, however, the Court further held that any losses incurred by the applicants in attempting to mitigate their loss would not be recoverable on the basis that there was no direct link between that loss and the unlawful Community rules.

(d) Damage

Claim for damages The applicant must set out clearly in its application to the Court the nature of the damage suffered. The damage for which compensation is sought must be actual and certain.[124] A claim for damages at large, where no specific heads of damage are identified, will be regarded as inadmissible. However, the fact that the amount of damages cannot be precisely quantified in

---

[120] Case C-358/90R *Compagnia Italiana Alcool v Commission* [1992] ECR I-2457 para 47; Case T-230/94 *Farrugia v Commission* [1996] ECR II-195 paras 42–46.

[121] Joined Cases 64/76, 113/76 and others *Dumortier Frères v Council* [1979] ECR 3091 para 15.

[122] Case 58/75 *Sergy v Commission* [1976] ECR 1139 para 45. See also Joined Cases C-46/93 and 48/93 *Brasserie du Pêcheur and Factortame* [1996] ECR I-1029 para 84, and particularly para 100 of the Opinion of Advocate-General Tesauro.

[123] [1992] ECR I-3061.

[124] Case T-478/93 *Wafer Zoo v Commission* [1995] ECR II-1479 para 49.

the application will not render the claim inadmissible.[125] Thus, a claim will be admissible where it sets out 'imminent damage foreseeable with sufficient certainty even if the damage cannot yet be precisely assessed'. For example, in Joined Cases 56 and 60/74 *Kampffmeyer v Commission*[126] German meal producers claimed that a system of aid to durum wheat growers wrongfully put them at a disadvantage *vis-à-vis* their French competitors, the production of durum wheat being localised in France (durum wheat is ground into meal which is then used to make pasta). They claimed damages for loss of profit which they would suffer in the future. The Court of Justice held that such a claim was admissible, stating that such loss was imminent and that the applicants could reserve the right to quantify the amount at a later stage, restricting themselves in the application to asking for a finding of the Community's liability. This possibility is important because it may be necessary to bring the matter before the Court as soon as the cause of damage is certain, in order to prevent even greater damage.

Proof of damage The EC courts have an unfettered discretion in assessing all the evidence submitted to them.[127] Thus, experts' reports, statistics, accounts and invoices have all been relied on to prove loss. The burden of proving the existence of damage rests with the applicant.[128] Conclusive proof must be adduced, and the nature and extent of the loss suffered must be particularised, otherwise the Court will refuse, of its own motion, to hear the application.[129] Moreover, a lack of particularity cannot be made good by a request from the applicant that the Court appoint an expert for the purpose of determining the loss alleged to have been suffered.[130]

Heads of damage Damages may be claimed for loss of earnings,[131] for penalties paid for repudiation of contracts,[132] for lost profit on concluded or foreseeable contracts,[133] for the wrongful abolition of production refunds,[134] for

---

[125] Case 5/71 *Schöppenstedt v Council* [1971] ECR 975 para 9.
[126] [1976] ECR 711 para 8; Case 44/76 *Eier Kontor v Council and Commission* [1977] ECR 393 para 8; Case 281/84 *Zuckerfabrik v Council and Commission* [1987] ECR 49 para 14.
[127] Case 261/78 *Interquell Stärke-Chemie v EEC* [1982] ECR 3271 para 11.
[128] Case T-571/93 *Lefebvre v Commission* [1995] ECR II-2379 para 85; Case T-575/93 *Koelman v Commission* [1996] ECR II-1 para 97.
[129] Case 74/74 *CNTA v Commission* [1976] ECR 797 paras 15–16; Case 49/79 *Pool v Council* [1980] ECR 569 para 12; Case 253/84 *GAEC v Council and Commission* [1987] ECR 123 para 12; Joined Cases T-481/93 and T-483/93 *Exporteurs in Levende Varkens v Commission* [1995] ECR II-2941 para 75.
[130] Case T-53/96 *Syndicat des Producteurs de Viande Bovine v Commission* [1996] ECR II-1579 para 26.
[131] Joined Cases C-104/89 and C-37/90 *Mulder v Council* [1992] ECR I-3061; Case C-308/87 *Grifoni v EAEC* [1994] ECR I-341.
[132] Joined Cases 5/66, 7/66 and others *Kampffmeyer v Commission* [1967] ECR 245 at 265.
[133] Ibid at pp 266–267; Case 74/74 *CNTA v Commission* [1975] ECR 533; Case 152/88 *Sofrimport v Commission* [1990] ECR I-2477.
[134] Case 238/78 *Ireks Arkady v Council* [1979] ECR 2955 (interlocutory order); Joined Cases 241/78 and others *DGV v Council* [1979] ECR 3017 (interlocutory order); Joined Cases 261/78 and 262/78 *Interquell Stärke-Chemie v EEC* [1979] ECR 3045 (interlocutory order), [1982] ECR 3271 (award); Joined Cases 64/76, 113/76 and others *Dumortier Frères v Council* [1979]

nominal damages,[135] for personal injuries and pain and suffering,[136] for loss of a chance of being employed[137] and for lost interest on late payments.[138]

Award of damages Where a claim is successful, the EC courts will make an interlocutory judgment ordering the parties to agree on the damage suffered, with liberty to apply to the Court failing agreement. Where damages are expressed in ECU (the European Currency Unit), the relevant date for converting the ECU to national currencies is the date of the interlocutory judgment.[139]

Interest Interest is payable on the amount of compensation due as from the date of judgment. Interest has been awarded at the rate of 8 per cent, unless the applicant has pleaded a lesser rate.[140]

ECR 3091 (interlocutory order), [1982] ECR 1733 (award).
[135] Case T-485/93 *Dreyfus v Commission* [1996] ECR II-1101 paras 71–75 (1 ECU for damage to reputation).
[136] Joined Cases 169/83 and 136/84 *Leussink v Commission* [1986] ECR 2801; Case 145/83 *Adams v Commission* [1985] ECR 3539.
[137] Case T-47/93 *C v Commission* [1996] ECR-SC II-743 (summarised at I-A-233).
[138] Case T-514/93 *Cobrecaf v Commission* [1995] ECR II-621 para 72.
[139] Joined Cases 64/76, 113/76 and others *Dumortier Frères v Council* [1982] ECR 1733; Joined Cases 256/80 and 5/81 *Birra Wührer v Council and Commission* [1984] ECR 3693 para 34.
[140] Case C-152/88 *Sofrimport v Commission* [1990] ECR I-2477 para 32; Joined Cases C-104/89 and C-37/90 *Mulder v Council* [1992] ECR I-3061 para 35.

Chapter 17

Interim Relief

1. NATURE OF INTERIM RELIEF

Purpose The purpose of interim relief is:[1]

> to safeguard the interests of one of the parties to the proceedings in order to prevent the judgment in the main proceedings from being rendered illusory by being deprived of any practical effect.

Any interim relief granted must be provisional and cannot affect or prejudge the final decision of the Court in any way.[2]

(a) Suspending the operation of Community acts

Article 185 Article 185 of the EC Treaty [new art 242] provides that:

> Actions brought before the Court of Justice shall not have suspensory effect. The Court of Justice may, however, if it considers that circumstances so require, order that application of the contested act be suspended.

Acts which may be suspended Article 185 may only be invoked to suspend the operation of a measure adopted by a Community institution. Only measures which are being specifically challenged in proceedings before the Court may be suspended under article 185.[3] An applicant may seek the suspension of part only of a measure, even if the validity of the whole measure is being challenged in the main action.[4]

---

[1] Case C-313/90R *CIRFS v Commission* [1991] ECR I-2557 para 24.
[2] Article 36 of the Statute of the Court of Justice; ECJ Rules of Procedure, article 86(4); CFI Rules of Procedure, article 107(4). Joined Cases 60/81 and 190/81R *IBM v Commission* [1981] ECR 1857 para 4; Case 231/86R *Breda-Geomineraria v Commission* [1986] ECR 2639 para 18; Case 176/88R *Hanning v Parliament* [1988] ECR 3915 para 8; Case 321/88R *Sparr v Commission* [1988] ECR 6405 para 9; Case 352/88R *Commission v Italy* [1989] ECR 267 para 22; Case 229/88R *Cargill v Commission* [1988] ECR 5183 para 14.
[3] ECJ Rules of Procedure, article 83(1); CFI Rules of Procedure, article 104(1).
[4] For example, see Case 20/74R *Kali-Chemie v Commission* [1974] ECR 337; Case 27/76R *United Brands Co v Commission* [1976] ECR 425.

Parties who may apply Article 185 may only be invoked by an applicant who is challenging the particular Community measure in proceedings before the Court.[5] The right to seek suspension of a contested measure is granted to applicants for the purpose of protecting their own interests and they cannot rely on disadvantages to third parties in support of their applications.[6] Furthermore, the validity of the measure must be open to challenge by the particular applicant. Thus, where a private party seeks the suspension of a measure of general application which is clearly not of direct and individual concern to him, the Court will reject the application for interim measures.[7]

(b) Other interim relief

Article 186 Article 186 of the EC Treaty [new art 243] provides that:

> The Court of Justice may in any cases before it prescribe any necessary interim measures.

Parties who may apply An application for interim measures under article 186 may be made by any party to a case before the Court. The measure sought must relate to the case before the Court.[8]

Nature of interim orders The Court has a wide discretion as to the nature of the interim measures it may order under article 186. In some cases, it may simply order a party to take 'the measures necessary' to achieve a particular result.[9] In Case 293/85R *Commission v Belgium*[10] the Commission sought the suspension of a Belgian law which required students who were nationals of other Member States to pay a supplementary enrolment fee (*minerval*) to universities. Belgian students were not required to pay the *minerval*. The Court of Justice ordered that students of other Member States should be entitled to enrol in Belgian universities without paying the *minerval*, but on condition that they gave a personal undertaking, in writing, to pay the *minerval* if the Belgian Government successfully defended the main action brought against it under article 169 [new art 226].

The Court also has power to order a party to take positive action. In Case 65/87R *Pfizer International v Commission*[11] the Court of Justice ordered the Commission to take certain steps to ensure that the additive Carbadox could be legally marketed in the Community.

---

[5] ECJ Rules of Procedure, article 83(1); CFI Rules of Procedure, article 104(1).
[6] Case 269/84R *Fabbro v Commission* [1984] ECR 4333 paras 9–10; Case 292/84R *Scharf v Commission* [1984] ECR 4349 para 12.
[7] Case 82/87R *Autexpo v Commission* [1987] ECR 2131 paras 13–16; Case 160/88R *Fedesa v Council* [1988] ECR 4121.
[8] ECJ Rules of Procedure, article 83(1); CFI Rules of Procedure, article 104(1).
[9] Case 154/85R *Commission v Italy* [1985] ECR 1753 para 21.
[10] [1985] ECR 3521. In Case 318/81R *Commission v CODEMI* [1982] ECR 1325 (EAEC) the Court ordered that a technical expert should be appointed to carry out certain tasks and that the Commission should pay the expert's costs.
[11] [1987] ECR 1691. See also Case T-203/95R *Connolly v Commission* [1995] ECR II-2919 paras 24–25.

In the context of an application for interim measures under article 186, the EC courts have power to order the suspension of the operation of an act other than the act challenged in the main proceedings. Generally, the courts will not exercise that jurisdiction unless the acts in question emanate from the same institution *and* that institution is a party to the proceedings.[12] However, in Case 23/86R *United Kingdom v Parliament*[13] the United Kingdom, in the context of an application under article 173 of the EC Treaty [new art 230] against the European Parliament, successfully sought interim measures against the Commission in respect of its implementation of the budget. The Commission, although not formally a party to the proceedings, was represented at the hearing and indicated that it would comply with any order which the Court addressed to it.[14]

Interim payments In Case C-393/96P(R) *Antonissen v Council*[15] the President of the Court indicated that, in certain cases, it might be appropriate to order a Community institution to make an interim payment to an applicant pending final judgment on the applicant's claim for damages against that institution. The President indicated that such an order should be confined to cases where the *prima facie* case appears particularly strong, and the urgency of the measures sought is undeniable.[16]

Quia timet **orders** In Case T-395/94 R(II) *Atlantic Container Line v Commission*[17] the President of the Court of First Instance rejected an application for a *quia timet* order whereby the applicant sought to prevent the Commission from adopting a particular decision. The President held that such an order could be made only in cases where the intended decision would immediately create rights for third parties and produce irreversible effects. In other cases, such as the one under consideration, the applicant was obliged to wait for the adoption of the decision, following which it could seek to have it annulled under article 173 of the EC Treaty whilst seeking interim relief in the context of that action.

---

[12] Case 133/87R *Nashua Corporation v Commission* [1987] ECR 2883 paras 7–8.

[13] [1986] ECR 1085 paras 22–24.

[14] Contrast the potentially narrower approach adopted by the Court of First Instance in Case T-543/93R *Gestevisión Telecinco v Commission* [1993] ECR II-1409 para 25; Case T-322/94R *Union Carbide v Commission* [1994] ECR II-1159 para 28; and Case T-6/95R *Cantine dei colli Berici v Commission* [1995] ECR II-647 para 30, where it stated that an application for interim measures is, in principle, admissible only if the measures sought fall within the scope of the final decision which the Court is capable of making.

[15] [1997] ECR I-441 paras 35–43. See also Case T-203/95R *Connolly v Commission* [1995] ECR II-2919 para 45, where the President of the Court of First Instance rejected a claim for the imposition of a periodic penalty on a Community institution in the context of an application for interim measures.

[16] When the matter was reconsidered by the President of the Court of First Instance he found that the applicant had failed to establish the existence of a particularly strong *prima facie* case and dismissed the application: Case T-179/96R *Antonissen v Council* [1996] ECR II-1641 paras 52–54.

[17] [1995] ECR II-2893 paras 39–41 and 48–50, upheld on appeal in Case C-149/95P(R) *Commission v Atlantic Container Line* [1995] ECR I-2163 paras 35–40. See also Case T-52/96R *Sogecable v Commission* [1996] ECR II-797 paras 39–41.

Preparatory inquiries It is not appropriate to ask the EC courts to order preparatory inquiries by means of a separate application under article 186 of the EC Treaty.[18]

Interim measures and article 169 In the context of proceedings against a Member State for breach of Community law under article 169 of the EC Treaty [new art 226], the Commission may make an application under article 186 seeking an interim order that the relevant national measures should be suspended, pending the final judgment of the Court.[19] Where the Court has already made a judgment against a Member State under article 169 and the Commission brings fresh proceedings for failure to comply with article 171 [new art 228], the Court will not grant interim measures where this would simply have the same effect as the original judgment, that is imposing an obligation on the Member State to put an end to the original breach.[20]

Interim measures and article 175 Interim measures are, in principle, available in actions brought under article 175 of the EC Treaty [new art 232].[21]

Interim measures and article 215 In principle, interim measures are available in the context of proceedings against the Community seeking damages under articles 178 and 215 of the EC Treaty [new arts 235 and 288].[22] However, in practice, given the reluctance of the EC courts and, in particular, the Court of First Instance, to recognise financial loss as constituting serious and irreparable harm, it will usually be very difficult to satisfy the conditions for the grant of interim relief.[23]

Interim measures and article 177 **[new art 234]** The general view is that the Court of Justice does not have power to grant interim measures in the context of preliminary reference proceedings.[24] However, the Court has never been called upon to determine the issue.

---

[18] Case T-18/96R *SCK and FNK v Commission* [1996] ECR II-407 para 41 (application for access to the Commission's file in a competition case). See Ch 18, pp 406–407 for a discussion of preparatory inquiries.

[19] For example, see Case 61/77R *Commission v Ireland* [1977] ECR 1411; Case 293/85R *Commission v Belgium* [1985] ECR 3521; Case C-87/94R *Commission v Belgium* [1994] ECR I-1395 paras 30–31. See also Case C-120/94R *Commission v Greece* [1994] ECR I-3037, where interim measures were sought in the context of an application by the Commission under article 225 of the EC Treaty [new art 298].

[20] Joined Cases 24/80 and 97/80R *Commission v France* [1980] ECR 1319.

[21] Case C-68/95 *T. Port* [1996] ECR I-6065 para 60.

[22] For example, see Case T-203/95R *Connolly v Commission* [1995] ECR II-2919; Case C-393/96P(R) *Antonissen v Council and Commission* [1997] ECR I-441 paras 35–43. See also Joined Cases C-51/90R and C-59/90R *Cosmos-Tank v Commission* [1990] ECR I-2167 para 33.

[23] For example, see Case T-228/95R *Lehrfreund v Council and Commission* [1996] ECR II-111 paras 67–71. See below at pp 379–380 and Hoskins, 'The Relationship between the Action for Damages and the Award of Interim Measures', in Heukels and McDonnell, *The Action for Damages in Community Law* (Kluwer, 1997).

[24] For example, see Anderson, *References to the European Court* (Sweet & Maxwell, 1995) at para 7–058.

2. CONDITIONS FOR GRANT OF INTERIM RELIEF

Conditions In deciding whether to grant interim relief, the following principles apply:[25]

(1) the applicant must show that it has a *prima facie* case as a matter of fact and law;

(2) the applicant must also show that the interim measures sought are necessary, as a matter of urgency, in order to avoid serious and irreparable damage to his interests;

(3) where appropriate, the Court is entitled to balance the interests of the parties which are at stake in deciding whether or not to grant interim relief;

(4) the interim order sought must be provisional in the sense that it must not prejudge any points of law or fact at issue in the main proceedings and it must not neutralise in advance the effects of the decision subsequently to be given in the main proceedings;[26]

(5) the judge dealing with the application has a broad discretion as to how to apply these criteria in the specific circumstances of each case.

The EC courts will refuse to grant interim measures where it is apparent that the measures sought by the applicant would not actually be of benefit to him.[27]

Furthermore, the Court may refuse to grant interim measures where the applicant has delayed in making its application.[28]

Burden of proof It is for the applicant to provide adequate evidence that the conditions for the grant of interim relief are satisfied.[29]

***Prima facie* case** The applicant must show that he has a *prima facie* case in the main action, not simply in relation to the application for interim relief itself.[30] Thus, for example, where the main action is inadmissible,[31] the application for interim relief will be dismissed.

---

[25] ECJ Rules of Procedure, article 83(2); CFI Rules of Procedure, article 104(2); Case C-149/95P(R) *Commission v Atlantic Container Line* [1995] ECR I-2163 paras 21–23; Case C-180/96R *United Kingdom v Commission* [1996] ECR I-3903 paras 44–45; Joined Cases C-239/96R and C-240/96R *United Kingdom v Commission* [1996] ECR I-4475 para 31; Case C-393/96P(R) *Antonissen v Council and Commission* [1997] ECR I-441 paras 27–28.

[26] Article 36 of the Statute of the Court of Justice; ECJ Rules of Procedure, article 86(4); CFI Rules of Procedure, article 107(4).

[27] Case T-164/96R *Moccia Irme v Commission* [1996] ECR II-2261 para 26; Case C-89/97P(R) *Moccia Irme v Commission* [1997] ECR I-2327 paras 43–46. See also Case T-2/95R *Industrie des poudres sphériques v Council* [1995] ECR II-485 para 35.

[28] Case C-87/94R *Commission v Belgium* [1994] ECR I-1395 paras 38 and 42–43.

[29] Case 250/85R *Brother Industries v Council* [1985] ECR 3459 paras 15–18; Case C-356/90R *Belgium v Commission* [1991] ECR I-2423 para 23; Case T-168/95R *Eridania v Council* [1995] ECR II-2817 para 33; Case T-155/96R *Mainz v Commission* [1996] ECR II-1655 para 19.

[30] Case 148/88R *Albani v Commission* [1988] ECR 3361; Case 108/88R *Cendoya v Commission* [1988] ECR 2585 para 21.

[31] Case 376/87R *Distrivet v Council* [1988] ECR 209; Case 160/88R *Fedesa v Council* [1988] ECR 4121.

The Court will, generally, refuse to examine the admissibility of the main application in the context of an application for interim relief.[32] However, if a party contends that the main action is manifestly inadmissible, the Court of Justice has consistently held that it will consider whether the main application reveals *prima facie* grounds for concluding that it is admissible.[33] The Court of First Instance has adopted a similar approach in holding that the question of admissibility should be reserved for the examination of the main application 'unless it is apparent at first sight that the latter is manifestly inadmissible'.[34]

Urgency The party seeking interim relief must furnish proof that he cannot wait until the conclusion of the main action without personally suffering damage which would have serious and irreparable effects for him[35] or that the immediate harm which he would suffer would be disproportionate to the interest of the institution in having the measure implemented.[36] Where the applicant has delayed before bringing the main action and the application for interim relief, the Court may be reluctant to find that the condition of urgency is satisfied.[37] However, in Case 23/87R *Tziovas v Parliament*[38] the Court of Justice held that:

> ... urgency is not determined by the speed with which a measure is to be applied for and taken but by the extent to which a person may need to obtain the adoption of a measure which is necessary at the present time to avoid certain damage.

The Court of Justice has held that it is not necessary for the applicant to establish with absolute certainty that serious and irreparable damage is imminent. It is sufficient that the likelihood of such damage being suffered is foreseeable with a sufficient degree of probability, particularly where it depends on the occurrence of a number of factors.[39]

---

[32] Case 75/72R *Perinciolo v Council* [1972] ECR 1201 para 7; Case 23/86R *United Kingdom v Parliament* [1986] ECR 1085 para 21; Case 65/87R *Pfizer International v Commission* [1987] ECR 1691 para 15.

[33] Case 118/83R *CMC v Commission* [1983] ECR 2583 para 37; Case 221/86R *Group of the European Right v Parliament* [1986] ECR 2969 para 19; Case 82/87R *Autexpo v Commission* [1987] ECR 2131 para 15; Joined Cases C-239/96R and C-240/96R *United Kingdom v Commission* [1996] ECR I-4475 para 37.

[34] Case T-168/95R *Eridania v Council* [1995] ECR II-2817 para 27; Case T-219/95R *Danielsson v Commission* [1995] ECR II-3051 para 58; Case T-155/96R *Mainz v Commission* [1996] ECR II-1655 para 8.

[35] Case 142/87R *Belgium v Commission* [1987] ECR 2589 para 23; Case C-356/90R *Belgium v Commission* [1991] ECR I-2423 para 23.

[36] Case T-191/96R *Succhi di Frutta v Commission* [1997] ECR II-211 para 31.

[37] Case C-57/89R *Commission v Germany* [1989] ECR 2849 paras 16–18.

[38] [1987] ECR 2841 paras 10–13.

[39] Case C-149/95P(R) *Commission v Atlantic Container Line* [1995] ECR I-2163 para 38; Case C-130/95 *Giloy v Hauptzollamt Frankfurt am Main-Ost* [1997] ECR I-4291 para 39. The Court of First Instance appeared to adopt a stricter approach, for example, in Case T-41/97R *Antillean Rice Mills v Council* [1997] ECR II-447 paras 46 and 58, where the President refused to grant interim measures as the applicant had failed to establish that there was an 'undeniable risk of serious and irreversible harm'.

Serious and irreparable harm Except in exceptional circumstances, purely financial loss will not be regarded as irreparable where it could be remedied by financial compensation at a later date.[40] Financial loss may be considered serious and irreparable if, *inter alia*:

(1) it would lead to the winding-up[41] or dissolution[42] of a company;
(2) it would require an individual to sell certain property;[43]
(3) the damage, if it occurs, could not be quantified;[44] or
(4) compensation could not restore the applicant to the position he was in prior to the occurrence of the damage, for example, because the contested measure would bring about irremediable changes in market shares[45] or would defame the reputation of the applicant.[46]

The Court will not grant interim relief where the final judgment of the Court in relation to the main application is likely to be given before any serious harm could occur.[47] Furthermore, the Court is reluctant to conclude that an applicant will suffer serious and irreparable harm where it is within the applicant's own power to ensure that no such harm occurs. In Case T-19/91R *Vichy v Commission*[48] the Court of First Instance refused to suspend a decision of the Commission to withdraw Vichy's immunity from fines pending the Commission's investigation of its revised distribution system under the Community competition rules. The Court held that the Commission's decision did not cause serious and irreparable harm because Vichy could put an end to the risk of being fined at any time by not pursuing its revised distribution system.

A Member State may rely on national interests, especially economic and social interests, in seeking interim relief, for example, where there is a threat to employment levels or the cost of living.[49] However, a Member State may not

---

[40] Case 229/88R *Cargill v Commission* [1988] ECR 5183 paras 17–18; Case T-51/91R *Hoyer v Commission* [1991] ECR II-679 para 19; Case C-213/91R *Abertal v Commission* [1991] ECR I-5109 para 24; Case T-168/95R *Eridania v Council* [1995] ECR II-2817 para 42. The Court of First Instance has adopted a very restrictive approach to arguments that financial loss to an undertaking would constitute irreparable harm: see Case T-228/95R *Lehrfreund v Council and Commission* [1996] ECR II-111 paras 68–69; Case T-84/96R *Cipeke v Commission* [1996] ECR II-1313 paras 40–46; Case T-41/97R *Antillean Rice Mills v Council* [1997] ECR II-447 paras 47–58.

[41] Case 310/85R *Deufil v Commission* [1986] ECR 537 paras 23–25; Case 152/88R *Sofrimport v Commission* [1988] ECR 2931 paras 31–32; Cases C-51/90R and C-59/90R *Cosmos-Tank v Commission* [1990] ECR I-2167 para 24; Case C-130/95 *Giloy v Hauptzollamt Frankfurt am Main-Ost* [1997] ECR I-4291 paras 37–38.

[42] Case T-88/94R *SCPA and EMC v Commission* [1994] ECR II-401 para 33.

[43] Case C-130/95 *Giloy v Hauptzollamt Frankfurt am Main-Ost* [1997] ECR I-4291 paras 37–38.

[44] Cases C-51/90R and C-59/90R *Cosmos-Tank v Commission* [1990] ECR II-2167 para 24.

[45] Case C-195/90R *Commission v Germany* [1990] ECR I-3351 paras 38–40. See also Case 65/87R *Pfizer International v Commission* [1987] ECR 1691 paras 16–19.

[46] Case T-203/95R *Connolly v Commission* [1995] ECR II-2919 paras 41–42.

[47] Case C-225/91R *Matra v Commission* [1991] ECR I-5823 paras 22–25.

[48] [1991] ECR II-265 paras 15–20. Cf Case C-149/95P(R) *Commission v Atlantic Container Line* [1995] ECR I-2163 paras 41–43.

[49] Case C-280/93R *Germany v Council* [1993] ECR I-3667 paras 22–28; Case C-180/96R *United*

rely on financial harm to national undertakings unless it can show that this would cause damage to the national economy as a whole.[50] Furthermore, in Joined Cases C-239/96R and C-240/96R *United Kingdom v Commission*[51] the President of the Court of Justice held that the United Kingdom was entitled to rely on financial damage which might be suffered by the Community and all of the Member States taken as a whole as a result of the contested Commission act.

The Commission, as guardian of the EC Treaty, may seek interim relief in order to prevent a flagrant breach of Community law.[52] In Case C-246/89R *Commission v United Kingdom*[53] the Commission obtained interim relief requiring the United Kingdom to suspend the application of certain provisions of the Merchant Shipping Act 1988, on the grounds that the provisions discriminated against EC nationals on the basis of their nationality. The Commission was concerned that certain Spanish fishermen would become insolvent as a result of the adoption of the Act, which prevented them from registering their ships in the United Kingdom.

Disproportionate harm The criteria of urgency will also be satisfied where the immediate harm to the applicant (albeit of a provisional nature because it could be remedied after judgment) would be disproportionate to the interests of the institution in having its acts applied, even where they are being challenged before the courts.[54] Conversely, the nature of the interim relief sought must not be out of proportion to the defendant institution's interest in having its acts implemented.[55]

Balance of interests In certain cases, particularly where the grant or refusal of interim relief would have the practical effect of substantively deciding the action, the Court will balance the prejudice which one party will suffer if the relief is granted, against the prejudice which the other party will suffer if the relief is denied.[56] For example, in Case C-272/91R *Commission v Italy*[57] (an application for interim relief by the Commission), the Court balanced the

---

Kingdom v Commission [1996] ECR I-3903 para 85.

[50] Case 142/87R *Belgium v Commission* [1987] ECR 2589 para 24; Case 111/88R *Greece v Commission* [1988] ECR 2591 paras 13–19; Case 303/88R *Italy v Commission* [1989] ECR 801; Case C-32/89R *Greece v Commission* [1989] ECR 985 paras 16–18.

[51] [1996] ECR I-4475 paras 62–66.

[52] Case C-272/91R *Commission v Italy* [1992] ECR I-457 paras 25–29.

[53] [1989] ECR 3125 paras 34–38, part of the *Factortame* litigation.

[54] Case 174/80R *Reichardt v Commission* [1980] ECR 2665 para 1; Case 141/84R *De Compte v Parliament* [1984] ECR 2575 para 4; Case 44/88R *De Compte v Parliament* [1988] ECR 1669 para 31; Case 176/88R *Hanning v Parliament* [1988] ECR 3915 para 9; Case T-84/96R *Cipeke v Commission* [1996] ECR II-1313 para 39; Case T-155/96R *Mainz v Commission* [1996] ECR II-1655 para 19. See also Case T-41/96R *Bayer v Commission* [1996] ECR II-381 paras 53–62.

[55] Case T-146/95R *Bernardi v Parliament* [1995] ECR II-2255 para 19.

[56] Case 278/84R *Germany v Commission* [1984] ECR 4341 para 20; Case 293/85R *Commission v Belgium* [1985] ECR 3521 para 24; Case 194/88R *Commission v Italy* [1988] ECR 4547 para 16; Case C-358/90R *Compagnia Italiana Alcool v Commission* [1990] ECR I-4887 para 29; Case T-45/90R *Speybrouck v Parliament* [1990] ECR II-705 para 36; Joined Cases T-24/92 and T-28/92R *Langnese-Iglo and Schöller Lebensmittel v Commission* [1992] ECR II-1839 paras 26–30; Case T-29/92R *SPO v Commission* [1992] ECR II-2161 paras 37–39.

[57] [1992] ECR I-457 paras 25–29.

Commission's interest in preventing an infraction of Community law against the Italian State's interest in achieving a rapid automisation of the national lottery system. The Italian State argued that, if it was prevented from introducing the new system, illegal gambling would flourish and the State would suffer a substantial loss in revenue. The Court emphasised that, if it refused interim relief and the Commission was successful in the main action, the final judgment would be deprived of effect because it would not be possible to reverse the steps taken by the Italian State. Therefore, the Court found in favour of the Commission and ordered the Italian State to take 'all the necessary measures' to suspend the introduction of the new system.

In Case 45/87R *Commission v Ireland*[58] the Court of Justice refused to grant the interim relief sought by the Commission, even though it had established a *prima facie* case that Ireland was in breach of Community public procurement legislation. The Court held that the risk of aggravating existing health and safety hazards if the award of the contract at issue were delayed outweighed the Commission's interest in ensuring the observance of Community law. Similarly, in Case C-180/96R *United Kingdom v Commission*,[59] which concerned the ban on the export of British meat as a result of the BSE problem, the Court of Justice held that the serious harm to public health which was liable to be caused by suspension of the ban outweighed the damage to commercial and social interests likely to result from maintaining the ban in force.

In Joined Cases 76/89, 77/89 and 91/89R *RTE v Commission*,[60] a competition case, the Court took into account whether the grant or refusal of interim relief would have the practical effect of substantively deciding the action because the resultant position could not be reversed.

Security The granting of interim measures may be made conditional on the lodging of security by the applicant.[61] Generally, an applicant will only be ordered to provide security where it would be liable for the sums which the security is intended to cover and there is a risk of it becoming insolvent[62] or of otherwise having insufficient funds.[63]

However, where the measure being challenged is a decision imposing a fine, the Court will require the applicant to provide a bank guarantee in the amount of the fine as security pending resolution of the main action, unless the applicant can demonstrate that exceptional circumstances exist.[64] Exceptional circumstances will exist where the requirement to provide a bank guarantee would, in

---

[58] [1987] ECR 1369 paras 32–33.
[59] [1996] ECR I-3903 paras 89–94.
[60] [1989] ECR 1141 para 15. See also Case C-246/89R *Commission v United Kingdom* [1989] ECR 3125 paras 39–42; Case C-149/95P(R) *Commission v Atlantic Container Line* [1995] ECR I-2163 paras 48–52.
[61] ECJ Rules of Procedure, article 86(2); CFI Rules of Procedure, article 107(2).
[62] Case C-195/90R *Commission v Germany* [1990] ECR I-3351 paras 48–50. See also Case 160/84R *Oryzomyli Kavallas v Commission* [1984] ECR 3217, including para 14 of the Report for the Hearing.
[63] Case C-12/95P *Tramasa v Commission* [1995] ECR I-467 para 22.
[64] Case 107/82R *AEG v Commission* [1982] ECR 1549 (competition case); Case 86/82R

itself, cause the applicant serious and irreparable damage.[65] In assessing the ability of an undertaking to furnish a bank guarantee as security, regard must be had not only to the financial circumstances of that undertaking but also those of its shareholders and the group of undertakings to which it belongs.[66] In Case T-308/94R *Cascades v Commission*[67] the applicant was given a period of six months to provide a bank guarantee on condition, *inter alia*, that it provided the Commission with regular information concerning its financial position.

Voluntary undertaking The Court will not grant interim relief where a party voluntarily undertakes to adopt the measures necessary to preserve the *status quo* pending the final resolution of the action.[68]

Anti-dumping cases Where an applicant is seeking to suspend the application of an anti-dumping duty, it must adduce evidence showing, first, that the damage suffered by it as a result of the imposition of the duty is particular to it and, secondly, that the balance of interests is in its favour, in the sense that the grant of the interim measures requested would not cause appreciable harm to the Community industry.[69] It is not sufficient merely to rely on the effects which are inherent in the imposition of anti-dumping duties, that is, a rise in the price of the product affected by the duty and a corresponding diminution in the share of the Community market.[70]

If the Court does decide to grant interim measures, this will generally be made conditional on the provision of security by the applicant equivalent to the amount of duty which would be due from it under the contested measure.[71]

3. PROCEDURE

Application The Rules of Procedure provide that an application for interim relief must be made by a party to a case before the Court.[72] This indicates that an

Hasselblad (GB) v Commission [1982] ECR 1555 (competition case); Case 263/82R *Klöckner-Werke v Commission* [1982] ECR 3995 (ECSC); Case 392/85R *Finisider v Commission* [1986] ECR 959 paras 12–19 (ECSC); Case 213/86R *Montedipe v Commission* [1986] ECR 2623 (competition case); Case T-104/95R *Chalkidos v Commission* [1995] ECR II-2235 paras 18–25 (competition case).

[65] For example, see Case 234/82R *Ferriere di Roè Volciano v Commission* [1983] ECR 725 (ECSC); Case T-18/96R *SCK and FNK v Commission* [1996] ECR II-407 paras 31–40. Cf Case 392/85R *Finisider v Commission* [1986] ECR 959 paras 14–19 (ECSC).

[66] Case T-295/94R *Buchmann v Commission* [1994] ECR II-1265 para 26; Case T-308/94R *Cascades v Commission* [1995] ECR II-265 paras 41–55; Case C-12/95P *Tramasa v Commission* [1995] ECR I-467 para 12.

[67] [1995] ECR II-265 para 56 (competition case).

[68] Case 45/84R *EISA v Commission* [1984] ECR 1759 paras 11–14; Case 64/86R *Sergio v Commission* [1986] ECR 1081 para 9; Case 322/87R *Frank v Court of Auditors* [1987] ECR 4375 para 19; Case C-40/92R *Commission v United Kingdom* [1992] ECR I-3389. See also Case C-385/89R *Greece v Commission* [1990] ECR I-561.

[69] Case 77/87R *Technointorg v Council* [1987] ECR 1793 para 17.

[70] Case C-6/94R *Descom v Council* [1994] ECR I-867 para 16.

[71] Case T-2/95R *Industrie des poudres sphériques v Council* [1995] ECR II-485 para 35.

[72] ECJ Rules of Procedure, article 83(1); CFI Rules of Procedure, article 104(1).

application for interim relief may not be made before the application in the main action has been lodged with the Court. However, it is permissible to lodge the application for interim measures at the same time as the main application.

An application for interim measures must be made by lodging a separate document in accordance with the general rules for written applications.[73] Any application for interim measures which is made in the main application to the Court rather than by a separate document will be declared inadmissible.[74] The application for interim measures should be a self-contained document, providing the information necessary to decide the interlocutory application without referring to the main application. However, in view of the need for urgency and rapid translation, the application should be drafted succinctly.[75]

The application must state:[76]

(1) the name and permanent address of the applicant;
(2) an address for service in Luxembourg and the name of the person authorised to accept service;[77]
(3) the identity of the defendant;
(4) the subject-matter of the proceedings, the circumstances giving rise to urgency and the pleas of fact and law establishing a *prima facie* case for the interim measures applied for;[78]
(5) the form of order sought by the applicant;
(6) where appropriate, the nature of any evidence offered in support;
(7) a claim for costs.

The original of the application must be signed by the party's agent or lawyer[79] and should be dated.

Relief sought It is possible to seek relief under both articles 185 and 186 [new arts 242 and 243] in the same application. However, the applicant must specify the nature of the relief which he is seeking, stating alternatives where appropriate. A general request for 'such further or other relief as the Court deems necessary or appropriate' will be declared inadmissible.[80]

---

[73] ECJ Rules of Procedure, article 83(3); CFI Rules of Procedure, article 104(3). The general rules applicable to written applications are discussed at p 523.

[74] Case T-146/95 *Bernardi v Parliament* [1996] ECR II-769 paras 29–30; confirmed on appeal in Case C-303/96P *Bernardi v Parliament* [1997] ECR I-1239 paras 30–31 and 47. See also Case T-107/94 *Kik v Council and Commission* [1995] ECR II-1717 para 38.

[75] *Notes for the guidance of Counsel in written and oral proceedings before the Court of Justice*, p 564.

[76] ECJ Rules of Procedure, article 38; CFI Rules of Procedure, article 44.

[77] It is usual to instruct a lawyer in Luxembourg for this purpose. If no address for service is given, pleadings are sent by registered post to counsel for the party concerned: see *Notes for the guidance of Counsel in written and oral proceedings before the Court of Justice*, p 561.

[78] ECJ Rules of Procedure, article 83(2); CFI Rules of Procedure, article 104(2).

[79] The application should also give a description of the signatory (Statute of the Court of Justice, article 19), for example, 'barrister'.

[80] Case T-228/95R *Lehrfreund v Council and Commission* [1996] ECR II-111 para 58.

Annexes The following documents should be annexed to the application:[81]

(1) A file containing the documents relied on as evidence, together with a schedule listing them.

(2) A certificate establishing that the lawyer acting for the applicant is entitled to act before a court of a Member State or of a State which is a party to the EEA Agreement.[82]

(3) Where the applicant is 'a legal person governed by private law', for example a company:

    (*a*) proof of its existence in law (for an English company, copies of the memorandum and articles of association or an extract from the Companies Register); and

    (*b*) proof that the applicant's lawyer is properly authorised to act (for example, a resolution of the board of directors or a declaration sworn before a notary).[83]

(4) In applications under article 173 [new art 230], a copy of the act challenged.[84]

(5) In applications under article 175 [new art 232], documentary evidence of the date on which the relevant institution was called upon to act.[85]

(6) In applications under article 181 or 182 [new arts 238 and 239], a copy of the relevant arbitration clause or special agreement (in the Court of Justice) or a copy of the contract which contains the arbitration clause (in the Court of First Instance).[86]

Lodging with the Court The original of the application for interim measures, including annexes, should be lodged with the Registrar of the Court of Justice or Court of First Instance, as appropriate, together with five certified copies for the Court and a copy for every other party to the proceedings.[87] Documents may be lodged with the security officers at the entrances to the Court buildings at any time of the day or night.[88] As the Rules of Procedure require that the original of the application must be signed by a party's agent or lawyer, the application may not be lodged with the Registry by fax.[89]

Applications for interim relief are allotted the case number of the main application with the suffix 'R', for example, 'Case C-272/91R'.

---

[81] Statute of the Court of Justice, article 19; ECJ Rules of Procedure, articles 37–38; CFI Rules of Procedure, articles 43–44.

[82] A copy of the Lawyer's Professional Identity Card (issued by the CCBE) is accepted for this purpose. A lawyer is not required to lodge a certificate each time he appears before the Court of Justice or the Court of First Instance. Each Registry is prepared to make reference to a certificate lodged in a previous case before that Court: CFI Instructions to Registrar, article 7(2).

[83] A lawyer representing a natural person is not required to provide proof of his authority to act when lodging the application, but must be able to provide such proof if his authority to act is challenged. See Case 14/64 *Gualco v High Authority* [1965] ECR 51 at 57 (ECSC).

[84] Statute of the Court of Justice, article 19.

[85] Ibid.

[86] ECJ Rules of Procedure, article 38(6); CFI Rules of Procedure, article 44(5a).

[87] ECJ Rules of Procedure, article 37; CFI Rules of Procedure, article 43.

[88] ECJ Instructions to Registrar, article 1(1); CFI Instructions to Registrar, article 2(3).

[89] CFI Instructions to Registrar, articles 6(3) and 10(3).

Subsequent procedure The application is served by the Registrar on the other parties concerned, and the President then prescribes a short period within which those parties may submit written or oral observations.[90] Although the President has power to order a preparatory inquiry, this is rarely done.[91] It is normal for an oral hearing to be held before any decision is made.[92]

Where there is extreme urgency, the President may grant the application even before the observations of the opposite party have been submitted or heard. Such a decision may be varied or cancelled without any application being made by any party.[93]

Order/judgment The President may decide the application himself or refer it to the Court.[94] Unless the decision specifies a date on which the order is to lapse, the order will lapse only when final judgment is delivered.[95] However, a party may apply, at any time, for an order to be varied or cancelled on account of a change in circumstances.[96] Furthermore, where an application for interim measures is rejected, the party who made it is not precluded from making a further application on the basis of new facts.[97]

Effect of order/judgment In *R v Secretary of State for Transport, ex p Factortame Limited*[98] the English Divisional Court analysed the effect of an order of the President of the Court of Justice granting interim measures in the following terms:

> ... it is an Order which is expressed in mandatory terms and which takes immediate effect. Under Community law the Order of the President has the same force and direct effect as any other order of the court or provision of Community law. The Order has direct effect. It must immediately be complied with by the party to which it is addressed (the United Kingdom) and the agencies of that party and failure to do so is a breach of Community law.

Costs The question of costs will normally be reserved until the final judgment. Any interlocutory application or response should contain a separate

---

[90] ECJ Rules of Procedure, article 84(1); CFI Rules of Procedure, article 105(1). In the Court of Justice, parties are usually given approximately one month to submit written observations in response to the application (see *Notes for the guidance of Counsel in written and oral proceedings before the Court of Justice*, reproduced at Appendix E, p 555).

[91] ECJ Rules of Procedure, article 84(2); CFI Rules of Procedure, article 105(2).

[92] For a brief description of the form of such hearings, see *Notes for the guidance of Counsel in written and oral proceedings before the Court of Justice* (reproduced at Appendix E, p 555). Lawyers are not required to wear robes at hearings for interim measures: ibid p 570.

[93] ECJ Rules of Procedure, article 84(2); CFI Rules of Procedure, article 105(2). For the procedure followed in the Court of Justice in such cases, see *Notes for the guidance of Counsel in written and oral proceedings before the Court of Justice* (reproduced at Appendix E, p 555). See also Case 45/87R *Commission v Ireland* [1987] ECR 783; Case C-195/90R *Commission v Germany* [1990] ECR I-2715; Case C-110/97R *Netherlands v Council* [1997] ECR I-1795 paras 27–30 and 33.

[94] ECJ Rules of Procedure, article 85; CFI Rules of Procedure, article 106.

[95] ECJ Rules of Procedure, article 86(3); CFI Rules of Procedure, article 107(3).

[96] ECJ Rules of Procedure, article 87; CFI Rules of Procedure, article 108. Case C-272/91R *Commission v Italy* [1992] ECR I-3929; Case T-104/95R *Chalkidos v Commission* [1995] ECR II-2235 para 26.

[97] ECJ Rules of Procedure, article 88; CFI Rules of Procedure, article 109.

[98] [1997] EuLR 475 at 523G.

claim for costs in the written pleadings. Failure to claim costs will mean that the Court will be obliged to award all of the costs to the successful party in the final judgment, without taking separate account of the outcome of any interlocutory applications.[99]

4. APPEALS

Availability/time-limits No appeal lies from a decision of the Court of Justice. However, parties may appeal to the Court against any judgment of the Court of First Instance concerning interim measures, within two months of the notification of the judgment to them.[100]

Application for appeal An appeal is brought by lodging an application with the Registry of the Court of Justice or the Registry of the Court of First Instance.[101] The appeal must include:[102]

 (1) the name and permanent address of the appellant;
 (2) an address for service in Luxembourg and the name of the person authorised to accept service;[103]
 (3) the names of the other parties to the proceedings before the Court of First Instance;
 (4) the date on which the decision appealed against was notified to the appellant;
 (5) the pleas in law and legal arguments relied on;[104]
 (6) the form of order sought by the appellant, either:
   (*a*) to set aside, in whole or in part, the decision of the Court of First Instance; or
   (*b*) the same form of order, in whole or in part, as that sought at first instance. The appeal may not seek a different form of order;[105]
 (7) a claim for costs.

Annexes The following documents should be annexed to the appeal:[106]

 (1) the decision of the Court of First Instance appealed against;
 (2) a certificate establishing that the lawyer acting for the appellant is entitled to act before a court of a Member State or of a State which is a party to the EEA Agreement.

---

[99] Case T-50/89 *Sparr v Commission* [1990] ECR II-539 para 9.

[100] Statute of the Court of Justice, article 50.

[101] ECJ Rules of Procedure, article 111.

[102] Ibid, article 112.

[103] It is usual to instruct a lawyer in Luxembourg for this purpose. The giving of an address for service is optional. If no address for service is given, pleadings are sent by registered post to counsel for the party concerned (see *Notes for the guidance of Counsel in written and oral proceedings before the Court of Justice*, reproduced at Appendix E, p 555).

[104] An appeal which fails to set out the grounds of appeal relied on in a coherent and comprehensible statement will be dismissed as inadmissible: Case C-78/97P(R) *Goldstein v Commission* (unreported, order of 10 March 1997) paras 20–24.

[105] ECJ Rules of Procedure, article 113.

[106] Ibid, article 112.

Grounds of appeal Appeals concerning interim measures are limited to points of law and may not call into question the way in which the Court of First Instance assessed facts.[107] Thus, an appeal will lie only on grounds of lack of competence of the Court of First Instance, a breach of procedure which adversely affected the interests of the appellants, or an error of Community law.[108]

In Case C-149/95P(R) *Commission v Atlantic Container Line*[109] the Commission argued that the interim measures granted by the President of the Court of First Instance were disproportionate. This was rejected by the President of the Court of Justice on the basis that the measures ordered were not *manifestly* disproportionate. This suggests that the Court of Justice will be reluctant simply to substitute its view of what is appropriate and will only interfere where the order of the Court of First Instance is obviously flawed.

In giving its reasons for its decision, the Court of First Instance is not required to reply explicitly to all the points of fact and law raised in the course of the interlocutory proceedings before it. It is sufficient that the reasons given justify the order in the circumstances of the case and enable the Court of Justice to exercise its powers of review.[110]

Order/judgment Appeals in respect of applications for interim relief may be decided by the President of the Court in accordance with the summary procedure applicable when an application for interim relief is made directly to the Court of Justice in a case pending before it.[111] If the appeal is well founded, the Court of Justice may decide the application for interim measures itself, or may refer the case back to the Court of First Instance.[112] Where an appeal is clearly inadmissible or unfounded, the Court of Justice may dismiss it by reasoned order at any time.[113]

---

[107] Case C-149/95P(R) *Commission v Atlantic Container Line* [1995] ECR I-2163 paras 16–18 and 39. Statute of the Court of Justice, article 51.

[108] Case C-268/96P(R) *SCK and FNK v Commission* [1996] ECR I-4971 paras 43–44; EC Treaty, article 168a [new art 225]; Statute of the Court of Justice, article 51.

[109] [1995] ECR I-2163 paras 54–56.

[110] Case C-149/95P(R) *Commission v Atlantic Container Line* [1995] ECR I-2163 paras 57–58; Case C-148/96P(R) *Goldstein v Commission* [1996] ECR I-3883 para 25; Case C-268/96P(R) *SCK and FNK v Commission* [1996] ECR I-4971 para 52.

[111] Statute of the Court of Justice, article 50; ECJ Rules of Procedure, articles 84–86 and 89. The relevant procedure is described above at pp 384–386.

[112] Case C-393/96P(R) *Antonissen v Council and Commission* [1997] ECR I-441 paras 44–45; Statute of the Court of Justice, article 54.

[113] Case C-78/97P(R) *Goldstein v Commission* (unreported, order of 10 March 1997) paras 11–13 ECJ Rules of Procedure, article 119.

5. POWERS OF THE COMMISSION

Powers of the Commission The Commission has the power to adopt interim measures in relation to competition[114] and State aid matters.[115] In relation to competition matters, interim measures may be adopted where there is a *prima facie* breach of the competition rules and where interim measures are required, as a matter of urgency, in order to avoid a situation likely to cause serious and irreparable damage to the party seeking their adoption, or which is intolerable in the public interest. The measures adopted must be of a temporary nature, designed to preserve the *status quo*, and restricted to what is necessary to ensure that the Commission's final decision is not deprived of any practical effect. Therefore, interim measures must not go beyond what can be ordered in the final decision. When adopting interim measures the Commission must respect the essential safeguards accorded to parties under Regulation 17/62,[116] in particular, the right to be heard. Decisions granting or refusing interim measures must be made in such a form as to be amenable to review by the EC courts.[117] The EC courts will not entertain applications for interim relief with which the Commission has primary jurisdiction to deal. In such cases, the role of the EC courts is limited to judicial review of any such decisions adopted by the Commission.[118]

---

[114] See Bellamy and Child, *The Common Market Law of Competition*, 4th edn (Sweet & Maxwell, 1993), pp 740–743; Kerse, *EC Antitrust Procedure*, 3rd edn (Sweet & Maxwell, 1994), pp 191–200.

[115] Case T-107/96R *Pantochim v Commission* [1996] ECR II-1361 paras 32–45.

[116] Council Regulation 17/62 of 6 February 1962, First Regulation implementing articles 85, 86 of the EEC Treaty (OJ 1962 13 p 204) (English Special Edition, OJ 1962 p 87) (as amended).

[117] Case 792/79R *Camera Care v Commission* [1980] ECR 119 paras 18–20; Joined Cases 228/82 and 229/82 *Ford of Europe v Commission* [1984] ECR 1129; Case T-23/90 *Peugeot v Commission* [1991] ECR II-653; Case T-44/90 *La Cinq v Commission* [1992] ECR II-1.

[118] Case 792/79R *Camera Care v Commission* [1980] ECR 119 paras 20–21; Case T-23/90R *Peugeot v Commission* [1990] ECR II-195; Case T-322/94R *Union Carbide v Commission* [1994] ECR II-1159 paras 26–27. See also Case 109/75R *National Carbonising Co v Commission* [1975] ECR 1193.

Chapter 18

Procedure Before the EC Courts

1. THE COURT OF JUSTICE AND THE COURT OF FIRST INSTANCE

Role of the Court Article 164 of the EC Treaty [new art 220] provides that:

The Court of Justice shall ensure that in the interpretation and application of this Treaty the law is observed.

Procedural rules The composition, organisation and procedure of the EC courts are governed by the Statute of the Court of Justice (EC)[1] and by the Rules of Procedure of the Court of Justice[2] and of the Court of First Instance.[3] The Rules of Procedure are substantially the same for both Courts.[4] The Rules of Procedure are supplemented by the Instructions to the Registrar of the Court of Justice[5] and the Instructions to the Registrar of the Court of First Instance.[6]

Guidance to parties The Court of Justice has issued a document entitled *Notes for the guidance of counsel in written and oral proceedings before the Court of Justice of the European Communities.*[7] The Court of First Instance has issued documents entitled *Advice for lawyers and agents regarding the written procedure before the Court of First Instance*[8] and *Notes for the guidance of counsel for the parties at the hearing of oral argument.*[9] In addition, parties may

---

[1] Protocol on the Statute of the Court of Justice of the European Economic Community, signed at Brussels on 17 April 1957, as amended. A consolidated version of the EC Statute of the Court of Justice is reproduced in Appendix B.

[2] Rules of Procedure of the Court of Justice of the European Communities of 19 June 1991 (OJ 1991 L176 p 7) (corrigendum in OJ 1992 L383 p 117). A consolidated version is reproduced in Appendix C.

[3] Rules of Procedure of the Court of First Instance of the European Communities of 2 May 1991 (OJ 1991 L136 p 1) (corrigendum in OJ 1991 L317 p 34). A consolidated version is reproduced in Appendix D.

[4] For a comprehensive review of procedure before the Court of Justice, see KPE Lasok, *The European Court of Justice, Practice and Procedure*, 2nd edn (Butterworths, 1993); and R Plender, *European Courts Practice and Precedents* (Sweet & Maxwell, 1997).

[5] OJ 1982 L39 p 35.

[6] OJ 1994 L78 p 32.

[7] Reproduced at Appendix E.

[8] OJ 1994 C120 p 16. Reproduced at Appendix F.

[9] Reproduced at Appendix G.

contact the Registry of either Court to seek advice as to the appropriate practice to be followed.[10]

Court of Justice[11] The Court of Justice consists of 15 judges and nine Advocates-General.[12] The Court of Justice sits in plenary session (of 15 or 11) or in chambers of three or five judges. The Court of Justice must sit in plenary session when it is requested to do so by a Member State or Community institution which is a party to the proceedings.[13] Only one Advocate-General sits in each case.[14] The function of the Advocate-General is to present reasoned submissions to the Court in the form of an Opinion, in order to assist the Court in reaching its judgment.[15] The Opinion is not binding in any way on the Court.[16]

Court of First Instance In view of the increasing workload of the Court of Justice, the Single European Act empowered the Council to create a Court of First Instance attached to the Court of Justice.[17] The Court of First Instance has 15 judges. There are no permanent Advocates-General, although one of the judges may be called upon to perform the task of Advocate-General in a particular case. The Court of First Instance usually sits in chambers of three or five judges, although it may sit in plenary session.[18] The Court of First Instance must assign a case to a chamber of five judges where this is requested by a Member State or a Community institution which is a party to the proceedings.[19] Decisions of the Court of First Instance are subject to appeals to the Court of Justice.[20]

A judgment of the Court of First Instance becomes definitive when either the time for appeal has expired without an appeal being lodged or, if an appeal is lodged, from the date of the judgment rejecting the appeal.[21]

The Court of First Instance is only bound by judgments of the Court of Justice, first, where the Court of Justice quashes a decision of the Court of First Instance on appeal and refers the case back to the latter court for judgment and, secondly, pursuant to the principle of *res judicata*.[22] However, in practice the

---

[10] CFI Instructions to Registrar, article 18(3).
[11] See David Edward, 'How the Court of Justice Works' (1995) 20 EL Rev 539.
[12] Article 165 of the EC Treaty [new art 221]. From 6 October 2000 there will be eight Advocates-General.
[13] Article 165 of the EC Treaty; ECJ Rules of Procedure, article 95.
[14] Except where the Court of Justice is requested to give an Opinion under article 228 of the EC Treaty. See ECJ Rules of Procedure, article 108(2).
[15] Article 166 of the EC Treaty [new art 222].
[16] See further at Ch 1, p 20.
[17] Article 168a of the EC Treaty [new art 225], added by article 11 of the Single European Act. The Court of First Instance was established by Council Decision 88/591 of 24 October 1988 (OJ 1989 C215 p 1). The President of the Court of Justice issued a decision dated 11 October 1989, declaring that the Court of First Instance had been duly established (OJ 1989 L317 p 48).
[18] Article 2 of Council Decision 88/591 of 24 October 1988 (OJ 1989 C215 p 1); CFI Rules of Procedure, articles 10–19. See also Decision laying down criteria for allocating cases between the Chambers (OJ 1994 C304 p 14).
[19] CFI Rules of Procedure, article 51(2).
[20] See below at pp 417–423.
[21] Case T-61/92 *De Compte v Parliament* [1995] ECR-SC II-449 para 16 (staff case).
[22] Case T-162/94 *NMB v Commission* [1996] ECR II-427 para 36. The principle of *res judicata* is

Court of First Instance does follow judgments of the Court of Justice, presumably in view of the automatic right of appeal to that Court.

President of the Court The judges of each Court elect a President from their number, who is responsible for the overall administration of that Court.[23]

Jurisdiction The Court of First Instance has jurisdiction to hear actions by natural or legal persons under articles 173, 175, 178 and 181 [new arts 230, 232, 235 and 238][24] of the EC Treaty and staff cases under article 179 [new art 236].[25] Such actions must be brought before the Court of First Instance, not the Court of Justice. The Court of First Instance is not competent to hear questions referred for a preliminary ruling under article 177 of the EC Treaty [new art 234];[26] nor has it been granted jurisdiction to hear actions brought by Member States or Community institutions.[27] Such actions and all requests for preliminary references must therefore be brought before the Court of Justice.

Where the Court of First Instance is seised of a matter in which it has no jurisdiction, it must transfer the matter to the Court of Justice if that Court does have jurisdiction.[28] Where an action which is within the jurisdiction of the Court of First Instance is brought before the Court of Justice, the Court of Justice must refer that action to the Court of First Instance.[29]

Where the Court of Justice and the Court of First Instance are seised of cases in which the same relief is sought, or the same issue of interpretation is raised, or the validity of the same act is challenged, the Court of First Instance may, after hearing the parties, stay the proceedings before it until the Court of Justice has delivered judgment. Equally, the Court of Justice is entitled to stay the proceedings before it to allow the proceedings before the Court of First Instance to continue. Where the validity of the same act is challenged before both Courts, the Court of First Instance may choose to decline jurisdiction to allow the Court of Justice to rule on the matter (rather than merely staying the action before it).[30]

---

dealt with below at p 392.

[23] ECJ Rules of Procedure, articles 7 and 8; CFI Rules of Procedure, articles 7 and 8.

[24] The Court of First Instance has jurisdiction in relation to actions brought under article 181 only where the contract was concluded after 1 August 1993. See article 3 of Council Decision 93/350 of 8 June 1993 (OJ 1993 L144 p 21).

[25] Article 3 of Council Decision 88/591 of 24 October 1988 (OJ 1989 C215 p 1); as substituted by Council Decision 93/350 of 8 June 1993 (OJ 1993 L144 p 21), as amended by Council Decision 94/149 of 7 March 1994 (OJ 1994 L66 p 29).

[26] Article 168a of the EC Treaty.

[27] Article 168a was amended by the Maastricht Treaty to give the Council (at the request of the Court of Justice) power to grant the Court of First Instance jurisdiction over actions brought by Member States and Community institutions. This power has not yet been exercised.

[28] Statute of the Court of Justice, article 47; CFI Rules of Procedure, article 112. See also Case C-72/90 *Asia Motor France v Commission* [1990] ECR I-2181 paras 16–21.

[29] Statute of the Court of Justice, article 47. See, for example, Case C-66/90 *PTT v Commission* [1991] ECR I-2723; Case C-95/97 *Région Wallonne v Commission* [1997] ECR I-1787.

[30] Statute of the Court of Justice, article 47. ECJ Rules of Procedure, article 82a; CFI Rules of Procedure, articles 77–80. For an example, see Case T-42/91 *PTT v Commission* [1991] ECR II-273.

Burden of proof The general rule is that it is for a party who seeks to rely on a particular fact to identify and produce the evidence which is necessary to establish the truth of that fact.[31]

Lis pendens Where the parties, subject-matter and submissions in two actions before the same Court are the same, the second action will be declared inadmissible.[32] The Court may raise the issue of *lis pendens* of its own motion.[33]

Res judicata The principle of *res judicata* is applicable to proceedings before the EC courts.[34] Thus, an action will be dismissed where the issues raised have been the subject of a previous judgment in proceedings which were between the same parties, had the same purpose and were based on the same submissions.[35] It follows that a judgment has the authority of *res judicata* only as between the parties to the proceedings which gave rise to that judgment.[36]

The principle applies only to matters of fact and law actually or necessarily settled by a judicial decision; it does not extend to arguments which could have been, but were not, put forward by the parties.[37] The EC courts may take into account the existence of *res judicata* of their own motion at any stage in the proceedings.[38]

2. PROCEDURE IN DIRECT ACTIONS

(a) General rules

Direct actions Direct actions, as their title suggests, are actions which may be brought directly before the EC courts without first commencing proceedings before a national court. The main types of direct actions are infraction proceedings against Member States under article 169 [new art 226], actions for annulment under article 173 [new art 230], actions for failure to act under article 175 [new art 232] and actions for damages under article 215 [new art 288]. In

---

[31] Paragraph 26 of the Opinion of Advocate-General Tesauro in Case C-362/95P *Blackspur DIY v Council and Commission* [1997] ECR I-4775. For a discussion of the different senses in which the term is used and its application in the EC Courts see Brealey 'The Burden of Proof before the European Court' (1985) 10 E. L. Rev 250.

[32] For example, see Joined Cases 358/85 and 51/86 *France v Parliament* [1988] ECR 4821 paras 6–12.

[33] Joined Cases 58/72 and 75/72 *Perinciolo v Council* [1973] ECR 511 para 5 (staff case); Case T-99/95 *Stott v Commission* [1996] ECR-SC II-2227 paras 22–24 (staff case).

[34] Joined Cases 79/63 and 82/63 *Reynier v Commission* [1964] ECR 259 at 266 (staff case); Case C-303/96P *Bernardi v Parliament* [1997] ECR I-1239 para 43.

[35] Joined Cases 159/84, 267/84, 12/85 and 264/85 *Ainsworth v Commission* [1987] ECR 1579 (staff case); T-162/94 *NMB v Commission* [1996] ECR II-427 para 37; Joined Cases T-177/94 and T-377/94 *Altmann v Commission* [1996] ECR II-2041 para 50 (staff case).

[36] Joined Cases C-151/97P(I) and C-157/97P(I) *National Power and PowerGen* [1997] ECR I-3491 para 73 (ECSC).

[37] C–281/89 *Italy v Commission* [1991] ECR I-347 paras 12–16; Case C-277/95P *Lenz v Commission* [1996] ECR I-6109 para 50.

[38] Paragraph 24 of the Opinion of Advocate-General Jacobs of 4 May 1994 in Case C-312/93 *Peterbroeck v Belgium* [1995] ECR I-4599.

contrast, references for preliminary rulings under article 177 [new art 234] come to the Court of Justice via proceedings which are already before the national courts.[39]

The Court of Justice has held that the provisions of the EC Treaty regarding the right of interested parties to bring an action before the EC courts should not be interpreted restrictively. Where the Treaty is silent on a point, the Court will not apply the relevant provisions in a way which imposes a limitation on that right.[40]

Special rules of procedure apply to cases before the Court of First Instance in proceedings brought against the Office for Harmonization in the Internal Market (Trade Marks and Designs) and against the Community Plant Variety Office.[41]

Rights of audience Private parties must be represented by a lawyer entitled to practise before a court of a Member State or of a State which is a party to the European Economic Area Agreement ('EEA Agreement'). A private party is not entitled to act in person in direct actions before the EC courts, even if he is authorised to plead before a national court or is a lawyer.[42] The Member States and the Community institutions are represented by agents appointed for each case.[43]

Language of the case The written and oral pleadings must be in the language of the case, as defined by the Rules of Procedure.[44] The language of the case must be chosen from one of the official Community languages, plus Irish.[45] Generally, the applicant may choose the language of the case.[46] However, in the Court of Justice, where the defendant is a Member State or a national of a Member State, the language of the case will be the official language of that State.[47] A Member State which intervenes in a case is entitled to use its own official language, in both the written and oral procedures.[48]

The EC courts may authorise the use of a different language at the joint request of the parties.[49] In addition, a particular party (including an intervener[50]) may apply to the Court to use a language which is different from the designated language of the case.[51] Any application must be accompanied by a detailed and

---

[39] The procedural rules which apply to preliminary rulings are discussed at Ch 11, pp 232–238.
[40] Case 25/62 *Plaumann v Commission* [1963] ECR 95 at 107; Case C-399/95R *Germany v Commission* [1996] ECR I-2441 para 45 (ECSC).
[41] CFI Rules of Procedure, articles 130–136.
[42] Case C-174/96P *Lopes v Court of Justice* [1996] ECR I-6401 paras 8–12.
[43] Statute of the Court of Justice, article 17.
[44] ECJ Rules of Procedure, articles 29–31; CFI Rules of Procedure, articles 35–37.
[45] ECJ Rules of Procedure, article 29(1); CFI Rules of Procedure, article 35(1).
[46] ECJ Rules of Procedure, article 29(2); CFI Rules of Procedure, article 35(2).
[47] ECJ Rules of Procedure, article 29(2)(*a*).
[48] ECJ Rules of Procedure, article 29(3); CFI Rules of Procedure, article 35(3).
[49] ECJ Rules of Procedure, article 29(2)(*b*); CFI Rules of Procedure, article 35(2)(*a*).
[50] Case T-290/94 *Kaysersberg v Commission* [1995] ECR II-2247.
[51] ECJ Rules of Procedure, article 29(2)(*c*); CFI Rules of Procedure, article 35(2)(*b*).

specific statement of reasons explaining why the derogation sought is necessary.[52]

Any supporting documents expressed in another language must be accompanied by a translation into the language of the case. In the case of lengthy documents, translations may be limited to extracts.[53] The EC courts will permit derogations from the rule requiring documents to be produced in the language of the case only in exceptional circumstances.[54]

Internal working language of the EC courts For reasons of procedural efficiency, the internal working language of the EC courts is French. All written pleadings must therefore be translated into French by the EC courts' translation service. Parties should bear this in mind when drafting pleadings and should endeavour to make them as concise and clear as possible. The Community institutions provide their own translations.

Lodging with the Court The original of all pleadings should be signed by the party's agent or lawyer[55] and should be dated. The original, including annexes, should be lodged with the appropriate Registrar, together with five certified copies for the Court and a copy for every other party to the proceedings.[56] All pleadings and correspondence with the Court should be sent to the Registrar of the Court of Justice or the Court of First Instance, as appropriate (and not to any individual judge or judges).[57] Documents may be lodged with the security officers at the entrances to the Court buildings at any time of the day or night.[58]

Where the Rules of Procedure require that the original of a pleading be signed by a party's agent or lawyer, that pleading may not be lodged with the Registry by fax.[59] This applies, *inter alia*, to originating applications, applications to intervene and appeals.[60]

Costs All applications, of whatever nature, should include a claim for costs. Failure to claim costs will mean that a party will have to bear his own costs, even if his application is successful.[61] However, it is not essential for the claim for costs to be made in the original application; it is sufficient if

---

[52] Case T-121/95 *EFMA v Council* [1997] ECR II-87.

[53] ECJ Rules of Procedure, article 29(3); CFI Rules of Procedure, article 35(3).

[54] Case T-11/95 *BP Chemicals v Commission* [1996] ECR II-599 paras 9–12.

[55] The application should also give a description of the signatory (Statute of the Court of Justice, article 19), for example 'barrister'.

[56] ECJ Rules of Procedure, article 37; CFI Rules of Procedure, article 43.

[57] Addresses: Registrar, Court of Justice of the European Communities, L–2925 Luxembourg; Registrar, Court of First Instance of the European Communities, L–2925 Luxembourg.

[58] ECJ Instructions to Registrar, article 1(1); CFI Instructions to Registrar, article 2(3).

[59] Ibid, articles 6(3) and 10(3).

[60] Case T-194/95(Intv II) *Area Cova v Council* [1996] ECR II-343 para 4 (an application to intervene). Certain communications with the Registry may be permitted by fax; for example, see Case T-395/94R *Atlantic Container Line v Commission* [1995] ECR II-595 para 6. Whenever there is a doubt, the party concerned should contact the Registry to verify whether service by fax is acceptable.

[61] ECJ Rules of Procedure, article 69(2); CFI Rules of Procedure, article 87(2). Case T-50/89 *Sparr v Commission* [1990] ECR II-539 para 9 (interlocutory applications).

it is made in subsequent written pleadings or at the oral hearing.[62]

Time-limits Detailed rules for reckoning periods of time are set out in the Rules of Procedure.[63] Time periods include official holidays, Sundays and Saturdays, and are not suspended during judicial vacations. However, if a time period ends on a Saturday, Sunday or official holiday[64] it is automatically extended to the end of the first following working day. A general extension of ten days exists for parties who are habitually resident in the United Kingdom[65] to take account of distance.[66] In addition, where the period of time allowed for initiating proceedings against a measure adopted by an institution runs from the publication of that measure, that period is calculated from the end of the fourteenth day after the publication of the measure in the *Official Journal.*[67] Time-limits cease to run when proceedings have been stayed by the EC courts, save in respect of applications to intervene in the Court of First Instance.[68] Time-limits before the EC courts are governed exclusively by Community law, and a party is not entitled to rely on provisions as to time under national law in cases before these courts.[69]

The EC courts apply the relevant time-limits very strictly in order to preserve legal certainty[70] and, if necessary, they will consider, of their own motion, whether the time-limits prescribed for bringing actions have been complied with.[71] The courts do not have a general discretion to extend the mandatory time-limits set down by the EC Treaty or Rules of Procedure.[72] It is the responsibility of the party alleging that an application is out of time to prove the date on which the measure was notified.[73]

---

[62] Case T-13/92 *Moat v Commission* [1993] ECR II-287 para 50; Joined Cases T-70/92 and T-71/92 *Florimex v Commission* [1997] ECR II-693 para 197.

[63] ECJ Rules of Procedure, articles 80–82; CFI Rules of Procedure, articles 101–103. See Case T-125/89 *Filtrona v Commission* [1990] ECR II-393; Case C-59/91 *France v Commission* [1992] ECR I-525 paras 3–7 (meaning of 'calendar month').

[64] The relevant official holidays are listed in Annex I of the ECJ Rules of Procedure.

[65] The application of the extension of time depends on where the applicant is habitually resident. The place of residence of the applicant's lawyer is irrelevant; see Case 28/65 *Fonzi v Commission* [1966] ECR 477. The Commission is entitled to an extension of two days on the basis that its seat is located in Brussels: Case C-137/92P *Commission v BASF* [1994] ECR I-2555 paras 38–42.

[66] ECJ Rules of Procedure, article 81(2); CFI Rules of Procedure, article 102(2). The relevant periods for each Member State are listed in Annex II, article 1 of the ECJ Rules of Procedure.

[67] ECJ Rules of Procedure, article 81(1); CFI Rules of Procedure, article 102(1).

[68] ECJ Rules of Procedure, article 82a(2); CFI Rules of Procedure, article 79(1).

[69] Case 209/83 *Valsabbia v Commission* [1984] ECR 3089 (ECSC); Case C-12/90 *Infortec v Commission* [1990] ECR I-4265 para 10.

[70] Case 152/85 *Misset v Council* [1987] ECR 223 para 11; Case 257/85 *Dufay v Parliament* [1987] ECR 1561 paras 9–10 (Court rejected an argument based on article 6 of the European Convention on Human Rights).

[71] Case 108/79 *Belfiore v Commission* [1980] ECR 1769 para 3.

[72] Case 4/67 *Muller v Commission* [1967] ECR 365 (ECSC); Joined Cases T-80/89 and others *BASF v Commission* [1995] ECR II-729 para 58.

[73] Joined Cases 32/58 and 33/58 *SNUPAT v High Authority* [1959] ECR 127 at 136 (ECSC); Case 42/58 *SAFE v High Authority* [1959] ECR 183 at 190 (ECSC); Joined Cases 193/87 and 194/87 *Maurissen v Court of Auditors* [1989] ECR 1045; Case T-1/90 *Pérez-Mínguez Casariego v Commission* [1991] ECR II-143 para 37. See also Case 152/85 *Misset v Council* [1987] ECR 223 para 7 (regardless of the time of day when a measure is notified, time does not begin to run until

A party's failure to comply with time-limits may be excused if he proves the existence of an excusable error, unforeseeable circumstances[74] or *force majeure*.[75] The concept of excusable error must be interpreted narrowly and will apply only in exceptional circumstances, for example where the conduct of the institution concerned was, either alone or to a decisive extent, such as to give rise to understandable confusion in the mind of a person acting in good faith and exercising normal care and attention.[76]

The concept of *force majeure* covers unusual circumstances which make it impossible for the relevant act to be carried out. Even though it does not require absolute impossibility, it does require abnormal difficulties, which are independent of the will of the person concerned and which are apparently inevitable, even if all due care is taken.[77] In Case C-195/91P *Bayer v Commission*[78] the Court of Justice held that the concept of *force majeure* contains an objective element relating to abnormal circumstances unconnected with the applicant in question, and a subjective element involving the obligation, on his part, to guard against the consequences of the abnormal event by taking appropriate steps without making unreasonable sacrifices. In particular, the applicant must pay close attention to the course of the procedure set in motion and demonstrate diligence in seeking to comply with the prescribed time-limits.

Four-stage procedure The procedure before the EC courts is divided into four main parts:

(1) the written procedure;
(2) preparatory inquiries;
(3) the oral procedure; and
(4) judgment.

---

the end of the day of notification. For the definition of 'notification', see Ch 1, pp 14–15 and Ch 13, p 326.

[74] See Joined Cases 25/65 and 26/65 *SIMET and FERAM v High Authority* [1967] ECR 33 (ECSC), where a postal delay was held to constitute an 'unforeseeable circumstance'. Contrast Case C-59/91 *France v Commission* [1992] ECR I-525 paras 8–12, where the applicants were not permitted to rely on a postal delay.

[75] Statute of the Court of Justice, article 42.

[76] Case T-12/90 *Bayer v Commission* [1991] ECR II-219 paras 28–29, upheld by the Court of Justice on appeal in Case C-195/91P *Bayer v Commission* [1994] ECR I-5619 paras 25–28; Case T-514/93 *Cobrecaf v Commission* [1995] ECR II-621 para 40. See also Case 25/68 *Schertzer v Parliament* [1977] ECR 1729 paras 10–21 (staff case); Case 117/78 *Orlandi v Commission* [1979] ECR 1613 paras 6–12 (staff case).

[77] Case 284/82 *Busseni v Commission* [1984] ECR 557 para 11 (ECSC); Case 224/83 *Vittoria v Commission* [1984] ECR 2349 (ECSC); Case 209/83 *Valsabbia v Commission* [1984] ECR 3089 (ECSC); Case 42/85 *Cockerill-Sambre v Commission* [1985] ECR 3749 (ECSC); Case T-12/90 *Bayer v Commission* [1991] ECR II-219 para 44, upheld by the Court of Justice on appeal in Case C-195/91P *Bayer v Commission* [1994] ECR I-5619 paras 30–33. A party may not rely on the malfunctioning of its own organisation: Case T-194/95 (Intv II) *Area Cova v Council* [1996] ECR II-343 para 6.

[78] [1994] ECR I-5619 para 32.

(b) Written procedure

Bringing an action An action is commenced by lodging[79] a written application with the Registrar of the Court of Justice or the Court of First Instance, as appropriate.[80]

Notice of the application is published in the *Official Journal*.[81]

Contents of application The application must state:[82]

(1) the name and permanent address of the applicant;[83]

(2) the identity of the defendant or defendants;

(3) the factual and legal background to the proceedings;

(4) where applicable, the nature of any evidence offered in support;

(5) the legal arguments relied on;

(6) the form of order sought by the applicant.

The application should also state an address for service in Luxembourg and the name of the person authorised to accept service.[84]

There is no set form for the application; however, it is normal practice to use appropriate sub-headings and numbered paragraphs.[85]

Costs/interest Every application should include a claim for costs. Failure to claim costs will mean that the applicant will have to bear his own costs, even if his application is successful.[86] In the context of monetary claims, the application should include a claim for interest which specifies the rate of interest claimed. The Court may reduce the interest claimed, but will not award interest at a rate higher than that claimed. In past cases, the Court has awarded interest at between 6 and 8 per cent.[87]

---

[79] For the rules relating to the lodging of documents, see above at p 394.

[80] Statute of the Court of Justice, article 19. For addresses, see fn 57 above.

[81] ECJ Rules of Procedure, article 16(6); CFI Rules of Procedure, article 24(6).

[82] Statute of the Court of Justice, article 19; ECJ Rules of Procedure, article 38(1); CFI Rules of Procedure, article 44(1).

[83] In Case 294/83 *Parti écologiste 'Les Verts' v Parliament* [1986] ECR 1339 paras 1–18 the applicant merged with other associations to form a new body, which was allowed to continue the original action.

[84] ECJ Rules of Procedure, article 38(2); CFI Rules of Procedure, article 44(2). It is usual to instruct a lawyer in Luxembourg for this purpose. The giving of an address for service is optional. If no address for service is given, pleadings are sent by registered post to counsel for the party concerned: see *Notes for the guidance of counsel in written and oral proceedings before the Court of Justice of the European Communities* (reproduced at Appendix E) Part B, para 4 (b).

[85] See Precedent H. See *Notes for the guidance of counsel in written and oral proceedings before the Court of Justice of the European Communities* (reproduced at Appendix E) Part B, para 13 (a).

[86] ECJ Rules of Procedure, article 69(2); CFI Rules of Procedure, article 87(2). It is not essential for the claim for costs to be made in the original application; it is sufficient if it is made in subsequent written pleadings or at the oral hearing: see Case T-13/92 *Moat v Commission* [1993] ECR II-287 para 50; Joined Cases T-70/92 and T-71/92 *Florimex v Commission* [1997] ECR II-693 para 197.

[87] For example, see Case 261/78 *Interquell Stärke-Chemie v EEC* [1982] ECR 3271; Joined Cases 64/76 and 113/76 and others *Dumortier Frères v Council* [1982] ECR 1733; Joined Cases C-104/89 and C-37/90 *Mulder v Council* [1992] ECR I-3061.

Co-defendants An application may be made against co-defendants.[88] However, a new defendant cannot be joined to the original application once proceedings have commenced. In Case 90/77 *Stimming v Commission*[89] the applicant brought an action for damages against the Commission and, in its reply, sought to join the Council as a co-defendant. This attempt was rejected by the Court of Justice, which emphasised that the Rules of Procedure do not allow such an alteration in the person of the defendant.

Pleas of fact and law The application must be sufficiently clear and precise to enable the defendant to prepare his defence and the Court to decide the case, if appropriate without other information. The pleas of fact and law must be sufficiently particularised. If the application is not sufficiently clear, or fails to provide essential information, it will be declared inadmissible, if necessary by the Court acting of its own motion.[90] In general, it is not permissible for an applicant to refer to the submissions made in another, related case.[91]

In considering the question of admissibility, the Court is entitled to take account of further information provided during the course of proceedings by the applicant (for example in the reply or in response to questions put by the Court).[92] However, the applicant should ensure that he sets out his case fully in the application. Although the Court will permit clarification of issues already raised in the application, it will not allow new issues of fact and law to be raised subsequently, even in the reply, which seek to extend the subject-matter of the proceedings beyond that defined in the application.[93] The only exception to this rule is in respect of new issues which are based on matters of law or fact and which have come to light in the course of the proceedings.[94]

Rectification of minor errors The EC courts will permit correction of mere clerical errors[95] and, in appropriate cases, may do so of their own motion.[96]

Form of order sought The applicant must state the precise form of order it seeks from the Court.[97] Any alternative forms of order should also be stated with precision. The EC courts have held that formulations such as 'any other

---

[88] For example, see Case 264/82 *Timex Corporation v Council and Commission* [1985] ECR 849.
[89] [1977] ECR 2113.
[90] Case T-387/94 *Asia Motor France v Commission* [1996] ECR II-961 paras 106–111; Case T-53/96 *Syndicat des Producteurs de Viande Bovine v Commission* [1996] ECR II-1579 paras 20–26; Case T-64/96 *De Jorio v Council* [1997] ECR II-127 paras 31–33.
[91] Joined Cases 19/63 and 65/63 *Prakash v Commission* [1965] ECR 533 at 546 (EAEC). However, see Case T-37/91 *ICI v Commission* [1995] ECR II-1901 paras 45–47, where the Court of First Instance allowed an applicant to cross-refer to another, closely related, pending case.
[92] Case 74/74 *CNTA v Commission* [1975] ECR 533 paras 2–6; Case T-18/90 *Jongen v Commission* [1991] ECR II-187 para 13; Case T-21/90 *Generlich v Commission* [1991] ECR II-1323 paras 32–33.
[93] Case 191/84 *Barcella v Commission* [1986] ECR 1541 paras 5–6; Case T-41/89 *Schwedler v Parliament* [1990] ECR II-79 para 34.
[94] See 'Amendment/new pleas in law' below at pp 402–403.
[95] Case C-149/95P(R) *Commission v Atlantic Container Line* [1995] ECR I-2163 paras 12–15.
[96] Case T-572/93 *Odigitria v Council* [1995] ECR II-2025 paras 15 and 22.
[97] In certain circumstances the failure to specify the form of order sought may be remedied by the

appropriate orders' are insufficiently precise and will be declared inadmissible.[98]

Annexes The following documents should be annexed to the application:[99]

(1) A file containing the documents relied on as evidence, together with a schedule listing them.

(2) A certificate establishing that the lawyer acting for the applicant is entitled to act before a court of a Member State or of a State which is a party to the EEA Agreement.[100]

(3) Where the applicant is 'a legal person governed by private law', for example a company:

    (a) proof of its existence in law[101] (for an English company, copies of the memorandum and articles of association or an extract from the Companies' Register should be produced); and

    (b) proof that the applicant's lawyer is authorised to act (for example a resolution of the board of directors or a declaration sworn before a notary).[102]

(4) In applications under article 173 of the EC Treaty [new art 230], a copy of the act challenged.[103]

(5) In applications under article 175 of the EC Treaty [new art 232], documentary evidence of the date on which the relevant institution was called upon to act.[104]

(6) In applications under article 181 [new art 238] or 182 [new art 239] of the EC Treaty, a copy of the relevant arbitration clause or special agreement (in the Court of Justice) or a copy of the contract which contains the arbitration clause (in the Court of First Instance).[105]

Court where the appropriate form of order can be inferred from the arguments contained in the application: see T-64/96 *De Jorio v Council* [1997] ECR II-127 paras 34–35.

[98] Case T-575/93 *Koelman v Commission* [1996] ECR II-1 para 31; Case T-228/95R *Lehrfreund v Council and Commission* [1996] ECR II-111 para 58; Case T-146/95 *Bernardi v Parliament* [1996] ECR II-769 para 27.

[99] ECJ Rules of Procedure, articles 37–38; CFI Rules of Procedure, articles 43–44. Statute of the Court of Justice, article 19.

[100] A copy of the Lawyer's Professional Identity Card (issued by the CCBE) is accepted for this purpose. A lawyer is not required to lodge a certificate each time he appears before the Court of Justice or the Court of First Instance. Each Registry is prepared to make reference to a certificate lodged in a previous case before that Court. See CFI Instructions to Registrar, article 7(2).

[101] Joined Cases T-551/93 and others *Industrias Pesqueras Campos v Commission* [1996] ECR II-247 paras 49–52 (company in liquidation); Case T-161/94 *Sinochem Heilongjiang v Council* [1996] ECR II-695 paras 31–35 (a Chinese company).

[102] A lawyer representing a natural person is not required to provide proof of his authority to act when lodging the application, but must be able to provide such proof if his authority to act is challenged. See Case 14/64 *Gualco v High Authority* [1965] ECR 51 at 57 (ECSC).

[103] Statute of the Court of Justice, article 19.

[104] Ibid.

[105] ECJ Rules of Procedure, article 38(6); CFI Rules of Procedure, article 44(5a).

Evidence There are no formal rules for the form in which evidence should be submitted;[106] it is sufficient to annex relevant documents to the pleading.[107] Such documents do not need to be exhibited to an affidavit or any other form of sworn statement.[108] In most cases, the annexed documents will not be translated. Important passages on which a party wishes to rely should therefore be set out in the pleading itself (which will be translated).

Confidential documents A party may request that confidential documents forming part of the pleadings should be placed in a special file, to be disclosed only to the principal parties and officers of the Court.[109]

Case numbers Cases are assigned a docket number when they are first lodged with the Courts' Registries. Since the establishment of the Court of First Instance in 1989, cases before the Court of Justice have borne the prefix 'C-'; cases before the Court of First Instance are denoted by the prefix 'T-'.[110] Each case is given a case number, which includes the year of registration, for example 'Case C-275/97' (the 275th case registered in the Court of Justice in 1997).

Judge-Rapporteur After an application has been lodged, the President of the Court designates a 'Judge-Rapporteur' ('juge rapporteur' in French) for that case, whose function is to ensure that the proper procedure is complied with, and to oversee the general conduct of the case.[111]

Service Once the Registrar is satisfied that the application is in order he serves it on the defendant.[112] In addition, copies of the application (and defence) are sent to the Council and the Commission, even where they are not named as parties in the application.[113]

Defence The defendant must lodge a defence within one month after service of the application. The time-limit may be extended by the President of the Court following an application by the defendant.[114] The defence must contain the following information:[115]

    (1) the name and permanent address of the defendant;

---

[106] Although see *Notes for the guidance of counsel in written and oral proceedings before the Court of Justice of the European Communities* (reproduced at Appendix E) Part B, para 13 (b) and *CFI: Advice for Lawyers and Agents regarding the written procedure* (reproduced at Appendix F) Part IV.

[107] *CFI, Notes for the guidance of counsel for the parties at the hearing* (reproduced at Appendix G), Part III, para 3.

[108] See paras 24–25 of the Opinion of Advocate-General Tesauro in Case C-44/94 *R v MAFF, ex p National Federation of Fishermen's Organizations* [1995] ECR I-3115.

[109] Case 236/81 *Celanese Chemical Co v Council and Commission* [1982] ECR 1183; Joined Cases T-134/94 and others *NMH Stahlwerke v Commission* [1996] ECR II-537 (ECSC). For the procedure to be followed in making an application to treat certain documents as confidential, see CFI Instructions to Registrar, article 5(4).

[110] This reflects the Court of First Instance's French title 'le Tribunal de première instance'.

[111] ECJ Rules of Procedure, article 9(2); CFI Rules of Procedure, article 13(2).

[112] ECJ Rules of Procedure, articles 39 and 79; CFI Rules of Procedure, articles 45 and 100.

[113] ECJ Rules of Procedure, article 16(7); CFI Rules of Procedure, article 24(7).

[114] ECJ Rules of Procedure, article 40(2); CFI Rules of Procedure, article 46(3).

[115] ECJ Rules of Procedure, article 40(1); CFI Rules of Procedure, article 46(1).

(2) an address for service in Luxembourg; and the name of the person authorised to accept service;[116]

(3) the arguments of fact and law relied on;

(4) the form of order sought by the defendant (this will usually ask for the rejection of the application and costs);

(5) the nature of any evidence offered.

There is no set form for the defence. However, it is normal practice to use appropriate sub-headings and numbered paragraphs. The defendant should ensure that he sets out his case fully in the defence. The Court will not allow later amendments, even in the rejoinder, which seek to extend the subject-matter of the proceedings as defined in the application and defence.[117] The defence should also include a claim for costs; failure to do so will mean that the defendant will have to bear his own costs, even if his defence is successful.[118]

Annexes The following documents should be annexed to the defence:[119]

(1) A file containing the documents relied on as evidence, together with a schedule listing them.[120]

(2) A certificate establishing that the lawyer acting for the defendant is entitled to act before a court of a Member State or of a State which is a party to the EEA Agreement.

(3) Where the defendant is 'a legal person governed by private law', for example a company:

    (*a*) proof of its existence in law (for an English company, copies of the memorandum and articles of association or an extract from the Companies' Register should be produced); and

    (*b*) proof that the applicant's lawyer is authorised to act (for example a resolution of the board of directors or a declaration sworn before a notary).

Default judgment The Rules of Procedure provide for judgment in default where a defendant fails to lodge a defence in the proper form within the time prescribed. Before giving judgment in default, the Court is required to consider

---

[116] The giving of an address for service is optional. If no address for service is given, pleadings are sent by registered post to counsel for the party concerned: see *Notes for the guidance of counsel in written and oral proceedings before the Court of Justice of the European Communities* (reproduced at Appendix E), Part B, para 4 (b).

[117] See below at pp 402–403.

[118] ECJ Rules of Procedure, article 69(2); CFI Rules of Procedure, article 87(2).

[119] ECJ Rules of Procedure, articles 37(4) and 40(1); CFI Rules of Procedure, articles 43(4) and 46(1). Statute of the Court of Justice, article 19.

[120] See above at p 400 under 'Evidence'.

whether the application is admissible, whether the appropriate formalities have been complied with, and whether the application appears well founded. The defendant is entitled to apply for the default judgment to be set aside.[121]

Reply and rejoinder The application and the defence may be supplemented by a reply from the applicant and by a rejoinder from the defendant. The lodgement of a reply or rejoinder is purely optional.[122] The President of the Court fixes the time-limits within which these pleadings are to be lodged.[123] The applicant is entitled to expand in his reply upon points made in his application.[124] Further evidence may be put forward in the reply or rejoinder, provided reasons are given for the delay in offering it.[125] However, no new plea in law may be introduced unless it is based on matters of law or fact which have come to light in the course of the procedure.[126]

Amendment/new pleas in law The Rules of Procedure provide that an applicant must state the pleas on which he relies in his application,[127] and the defendant must do likewise in his defence.[128] No new plea in law may be introduced in the course of proceedings unless it is based on matters of law or fact which have come to light in the course of the procedure.[129] A plea in law will be considered to be new only if it has not been mentioned directly or indirectly in the application or defence.[130] For a new fact to justify the raising of a fresh issue during the proceedings, it must not have existed or must not have been known to the applicant when the action was commenced.[131]

---

[121] ECJ Rules of Procedure, article 94; CFI Rules of Procedure, article 122. See Case T-85/94 *Branco v Commission* [1995] ECR II-45 paras 18–22 (procedure followed for default judgment); Case T-85/94(122) *Commission v Branco* [1995] ECR II-2993 (application to set aside default judgment); Case C-274/93 *Commission v Luxembourg* [1996] ECR I-2019 (application for default judgment dismissed as inadmissible).

[122] See *Notes for guidance of counsel in written and oral proceedings before the Court of Justice of the European Communities* (reproduced at Appendix E) Part B, para 8 (b).

[123] ECJ Rules of Procedure, article 41; CFI Rules of Procedure, article 47. An extension of the time allowed for lodging replies and rejoinders is granted only in exceptional circumstances: *Notes for guidance of counsel in written and oral proceedings before the Court of Justice of the European Communities* (reproduced at Appendix E) Part B, para 8 (b).

[124] Case T-21/90 *Generlich v Commission* [1991] ECR II-1323 para 32; Case T-106/95 *FFSA v Commission* [1997] ECR II-229 paras 124–125.

[125] ECJ Rules of Procedure, article 42(1); CFI Rules of Procedure, article 48(1).

[126] ECJ Rules of Procedure, article 42(2); CFI Rules of Procedure, article 48(2). Case C-135/92 *Fiskano v Commission* [1994] ECR I-2885 paras 31–32; Case T-171/94 *Descom Scales Manufacturing Co v Council* [1995] ECR II-2413 para 98; Case T-146/95 *Bernardi v Parliament* [1996] ECR II-769 para 31.

[127] ECJ Rules of Procedure, article 38(1)(*c*); CFI Rules of Procedure, article 44(1)(*c*).

[128] ECJ Rules of Procedure, article 40(1)(*b*); CFI Rules of Procedure, article 46(1)(*b*).

[129] ECJ Rules of Procedure, article 42(2); CFI Rules of Procedure, article 48(2). These rules will also prevent the introduction of a new head of relief. For example, in Case T-4/96 *S v Court of Justice* [1997] ECR II-1125 paras 104–105 an applicant was not permitted to add a claim for compensation to her original application for annulment.

[130] Joined Cases C-71/95, C-155/95 and C-271/95 *Belgium v Commission* [1997] ECR I-687 paras 29–31.

[131] Case 11/81 *Dürbeck v Commission* [1982] ECR 1251 para 17; Case T-435/93 *ASPEC v Commission* [1995] ECR II-1281 paras 96–99.

The EC courts have taken a strict approach to amendments and have consistently held that an amendment may not seek to extend the subject-matter of the proceedings as established in the application and defence.[132] An amendment may be permitted, for example, where the decision originally challenged in the application has been replaced by another decision with the same subject-matter,[133] or where the scope of the original decision has been extended without affecting the general principle to which it gives effect.[134] Equally, a later submission, which amplifies a submission, express or implied, previously made in the original application, will also be permitted.[135] The Court of First Instance has held that a subsequent judgment of the EC courts cannot be relied on as a new matter allowing a new legal ground to be introduced because such judgments have effect *ex tunc* (ie they declare the law as it has always been).[136]

The Rules of Procedure do not lay down either a time-limit or any particular formalities for the submission of a new plea in law, and the Court of First Instance has indicated that it would be inappropriate to impose any form of time-bar.[137] In appropriate circumstances, new pleas in law may even be raised at the oral hearing.[138]

Joinder of cases The Court may, at any time, order that cases concerning the same subject-matter should be joined for the written or oral procedure or for final judgment.[139] Joint applications may be permitted where the applicants' conclusions refer only to identical measures or to measures which concern them all equally.[140]

Intervention[141] Member States and Community institutions are entitled to intervene as of right in cases before the EC courts. They are not required to demonstrate that they have an interest in the result of the case.[142] All other

---

[132] Case 232/78 *Commission v France* [1979] ECR 2729 paras 2–3; Case 125/78 *GEMA v Commission* [1979] ECR 3173 para 26; Case 124/81 *Commission v United Kingdom* [1983] ECR 203 para 6; Case T-64/89 *Automec v Commission* [1990] ECR II-367 paras 66–70. Cf Joined Cases 82 and 83/85R *Eurasian Corporation v Commission* [1985] ECR 1191, where amendments to an application for interim measures were permitted as, on the facts of the case, the Commission's opportunity to defend itself was not affected thereby.

[133] Case 14/81 *Alpha Steel v Commission* [1982] ECR 749 paras 7–8 (ECSC); Case 103/85 *Stahlwerke Peine-Salzgitter v Commission* [1988] ECR 4131 paras 10–13 (ECSC); Case T-22/96 *Langdon v Commission* [1996] ECR II-1009 para 16.

[134] Joined Cases 351/85 and 360/85 *Fabrique de fer de Charleroi v Commission* [1987] ECR 3639 paras 8–11 (ECSC).

[135] Case 306/81 *Verros v Parliament* [1983] ECR 1755 para 9.

[136] Case T-521/93 *Atlanta v European Communities* [1996] ECR II-1707 para 39; Case T-106/95 *FFSA v Commission* [1997] ECR II-229 paras 54–60.

[137] Case T-37/91 *ICI v Commission* [1995] ECR II-1901 para 84.

[138] Case T-508/93 *Mancini v Commission* [1994] ECR-SC II-761 paras 33–34.

[139] ECJ Rules of Procedure, article 43; CFI Rules of Procedure, article 50.

[140] Joined Cases 18/64 and 19/64 *Alvino v Commission* [1965] ECR 789 at 796.

[141] Statute of the Court of Justice, article 37; ECJ Rules of Procedure, article 93; *Notes for the guidance of counsel in written and oral proceedings before the Court of Justice of the European Communities* (reproduced at Appendix E) Part B, para 12; CFI Rules of Procedure, articles 115–116. Intervention is permissible only on the basis of these procedural rules; see Case T-1/90 *Pérez-Mínguez Casariego v Commission* [1991] ECR II-143 paras 41–44.

[142] See Case 138/79 *Roquette Frères v Council* [1980] ECR 3333 paras 17–21.

persons[143] are not permitted to intervene in cases between Member States, between institutions of the Community or between Member States and institutions of the Community, and may intervene in other cases only where they can establish that they have an interest in the result.[144]

An application to intervene must be made within three months of the publication of the notice in the *Official Journal* that the case has been registered.[145] Save for Member States,[146] interveners must use the language of the case determined by the main parties unless they obtain an order from the Court permitting them to use a different language.[147] The application must state:[148]

(1) the relevant case number and the identity of the parties;
(2) the name and address of the intervener;
(3) an address for service in Luxembourg and the name of the person authorised to accept service;[149]
(4) the form of order which the intervener wishes to support (this must be a form of order sought by one of the original parties to the proceedings); and
(5) except in the case of applications to intervene by a Member State or Community institution, the reasons establishing the intervener's right to intervene.

The original of the application to intervene must be signed by the party's agent or lawyer and must be dated. The original should be lodged with the appropriate Registrar, together with five certified copies for the Court and a copy for every other party to the proceedings.[150] The application to intervene should be accompanied by a certificate establishing that the lawyer acting for the intervener is entitled to act before a court of a Member State or of a State which is a party to the EEA Agreement. In addition, where the applicant is 'a

---

[143] In Joined Cases 41/73, 43–48/73 and others *Sucrière v Commission* [1973] ECR 1465 the Court of Justice held that a body without legal personality (the National Union of Italian Consumers) was entitled to intervene in an action. The Consultative Committee of the Bars and Law Societies of the European Community ('CCBE') was allowed to intervene in Case 155/79 *AM & S Europe v Commission* [1982] ECR 1575 para 8. In Joined Cases 91/82 and 200/82 *Chris International Foods v Commission* [1983] ECR 417 a non-Member State (Dominica) was permitted to intervene in an action. Trade union organisations are generally allowed to intervene in staff cases where the judgment is likely to affect collective interests: Case T-84/91 *Meskens v Parliament* [1992] II-1565 para 9.

[144] Statute of the Court of Justice, article 37.

[145] ECJ Rules of Procedure, article 93(1); CFI Rules of Procedure, article 115(1).

[146] ECJ Rules of Procedure, article 29(3); CFI Rules of Procedure, article 35(3).

[147] ECJ Rules of Procedure, article 29(2)(*c*); CFI Rules of Procedure, article 35(2)(*b*). Case T-290/94 *Kayersberg v Commission* [1995] ECR II-2247 paras 6–8.

[148] ECJ Rules of Procedure, article 93(1); CFI Rules of Procedure, article 115(2).

[149] It is usual to instruct a lawyer in Luxembourg for this purpose. The giving of an address for service is optional. If no address for service is given, pleadings are sent by registered post to counsel for the party concerned: see *Notes for the guidance of counsel in written and oral proceedings before the Court of Justice of the European Communities* (reproduced at Appendix E) Part B, para 4 (b).

[150] ECJ Rules of Procedure, article 93(1) provides that articles 37 and 38 of those Rules apply to applications to intervene; CFI Rules of Procedure, article 115(2) provides that articles 43 and 44 of those Rules apply to applications to intervene.

legal person governed by private law', for example, a company: (*a*) proof of its existence in law (for an English company, copies of the memorandum and articles of association or an extract from the Companies' Register); and (*b*) proof that the applicant's lawyer is authorised to act (for example a resolution of the board of directors or a declaration sworn before a notary) should be produced. It is not permissible to make an application to intervene simply by sending a fax to the relevant Registry.[151]

In order to establish a sufficient interest to intervene, an individual applicant must demonstrate that it will be directly affected by the form of orders being sought by the parties. An indirect interest in the outcome of the case, for example by reason of similarities between the situation of the applicant and one of the parties, will not suffice; nor will a mere interest in the legal submissions being put forward by the parties where there is no direct and existing interest in the grant by the Court of the order as sought.[152] The EC courts adopt a more liberal approach in relation to representative organisations or associations. In practice, a representative body will be permitted to intervene if: (*a*) it represents an appreciable number of undertakings active in the sector concerned; (*b*) its objects include that of protecting its members' interests; (*c*) the case may raise questions of principle affecting the functioning of the sector concerned; and (*d*) the interests of its members may therefore be affected to an appreciable extent by the judgment.[153]

The Registrar serves the application to intervene on the other parties and, after they have been given an opportunity to make submissions, the President or the Court usually gives a decision in the form of an order.[154] If the Court allows the intervention, the President prescribes a period within which the intervener must submit his statement in intervention and the intervener receives a copy of all the documents served on the parties, unless one of the parties makes an application for the omission of secret or confidential information.[155]

The statement in intervention must contain:[156]

(1) a statement of the form of order sought, which must support or oppose, in whole or in part, the order already sought by one of the parties;

(2) the pleas in law and arguments relied on;

(3) where relevant, the nature of any evidence put forward.

---

[151] Case T-194/95(Intv II) *Area Cova v Council* [1996] ECR II-343 paras 2–4.

[152] Case T-108/94 *Candiotte v Council* [1994] ECR II-863 para 5; Joined Cases C-151/97P(I) and C-157/97P(I) *National Power and PowerGen* [1997] ECR I-3491 para 53 (ECSC). See also Case T-35/91 *Eurosport Consortium v Commission* [1991] ECR II-1359 (competition case).

[153] Case T-87/92 *Kruidvat v Commission* [1993] ECR II-1375 para 14; Joined Cases C-151/97P(I) and C-157/97P(I) *National Power and PowerGen* [1997] ECR I-3491 para 66 (ECSC).

[154] ECJ Rules of Procedure, article 93(2); CFI Rules of Procedure, article 116(1).

[155] ECJ Rules of Procedure, article 93(3); CFI Rules of Procedure, article 116(2). See Joined Cases T-24/92R and T-28/92R *Langnese-Iglo and Schöller Lebensmittel v Commission* [1992] ECR II-1713 paras 5–10; Case T-395/94R *Atlantic Container Line v Commission* [1995] ECR II-595 paras 6 and 30; Case T-102/96 *Gencor v Commission* [1997] ECR II-879.

[156] ECJ Rules of Procedure, article 93(5); CFI Rules of Procedure, article 116(4).

Submissions made by an intervener are limited to supporting the form of order sought by one of the parties.[157] This does not prevent an intervener from presenting arguments which differ from those put forward by the party which it is supporting.[158]

The original of the statement in intervention must be signed by the party's agent or lawyer and must be dated. The original should be lodged with the appropriate Registrar, together with five certified copies for the Court, and a copy for every other party to the proceedings.

After the statement in intervention has been lodged, the parties will generally be given an opportunity to reply to that statement in writing.[159]

Member States and Community institutions which intervene must bear their own costs. The Court may order other interveners to bear their own costs.[160]

Judge-Rapporteur's preliminary report[161] After the close of written pleadings, all of the pleadings are translated into French. The Judge-Rapporteur then prepares his preliminary report. In the Court of Justice, this report summarises the subject-matter of the case and may contain indications as to how the case might be decided. In the Court of First Instance, the report contains a more detailed analysis of the fact and law. The report also makes recommendations as to whether any preparatory inquiries are necessary and whether the case should be referred to a chamber. The Court of Justice holds a weekly general meeting at which all of the members of the Court discuss the future conduct of each case on the basis of the preliminary report submitted by the Judge-Rapporteur. In the Court of First Instance, the preliminary reports are examined only by the members of the chamber to which the case has been initially allocated. The preliminary report is a purely internal document: copies are not provided to the parties.

(c) Preparatory inquiries

Obtaining further evidence The EC courts have wide powers for obtaining further evidence, exercisable both of their own motion or on an application by one of the parties.[162] Either Court may adopt the following measures of inquiry:

---

[157] Statute of the Court of Justice, article 37.

[158] Case 30/59 *Steenkolenmijnen v High Authority* [1961] ECR 1 at 17–18 (ECSC); Case T-459/93 *Siemens v Commission* [1995] ECR II-1675 paras 22–23; Case C-156/93 *Parliament v Commission* [1995] ECR I-2019 paras 14–15; Case C-360/93 *Parliament v Council* [1996] ECR I-1195 paras 20–22. Contrast Case C-155/91 *Commission v Council* [1993] ECR I-939 paras 22–24, commented on in para 12 of the Opinion of Advocate-General Tesauro in Case C-58/94 *Netherlands v Council* [1996] ECR I-2169.

[159] ECJ Rules of Procedure, article 93(6); CFI Rules of Procedure, article 116(5).

[160] ECJ Rules of Procedure, article 69(4); CFI Rules of Procedure, article 87(4).

[161] ECJ Rules of Procedure, article 44; CFI Rules of Procedure, article 52.

[162] See, generally, Statute of the Court of Justice, articles 21–27; ECJ Rules of Procedure, articles 45–54 and 124; CFI Rules of Procedure, articles 64–76. Preparatory measures can be ordered only by the Court and cannot be ordered by the President in the context of an interlocutory application: see Case C-358/89R *Extramet Industrie v Council* [1990] ECR I-431.

(1) The Court may require the parties to produce documents and information which it considers desirable.[163] It may require Member States and Community institutions which are not parties to the case to supply all information necessary for the proceedings.[164]

(2) The Court may summon and orally examine witnesses, whether parties or non-parties.[165]

(3) The Court may order that an expert's report be obtained.[166]

(4) The Court may issue letters rogatory for the examination of witnesses or experts.[167]

(5) The Court may inspect the place or thing in question.[168]

In addition, the Court of First Instance may invite the parties to make written or oral submissions on certain aspects of the proceedings and may summon the parties or their agents to meetings.[169]

Where a party makes an application for the adoption of measures of inquiry, he must provide evidence of why such measures are necessary.[170] The purpose of preparatory inquiries is to prove alleged facts. They may not be ordered to remedy a pleading in circumstances where a party has failed to provide any particulars whatsoever on a particular matter.[171]

In practice, the most common form of inquiry is for the Court to put questions in writing to the parties to clarify or expand on certain points raised in the pleadings.[172] This sort of inquiry is not technically a 'preparatory inquiry', as it is carried out on a more informal basis. This form of inquiry is known as a 'measure of organisation of procedure'.

Following completion of the preparatory inquiry, the President will usually fix the date for the opening of the oral procedure.[173]

---

[163] See Joined Cases 121/86 and 122/86R *Epicheiriseon v Council and Commission* [1987] ECR 833 on the appropriate procedure to be followed by a party to obtain discovery of documents.

[164] Statute of the Court of Justice, article 21.

[165] Statute of the Court of Justice, article 23; ECJ Rules of Procedure, articles 47–48; CFI Rules of Procedure, articles 68–69.

[166] Statute of the Court of Justice, article 22; ECJ Rules of Procedure, article 49; CFI Rules of Procedure, article 70.

[167] Statute of the Court of Justice, article 26. ECJ Rules of Procedure, article 52; Supplementary Rules, articles 1–3 (OJ 1974 L350 p 29, as amended by OJ 1987 L165 p 4). CFI Rules of Procedure, article 75. For example, see Case 160/84 *Oryzomyli Kavallas v Commission* [1985] ECR 675.

[168] ECJ Rules of Procedure, article 45(2)(*e*); CFI Rules of Procedure, article 65(*e*).

[169] CFI Rules of Procedure, article 64(3).

[170] Case 51/65 *ILFO v High Authority* [1966] ECR 87 (ECSC).

[171] Case T-53/96 *Syndicat des Producteurs de Viande Bovine v Commission* [1996] ECR II-1579 paras 25–26.

[172] See Joined Cases T-244/93 and T-486/93 *TWD v Commission* [1995] ECR II-2265 para 13.

[173] ECJ Rules of Procedure, article 54. See Case 77/70 *Prelle v Commission* [1971] ECR 561 paras 6–7, where the Court of Justice indicated that a party could make an application for a measure of inquiry after the oral procedure had closed, but only if it related to facts which were capable of having a decisive influence and which the party concerned was not able to put forward before the closure of the oral procedure.

(d) Interlocutory matters

Admissibility A challenge to the admissibility of an application may be raised in the defence, in which case it will normally be considered by the Court in its final judgment. Alternatively, a party may raise the question of admissibility as a preliminary issue by making an application to the Court setting out the pleas of fact and law relied on and the form of order sought by the applicant.[174] Any supporting documents must be annexed to the application. Having given the other party the opportunity to make written submissions on the matter, there may then be an oral hearing,[175] following which the Court will decide the question of admissibility as an interlocutory matter, or reserve its decision until the final substantive judgment.

Where the Court of Justice or the Court of First Instance has no jurisdiction on the matter or where the action is manifestly inadmissible, it may decide the matter by adopting a reasoned order to that effect.[176] An action which is manifestly lacking any foundation in law may also be dismissed by the Court of First Instance by reasoned order.[177]

The EC courts may raise of their own motion at any time an absolute bar to proceeding with a case.[178] The admissibility of an action is an issue of public policy which may be raised by the Court of its own motion; its review is not confined to objections of inadmissibility raised by the parties.[179] In addition, the EC courts may at any time, of their own motion, declare, after hearing the parties, that the action has become devoid of purpose and that there is no need to adjudicate upon it.[180]

The admissibility of an action is judged as of the date when the application was lodged. If, at that time, the conditions for an action to be brought are not fulfilled, the action is inadmissible, unless the defect is rectified within the period prescribed for proceedings to be instituted. In Case 50/84 *Bensider v Commission*[181] an application made on the last day of the prescribed period was declared to be inadmissible, as the applicant, a company, had not acquired legal personality under its national law at that date and was not, therefore, entitled to bring legal proceedings.

Interim measures The substantive and procedural law relating to interim measures is considered in Chapter 17.

---

[174] ECJ Rules of Procedure, article 91; CFI Rules of Procedure, article 114.

[175] The EC courts are entitled to decide that an oral hearing is not necessary: see ECJ Rules of Procedure, article 91(3); CFI Rules of Procedure, article 114(3).

[176] ECJ Rules of Procedure, article 92(1); CFI Rules of Procedure, article 111.

[177] CFI Rules of Procedure, article 111.

[178] ECJ Rules of Procedure, article 92(2); CFI Rules of Procedure, article 113.

[179] Case T-146/95 *Bernardi v Parliament* [1996] ECR II-769 para 22; Case T-99/95 *Stott v Commission* [1996] ECR-SC 2227 para 22. See also para 12 of the Opinion of Advocate-General Fennelly in Case C-334/94 *Commission v France* [1996] ECR I-1307, where he stated that the Court *must* raise of its own motion issues which go to its jurisdiction.

[180] ECJ Rules of Procedure, article 92(2); CFI Rules of Procedure, article 113.

[181] [1984] ECR 3991 (ECSC).

Expedition The general rule is that cases are dealt with in the order in which their preparatory inquiries have been completed. However, the President may, in special circumstances, order that a case be given priority over others.[182]

Stay of proceedings The Court of Justice has a general power to stay proceedings subject to the conditions established in its Rules of Procedure.[183] In contrast, the Court of First Instance may stay proceedings only in specific instances, for example at the joint request of the parties.[184] Time-limits cease to run when proceedings have been stayed, save in respect of applications to intervene in the Court of First Instance.[185]

Costs in interlocutory applications Any interlocutory application or response should contain a separate claim for costs. Failure to do so will mean that the Court is obliged to award all of the costs in the action to the successful party in the final judgment, without taking separate account of the outcome of any interlocutory applications.[186]

Discontinuance A case may be withdrawn from the register if the parties agree a settlement (except in applications under article 173 or 175 of the EC Treaty [new arts 230 and 232]) or if the applicant informs the Court, in writing, that he wishes to discontinue the proceedings.[187] In these circumstances, the President will give a decision on costs in accordance with the specific provisions set down in the Rules of Procedure.[188] The general rule is that the party who discontinues or withdraws from the proceedings must pay the other party's costs if they have been applied for in the observations of the other party on the discontinuance, subject to any agreement between the parties themselves as to costs. However, upon application by the party who discontinues or withdraws, the Court has power to order that the costs should be borne by the other party if this appears justified.[189] If costs are not applied for, the parties bear their own costs.

(e) Oral procedure

Oral hearing The Court of Justice, with the express consent of the parties, may decide to dispense with the oral procedure.[190]

Report for the hearing The Judge-Rapporteur prepares a report for the hearing. The report is a wholly neutral document, summarising the facts of the case and the arguments contained in the written pleadings. The report is

---

[182] ECJ Rules of Procedure, article 55; CFI Rules of Procedure, article 55.
[183] ECJ Rules of Procedure, article 82a; Statute of the Court of Justice, article 47.
[184] CFI Rules of Procedure, articles 77–79, 123(4), 128 and 129(4); Statute of the Court of Justice, article 47.
[185] ECJ Rules of Procedure, article 82a(2); CFI Rules of Procedure, article 79(1).
[186] Case T-50/89 *Sparr v Commission* [1990] ECR II-539 para 9.
[187] ECJ Rules of Procedure, articles 77–78; CFI Rules of Procedure, articles 98–99.
[188] ECJ Rules of Procedure, article 69(5); CFI Rules of Procedure, article 87(5).
[189] See Case C-120/94 *Commission v Greece* [1996] ECR I-1513.
[190] ECJ Rules of Procedure, article 44(a).

circulated to the members of the Court, the parties and any interveners prior to the hearing. Where there is to be no oral hearing, the report for the hearing is known as the 'report of the Judge-Rapporteur'. If a party considers that the report for the hearing (or the report of the Judge-Rapporteur) does not accurately set out the facts or the arguments, he should inform the Registrar of this before the hearing in writing and suggest appropriate amendments. For the purposes of the oral hearing, the parties should assume that all the members of the Court are aware of the contents of the report for the hearing.

Public hearing The oral hearing will be a public hearing, unless the Court, of its own motion or on application by the parties, decides otherwise.[191]

Conduct of the oral hearing The main purpose of the oral hearing is not to repeat the written observations already made, but to supplement the written procedure. It should be used to highlight points of importance, to clarify difficult issues and to respond to arguments raised by other parties.

Lawyers and agents wear their national robes. Barristers usually address the Court as 'My Lords'. A party may address the Court only through his agent, adviser or lawyer.[192]

The Court encourages advocates to provide copies of the notes upon which their speech will be based to the interpreters prior to the hearing. This facilitates the simultaneous interpretation of the advocate's speech.[193] Because of the use of simultaneous interpretation, it is vital that advocates should address the Court in short sentences using simple terms and should not speak too quickly.

Before the oral hearing begins, the legal representatives are usually invited to a room behind the Court to deal with any particular arrangements for the hearing. The Judge-Rapporteur or the Advocate-General may indicate particular matters which they would like to be developed in the oral submissions.

As a general rule, the time allowed for the speeches is usually a maximum of 30 minutes for each main party, except in cases before chambers of three judges, where the time permitted is usually limited to 15 minutes. Interveners are limited to a maximum of 15 minutes. These time-limits are rigorously enforced by the President; however, an allowance is made for any time used to reply to questions put by the Court. A party may apply for a longer period by sending a request to the Registrar at least 15 days before the hearing. The request must detail the reasons on which it is based and should indicate the amount of time being sought.[194]

---

[191] Statute of the Court of Justice, article 28.

[192] Ibid, article 29; ECJ Rules of Procedure, article 58; CFI Rules of Procedure, article 59.

[193] In addition, the interpreters read the case papers and relevant authorities cited in the written submissions prior to the hearing.

[194] *Notes for the guidance of counsel in written and oral proceedings before the Court of Justice of the European Communities* (reproduced at Appendix E) Part C, para 5; *CFI, Notes for the guidance of counsel for the parties at the hearing* (reproduced at Appendix G), Part 4.

After submissions have been made on behalf of each party, the judges and Advocate-General may ask questions.[195] Each speaker will then be given the opportunity to make a short reply. At the end of the oral hearing, the Advocate-General will usually indicate the date on which he intends to deliver his Opinion.

Advocate-General's Opinion In the Court of Justice the Advocate-General delivers the conclusions of his Opinion orally, some time following the oral hearing. It is not necessary for the parties to attend. Once the Opinion has been delivered the oral procedure is declared closed.[196] In the Court of First Instance the oral procedure is generally declared closed at the end of the oral hearing.[197]

(f) Judgment

Secret deliberation The Court reaches its judgment by deliberation in closed session. Only the judges who were present at the oral hearing take part in the deliberations. If necessary, decisions are reached by majority following a vote. Only one judgment is delivered; there are no dissenting judgments. The conduct of the deliberations is confidential.[198]

Delivery of judgment Judgment is delivered in open court. The parties need not attend. All parties to the action are served with certified copies of the judgment,[199] which is binding as from its date of delivery.[200] The texts of judgments are available on the Court of Justice's web site on the Internet at www.curia.eu.int.

Length of proceedings In 1996, the average length of proceedings for direct actions in the Court of Justice (from lodging of the application to judgment) was 19.6 months.[201]

Slip rule/rectification of errors The Court may rectify clerical mistakes, errors in calculation or obvious slips in any judgment, either of its own motion or on application by a party within two weeks of the delivery of the judgment.[202]

---

[195] ECJ Rules of Procedure, article 57; CFI Rules of Procedure, article 58.

[196] ECJ Rules of Procedure, article 59. In the Court of First Instance, where an Advocate-General has been appointed he need not deliver his reasoned submissions orally: Statute of the Court of Justice, article 46.

[197] CFI Rules of Procedure, articles 60–62.

[198] Statute of the Court of Justice, articles 32–34. ECJ Rules of Procedure, articles 27 and 63–65; CFI Rules of Procedure, articles 33 and 81–83.

[199] ECJ Rules of Procedure, article 64; CFI Rules of Procedure, article 82.

[200] ECJ Rules of Procedure, article 65; CFI Rules of Procedure, article 82. See the exception in relation to decisions of the Court of First Instance declaring regulations to be void in the Statute of the Court of Justice, article 53.

[201] These figures are taken from the *Weekly Summaries of the Court of Justice*, Number 36 of 1996.

[202] ECJ Rules of Procedure, article 66; CFI Rules of Procedure, article 84. For example, see Joined Cases C-89/85 and others *Ahlström v Commission* [1994] ECR I-99; Case C-19/93P *Rendo v Commission* [1996] ECR I-1997.

Omissions If the Court omits to make a decision on any head of the claim or on costs, a party can apply to the Court to supplement its judgment within one month after service of the judgment.[203]

Interpretation of judgments Any party or any Community institution with an interest can make an application to the Court to clarify the meaning or scope of a judgment.[204] A person who was not a party to the case cannot make an application for interpretation.[205] Where several actions are brought against the same measure and where, as a result of one of those actions, the measure is annulled, the applicants in the other actions may be entitled to make an application for interpretation of the judgment, provided those applicants had put forward the same reasons for annulment in their own application as the Court relied on in its judgment.[206] Interveners may also submit an application for interpretation, even if the party whose conclusions they supported does not do so.[207]

An application for interpretation must be based on the obscurity or ambiguity of the judgment in question, and may not raise questions on the effect of the judgment.[208] An interpreting judgment is binding not only on the applicants, but also on any other party, insofar as that party is affected by the passage in the judgment which the Court is asked to interpret or by a passage which is exactly similar thereto.[209]

Revision of judgments Revision[210] is not an appeal procedure but an exceptional review procedure which allows an applicant to ask the Court to reconsider a judgment where there has been a discovery of elements of a factual nature which existed prior to the judgment but which were unknown at that time to the Court which delivered it as well as to the party applying for revision[211] and which, had the Court been able to take them into consideration, could have led it to a different determination of the proceedings. The conditions of review are construed strictly by the Court, since revision is an exceptional procedure

---

[203] ECJ Rules of Procedure, article 67; CFI Rules of Procedure, article 85 (limited to a failure to give a decision on costs). For example, see Joined Cases C-89/85 and others *Ahlström v Commission* [1994] ECR I-99.

[204] Statute of the Court of Justice, article 40; ECJ Rules of Procedure, article 102; CFI Rules of Procedure, article 129.

[205] Case 24/66bis *Getreidehandel v Commission* [1973] ECR 1599.

[206] Case 5/55 *ASSIDER v High Authority* [1955] ECR 135 at 141 (ECSC).

[207] Joined Cases 146/85 and 431/85 *Maindiaux v Economic and Social Committee* [1988] ECR 2003 para 4.

[208] Case 5/55 *ASSIDER v High Authority* [1955] ECR 135 at 142 (ECSC); Case 70/63A *High Authority v Collotti and Court of Justice* [1965] ECR 275 (ECSC); Case 110/63 *Willame v Commission* [1966] ECR 287; Case 9/81 *Court of Auditors v Williams* [1983] ECR 2859 para 12; Case 206/81A *Alvarez v Parliament* [1983] ECR 2865.

[209] Joined Cases 41/73, 43/73 and 44/73 *Sucrière v Commission* [1977] ECR 445 paras 27–30.

[210] Statute of the Court of Justice, article 41; ECJ Rules of Procedure, articles 98–100; CFI Rules of Procedure, articles 125–128. Case T-4/89Rev *BASF v Commission* [1992] ECR II-1591 para 9; Case C-130/91 RevII *ISAE/VP and Interdata v Commission* [1996] ECR I-65 para 6.

[211] Case 56/70 *Mandelli v Commission* [1971] ECR 1 (ECSC).

which may render the principle of *res judicata* inapplicable.[212] Revision is not available in respect of a judgment on points of law only.[213]

An application for review must be made within three months of the date on which the facts on which the application is based came to the applicant's knowledge.[214] Furthermore, no application for revision can be made later than ten years from the date of the judgment.[215]

Review at the request of third parties Member States, Community institutions and any private party may, subject to the conditions set out in the Rules of Procedure, institute third party proceedings to contest a judgment which was rendered without their being heard, where the judgment is prejudicial to their rights.[216] This is an exceptional procedure and is subject to strict control by the Court in order to protect legal certainty in respect of judgments.

Enforcement Enforcement of judgments is governed by the rules of civil procedure in force in the State in which enforcement is carried out.[217] Enforcement may only be suspended by means of an application to the Court of Justice or the Court of First Instance, as appropriate.[218] Enforcement proceedings against the property and assets of the Community institutions may be carried out only with the authorisation of the EC courts.[219] However, it is not necessary to obtain such authorisation where the relevant institution does not object to such proceedings.[220]

---

[212] Case 116/78Rev *Bellintani v Commission* [1980] ECR 23; Case 267/80Rev *Riseria Modenese v Council and Commission and Birra Peroni* [1985] ECR 3499 para 10. See also Case 235/82Rev *Ferriere San Carlo v Commission* [1986] ECR 1799 (ECSC) (applicant failed to indicate which points of the judgment it contested).

[213] Case C-185/90P-Rev *Gill v Commission* [1992] ECR I-993 paras 11–16.

[214] ECJ Rules of Procedure, article 98; CFI Rules of Procedure, article 125.

[215] Statute of the Court of Justice, article 41.

[216] Statute of the Court of Justice, article 39; ECJ Rules of Procedure, article 97; CFI Rules of Procedure, articles 123–124. See Case T-35/89 *Zubizarreta v Albani* [1992] ECR II-1599. See also Joined Cases 9/60 and 12/60 *Belgium v Vloeberghs and High Authority* [1962] ECR 171 (ECSC); Joined Cases 42/59 and 49/59 (third party proceedings) *Breedband v SNUPAT* [1962] ECR 145 (ECSC); Case 267/80TO *Birra Dreher v Riseria Modenese, Council and Commission* [1986] ECR 3901; Case 292/84TP *Bolognese v Scharf and Commission* [1987] ECR 3563 paras 7–10; Case 147/86TO 1–3 *POIFXG v Greece and Commission* [1989] ECR 4103.

[217] Articles 187 [new art 244] and 192 [new art 256] of the EC Treaty. It is for the appropriate national authority to oversee the enforcement process; see Case 4/73 (Enforcement) *Nold v Ruhrkohle* [1977] ECR 1 (ECSC).

[218] Article 192 of the EC Treaty. Statute of the Court of Justice, article 36; ECJ Rules of Procedure, articles 89 and 97(2); CFI Rules of Procedure, articles 110 and 123(2).

[219] Article 1 of the Protocol on the Privileges and Immunities of the European Communities; Case C-2/94SA *ENU v Commission* [1995] ECR I-2767.

[220] Case 1/87SA *Universe Tankship v Commission* [1987] ECR 2807; Case T-497/93 *Hogan v Court of Justice* [1995] ECR II-703 paras 48–49.

(g) Costs

Order as to costs The rules as to costs are set out in the Rules of Procedure.[221] The final judgment or order closing the proceedings must contain a decision as to costs.[222] However, the Court may only make an order as to the costs incurred in those particular proceedings (and not other related proceedings).[223] The general rule is that the unsuccessful party must bear all the costs of the action if they have been applied for by the successful party. If costs are not claimed by the successful party, both parties must bear their own costs.[224] It is not essential for the claim for costs to be made in the original application; it is sufficient if it is made in subsequent written pleadings or at the oral hearing.[225]

Where there are several unsuccessful parties, the Court has a discretion as to how the costs are to be shared.[226] Where each party succeeds on some heads and fails on others, or where the circumstances are exceptional, the Court may order that the costs be shared or that the parties bear their own costs.[227] In Case T-96/92 *CCE de la Société Générale des Grandes Sources v Commission*[228] the Court of First Instance held that there were 'exceptional circumstances' where the relevant application had been the first of its type.

The Court may order a successful party to pay costs which it considers that party to have 'unreasonably or vexatiously' caused the opposite party to incur.[229] In Case 14/63 *Clabecq v High Authority*[230] the Court of Justice held that where defective drafting of a measure by a Community institution was the decisive factor in the making of an application which was dismissed, it was appropriate to order that the parties should bear their own costs. In Joined Cases 5/60, 7/60 and 8/60 *Meroni, FERAM and SIMET v High Authority*[231] the High Authority revoked the contested decisions during the course of the proceedings. The successful parties were ordered to pay the costs incurred after the

---

[221] ECJ Rules of Procedure, articles 69–75; CFI Rules of Procedure, articles 87–93. See also Statute of the Court of Justice, article 35. See generally André Fiebig, 'The Indemnification of Costs in Proceedings before the European Courts' [1997] 34 CML Rev 89.

[222] ECJ Rules of Procedure, article 69(1); CFI Rules of Procedure, article 87(1).

[223] Case T-387/94 *Asia Motor France v Commission* [1996] ECR II-961 paras 113–114.

[224] ECJ Rules of Procedure, article 69(2); CFI Rules of Procedure, article 87(2). See also Joined Cases 23/63, 24/63 and 52/63 *Usines Henricot v High Authority* [1963] ECR 217 at 225 (ECSC); Joined Cases 53/63 and 54/63 *Lemmerz-Werke v High Authority* [1963] ECR 239 at 248–249 (ECSC).

[225] Case T-13/92 *Moat v Commission* [1993] ECR II-287 para 50; Joined Cases T-70/92 and T-71/92 *Florimex v Commission* [1997] ECR II-693 para 197.

[226] ECJ Rules of Procedure, article 69(2); CFI Rules of Procedure, article 87(2).

[227] ECJ Rules of Procedure, article 69(3); CFI Rules of Procedure, article 87(3).

[228] [1995] ECR II-1213 paras 67–68. *Cf* Case C-58/94 *Netherlands v Commission* [1996] ECR I-2169, where a similar approach was proposed by Advocate-General Tesauro at para 24 of his Opinion but not followed by the Court in its judgment.

[229] ECJ Rules of Procedure, article 69(3); CFI Rules of Procedure, article 87(3).

[230] [1963] ECR 357 at 374 (ECSC). See also Case 49/64 *Stipperger v High Authority* [1965] ECR 521 at 527.

[231] [1961] ECR 107 (ECSC).

the revocation since they had chosen to continue the proceedings, even though they no longer had an interest in doing so.

Member States and institutions which intervene in proceedings must bear their own costs. The Court may order any other intervener to bear its own costs.[232]

The party which is awarded costs should send an account of the costs which it claims to the other party within a reasonable period.[233]

Interlocutory applications Any interlocutory application should contain a separate claim for costs. Failure to do so will mean that the Court is obliged to award all of the costs in the action to the successful party in the final judgment, without taking separate account of the outcome of any interlocutory applications.[234]

Taxation If there is a dispute concerning the amount of costs, a party can apply for the matter to be settled by the Court.[235] The EC courts have no power to tax the fees payable by parties to their own lawyers, but only to determine the amount of those fees which may be recovered from the party ordered to pay the costs. As Community law contains no provisions laying down a scale of fees, the Court will consider all the facts of the case, taking into account the purpose and nature of the proceedings, their significance from the point of view of Community law, the difficulty of the case, the amount of work required to be carried out by the lawyers involved and the financial interest the parties had in the proceedings.[236] The Court is not obliged to take account of any national scales of lawyers' fees or any agreement concluded in that regard between the party concerned and his agents or advisers.[237]

Recoverable costs The Rules of Procedure provide that expenses necessarily incurred by the parties for the purpose of the proceedings, in particular the travel and subsistence expenses and the remuneration of agents, advisers or lawyers, are to be regarded as recoverable costs.[238] Only costs relating to the actual

---

[232] ECJ Rules of Procedure, article 69(4); CFI Rules of Procedure, article 87(4). These rules were introduced in 1991.

[233] In Case 126/76 (Costs) *Dietz v Commission* [1979] ECR 2131 six months was not considered unreasonable. In Case T-2/93(92) *Air France v Commission* [1996] ECR II-235 para 12 one year was held not to exceed a reasonable period.

[234] Case T-50/89 *Sparr v Commission* [1990] ECR II-539 para 9.

[235] ECJ Rules of Procedure, article 74(1); CFI Rules of Procedure, article 92(1). National courts have no jurisdiction to tax costs incurred in direct actions before the EC courts: Case C-2/94SA *ENU v Commission* [1995] ECR I-2767 para 10. The Court will tax the costs only if they are disputed: see Case 25/65 *SIMET v High Authority* [1967] ECR 113 (ECSC); Joined Cases 9/65 and 58/65 *San Michele v High Authority* [1968] ECR 259 (ECSC). See also Case 6/72 (Costs) *Europemballage and Continental Can v Commission* [1975] ECR 495 (costs must be fixed in the national currency of a Member State or an EEA member).

[236] Case 318/82 *Leeuwarder Papierwarenfabriek v Commission* [1985] ECR 809; Case C-294/90DEP *British Aerospace v Commission* [1994] ECR I-5423 paras 10–14.

[237] Case T-2/93(92) *Air France v Commission* [1996] ECR II-235 para 21.

[238] ECJ Rules of Procedure, article 73(b); CFI Rules of Procedure, article 91(b).

proceedings may be recovered. Thus, costs incurred in proceedings before the Commission will not be recoverable.[239]

In addition, the following have been held to be recoverable as costs:

(1) postal, telephone, telex and photocopying charges;[240]

(2) travel and subsistence costs of the applicant if his presence at the oral hearing is necessary for the purpose of the proceedings.[241]

Where a Community institution has been represented by one of its own officials, it is not entitled to recover any costs in respect of legal fees; it will generally be limited to claiming only the travel and subsistence expenses incurred.[242]

The EC courts have held that the following are not recoverable as costs:

(1) remuneration paid by an undertaking to its in-house lawyers;[243]

(2) expenses incurred in translating documents (except where this allowed a party to reduce his overall legal costs, for example by retaining lawyers already familiar with the matter);[244]

(3) the expense of providing a bank guarantee in respect of a competition fine pending resolution of proceedings.[245]

(h) Legal aid

A party, or prospective party, who is wholly or in part unable to meet the costs of proceedings may apply directly to the Court, at any time, for legal aid.[246] An application for legal aid does not need to be presented by a lawyer.[247] The application must be accompanied by evidence of the applicant's need for assistance, in particular a document from a competent authority certifying his lack of means.[248]

Before granting legal aid, the Court must consider whether there is manifestly no cause of action.[249] Therefore, where the application for legal aid is

---

[239] Case C-222/92DEP *SFEI v Commission* [1994] ECR I-5431.

[240] Case 238/78 *Ireks-Arkady v EEC* [1981] ECR 1723 para 5.

[241] Case 24/79 *Oberthür v Commission* [1981] ECR 2229.

[242] Case 126/76 (Costs) *Dietz v Commission* [1979] ECR 2131. The position is different where the institution elects to be represented by a lawyer or agent who is not employed by that institution: Case C-370/89DEP *EIB v SGEEM* (Order of 15 September 1994), para 9 (unreported); Case T-460/93DEP *Etienne Tête v EIB* [1995] ECR II-229.

[243] Case C-104/85DEP *Bowater v Commission* (Order of 15 February 1995), para 10 (unreported).

[244] Case T-2/93(92) *Air France v Commission* ECR II-235 para 26.

[245] Case T-77/92 *Parker Pen v Commission* [1994] ECR II-549 paras 99–101.

[246] ECJ Rules of Procedure, article 76; Supplementary Rules, articles 4–5 (OJ 1974 L350 p 29) (as amended by OJ 1987 L165 p 4); CFI Rules of Procedure, articles 94–97. See Tom Kennedy, 'Paying the Piper: Legal Aid in Proceedings before the Court of Justice' [1988] CML Rev 559.

[247] ECJ Rules of Procedure, article 76(2); CFI Rules of Procedure, article 94(2); Case T-157/96AJ *Affatato v Commission* [1997] ECR II-155.

[248] ECJ Rules of Procedure, article 76(1); CFI Rules of Procedure, article 94(1). See Case T-157/96AJ *Affatato v Commission* [1997] ECR II-155 for the types of documents which might be acceptable to the Court.

[249] ECJ Rules of Procedure, article 76(3); CFI Rules of Procedure, article 94(2). Case T-13/91R *Harrison v Commission* [1991] ECR II-179 para 27; Case T-30/96 *Gomes de Sá Pereira v Council* [1996] ECR II-785 paras 33–34.

made before the commencement of proceedings, the applicant must give a brief description of the subject-matter of the application.[250]

3. APPEALS AGAINST DECISIONS OF THE COURT OF FIRST INSTANCE

Availability of appeals The following judgments and orders of the Court of First Instance may be appealed to the Court of Justice:[251]

(1) final judgments;

(2) decisions disposing of substantive issues in part only;

(3) decisions disposing of procedural issues concerning lack of competence or inadmissibility.

In addition, the following interlocutory matters may be appealed to the Court of Justice:[252]

(1) decisions dismissing applications to intervene;

(2) decisions concerning interim measures (articles 185 [new art 242] and 186 [new art 243] of the EC Treaty);

(3) decisions concerning the suspension of enforcement of decisions of the Council or Commission which impose a pecuniary obligation on persons other than States (article 192, para 4, of the EC Treaty [new art 256]).

There is no need to obtain leave to appeal from either the Court of First Instance or the Court of Justice before lodging an appeal. However, the Court of Justice may of its own motion declare that an appeal is inadmissible or devoid of purpose on the ground that the appellant no longer has an interest in bringing or in maintaining the appeal where an event subsequent to the judgment of the Court of First Instance has removed the prejudicial effect of that judgment as regards the appellant. For an appellant to have an interest in bringing proceedings, the appeal must be likely, if successful, to procure an advantage to the party bringing it.[253]

(a) Appeal from final judgments/decisions disposing of substantive issues in part only/decisions concerning lack of competence or inadmissibility

(i) Nature of appeal

Notification Final judgments of the Court of First Instance, decisions disposing of substantive issues in part only and decisions disposing of procedural issues concerning lack of competence or inadmissibility are notified by the Registrar of the Court of First Instance to all parties, as well as to all the

---

[250] *Notes for the guidance of counsel in written and oral proceedings before the Court of Justice of the European Communities* (reproduced at Appendix E) Part A, para 4 (b).

[251] Statute of the Court of Justice, article 49.

[252] Ibid, article 50.

[253] Case C-19/93P *Rendo v Commission* [1995] ECR I-3319 para 13.

Member States and Community institutions, even if they did not intervene in the case.[254]

Parties entitled to appeal An appeal on any of the above matters may be brought before the Court of Justice by any party which has been wholly, or partly, unsuccessful. Interveners, other than Member States or Community institutions, may only appeal against decisions which directly affect them. An appeal may be brought by a Member State or Community institution which did not intervene at first instance (except in staff cases).[255]

Time-limits for appeal Any appeal must be brought within two months of notification.[256]

Cross-appeal A party may raise a cross-appeal in its response.[257] The cross-appeal may not rely on new pleas which were not raised in the proceedings before the Court of First Instance.[258]

Grounds of appeal Appeals to the Court of Justice are limited to points of law, ie:

(1) lack of competence of the Court of First Instance;
(2) breach of procedure which adversely affects the interests of the appellant; and
(3) infringement of Community law by the Court of First Instance.[259]

New pleas which were not part of the original proceedings before the Court of First Instance cannot be raised for the first time in the appeal.[260] An appellant will not be permitted to introduce new evidence before the Court of Justice, even if it came to his attention after the judgment of the Court of First Instance.[261]

Appeals are limited to points of law. The Court of Justice has no jurisdiction to establish facts on appeal or, in principle, to examine the evidence which the Court of First Instance accepted in support of those facts.[262] Provided that the evidence has been properly obtained and the general principles of law and the rules of procedure in relation to the burden of proof and the taking of evidence

---

[254] Statute of the Court of Justice, article 48.

[255] Ibid, article 49; see also article 54(3) for the effect of such appeals.

[256] Ibid, article 49.

[257] ECJ Rules of Procedure, article 116(1); Case C-346/90P *F v Commission* [1992] ECR I-2691 para 4.

[258] ECJ Rules of Procedure, article 116(2).

[259] Statute of the Court of Justice, article 51. See para 2 of the Opinion of Advocate-General Tesauro in Case C-132/90P *Schwedler v Parliament* [1991] ECR I-5745 for a general analysis of the appellate function of the Court of Justice.

[260] Case C-76/93P *Scaramuzza v Commission* [1994] ECR I-5173 paras 15–19; Case C-19/95P *San Marco v Commission* [1996] ECR I-4435 paras 47–52. ECJ Rules of Procedure, articles 113(2) and 116(2). At paras 27–29 of his Opinion in Case C-357/95P *ENU v Commission* [1997] ECR I-1329 (EAEC) Advocate-General Fennelly took the view that the Court of Justice could consider of its own motion issues concerning the competence of the Court of First Instance, even where these had not been raised by the parties in the proceedings before that Court.

[261] Case C-396/93P *Henrichs v Commission* [1995] ECR I-2611 paras 9 and 14.

[262] Case C-320/92P *Finsider v Commission* [1994] ECR I-5697 para 28 (ECSC); Case C-19/95P *San Marco v Commission* [1996] ECR I-4435 para 40.

have been observed, it is for the Court of First Instance alone to assess the value which should be attached to the evidence produced to it.[263] However, the Court of Justice does have jurisdiction to overturn the Court of First Instance's findings of fact where an error of assessment is apparent from the documents submitted to the Court of First Instance.[264] Furthermore, the Court of Justice has jurisdiction to review the legal assessment of facts by the Court of First Instance and the legal conclusions it has drawn from them.[265]

The Court of Justice is not entitled to substitute, on grounds of fairness, its own assessment for that of the Court of First Instance as to the appropriate level of fines to be imposed on undertakings for infringements of Community law.[266] However, it is entitled to consider whether the Court of First Instance has taken sufficient account of the arguments raised as to the level of fines imposed.[267]

An appeal must indicate the precise grounds upon which it is brought. An appeal which merely repeats or reproduces word for word the pleas in law and arguments previously submitted to the Court of First Instance will be declared to be inadmissible.[268]

Any challenge to grounds given in a judgment of the Court of First Instance which went beyond what was necessary for it to give its judgment ('supererogatory grounds') will be declared to be inadmissible.[269]

Appeals as to costs There is no right to appeal solely as to the amount of costs awarded or the party ordered to pay them.[270] Thus, where the Court of Justice dismisses all the other pleas in law made by the appellant, it will declare any remaining plea as to costs inadmissible.[271]

---

[263] Case C-19/95P *San Marco v Commission* [1996] ECR I-4435 para 40.

[264] Case C-53/92P *Hilti v Commission* [1994] ECR I-667 para 42; Case C-136/92P *Commission v Lualdi* [1994] ECR I-1981 paras 48–50; Case C-19/95P *San Marco v Commission* [1996] ECR I-4435 para 39; Case C-362/95P *Blackspur DIY v Council and Commission* [1997] ECR I-4775 para 29.

[265] Case C-19/95P *San Marco v Commission* [1996] ECR I-4435 para 39; Case C-89/97P(R) *Moccia Irme v Commission* [1997] ECR I-2329 para 39; Case C-278/95P *Siemens v Commission* [1997] ECR I-2507 paras 42–45. See also Case C-19/93P *Rendo v Commission* [1995] ECR I-3319 para 26. For a discussion of the appropriate approach in competition cases, see paras 8–12 and 46–49 of the Opinion of Advocate-General Jacobs in Case C-53/92P *Hilti v Commission* [1994] ECR I-667.

[266] Case C-320/92P *Finanziaria Siderurgica Finsider v Commission* [1994] ECR I-5697 para 46 (ECSC); Case C-310/93P *BPB Industries and British Gypsum v Commission* [1995] ECR I-865 para 34.

[267] Case C-219/95P *Ferriere Nord v Commission* [1997] ECR I-4411 para 31.

[268] Case C-87/95P *CNPAAP v Commission* [1996] ECR I-2003 paras 29–31; Case C-19/95P *San Marco v Commission* [1996] ECR I-4435 paras 36–38; Case C-293/95P *Odigitria v Council* [1996] ECR I-6129 paras 44–45.

[269] Case C-137/95P *Samenwerkende Prijsregelende Organisaties in de Bouwnijverheid v Commission* [1996] ECR I-1611 para 47; Case C-264/95P *Commission v UIC* [1997] ECR I-1287 para 48; Case C-395/95P *Geotronics v Commission* [1997] ECR I-2271 para 23.

[270] Statute of the Court of Justice, article 51.

[271] Case C-253/94P *Roujansky v Council* [1995] ECR I-7 paras 12–14; Case C-396/93P *Henrichs v Commission* [1995] ECR I-2611 paras 64–66; Case C-303/96P *Bernardi v Parliament* [1997] ECR I-1239 para 49.

(ii) Procedure

Application for appeal An appeal is brought by lodging an application with the Registry of the Court of Justice or the Registry of the Court of First Instance.[272] The appeal must state:[273]

(1) the name and permanent address of the appellant;

(2) an address for service in Luxembourg and the name of the person authorised to accept service;[274]

(3) the names of the other parties to the proceedings before the Court of First Instance;

(4) the date on which the decision appealed against was notified to the appellant;

(5) the pleas in law and legal arguments relied on;[275]

(6) the form of order sought by the appellant, either:[276]

   (*a*) to set aside, in whole or in part, the decision of the Court of First Instance; or

   (*b*) the same form of order, in whole or in part, as that sought at first instance. The appeal may not seek a different form of order.[277] In addition, the appeal should include a claim for costs. Failure to claim costs will mean that the appellant will not be entitled to recover any costs, even if his appeal is successful.[278]

Language of the case The language of the case in an appeal is the same as the language of the case in the proceedings before the Court of First Instance.[279]

Annexes The following documents should be annexed to the appeal:[280]

(1) the decision of the Court of First Instance appealed against;

(2) a certificate establishing that the lawyer acting for the appellant is entitled to act before a court of a Member State or of a State which is a party to the EEA Agreement.

---

[272] ECJ Rules of Procedure, article 111.

[273] Ibid, article 112.

[274] It is usual to instruct a lawyer in Luxembourg for this purpose. The giving of an address for service is optional. If no address for service is given, pleadings are sent by registered post to counsel for the party concerned: see *Notes for the guidance of counsel in written and oral proceedings before the Court of Justice of the European Communities* (reproduced at Appendix E) Part B, para 4 (b).

[275] An appeal which fails to set out the grounds of appeal relied on in a coherent and comprehensible statement will be dismissed as inadmissible: Case C-51/95P *Unifruit Hellas v Commission* [1997] ECR I-727 paras 31–33; Case C-78/97P(R) *Goldstein v Commission* (unreported order of 10 March 1997).

[276] ECJ Rules of Procedure, article 113. The subject-matter of the proceedings before the Court of First Instance may not be changed in the appeal.

[277] Case C-53/92P *Hilti v Commission* [1994] ECR I-667 paras 48–50.

[278] Case C-253/94P *Roujansky v Council* [1995] ECR I-7 para 16.

[279] ECJ Rules of Procedure, article 110. Parties may apply to the Court to use a different language, and Member States may intervene in their own language.

[280] ECJ Rules of Procedure, article 112.

Lodging with the Court The original of the appeal must be signed by the appellant's agent or lawyer and should be dated. The original, including annexes, should be lodged with the Registrar, together with five certified copies for the Court and a copy for every other party to the proceedings.[281] Upon registration, appeals from the Court of First Instance are assigned a case number in the form 'C–345/90P'.[282] Notice of the appeal is served on all the parties to the proceedings before the Court of First Instance.[283]

Further pleadings Any party to the proceedings before the Court of First Instance may lodge a response within two months after service on him of the notice of appeal.[284] This may be followed by a reply and rejoinder or any other pleading where the President expressly allows it. A party who wishes to submit a reply or rejoinder must make an application to that effect within seven days of service of the response or reply.[285]

Further procedure Following the written pleadings, the procedure followed by the Court of Justice on an appeal is similar to the procedure in other cases. In particular, the same rules apply in relation to:[286]

(1) stay of proceedings;
(2) discontinuance;
(3) the slip rule;
(4) rectification of omissions;
(5) interpretation of judgments;
(6) revision of judgments;
(7) review at the request of third parties;
(8) legal aid.

Intervention The general rules as to intervention apply also to appeals.[287] However, an application to intervene in appeal proceedings must be lodged within one month of the date on which notice of the appeal is published in the *Official Journal of the European Communities*.[288] The right to intervene in appeals is not limited to those who intervened in the proceedings before the Court of First Instance.[289] Persons who intervened in the proceedings before the Court of First Instance are treated as parties to those proceedings and have an automatic right to participate in any appeal proceedings. They are not required to submit a fresh application to intervene in the appeal proceedings.[290]

---

[281] Ibid, article 112.
[282] The 'P' derives from the French word for appeal, 'pourvoi'.
[283] ECJ Rules of Procedure, article 114.
[284] Ibid, articles 115–116.
[285] Ibid, article 117.
[286] Ibid, article 118. Note that the powers to order preparatory inquiries do not apply to appeals.
[287] Ibid, article 118 and article 93. Case C-245/95P (Intervention II) *Commission v NTN Corporation and Koyo Seiko Co* [1996] ECR I-559. The general rules concerning intervention are discussed above at pp 403–406.
[288] ECJ Rules of Procedure, article 123.
[289] ECJ Rules of Procedure, article 118 and article 93.
[290] Case C-244/91P *Pincherle v Commission* [1993] ECR I-6965 paras 14–17; Case C-245/95P (Intervention I) *Commission v NTN Corporation and Koyo Seiko Co* [1996] ECR I-553.

Interim measures An appeal does not have suspensory effect. However, articles 185 and 186 of the EC Treaty [new arts 242 and 243] are applicable to appeals, and a party may pursuant to these articles apply to the Court of Justice to suspend the application of a judgment of the Court of First Instance, pending an appeal to the Court of Justice.[291]

Inadmissibility The Court of Justice may, of its own motion, dismiss an appeal in whole or in part where it is clearly inadmissible or clearly unfounded.[292]

Oral hearing The Court of Justice may decide to dispense with the oral part of the procedure unless one of the parties objects on the ground that the written procedure did not enable him fully to defend his point of view.[293] If an oral hearing is held, it will follow the same procedure as in other actions.[294]

(iii) Judgment

Nature of judgment Where an appeal is well founded, the Court of Justice will quash the decision of the Court of First Instance. It may give final judgment in the matter, where the state of the proceedings so permits, or refer the case back to the Court of First Instance for judgment. If the matter is referred back to the Court of First Instance, that Court is bound by any decisions of the Court of Justice on points of law.[295]

Where the Court of First Instance has adopted reasoning which is incorrect, but the decision can be justified on other, valid grounds, an appeal against that decision will be rejected.[296]

Length of proceedings In 1996, the average length of proceedings for an appeal (from lodging of the appeal to judgment) was 14 months.[297]

(iv) Costs

The general rules as to costs apply.[298] Where the appeal fails, or where the appeal succeeds and the Court of Justice gives final judgment, the Court of Justice will make an order as to costs.[299] Where the case is referred back to the Court of First Instance, that Court makes an order covering the costs of the

---

[291] Statute of the Court of Justice, article 53; ECJ Rules of Procedure, article 118. Case C-345/90PR *Parliament v Hanning* [1991] ECR I-231; Case T-77/91R *Hochbaum v Commission* [1991] ECR II-1285 paras 19–22; Case C-254/95PR *Parliament v Innamorati* [1995] ECR I-2707 para 14.

[292] ECJ Rules of Procedure, article 119.

[293] Statute of the Court of Justice, article 52; ECJ Rules of Procedure, articles 120 and 121.

[294] Ibid, article 118.

[295] Statute of the Court of Justice, article 54. The procedure to be followed where a case is referred back to the Court of First Instance is contained in the CFI Rules of Procedure, articles 117–121.

[296] Case C-30/91 *Lestelle v Commission* [1992] ECR I-3755 para 28 (ECSC); Case C-36/92P *SEP v Commission* [1994] ECR I-1911 para 33; Case C-480/93P *Zunis Holding v Commission* [1996] ECR I-1 para 15.

[297] These figures are taken from the *Weekly Summaries of the Court of Justice*, Number 36 of 1996.

[298] ECJ Rules of Procedure, article 118. The general rules as to costs are discussed above at pp 414–416.

[299] ECJ Rules of Procedure, article 122.

proceedings instituted before it, as well as the costs of the appeal proceedings before the Court of Justice.[300] Every appeal lodged should include a claim for costs. Failure to do so will mean that the appellant will not be entitled to recover any costs, even if his appeal is successful.[301]

(b) Appeal from decisions dismissing applications to intervene/ decisions concerning interim measures/decisions concerning suspension of enforcement

Interim measures/suspension of enforcement Parties may appeal to the Court of Justice against any decision of the Court of First Instance concerning interim measures (under article 185 or 186 of the EC Treaty [new arts 242 and 243]) or concerning the suspension of enforcement of decisions of the Council or Commission imposing a pecuniary obligation on persons other than States (article 192, para 4, of the EC Treaty [new art 256]) within two months of the notification of the Court's decision to the parties.[302]

Decisions refusing intervention Any person whose application to intervene has been dismissed by the Court of First Instance may appeal to the Court of Justice within two weeks of the notification of the decision dismissing the application.[303]

Procedure Appeals on these matters do not follow the normal appeal procedure; instead, they follow the procedure adopted by the Court of Justice when dealing with applications for interim measures in cases before it.[304]

---

[300] CFI Rules of Procedure, article 121.
[301] Case C-253/94P *Roujansky v Council* [1995] ECR I-7 para 16.
[302] Statute of the Court of Justice, article 50.
[303] Ibid.
[304] ECJ Rules of Procedure, articles 83–86, applicable by virtue of Statute of the Court of Justice, article 50 and article 36. These rules are discussed at Ch 17, pp 382–386.

Part V

Precedents

Precedent A
Damages Against a Private Party—
Statement of Claim

IN THE HIGH COURT OF JUSTICE   199——— A No ———
QUEEN'S BENCH DIVISION

BETWEEN

AB LIMITED   Plaintiff

—and—

CD LIMITED   Defendant

STATEMENT OF CLAIM

1. The Plaintiff carries on business in the United Kingdom and Italy as an exporter/importer and retailer of computer games and has a registered office at [*insert address*].

2. The Defendant is a manufacturer of computer games and has a registered office at [*insert address*].

3. In or about June 1996 the Plaintiff sought to export computer games manufactured by the Defendant from the United Kingdom to Italy. The Plaintiff intended to resell the computer games in Italy.

4. The Plaintiff was prevented from exporting computer games to Italy as the Defendant instructed all of its authorised distributors in the United Kingdom not to sell computer games to the Plaintiff.

5. At all material times the Defendant was in a dominant position in a substantial part of the Common Market within the meaning of article 86 of the EC Treaty. In support of this contention the Plaintiff relies on the following facts and matters:
[*specify supporting facts and matters*]

6. The Defendant has abused its dominant position contrary to article 86 of the EC Treaty. In support of this contention the Plaintiff relies on the following facts and matters:
   [*specify supporting facts and matters*]

7. The above abuses of a dominant position have had an appreciable effect on trade between Member States. In support of this contention the Plaintiff relies on the following facts and matters:
   [*specify supporting facts and matters*]

8. The Defendant owes to the Plaintiff a statutory duty under the European Communities Act 1972 and further or alternatively a duty arising under European Community law to comply with the provisions of the EC Treaty and in particular article 86 thereof.

9. For the reasons set out above the Defendant has acted in breach of the said duty.

10. Further or alternatively, the Defendant has acted unlawfully with the intention of harming the business of the Plaintiff. Alternatively, the Defendant should reasonably have foreseen that its conduct as set out above would harm the business of the Plaintiff.

11. In the premises the conduct of the Defendant constitutes unlawful interference by the Defendant with the business of the Plaintiff.

12. The Plaintiff has suffered loss and damage as a result of the said breach of duty and/or unlawful interference.

PARTICULARS

[*give particulars of loss*]

13. The Plaintiff is entitled to interest pursuant to s 35A of the Supreme Court Act 1981 on such sums and at such rate and for such period as the Court deems fit.

AND the Plaintiff claims:

(1) damages;
(2) interest pursuant to s 35A of the Supreme Court Act 1981.

[*name of counsel*]

SERVED this ——————— day of ——————— 199—— by [*firm name*] of [*address*], Solicitors to the Plaintiff.

Precedent B
Damages Against the State—
Statement of Claim

IN THE HIGH COURT OF JUSTICE   199—— A No ————
QUEEN'S BENCH DIVISION

BETWEEN

AB LIMITED   Plaintiff

—and—

MINISTER OF AGRICULTURE,
FISHERIES AND FOOD   Defendant

STATEMENT OF CLAIM

1. The Plaintiff carries on business in the United Kingdom as a breeder and importer of cattle for resale.

2. In June 1994 the Plaintiff commenced the importation of cattle from Belgium into the United Kingdom for breeding and resale purposes.

3. By the Import of Cattle from Belgium (Animal Health) Regulations 1996 (SI 1996/000) ('the Regulations') the Defendant prohibited the importation into the United Kingdom of cattle from Belgium with effect from 1 February 1996.

4. The Regulations constitute a measure having equivalent effect to a quantitative restriction and are contrary to article 30 of the EC Treaty.

5. Article 30 of the EC Treaty has direct effect and is intended to confer rights on individuals.

6. The breach of article 30 of the EC Treaty is sufficiently serious to give rise to liability in damages on the part of the United Kingdom.

PARTICULARS

[*insert particulars*]

7. The Plaintiff has suffered loss and damage as a direct result of the Defendant's breach of article 30 of the EC Treaty.

PARTICULARS

[*insert particulars*]

8. The Defendant owes the Plaintiff a statutory duty under the European Communities Act 1972 and further or alternatively a duty arising under European Community law to comply with the provisions of the EC Treaty and in particular article 30 thereof.

9. For the reasons set out above the Defendant has acted in breach of the said duty.

10. The Plaintiff is entitled to interest pursuant to s 35A of the Supreme Court Act 1981 on such sums and at such rate and for such period as the Court deems fit.

AND the Plaintiff claims:

(1) damages;
(2) interest pursuant to s 35A of the Supreme Court Act 1981.

[*name of counsel*]

SERVED this ——————— day of ——————— 199—— by [*firm name*] of [*address*], Solicitors to the Plaintiff.

Precedent C
Preliminary Reference—Notice of Motion

IN THE HIGH COURT OF JUSTICE   199——— A No ————
[QUEEN'S BENCH DIVISION/CHANCERY DIVISION]

BETWEEN

AB LIMITED   Plaintiff

—and—

CD LIMITED   Defendant

NOTICE OF MOTION

TAKE NOTICE that this Honourable Court will be moved before Mr Justice ————————— at the Royal Courts of Justice, Strand, London WC2A 2LL, on the ————————— day of ————————— 199—— at ——— o'clock in the [fore/after]noon or so soon thereafter as Counsel can be heard for an order that:

(1) the questions set out in the draft Schedule hereto concerning the [interpretation /validity] of Commission Directive 000/93 of 24 June 1993 on the approximation of the laws of the Member States relating to the labelling of foodstuffs be referred to the Court of Justice of the European Communities for a preliminary ruling in accordance with article 177 of the EC Treaty;

(2) all further proceedings in this action be stayed until after the Court of Justice shall have given its ruling on the said question or until further Order in the meantime;

(3) the costs of this Motion be costs reserved.

[*signature*]
Solicitors to the Plaintiff

DATED this ————————— day of ————————— 199——.

PRECEDENTS

To the Defendant
and to [*name*] of [*address*], Solicitors to the Defendant.

SCHEDULE

REQUEST FOR A PRELIMINARY RULING OF THE COURT OF JUSTICE OF THE EUROPEAN COMMUNITIES

[*The Schedule should contain the following:*

   (a) description of the parties;
   (b) facts of the case;
   (c) details of any judgment of a lower court;
   (d) description of relevant provisions of English law;
   (e) description of relevant provisions of Community law;
   (f) reasons why preliminary reference is necessary;
   (g) arguments of the parties on issues of Community law.]

The preliminary ruling of the Court of Justice is accordingly requested on the following questions:

[*list questions*]

Precedent D
Preliminary Reference—Order

IN THE HIGH COURT OF JUSTICE   199—— A No ————
[QUEEN'S BENCH DIVISION/CHANCERY DIVISION]
THE HONOURABLE MR JUSTICE ——————

BETWEEN

AB LIMITED   Plaintiff

—and—

CD LIMITED   Defendant

ORDER

UPON READING the Notice of Motion herein dated the ——————— day of —————— 199—— filed on behalf of the Plaintiff.

AND UPON READING the affidavit[s] of ——————— sworn on ——————— together with the exhibits referred to therein filed on behalf of the Plaintiff and the Statement of Facts set out in the Schedule thereto.

AND UPON READING the affidavit[s] of ——————— sworn on ——————— together with the exhibits referred to therein filed on behalf of the Defendant.

AND UPON HEARING counsel for the Plaintiff and for the Defendant.

IT IS ORDERED THAT:

(1) the questions set out in the Schedule hereto concerning the [interpretation/ validity] of Commission Directive 000/93 of 24 June 1993 on the approximation of the laws of the Member States relating to the labelling of foodstuffs be referred to the Court of Justice of the European Communities for a preliminary ruling in accordance with article 177 of the EC Treaty;

(2) all further proceedings in this action be stayed until after the Court of Justice shall have given its ruling on the said question or until further Order in the meantime;

[(3) the Senior Master of the Queen's Bench Division do send a copy of this Order to the Registrar of the Court of Justice without waiting for the expiry of the time to appeal against this Order pursuant to RSC Ord 114, r 5;][1]

(4) the costs of this Motion be costs reserved.

SCHEDULE

REQUEST FOR A PRELIMINARY RULING OF THE COURT OF JUSTICE OF THE EUROPEAN COMMUNITIES

[*The Schedule should contain the following:*

(h) *description of the parties;*
(i) *facts of the case;*
(j) *details of any judgment of a lower court;*
(k) *description of relevant provisions of English law;*
(l) *description of relevant provisions of Community law;*
(m) *reasons why preliminary reference is necessary;*
(n) *arguments of the parties on issues of Community law.*]

The preliminary ruling of the Court of Justice is accordingly requested on the following questions:

[*list questions*]

DATED this ——————— day of ——————— 199——.

---

[1] All parties may agree to waive their rights to appeal. See further at p 146.

Precedent E
Preliminary Reference—Notice of Appeal

IN THE COURT OF APPEAL   199—— A No ————
ON APPEAL FROM THE HIGH COURT OF JUSTICE
[QUEEN'S BENCH DIVISION/CHANCERY DIVISION]

BETWEEN:

AB LIMITED   Plaintiff

—and—

CD LIMITED   Defendant

NOTICE OF APPEAL

TAKE NOTICE that the Court of Appeal will be moved as soon as Counsel can be heard on behalf of the above-named [Defendant] on appeal from the judgment and order of Mr Justice ———————— given at the hearing of the [Plaintiff's] Motion on the ———————— day of ———————— 199—— whereby on the [Plaintiff's] application under RSC Ord 114 the Court ordered that there be referred to the Court of Justice of the European Communities for a preliminary ruling under article 177 of the EC Treaty the following questions:

[*reproduce questions*]

FOR AN ORDER that the said judgment be set aside AND for an Order that the [Plaintiff] pay to the [Defendant] the costs of this appeal.

AND FURTHER TAKE NOTICE that the grounds of the appeal are:

[*specify grounds of appeal*]

DATED this ———————— day of ———————— 199——.

[*name of solicitors*]
Solicitors to the Defendant.

To the Plaintiff and [*name of solicitors*], Solicitors to the Plaintiff.

Precedent F
Preliminary Reference—
Observations to the Court of Justice

IN THE COURT OF JUSTICE OF THE EUROPEAN COMMUNITIES

CASE C-000/94

ON A REFERENCE FOR A PRELIMINARY RULING UNDER ARTICLE 177 OF THE EC TREATY MADE BY THE [QUEEN'S BENCH DIVISION OF THE HIGH COURT OF JUSTICE OF ENGLAND AND WALES], IN THE CASE PENDING BEFORE IT

BETWEEN

AB LIMITED

—and—

CD LIMITED

WRITTEN OBSERVATIONS OF CD LIMITED

FACTS

[*set out additional facts not sufficiently dealt with in reference or indicate agreement with facts as set out in reference*]

LEGAL SUBMISSIONS

First Question

[*Set out submissions*]

Consequently, CD Limited submits that the Court of Justice should answer the first question as follows:

[*For example, 'Article 5 of Commission Directive 000/93 of 24 June 1993 on the approximation of the laws of the Member States relating to the labelling of*

*foodstuffs precludes a national law from requiring the exclusive use of a
specific language for the labelling of foodstuffs'.]*

Second Question

Third Question

DATED this ——————— day of ——————— 199———.

Signed [*counsel*], instructed by ———————, Solicitors of [*address*].

Precedent G
Article 169—Complaint to the Commission
(OJ No C26/6, 1 February 1989)

The Commission is issuing this standard complaint form to assist complainants in cases of failure to comply with Community law.

COMPLAINT TO THE COMMISSION OF THE EUROPEAN COMMUNITIES FOR FAILURE TO COMPLY WITH COMMUNITY LAW

(89/C 26/07)

Name of complainant([1]):

Nationality:

Address or registered office:

Sphere of activity:

Member State, body or undertaking which has failed to comply with Community law:

Subject-matter of complaint and damage suffered, if any:

Steps taken before national or Community authorities:

— Administrative steps:

---

[1] The Commission undertakes to observe the customary rules of confidentiality when investigating the complaint.

— Proceedings, if any, before courts or tribunals:

Documentary or other evidence available in support of the complaint:

(Note to appear on the back of the form)

The Commission of the European Communities is responsible under the Treaties for ensuring the correct application of their provisions and of measures taken by the Community institutions.

Any individual may lodge a complaint with the Commission concerning a practice or a measure which, in his opinion, infringes a Community provision.

The complaint may be made on this form. It may either be sent direct to Brussels (Commission of the European Communities, 200 rue de la Loi, B–1049 Brussels) or be handed in at one of the Commission's information offices.

The following administrative safeguards exist for the complainant's benefit:

— an acknowledgement of receipt will be sent to the complainant as soon as the complaint is registered;

— the complainant will be informed of the action taken in response to his complaint, including representations made to the national authorities, Community bodies or undertakings concerned;

— the complainant will be informed of any infringement proceedings that the Commission intends to institute against a Member State as a result of the complaint and of any legal action it intends to take against an undertaking. Where appropriate, the complainant will be informed of proceedings that have already been instituted in relation to the subject-matter of the complaint.

Precedent H
Article 173—Application to the Court of First Instance

IN THE COURT OF FIRST INSTANCE OF THE EUROPEAN COMMUNITIES

X Limited, a company incorporated in England, of [registered office], represented by ——————, barrister of Gray's Inn, instructed by [name], solicitor, with an address for service at [name of Luxembourg agent and Luxembourg address for service]

Applicant

—and—

The Commission of the European Communities   Defendant

APPLICATION under article 173 of the EC Treaty for a declaration that Commission Decision 000/96 of 23 October 1996 relating to a proceeding under article 85 of the EC Treaty is void

---

FACTS

[insert]

LEGAL ARGUMENTS

[insert]

ORDER SOUGHT

AB Limited respectfully asks the Court:

(1) to declare that Commission Decision 000/96 of 23 October 1996 is void;
(2) to order the Commission to pay costs.

Signed: [*signature of legal representative*]

DATED the ——————— day of ——————— 199——.

[*plus necessary annexes*]

Appendices

Appendix A

List of Directly Effective Treaty Articles (OJ No C177/13, 4 July 1983)

1. Treaty Articles which have direct effect

Article 7 [new art 12] — Case 22/80 *Boussac Saint-Frères SA v Gerstenmeier* [1980] ECR 3427

Article 9 [new art 23] — Cases 2 and 3/69 *Sociaal Fonds voor de Diamantarbeiders v SA Ch Brachfeld & Sons* [1969] ECR 211

Article 12 [new art 25] — Case 26/62 *NV Algemene Transport-en Expeditie Onderneming van Genden Loos v Nederlandse Tarief Commissie* [1963] ECR 1

Article 13 (2) [repealed by Amsterdam Treaty] — Case 33/70 *SACE SpA v Italian Ministry for Finance* [1970] ECR 1213

Article 16 [repealed by Amsterdam treaty] — Case 18/71 *Eunomia di Porro e C v Italian Ministry for Education* [1971] ECR 811

Article 30 [new art 28] — Case 74/76 *Iannelli and Volpi SpA v Meroni* [1977] ECR 557

Article 31 and first paragraph of Article 32 [both repealed by Amsterdam Treaty] — Case 13/68 *Salgoil SpA v Italian Ministry for Foreign Trade* [1968] ECR 453

Article 34 [new art 29] — Case 83/78 *Pigs Marketing Board v Redmond* [1978] ECR 2347

Article 37 (1) [new art 31] — Case 59/75 *Pubblico Ministero v Manghera* [1976] ECR 91

Article 37 (2) [new art 31] — Case 6/64 *Costa v ENEL* [1964] ECR 585

Article 48 (2) [new art 39] — Case 167/73 *EC Commission v France* [1974] ECR 359

Article 52 [new art 43] — Case 2/74 *Reyners v Belgium* [1974] ECR 631

Article 53 [repealed by Amsterdam Treaty] — Case 6/64 *Costa v ENEL* [1964] ECR 585

First paragraph of Article 59 [new art 49] and third paragraph of Article 60 [new art 50] — Case 33/74 *Van Binsbergen v Bestuur van de Bedrijfsvereniging voor de Metaalnijverheid* [1974] ECR 1299

Article 85 [new art 81] — Case 13/61 *Kledingverkoopbedrijf de Geus un Uitdenbogerd v Robert Bosch GmbH* [1962] ECR 45

Article 86 [new art 82] (in conjunction with Article 90 [new art 86]) — Case 155/73 *Sacchi* [1974] ECR 409

Final sentence of Article 93 (3) [new art 88] — Case 6/64 *Costa v ENEL* [1964] ECR 585

445

First paragraph of Article 95 [new art 90] — Case 57/65 *Lütticke GmbH v Hauptzollamt Saarlouis* [1966] ECR 205

Second paragraph of Article 95 [new art 90] — Case 27/67 *Fink-Frucht GmbH v Hauptzollamt München-Landsbergerstraße* [1968] ECR 223

Article 119 [new art 141] — Case 43/75 *Defrenne v SA Belge de Navigation Aérienne* [1976] ECR 455

Except for Article 119, which is an exception from the general rule for specific reasons, the date on which a provision of the Treaty becomes directly applicable does not depend on the date of the Court judgment.

2. Treaty Articles which do not have direct effect

Second paragraph of Article 32 — Case 13/68 *Salgoil SpA v Italian Ministry for Foreign Trade* [1968] ECR 453

Article 33 [repealed by Amsterdam Treaty] — Ibid.

Article 67 [repealed by Amsterdam Treaty] — Case 203/80 *Casati* [1981] ECR 2595

First paragraph of Article 71 — Case 203/80 *Casati* [1981] ECR 2595

Article 90 (2) [new art 86] — Case 10/71 *Ministère Public of Luxembourg v Muller* [1971] ECR 723

Article 97 [repealed by Amsterdam Treaty] — Case 57/65 *Lütticke GmbH v Hauptzollamt Saarlouis* [1966] ECR 205

Article 102 [new art 97] — Case 6/64 *Costa v ENEL* [1964] ECR 585

Articles 5 [new art 10] and 107 [new art 108] — Case 9/73 *Schlüter v Hauptzollamt Lörrach* [1973] ECR 1135

Appendix B

Statute of the Court of Justice (EC Statute)[1]

Article 1

The Court established by Article 4 of this Treaty shall be constituted and shall function in accordance with the provisions of this Treaty and of this Statute.

TITLE I

Judges and Advocates-General

Article 2

Before taking up his duties each Judge shall, in open court, take an oath to perform his duties impartially and conscientiously and to preserve the secrecy of the deliberations of the Court.

Article 3

The Judges shall be immune from legal proceedings. After they have ceased to hold office, they shall continue to enjoy immunity in respect of acts performed by them in their official capacity, including words spoken or written.

The Court, sitting in plenary session, may waive the immunity.

Where immunity has been waived and criminal proceedings are instituted against a Judge, he shall be tried, in any of the Member States, only by the Court competent to judge the members of the highest national judiciary.

Article 4

The Judges may not hold any political or administrative office.

They may not engage in any occupation, whether gainful or not, unless exemption is exceptionally granted by the Council.

When taking up their duties, they shall give a solemn undertaking that, both during and after their term of office, they will respect the obligations arising therefrom, in particular the duty to behave with integrity and discretion as regards the acceptance, after they have ceased to hold office, of certain appointments or benefits.

Any doubt on this point shall be settled by decision of the Court.

---

[1] Protocol of the Statute of the Court of Justice, signed at Brussels on 17 April 1957. Consolidated version as at September 1997.

Article 5

Apart from normal replacement, or death, the duties of a Judge shall end when he resigns.

Where a Judge resigns, his letter of resignation shall be addressed to the President of the Court for transmission to the President of the Council. Upon this notification a vacancy shall arise on the bench.

Save where Article 6 applies, a Judge shall continue to hold office until his successor takes up his duties.

Article 6

A Judge may be deprived of his office or of his right to a pension or other benefits in its stead only if, in the unanimous opinion of the Judges and Advocates-General of the Court, he no longer fulfils the requisite conditions or meets the obligations arising from his office. The Judge concerned shall not take part in any such deliberations.

The Registrar of the Court shall communicate the decision of the Court to the President of the European Parliament and to the President of the Commission and shall notify it to the President of the Council.

In the case of a decision depriving a Judge of his office, a vacancy shall arise on the bench upon this latter notification.

Article 7

A Judge who is to replace a member of the Court whose term of office has not expired shall be appointed for the remainder of his predecessor's term.

Article 8

The provisions of Articles 2 to 7 shall apply to the Advocates-General.

TITLE II

Organization

Article 9

The Registrar shall take an oath before the Court to perform his duties impartially and conscientiously and to preserve the secrecy of the deliberations of the Court.

Article 10

The Court shall arrange for replacement of the Registrar on occasions when he is prevented from attending the Court.

Article 11

Officials and other servants shall be attached to the Court to enable it to function. They shall be responsible to the Registrar under the authority of the President.

Article 12

On a proposal from the Court, the Council may, acting unanimously, provide for the appointment of Assistant Rapporteurs and lay down the rules governing their service. The Assistant Rapporteurs may be required, under conditions laid down in the rules of procedure, to participate in preparatory inquiries in cases pending before the Court and to cooperate with the Judge who acts as Rapporteur.

The Assistant Rapporteurs shall be chosen from persons whose independence is beyond doubt and who possess the necessary legal qualifications; they shall be appointed by the Council. They shall take an oath before the Court to perform their duties impartially and conscientiously and to preserve the secrecy of the deliberations of the Court.

Article 13

The Judges, the Advocates-General and the Registrar shall be required to reside at the place where the Court has its seat.

Article 14

The Court shall remain permanently in session. The duration of the judicial vacations shall be determined by the Court with due regard to the needs of its business.

Article 15

Decisions of the Court shall be valid only when an uneven number of its members is sitting in the deliberations. Decisions of the full Court shall be valid if nine members are sitting. Decisions of the Chambers consisting of three or five Judges shall be valid only if three Judges are sitting. Decisions of the Chambers consisting of seven Judges shall be valid only if five Judges are sitting. In the event of one of the Judges of a Chamber being prevented from attending, a Judge of another Chamber may be called upon to sit in accordance with conditions laid down in the rules of procedure.

Article 16

No Judge or Advocate-General may take part in the disposal of any case in which he has previously taken part as agent or adviser or has acted for one of the parties, or in which he has been called upon to pronounce as a Member of a court or tribunal, of a commission of inquiry or in any other capacity.

If, for some special reason, any Judge or Advocate-General considers that he should not take part in the judgment or examination of a particular case, he shall so inform the President. If, for some special reason, the President considers that any Judge or Advocate-General should not sit or make submissions in a particular case, he shall notify him accordingly.

Any difficulty arising as to the application of this Article shall be settled by decision of the Court.

A party may not apply for a change in the composition of the Court or of one of its Chambers on the grounds of either the nationality of a Judge or the absence from the Court or from the Chamber of a Judge of the nationality of that party.

TITLE III

Procedure

Article 17

The States and the institutions of the Community shall be represented before the Court by an agent appointed for each case: the agent may be assisted by an adviser or by a lawyer.

The States, other than the Member States, which are parties to the Agreement on the European Economic Area, and also the EFTA Surveillance Authority referred to in that Agreement, shall be represented in same manner.

Other parties must be represented by a lawyer.

Only a lawyer authorized to practise before a court of a Member State or of another State which is a party to the Agreement on the European Economic Area may represent or assist a party before the Court.

Such agents, advisers and lawyers shall, when they appear before the Court, enjoy the rights and immunities necessary to the independent exercise of their duties, under conditions laid down in the rules of procedure.

As regards such advisers and lawyers who appear before it, the Court shall have the powers normally accorded to courts of law, under conditions laid down in the rules of procedure.

University teachers being nationals of a Member State whose law accords them a right of audience shall have the same rights before the Court as are accorded by this Article to lawyers entitled to practise before a court of a Member State.

Article 18

The procedure before the Court shall consist of two parts: written and oral.

The written procedure shall consist of the communication to the parties and to the institutions of the Community whose decisions are in dispute, of applications, statements of case, defences and observations, and of replies, if any, as well as of all papers and documents in support or of certified copies of them.

Communications shall be made by the Registrar in the order and within the time laid down in the rules of procedure.

The oral procedure shall consist of the reading of the report presented by a Judge acting as Rapporteur, the hearing by the Court of agents, advisers and lawyers entitled to practise before a court of a Member State and of the submissions of the Advocate-General, as well as the hearing, if any, of witnesses and experts.

Article 19

A case shall be brought before the Court by a written application addressed to the Registrar. The application shall contain the applicant's name and permanent address and the description of the signatory, the name of the party or names of the parties against whom the application is made, the subject-matter of the dispute, the form of order sought and a brief statement of the pleas in law on which the application is based.

The application shall be accompanied, where appropriate, by the measure the annulment of which is sought or, in the circumstances referred to in Article 175 of this Treaty, by documentary evidence of the date on which an institution was, in accordance with that Article, requested to act. If the documents are not submitted with the application, the Registrar shall ask the party concerned to produce them within a reasonable period, but in that event the rights of the party shall not lapse even if such documents are produced after the time-limit for bringing proceedings.

Article 20

In the cases governed by Article 177 of this Treaty, the decision of the court or tribunal of a Member State which suspends its proceedings and refers a case to the Court shall be notified to the Court by the court or tribunal concerned. The decision shall then be notified by the Registrar of the Court to the parties, to the Member States and to the Commission, and also to the Council or to the European Central Bank if the act the validity or interpretation of which is in dispute originates from one of them, and to the

European Parliament and the Council if the act the validity or interpretation of which is in dispute was adopted jointly by those two institutions.

Within two months of this notification, the parties, the Member States, the Commission and, where appropriate, the European Parliament, the Council and the European Central Bank, shall be entitled to submit statements of case or written observations to the Court.

The decision of the aforesaid court or tribunal shall, moreover, be notified by the Registrar of the Court to the States, other than the Member States, which are parties to the Agreement on the European Economic Area and also to the EFTA Surveillance Authority referred to in that Agreement which may, within two months of notification, where one of the fields of application of that Agreement is concerned, submit statements of case or written observations to the Court.

Article 21

The Court may require the parties to produce all documents and to supply all information which the Court considers desirable. Formal note shall be taken of any refusal.

The Court may also require the Member States and institutions not being parties to the case to supply all information which the Court considers necessary for the proceedings.

Article 22

The Court may at any time entrust any individual, body, authority, committee or other organization it chooses with the task of giving an expert opinion.

Article 23

Witnesses may be heard under conditions laid down in the rules of procedure.

Article 24

With respect to defaulting witnesses the Court shall have the powers generally granted to courts and tribunals and may impose pecuniary penalties under conditions laid down in the rules of procedure.

Article 25

Witnesses and experts may be heard on oath taken in the form laid down in the rules of procedure or in the manner laid down by the law of the country of the witness or expert.

Article 26

The Court may order that a witness or expert be heard by the judicial authority of his place of permanent residence.

The order shall be sent for implementation to the competent judicial authority under conditions laid down in the rules of procedure. The documents drawn up in compliance with the letters rogatory shall be returned to the Court under the same conditions.

The Court shall defray the expenses, without prejudice to the right to charge them, where appropriate, to the parties.

Article 27

A Member State shall treat any violation of an oath by a witness or expert in the same manner as if the offence had been committed before one of its courts with jurisdiction in civil proceedings. At the instance of the Court, the Member State concerned shall prosecute the offender before its competent court.

Article 28

The hearing in court shall be public, unless the Court, of its own motion or on application by the parties, decides otherwise for serious reasons.

Article 29

During the hearings the Court may examine the experts, the witnesses and the parties themselves. The latter, however, may address the Court only through their representatives.

Article 30

Minutes shall be made of each hearing and signed by the President and the Registrar.

Article 31

The case list shall be established by the President.

Article 32

The deliberations of the Court shall be and shall remain secret.

Article 33

Judgments shall state the reasons on which they are based. They shall contain the names of the Judges who took part in the deliberations.

Article 34

Judgments shall be signed by the President and the Registrar. They shall be read in open court.

Article 35

The Court shall adjudicate upon costs.

Article 36

The President of the Court may, by way of summary procedure, which may, in so far as necessary, differ from some of the rules contained in this Statute and which shall be laid down in the rules of procedure, adjudicate upon applications to suspend execution, as provided for in Article 185 of this Treaty, or to prescribe interim measures in pursuance of Article 186 or to suspend enforcement in accordance with the last paragraph of Article 192.

Should the President be prevented from attending, his place shall be taken by another Judge under conditions laid down in the rules of procedure.

The ruling of the President or of the Judge replacing him shall be provisional and shall in no way prejudice the decision of the Court on the substance of the case.

Article 37

Member States and institutions of the Community may intervene in cases before the Court.

The same right shall be open to any other person establishing an interest in the result of any case submitted to the Court, save in cases between Member States, between institutions of the Community or between Member States and institutions of the Community.

Without prejudice to the preceding paragraph, the States, other than the Member States, which are parties to the Agreement on the European Economic Area, and also the EFTA Surveillance Authority referred to in that Agreement, may intervene in cases before the Court where one of the fields of application of that Agreement is concerned.

An application to intervene shall be limited to supporting the form of order sought by one of the parties.

Article 38

Where the defending party, after having been duly summoned, fails to file written submissions in defence, judgment shall be given against that party by default. An objection may be lodged against the judgment within one month of it being notified. The objection shall not have the effect of staying enforcement of the judgment by default unless the Court decides otherwise.

Article 39

Member States, institutions of the Community and any other natural or legal persons may, in cases and under conditions to be determined by the rules of procedure, institute third-party proceedings to contest a judgment rendered without their being heard, where the judgment is prejudicial to their rights.

Article 40

If the meaning or scope of a judgment is in doubt, the Court shall construe it on application by any party or any institution of the Community establishing an interest therein.

Article 41

An application for revision of a judgment may be made to the Court only on discovery of a fact which is of such a nature as to be a decisive factor, and which, when the judgment was given, was unknown to the Court and to the party claiming the revision.

The revision shall be opened by a judgment of the Court expressly, recording the existence of a new fact, recognizing that it is of such a character as to lay the case open to revision and declaring the application admissible on this ground.

No application for revision may be made after the lapse of 10 years from the date of the judgment.

Article 42

Periods of grace based on considerations of distance shall be determined by the rules of procedure.

No right shall be prejudiced in consequence of the expiry of a time-limit if the party concerned proves the existence of unforeseeable circumstances or of *force majeure*.

Article 43

Proceedings against the Community in matters arising from non-contractual liability shall be barred after a period of five years from the occurrence of the event giving rise thereto. The period of limitation shall be interrupted if proceedings are instituted before the Court or if prior to such proceedings an application is made by the aggrieved party to the relevant institution of the Community. In the latter event the proceedings must be instituted within the period of two months provided for in Article 173; the provisions of the second paragraph of Article 175 shall apply where appropriate.

TITLE IV

The Court of First Instance of the European Communities

Article 44

Articles 2 to 8, and 13 to 16 of this Statute shall apply to the Court of First Instance and its members. The oath referred to in Article 2 shall be taken before the Court of Justice and the decisions referred to in Articles 3, 4 and 6 shall be adopted by that Court after hearing the Court of First Instance.

Article 45

The Court of First Instance shall appoint its Registrar and lay down the rules governing his service. Articles 9, 10 and 13 of this Statute shall apply to the Registrar of the Court of First Instance *mutatis mutandis*.

The President of the Court of Justice and the President of the Court of First Instance shall determine, by common accord, the conditions under which officials and other servants attached to the Court of Justice shall render their services to the Court of First Instance to enable it to function. Certain officials or other servants shall be responsible to the Registrar of the Court of First Instance under the authority of the President of the Court of First Instance.

Article 46

The procedure before the Court of First Instance shall be governed by Title III of this Statute, with the exception of Article 20.

Such further and more detailed provisions as may be necessary shall be laid down in the Rules of Procedure established in accordance with Article 168a (4) of the Treaty. The Rules of Procedure may derogate from the fourth paragraph of Article 37 and from Article 38 of this Statute in order to take account of the specific features of litigation in the field of intellectual property.

Notwithstanding the fourth paragraph of Article 18 of this Statute, the Advocate-General may make his reasoned submissions in writing.

Article 47

Where an application or other procedural document addressed to the Court of First Instance is lodged by mistake with the Registrar of the Court of Justice, it shall be transmitted immediately by that Registrar to the Registrar of the Court of First Instance; likewise, where an application or other procedural document addressed to the Court of Justice is lodged by mistake with the Registrar of the Court of First Instance, it shall be transmitted immediately by that Registrar to the Registrar of the Court of Justice.

Where the Court of First Instance finds that it does not have jurisdiction to hear and determine an action in respect of which the Court of Justice has jurisdiction, it shall refer that action to the Court of Justice; likewise, where the Court of Justice finds that an action falls within the jurisdiction of the Court of First Instance, it shall refer that action to the Court of First Instance, whereupon that Court may not decline jurisdiction.

Where the Court of Justice and the Court of First Instance are seised of cases in which the same relief is sought, the same issue of interpretation is raised or the validity of the same act is called in question, the Court of First Instance may, after hearing the parties, stay the proceedings before it until such time as the Court of Justice shall have delivered judgment. Where applications are made for the same act to be declared void, the Court of

First Instance may also decline jurisdiction in order that the Court of Justice may rule on such applications. In the cases referred to in this subparagraph, the Court of Justice may also decide to stay the proceedings before it; in that event, the proceedings before the Court of First Instance shall continue.

Article 48

Final decisions of the Court of First Instance, decisions disposing of the substantive issues in part only or disposing of a procedural issue concerning a plea of lack of competence or inadmissibility, shall be notified by the Registrar of the Court of First Instance to all parties as well as all Member States and the Community institutions even if they did not intervene in the case before the Court of First Instance.

Article 49

An appeal may be brought before the Court of Justice, within two months of the notification of the decision appealed against, against final decisions of the Court of First Instance and decisions of that Court disposing of the substantive issues in part only or disposing of a procedural issue concerning a plea of lack of competence or inadmissibility.

Such an appeal may be brought by any party which has been unsuccessful, in whole or in part, in its submissions. However, interveners other than the Member States and the Community institutions may bring such an appeal only where the decision of the Court of First Instance directly affects them.

With the exception of cases relating to disputes between the Community and its servants, an appeal may also be brought by Member States and Community institutions which did not intervene in the proceedings before the Court of First Instance. Such Member States and institutions shall be in the same position as Member States or institutions which intervened at first instance.

Article 50

Any person whose application to intervene has been dismissed by the Court of First Instance may appeal to the Court of Justice within two weeks of the notification of the decision dismissing the application.

The parties to the proceedings may appeal to the Court of Justice against any decision of the Court of First Instance made pursuant to Article 185 or 186 or the fourth paragraph of Article 192 of this Treaty within two months from their notification.

The appeal referred to in the first two paragraphs of this Article shall be heard and determined under the procedure referred to in Article 36 of this Statute.

Article 51

An appeal to the Court of Justice shall be limited to points of law. It shall lie on the grounds of lack of competence of the Court of First Instance, a breach of procedure before it which adversely affects the interests of the appellant as well as the infringement of Community law by the Court of First Instance.

No appeal shall lie regarding only the amount of the costs or the party ordered to pay them.

Article 52

Where an appeal is brought against a decision of the Court of First Instance, the procedure before the Court of Justice shall consist of a written part and an oral part. In accordance with conditions laid down in the rules of procedure, the Court of Justice, having heard the Advocate-General and the parties, may dispense with the oral procedure.

Article 53

Without prejudice to Articles 185 and 186 of this Treaty, an appeal shall not have suspensory effect.

By way of derogation from Article 187 of this Treaty, decisions of the Court of First Instance declaring a regulation to be void shall take effect only as from the date of expiry of the period referred to in the first paragraph of Article 49 of this Statute or, if an appeal shall have been brought within that period, as from the date of dismissal of the appeal, without prejudice, however, to the right of a party to apply to the Court of Justice, pursuant to Articles 185 and 186 of this Treaty, for the suspension of the effects of the regulation which has been declared void or for the prescription of any other interim measure.

Article 54

If the appeal is well founded, the Court of Justice shall quash the decision of the Court of First Instance. It may itself give final judgment in the matter, where the state of the proceedings so permits, or refer the case back to the Court of First Instance for judgment.

Where a case is referred back to the Court of First Instance, that Court shall be bound by the decision of the Court of Justice on points of law.

When an appeal brought by a Member State or a Community institution, which did not intervene in the proceedings before the Court of First Instance, is well founded the Court of Justice may, if it considers this necessary, state which of the effects of the decision of the Court of First Instance which has been quashed shall be considered as definitive in respect of the parties to the litigation.

Article 55

The rules of procedure of the Court provided for in Article 188 of this Treaty shall contain, apart from the provisions contemplated by this Statute, any other provisions necessary for applying and, where required, supplementing it.

Article 56

The Council may, acting unanimously, make such further adjustments to the provisions of this Statute as may be required by reason of measures taken by the Council in accordance with the last paragraph of Article 165 of this Treaty.

Article 57

(text not reproduced)

Appendix C

Rules of Procedure—Court of Justice

RULES OF PROCEDURE OF THE COURT OF JUSTICE OF THE EUROPEAN COMMUNITIES OF 19 JUNE 1991[1]

CONTENTS

---

[1] Consolidated version as at September 1997.

THE COURT OF JUSTICE,

Having regard to the powers conferred on the Court of Justice by the Treaty establishing the European Coal and Steel Community, the Treaty establishing the European Economic Community and the Treaty establishing the European Atomic Energy Community (Euratom),

Having regard to Article 55 of the Protocol on the Statute of the Court of Justice of the European Coal and Steel Community,

Having regard to the third paragraph of Article 188 of the Treaty establishing the European Economic Community,

Having regard to the third paragraph of Article 160 of the Treaty establishing the European Atomic Energy Community (Euratom),

Whereas it is necessary to revise the text of its Rules of Procedure in the various languages in order to ensure coherence and uniformity between those language versions;

With the unanimous approval of that revision, given by the Council on 29 April 1991;

And whereas, after the numerous amendments to its Rules of Procedure, it is necessary, in the interests of clarity and simplicity, to establish a coherent authentic text,

With the unanimous approval of the Council, given on 7 June 1991,

REPLACES ITS RULES OF PROCEDURE BY THE FOLLOWING RULES:

Interpretation

Article 1

In these Rules:

'EC Treaty' means the Treaty establishing the European Community;

'EC Statute' means the Protocol on the Statute of the Court of Justice of the European Community;

'ECSC Treaty' means the Treaty establishing the European Coal and Steel Community;

'ECSC Statute' means the Protocol on the Statute of the Court of Justice of the European Coal and Steel Community;

'Euratom Treaty' means the Treaty establishing the European Atomic Energy Community (Euratom);

'Euratom Statute' means the Protocol on the Statute of the Court of Justice of the European Atomic Energy Community;

'EEA Agreement' means the Agreement on the European Economic Area.

For the purposes of these Rules:

'institutions' means the institutions of the Communities and bodies which are established by the Treaties, or by an act adopted in implementation thereof, and which may be parties before the Court;

'EFTA Surveillance Authority' means the surveillance authority referred to in the EEA Agreement.

APPENDIX C

TITLE 1

Organization of the Court

Chapter 1

JUDGES AND ADVOCATES-GENERAL

Article 2

The term of office of a Judge shall begin on the date laid down in his instrument of appointment. In the absence of any provisions regarding the date, the term shall begin on the date of the instrument.

Article 3

1. Before taking up his duties, a Judge shall at the first public sitting of the Court which he attends after his appointment take the following oath:

'I swear that I will perform my duties impartially and conscientiously; I swear that I will preserve the secrecy of the deliberations of the Court'.

2. Immediately after taking the oath, a Judge shall sign a declaration by which he solemnly undertakes that, both during and after his term of office, he will respect the obligations arising therefrom, and in particular the duty to behave with integrity and discretion as regards the acceptance, after he has ceased to hold office, of certain appointments and benefits.

Article 4

When the Court is called upon to decide whether a Judge no longer fulfils the requisite conditions or no longer meets the obligations arising from his office, the President shall invite the Judge concerned to make representations to the Court, in closed session and in the absence of the Registrar.

Article 5

Articles 2, 3 and 4 of these Rules shall apply in a corresponding manner to Advocates-General.

Article 6

Judges and Advocates-General shall rank equally in precedence according to their seniority in office.

Where there is equal seniority in office, precedence shall be determined by age.

Retiring Judges and Advocates-General who are reappointed shall retain their former precedence.

Chapter 2

PRESIDENCY OF THE COURT AND CONSTITUTION OF THE CHAMBERS

Article 7

1. The Judges shall, immediately after the partial replacement provided for in Article 167 of the EC Treaty, Article 32b of the ECSC Treaty and Article 139 of the Euratom Treaty, elect one of their number as President of the Court for a term of three years.

2. If the office of the President of the Court falls vacant before the normal date of expiry thereof, the Court shall elect a successor for the remainder of the term.

3. The elections provided for in this Article shall be by secret ballot. If a Judge obtains an absolute majority he shall be elected. If no Judge obtains an absolute majority, a second ballot shall be held and the Judge obtaining the most votes shall be elected. Where two or more Judges obtain an equal number of votes the oldest of them shall be deemed elected.

Article 8

The President shall direct the judicial business and the administration of the Court; he shall preside at hearings and deliberations.

Article 9

1. The Court shall set up Chambers in accordance with the provisions of the second paragraph of Article 165 of the EC Treaty, the second paragraph of Article 32 of the ECSC Treaty and the second paragraph of Article 137 of the Euratom Treaty and shall decide which Judges shall be attached to them.

The composition of the Chambers shall be published in the *Official Journal of the European Communities.*

2. As soon as an application initiating proceedings has been lodged, the President shall assign the case to one of the Chambers for any preparatory inquiries and shall designate a Judge from that Chamber to act as Rapporteur.

3. The Court shall lay down criteria by which, as a rule, cases are to be assigned to Chambers.

4. These Rules shall apply to proceedings before the Chambers.

In cases assigned to a Chamber the powers of the President of the Court shall be exercised by the President of the Chamber.

Article 10

1. The Court shall appoint for a period of one year the Presidents of the Chambers and the First Advocate-General.

The provisions of Article 7 (2) and (3) shall apply.

Appointments made in pursuance of this paragraph shall be published in the *Official Journal of the European Communities.*

2. The First Advocate-General shall assign each case to an Advocate-General as soon as the Judge-Rapporteur has been designated by the President. He shall take the necessary steps if an Advocate-General is absent or prevented from acting.

Article 11

When the President of the Court is absent or prevented from attending or when the office of President is vacant, the functions of President shall be exercised by a President of a Chamber according to the order of precedence laid down in Article 6 of these Rules.

If the President of the Court and the President of the Chambers are all prevented from attending at the same time, or their posts are vacant at the same time, the functions of President shall be exercised by one of the other Judges according to the order of precedence laid down in Article 6 of these Rules.

APPENDIX C

Chapter 3

REGISTRY

Section 1—The Registrar and Assistant Registrars

Article 12

1. The Court shall appoint the Registrar. Two weeks before the date fixed for making the appointment, the President shall inform the Members of the Court of the applications which have been made for the post.

2. An application shall be accompanied by full details of the candidate's age, nationality, university degrees, knowledge of any languages, present and past occupations and experience, if any, in judicial and international fields.

3. The appointment shall be made following the procedure laid down in Article 7 (3) of these Rules.

4. The Registrar shall be appointed for a term of six years. He may be reappointed.

5. The Registrar shall take the oath in accordance with Article 3 of these Rules.

6. The Registrar may be deprived of his office only if he no longer fulfils the requisite conditions or no longer meets the obligations arising from his office; the Court shall take its decision after giving the Registrar an opportunity to make representations.

7. If the office of Registrar falls vacant before the normal date of expiry of the term thereof, the Court shall appoint a new Registrar for a term of six years.

Article 13

The Court may, following the procedure laid down in respect of the Registrar, appoint one or more Assistant Registrars to assist the Registrar and to take his place in so far as the Instructions to the Registrar referred to in Article 15 of these Rules allow.

Article 14

Where the Registrar and Assistant Registrar are absent or prevented from attending or their posts are vacant, the President shall designate an official to carry out temporarily the duties of Registrar.

Article 15

Instructions to the Registrar shall be adopted by the Court acting on a proposal from the President.

Article 16

1. There shall be kept in the Registry, under the control of the Registrar, a register initialled by the President, in which all pleadings and supporting documents shall be entered in the order in which they are lodged.

2. When a document has been registered, the Registrar shall make a note to that effect on the original and, if a party so requests, on any copy submitted for the purpose.

3. Entries in the register and the notes provided for in the preceding paragraph shall be authentic.

4. Rules for keeping the register shall be prescribed by the Instructions to the Registrar referred to in Article 15 of the Rules.

5. Persons having an interest may consult the register at the Registry and may obtain copies or extracts on payment of a charge on a scale fixed by the Court on a proposal from the Registrar.

The parties to a case may on payment of the appropriate charge also obtain copies of pleadings and authenticated copies of judgments and orders.

6. Notice shall be given in the *Official Journal of the European Communities* of the date of registration of an application initiating proceedings, the names and addresses of the parties, the subject-matter of the proceedings, the form of order sought by the applicant and a summary of the pleas in law and of the main supporting arguments.

7. Where the Council or the Commission is not a party to a case, the Court shall send to it copies of the application and of the defence, without the annexes thereto, to enable it to assess whether the inapplicability of one of its acts is being invoked under Article 184 of the EC Treaty, the third paragraph of Article 36 of the ECSC Treaty or Article 156 of the Euratom Treaty.

Article 17

1. The Registrar shall be responsible, under the authority of the President, for the acceptance, transmission and custody of documents and for effecting service as provided for by these Rules.

2. The Registrar shall assist the Court, the Chambers, the President and the Judges in all their official functions.

Article 18

The Registrar shall have custody of the seals. He shall be responsible for the records and be in charge of the publications of the Court.

Article 19

Subject to Articles 4 and 27 of these Rules, the Registrar shall attend the sittings of the Court and of the Chambers.

Section 2—Other departments

Article 20

1. The official and other servants of the Court shall be appointed in accordance with the provisions of the Staff Regulations.

2. Before taking up his duties, an official shall take the following oath before the President, in the presence of the Registrar:

'I swear that I will perform loyally, discreetly and conscientiously the duties assigned to me by the Court of Justice of the European Communities'.

Article 21

The organization of the departments of the Court shall be laid down, and may be modified, by the Court on a proposal from the Registrar.

Article 22

The Court shall set up a translating service staffed by experts with adequate legal training and a thorough knowledge of several official languages of the Court.

Article 23

The Registrar shall be responsible, under the authority of the President, for the administration of the Court, its financial management and its accounts; he shall be assisted in this by an administrator.

Chapter 4

ASSISTANT RAPPORTEURS

Article 24

1. Where the Court is of the opinion that the consideration of and preparatory inquiries in cases before it so require, it shall, pursuant to Article 12 of the EC Statute, Article 16 of the ECSC Statute and Article 12 of the Euratom Statute, propose the appointment of Assistant Rapporteurs.

2. Assistant Rapporteurs shall in particular assist the President in connection with applications for the adoption of interim measures and assist the Judge-Rapporteurs in their work.

3. In the performance of their duties the Assistant Rapporteurs shall be responsible to the President of the Court, the President of a Chamber or a Judge-Rapporteur, as the case may be.

4. Before taking up his duties, an Assistant Rapporteur shall take before the Court the oath set out in Article 3 of these Rules.

Chapter 5

THE WORKING OF THE COURT

Article 25

1. The dates and times of the sittings of the Court shall be fixed by the President.

2. The dates and times of the sittings of the Chambers shall be fixed by their respective Presidents.

3. The Court and the Chambers may choose to hold one or more sittings in a place other than that in which the Court has its seat.

Article 26

1. Where, by reason of a Judge being absent or prevented from attending, there is an even number of Judges, the most junior Judge within the meaning of Article 6 of these Rules shall abstain from taking part in the deliberations unless he is the Judge-Rapporteur. In that case the Judge immediately senior to him shall abstain from taking part in the deliberations.

2. If, after the Court has been convened, it is found that the quorum referred to in Article 15 of the EC Statute, Article 18 of the ECSC Statute and Article 15 of the Euratom Statute has not been attained, the President shall adjourn the sitting until there is a quorum.

3. If, in any Chamber, the quorum referred to in Article 15 of the EC Statute, Article 18 of the ECSC Statute and Article 15 of the Euratom Statute has not been attained, the President of that Chamber shall so inform the President of the Court, who shall designate another Judge to complete the Chamber.

Article 27

1. The Court and Chambers shall deliberate in closed session.

2. Only those Judges who were present at the oral proceedings and the Assistant Rapporteur, if any, entrusted with the consideration of the case may take part in the deliberations.

3. Every Judge taking part in the deliberations shall state his opinion and the reasons for it.

4. Any Judge may require that any questions be formulated in the language of his choice and communicated in writing to the Court or Chamber before being put to the vote.

5. The conclusions reached by the majority of the Judges after final discussion shall determine the decision of the Court. Votes shall be cast in reverse order to the order of precedence laid down in Article 6 of these Rules.

6. Differences of view on the substance, wording or order of questions, or on the interpretation of the voting, shall be settled by decision of the Court or Chamber.

7. Where the deliberations of the Court concern questions of its own administration, the Advocates-General shall take part and have a vote. The Registrar shall be present, unless the Court decides to the contrary.

8. Where the Court sits without the Registrar being present it shall, if necessary, instruct the most junior Judge within the meaning of Article 6 of these Rules to draw up minutes. The minutes shall be signed by this Judge and by the President.

Article 28

1. Subject to any special decision of the Court, its vacations shall be as follows:

— from 18 December to 10 January,

— from the Sunday before Easter to the second Sunday after Easter,

— from 15 July to 15 September.

During vacations, the functions of President shall be exercised at the place where the Court has its seat either by the President himself, keeping in touch with the Registrar, or by a President of Chamber or other Judge invited by the President to take his place.

2. In a case of urgency, the President may convene the Judges and the Advocates-General during the vacations.

3. The Court shall observe the official holidays of the place where it has its seat.

4. The Court may, in proper circumstances, grant leave of absence to any Judge or Advocate-General.

Chapter 6

LANGUAGES

Article 29

1. The language of a case shall be Danish, Dutch, English, Finnish, French, German, Greek, Irish, Italian, Portuguese, Spanish or Swedish.

2. The language of the case shall be chosen by the applicant, except that:

(a) where the defendant is a Member State or a natural or legal person having the nationality of a Member State, the language of the case shall be the official language of that State; where that State has more than one official language, the applicant may choose between them;

(b) at the joint request of the parties, the use of another of the languages mentioned in paragraph 1 for all or part of the proceedings may be authorized;

(c) at the request of one of the parties, and after the opposite party and the Advocate-General have been heard, the use of another of the languages mentioned in paragraph 1 as the language of the case for all or part of the proceedings may be authorized by way of derogation from subparagraphs (a) and (b).

In cases to which Article 103 of these Rules applies, the language of the case shall be the language of the national court or tribunal which refers the matter to the Court. At the duly substantiated request of one of the parties to the main proceedings, and after the opposite party and the Advocate-General have been heard, the use of another of the languages mentioned in paragraph 1 may be authorized for the oral procedure.

Requests as above may be decided on by the President; the latter may and, where he wishes to accede to a request without the agreement of all the parties, must refer the request to the Court.

3. The language of the case shall be used in the written and oral pleadings of the parties and in supporting documents, and also in the minutes and decisions of the Court.

Any supporting documents expressed in another language must be accompanied by a translation into the language of the case.

In the case of lengthy documents, translations may be confined to extracts. However, the Court or Chamber may, of its own motion or at the request of a party, at any time call for a complete or fuller translation.

Notwithstanding the foregoing provisions, a Member State shall be entitled to use its official language when intervening in a case before the Court or when taking part in any reference of a kind mentioned in Article 103. This provision shall apply both to written statements and to oral addresses. The Registrar shall cause any such statement or address to be translated into the language of the case.

The States, other than the Member States, which are parties to the EEA Agreement, and also the EFTA Surveillance Authority, may be authorized to use one of the languages mentioned in paragraph 1, other than the language of the case, when they intervene in a case before the Court or participate in preliminary ruling proceedings envisaged by Article 20 of the EC Statute. This provision shall apply both to written statements and oral addresses. The Registrar shall cause any such statement or address to be translated into the language of the case.

4. Where a witness or expert states that he is unable adequately to express himself in one of the languages referred to in paragraph (1) of this Article, the Court or Chamber may authorize him to give his evidence in another language. The Registrar shall arrange for translation into the language of the case.

5. The President of the Court and the Presidents of Chambers in conducting oral proceedings, the Judge-Rapporteur both in his preliminary report and in his report for the hearing, Judges and Advocates-General in putting questions and Advocates-General in delivering their opinions may use one of the languages referred to in paragraph (1) of this Article other than the language of the case. The Registrar shall arrange for translation into the language of the case.

Article 30

1. The Registrar shall, at the request of any Judge, of the Advocate-General or of a party, arrange for anything said or written in the course of the proceedings before the Court or a Chamber to be translated into the languages he chooses from those referred to in Article 29 (1).

2. Publications of the Court shall be issued in the languages referred to in Article 1 of Council Regulation No. 1.

Article 31

The texts of documents drawn up in the language of the case or in any other language authorized by the Court pursuant to Article 29 of these Rules shall be authentic.

Chapter 7

RIGHTS AND OBLIGATIONS OF AGENTS, ADVISERS AND LAWYERS

Article 32

1. Agents, advisers and lawyers appearing before the Court or before any judicial authority to which the Court has addressed letters rogatory shall enjoy immunity in respect of words spoken or written by them concerning the case or the parties.

2. Agents, advisers and lawyers shall enjoy the following further privileges and facilities:

(a) papers and documents relating to the proceedings shall be exempt from both search and seizure; in the event of a dispute the customs officials or police may seal those papers and documents; they shall then be immediately forwarded to the Court for inspection in the presence of the Registrar and of the person concerned;

(b) agents, advisers and lawyers shall be entitled to such allocation of foreign currency as may be necessary for the performance of their duties;

(c) agents, advisers and lawyers shall be entitled to travel in the course of duty without hindrance.

Article 33

In order to qualify for the privileges, immunities and facilities specified in Article 32, persons entitled to them shall furnish proof of their status as follows:

(a) agents shall produce an official document issued by the party for whom they act, and shall forward without delay a copy thereof to the Registrar;

(b) advisers and lawyers shall produce a certificate signed by the Registrar. The validity of this certificate shall be limited to a specified period, which may be extended or curtailed according to the length of the proceedings.

Article 34

The privileges, immunities and facilities specified in Article 32 of these Rules are granted exclusively in the interests of the proper conduct of proceedings.

The Court may waive the immunity where it considers that the proper conduct of proceedings will not be hindered thereby.

Article 35

1. Any adviser or lawyer whose conduct towards the Court, a Chamber, a Judge, an Advocate-General or the Registrar is incompatible with the dignity of the Court, or who uses his rights for purposes other than those for which they were granted, may at any time be excluded from the proceedings by an order of the Court or Chamber, after the Advocate-General has been heard; the person concerned shall be given an opportunity to defend himself.

The order shall have immediate effect.

2. Where an adviser or lawyer is excluded from the proceedings, the proceedings shall be suspended for a period fixed by the President in order to allow the party concerned to appoint another adviser or lawyer.

3. Decisions taken under this Article may be rescinded.

Article 36

The provisions of this Chapter shall apply to university teachers who have a right of audience before the Court in accordance with Article 17 of the EC Statute, Article 20 of the ECSC Statute and Article 17 of the Euratom Statute.

TITLE II

Procedure

Chapter 1

WRITTEN PROCEDURE

Article 37

1. The original of every pleading must be signed by the party's agent or lawyer.

The original, accompanied by all annexes referred to therein, shall be lodged together with five copies for the Court and a copy for every other party to the proceedings. Copies shall be certified by the party lodging them.

2. Institutions shall in addition produce, within time-limits laid down by the Court, translations of all pleadings into the other languages provided for by Article 1 of Council Regulation No. 1. The second subparagraph of paragraph (1) of this Article shall apply.

3. All pleadings shall bear a date. In the reckoning of time-limits for taking steps in proceedings, only the date of lodgment at the Registry shall be taken into account.

4. To every pleading there shall be annexed a file containing the documents relied on in support of it, together with a schedule listing them.

5. Where, in view of the length of a document, only extracts from it are annexed to the pleading, the whole document or a full copy of it shall be lodged at the Registry.

Article 38

1. An application of the kind referred to in Article 19 of the EC Statute, Article 22 of the ECSC Statute and Article 19 of the Euratom Statute shall state:

(a) the name and address of the applicant;

(b) the designation of the party against whom the application is made;

(c) the subject-matter of the proceedings and a summary of the pleas in law on which the application is based;

(d) the form of order sought by the applicant;

(e) where appropriate, the nature of any evidence offered in support.

2. For the purpose of the proceedings, the application shall state an address for service in the place where the Court has its seat and the name of the person who is authorized and has expressed willingness to accept service.

If the application does not comply with these requirements, all service on the party concerned for the purpose of the proceedings shall be effected, for so long as the defect has not been cured, by registered letter addressed to the agent or lawyer of that party. By way of derogation from Article 79, service shall then be deemed to be duly effected by the lodging of the registered letter at the post office of the place where the Court has its seat.

3. The lawyer acting for a party must lodge at the Registry a certificate that he is authorized to practise before a court of a Member State or of another State which is a party to the EEA Agreement.

4. The application shall be accompanied, where appropriate, by the documents specified in the second paragraph of Article 19 of the EC Statute, in the second paragraph of Article 22 of the ECSC Statute and in the second paragraph of Article 19 of the Euratom Statute.

5. An application made by a legal person governed by private law shall be accompanied by:

(a) the instrument or instruments constituting or regulating that legal person or a recent extract from the register of companies, firms or associations or any other proof of its existence in law;

(b) proof that the authority granted to the applicant's lawyer has been properly conferred on him by someone authorized for the purpose.

6. An application submitted under Articles 181 and 182 of the EC Treaty, Articles 42 and 89 of the ECSC Treaty and Articles 153 and 154 of the Euratom Treaty shall be accompanied by a copy of the arbitration clause contained in the contract governed by private or public law entered into by the Communities or on their behalf, or, as the case may be, by a copy of the special agreement concluded between the Member States concerned.

7. If an application does not comply with the requirements set out in paragraphs (3) to (6) of this Article, the Registrar shall prescribe a reasonable period within which the applicant is to comply with them whether by putting the application itself in order or by producing any of the abovementioned documents. If the applicant fails to put the application in order or to produce the required documents within the time prescribed, the Court shall, after hearing the Advocate-General, decide whether the non-compliance with these conditions renders the application formally inadmissible.

Article 39

The application shall be served on the defendant. In a case where Article 38 (7) applies, service shall be effected as soon as the application has been put in order or the Court has declared it admissible notwithstanding the failure to observe the formal requirements set out in that Article.

Article 40

1. Within one month after service on him of the application, the defendant shall lodge a defence, stating:

(a) the name and address of the defendant;

(b) the arguments of fact and law relied on;

(c) the form of order sought by the defendant;

(d) the nature of any evidence offered by him.

The provisions of Article 38 (2) to (5) of these Rules shall apply to the defence.

2. The time-limit laid down in paragraph (1) of this Article may be extended by the President on a reasoned application by the defendant.

Article 41

1. The application initiating the proceedings and the defence may be supplemented by a reply from the applicant and by a rejoinder from the defendant.

2. The President shall fix the time-limits within which these pleadings are to be lodged.

Article 42

1. In reply or rejoinder a party may offer further evidence. The party must, however, give reasons for the delay in offering it.

2. No new plea in law may be introduced in the course of proceedings unless it is based on matters of law or of fact which come to light in the course of the procedure.

If in the course of the procedure one of the parties puts forward a new plea in law which is so based, the President may, even after the expiry of the normal procedural time-limits, acting on a report of the Judge-Rapporteur and after hearing the Advocate-General, allow the other party time to answer on that plea.

The decision on the admissibility of the plea shall be reserved for the final judgment.

Article 43

The Court may, at any time, after hearing the parties and the Advocate-General, if the assignment referred to in Article 10 (2) has taken place, order that two or more cases concerning the same subject-matter shall, on account of the connection between them, be joined for the purposes of the written or oral procedure or of the final judgment. The cases may subsequently be disjoined. The President may refer these matters to the Court.

Article 44

1. After the rejoinder provided for in Article 41 (1) of these Rules has been lodged, the President shall fix a date on which the Judge-Rapporteur is to present his preliminary report to the Court. The report shall contain recommendations as to whether a preparatory inquiry or any other preparatory step should be undertaken and whether the case should be referred to the Chamber to which it has been assigned under Article 9 (2).

The Court shall decide, after hearing the Advocate-General, what action to take upon the recommendations of the Judge-Rapporteur.

The same procedure shall apply:

(a) where no reply or no rejoinder has been lodged within the time-limit fixed in accordance with Article 41 (2) of these Rules;

(b) where the party concerned waives his right to lodge a reply or rejoinder.

2. Where the Court orders a preparatory inquiry and does not undertake it itself, it shall assign the inquiry to the Chamber.

Where the Court decides to open the oral procedure without an inquiry, the President shall fix the opening date.

Article 44(a)

Without prejudice to any special provisions laid down in these Rules, and except in the specific cases in which, after the pleading referred to in Article 40 (1) and, as the case may be, in Article 41 (1) have been lodged, the Court, acting on a report from the Judge-Rapporteur, after hearing the Advocate-General and with the express consent of the parties, decides otherwise, the procedure before the Court shall also include an oral part.

Chapter 2

PREPARATORY INQUIRIES

Section 1—Measures of inquiry

Article 45

1. The Court, after hearing the Advocate-General, shall prescribe the measures of inquiry that it considers appropriate by means of an order setting out the facts to be proved. Before the Court decides on the measures of inquiry referred to in paragraph (2) (c), (d) and (e) the parties shall be heard.

The order shall be served on the parties.

2. Without prejudice to Articles 21 and 22 of the EC Statute, Articles 24 and 25 of the ECSC Statute or Articles 22 and 23 of the Euratom Statute, the following measures of inquiry may be adopted:

(a) the personal appearance of the parties;

(b) a request for information and production of documents;

(c) oral testimony;

(d) the commissioning of an expert's report;

(e) an inspection of the place or thing in question.

3. The measures of inquiry which the Court has ordered may be conducted by the Court itself, or be assigned to the Judge-Rapporteur.

The Advocate-General shall take part in the measures of inquiry.

4. Evidence may be submitted in rebuttal and previous evidence may be amplified.

Article 46

1. A Chamber to which a preparatory inquiry has been assigned may exercise the powers vested in the Court by Articles 45 and 47 to 53 of these Rules; the powers vested in the President of the Court may be exercised by the President of the Chamber.

2. Articles 56 and 57 of the Rules shall apply in a corresponding manner to proceedings before the Chamber.

3. The parties shall be entitled to attend the measures of inquiry.

Section 2—The summoning and examination of witnesses and experts

Article 47

1. The Court may, either of its own motion or on application by a party, and after hearing the Advocate-General, order that certain facts be proved by witnesses. The order of the Court shall set out the facts to be established.

The Court may summon a witness of its own motion or on application by a party or at the instance of the Advocate-General.

An application by a party for the examination of a witness shall state precisely about what facts and for what reasons the witness should be examined.

2. The witness shall be summoned by an order of the Court containing the following information:

(a) the surname, forenames, description and address of the witness;

(b) an indication of the facts about which the witness is to be examined;

(c) where appropriate, particulars of the arrangements made by the Court for reimbursement of expenses incurred by the witness, and of the penalties which may be imposed on defaulting witnesses.

The order shall be served on the parties and the witnesses.

3. The Court may make the summoning of a witness for whose examination a party has applied conditional upon the deposit with the cashier of the Court of a sum sufficient to cover the taxed costs thereof; the Court shall fix the amount of the payment.

The cashier shall advance the funds necessary in connection with the examination of any witness summoned by the Court of its own motion.

4. After the identity of the witness has been established, the President shall inform him that he will be required to vouch the truth of his evidence in the manner laid down in these Rules.

The witness shall give his evidence to the Court, the parties having been given notice to attend. After the witness has given his main evidence the President may, at the request of a party or of his own motion, put questions to him.

The other Judges and the Advocate-General may do likewise.

Subject to the control of the President, questions may be put to witnesses by the representatives of the parties.

5. After giving his evidence, the witness shall take the following oath:

'I swear that I have spoken the truth, the whole truth and nothing but the truth.'

The Court may, after hearing the parties, exempt a witness from taking the oath.

6. The Registrar shall draw up minutes in which the evidence of each witness is reproduced.

The minutes shall be signed by the President or by the Judge-Rapporteur responsible for conducting the examination of the witness, and by the Registrar. Before the minutes are thus signed, witnesses must be given an opportunity to check the content of the minutes and to sign them.

The minutes shall constitute an official record.

Article 48

1. Witnesses who have been duly summoned shall obey the summons and attend for examination.

2. If a witness who has been duly summoned fails to appear before the Court, the Court may impose upon him a pecuniary penalty not exceeding ECU 5 000 and may order that a further summons be served on the witness at his own expense.

The same penalty may be imposed upon a witness who, without good reason, refuses to give evidence or to take the oath or where appropriate to make a solemn affirmation equivalent thereto.

3. If the witness proffers a valid excuse to the Court, the pecuniary penalty imposed on him may be cancelled. The pecuniary penalty imposed may be reduced at the request of the witness where he establishes that it is disproportionate to his income.

4. Penalties imposed and other measures ordered under this Article shall be enforced in accordance with Articles 187 and 192 of the EC Treaty, Articles 44 and 92 of the ECSC Treaty and Articles 159 and 164 of the Euratom Treaty.

Article 49

1. The Court may order that an expert's report be obtained. The order appointing the expert shall define his task and set a time-limit within which he is to make his report.

2. The expert shall receive a copy of the order, together with all the documents necessary for carrying out his task. He shall be under the supervision of the Judge-Rapporteur, who may be present during his investigation and who shall be kept informed of his progress in carrying out his task.

The Court may request the parties or one of them to lodge security for the costs of the expert's report.

3. At the request of the expert, the Court may order the examination of witnesses. Their examination shall be carried out in accordance with Article 47 of these Rules.

4. The expert may give his opinion only on points which have been expressly referred to him.

5. After the expert has made his report, the Court may order that he be examined, the parties having been given notice to attend.

Subject to the control of the President, questions may be put to the expert by the representatives of the parties.

6. After making his report, the expert shall take the following oath before the Court:

'I swear that I have conscientiously and impartially carried out my task.'

The Court may, after hearing the parties, exempt the expert from taking the oath.

Article 50

1. If one of the parties objects to a witness or to an expert on the ground that he is not a competent or proper person to act as witness or expert or for any other reason, or if a witness or expert refuses to give evidence, to take the oath or to make a solemn affirmation equivalent thereto, the matter shall be resolved by the Court.

2. An objection to a witness or to an expert shall be raised within two weeks after service of the order summoning the witness or appointing the expert; the statement of objection must set out the grounds of objection and indicate the nature of any evidence offered.

Article 51

1. Witnesses and experts shall be entitled to reimbursement of their travel and subsistence expenses. The cashier of the Court may make a payment to them towards these expenses in advance.

2. Witnesses shall be entitled to compensation for loss of earnings, and experts to fees for their services. The cashier of the Court shall pay witnesses and experts their compensation or fees after they have carried out their respective duties or tasks.

Article 52

The Court may, on application by a party or of its own motion, issue letters rogatory for the examination of witnesses or experts, as provided for in the supplementary rules mentioned in Article 125 of these Rules.

Article 53

1. The Registrar shall draw up minutes of every hearing. The minutes shall be signed by the President and by the Registrar and shall constitute an official record.

2. The parties may inspect the minutes and any expert's report at the Registry and obtain copies at their own expense.

Section 3—Closure of the preparatory inquiry

Article 54

Unless the Court prescribes a period within which the parties may lodge written observations, the President shall fix the date for the opening of the oral procedure after the preparatory inquiry has been completed.

Where a period had been prescribed for the lodging of written observations, the President shall fix the date for the opening of the oral procedure after that period has expired.

Chapter 3

ORAL PROCEDURE

Article 55

1. Subject to the priority of decisions provided for in Article 85 of these Rules, the Court shall deal with the cases before it in the order in which the preparatory inquiries in them have been completed. Where the preparatory inquiries in several cases are completed simultaneously, the order in which they are to be dealt with shall be determined by the dates of entry in the register of the applications initiating them respectively.

2. The President may in special circumstances order that a case be given priority over others.

The President may in special circumstances, after hearing the parties and the Advocate-General, either on his own initiative or at the request of one of the parties, defer a case to be dealt with at a later date. On a joint application by the parties the President may order that a case be deferred.

Article 56

1. The proceedings shall be opened and directed by the President, who shall be responsible for the proper conduct of the hearing.

2. The oral proceedings in cases heard *in camera* shall not be published.

Article 57

The President may in the course of the hearing put questions to the agents, advisers or lawyers of the parties.

The other Judges and the Advocate-General may do likewise.

Article 58

A party may address the Court only through his agent, adviser or lawyer.

Article 59

1. The Advocate-General shall deliver his opinion orally at the end of the oral procedure.

2. After the Advocate-General has delivered his opinion, the President shall declare the oral procedure closed.

Article 60

The Court may at any time, in accordance with Article 45 (1), after hearing the Advocate-General, order any measure of inquiry to be taken or that a previous inquiry be repeated or expanded. The Court may direct the Chamber or the Judge-Rapporteur to carry out the measures so ordered.

Article 61

The Court may, after hearing the Advocate-General, order the reopening of the oral procedure.

Article 62

1. The Registrar shall draw up minutes of every hearing. The minutes shall be signed by the President and by the Registrar and shall constitute an official record.

2. The parties may inspect the minutes at the Registry and obtain copies at their own expense.

Chapter 4

JUDGMENTS

Article 63

The judgment shall contain:

— a statement that it is the judgment of the Court,

— the date of its delivery,

— the names of the President and of the Judges taking part in it,

— the name of the Advocate-General,

— the name of the Registrar,

— the description of the parties,

— the names of the agents, advisers and lawyers of the parties,

— a statement of the forms of order sought by the parties,

— a statement that the Advocate-General has been heard,

— a summary of the facts,

— the grounds for the decision,

— the operative part of the judgment, including the decision as to costs.

Article 64

1. The judgment shall be delivered in open court; the parties shall be given notice to attend to hear it.

2. The original of the judgment, signed by the President, by the Judges who took part in the deliberations and by the Registrar, shall be sealed and deposited at the Registry; the parties shall be served with certified copies of the judgment.

3. The Registrar shall record on the original of the judgment the date on which it was delivered.

Article 65

The judgment shall be binding from the date of its delivery.

Article 66

1. Without prejudice to the provisions relating to the interpretation of judgments the Court may, of its own motion or on application by a party made within two weeks after the delivery of a judgment, rectify clerical mistakes, errors in calculation and obvious slips in it.

2. The parties, whom the Registrar shall duly notify, may lodge written observations within a period prescribed by the President.

3. The Court shall take its decision in closed session after hearing the Advocate-General.

4. The original of the rectification order shall be annexed to the original of the rectified judgment. A note of this order shall be made in the margin of the original of the rectified judgment.

Article 67

If the Court should omit to give a decision on a specific head or claim or on costs, any party may within a month after service of the judgment apply to the Court to supplement its judgment.

The application shall be served on the opposite party and the President shall prescribe a period within which that party may lodge written observations.

After these observations have been lodged, the Court shall, after hearing the Advocate-General, decide both on the admissibility and on the substance of the application.

Article 68

The Registrar shall arrange for the publication of reports of cases before the Court.

Chapter 5

COSTS

Article 69

1. A decision as to costs shall be given in the final judgment or in the order which closes the proceedings.

2. The unsuccessful party shall be ordered to pay the costs if they have been applied for in the successful party's pleadings.

Where there are several unsuccessful parties the Court shall decide how the costs are to be shared.

3. Where each party succeeds on some and fails on other heads, or where the circumstances are exceptional, the Court may order that the costs be shared or that the parties bear their own costs.

The Court may order a party, even if successful, to pay costs which the Court considers that party to have unreasonably or vexatiously caused the opposite party to incur.

4. The Member States and institutions which intervene in the proceedings shall bear their own costs.

The States, other than the Member States, which are parties to the EEA Agreement, and also the EFTA Surveillance Authority, shall bear their own costs if they intervene in the proceedings.

The Court may order an intervener other than those mentioned in the preceding subparagraphs to bear his own costs.

5. A party who discontinues or withdraws from proceedings shall be ordered to pay the costs if they have been applied for in the other party's observations on the discontinuance pleadings. However, upon application by the party who discontinues or withdraws from proceedings, the costs shall be borne by the other party if this appears justified by the conduct of that party.

Where the parties have come to an agreement on costs, the decision as to costs shall be in accordance with that agreement.

If costs are not applied for, the parties shall bear their own costs.

6. Where a case does not proceed to judgment the costs shall be in the discretion of the Court.

Article 70

Without prejudice to the second subparagraph of Article 69 (3) of these Rules, in proceedings between the Communities and their servants the institutions shall bear their own costs.

Article 71

Costs necessarily incurred by a party in enforcing a judgment or order of the Court shall be refunded by the opposite party on the scale in force in the State where the enforcement takes place.

Article 72

Proceedings before the Court shall be free of charge, except that:

(a) where a party has caused the Court to incur avoidable costs the Court may, after hearing the Advocate-General, order that party to refund them;

(b) where copying or translation work is carried out at the request of a party, the cost shall, in so far as the Registrar considers it excessive, be paid for by that party on the scale of charges referred to in Article 16 (5) of these Rules.

Article 73

Without prejudice to the preceding Article, the following shall be regarded as recoverable costs:

(a) sums payable to witnesses and experts under Article 51 of these Rules;

(b) expenses necessarily incurred by the parties for the purpose of the proceedings, in particular the travel and subsistence expenses and the remuneration of agents, advisers or lawyers.

Article 74

1. If there is a dispute concerning the costs to be recovered, the Chamber to which the case has been assigned shall, on application by the party concerned and after hearing the opposite party and the Advocate-General, make an order, from which no appeal shall lie.

2. The parties may, for the purposes of enforcement, apply for an authenticated copy of the order.

Article 75

1. Sums due from the cashier of the Court shall be paid in the currency of the country where the Court has its seat.

At the request of the person entitled to any sum, it shall be paid in the currency of the country where the expenses to be refunded were incurred or where the steps in respect of which payment is due were taken.

2. Other debtors shall make payment in the currency of their country of origin.

3. Conversions of currency shall be made at the official rates of exchange ruling on the day of payment in the country where the Court has its seat.

Chapter 6

LEGAL AID

Article 76

1. A party who is wholly or in part unable to meet the costs of the proceedings may at any time apply for legal aid.

The application shall be accompanied by evidence of the applicant's need of assistance, and in particular by a document from the competent authority certifying his lack of means.

2. If the application is made prior to proceedings which the applicant wishes to commence, it shall briefly state the subject of such proceedings.

The application need not be made through a lawyer.

3. The President shall designate a Judge to act as Rapporteur. The Chamber to which the latter belongs shall, after considering the written observations of the opposite party and

after hearing the Advocate-General, decide whether legal aid should be granted in full or in part, or whether it should be refused. The Chamber shall consider whether there is manifestly no cause of action.

The Chamber shall make an order without giving reasons, and no appeal shall lie therefrom.

4. The Chamber may at any time, either of its own motion or on application, withdraw legal aid if the circumstances which led to its being granted alter during the proceedings.

5. Where legal aid is granted, the cashier of the Court shall advance the funds necessary to meet the expenses.

In its decision as to costs the Court may order the payment to the cashier of the Court of the whole or any part of amounts advanced as legal aid.

The Registrar shall take steps to obtain the recovery of these sums from the party ordered to pay them.

Chapter 7

DISCONTINUANCE

Article 77

If, before the Court has given its decision, the parties reach a settlement of their dispute and intimate to the Court the abandonment of their claims, the President shall order the case to be removed from the register and shall give a decision as to costs in accordance with Article 69 (5), having regard to any proposals made by the parties on the matter.

This provision shall not apply to proceedings under Articles 173 and 175 of the EC Treaty, Articles 33 and 35 of the ECSC Treaty, and Articles 146 and 148 of the Euratom Treaty.

Article 78

If the applicant informs the Court in writing that he wishes to discontinue the proceedings, the President shall order the case to be removed from the register and shall give a decision as to costs in accordance with Article 69 (5).

Chapter 8

SERVICE

Article 79

Where these Rules require that a document be served on a person, the Registrar shall ensure that service is effected at that person's address for service either by the dispatch of a copy of the document by registered post with a form for acknowledgement of receipt or by personal delivery of the copy against a receipt.

The Registrar shall prepare and certify the copies of documents to be served, save where the parties themselves supply the copies in accordance with Article 37 (1) of these Rules.

Chapter 9

TIME LIMITS

Article 80

1. Any period of time prescribed by the EC, ECSC or Euratom Treaties, the Statutes of the Court or these Rules for the taking of any procedural step shall be reckoned as follows:

(a) where a period expressed in days, weeks, months or years is to be calculated from the moment at which an event occurs or an action takes place, the day during which that event occurs or that action takes place shall not be counted as falling within the period in question;

(b) a period expressed in weeks, months or in years shall end with the expiry of whichever day in the last week, month or year is the same day of the week, or falls on the same date, as the day during which the event or action from which the period is to be calculated occurred or took place. If, in a period expressed in months or in years, the day on which it should expire does not occur in the last month, the period shall end with the expiry of the last day of that month;

(c) where a period is expressed in months and days, it shall first be reckoned in whole months, then in days;

(d) periods shall include official holidays, Sundays and Saturdays;

(e) periods shall not be suspended during the judicial vacations.

2. If the period would otherwise end on a Saturday, Sunday or an official holiday, it shall be extended until the end of the first following working day.

A list of official holidays drawn up by the Court shall be published in the *Official Journal of the European Communities*.

Article 81

1. Where the period of time allowed for initiating proceedings against a measure adopted by an institution runs from the publication of that measure, that period shall be calculated, for the purposes of Article 80(1)(a), from the end of the 14th day after publication thereof in the *Official Journal of the European Communities*.

2. The extensions, on account of distance, of prescribed time limits shall be provided for in a decision of the Court which shall be published in the *Official Journal of the European Communities*.

Article 82

Any time limit prescribed pursuant to these Rules may be extended by whoever prescribed it.

The President and the Presidents of Chambers may delegate to the Registrar power of signature for the purpose of fixing time limits which, pursuant to these Rules, it falls to them to prescribe or of extending such time limits.

Chapter 10

STAY OF PROCEEDINGS

Article 82a

1. The proceedings may be stayed:

(a) in the circumstances specified in the third paragraph of Article 47 of the EC Statute, the third paragraph of Article 47 of the ECSC Statute and the third paragraph of Article 48 of the Euratom Statute, by order of the Court or of the Chamber to which the case has been assigned, made after hearing the Advocate-General;

(b) in all other cases, by decision of the President adopted after hearing the Advocate-General and, save in the case of references for a preliminary ruling as referred to in Article 103, the parties.

The proceedings may be resumed by order or decision, following the same procedure.

The orders or decisions referred to in this paragraph shall be served on the parties.

2. The stay of proceedings shall take effect on the date indicated in the order or decision of stay or, in the absence of such indication, on the date of that order or decision.

While proceedings are stayed time shall cease to run for the purposes of prescribed time limits for all parties.

3. Where the order or decision of stay does not fix the length of stay, it shall end on the date indicated in the order or decision of resumption or, in the absence of such indication, on the date of the order or decision of resumption.

From the date of resumption time shall begin to run afresh for the purposes of the time limits.

TITLE III

Special Forms of Procedure

Chapter 1

SUSPENSION OF OPERATION OR ENFORCEMENT AND OTHER INTERIM MEASURES

Article 83

1. An application to suspend the operation of any measure adopted by an institution, made pursuant to Article 185 of the EC Treaty, the second paragraph of Article 39 of the ECSC Treaty or Article 157 of the Euratom Treaty, shall be admissible only if the applicant is challenging that measure in proceedings before the Court.

An application for the adoption of any other interim measure referred to in Article 186 of the EC Treaty, the third paragraph of Article 39 of the ECSC Treaty and Article 158 of the Euratom Treaty shall be admissible only if it is made by a party to a case before the Court and relates to that case.

2. Any application of a kind referred to in paragraph (1) of this Article shall state the subject-matter of the proceedings, the circumstances giving rise to urgency and the pleas of fact and law establishing a *prima facie* case for the interim measures applied for.

3. The application shall be made by a separate document and in accordance with the provisions of Articles 37 and 38 of these Rules.

Article 84

1. The application shall be served on the opposite party, and the President shall prescribe a short period within which that party may submit written or oral observations.

2. The President may order a preparatory inquiry.

The President may grant the application even before the observations of the opposite party have been submitted. This decision may be varied or cancelled even without any application being made by any party.

Article 85

The President shall either decide on the application himself or refer it to the Court.

If the President is absent or prevented from attending, Article 11 of these Rules shall apply.

Where the application is referred to it, the Court shall postpone all other cases, and shall give a decision after hearing the Advocate-General. Article 84 shall apply.

Article 86

1. The decision on the application shall take the form of a reasoned order, from which no appeal shall lie. The order shall be served on the parties forthwith.

2. The enforcement of the order may be made conditional on the lodging by the applicant of security, of an amount and nature to be fixed in the light of the circumstances.

3. Unless the order fixes the date on which the interim measure is to lapse, the measure shall lapse when final judgment is delivered.

4. The order shall have only an interim effect, and shall be without prejudice to the decision of the Court on the substance of the case.

Article 87

On application by a party, the order may at any time be varied or cancelled on account of a change in circumstances.

Article 88

Rejection of an application for an interim measure shall not bar the party who made it from making a further application on the basis of new facts.

Article 89

The provisions of this Chapter shall apply to applications to suspend the enforcement of a decision of the Court or of any measure adopted by another institution, submitted pursuant to Articles 187 and 192 of the EC Treaty, Articles 44 and 92 of the ECSC Treaty or Articles 159 and 164 of the Euratom Treaty.

The order granting the application shall fix, where appropriate, a date on which the interim measure is to lapse.

Article 90

1. An application of a kind referred to in the third and fourth paragraphs of Article 81 of the Euratom Treaty shall contain:

(a) the names and addresses of the persons or undertakings to be inspected;

(b) an indication of what is to be inspected and of the purpose of the inspection.

2. The President shall give his decision in the form of an order. Article 86 of these Rules shall apply.

If the President is absent or prevented from attending, Article 11 of these Rules shall apply.

Chapter 2

PRELIMINARY ISSUES

Article 91

1. A party applying to the Court for a decision on a preliminary objection or other preliminary plea not going to the substance of the case shall make the application by a separate document.

The application must state the pleas of fact and law relied on and the form of order sought by the applicant; any supporting documents must be annexed to it.

2. As soon as the application has been lodged, the President shall prescribe a period within which the opposite party may lodge a document containing a statement of the form of order sought by that party and its pleas in law.

3. Unless the Court decides otherwise, the remainder of the proceedings shall be oral.

4. The Court shall, after hearing the Advocate-General, decide on the application or reserve its decision for the final judgment.

If the Court refuses the application or reserves its decision, the President shall prescribe new time-limits for the further steps in the proceedings.

Article 92

1. Where it is clear that the Court has no jurisdiction to take cognizance of an action or where the action is manifestly inadmissible, the Court may, by reasoned order, after hearing the Advocate-General and without taking further steps in the proceedings, give a decision on the action.

2. The Court may at any time of its own motion consider whether there exists any absolute bar to proceeding with a case or declare, after hearing the parties, that the action has become devoid of purpose and that there is no need to adjudicate on it; it shall give its decision in accordance with Article 91 (3) and (4) of these Rules.

Chapter 3

INTERVENTION

Article 93

1. An application to intervene must be made within three months of the publication of the notice referred to in Article 16 (6) of these Rules.

The application shall contain:

(a) the description of the case;

(b) the description of the parties;

(c) the name and address of the intervener;

(d) the intervener's address for service at the place where the Court has its seat;

(e) the form of order sought, by one or more of the parties, in support of which the intervener is applying for leave to intervene;

(f) a statement of the circumstances establishing the right to intervene, where the application is submitted pursuant to the second or third paragraph of Article 37 of the EC Statute, Article 34 of the ECSC Statute or the second paragraph of Article 38 of the Euratom Statute.

The intervener shall be represented in accordance with Article 17 of the EC Statute, Article 20 of the ECSC Statute and Article 17 of the Euratom Statute.

Articles 37 and 38 of these Rules shall apply.

2. The application shall be served on the parties.

The President shall give the parties an opportunity to submit their written or oral observations before deciding on the application.

The President shall decide on the application by order or shall refer the application to the Court.

3. If the President allows the intervention, the intervener shall receive a copy of every document served on the parties. The President may, however, on application by one of the parties, omit secret or confidential documents.

4. The intervener must accept the case as he finds it at the time of his intervention.

5. The President shall prescribe a period within which the intervener may submit a statement in intervention.

The statement in intervention shall contain:

(a) a statement of the form of order sought by the intervener in support of or opposing, in whole or in part, the form of order sought by one of the parties;

(b) the pleas in law and arguments relied on by the intervener;

(c) where appropriate, the nature of any evidence offered.

6. After the statement in intervention has been lodged, the President shall, where necessary, prescribe a time-limit within which the parties may reply to that statement.

Chapter 4

JUDGMENTS BY DEFAULT AND APPLICATIONS TO SET THEM ASIDE

Article 94

1. If a defendant on whom an application initiating proceedings has been duly served fails to lodge a defence to the application in the proper form within the time prescribed, the applicant may apply for judgment by default.

The application shall be served on the defendant. The Court may decide to open the oral procedure on the application.

2. Before giving judgment by default the Court shall, after hearing the Advocate-General, consider whether the application initiating proceedings is admissible, whether

the appropriate formalities have been complied with, and whether the application appears well founded. The Court may order a preparatory inquiry.

3. A judgment by default shall be enforceable. The Court may, however, grant a stay of execution until the Court has given its decision on any application under paragraph (4) to set aside the judgment, or it may make execution subject to the provision of security of an amount and nature to be fixed in the light of the circumstances; this security shall be released if no such application is made or if the application fails.

4. Application may be made to set aside a judgment by default.

The application to set aside the judgment must be made within one month from the date of service of the judgment and must be lodged in the form prescribed by Articles 37 and 38 of these Rules.

5. After the application has been served, the President shall prescribe a period within which the other party may submit his written observations.

The proceedings shall be conducted in accordance with Articles 44 *et seq.* of these Rules.

6. The Court shall decide by way of a judgment which may not be set aside. The original of this judgment shall be annexed to the original of the judgment by default. A note of the judgment on the application to set aside shall be made in the margin of the original of the judgment by default.

Chapter 5

CASES ASSIGNED TO CHAMBERS

Article 95

1. The Court may assign any case brought before it to a Chamber insofar as the difficulty or the importance of the case or particular circumstances are not such as to require that the Court decide it in plenary session.

2. The decision so to assign a case shall be taken by the Court at the end of the written procedure upon consideration of the preliminary report presented by the Judge-Rapporteur and after the Advocate-General has been heard.

However, a case may not be so assigned if a Member State or an institution of the Communities, being a party to the proceedings, has requested that the case be decided in plenary session. In this subparagraph the expression 'party to the proceedings' means any Member State or any institution which is a party to or an intervener in the proceedings or which has submitted written observations in any reference of a kind mentioned in Article 103 of these Rules.

The request referred to in the preceding subparagraph may not be made in proceedings between the Communities and their servants.

3. A Chamber may at any stage refer a case back to the Court.

Article 96

(repealed)

Chapter 6

EXCEPTIONAL REVIEW PROCEDURES

Section 1—Third-party proceedings

Article 97

1. Articles 37 and 38 of these Rules shall apply to an application initiating third-party proceedings. In addition such an application shall:

(a) specify the judgment contested;

(b) state how that judgment is prejudicial to the rights of the third party;

(c) indicate the reasons for which the third party was unable to take part in the original case.

The application must be made against all the parties to the original case.

Where the judgment has been published in the *Official Journal of the European Communities*, the application must be lodged within two months of the publication.

2. The Court may, on application by the third party, order a stay of execution of the judgment. The provisions of Title III, Chapter I, of these Rules shall apply.

3. The contested judgment shall be varied on the points on which the submissions of the third party are upheld.

The original of the judgment in the third-party proceedings shall be annexed to the original of the contested judgment. A note of the judgment in the third-party proceedings shall be made in the margin of the original of the contested judgment.

Section 2—Revision

Article 98

An application for revision of a judgment shall be made within three months of the date on which the facts on which the application is based came to the applicant's knowledge.

Article 99

1. Articles 37 and 38 of these Rules shall apply to an application for revision. In addition such an application shall:

(a) specify the judgment contested;

(b) indicate the points on which the judgment is contested;

(c) set out the facts on which the application is based;

(d) indicate the nature of the evidence to show that there are facts justifying revision of the judgment, and that the time-limit laid down in Article 98 has been observed.

2. The application must be made against all parties to the case in which the contested judgment was given.

Article 100

1. Without prejudice to its decision on the substance, the Court, in closed session, shall, after hearing the Advocate-General and having regard to the written observations of the parties, give in the form of a judgment its decision on the admissibility of the application.

2. If the Court finds the application admissible, it shall proceed to consider the substance of the application and shall give its decision in the form of a judgment in accordance with these Rules.

3. The original of the revising judgment shall be annexed to the original of the judgment revised. A note of the revising judgment shall be made in the margin of the original of the judgment revised.

Chapter 7

APPEALS AGAINST DECISIONS OF THE ARBITRATION COMMITTEE

Article 101

1. An application initiating an appeal under the second paragraph of Article 18 of the Euratom Treaty shall state:

(a) the name and address of the applicant;

(b) the description of the signatory;

(c) a reference to the arbitration committee's decision against which the appeal is made;

(d) the description of the parties;

(e) a summary of the facts;

(f) the pleas in law of and the form of order sought by the applicant.

2. Articles 37 (3) and (4) and 38 (2), (3) and (5) of these Rules shall apply.

A certified copy of the contested decision shall be annexed to the application.

3. As soon as the application has been lodged, the Registrar of the Court shall request the arbitration committee registry to transmit to the Court the papers in the case.

4. Articles 39, 40, 55 *et seq.* of these Rules shall apply to these proceedings.

5. The Court shall give its decision in the form of a judgment. Where the Court sets aside the decision of the arbitration committee it may refer the case back to the committee.

Chapter 8

INTERPRETATION OF JUDGMENTS

Article 102

1. An application for interpretation of a judgment shall be made in accordance with Articles 37 and 38 of these Rules. In addition it shall specify:

(a) the judgment in question;

(b) the passages of which interpretation is sought.

The application must be made against all the parties to the case in which the judgment was given.

2. The Court shall give its decision in the form of a judgment after having given the parties an opportunity to submit their observations and after hearing the Advocate-General.

The original of the interpreting judgment shall be annexed to the original of the judgment interpreted. A note of the interpreting judgment shall be made in the margin of the original of the judgment interpreted.

Chapter 9

PRELIMINARY RULINGS AND OTHER REFERENCES FOR INTERPRETATION

Article 103

1. In cases governed by Article 20 of the EC Statute and Article 21 of the Euratom Statute, the procedure shall be governed by the provisions of these Rules, subject to adaptations necessitated by the nature of the reference for a preliminary ruling.

2. The provisions of paragraph (1) shall apply to the references for a preliminary ruling provided for in the Protocol concerning the interpretation by the Court of Justice of the Convention of 29 February 1968 on the mutual recognition of companies and legal persons and the Protocol concerning the interpretation by the Court of Justice of the Convention of 27 September 1968 on jurisdiction and the enforcement of judgments in civil and commercial matters, signed at Luxembourg on 3 June 1971, and to the references provided for by Article 4 of the latter Protocol.

The provisions of paragraph (1) shall apply also to references for interpretation provided for by other existing or future agreements.

3. In cases provided for in Article 41 of the ECSC Treaty, the text of the decision to refer the matter shall be served on the parties in the case, the Member States, the Commission and the Council.

These parties, States and institutions may, within two months from the date of such service, lodge written statements of case or written observations.

The provisions of paragraph (1) shall apply.

Article 104

1. The decisions of national courts or tribunals referred to in Article 103 shall be communicated to the Member States in the original version, accompanied by a translation into the official language of the State to which they are addressed.

In the cases governed by Article 20 of the EC Statute, the decisions of national courts or tribunals shall be notified to the States, other than the Member States, which are parties to the EEA Agreement, and also to the EFTA Surveillance Authority, in the original version, accompanied by a translation into one of the languages mentioned in Article 29 (1), to be chosen by the addressee of the notification.

2. As regards the representation and attendance of the parties to the main proceedings in the preliminary ruling procedure the Court shall take account of the rules of procedure of the national court or tribunal which made the reference.

3. Where a question referred to the Court for a preliminary ruling is manifestly identical to a question on which the Court has already ruled, the Court may, after informing the court or tribunal which referred the question to it, hearing any observations submitted by the persons referred to in Article 20 of the EC Statute, Article 21 of the Euratom Statute and Article 103 (3) of these Rules and hearing the Advocate-General, give its decision by reasoned order in which reference is made to its previous judgment.

4. Without prejudice to paragraph (3) of this Article, the procedure before the Court in the case of a reference for a preliminary ruling shall also include an oral part. However, after the statements of case or written observations referred to in Article 20 of the EC Statute, Article 21 of the Euratom Statute and Article 103 (3) of these Rules have been submitted, the Court, acting on a report from the Judge-Rapporteur, after informing the

persons who under the aforementioned provisions are entitled to submit such statements or observations, may, after hearing the Advocate-General, decide otherwise, provided that none of those persons has asked to present oral argument.

5. It shall be for the national court or tribunal to decide as to the costs of the reference.

In special circumstances the Court may grant, by way of legal aid, assistance for the purpose of facilitating the representation or attendance of a party.

Chapter 10

SPECIAL PROCEDURES UNDER ARTICLES 103 TO 105 OF THE EURATOM TREATY

Article 105

1. Four certified copies shall be lodged of an application under the third paragraph of Article 103 of the Euratom Treaty. The Commission shall be served with a copy.

2. The application shall be accompanied by the draft of the agreement or contract in question, by the observations of the Commission addressed to the State concerned and by all other supporting documents.

The Commission shall submit its observations to the Court within a period of 10 days, which may be extended by the President after the State concerned has been heard.

A certified copy of the observations shall be served on that State.

3. As soon as the application has been lodged the President shall designate a Judge to act as Rapporteur. The First Advocate-General shall assign the case to an Advocate-General as soon as the Judge-Rapporteur has been designated.

4. The decision shall be taken in closed session after the Advocate-General has been heard.

The agents and advisers of the State concerned and of the Commission shall be heard if they so request.

Article 106

1. In cases provided for in the last paragraph of Article 104 and the last paragraph of Article 105 of the Euratom Treaty, the provisions of Articles 37 *et seq.* of these Rules shall apply.

2. The application shall be served on the State to which the respondent person or undertaking belongs.

Chapter 11

OPINIONS

Article 107

1. A request by the Council for an Opinion pursuant to Article 228 of the EC Treaty shall be served on the Commission and on the European Parliament. Such a request by the Commission shall be served on the Council, on the European Parliament and on the Member States. Such a request by a Member State shall be served on the Council, on the Commission, on the European Parliament and on the other Member States.

The President shall prescribe a period within which the institutions and Member States which have been served with a request may submit their written observations.

2. The Opinion may deal not only with the question whether the envisaged agreement is compatible with the provisions of the EC Treaty but also with the question whether the Community or any Community institution has the power to enter into that agreement.

Article 108

1. As soon as the request for an Opinion has been lodged, the President shall designate a Judge to act as Rapporteur.

2. The Court sitting in closed session shall, after hearing the Advocates-General, deliver a reasoned Opinion.

3. The Opinion, signed by the President, by the Judges who took part in the deliberations and by the Registrar, shall be served on the Council, the Commission, the European Parliament and the Member States.

Article 109

Requests for the Opinion of the Court under the fourth paragraph of Article 95 of the ECSC Treaty shall be submitted jointly by the Commission and the Council.

The Opinion shall be delivered in accordance with the provisions of the preceding Article. It shall be communicated to the Commission, the Council and the European Parliament.

TITLE IV

Appeals against decisions of the Court of First Instance

Article 110

Without prejudice to the arrangements laid down in Article 29 (2) (b) and (c) and the fourth subparagraph of Article 29 (3) of these Rules, in appeals against decisions of the Court of First Instance as referred to in Articles 49 and 50 of the EC Statute, Articles 49 and 50 of the ECSC Statute and Articles 50 and 51 of the Euratom Statute, the language of the case shall be the language of the decision of the Court of First Instance against which the appeal is brought.

Article 111

1. An appeal shall be brought by lodging an application at the Registry of the Court of Justice or of the Court of First Instance.

2. The Registry of the Court of First Instance shall immediately transmit to the Registry of the Court of Justice the papers in the case at first instance and, where necessary, the appeal.

Article 112

1. An appeal shall contain:

(a) the name and address of the appellant;

(b) the names of the other parties to the proceedings before the Court of First Instance;

(c) the pleas in law and legal arguments relied on;

(d) the form or order sought by the appellant.

Article 37 and Article 38 (2) and (3) of these Rules shall apply to appeals.

2. The decision of the Court of First Instance appealed against shall be attached to the appeal. The appeal shall state the date on which the decision appealed against was notified to the appellant.

3. If an appeal does not comply with Article 38 (3) or with paragraph (2) of this Article, Article 38 (7) of these Rules shall apply.

Article 113

1. An appeal may seek:

— to set aside, in whole or in part, the decision of the Court of First Instance;

— the same form of order, in whole or in part, as that sought at first instance and shall not seek a different form of order.

2. The subject-matter of the proceedings before the Court of First Instance may not be changed in the appeal.

Article 114

Notice of the appeal shall be served on all the parties to the proceedings before the Court of First Instance. Article 39 of these Rules shall apply.

Article 115

1. Any party to the proceedings before the Court of First Instance may lodge a response within two months after service on him of notice of the appeal. The time-limit for lodging a response shall not be extended.

2. A response shall contain:

(a) the name and address of the party lodging it;

(b) the date on which notice of the appeal was served on him;

(c) the pleas in law and legal arguments relied on;

(d) the form of order sought by the respondent.

Article 38 (2) and (3) of these Rules shall apply.

Article 116

1. A response may seek:

— to dismiss, in whole or in part, the appeal or to set aside, in whole or in part, the decision of the Court of First Instance;

— the same form of order, in whole or in part, as that sought at first instance and shall not seek a different form of order.

2. The subject-matter of the proceedings before the Court of First Instance may not be changed in the response.

Article 117

1. The appeal and the response may be supplemented by a reply and a rejoinder or any other pleading, where the President expressly, on application made within seven days of service of the response or of the reply, considers such further pleading necessary and expressly allows it in order to enable the party concerned to put forward its point of view or in order to provide a basis for the decision on the appeal.

2. Where the response seeks to set aside, in whole or in part, the decision of the Court of First Instance on a plea in law which was not raised in the appeal, the appellant or any other party may submit a reply on that plea alone within two months of the service of the response in question. Paragraph (1) shall apply to any further pleading following such a reply.

3. Where the President allows the lodging of a reply and a rejoinder, or any other pleading, he shall prescribe the period within which they are to be submitted.

Article 118

Subject to the following provisions, Articles 42 (2), 43, 44, 55 to 90, 93, 95 to 100 and 102 of these Rules shall apply to the procedure before the Court of Justice on appeal from a decision from the Court of First Instance.

Article 119

Where the appeal is, in whole or in part, clearly inadmissible or clearly unfounded, the Court may at any time, acting on a report from the Judge-Rapporteur and after hearing the Advocate-General, by reasoned order dismiss the appeal in whole or in part.

Article 120

After the submission of pleadings as provided for in Articles 115 (1) and, if any, Article 117 (1) and (2) of these Rules, the Court may, acting on a report from the Judge-Rapporteur and after hearing the Advocate-General and the parties, decide to dispense with the oral part of the procedure unless one of the parties objects on the ground that the written procedure did not enable him fully to defend his point of view.

Article 121

The report referred to in Article 44 (1) shall be presented to the Court after the pleadings provided for in Article 115 (1) and Article 117 (1) and (2) of these Rules have been lodged. The report shall contain, in addition to the recommendations provided for in Article 44 (1), a recommendation as to whether Article 120 of these Rules should be applied. Where no such pleadings are lodged, the same procedure shall apply after the expiry of the period prescribed for lodging them.

Article 122

Where the appeal is unfounded or where the appeal is well founded and the Court itself gives final judgment in the case, the Court shall make a decision as to costs.

In proceedings between the Communities and their servants:

— Article 70 of these Rules shall apply only to appeals brought by institutions;

— by way of derogation from Article 69 (2) of these Rules, the Court may, in appeals brought by officials or other servants of an institution, order the parties to share the costs where equity so requires.

If the appeal is withdrawn Article 69 (5) shall apply.

When an appeal brought by a Member State or an institution which did not intervene in the proceedings before the Court of First Instance is well founded, the Court of Justice may order that the parties share the costs or that the successful appellant pay the costs which the appeal has caused an unsuccessful party to incur.

Article 123

An application to intervene made to the Court in appeal proceedings shall be lodged before the expiry of a period of one month running from the publication referred to in Article 16 (6).

TITLE V

(Procedures provided for by the EEA Agreement)

Article 123a

1. In the case governed by Article 111 (3) of the EEA Agreement,[2] the matter shall be brought before the Court by a request submitted by the Contracting Parties to the dispute. The request shall be served on the other Contracting Parties, on the Commission, on the EFTA Surveillance Authority and, where appropriate, on the other persons to whom a reference for a preliminary ruling raising the same question of interpretation of Community legislation would be notified.

The President shall prescribe a period within which the Contracting Parties and the other persons on whom the request has been served may submit written observations.

The request shall be made in one of the languages mentioned in Article 29 (1). Paragraphs (3) and (5) of that Article shall apply. The provisions of Article 104 (1) shall apply *mutatis mutandis*.

2. As soon as the request referred to in paragraph 1 of this Article has been submitted, the President shall appoint a Judge-Rapporteur. The First Advocate-General shall, immediately afterwards, assign the request to an Advocate-General.

The Court shall, after hearing the Advocate-General, give a reasoned decision on the request in closed session.

3. The decision of the Court, signed by the President, by the Judges who took part in the deliberations and by the Registrar, shall be served on the Contracting Parties and on the other persons referred to in paragraph 1.

Article 123b

In the case governed by Article 1 of Protocol 34 to the EEA Agreement, the request of a court or tribunal of an EFTA State shall be served on the parties to the case, on the Contracting Parties, on the Commission, on the EFTA Surveillance Authority and, where appropriate, on the other persons to whom a reference for a preliminary ruling raising the same question of interpretation of Community legislation would be notified.

If the request is not submitted in one of the languages mentioned in Article 29 (1), it shall be accompanied by a translation into one of those languages.

Within two months of this notification, the parties to the case, the Contracting Parties and the other persons referred to in the first paragraph shall be entitled to submit statements of case or written observations.

The procedure shall be governed by the provisions of these Rules, subject to the adaptations called for by the nature of the request.

Miscellaneous Provisions

Article 124

1. The President shall instruct any person who is required to take an oath before the Court, as witness or expert, to tell the truth or to carry out his task conscientiously and impartially, as the case may be, and shall warn him of the criminal liability provided for in his national law in the event of any breach of this duty.

---

[2] OJ No L 1, 3 January 1994, p 27.

2. The witness shall take the oath either in accordance with the first subparagraph of Article 47 (5) of these Rules or in the manner laid down by his national law.

Where his national law provides the opportunity to make, in judicial proceedings, a solemn affirmation equivalent to an oath as well as or instead of taking an oath, the witness may make such an affirmation under the conditions and in the form prescribed in his national law.

Where his national law provides neither for taking an oath nor for making a solemn affirmation, the procedure described in paragraph (1) shall be followed.

3. Paragraph (2) shall apply *mutatis mutandis* to experts, a reference to the first subparagraph of Article 49 (6) replacing in this case the reference to the first subparagraph of Article 47 (5) of these Rules.

Article 125

Subject to the provisions of Article 188 of the EC Treaty and Article 160 of the Euratom Treaty and after consultation with the Governments concerned, the Court shall adopt supplementary rules concerning its practice in relation to:

(a) letters rogatory; .

(b) applications for legal aid;

(c) reports of perjury by witnesses or experts, delivered pursuant to Article 27 of the EC Statute and Article 28 of the ECSC and Euratom Statutes.

Article 126

These Rules replace the Rules of Procedure of the Court of Justice of the European Communities adopted on 4 December 1974 (*Official Journal of the European Communities* No L 350 of 28 December 1974, p. 1), as last amended on 15 May 1991.

Article 127

These Rules, which are authentic in the languages mentioned in Article 29 (1) of these Rules, shall be published in the *Official Journal of the European Communities* and shall enter into force on the first day of the second month following their publication.

Done at Luxembourg, 19 June 1991.

ANNEX I

Decision on Official Holidays

THE COURT OF JUSTICE OF THE EUROPEAN COMMUNITIES,

Having regard to Article 80 (2) of the Rules of Procedure, which requires the Court to draw up a list of official holidays;

DECIDES

Article 1

For the purposes of Article 80 (2) of the Rules of Procedure the following shall be official holidays:

New Year's Day;

Easter Monday;

1 May;

Ascension Day;

Whit Monday;

23 June;

24 June, where 23 June is a Sunday;

15 August;

1 November;

25 December;

26 December.

The official holidays referred to in the first paragraph hereof shall be those observed at the place where the Court of Justice has its seat.

Article 2

Article 80 (2) of the Rules of Procedure shall apply only to the official holidays mentioned in Article 1 of this Decision.

Article 3

This Decision, which shall constitute Annex I to the Rules of Procedure, shall enter into force on the same day as those Rules.

It shall be published in the *Official Journal of the European Communities*.

Done at Luxembourg, 19 June 1991.

APPENDIX C

ANNEX II

Decision on Extension of Time Limits on Account of Distance

THE COURT OF JUSTICE OF THE EUROPEAN COMMUNITIES,

Having regard to Article 81 (2) of the Rules of Procedure relating to the extension, on account of distance, of prescribed time limits;

DECIDES

Article 1

In order to take account of distance, procedural time limits for all parties save those habitually resident in the Grand Duchy of Luxembourg shall be extended as follows:

— for the Kingdom of Belgium: two days,

— for the Federal Republic of Germany, the European territory of the French Republic and the European territory of the Kingdom of the Netherlands: six days,

— for the European territory of the Kingdom of Denmark, for the Kingdom of Spain, for Ireland, for the Hellenic Republic, for the Italian Republic, for the Republic of Austria, for the Portuguese Republic (with the exception of the Azores and Madeira), for the Republic of Finland, for the Kingdom of Sweden and for the United Kingdom: 10 days,

— for other European countries and territories: two weeks,

— for the autonomous regions of the Azores and Madeira of the Portuguese Republic: three weeks,

— for other countries, departments and territories: one month.

Article 2

This Decision, which shall constitute Annex II to the Rules of Procedure, shall enter into force on the same day as those Rules.

It shall be published in the *Official Journal of the European Communities*.

Done at Luxembourg, 19 June 1991.

SUPPLEMENTARY RULES

Chapter I

LETTERS ROGATORY

Article 1

Letters rogatory shall be issued in the form of an order which shall contain the names, forenames, description and address of the witness or expert, set out the facts on which the witness or expert is to be examined, name the parties, their agents, lawyers or advisers, indicate their addresses for service and briefly describe the subject-matter of the proceedings.

Notice of the order shall be served on the parties by the Registrar.

Article 2

The Registrar shall send the order to the competent authority named in Annex I of the Member State in whose territory the witness or expert is to be examined. Where necessary, the order shall be accompanied by a translation into the official languages of the Member State to which it is addressed.

The authority named pursuant to the first paragraph shall pass on the order to the judicial authority which is competent according to its national law.

The competent judicial authority shall give effect to the letters rogatory in accordance with its national law. After implementation the competent judicial authority shall transmit to the authority named pursuant to the first paragraph the order embodying the letters rogatory, any documents arising from the implementation and a detailed statement of costs. These documents shall be sent to the Registrar of the Court.

The Registrar shall be responsible for the translation of the documents into the language of the case.

Article 3

The Court shall defray the expenses occasioned by the letters rogatory without prejudice to the right to charge them, where appropriate, to the parties.

Chapter II

LEGAL AID

Article 4

The Court, by any order by which it decides that a person is entitled to receive legal aid, shall order that a lawyer be appointed to act for him.

If the person does not indicate his choice of lawyer, or if the Court considers that his choice is unacceptable, the Registrar shall send a copy of the order and of the application for legal aid to the authority named in Annex II, being the competent authority of the State concerned.

The Court, in the light of the suggestions made by that authority, shall of its own motion appoint a lawyer to act for the person concerned.

Article 5

The Court shall advance the funds necessary to meet expenses.

It shall adjudicate on the lawyer's disbursements and fees; the President may, on application by the lawyer, order that he receive an advance.

Chapter III

REPORTS OF PERJURY BY A WITNESS OR EXPERT

Article 6

The Court, after hearing the Advocate-General, may decide to report to the competent authority referred to in Annex III of the Member State whose courts have penal jurisdiction in any case of perjury on the part of a witness or expert before the Court, account being taken of the provisions of Article 124 of the Rules of Procedure.

Article 7

The Registrar shall be responsible for communicating the decision of the Court.

The decision shall set out the facts and circumstances on which the report is based.

FINAL PROVISIONS

Article 8

These Supplementary Rules replace the Supplementary Rules of 9 March 1962 (OJ, 1962, p. 1113).

Article 9

These Rules, which shall be authentic in the languages referred to in Article 29 (1) of the Rules of Procedure, shall be published in the *Official Journal of the European Communities*.

These Rules shall enter into force on the date of their publication.

ANNEX I

LIST REFERRED TO IN THE FIRST PARAGRAPH OF ARTICLE 2

Belgium
The Minister for Justice
Denmark
The Minister for Justice
Germany
The Federal Minister for Justice
Greece
The Minister for Justice
Spain
The Minister for Justice
France
The Minister for Justice
Ireland
The Minister for Justice
Italy
The Minister for Justice
Luxembourg
The Minister for Justice
Netherlands
The Minister for Justice
Austria
The Federal Minister for Justice
Portugal
The Minister for Justice
Finland
The Ministry of Justice
Sweden
The Ministry of Justice
United Kingdom
The Secretary of State

APPENDIX C

ANNEX II

LIST REFERRED TO IN THE SECOND PARAGRAPH OF ARTICLE 4

Belgium
The Minister for Justice
Denmark
The Minister for Justice
Germany
Bundesrechtsanwaltskammer
Greece
The Minister for Justice
Spain
The Minister for Justice
France
The Minister for Justice
Ireland
The Minister for Justice
Italy
The Minister for Justice
Luxembourg
The Minister for Justice
Netherlands
Algemene Raad van de Nederlandse Orde van Advocaten
Austria
The Federal Minister for Justice
Portugal
The Minister for Justice
Finland
The Ministry of Justice
Sweden
Sveriges Advokatsamfund
United Kingdom
The Law Society, London (for applicants resident in England or Wales)
The Law Society of Scotland, Edinburgh (for applicants resident in Scotland)
The Incorporated Law Society of Northern Ireland, Belfast (for applicants resident in Northern Ireland)

ANNEX III

LIST REFERRED TO IN ARTICLE 6

Belgium
The Minister for Justice
Denmark
The Minister for Justice
Germany
The Federal Minister for Justice
Greece
The Minister for Justice
Spain
The Minister for Justice
France
The Minister for Justice
Ireland
The Attorney-General
Italy
The Minister for Justice
Luxembourg
The Minister for Justice
Netherlands
The Minister for Justice
Austria
The Federal Minister for Justice
Portugal
The Minister for Justice
Finland
The Ministry of Justice
Sweden
Riksaklågaren
United Kingdom
Her Majesty's Attorney-General (for witnesses or experts resident in England or Wales)
Her Majesty's Advocate (for witnesses or experts resident in Scotland)
Her Majesty's Attorney-General (for witnesses or experts resident in Northern Ireland)

PROTOCOL ON THE INTERPRETATION BY THE COURT OF JUSTICE OF THE CONVENTION OF 27 SEPTEMBER 1968 ON JURISDICTION AND THE ENFORCEMENT OF JUDGMENTS IN CIVIL AND COMMERCIAL MATTERS

Article 1

The Court of Justice of the European Communities shall have jurisdiction to give rulings on the interpretation of the Convention on jurisdiction and the enforcement of judgments in civil and commercial matters and the Protocol annexed to that Convention, signed at Brussels on 27 September 1968, and also on the interpretation of the present Protocol.

The Court of Justice of the European Communities shall also have jurisdiction to give rulings on the interpretation of the Convention on the accession of the Kingdom of Denmark, Ireland and the United Kingdom of Great Britain and Northern Ireland to the Convention of 27 September 1968 and to this Protocol.

The Court of Justice of the European Communities shall also have jurisdiction to give rulings on the interpretation of the Convention on the accession of the Hellenic Republic to the Convention of 27 September 1968 and to this Protocol, as adjusted by the 1978 Convention.

The Court of Justice of the European Communities shall also have jurisdiction to give rulings on the interpretation of the Convention on the accession of the Kingdom of Spain and the Portuguese Republic to the Convention of 27 September 1968 and to this Protocol, as adjusted by the 1978 Convention and the 1982 Convention.

Article 2

The following courts may request the Court of Justice to give preliminary rulings on questions of interpretation:

1— in Belgium: la Cour de Cassation (het Hof van Cassatie) and le Conseil d'Etat (de Raad van State),

— in Denmark: Højesteret,

— in the Federal Republic of Germany: die obersten Gerichtshöfe des Bundes,

— in Greece: the τα ανώτατα Δικαστήρια,

— in Spain: el Tribunal Supremo,

— in France: la Cour de Cassation and le Conseil d'Etat,

— in Ireland: the Supreme Court,

— in Italy: la Corte Suprema di Cassazione,

— in Luxembourg: la Cour Supérieure de Justice, when sitting as Cour de Cassation,

— in the Netherlands: de Hoge Raad,

— in Portugal: o Supremo Tribunal de Justiça and o Supremo Tribunal Administrativo,

— in the United Kingdom: the House of Lords and courts to which application has been made under the second paragraph of Article 37 or under Article 41 of the Convention;

2— the courts of the Contracting States when they are sitting in an appellate capacity;

3— in the cases provided for in Article 37 of the Convention, the courts referred to in that Article.

Article 3

1. Where a question of interpretation of the Convention or of one of the other instruments referred to in Article 1 is raised in a case pending before one of the courts listed in point 1 of Article 2, that court shall, if it considers that a decision on the question is necessary to enable it to give judgment, request the Court of Justice to give a ruling thereon.

2. Where such a question is raised before any court referred to in point 2 or 3 of Article 2, that court may, under the conditions laid down in paragraph 1, request the Court of Justice to give a ruling thereon.

Article 4

1. The competent authority of a Contracting State may request the Court of Justice to give a ruling on a question of interpretation of the Convention or of one of the other instruments referred to in Article 1 if judgments given by courts of that State conflict with the interpretation given either by the Court of Justice or in a judgment of one of the courts of another Contracting State referred to in point 1 or 2 of Article 2. The provisions of this paragraph shall apply only to judgments which have become *res judicata*.

2. The interpretation given by the Court of Justice in response to such a request shall not affect the judgments which gave rise to the request for interpretation.

3. The Procurators-General of the Courts of Cassation of the Contracting States, or any other authority designated by a Contracting State, shall be entitled to request the Court of Justice for a ruling on interpretation in accordance with paragraph 1.

4. The Registrar of the Court of Justice shall give notice of the request to the Contracting States, to the Commission and to the Council of the European Communities; they shall then be entitled within two months of the notification to submit statements of case or written observations to the Court.

5. No fees shall be levied or any costs or expenses awarded in respect of the proceedings provided for in this Article.

Article 5

1. Except where this Protocol otherwise provides, the provisions of the Treaty establishing the European Economic Community and those of the Protocol on the Statute of the Court of Justice annexed thereto, which are applicable when the Court is requested to give a preliminary ruling, shall also apply to any proceedings for the interpretation of the Convention and the other instruments referred to in Article 1.

2. The Rules of Procedure of the Court of Justice shall, if necessary, be adjusted and supplemented in accordance with Article 188 of the Treaty establishing the European Economic Community.

Article 11

The Contracting States shall communicate to the Secretary-General of the Council of the European Communities the texts of any provisions of their laws which necessitate an amendment to the list of courts in point 1 of Article 2.

Article 12

This Protocol is concluded for an unlimited period.

APPENDIX C

Article 14

This Protocol, drawn up in a single original in the Dutch, French, German and Italian languages, all four texts being equally authentic, shall be deposited in the archives of the Secretariat of the Council of the European Communities. The Secretary-General shall transmit a certified copy to the Government of each signatory State.

FIRST PROTOCOL ON THE INTERPRETATION BY THE COURT OF JUSTICE OF THE EUROPEAN COMMUNITIES OF THE CONVENTION ON THE LAW APPLICABLE TO CONTRACTUAL OBLIGATIONS, OPENED FOR SIGNATURE IN ROME ON 19 JUNE 1980

Article 1

The Court of Justice of the European Communities shall have jurisdiction to give rulings on the interpretation of:

(a) the Convention on the law applicable to contractual obligations, opened for signature in Rome on 19 June 1980, hereinafter referred to as 'the Rome Convention';

(b) the Convention on accession to the Rome Convention by the States which have become Members of the European Communities since the date on which it was opened for signature;

(c) this Protocol.

Article 2

Any of the courts referred to below may request the Court of Justice to give a preliminary ruling on a question raised in a case pending before it and concerning interpretation of the provisions contained in the instruments referred to in Article 1 if that court considers that a decision on the question is necessary to enable it to give judgment:

(a)— in Belgium: la Cour de Cassation (het Hof van Cassatie) and le Conseil d'Etat (de Raad van State),

— in Denmark: Højesteret,

— in the Federal Republic of Germany: die obersten Gerichtshöfe des Bundes,

— in Greece: τα ανώτατα Διχαστήρια,

— in Spain: el Tribunal Supremo,

— in France: la Cour de Cassation and le Conseil d'Etat,

— in Ireland: the Supreme Court,

— in Italy: la Corte Suprema di Cassazione and il Consiglio di Stato,

— in Luxembourg: la Cour Supérieure de Justice, when sitting as Cour de Cassation,

— in the Netherlands: de Hoge Raad,

— in Portugal: o Supremo Tribunal de Justiça and o Supremo Tribunal Administrativo,

— in the United Kingdom: the House of Lords and other courts from which no further appeal is possible;

(b)— the courts of the Contracting States when acting as appeal courts.

Article 3

1. The competent authority of a Contracting State may request the Court of Justice to give a ruling on a question of interpretation of the provisions contained in the instruments referred to in Article 1 if judgments given by courts of that State conflict with the interpretation given either by the Court of Justice or in a judgment of one of the

courts of another Contracting State referred to in Article 2. The provisions of this paragraph shall apply only to judgments which have become *res judicata*.

2. The interpretation given by the Court of Justice in response to such a request shall not affect the judgments which gave rise to the request for interpretation.

3. The Procurators-General of the Supreme Courts of Appeal of the Contracting States, or any other authority designated by a Contracting State, shall be entitled to request the Court of Justice for a ruling on interpretation in accordance with paragraph 1.

4. The Registrar of the Court of Justice shall give notice of the request to the Contracting States, to the Commission and to the Council of the European Communities; they shall then be entitled within two months of the notification to submit statements of case or written observations to the Court.

5. No fees shall be levied or any costs or expenses awarded in respect of the proceedings provided for in this Article.

Article 4

1. Except where this Protocol otherwise provides, the provisions of the Treaty establishing the European Economic Community and those of the Protocol on the Statute of the Court of Justice annexed thereto, which are applicable when the Court is requested to give a preliminary ruling, shall also apply to any proceedings for the interpretation of the instruments referred to in Article 1.

2. The Rules of Procedure of the Court of Justice shall, if necessary, be adjusted and supplemented in accordance with Article 188 of the Treaty establishing the European Economic Community.

Article 5

This Protocol shall be subject to ratification by the Signatory States. The instruments of ratification shall be deposited with the Secretary-General of the Council of the European Communities.

Article 6

1. To enter into force, this Protocol must be ratified by seven States in respect of which the Rome Convention is in force. This Protocol shall enter into force on the first day of the third month following the deposit of the instrument of ratification by the last such State to take this step. If, however, the Second Protocol conferring on the Court of Justice of the European Communities certain powers to interpret the Convention on the law applicable to contractual obligations, opened for signature in Rome on 19 June 1980, concluded in Brussels on 19 December 1988, enters into force on a later date, this Protocol shall enter into force on the date of entry into force of the Second Protocol.

2. Any ratification subsequent to the entry into force of this Protocol shall take effect on the first day of the third month following the deposit of the instrument of ratification, provided that the ratification, acceptance or approval of the Rome Convention by the State in question has become effective.

Article 7

The Secretary-General of the Council of the European Communities shall notify the Signatory States of:

(a) the deposit of each instrument of ratification;

(b) the date of entry into force of this Protocol;

(c) any designation communicated pursuant to Article 3 (3);

(d) any communication made pursuant to Article 8.

Article 8

The Contracting States shall communicate to the Secretary-General of the Council of the European Communities the texts of any provisions of their laws which necessitate an amendment to the list of courts in Article 2 (a).

Article 9

This Protocol shall have effect for as long as the Rome Convention remains in force under the conditions laid down in Article 30 of that Convention.

Article 11

This Protocol, drawn up in a single original in the Danish, Dutch, English, French, German, Greek, Irish, Italian, Portuguese and Spanish languages, all 10 texts being equally authentic, shall be deposited in the archives of the General Secretariat of the Council of the European Communities. The Secretary-General shall transmit a certified copy to the Government of each Signatory State.

Joint Declaration

The Governments of the Kingdom of Belgium, the Kingdom of Denmark, the Federal Republic of Germany, the Hellenic Republic, the Kingdom of Spain, the French Republic, Ireland, the Italian Republic, the Grand Duchy of Luxembourg, the Kingdom of the Netherlands, the Portuguese Republic and the United Kingdom of Great Britain and Northern Ireland,

On signing the First Protocol on the interpretation by the Court of Justice of the European Communities of the Convention on the law applicable to contractual obligations, opened for signature in Rome on 19 June 1980,

Desiring to ensure that the Convention is applied as effectively and as uniformly as possible,

Declare themselves ready to organize, in cooperation with the Court of Justice of the European Communities, an exchange of information on judgments which have become *res judicata* and have been handed down pursuant to the Convention on the law applicable to contractual obligations by the courts referred to in Article 2 of the said Protocol. The exchange of information will comprise:

— the forwarding to the Court of Justice by the competent national authorities of judgments handed down by the courts referred to in Article 2 (a) and significant judgments handed down by the courts referred to in Article 2 (b),

— the classification and the documentary exploitation of these judgments by the Court of Justice including, as far as necessary, the drawing up of abstracts and translations, and the publication of judgments of particular importance,

— the communication by the Court of Justice of the documentary material to the competent national authorities of the States parties to the Protocol and to the Commission and the Council of the European Communities.

APPENDIX C

SECOND PROTOCOL CONFERRING ON THE COURT OF JUSTICE OF THE EUROPEAN COMMUNITIES CERTAIN POWERS TO INTERPRET THE CONVENTION ON THE LAW APPLICABLE TO CONTRACTUAL OBLIGATIONS, OPENED FOR SIGNATURE IN ROME ON 19 JUNE 1980

Article 1

1. The Court of Justice of the European Communities shall, with respect to the Rome Convention, have the jurisdiction conferred upon it by the First Protocol on the interpretation by the Court of Justice of the European Communities of the Convention on the law applicable to contractual obligations, opened for signature in Rome on 19 June 1980, concluded in Brussels on 19 December 1988. The Protocol on the Statute of the Court of Justice of the European Communities and the Rules of Procedure of the Court of Justice shall apply.

2. The Rules of Procedure of the Court of Justice shall be adapted and supplemented as necessary in accordance with Article 188 of the Treaty establishing the European Economic Community.

Article 2

This Protocol shall be subject to ratification by the Signatory States. The instruments of ratification shall be deposited with the Secretary-General of the Council of the European Communities.

Article 3

This Protocol shall enter into force on the first day of the third month following the deposit of the instrument of ratification of the last Signatory State to complete that formality.

Article 4

This Protocol, drawn up in a single original in the Danish, Dutch, English, French, German, Greek, Irish, Italian, Portuguese and Spanish languages, all 10 texts being equally authentic, shall be deposited in the archives of the General Secretariat of the Council of the European Communities. The Secretary-General shall transmit a certified copy to the Government of each signatory.

Appendix D

Rules of Procedure—Court of First Instance

RULES OF PROCEDURE OF THE COURT OF FIRST INSTANCE OF THE EUROPEAN COMMUNITIES[1]

CONTENTS

[1] Consolidated version as at September 1997.

THE COURT OF FIRST INSTANCE OF THE EUROPEAN COMMUNITIES,

Having regard to Article 32d of the Treaty establishing the European Coal and Steel Community,

Having regard to Article 168a of the Treaty establishing the European Economic Community,

Having regard to Article 140a of the Treaty establishing the European Atomic Energy Community,

Having regard to the Protocol on the Statute of the Court of Justice of the European Coal and Steel Community, signed in Paris on 18 April 1951,

Having regard to the Protocol on the Statute of the Court of Justice of the European Community, signed in Brussels on 17 April 1957,

Having regard to the Protocol on the Statute of the Court of Justice of the European Atomic Energy Community, signed in Brussels on 17 April 1957,

Having regard to Council Decision 88/591 ECSC, EC, Euratom of 24 October 1988 establishing a Court of First Instance of the European Communities (OJ No L 319 of 25 November 1988, with corrigendum in OJ No L 241 of 17 August 1989), and in particular Article 11 thereof,

Having regard to the agreement of the Court of Justice,

Having regard to the unanimous approval of the Council, given on 21 December 1990 and 29 April 1991,

Whereas the Court of First Instance is to establish its rules of procedure in agreement with the Court of Justice and with the unanimous approval of the Council and to adopt them immediately upon its constitution;

Whereas it is necessary to adopt the provisions laid down for the functioning of the Court of First Instance by the Treaties, by the Protocols on the Statutes of the Court of Justice and by the Council Decision of 24 October 1988 establishing a Court of First Instance of the European Communities and to adopt any other provisions necessary for applying and, where required, supplementing those instruments;

Whereas it is necessary to lay down for the Court of First Instance procedures adapted to the duties of such a court and to the task entrusted to the Court of First Instance of ensuring effective judicial protection of individual interests in cases requiring close examination of complex facts;

Whereas it is, moreover, desirable that the rules applicable to the procedure before the Court of First Instance should not differ more than is necessary from the rules applicable to the procedure before the Court of Justice under its Rules of Procedure adopted on 4 December 1974 (OJ No L 350 of 28 December 1974), as subsequently amended,

adopts the following

RULES OF PROCEDURE

INTERPRETATION

Article 1

In these Rules:

'EC Treaty'　　　　means the Treaty establishing the European Community;

'EC Statute'	means the Protocol on the Statute of the Court of Justice of the European Community;
'ECSC Treaty'	means the Treaty establishing the European Coal and Steel Community;
'ECSC Statute'	means the Protocol on the Statute of the Court of Justice of the European Coal and Steel Community;
'Euratom Treaty'	means the Treaty establishing the European Atomic Energy Community (Euratom);
'Euratom Statute'	means the Protocol on the Statute of the Court of Justice of the European Atomic Energy Community;
'EEA Agreement'	means the Agreement on the European Economic Area.

For the purposes of these Rules:

'institutions'	means the institutions of the Communities and bodies which are established by the Treaties, or by an act adopted in implementation thereof, and which may be parties before the Court of First Instance;
'EFTA Surveillance Authority'	means the surveillance authority referred to in the EEA Agreement.

TITLE 1

Organization of the Court of First Instance

Chapter 1

PRESIDENT AND MEMBERS OF THE COURT OF FIRST INSTANCE

Article 2

§ 1

Every Member of the Court of First Instance shall, as a rule, perform the function of Judge.

Members of the Court of First Instance are hereinafter referred to as 'Judges'.

§ 2

Every Judge, with the exception of the President, may, in the circumstances specified in Articles 17 to 19, perform the function of Advocate-General in a particular case.

References to the Advocate-General in these Rules shall apply only where a Judge has been designated as Advocate-General.

Article 3

The term of office of a Judge shall begin on the date laid down in his instrument of appointment. In the absence of any provision regarding the date, the term shall begin on the date of the instrument.

Article 4

§ 1

Before taking up his duties, a Judge shall take the following oath before the Court of Justice of the European Communities:

'I swear that I will perform my duties impartially and conscientiously; I swear that I will preserve the secrecy of the deliberations of the Court.'

§ 2

Immediately after taking the oath, a Judge shall sign a declaration by which he solemnly undertakes that, both during and after his term of office, he will respect the obligations arising therefrom, and in particular the duty to behave with integrity and discretion as regards the acceptance, after he has ceased to hold office, of certain appointments and benefits.

Article 5

When the Court of Justice is called upon to decide, after consulting the Court of First Instance, whether a Judge of the Court of First Instance no longer fulfils the requisite conditions or no longer meets the obligations arising from his office, the President of the Court of First Instance shall invite the Judge concerned to make representations to the Court of First Instance, in closed session and in the absence of the Registrar.

The Court of First Instance shall state the reasons for its opinion.

An opinion to the effect that a Judge of the Court of First Instance no longer fulfils the requisite conditions or no longer meets the obligations arising from his office must receive the votes of at least seven Judges of the Court of First Instance. In that event, particulars of the voting shall be communicated to the Court of Justice.

Voting shall be by secret ballot; the Judge concerned shall not take part in the deliberations.

Article 6

With the exception of the President of the Court of First Instance and of the Presidents of the Chambers, the Judges shall rank equally in precedence according to their seniority in office.

Where there is equal seniority in office, precedence shall be determined by age.

Retiring Judges who are reappointed shall retain their former precedence.

Article 7

§ 1

The Judges shall, immediately after the partial replacement provided for in Article 168 a of the EC Treaty, Article 32 (d) of the ECSC Treaty and Article 140 a of the Euratom Treaty, elect one of their number as President of the Court of First Instance for a term of three years.

§ 2

If the office of President of the Court of First Instance falls vacant before the normal date of expiry thereof, the Court of First Instance shall elect a successor for the remainder of the term.

§ 3

The elections provided for in this Article shall be by secret ballot. If a Judge obtains an absolute majority he shall be elected. If no Judge obtains an absolute majority, a second ballot shall be held and the Judge obtaining the most votes shall be elected. Where two or more Judges obtain an equal number of votes the oldest of them shall be deemed elected.

Article 8

The President of the Court of First Instance shall direct the judicial business and the administration of the Court of First Instance. He shall preside at plenary sittings and deliberations.

Article 9

When the President of the Court of First Instance is absent or prevented from attending or when the office of President is vacant, the functions of President shall be exercised by a President of a Chamber according to the order of precedence laid down in Article 6.

If the President of the Court and the Presidents of the Chambers are all prevented from attending at the same time, or their posts are vacant at the same time, the functions of President shall be exercised by one of the other Judges according to the order of precedence laid down in Article 6.

Chapter 2

CONSTITUTION OF THE CHAMBERS AND DESIGNATION OF JUDGE-RAPPORTEURS AND ADVOCATES-GENERAL

Article 10

§ 1

The Court of First Instance shall set up Chambers composed of three or five Judges and shall decide which Judges shall be attached to them.

§ 2

The composition of the Chambers shall be published in the *Official Journal of the European Communities*.

Article 11

§ 1

Cases before the Court of First Instance shall be heard by Chambers composed in accordance with Article 10.

Cases may be heard by the Court of First Instance sitting in plenary session under the conditions laid down in Articles 14, 51, 106, 118, 124, 127 and 129.

§ 2

In cases coming before a Chamber, the term 'Court of First Instance' in these Rules shall designate that Chamber.

Article 12

The Court of First Instance shall lay down criteria by which cases are to be allocated among the Chambers.

The decision shall be published in the *Official Journal of the European Communities*.

Article 13

§ 1

As soon as the application initiating proceedings has been lodged, the President of the Court of First Instance shall assign the case to one of the Chambers.

§ 2

The President of the Chamber shall propose to the President of the Court of First Instance, in respect of each case assigned to the Chamber, the designation of a Judge to act as Rapporteur; the President of the Court of First Instance shall decide on the proposal.

Article 14

Whenever the legal difficulty or the importance of the case or special circumstances so justify, a case may be referred to the Court of First Instance sitting in plenary session or to a Chamber composed of a different number of Judges.

Any decision to refer a case shall be taken under the conditions laid down in Article 51.

Article 15

The Court of First Instance shall appoint for a period of one year the Presidents of the Chambers.

The provisions of Article 7 (2) and (3) shall apply.

The appointments made in pursuance of this Article shall be published in the *Official Journal of the European Communities*.

Article 16

In cases coming before a Chamber the powers of the President shall be exercised by the President of the Chamber.

Article 17

When the Court of First Instance sits in plenary session, it shall be assisted by an Advocate-General designated by the President of the Court of First Instance.

Article 18

A Chamber of the Court of First Instance may be assisted by an Advocate-General if it is considered that the legal difficulty or the factual complexity of the case so requires.

Article 19

The decision to designate an Advocate-General in a particular case shall be taken by the Court of First Instance sitting in plenary session at the request of the Chamber before which the case comes.

The President of the Court of First Instance shall designate the Judge called upon to perform the function of Advocate-General in that case.

APPENDIX D

Chapter 3

REGISTRY

Section 1—The Registrar

Article 20

§ 1

The Court of First Instance shall appoint the Registrar.

Two weeks before the date fixed for making the appointment, the President of the Court of First Instance shall inform the Judges of the applications which have been submitted for the post.

§ 2

An application shall be accompanied by full details of the candidate's age, nationality, university degrees, knowledge of any languages, present and past occupations and experience, if any, in judicial and international fields.

§ 3

The appointment shall be made following the procedure laid down in Article 7 (3).

§ 4

The Registrar shall be appointed for a term of six years. He may be reappointed.

§ 5

Before he takes up his duties the Registrar shall take the oath before the Court of First Instance in accordance with Article 4.

§ 6

The Registrar may be deprived of his office only if he no longer fulfils the requisite conditions or no longer meets the obligations arising from his office; the Court of First Instance shall take its decision after giving the Registrar an opportunity to make representations.

§ 7

If the office of Registrar falls vacant before the usual date of expiry of the term thereof, the Court of First Instance shall appoint a new Registrar for a term of six years.

Article 21

The Court of First Instance may, following the procedure laid down in respect of the Registrar, appoint one or more Assistant Registrars to assist the Registrar and to take his place in so far as the Instructions to the Registrar referred to in Article 23 allow.

Article 22

Where the Registrar is absent or prevented from attending and, if necessary, where the Assistant Registrar is absent or so prevented, or where their posts are vacant, the President of the Court of First Instance shall designate an official or servant to carry out the duties of Registrar.

Article 23

Instructions to the Registrar shall be adopted by the Court of First Instance acting on a proposal from the President of the Court of First Instance.

Article 24

§ 1

There shall be kept in the Registry, under the control of the Registrar, a register initialled by the President of the Court of First Instance, in which all pleadings and supporting documents shall be entered in the order in which they are lodged.

§ 2

When a document has been registered, the Registrar shall make a note to that effect on the original and, if a party so requests, on any copy submitted for the purpose.

§ 3

Entries in the register and the notes provided for in the preceding paragraph shall be authentic.

§ 4

Rules for keeping the register shall be prescribed by the Instructions to the Registrar referred to in Article 23.

§ 5

Persons having an interest may consult the register at the Registry and may obtain copies or extracts on payment of a charge on a scale fixed by the Court of First Instance on a proposal from the Registrar.

The parties to a case may, on payment of the appropriate charge, also obtain copies of pleadings and authenticated copies of orders and judgments.

§ 6

Notice shall be given in the *Official Journal of the European Communities* of the date of registration of an application initiating proceedings, the names and addresses of the parties, the subject-matter of the proceedings, the form of order sought by the applicant and a summary of the pleas in law and of the main supporting arguments.

§ 7

Where the Council or the Commission is not a party to a case, the Court of First Instance shall send to it copies of the application and of the defence without the annexes thereto, to enable it to assess whether the inapplicability of one of its acts is being invoked under Article 184 of the EC Treaty, the third paragraph of Article 36 of the ECSC Treaty or Article 156 of the Euratom Treaty.

Article 25

§ 1

The Registrar shall be responsible, under the authority of the President, for the acceptance, transmission and custody of documents and for effecting service as provided for by these Rules.

§ 2

The Registrar shall assist the Court of First Instance, the Chambers, the President and the Judges in all their official functions.

Article 26

The Registrar shall have custody of the seals. He shall be responsible for the records and be in charge of the publications of the Court of First Instance.

Article 27

Subject to Articles 5 and 33, the Registrar shall attend the sittings of the Court of First Instance and of the Chambers.

Section 2—Other Departments

Article 28

The officials and other servants whose task is to assist directly the President, the Judges and the Registrar shall be appointed in accordance with the Staff Regulations. They shall be responsible to the Registrar, under the authority of the President of the Court of First Instance.

Article 29

The officials and other servants referred to in Article 28 shall take the oath provided for in Article 20 (2) of the Rules of Procedure of the Court of Justice before the President of the Court of First Instance in the presence of the Registrar.

Article 30

The Registrar shall be responsible, under the authority of the President of the Court of First Instance, for the administration of the Court of First Instance, its financial management and its accounts; he shall be assisted in this by the departments of the Court of Justice.

Chapter 4

THE WORKING OF THE COURT OF FIRST INSTANCE

Article 31

§ 1

The dates and times of the sittings of the Court of First Instance shall be fixed by the President.

§ 2

The Court of First Instance may choose to hold one or more sittings in a place other than that in which the Court of First Instance has its seat.

Article 32

§ 1

Where, by reason of a Judge being absent or prevented from attending, there is an even number of Judges, the most junior Judge within the meaning of Article 6 shall abstain from taking part in the deliberations unless he is the Judge-Rapporteur. In this case, the Judge immediately senior to him shall abstain from taking part in the deliberations.

Where, following the designation of an Advocate-General pursuant to Article 17, there is an even number of Judges in the Court of First Instance sitting in plenary session, the President of the Court shall designate, before the hearing and in accordance with a rota established in advance by the Court of First Instance and published in the *Official Journal of the European Communities*, the Judge who will not take part in the judgment of the case.

§ 2

If, after the Court of First Instance has been convened in plenary session, it is found that the quorum of nine Judges has not been obtained, the President of the Court of First Instance shall adjourn the sitting until there is a quorum.

§ 3

If in any Chamber the quorum of three Judges has not been attained, the President of that Chamber shall so inform the President of the Court of First Instance, who shall designate another Judge to complete the Chamber.

§ 4

If in any Chamber of three or five Judges the number of Judges assigned to that Chamber is higher than three or five respectively, the President of the Chamber shall decide which of the Judges will be called upon to take part in the judgment of the case.

Article 33

§ 1

The Court of First Instance shall deliberate in closed session.

§ 2

Only those Judges who were present at the oral proceedings may take part in the deliberations.

§ 3

Every Judge taking part in the deliberations shall state his opinion and the reasons for it.

§ 4

Any Judge may require that any question be formulated in the language of his choice and communicated in writing to the other Judges before being put to the vote.

§ 5

The conclusions reached by the majority of the Judges after final discussion shall determine the decision of the Court of First Instance. Votes shall be cast in reverse order to the order of precedence laid down in Article 6.

§ 6

Differences of view on the substance, wording or order of questions, or on the interpretation of a vote shall be settled by decision of the Court of First Instance.

§ 7

Where the deliberations of the Court of First Instance concern questions of its own administration, the Registrar shall be present, unless the Court of First Instance decides to the contrary.

§ 8

Where the Court of First Instance sits without the Registrar being present it shall, if necessary, instruct the most junior Judge within the meaning of Article 6 to draw up minutes. The minutes shall be signed by this Judge and by the President.

Article 34

§ 1

Subject to any special decision of the Court of First Instance, its vacations shall be as follows:

— from 18 December to 10 January,

— from the Sunday before Easter to the second Sunday after Easter,

— from 15 July to 15 September.

During the vacations, the functions of President shall be exercised at the place where the Court of First Instance has its seat either by the President himself, keeping in touch with the Registrar, or by a President of Chamber or other Judge invited by the President to take his place.

§ 2

In a case of urgency, the President may convene the Judges during the vacations.

§ 3

The Court of First Instance shall observe the official holidays of the place where it has its seat.

§ 4

The Court of First Instance may, in proper circumstances, grant leave of absence to any Judge.

Chapter 5

LANGUAGES

Article 35

§ 1

The language of a case shall be Danish, Dutch, English, Finnish, French, German, Greek, Irish, Italian, Portuguese, Spanish or Swedish.

§ 2

The language of the case shall be chosen by the applicant, except that:

(a) at the joint request of the parties the use of another of the languages mentioned in paragraph 1 for all or part of the proceedings may be authorized;

(b) at the request of one of the parties, and after the opposite party and the Advocate-General have been heard, the use of another of the languages mentioned in paragraph 1 as the language of the case for all or part of the proceedings may be authorized by way of derogation from subparagraph (a).

Requests as above may be decided on by the President; the latter may and, where he proposes to accede to a request without the agreement of all the parties, must refer the request to the Court of First Instance.

§ 3

The language of the case shall be used in the written and oral pleadings of the parties and in supporting documents, and also in the minutes and decisions of the Court of First Instance.

Any supporting documents expressed in another language must be accompanied by a translation into the language of the case.

In the case of lengthy documents, translations may be confined to extracts. However, the Court of First Instance may, of its own motion or at the request of a party, at any time call for a complete or fuller translation.

Notwithstanding the foregoing provisions, a Member State shall be entitled to use its official language when intervening in a case before the Court of First Instance. This provision shall apply both to written statements and to oral addresses. The Registrar shall cause any such statement or address to be translated into the language of the case.

The States, other than the Member States, which are parties to the EEA Agreement, and also the EFTA Surveillance Authority, may be authorized to use one of the languages mentioned in paragraph 1, other than the language of the case, when they intervene in a case before the Court of First Instance. This provision shall apply both to written statements and oral addresses. The Registrar shall cause any such statement or address to be translated into the language of the case.

§ 4

Where a witness or expert states that he is unable adequately to express himself in one of the languages referred to in paragraph (1) of this Article, the Court of First Instance may authorize him to give his evidence in another language. The Registrar shall arrange for translation into the language of the case.

§ 5

The President in conducting oral proceedings, the Judge-Rapporteur both in his preliminary report and in his report for the hearing, Judges and the Advocate-General in putting questions and the Advocate-General in delivering his opinion may use one of the languages referred to in paragraph (1) of this Article other than the language of the case. The Registrar shall arrange for translation into the language of the case.

Article 36

§ 1

The Registrar shall, at the request of any Judge, of the Advocate-General or of a party, arrange for anything said or written in the course of the proceedings before the Court of First Instance to be translated into the languages he chooses from those referred to in Article 35 (1).

§ 2

Publications of the Court of First Instance shall be issued in the language referred to in Article 1 of Council Regulation No.1.

Article 37

The texts of documents drawn up in the language of the case or in any other language authorized by the Court of First Instance pursuant to Article 35 shall be authentic.

APPENDIX D

Chapter 6

RIGHTS AND OBLIGATIONS OF AGENTS, ADVISERS AND LAWYERS

Article 38

§ 1

Agents, advisers and lawyers, appearing before the Court of First Instance or before any judicial authority to which it has addressed letters rogatory, shall enjoy immunity in respect of words spoken or written by them concerning the case or the parties.

§ 2

Agents, advisers and lawyers shall enjoy the following further privileges and facilities:

(a) papers and documents relating to the proceedings shall be exempt from both search and seizure; in the event of a dispute the customs officials or police may seal those papers and documents; they shall then be immediately forwarded to the Court of First Instance for inspection in the presence of the Registrar and of the person concerned;

(b) agents, advisers and lawyers shall be entitled to such allocation of foreign currency as may be necessary for the performance of their duties;

(c) agents, advisers and lawyers shall be entitled to travel in the course of duty without hindrance.

Article 39

In order to qualify for the privileges, immunities and facilities specified in Article 38, persons entitled to them shall furnish proof of their status as follows:

(a) agents shall produce an official document issued by the party for whom they act and shall forward without delay a copy thereof to the Registrar;

(b) advisers and lawyers shall produce a certificate signed by the Registrar. The validity of this certificate shall be limited to a specified period, which may be extended or curtailed according to the length of the proceedings.

Article 40

The privileges, immunities and facilities specified in Article 38 are granted exclusively in the interests of the proper conduct of proceedings.

The Court of First Instance may waive the immunity where it considers that the proper conduct of proceedings will not be hindered thereby.

Article 41

§ 1

Any adviser or lawyer whose conduct towards the Court of First Instance, the President, a Judge or the Registrar is incompatible with the dignity of the Court of First Instance, or who uses his rights for purposes other than those for which they were granted, may at any time be excluded from the proceedings by an order of the Court of First Instance; the person concerned shall be given an opportunity to defend himself.

The order shall have immediate effect.

§ 2

Where an adviser or lawyer is excluded from the proceedings, the proceedings shall be suspended for a period fixed by the President in order to allow the party concerned to appoint another adviser or lawyer.

§ 3

Decisions taken under this Article may be rescinded.

Article 42

The provisions of this Chapter shall apply to university teachers who have a right of audience before the Court of First Instance in accordance with Article 17 of the EC Statute, Article 20 of the ECSC Statute and Article 17 of the Euratom Statute.

TITLE 2

Procedure

Chapter 1

WRITTEN PROCEDURE

Article 43

§ 1

The original of every pleading must be signed by the party's agent or lawyer.

The original, accompanied by all annexes referred to therein, shall be lodged together with five copies for the Court of First Instance and a copy for every other party to the proceedings. Copies shall be certified by the party lodging them.

§ 2

Institutions shall in addition produce, within time-limits laid down by the Court of First Instance, translations of all pleadings into the other languages provided for by Article 1 of Council Regulation No. 1. The second subparagraph of paragraph (1) of this Article shall apply.

§ 3

All pleadings shall bear a date. In the reckoning of time-limits for taking steps in proceedings only the date of lodgment at the Registry shall be taken into account.

§ 4

To every pleading there shall be annexed a file containing the documents relied on in support of it, together with a schedule listing them.

§ 5

Where, in view of the length of a document, only extracts from it are annexed to the pleading, the whole document or a full copy of it shall be lodged at the Registry.

Article 44

§ 1

An application of the kind referred to in Article 19 of the EC Statute, Article 22 of the ECSC Statute and Article 19 of the Euratom Statute shall state:

(a) the name and address of the applicant;

(b) the designation of the party against whom the application is made;

(c) the subject-matter of the proceedings and a summary of the pleas in law on which the application is based;

(d) the form of order sought by the applicant;

(e) where appropriate, the nature of any evidence offered in support.

§ 2

For the purpose of the proceedings, the application shall state an address for service in the place where the Court of First Instance has its seat and the name of the person who is authorized and has expressed willingness to accept service.

If the application does not comply with these requirements, all service on the party concerned for the purposes of the proceedings shall be effected, for so long as the defect has not been cured, by registered letter addressed to the agent or lawyer of that party. By way of derogation from Article 100, service shall then be deemed to have been duly effected by the lodging of the registered letter at the post office of the place where the Court of First Instance has its seat.

§ 3

The lawyer acting for a party must lodge at the Registry a certificate that he is authorized to practise before a Court of a Member State or of another State which is a party to the EEA Agreement.

§ 4

The application shall be accompanied, where appropriate, by the documents specified in the second paragraph of Article 19 of the EC Statute, in the second paragraph of Article 22 of the ECSC Statute and in the second paragraph of Article 19 of the Euratom Statute.

§ 5

An application made by a legal person governed by private law shall be accompanied by:

(a) the instrument or instruments constituting and regulating that legal person or a recent extract from the register of companies, firms or associations or any other proof of its existence in law;

(b) proof that the authority granted to the applicant's lawyer has been properly conferred on him by someone authorized for the purpose.

§ 5a

An application submitted under Article 181 of the EC Treaty, Article 42 of the ECSC Treaty or Article 153 of the Euratom Treaty pursuant to an arbitration clause contained in a contract governed by public or private law, entered into by the Community or on its behalf, shall be accompanied by a copy of the contract which contains that clause.

§ 6

If an application does not comply with the requirements set out in paragraphs (3) to (5) of this Article, the Registrar shall prescribe a reasonable period within which the applicant is to comply with them whether by putting the application itself in order or by producing any of the abovementioned documents. If the applicant fails to put the application in order or to produce the required documents within the time prescribed, the Court of First Instance shall decide whether the non-compliance with these conditions renders the application formally inadmissible.

Article 45

The application shall be served on the defendant. In a case where Article 44 (6) applies, service shall be effected as soon as the application has been put in order or the Court of First Instance has declared it admissible notwithstanding the failure to observe the formal requirements set out in that Article.

Article 46

§ 1

Within one month after service on him of the application, the defendant shall lodge a defence, stating:

(a) the name and address of the defendant;

(b) the arguments of fact and law relied on;

(c) the form of order sought by the defendant;

(d) the nature of any evidence offered by him.

The provisions of Article 44 (2) to (5) shall apply to the defence.

§ 2

In proceedings between the Communities and their servants the defence shall be accompanied by the complaint within the meaning of Article 90 (2) of the Staff Regulations of Officials and by the decision rejecting the complaint together with the dates on which the complaint was submitted and the decision notified.

§ 3

The time-limit laid down in paragraph (1) of this Article may be extended by the President on a reasoned application by the defendant.

Article 47

§ 1

The application initiating the proceedings and the defence may be supplemented by a reply from the applicant and by a rejoinder from the defendant.

§ 2

The President shall fix the time-limits within which these pleadings are to be lodged.

Article 48

§ 1

In reply or rejoinder a party may offer further evidence. The party must, however, give reasons for the delay in offering it.

§ 2

No new plea in law may be introduced in the course of proceedings unless it is based on matters of law or of fact which come to light in the course of the procedure.

If in the course of the procedure one of the parties puts forward a new plea in law which is so based, the President may, even after the expiry of the normal procedural time-limits, acting on a report of the Judge-Rapporteur and after hearing the Advocate-General, allow the other party time to answer on that plea.

Consideration of the admissibility of the plea shall be reserved for the final judgment.

Article 49

At any stage of the proceedings the Court of First Instance may, after hearing the Advocate-General, prescribe any measure of organization of procedure or any measure of inquiry referred to in Articles 64 and 65 or order that a previous inquiry be repeated or expanded.

Article 50

The President may, at any time, after hearing the parties and the Advocate-General, order that two or more cases concerning the same subject-matter shall, on account of the connection between them, be joined for the purposes of the written or oral procedure or of the final judgment. The cases may subsequently be disjoined. The President may refer those matters to the Court of First Instance.

Article 51

§ 1

In the cases specified in Article 14, and at any stage in the proceedings, the Chamber hearing the case may, either on its own initiative or at the request of one of the parties, propose to the Court of First Instance sitting in plenary session that the case be referred to the Court of First Instance sitting in plenary session or to a Chamber composed of a different number of Judges. The Court of First Instance sitting in plenary session shall, after hearing the parties and the Advocate-General, decide whether or not to refer a case.

§ 2

The case shall be maintained before or referred to a Chamber composed of five Judges where a Member State or an institution of the European Communities which is a party to the proceedings so requests.

Article 52

§ 1

Without prejudice to the application of Article 49, the President shall, after the rejoinder has been lodged, fix a date on which the Judge-Rapporteur is to present his preliminary report to the Court of First Instance. The report shall contain recommendations as to whether measures of organization of procedure or measures of inquiry should be undertaken and whether the case should be referred to the Court of First Instance sitting in plenary session or to a Chamber composed of a different number of Judges.

§ 2

The Court of First Instance shall decide, after hearing the Advocate-General, what action to take upon the recommendations of the Judge-Rapporteur.

The same procedure shall apply:

(a) where no reply or no rejoinder has been lodged within the time-limit fixed in accordance with Article 47 (2);

(b) where the party concerned waives his right to lodge a reply or rejoinder.

Article 53

Where the Court of First Instance decides to open the oral procedure without undertaking measures of organization of procedure or ordering a preparatory inquiry, the President of the Court of First Instance shall fix the opening date.

Article 54

Without prejudice to any measures of organization of procedure or measures of inquiry which may be arranged at the stage of the oral procedure, where, during the written procedure, measures of organization of procedure or measures of inquiry have been instituted and completed, the President shall fix the date for the opening of the oral procedure.

Chapter 2

ORAL PROCEDURE

Article 55

§ 1

Subject to the priority of decisions provided for in Article 106, the Court of First Instance shall deal with the cases before it in the order in which the preparatory inquiries in them have been completed. Where the preparatory inquiries in several cases are completed simultaneously, the order in which they are to be dealt with shall be determined by the dates of entry in the register of the applications initiating them respectively.

§ 2

The President may in special circumstances order that a case be given priority over others.

The President may in special circumstances, after hearing the parties and the Advocate-General, either on his own initiative or at the request of one of the parties, defer a case to be dealt with at a later date. On a joint application by the parties the President may order that a case be deferred.

Article 56

The proceedings shall be opened and directed by the President, who shall be responsible for the proper conduct of the hearing.

Article 57

The oral proceedings in cases heard *in camera* shall not be published.

Article 58

The President may, in the course of the hearing, put questions to the agents, advisers or lawyers of the parties.

The other Judges and the Advocate-General may do likewise.

Article 59

A party may address the Court of First Instance only through his agent, adviser or lawyer.

Article 60

Where an Advocate-General has not been designated in a case, the President shall declare the oral procedure closed at the end of the hearing.

Article 61

§ 1

Where the Advocate-General delivers his opinion in writing, he shall lodge it at the Registry, which shall communicate it to the parties.

§ 2

After the delivery, orally or in writing, of the opinion of the Advocate-General the President shall declare the oral procedure closed.

Article 62

The Court of First Instance may, after hearing the Advocate-General, order the re-opening of the oral procedure.

Article 63

§ 1

The Registrar shall draw up minutes of every hearing. The minutes shall be signed by the President and by the Registrar and shall constitute an official record.

§ 2

The parties may inspect the minutes at the Registry and obtain copies at their own expense.

Chapter 3

MEASURES OF ORGANIZATION OF PROCEDURE AND MEASURES OF INQUIRY

Section 1—Measures of organization of procedure

Article 64

§ 1

The purposes of measures of organization of procedure shall be to ensure that cases are prepared for hearing, procedures carried out and disputes resolved under the best possible conditions. They shall be prescribed by the Court of First Instance, after hearing the Advocate-General.

§ 2

Measures of organization of procedure shall, in particular, have as their purpose:

(a) to ensure efficient conduct of the written and oral procedure and to facilitate the taking of evidence;

(b) to determine the points on which the parties must present further argument or which call for measures of inquiry;

(c) to clarify the forms of order sought by the parties, their pleas in law and arguments and the points at issue between them;

(d) to facilitate the amicable settlement of proceedings.

§ 3

Measures of organization of procedure may, in particular, consist of:

(a) putting questions to the parties;

(b) inviting the parties to make written or oral submissions on certain aspects of the proceedings;

(c) asking the parties or third parties for information or particulars;

(d) asking for documents or any papers relating to the case to be produced;

(e) summoning the parties' agents or the parties in person to meetings.

§ 4

Each party may, at any stage of the procedure, propose the adoption or modification of measures of organization of procedure. In that case, the other parties shall be heard before those measures are prescribed.

Where the procedural circumstances so require, the Registrar shall inform the parties of the measures envisaged by the Court of First Instance and shall give them an opportunity to submit comments orally or in writing.

§ 5

If the Court of First Instance sitting in plenary session decides to prescribe measures of organization of procedure and does not undertake such measures itself, it shall entrust the task of so doing to the Chamber to which the case was originally assigned or to the Judge-Rapporteur.

If a Chamber prescribes measures of organization of procedure and does not undertake such measures itself, it shall entrust the task to the Judge-Rapporteur.

The Advocate-General shall take part in measures of organization of procedure.

Section 2—Measures of inquiry

Article 65

Without prejudice to Articles 21 and 22 of the EC Statute, Articles 24 and 25 of the ECSC Statute and Articles 22 and 23 of the Euratom Statute, the following measures of inquiry may be adopted:

(a) the personal appearance of the parties;

(b) a request for information and production of documents;

(c) oral testimony;

(d) the commissioning of an expert's report;

(e) an inspection of the place or thing in question.

Article 66

§ 1

The Court of First Instance, after hearing the Advocate-General, shall prescribe the measures of inquiry that it considers appropriate by means of an order setting out the facts to be proved. Before the Court of First Instance decides on the measures of inquiry referred to in Article 65 (c), (d) and (e) the parties shall be heard.

The order shall be served on the parties.

§ 2

Evidence may be submitted in rebuttal and previous evidence may be amplified.

Article 67

§ 1

Where the Court of First Instance sitting in plenary session orders a preparatory inquiry and does not undertake such an inquiry itself, it shall entrust the task of so doing to the Chamber to which the case was originally assigned or to the Judge-Rapporteur.

Where a Chamber orders a preparatory inquiry and does not undertake such an inquiry itself, it shall entrust the task of so doing to the Judge-Rapporteur.

The Advocate-General shall take part in the measures of inquiry.

§ 2

The parties may be present at the measures of inquiry.

Section 3—The summoning and examination of witnesses and experts

Article 68

§ 1

The Court of First Instance may, either of its own motion or on application by a party, and after hearing the Advocate-General and the parties, order that certain facts be proved by witnesses. The order shall set out the facts to be established.

The Court of First Instance may summon a witness of its own motion or on application by a party or at the instance of the Advocate-General.

An application by a party for the examination of a witness shall state precisely about what facts and for what reasons the witness should be examined.

§ 2

The witness shall be summoned by an order containing the following information:

(a) the surname, forenames, description and address of the witness;

(b) an indication of the facts about which the witness is to be examined;

(c) where appropriate, particulars of the arrangements made by the Court of First Instance for reimbursement of expenses incurred by the witness, and of the penalties which may be imposed on defaulting witnesses.

The order shall be served on the parties and the witnesses.

§ 3

The Court of First Instance may make the summoning of a witness for whose examination a party has applied conditional upon the deposit with the cashier of the Court of First Instance of a sum sufficient to cover the taxed costs thereof; the Court of First Instance shall fix the amount of the payment.

The cashier of the Court of First Instance shall advance the funds necessary in connection with the examination of any witness summoned by the Court of First Instance of its own motion.

§ 4

After the identity of the witness has been established, the President shall inform him that he will be required to vouch the truth of his evidence in the manner laid down in paragraph (5) of this Article and in Article 71.

The witness shall give his evidence to the Court of First Instance, the parties having been given notice to attend. After the witness has given his main evidence the President may, at the request of a party or of his own motion, put questions to him.

The other Judges and the Advocate-General may do likewise.

Subject to the control of the President, questions may be put to witnesses by the representatives of the parties.

§ 5

Subject to the provisions of Article 71, the witness shall, after giving his evidence, take the following oath:

'I swear that I have spoken the truth, the whole truth and nothing but the truth.'

The Court of First Instance may, after hearing the parties, exempt a witness from taking the oath.

§ 6

The Registrar shall draw up minutes in which the evidence of each witness is reproduced.

The minutes shall be signed by the President or by the Judge-Rapporteur responsible for conducting the examination of the witness, and by the Registrar. Before the minutes are thus signed, witnesses must be given an opportunity to check the content of the minutes and to sign them.

The minutes shall constitute an official record.

Article 69

§ 1

Witnesses who have been duly summoned shall obey the summons and attend for examination.

§ 2

If a witness who has been duly summoned fails to appear before the Court of First Instance, the latter may impose upon him a pecuniary penalty not exceeding 5 000 ECU and may order that a further summons be served on the witness at his own expense.

The same penalty may be imposed upon a witness who, without good reason, refuses to give evidence or to take the oath or where appropriate to make a solemn affirmation equivalent thereto.

§ 3

If the witness proffers a valid excuse to the Court of First Instance, the pecuniary penalty imposed on him may be cancelled. The pecuniary penalty imposed may be reduced at the request of the witness where he establishes that it is disproportionate to his income.

§ 4

Penalties imposed and other measures ordered under this Article shall be enforced in accordance with Articles 187 and 192 of the EC Treaty, Articles 44 and 92 of the ECSC Treaty and Articles 159 and 164 of the Euratom Treaty.

Article 70

§ 1

The Court of First Instance may order that an expert's report be obtained. The order appointing the expert shall define his task and set a time-limit within which he is to make his report.

§ 2

The expert shall receive a copy of the order, together with all the documents necessary for carrying out his task. He shall be under the supervision of the Judge-Rapporteur, who may be present during his investigation and who shall be kept informed of his progress in carrying out his task.

The Court of First Instance may request the parties or one of them to lodge security for the costs of the expert's report.

§ 3

At the request of the expert, the Court of First Instance may order the examination of witnesses. Their examination shall be carried out in accordance with Article 68.

§ 4

The expert may give his opinion only on points which have been expressly referred to him.

§ 5

After the expert has made his report, the Court of First Instance may order that he be examined, the parties having been given notice to attend.

Subject to the control of the President, questions may be put to the expert by the representatives of the parties.

§ 6

Subject to the provisions of Article 71, the expert shall, after making his report, take the following oath before the Court of First Instance:

'I swear that I have conscientiously and impartially carried out my task.'

The Court of First Instance may, after hearing the parties, exempt the expert from taking the oath.

Article 71

§ 1

The President shall instruct any person who is required to take an oath before the Court of First Instance, as witness or expert, to tell the truth or to carry out his task conscientiously and impartially, as the case may be, and shall warn him of the criminal liability provided for in his national law in the event of any breach of this duty.

§ 2

Witnesses and experts shall take the oath either in accordance with the first subparagraph of Article 68 (5) and the first subparagraph of Article 70 (6) or in the manner laid down by their national law.

§ 3

Where the national law provides the opportunity to make, in judicial proceedings, a solemn affirmation equivalent to an oath as well as or instead of taking an oath, the witnesses and experts may make such an affirmation under the conditions and in the form prescribed in their national law.

Where their national law provides neither for taking an oath nor for making a solemn affirmation, the procedure described in the first paragraph of this Article shall be followed.

Article 72

§ 1

The Court of First Instance may, after hearing the Advocate-General, decide to report to the competent authority referred to in Annex III to the Rules supplementing the Rules of Procedure of the Court of Justice of the Member State whose courts have penal jurisdiction in any case of perjury on the part of a witness or expert before the Court of First Instance, account being taken of the provisions of Article 71.

§ 2

The Registrar shall be responsible for communicating the decision of the Court of First Instance. The decision shall set out the facts and circumstances on which the report is based.

Article 73

§ 1

If one of the parties objects to a witness or to an expert on the ground that he is not a competent or proper person to act as witness or expert or for any other reason, or if a witness or expert refuses to give evidence, to take the oath or to make a solemn affirmation equivalent thereto, the matter shall be resolved by the Court of First Instance.

§ 2

An objection to a witness or to an expert shall be raised within two weeks after service of the order summoning the witness or appointing the expert; the statement of objection must set out the grounds of objection and indicate the nature of any evidence offered.

Article 74

§ 1

Witnesses and experts shall be entitled to reimbursement of their travel and subsistence expenses. The cashier of the Court of First Instance may make a payment to them towards these expenses in advance.

§ 2

Witnesses shall be entitled to compensation for loss of earnings, and experts to fees for their services. The cashier of the Court of First Instance shall pay witnesses and experts their compensation or fees after they have carried out their respective duties or tasks.

Article 75

§ 1

The Court of First Instance may, on application by a party or of its own motion, issue letters rogatory for the examination of witnesses or experts.

§ 2

Letters rogatory shall be issued in the form of an order which shall contain the name, forenames, description and address of the witness or expert, set out the facts on which the witness or expert is to be examined, name the parties, their agents, lawyers or advisers, indicate their addresses for service and briefly describe the subject-matter of the proceedings.

Notice of the order shall be served on the parties by the Registrar.

§ 3

The Registrar shall send the order to the competent authority named in Annex I to the Rules supplementing the Rules of Procedure of the Court of Justice of the Member State in whose territory the witness or expert is to be examined. Where necessary, the order shall be accompanied by a translation into the official language or languages of the Member State to which it is addressed.

The authority named pursuant to the first paragraph shall pass on the order to the judicial authority which is competent according to its national law.

The competent judicial authority shall give effect to the letters rogatory in accordance with its national law. After implementation the competent judicial authority shall transmit to the authority named pursuant to the first paragraph the order embodying the letters rogatory, any documents arising from the implementation and a detailed statement of costs. These documents shall be sent to the Registrar.

The Registrar shall be responsible for the translation of the documents into the language of the case.

§ 4

The Court of First Instance shall defray the expenses occasioned by the letters rogatory without prejudice to the right to charge them, where appropriate, to the parties.

Article 76

§ 1

The Registrar shall draw up minutes of every hearing. The minutes shall be signed by the President and by the Registrar and shall constitute an official record.

§ 2

The parties may inspect the minutes and any expert's report at the Registry and obtain copies at their own expense.

Chapter 4

STAY OF PROCEEDINGS AND DECLINING OF JURISDICTION BY THE COURT OF FIRST INSTANCE

Article 77

Without prejudice to Article 123 (4), Article 128 and Article 129 (4), proceedings may be stayed:

(a) in the circumstances specified in the third paragraph of Article 47 of the EC Statute, the third paragraph of Article 47 of the ECSC Statute and the third paragraph of Article 48 of the Euratom Statute;

(b) where an appeal is brought before the Court of Justice against a decision of the Court of First Instance disposing of the substantive issues in part only, disposing of a procedural issue concerning a plea of lack of competence or inadmissibility or dismissing an application to intervene;

(c) at the joint request of the parties.

Article 78

The decision to stay the proceedings shall be made by order of the President after hearing the parties and the Advocate-General; the President may refer the matter to the Court of First Instance. A decision ordering that the proceedings be resumed shall be adopted in accordance with the same procedure. The orders referred to in this Article shall be served on the parties.

Article 79

§ 1

The stay of proceedings shall take effect on the date indicated in the order of stay or, in the absence of such an indication, on the date of that order.

While proceedings are stayed time shall, except for the purposes of the time-limit prescribed in Article 115 (1) for an application to intervene, cease to run for the purposes of prescribed time-limits for all parties.

§ 2

Where the order of stay does not fix the length of the stay, it shall end on the date indicated in the order of resumption, or, in the absence of such indication, on the date of the order of resumption.

From the date of resumption time shall begin to run afresh for the purposes of the time-limits.

Article 80

Decisions declining jurisdiction in the circumstances specified in the third paragraph of Article 47 of the EC Statute, the third paragraph of Article 47 of the ECSC Statute and the third paragraph of Article 48 of the Euratom Statute shall be made by the Court of First Instance by way of an order which shall be served on the parties.

Chapter 5

JUDGMENTS

Article 81

The judgment shall contain:

— a statement that it is the judgment of the Court of First Instance,

— the date of its delivery,

— the names of the President and of the Judges taking part in it,

— the name of the Advocate-General, if designated,

— the name of the Registrar,

— the description of the parties,

— the names of the agents, advisers and lawyers of the parties,

— a statement of the forms of order sought by the parties,

— a statement, where appropriate, that the Advocate-General delivered his opinion,

— a summary of the facts,

— the grounds for the decision,

— the operative part of the judgment, including the decision as to costs.

Article 82

§ 1

The judgment shall be delivered in open court; the parties shall be given notice to attend to hear it.

§ 2

The original of the judgment, signed by the President, by the Judges who took part in the deliberations and by the Registrar, shall be sealed and deposited at the Registry; the parties shall be served with certified copies of the judgment.

§ 3

The Registrar shall record on the original of the judgment the date on which it was delivered.

Article 83

Subject to the provisions of the second paragraph of Article 53 of the EC Statute, the second paragraph of Article 53 of the ECSC Statute and the second paragraph of Article 54 of the Euratom Statute, the judgment shall be binding from the date of its delivery.

Article 84

§ 1

Without prejudice to the provisions relating to the interpretation of judgments, the Court of First Instance may, of its own motion or on application by a party made within two weeks after the delivery of a judgment, rectify clerical mistakes, errors in calculation and obvious slips in it.

§ 2

The parties, whom the Registrar shall duly notify, may lodge written observations within a period prescribed by the President.

§ 3

The Court of First Instance shall take its decision in closed session.

§ 4

The original of the rectification order shall be annexed to the original of the rectified judgment. A note of this order shall be made in the margin of the original of the rectified judgment.

Article 85

If the Court of First Instance should omit to give a decision on costs, any party may within a month after service of the judgment apply to the Court of First Instance to supplement its judgment.

The application shall be served on the opposite party and the President shall prescribe a period within which that party may lodge written observations.

After these observations have been lodged, the Court of First Instance shall decide both on the admissibility and on the substance of the application.

Article 86

The Registrar shall arrange for the publication of cases before the Court of First Instance.

Chapter 6

COSTS

Article 87

§ 1

A decision as to costs shall be given in the final judgment or in the order which closes the proceedings.

§ 2

The unsuccessful party shall be ordered to pay the costs if they have been applied for in the successful party's pleadings.

Where there are several unsuccessful parties the Court of First Instance shall decide how the costs are to be shared.

§ 3

Where each party succeeds on some and fails on other heads, or where the circumstances are exceptional, the Court of First Instance may order that the costs be shared or that each party bear its own costs.

The Court of First Instance may order a party, even if successful, to pay costs which it considers that party to have unreasonably or vexatiously caused the opposite party to incur.

§ 4

The Member States and institutions which intervened in the proceedings shall bear their own costs.

The States, other than the Member States, which are parties to the EEA Agreement, and also the EFTA Surveillance Authority, shall bear their own costs if they intervene in the proceedings.

The Court of First Instance may order an intervener other than those mentioned in the preceding subparagraph to bear his own costs.

§ 5

A party who discontinues or withdraws from proceedings shall be ordered to pay the costs if they have been applied for in the observations of the other party on the discontinuance. However, upon application by the party who discontinues or withdraws from proceedings, the costs shall be borne by the other party if this appears justified by the conduct of that party.

Where the parties have come to an agreement on costs, the decision as to costs shall be in accordance with that agreement.

If costs are not applied for, the parties shall bear their own costs.

§ 6

Where a case does not proceed to judgment, the costs shall be in the discretion of the Court of First Instance.

Article 88

Without prejudice to the second subparagraph of Article 87 (3), in proceedings between the Communities and their servants the institutions shall bear their own costs.

Article 89

Costs necessarily incurred by a party in enforcing a judgment or order of the Court of First Instance shall be refunded by the opposite party on the scale in force in the State where the enforcement takes place.

Article 90

Proceedings before the Court of First Instance shall be free of charge, except that:

(a) where a party has caused the Court of First Instance to incur avoidable costs, the Court of First Instance may order that party to refund them;

(b) where copying or translation work is carried out at the request of a party, the cost shall, in so far as the Registrar considers it excessive, be paid for by that party on the scale of charges referred to in Article 24 (5).

Article 91

Without prejudice to the preceding Article, the following shall be regarded as recoverable costs:

(a) sums payable to witnesses and experts under Article 74;

(b) expenses necessarily incurred by the parties for the purpose of the proceedings, in particular the travel and subsistence expenses and the remuneration of agents, advisers or lawyers.

Article 92

§ 1

If there is a dispute concerning the costs to be recovered, the Court of First Instance hearing the case shall, on application by the party concerned and after hearing the opposite party, make an order, from which no appeal shall lie.

§ 2

The parties may, for the purposes of enforcement, apply for an authenticated copy of the order.

Article 93

§ 1

Sums due from the cashier of the Court of First Instance shall be paid in the currency of the country where the Court of First Instance has its seat.

At the request of the person entitled to any sum, it shall be paid in the currency of the country where the expenses to be refunded were incurred or where the steps in respect of which the payment is due were taken.

§ 2

Other debtors shall make payment in the currency of their country of origin.

§ 3

Conversions of currency shall be made at the official rates of exchange ruling on the day of payment in the country where the Court of First Instance has its seat.

Chapter 7

LEGAL AID

Article 94

§ 1

A party who is wholly or in part unable to meet the costs of the proceedings may at any time apply for legal aid.

The application shall be accompanied by evidence of the applicant's need of assistance, and in particular by a document from the competent authority certifying his lack of means.

§ 2

If the application is made prior to proceedings which the applicant wishes to commence, it shall briefly state the subject of such proceedings.

The application need not be made through a lawyer.

The President shall, after considering the written observations of the opposite party, decide whether legal aid should be granted in full or in part, or whether it should be refused. He shall consider whether there is manifestly no cause of action. He may refer the matter to the Court of First Instance.

The decision shall be taken by way of an order without giving reasons, and no appeal shall lie therefrom.

Article 95

§ 1

The Court of First Instance, by any order by which it decides that a person is entitled to receive legal aid, shall order that a lawyer be appointed to act for him.

§ 2

If the person does not indicate his choice of lawyer, or if the Court of First Instance considers that his choice is unacceptable, the Registrar shall send a copy of the order and of the application for legal aid to the authority named in Annex II to the Rules supplementing the Rules of Procedure of the Court of Justice, being the competent authority of the State concerned.

§ 3

The Court of First Instance, in the light of the suggestions made by that authority, shall of its own motion appoint a lawyer to act for the person concerned.

§ 4

An order granting legal aid may specify an amount to be paid to the lawyer appointed to act for the person concerned or fix a limit which the lawyer's disbursements and fees may not, in principle, exceed.

Article 96

The Court of First Instance may at any time, either of its own motion or on application, withdraw legal aid if the circumstances which led to its being granted alter during the proceedings.

Article 97

§ 1

Where legal aid is granted, the cashier of the Court of First Instance shall advance the funds necessary to meet the expenses.

§ 2

The President, who may refer the matter to the Court of First Instance, shall adjudicate on the lawyer's disbursements and fees; he may, on application by the lawyer, order that he receive an advance.

§ 3

In its decision as to costs the Court of First Instance may order the payment to the cashier of the Court of First Instance of the whole or any part of amounts advanced as legal aid.

The Registrar shall take steps to obtain the recovery of these sums from the party ordered to pay them.

Chapter 8

DISCONTINUANCE

Article 98

If, before the Court of First Instance has given its decision, the parties reach a settlement of their dispute and intimate to the Court of First Instance the abandonment of their claims, the President shall order the case to be removed from the register and shall give a decision as to costs in accordance with Article 87 (5) having regard to any proposals made by the parties on the matter.

This provision shall not apply to proceedings under Articles 173 and 175 of the EC Treaty, Articles 33 and 35 of the ECSC Treaty and Articles 146 and 148 of the Euratom Treaty.

Article 99

If the applicant informs the Court of First Instance in writing that he wishes to discontinue the proceedings, the President shall order the case to be removed from the register and shall give a decision as to costs in accordance with Article 87 (5).

Chapter 9

SERVICE

Article 100

Where these Rules require that a document be served on a person, the Registrar shall ensure that service is effected at that person's address for service either by the dispatch of a copy of the document by registered post with a form for acknowledgement of receipt or by personal delivery of the copy against a receipt.

The Registrar shall prepare and certify the copies of documents to be served, save where the parties themselves supply the copies in accordance with Article 43 (1).

Chapter 10

TIME-LIMITS

Article 101

§ 1

Any period of time prescribed by the EC, ECSC and Euratom Treaties, the Statutes of the Court of Justice or these Rules for the taking of any procedural step shall be reckoned as follows:

(a) Where a period expressed in days, weeks, months or years is to be calculated from the moment at which an event occurs or an action takes place, the day during which that event occurs or that action takes place shall not be counted as falling within the period in question;

(b) A period expressed in weeks, months or in years shall end with the expiry of whichever day in the last week, month or year is the same day of the week, or falls on the same date, as the day during which the event or action from which the period is to be calculated occurred or took place. If, in a period expressed in months or in years, the day on which it should expire does not occur in the last month, the period shall end with the expiry of the last day of that month;

(c) Where a period is expressed in months and days, it shall first be reckoned in whole months, then in days;

(d) Periods shall include official holidays, Sundays and Saturdays;

(e) Periods shall not be suspended during the judicial vacations.

§ 2

If the period would otherwise end on a Saturday, Sunday or official holiday, it shall be extended until the end of the first following working day.

The list of official holidays drawn up by the Court of Justice and published in the *Official Journal of the European Communities* shall apply to the Court of First Instance.

Article 102

§ 1

Where the period of time allowed for commencing proceedings against a measure adopted by an institution runs from the publication of that measure, that period shall be calculated, for the purposes of Article 101(1), from the end of the 14th day after publication thereof in the *Official Journal of the European Communities.*

§ 2

The extensions, on account of distance, of prescribed time-limits provided for in a decision of the Court of Justice and published in the *Official Journal of the European Communities* shall apply to the Court of First Instance.

Article 103

§ 1

Any time-limit prescribed pursuant to these Rules may be extended by whoever prescribed it.

§ 2

The President may delegate power of signature to the Registrar for the purpose of fixing time-limits which, pursuant to these Rules, it falls to the President to prescribe, or of extending such time-limits.

TITLE 3

Special Forms of Procedure

Chapter 1

SUSPENSION OF OPERATION OR ENFORCEMENT AND OTHER INTERIM MEASURES

Article 104

§ 1

An application to suspend the operation of any measure adopted by an institution, made pursuant to Article 185 of the EC Treaty, the second paragraph of Article 39 of the ECSC Treaty and Article 157 of the Euratom Treaty shall be admissible only if the applicant is challenging that measure in proceedings before the Court of First Instance.

An application for the adoption of any other interim measure referred to in Article 186 of the EC Treaty, the third paragraph of Article 39 of the ECSC Treaty and Article 158 of the Euratom Treaty shall be admissible only if it is made by a party to a case before the Court of First Instance and relates to that case.

§ 2

An application of a kind referred to in paragraph (1) of this Article shall state the subject-matter of the proceedings, the circumstances giving rise to urgency and the pleas of fact and law establishing a *prima facie* case for the interim measures applied for.

§ 3

The application shall be made by a separate document and in accordance with the provisions of Articles 43 and 44.

Article 105

§ 1

The application shall be served on the opposite party, and the President of the Court of First Instance shall prescribe a short period within which that party may submit written or oral observations.

§ 2

The President of the Court of First Instance may order a preparatory inquiry.

The President of the Court of First Instance may grant the application even before the observations of the opposite party have been submitted. This decision may be varied or cancelled even without any application being made by any party.

Article 106

The President of the Court of First Instance shall either decide on the application himself or refer it to the Chamber to which the case has been assigned in the main proceedings or to the Court of First Instance sitting in plenary session if the case has been assigned to it.

If the President of the Court of First Instance is absent or prevented from attending, he shall be replaced by the President or the most senior Judge, within the meaning of Article 6, of the bench of the Court of First Instance to which the case has been assigned.

Where the application is referred to a bench of the Court of First Instance, that bench shall postpone all other cases and shall give a decision. Article 105 shall apply.

Article 107

§ 1

The decision on the application shall take the form of a reasoned order. The order shall be served on the parties forthwith.

§ 2

The enforcement of the order may be made conditional on the lodging by the applicant of security, of an amount and nature to be fixed in the light of the circumstances.

§ 3

Unless the order fixes the date on which the interim measure is to lapse, the measure shall lapse when final judgment is delivered.

§ 4

The order shall have only an interim effect, and shall be without prejudice to the decision on the substance of the case by the Court of First Instance.

Article 108

On application by a party, the order may at any time be varied or cancelled on account of a change in circumstances.

Article 109

Rejection of an application for an interim measure shall not bar the party who made it from making a further application on the basis of new facts.

Article 110

The provisions of this Chapter shall apply to applications to suspend the enforcement of a decision of the Court of First Instance or of any measure adopted by another institution, submitted pursuant to Articles 187 and 192 of the EC Treaty, Articles 44 and 92 of the ECSC Treaty and Articles 159 and 164 of the Euratom Treaty.

The order granting the application shall fix, where appropriate, a date on which the interim measure is to lapse.

Chapter 2

PRELIMINARY ISSUES

Article 111

Where it is clear that the Court of First Instance has no jurisdiction to take cognizance of an action or where the action is manifestly inadmissible or manifestly lacking any foundation in law, the Court of First Instance may, by reasoned order, after hearing the Advocate-General and without taking further steps in the proceedings, give a decision on the action.

Article 112

The decision to refer an action to the Court of Justice, pursuant to the second paragraph of Article 47 of the EC Statute, the second paragraph of Article 47 of the ECSC Statute and the second paragraph of Article 48 of the Euratom Statute, shall, in the case of manifest lack of competence, be made by reasoned order and without taking any further steps in the proceedings.

Article 113

The Court of First Instance may at any time, of its own motion, consider whether there exists any absolute bar to proceeding with an action or declare, after hearing the parties, that the action has become devoid of purpose and that there is no need to adjudicate on it; it shall give its decision in accordance with Article 114 (3) and (4).

Article 114

§ 1

A party applying to the Court of First Instance for a decision on admissibility, on lack of competence or other preliminary plea not going to the substance of the case shall make the application by a separate document.

The application must contain the pleas of fact and law relied on and the form of order sought by the applicant; any supporting documents must be annexed to it.

§ 2

As soon as the application has been lodged, the President shall prescribe a period within which the opposite party may lodge a document containing a statement of the form of order sought by that party and its pleas in law.

§ 3

Unless the Court of First Instance otherwise decides, the remainder of the proceedings shall be oral.

§ 4

The Court of First Instance shall, after hearing the Advocate-General, decide on the application or reserve its decision for the final judgment. It shall refer the case to the Court of Justice if the case falls within the jurisdiction of that Court.

If the Court of First Instance refuses the application or reserves its decision, the President shall prescribe new time-limits for further steps in the proceedings.

Chapter 3

INTERVENTION

Article 115

§ 1

An application to intervene must be made within three months of the publication of the notice referred to in Article 24 (6).

§ 2

The application shall contain:

(a) the description of the case;

(b) the description of the parties;

(c) the name and address of the intervener;

(d) the intervener's address for service at the place where the Court of First Instance has its seat;

(e) the form of order sought, by one or more of the parties, in support of which the intervener is applying for leave to intervene;

(f) a statement of the circumstances establishing the right to intervene, where the application is submitted pursuant to the second or third paragraph of Article 37 of the EC Statute, Article 34 of the ECSC Statute or the second paragraph of Article 38 of the Euratom Statute.

Articles 43 and 44 shall apply.

§ 3

The intervener shall be represented in accordance with Article 17 of the EC Statute, the first and second paragraphs of Article 20 of the ECSC Statute and Article 17 of the Euratom Statute.

Article 116

§ 1

The application shall be served on the parties.

The President shall give the parties an opportunity to submit their written or oral observations before deciding on the application.

The President shall decide on the application by order or shall refer the decision to the Court of First Instance. The order must be reasoned if the application is dismissed.

§ 2

If the President allows the intervention, the intervener shall receive a copy of every document served on the parties. The President may, however, on application by one of the parties, omit secret or confidential documents.

§ 3

The intervener must accept the case as he finds it at the time of his intervention.

§ 4

The President shall prescribe a period within which the intervener may submit a statement in intervention.

The statement in intervention shall contain:

(a) a statement of the form of order sought by the intervener in support of or opposing, in whole or in part, the form of order sought by one of the parties;

(b) the pleas in law and arguments relied on by the intervener;

(c) where appropriate, the nature of any evidence offered.

§ 5

After the statement in intervention has been lodged, the President shall, where necessary, prescribe a time-limit within which the parties may reply to that statement.

Chapter 4

JUDGMENTS OF THE COURT OF FIRST INSTANCE DELIVERED AFTER ITS DECISION HAS BEEN SET ASIDE AND THE CASE REFERRED BACK TO IT

Article 117

Where the Court of Justice sets aside a judgment or an order of the Court of First Instance and refers the case back to that Court, the latter shall be seised of the case by the judgment so referring it.

Article 118

§ 1

Where the Court of Justice sets aside a judgment or an order of a Chamber, the President of the Court of First Instance may assign the case to another Chamber composed of the same number of Judges.

§ 2

Where the Court of Justice sets aside a judgment delivered or an order made by the Court of First Instance sitting in plenary session, the case shall be assigned to that Court as so constituted.

§ 3

In the cases provided for in paragraphs (1) and (2) of this Article, Articles 13 (2), 14 and 51 shall apply.

Article 119

§ 1

Where the written procedure before the Court of First Instance has been completed when the judgment referring the case back to it is delivered, the course of the procedure shall be as follows:

(a) Within two months from the service upon him of the judgment of the Court of Justice the applicant may lodge a statement of written observations.

(b) In the month following the communication to him of that statement, the defendant may lodge a statement of written observations. The time allowed to the defendant for lodging it may in no case be less than two months from the service upon him of the judgment of the Court of Justice.

(c) In the month following the simultaneous communication to the intervener of the observations of the applicant and the defendant, the intervener may lodge a statement of written observations. The time allowed to the intervener for lodging it may in no case be less than two months from the service upon him of the judgment of the Court of Justice.

§ 2

Where the written procedure before the Court of First Instance had not been completed when the judgment referring the case back to the Court of First Instance was delivered, it shall be resumed, at the stage which it had reached, by means of measures of organization of procedure adopted by the Court of First Instance.

§ 3

The Court of First Instance may, if the circumstances so justify, allow supplementary statements of written observations to be lodged.

Article 120

The procedure shall be conducted in accordance with the provisions of Title II of these Rules.

Article 121

The Court of First Instance shall decide on the costs relating to the proceedings instituted before it and to the proceedings on the appeal before the Court of Justice.

Chapter 5

JUDGMENTS BY DEFAULT AND APPLICATIONS TO SET THEM ASIDE

Article 122

§ 1

If a defendant on whom an application initiating proceedings has been duly served fails to lodge a defence to the application in the proper form within the time prescribed, the applicant may apply to the Court of First Instance for judgment by default.

The application shall be served on the defendant. The Court of First Instance may decide to open the oral procedure on the application.

§ 2

Before giving judgment by default the Court of First Instance shall consider whether the application initiating proceedings is admissible, whether the appropriate formalities have been complied with, and whether the application appears well founded. It may order a preparatory inquiry.

§ 3

A judgment by default shall be enforceable. The Court of First Instance may, however, grant a stay of execution until it has given its decision on any application under paragraph (4) of this Article to set aside the judgment, or it may make execution subject to the provision of security of an amount and nature to be fixed in the light of the circumstances; this security shall be released if no such application is made or if the application fails.

§ 4

Application may be made to set aside a judgment by default.

The application to set aside the judgment must be made within one month from the date of service of the judgment and must be lodged in the form prescribed by Articles 43 and 44.

§ 5

After the application has been served, the President shall prescribe a period within which the other party may submit his written observations.

The proceedings shall be conducted in accordance with the provisions of Title II of these Rules.

§ 6

The Court of First Instance shall decide by way of a judgment which may not be set aside. The original of this judgment shall be annexed to the original of the judgment by default. A note of the judgment on the application to set aside shall be made in the margin of the original of the judgment by default.

Chapter 6

EXCEPTIONAL REVIEW PROCEDURES

Section 1—Third-party proceedings

Article 123

§ 1

Articles 43 and 44 shall apply to an application initiating third-party proceedings. In addition such an application shall:

(a) specify the judgment contested;

(b) state how that judgment is prejudicial to the rights of the third party;

(c) indicate the reasons for which the third party was unable to take part in the original case before the Court of First Instance.

The application must be made against all the parties to the original case.

Where the judgment has been published in the *Official Journal of the European Communities*, the application must be lodged within two months of the publication.

§ 2

The Court of First Instance may, on application by the third party, order a stay of execution of the judgment. The provisions of Title III, Chapter 1, shall apply.

§ 3

The contested judgment shall be varied on the points on which the submissions of the third party are upheld.

The original of the judgment in the third-party proceedings shall be annexed to the original of the contested judgment. A note of the judgment in the third-party proceedings shall be made in the margin of the original of the contested judgment.

§ 4

Where an appeal before the Court of Justice and an application initiating third-party proceedings before the Court of First Instance contest the same judgment of the Court of First Instance, the Court of First Instance may, after hearing the parties, stay the proceedings until the Court of Justice has delivered its judgment.

Article 124

The application initiating third-party proceedings shall be assigned to the Chamber which delivered the judgment which is the subject of the application; if the Court of First Instance sitting in plenary session delivered the judgment, the application shall be assigned to it.

Section 2—Revision

Article 125

Without prejudice to the period of ten years prescribed in the third paragraph of Article 41 of the EC Statute, the third paragraph of Article 38 of the ECSC Statute and the third paragraph of Article 42 of the Euratom Statute, an application for revision of a judgment shall be made within three months of the date on which the facts on which the application is based came to the applicant's knowledge.

Article 126

§ 1

Articles 43 and 44 shall apply to an application for revision. In addition such an application shall:

(a) specify the judgment contested;

(b) indicate the points on which the application is based;

(c) set out the facts on which the application is based;

(d) indicate the nature of the evidence to show that there are facts justifying revision of the judgment, and that the time-limits laid down in Article 125 have been observed.

§ 2

The application must be made against all parties to the case in which the contested judgment was given.

Article 127

§ 1

The application for revision shall be assigned to the Chamber which delivered the judgment which is the subject of the application; if the Court of First Instance sitting in plenary session delivered the judgment, the application shall be assigned to it.

§ 2

Without prejudice to its decision on the substance, the Court of First Instance shall, after hearing the Advocate-General, having regard to the written observations of the parties, give its decision on the admissibility of the application.

§ 3

If the Court of First Instance finds the application admissible, it shall proceed to consider the substance of the application and shall give its decision in the form of a judgment in accordance with these Rules.

§ 4

The original of the revising judgment shall be annexed to the original of the judgment revised. A note of the revising judgment shall be made in the margin of the original of the judgment revised.

Article 128

Where an appeal before the Court of Justice and an application for revision before the Court of First Instance concern the same judgment of the Court of First Instance, the Court of First Instance may, after hearing the parties, stay the proceedings until the Court of Justice has delivered its judgment.

Section 3—Interpretation of judgments

Article 129

§ 1

An application for interpretation of a judgment shall be made in accordance with Articles 43 and 44. In addition it shall specify:

(a) the judgment in question;

(b) the passages of which interpretation is sought.

The application must be made against all the parties to the case in which the judgment was given.

§ 2

The application for interpretation shall be assigned to the Chamber which delivered the judgment which is the subject of the application; if the Court of First Instance sitting in plenary session delivered the judgment, the application shall be assigned to it.

§ 3

The Court of First Instance shall give its decision in the form of a judgment after having given the parties an opportunity to submit their observations and after hearing the Advocate-General.

The original of the interpreting judgment shall be annexed to the original of the judgment interpreted. A note of the interpreting judgment shall be made in the margin of the original of the judgment interpreted.

§ 4

Where an appeal before the Court of Justice and an application for interpretation before the Court of First Instance concern the same judgment of the Court of First Instance, the Court of First Instance may, after hearing the parties, stay the proceedings until the Court of Justice has delivered its judgment.

TITLE 4

Proceedings relating to Intellectual Property Rights

Article 130

§ 1

Subject to the special provisions of this Title, the provisions of these Rules of Procedure shall apply to proceedings brought against the Office for Harmonization in the Internal Market (Trade Marks and Designs) and against the Community Plant Variety Office (both hereinafter referred to as 'the Office'), and concerning the application of the rules relating to an intellectual property regime.

§ 2

The provisions of this Title shall not apply to actions brought directly against the Office without prior proceedings before a Board of Appeal.

Article 131

§ 1

The application shall be drafted in one of the languages described in Article 35 (1), according to the applicant's choice.

§ 2

The language in which the application is drafted shall become the language of the case if the applicant was the only party to the proceedings before the Board of Appeal or if another party to those proceedings does not object to this within a period laid down for that purpose by the Registrar after the application has been lodged.

If, within that period, the parties to the proceedings before the Board of Appeal inform the Registrar of their agreement on the choice, as the language of the case, of one of the languages referred to in Article 35 (1), that language shall become the language of the case before the Court of First Instance.

In the event of an objection to the choice of the language of the case made by the applicant within the period referred to above and in the absence of an agreement on the matter between the parties to the proceedings before the Board of Appeal, the language in which the application for registration in question was filed at the Office shall become the language of the case. If, however, on a reasoned request by any party and after hearing the other parties, the President finds that the use of that language would not enable all parties to the proceedings before the Board of Appeal to follow the proceedings and defend their interests and that only the use of another language from among those mentioned in Article 35 (1) makes it possible to remedy that situation, he may designate that other language as the language of the case; the President may refer the matter to the Court of First Instance.

§ 3

In the pleadings and other documents addressed to the Court of First Instance and during the oral procedure, the applicant may use the language chosen by him in accordance with paragraph 1 and each of the other parties may use a language chosen by that party from those mentioned in Article 35 (1).

§ 4

If, by virtue of paragraph 2, a language other than that in which the application is drafted becomes the language of the case, the Registrar shall cause the application to be translated into the language of the case.

Each party shall be required, within a reasonable period to be prescribed for that purpose by the Registrar, to produce a translation into the language of the case of the pleadings or documents other than the application that are lodged by that party in a language other than the language of the case pursuant to paragraph 3. The party producing the translation, which shall be authentic within the meaning of Article 37, shall certify its accuracy. If the translation is not produced within the period prescribed, the pleading or the procedural document in question shall be removed from the file.

The Registrar shall cause everything said during the oral procedure to be translated into the language of the case and, at the request of any party, into the language used by that party in accordance with paragraph 3.

Article 132

§ 1

Without prejudice to Article 44, the application shall contain the names of all the parties to the proceedings before the Board of Appeal and the addresses which they had given for the purposes of the notifications to be effected in the course of those proceedings.

The contested decision of the Board of Appeal shall be appended to the application. The date on which the applicant was notified of that decision must be indicated.

§ 2

If the application does not comply with paragraph 1, Article 44 (6) shall apply.

Article 133

§ 1

The Registrar shall inform the Office and all the parties to the proceedings before the Board of Appeal of the lodging of the application. He shall arrange for service of the application after determining the language of the case in accordance with Article 131 (2).

§ 2

The application shall be served on the Office, as defendant, and on the parties to the proceedings before the Board of Appeal other than the applicant. Service shall be effected in the language of the case.

Service of the application on a party to the proceedings before the Board of Appeal shall be effected by registered post with a form of acknowledgment of receipt at the address given by the party concerned for the purposes of the notifications to be effected in the course of the proceedings before the Board of Appeal.

§ 3

Once the application has been served, the Office shall forward to the Court of First Instance the file relating to the proceedings before the Board of Appeal.

Article 134

§ 1

The parties to the proceedings before the Board of Appeal other than the applicant may participate, as interveners, in the proceedings before the Court of First Instance.

§ 2

The interveners referred to in paragraph 1 shall have the same procedural rights as the main parties.

They may support the form of order sought by a main party and they may apply for a form of order and put forward pleas in law independently of those applied for and put forward by the main parties.

§ 3

An intervener, as referred to in paragraph 1, may, in his response lodged in accordance with Article 135 (1), seek an order annulling or altering the decision of the Board of Appeal on a point not raised in the application and put forward pleas in law not raised in the application.

Such submissions seeking orders or putting forward pleas in law in the intervener's response shall cease to have effect should the applicant discontinue the proceedings.

§ 4

In derogation from Article 122, the default procedure shall not apply where an intervener, as referred to in paragraph 1 of this Article, has responded to the application in the manner and within the period prescribed.

Article 135

§ 1

The Office and the interveners referred to in Article 134 (1) may submit responses to the application within a period of two months from the service of the application.

Article 46 shall apply to the responses.

§ 2

The application and the responses may be supplemented by replies and rejoinders by the parties, including the interveners referred to in Article 134 (1), where the President, on a reasoned application made within two weeks of service of the responses or replies, considers such further pleading necessary and allows it in order to enable the party concerned to put forward its point of view.

The President shall prescribe the period within which such pleadings are to be submitted.

§ 3

Without prejudice to the foregoing, in the cases referred to in Article 134 (3), the other parties may, within a period of two months of service upon them of the response, submit a pleading confined to responding to the form of order sought and the pleas in law submitted for the first time in the response of an intervener. That period may be extended by the President on a reasoned application from the party concerned.

§ 4

The parties' pleadings may not change the subject-matter of the proceedings before the Board of Appeal.

Article 136

§ 1

Where an action against a decision of a Board of Appeal is successful, the Court of First Instance may order the Office to bear only its own costs.

§ 2

Costs necessarily incurred by the parties for the purposes of the proceedings before the Board of Appeal and costs incurred for the purposes of the production, prescribed by the second subparagraph of Article 131 (4), of translations of pleadings or other documents into the language of the case shall be regarded as recoverable costs.

In the event of inaccurate translations being produced, the second subparagraph of Article 87 (3) shall apply.

Miscellaneous Provisions

Article 137

These Rules, which are authentic in the languages mentioned in Article 35 (1), shall be published in the *Official Journal of the European Communities*. They shall enter into force on the first day of the second month from the date of their publication.

Done at Luxembourg on 2 May 1991.

H. JUNG

Registrar

JL CRUZ VILAÇA

President

Notes for the Guidance of Counsel[1] in Written and Oral Proceedings before the Court of Justice of the European Communities[2]

Introduction

Two factors distinguish proceedings before the Court of Justice from those before certain national supreme courts. Firstly, proceedings before the Court of Justice are governed by strict rules of law contained in the Treaties, the Protocols on the Statute of the Court and its Rules of Procedure. The Court is thus not in a position to make exceptions to them. Secondly, proceedings before the Court are subject to rules on the use of languages appropriate to a multilingual Community, a fact which influences the nature and purpose of both the written and the oral procedure (see A.3 and C.4 below).

Accordingly, this guide is designed to explain to Counsel the purpose of proceedings before the Court, in order to enhance the quality of judicial protection within the Community legal order and ensure the rapid and effective conduct of cases.

This guide should therefore be seen as a working tool intended to enable Counsel to present their written and oral pleadings in the form which the Court of Justice considers most fitting. At the same time, attention will be drawn to the Court's procedural practice. However, this guide is intended neither to lay down legal rules in itself nor to override the relevant provisions in force.

In these notes, references to 'the Statute' and 'the RP' are respectively references to the Statute of the Court of Justice of the EEC and of the Rules of Procedure of the Court. The version of the Rules of Procedure at present in force was adopted on 19 June 1991 (OJ 1991 L176 p 1). A publication entitled *Selected Instruments relating to the organization, jurisdiction and procedure of the Court* can be purchased from the Office of Official Publications of the European Communities, L-2985, Luxembourg.

---

[1] The word 'Counsel' is used in a non-technical sense so as to include all those appearing before the Court and acting as advocate, whatever their capacity or professional status.

[2] Postal address: Court of Justice of the European Communities, L2925, Luxembourg. Telephone (switchboard) 43031. Fax: Switchboard—4303 2600; Registry—433766; Interpreters—4303 3697; Press Office—4303 2500.

APPENDIX E

CONTENTS

APPENDIX E

A. GENERAL POINTS

1. The various stages of proceedings before the Court of Justice

Proceedings before the Court comprise a written phase followed by an oral phase (see the first paragraph of Article 18 of the Statute).

The oral procedure includes the presentation of oral argument at the hearing and the Advocate-General's Opinion, which is delivered in open court. The only part of the oral procedure that is compulsory in all cases is the Advocate-General's Opinion (see C.7 below).

The active participation of Counsel for parties to the proceedings concludes with the hearing at which oral argument is presented.

2. Representation of the parties

a. The rule

The requirement that parties be represented is laid down in Article 17 of the Statute. Apart from Member States and Community institutions, which are represented by their Agents, parties must be represented in all proceedings except applications for legal aid (see A.4.b below), and, in certain circumstances, preliminary-ruling proceedings (see b below), by a lawyer registered as having a right of audience before the courts of one of the Member States.

University professors who are nationals of Member States whose law allows them to plead before courts are treated as Counsel by virtue of the fifth paragraph of Article 17 of the Statute.

Pursuant to Article 38(3) of the RP, Counsel are required, when lodging an application, to attach a certificate as to their right of audience before the courts of one of the Member States. A copy of the Lawyer's Professional Identity Card (issued by the CCBE) is accepted for this purpose.

b. Representation in preliminary-ruling proceedings

The requirement of representation differs slightly in preliminary-ruling proceedings (Article 104(2) of the RP). Any person empowered to represent or assist a party in the proceedings before the national court may also do so before the Court of Justice. Consequently, if the rules of procedure applicable to proceedings before the national court do not require parties to be represented, the parties to those proceedings are entitled to submit their own written and oral observations.

3. Use of languages

A clear distinction must be drawn between the language of the case, which is governed by Article 29 et seq of the RP, and the working language used within the Court.

All the official languages of the Member States of the EC can be the language of the case. However, each case has its 'own' language. Only one language may therefore be chosen as the language of the case. An exception is made to this rule where cases are joined and the language of the case is different for each: in such circumstances all the languages involved may be used.

The provisions of Article 29 of the RP concerning that choice are very detailed but can be summarised in three sentences.

— In direct actions the applicant has the right to choose the language of the case unless the defendant is a Member State or a natural or legal person who is a national of a Member State; in such cases, the language of the case is the official language (or one of the official languages where there are more than one) of that State.

— In preliminary rulings, the language of the case is always that of the national court making the reference.
— The Member States may use their own language where they intervene in a direct action or take part in preliminary-ruling proceedings.

The Judges and Advocates-General are not required to use the language of the case. They are therefore at liberty to ask questions at the hearing in any of the official languages of the Communities even if it is not the language of the case.

The working language of the Court is the language used by the Members of the Court and its staff for day-to-day internal communication and work produced jointly. At present, the working language is French. Consequently, pleadings submitted in a language other than French are translated into French for the Court's internal purposes.

4. Costs and legal aid

a. Costs

Proceedings before the Court are free, in that no charge or fee of any kind is payable to the Court.

The costs referred to in Article 63 et seq of the RP are only those costs which are described as 'recoverable', namely lawyers' fees, payments to witnesses, post and telephone costs, and so forth, incurred by the parties themselves.

The rule concerning the award of costs is simple: the unsuccessful party is ordered to pay the costs and thus bears its own costs and those of the other parties, except Member States and institutions, which, when intervening, bear their own costs. For costs to be awarded on that basis, a request to that effect must be included as one of the orders sought ('conclusions')—if no such request is made the parties bear their own costs.

However, the Court may, according to the circumstances of the case, either order that the parties bear their own costs wholly or in part or even award costs against the successful party.

Special conditions apply to proceedings brought by officials (see Article 70 of the RP).

The Court gives a decision on costs in the judgment or order which brings the proceedings to an end.

With regard to costs incurred in preliminary-ruling cases, the Court's decision incorporates a standard form of words referring to the final decision to be taken by the national court which made the reference to the Court of Justice. Institutions and Member States which submit observations bear their own costs.

b. Legal aid

Article 76 of the RP provides for legal aid. The Court has a limited budget for that purpose.

Any party may at any time apply for legal aid if he is 'wholly or in part unable to meet the costs of the proceedings'. The right to make such an application is not conditional upon the nature of the action or procedure. Thus, legal aid may also be applied for in a preliminary-ruling case. However, in such a case, the party concerned must first seek legal aid from the competent authorities in his own country. In order to establish his lack of means, the person concerned must provide the Court with all relevant information, in particular a certificate from the competent authority to that effect.

Where legal aid is applied for before the commencement of proceedings, the party must give a brief description of the subject-matter of the application in order to enable the Court to consider whether the application is not manifestly unfounded.

The obligation to be represented by Counsel does not apply to applications for legal aid.

An order granting or withholding legal aid does not state the reasons on which it is based and is not subject to appeal.

It must be emphasised that the grant of legal aid does not mean that the recipient of it cannot, if appropriate, be ordered to pay the costs. Moreover, the Court may take action to recover sums disbursed by way of legal aid.

B. THE WRITTEN PROCEDURE

1. The purpose of the written procedure

Regardless of the nature of the proceedings concerned (direct action, reference for a preliminary ruling, appeal), the purpose of the written procedure is always the same, namely to put before the Court, the Judges and the Advocate-General an exhaustive account of the facts, pleas and arguments of the parties and the forms of order sought.

In that connection, it is important to note that the entire procedure before the Court, in particular the written phase, is governed by the principle whereby new pleas may not be raised in the course of the proceedings, with the sole exception of those based on matters of law and fact which come to light in the course of the procedure.

The procedure before the Court does not therefore have the same flexibility as that allowed by certain national rules of procedure.

2. The conduct of the written procedure

The course of the written procedure differs according to the nature of the proceedings.

a. Direct actions

In direct actions, each litigant may submit two sets of pleadings: the application and the reply in the case of the applicant, and the defence and rejoinder in the case of the defendant.

b. Appeals

In an appeal against a decision of the Court of First Instance, the parties may, in principle, submit only one set of pleadings, the application or response, depending on their respective roles. The possibility of a reply or rejoinder is subject to express authorisation from the President of the Court of Justice (see B.8.c below).

c. Preliminary-ruling proceedings

In preliminary-ruling proceedings the persons referred to in Article 20 of the Statute may, *within a mandatory period of two months after notification of the order for reference*, submit their written observations (see B.9 below).

3. The lodgement of pleadings

All pleadings must be sent to the Registry of the Court in order to be registered in accordance with Article 37 of the RP. The original must be signed by Counsel for the party concerned. Copies must be certified by the party lodging them.

All documents relied on must be annexed to the relevant pleading, which must be accompanied by a schedule listing them.

In direct actions, the original pleading and all the annexes to it must be lodged together with five copies for the Court and, for the purposes of notification (see B.4 below), a copy for every other party to the proceedings.

Any pleading may be delivered by hand to the Court Registry or, outside the working hours of the Registry, to the security officer on duty at the main entrance to the Court building (Boulevard Konrad Adenauer, Plateau du Kirchberg). The Court building is open 24 hours a day.

If pleadings are sent by post, the envelope must bear the following address *and nothing else*:

Court of Justice of the European Communities
—Registry—
L-2925 Luxembourg

4. Notification

a. The addressees

In direct actions, the following, *inter alia*, are notified to the parties concerned: applications, appeals, defences, replies, rejoinders, applications for interim measures and applications for leave to intervene.

References for a preliminary ruling from national courts, and the observations of those entitled to submit them under Article 20 of the Statute, are notified to the parties to the proceedings, the Member States, the Commission and, if appropriate, the Council.

In all cases, the Report for the Hearing (or the Report of the Judge-Rapporteur), the Opinion of the Advocate-General and the Judgment are notified to those taking part in the proceedings before the Court.

b. Address for service

In the case of direct actions, Article 38(2) of the RP provides that parties are to give an address for service in Luxembourg; the address given may be that of any natural person residing in Luxembourg, with the exception of officials of the Court of Justice. In such cases, due notification is deemed to take place upon receipt of the document in question by the person whose address has been given as the address for service.

However, the giving of an address for service is optional. If no address for service is given, pleadings are sent by registered post to Counsel for the party concerned.

In the case of preliminary-ruling proceedings, as there is no obligation to give an address for service, service is effected by registered post with a form of acknowledge-ment of receipt.

5. Procedural time-limits

Procedural time-limits are calculated in accordance with Article 80 et seq of the RP. It must be emphasised that certain of those time-limits cannot be extended—such as, for example, the time-limits provided for in Articles 173 and 175 of the EC Treaty [new arts 230 and 232] and Article 20 of the Statute.

a. Calculation of time-limits

Where documents are sent by registered post, the rule is that *time starts to run from the date on which they are handed to the postal authorities*. However, for the lodgment of observations in preliminary-ruling proceedings, as provided for in Article 20 of the Statute, time does not start running until the copy of the order for reference is received. The date of receipt is evidenced by the record of acknowledgment of receipt returned to the Court Registry by the postal authorities.

b. Extension of time-limits on account of distance

Time-limits are extended on account of distance by the periods laid down by the Court in the decision set out in Annex II to the RP. The additional time is calculated by reference to the place of establishment or habitual residence of the person concerned.

In letters accompanying pleadings notified or served by it, the Registry indicates the latest date on which the pleading in response to it may be lodged, either in general terms or by specifying the exact date.

c. Extension of time-limits for other reasons

Certain time-limits laid down by the Rules of Procedure may be extended under Article 82 thereof, such as the period within which a defence must be lodged. An application for any such extension must be made in every case by the party concerned. *The application must be made before the prescribed period has expired and reasons for the application must be given.* For that purpose, it is helpful if the consent of the opposite party is lodged at the same time as the application for extension.

6. Originating applications

a. The application in direct actions

The originating application must be submitted in accordance with Articles 37 and 38 of the RP. It is important to note that Article 38(1) of the RP is strictly applied (see Article 38(7) of the RP). Failure to observe mandatory conditions may, in certain cases, render the application formally inadmissible.

In principle, the language of the case is chosen by the applicant (Article 29 of the RP).

b. Applications initiating appeal proceedings

The conditions applicable to applications initiating appeal proceedings are laid down in Article 112 of the RP. Article 112(1) of the RP is strictly applied (see Article 112(2) of the RP).

The language of the case is that of the decision of the Court of First Instance against which the appeal is brought (see Article 110 of the RP).

c. The purpose common to all originating applications

Originating applications must place before the Court all matters of fact and law which justify the commencement of proceedings. At the same time, the application defines the scope of the proceedings—in principle, it is not permitted to raise new issues or add to the forms of order sought in the course of the proceedings (see also B.13.a above).

d. Summary of pleas and arguments

It is desirable for all pleadings to be accompanied by a summary, comprising no more than two pages, of the pleas and arguments put forward. The summary ensures that the pleas and arguments relied upon are clearly identified for the purpose, in particular, of preparation of the Report for the Hearing by the Judge-Rapporteur.

7. References for preliminary rulings

In preliminary rulings, proceedings before the Court are set in motion by the national court's decision to stay the proceedings before it and submit questions on Community law. The litigants before the national court are not entitled to make a reference to the Court of Justice on their own initiative, nor are they under any obligation to take any action before they are served with a copy of the order for reference by the Registry of the Court of Justice (see B.2.c and B.4 above).

The order for reference, the form of which is governed by the rules of the national jurisdiction, is forwarded to the Court of Justice either by the registry of the national court or by the Judge himself. It may be sent by ordinary post.

If Counsel propose the text of the order for reference, it is important that they give a clear account of the factual and legislative background so that the meaning of the questions is clear.

8. The other documents submitted in direct actions and appeals

a. The defence

The substantive conditions governing the defence are set out in Article 40 of the RP. In view of the prohibition of putting forward new pleas in law, which applies to all stages of the proceedings, the defendant must set out all matters of law and of fact available to him when drafting the defence.

b. The reply and the rejoinder

The reply is intended merely to *respond* to the pleas and arguments raised in the defence. All unnecessary repetition must be avoided.

Similarly, the sole purpose of the rejoinder is to *respond* to the pleas and arguments put forward in the reply.

Both replies and rejoinders are subject to the requirements of Article 42 of the RP and may not, in principle, put forward new pleas in law.

The lodgement of a reply or rejoinder is purely optional. With a view to expediting the written procedure, the parties are requested seriously to consider the possibility of waiving the right to lodge them.

An extension of the time allowed for lodging replies and rejoinders is granted only in exceptional circumstances.

c. The response, reply and rejoinder in appeal proceedings

The response to an appeal must fulfil the requirements of Article 115 of the RP. A reply and rejoinder may be lodged only with the express prior consent of the President following an application from the person concerned. That application must without fail be lodged within a period of seven days as from notification of the response or reply. With a view to completion of the written procedure within the shortest possible time, parties are requested as far as possible to refrain from making such applications.

d. Summaries of pleas in law and arguments

It is desirable for the defence and other pleadings to be accompanied, in the same way as originating applications, by a summary, not exceeding two pages in length, of the pleas in law and arguments put forward.

9. Written observations in preliminary-ruling proceedings

After receiving a copy from the Court Registry of the request for a preliminary ruling, the 'interested parties'—the litigants before the national court, the Member States, the Commission and, if appropriate, the Council—may submit a document, referred to as written observations, *within a period of two months (which may be extended, if appropriate, on account of distance in accordance with the decision set out in Annex II of the RP). This time-limit is mandatory and cannot therefore be extended.*

The purpose of the written observations is to suggest the answers which the Court should give to the questions referred to it, and to set out succinctly, but completely, the reasoning on which those answers are based. It is important to bring to the attention of the Court all the factual circumstances of the case before the national court and the relevant provisions of the national legislation at issue.

It must be emphasised that none of the parties is entitled to reply in writing to the written observations submitted by the others. Any response to the written observations of other parties must be made orally at the hearing. For that purpose, the written observations are notified to all the parties once the written procedure is completed and the necessary translations have been made.

The submission of written observations is strongly recommended since the time allowed for oral argument at the hearing is strictly limited. However, any party who has not submitted written observations retains the right to present oral argument, in particular his responses to the written arguments, at the hearing, if a hearing is held.

10. Stay of proceedings

Pursuant to Article 82a of the RP, the proceedings may be stayed:

— in the circumstances specified in Article 47 of the Statute where the Court of Justice and the Court of First Instance are called on to adjudicate at the same time on the same subject-matter; the decision to stay the proceedings is a matter for the Court of Justice and the parties will not necessarily be given an opportunity to express their views;

— in all other cases, the decision is a matter for the President. The decision is taken after the views of the Advocate-General have been heard and, save in the case of references for a preliminary ruling, those of the parties.

Whilst the proceedings are suspended, no period prescribed for any procedural steps by the parties will expire.

11. Applications for interim measures

Applications for interim measures can be entertained only if they are made by a party to proceedings pending before the Court of Justice and relate to those proceedings. Notwithstanding that connection with the main proceedings, *the application for interim measures must always be made in a separate document* and must meet the conditions laid down by Article 83 of the RP. It may be presented at the same time as the originating application.

In view of the fact that applications for interim measures are made as a matter of urgency and of the need for rapid translation, applicants are requested to set out succinctly in their applications the pleas in fact and law on which their application is based. The application for interim measures should itself provide all the details needed to enable the President or the Court, as the case may be, to decide whether there are good grounds for the requested measures to be granted.

Once the application for interim measures has been served on him, the other party is traditionally allowed to submit written observations within a brief period, approximately one month.

It is only after those observations have been lodged that the President, with the Judge-Rapporteur and Advocate-General in attendance, hears the parties concerned (in public) and makes an order.

In cases of extreme urgency, the President may make an order immediately, that is to say within three or four days after the application for interim measures is made and without awaiting written observations from the other party. In such cases, the order is provisional, in that it does not bring the procedure on the interlocutory application to an end. The other party is then invited to submit written observations. The final stage, after the hearing, is a (second) order concluding the interlocutory proceedings which confirms or amends the first (provisional) order.

12. Intervention

Intervention is allowed only in direct actions and appeals. The forms of order sought in the application to intervene must be limited to supporting the submissions of one or other of the parties. It must be borne in mind that the intervener is required to accept the case as it stands at the time of intervention.

The intervention procedure is twofold, comprising: (a) the action taken in order to obtain leave to intervene and (b) the actual participation of the intervener in the proceedings.

a. Action taken to obtain leave to intervene

A person wishing to intervene in a direct action must submit an application to intervene. That document must contain all the information needed to enable the President or, in certain cases, the Court to make an order granting leave to intervene. Before the Court or the President makes an order, the original litigants are invited to submit written observations, and in exceptional cases even oral observations, as to whether or not intervention is admissible and appropriate. At the same time, they are asked to inform the Court whether they intend availing themselves of the right of confidentiality. If leave to intervene is granted, the intervener is invited to lodge non-confidential versions of its observations.

The application to intervene need not be in the language of the case.

b. The intervener's participation in the proceedings

Once leave to intervene has been granted, the intervener submits a statement in intervention. At that stage, the language of the case must be used, unless the intervener is a Member State.

The statement in intervention may be followed by a statement in reply.

13. Practical advice

a. The drafting and scheme of pleadings

There are no formal requirements applicable to pleadings (subject to compliance with rules laid down elsewhere); but they must be clear, concise and complete.

In view of the translation workload, in particular, and the time involved in translation, repetition must be avoided. The Court should be able, on a single reading, to apprehend the essential matters of fact and law.

Since in most cases pleadings will be read by the Judges and the Advocate-General in a language other than that in which they are drafted, Counsel must always bear in mind that, if the meaning of a text is obscure in the original language, there is a risk that the translation will deepen the obscurity. That risk is aggravated by the fact that it is not always possible, in the transition from one language to another, to find a satisfactory, or even accurate, translation of the 'legal jargon' which may be used before national courts.

Counsel should also remember the strict rule concerning the introduction of fresh pleas in law (see B.1, B.6.c and B.8.a above); they are not entitled to 'reserve', even conditionally, pleas or arguments for subsequent pleadings or the hearing.

Ideally, the structure of pleadings should be clear and logical and they should be divided into separate parts with titles and paragraph numbers. In addition to a summary of the pleas in law and arguments, a table of contents may be useful in complex cases.

The pattern of originating applications may be outlined as follows:

— details of the type of dispute involved, and of the kind of decision sought: action for annulment, application for interim measures, and so on;
— a brief account of the relevant facts;
— all the pleas in law on which the application is based;
— the arguments in support of each plea in law. They must include relevant references to the case-law of the Court;
— the forms of order sought, based on the pleas in law and arguments.

In appeals, the forms of order sought are limited by Article 113 of the RP.

It is desirable for the defence and similar documents to follow closely the structure of the reasoning set out in the pleadings to which they constitute a response.

Written observations in preliminary rulings must set out:

— the relevant facts and the relevant provisions of national law;

— legal argument, including references to the case-law of the Court;
— proposals for answers to be given by the Court to the questions submitted by the national court.

However, if the party concerned accepts the facts of the case as set out in the order for reference, he need merely say so.

b. Documents annexed to pleadings

It must be borne in mind that, pursuant to Article 37 of the RP, documents relied on by the parties must be annexed to pleadings. Unless there are exceptional circumstances and the parties consent, the Court will not take account of documents submitted outside the prescribed time-limits or produced at the hearing.

Only relevant documents, on which the parties base their arguments, must be annexed to pleadings. Where documents are of some length, it is not only permissible, but indeed desirable, for the relevant extracts only to be annexed to the pleading and for a copy of the complete document to be lodged at the Registry.

Since annexes are not translated by the Court unless a Member of the Court so requests, the relevance of every document must be clearly indicated in the body of the pleading to which it is annexed.

The Court does not accept notes on which oral argument is to be based for inclusion in the file on the case. The parties are not allowed access to the recording of the oral argument, this being available only for the Court's internal requirements. (See C.4 below regarding the forwarding to the Interpretation Division of notes on which oral submissions are to be based.)

However, Counsel may in all cases send unofficial translations of pleadings and annexes, although, by virtue of Article 31 of the RP, such translations are not authentic.

c. Facts and evidence

The initial pleadings must indicate all evidence in support of each of the points of fact at issue. However, new evidence may be put forward subsequently (in contrast to the rule excluding new pleas in law), provided that adequate reasons are given to justify the delay.

The various forms of evidence upon which parties may rely are set out in Article 45(2) of the RP.

d. Citations

Counsel are requested, when citing a judgment of the Court, to give full details, including the names of the parties or, at least, the name of the applicant. In addition, when citing a passage from a judgment of the Court or from an Opinion of an Advocate-General, they are requested to specify the page number and the number of the paragraph in which the passage in question is to be found.

To facilitate its work, the Court suggests as an appropriate form of citation that used in the judgments of the Court, for example: 'judgment in Case 152/85 *Misset* [1987] ECR 223, paragraph . . .'.

C. ORAL PROCEDURE

1. Preparation for the main hearing

Once the written procedure is completed and the necessary translations have been made, the Judge-Rapporteur places the preliminary report before the administrative meeting, in which all the Members of the Court take part. At that meeting, the Judge-Rapporteur, in consultation with the Advocate-General, proposes any procedural or preparatory measures to be taken by the Court.

In most cases, the Court, at the suggestion of the Judge-Rapporteur, decides to open the oral procedure without any preparatory inquiries. The exact date is fixed by the President.

a. Preparatory measures

At the same time, the Court decides on any preparatory measures to be taken, on a proposal from the Judge-Rapporteur in consultation with the Advocate-General. Accordingly, in some cases the parties may be asked, before the hearing, either to provide better particulars of the forms of order sought by them and of their pleas in law in order to clarify obscure points, or to examine in greater detail issues which have not been adequately canvassed, or to concentrate their pleadings on the decisive issues or to commence their oral submissions by answering certain questions put to them by the Court. The parties' replies to those questions should be given either in writing before the hearing within a period laid down for that purpose, or in writing on the date of the hearing or orally during the hearing. Exceptionally, preparatory measures may be decided upon at a later stage by the Judge-Rapporteur and the Advocate-General in consultation with the presiding Judge, but within a reasonable period, before Counsel have prepared their oral submissions.

A situation sometimes arises where the Court considers it appropriate to request coordination of oral submissions by several Counsel who are putting forward essentially the same views or of those of the Counsel called on to put forward the same views several times at the same hearing (for example in a direct action and related preliminary-ruling proceedings).

Counsel are requested in all cases to take the initiative themselves to coordinate their oral submissions with a view to limiting the duration of the oral procedure.

b. The Report for the Hearing and the Report of the Judge-Rapporteur

About three weeks before the hearing, the Report for the Hearing is sent to Counsel for the parties to the proceedings, each Member State and Community institution that has submitted observations and the other participants in the proceedings. The Report for the Hearing, drawn up by the Judge-Rapporteur, summarizes the facts and the pleas and arguments in direct actions and the facts and the observations lodged in preliminary-ruling proceedings.

Where there is to be no oral procedure (see C.7 below), the Report for the Hearing becomes the Report of the Judge-Rapporteur. Apart from the name, there is no difference between a Report for the Hearing and a Report of the Judge-Rapporteur.

After receiving the Report for the Hearing or, in certain cases, the Report of the Judge-Rapporteur, the parties are invited to satisfy themselves that the basic arguments have been correctly summarised and that the report faithfully reflects the views of the parties as expressed in the pleadings. If the report does not faithfully reflect the essential reasoning of the parties, Counsel are requested to inform the Registrar—before the hearing in the case of a Report for the Hearing—and to suggest such drafting amendments as they consider appropriate. It must, however, be emphasized that the Report for the Hearing is, by its very nature, a report presented by the Judge-Rapporteur to the other Members of the Court and that it is for him to decide whether it need be amended.

2. The purpose of the oral procedure

In all cases (both direct actions and preliminary rulings), the purpose of the oral procedure is:

— to answer the questions put by the Court;

— to recall, if necessary, by way of a highly condensed summary, the positions taken by the parties, with emphasis on the essential submissions in support of which written argument has been presented;
— to submit any new arguments prompted by recent events occurring after the close of the written procedure which, for that reason, could not be set out in the pleadings;
— to explain and expound the more complex points and those which are more difficult to grasp, and to highlight the most important points.

In preliminary rulings, the oral procedure enables lawyers to reply briefly to the main arguments set out in other written observations.

The oral procedure must, however, be seen as *supplementing the written procedure* and should involve no repetition of what has already been stated in writing.

3. Conduct of the oral procedure

Before the sitting commences, the Court invites Counsel to a brief private meeting in order to settle arrangements for the hearing. In some cases, at this early stage, the Judge-Rapporteur or the Advocate-General, or both, may indicate the matters which they would like to be developed in the oral observations.

As a rule, the hearing starts with oral argument from Counsel for the parties. This is followed by questions put to Counsel by the Members of the Court. The hearing concludes with brief replies from those Counsel who wish to make them.

The Members of the Court frequently interrupt Counsel when they are speaking in order to clarify points which appear to them to be of particular relevance.

4. The constraints of simultaneous interpretation

The Members of the Court do not necessarily follow the oral submissions in the language in which they are made but often listen to the simultaneous interpretation. This imposes certain constraints to which Counsel should, in their own interests, be attentive in order to ensure that what they say is perfectly understood by the Members of the Court. Counsel must therefore regard the interpreters as essential partners in presentation of their argument.

In the first place, it is highly inadvisable to read a text prepared in advance. The reason for this is that an address prepared in writing is made up of longer and more complicated sentences and is delivered at greater speed than one which is largely extemporaneous. It is preferable to speak on the basis of well-structured notes, using simple terms and short sentences.

In cases where Counsel prefers to follow a text, the same advice applies: simple terms and short sentences should be used and the text should be read at normal talking speed.

For the same reasons, it is desirable for Counsel to give details of the proposed structure of their submissions before dealing with any matter in detail.

Before attending the hearing, the interpreters carefully study the entire file on the case. If, as soon as possible, Counsel forward all relevant information concerning the probable content of their oral submissions (possibly the notes on which they are to be based), the interpreters will be able to complete their preparatory work, give a better rendering of the oral submissions and ensure that they are not disconcerted by technical terms, citations of texts or figures.

It is preferable to send such information by fax (Luxembourg (352) 4303-3697). Needless to say, the confidentiality of texts will be preserved. To obviate any misunderstanding, the name of the party must be indicated in the text.

Finally, it should be borne in mind that Counsel will not be heard unless they speak directly into the microphone.

5. Time allowed for addressing the Court

As a general rule, the period initially allowed to each main party is limited to *a maximum of 30 minutes* before the Court sitting in plenary session and Chambers composed of five Judges and *a maximum of 15 minutes* before Chambers composed of three Judges. The time allowed to interveners is limited to *a maximum of 15 minutes*. (This limitation applies only to oral argument properly so called and does not include the time taken to reply to questions put by Members of the Court.)

Exceptions to this rule may be allowed by the Court in order to put the parties on an equal footing. For that purpose, an application must be sent to the Registrar of the Court, giving a detailed explanation and indicating the time considered necessary. In order to be taken into account, *such applications must reach the Court at least 15 days before the date of the hearing*. The decision on the application will be notified to the applicant at least one week before the hearing.

Any party who indicates that a shorter period will be sufficient must keep to the period allowed.

Where a party is represented by more than one Counsel, no more than two of them may present oral argument and their combined speaking time must not exceed the time-limits indicated above. The answers to the questions put by Members of the Court and replies to the observations of other Counsel may however be given by Counsel other than those who addressed the Court.

Where several parties defend the same point of view before the Court (a situation which arises particularly where there are interventions or cases are joined), their Counsel are invited to confer with each other before the hearing so as to avoid any repetition.

The President of the Court or Chamber hearing the case will seek to ensure observance of the principles set out above, as regards both the purpose of the oral procedure, that is to say the actual content of the oral submissions, and the time allowed for addressing the Court.

6. The need for oral submissions

It is for each Counsel to judge, in the light of the purpose of the oral procedure, as defined above, whether oral argument is really necessary or whether a simple reference to the written observations or pleadings would suffice. The Court would like to stress that if a party refrains from presenting oral argument, this will never be construed as constituting acquiescence in the oral argument presented by another party.

In that connection, it goes without saying that the Court takes account of the procedural constraints inherent in preliminary-ruling cases, in which only the oral procedure gives the parties an opportunity to respond to the written observations of another 'interested party' and, if necessary, to take a position regarding new developments.

7. Omission of the hearing

Article 44a of the RP (in the case of direct actions), Article 104(4) of the RP (for preliminary rulings) and Article 120 of the RP (for appeals) allow the oral procedure to be dispensed with.

The Court's practice regarding consultation of the parties for that purpose is at present that, in all cases, the litigants (in direct actions and appeals) or all the participants in the proceedings (in preliminary rulings) are automatically asked by the Registry to state their views as to the need for a hearing.

8. The hearing of applications for interim measures

As a general rule, before an order granting interim measures is made, the views of the parties concerned are heard by the President, the Judge-Rapporteur and the Advocate-

General. The hearing is public and takes place about two to four weeks before the President, or, where appropriate, the Court, makes an order on the application. Such hearings are much less formal than the main hearing. In practice, the President starts by summarizing, orally, the difficulties involved in the case. He then invites the parties to express their views on those difficulties. The hearing ends with questions put to the parties.

Where the matter is referred to the full Court, a more formal hearing of the traditional type is held.

It must be borne in mind that such hearings are not intended to enable the parties to address the merits of the case.

9. Practical advice

a. Postponement of hearings

The Court grants requests for postponement only for compelling reasons.

b. Entrance to the building

As a security measure, access to the Court building is controlled. Counsel are therefore requested kindly to produce their professional card, identity card, passport or some other means of identification.

c. Dress

Lawyers are required to appear before the Court in their robes. The Court always has a number of plain robes to help out those who have forgotten their own. This rule regarding dress does not apply to hearings of applications for interim measures: at such hearings neither the Members of the Court nor the lawyers wear robes.

Index to Appendix E

(The figures refer to pages)

Court of First Instance: Advice for Lawyers and Agents Regarding the Written Procedure

I. THE PURPOSE OF THE WRITTEN PROCEDURE

The purpose of the written procedure before the Court of First Instance is to define the subject-matter of the action and to put before the Court all the claims of the parties by informing it of the relevant facts, forms of order sought, and the pleas and arguments of the parties so as to enable the Court to give judgment in the action.

II. THE PRESENTATION AND DRAFTING OF PLEADINGS

1. Pleadings should have a clear structure: each section should have a title and paragraphs should be numbered consecutively. In the case of lengthy pleadings, it is desirable to introduce each section with a brief summary of its contents and to include a table of contents in the pleading.

2. Since the number of pleadings which each party may submit to the Court is limited (see Article 47 of the Rules of Procedure of the Court of First Instance) and new pleas may not be raised in the course of the proceedings except in certain limited circumstances (see Article 48 of the Rules of Procedure), it is advisable that a party should set out its entire case as fully as possible in its first pleading (the application or the defence).

3. In view of the fact that the Judges will often study a set of pleadings by reading translations of them into another language, it is advisable to draft pleadings in a simple, straightforward and concise style which facilitates translation and to limit the number of pages to what is strictly necessary.

4. When pleadings are drafted documents to which reference is made in them should be clearly identified and care should also be taken to ensure that all important documents are submitted. Documents should be identified by indicating, each time reference is made to them, the pleading to which the documents concerned is annexed, with an indication of the annex number as it appears in the schedule of annexes attached to that pleading. It is desirable for each document to be identified in the same way throughout both the written and oral proceedings. Attaching to a pleading documents already submitted to the Court as annexes to another pleading needlessly increases the volume of written evidence to be considered by the Court and may cause confusion.

5. When addressing the arguments of another party it is advisable to refer to the relevant pages of the other party's pleading.

III. THE STRUCTURE OF PLEADINGS

1. Originating applications must comply with Article 44 of the Rules of Procedure. Ideally, they should be structured as follows:

(1) Indication of the parties
    See Article 44(1)(*a*) and (*b*) and (2) of the Rules of Procedure.
(2) Details of the type of dispute involved
    For example: 'Application under Article 173 of the EC Treaty [new art 230] for the annulment of a decision of [the institution concerned] . . .'
(3) A summary of the relevant facts
    Supported by references to the documents and offers of evidence
(4) Any considerations relating to the admissibility of the action
(5) A brief statement of all the pleas in law on which the action is based
(6) A summary of the arguments put forward in support of each plea in law
    Including, where appropriate, references to the relevant case-law of the Court of Justice and of the Court of First Instance
(7) Form of order sought
    Parties must set out the precise terms of the operative part of the order or judgment which they seek (for example: '(1) Annul the defendant's decision of . . . ; (2) Order the defendant to pay the costs'). When drawing up the form of order sought, those acting for applicants should bear in mind what is laid down in Article 176 of the EC Treaty [new art 233] in the form of order sought pleas and arguments set out earlier in the application (for example, the following types of formulation should be avoided: '. . . declare that the action is admissible and well-founded; declare that the contested decision does not state the reasons on which it is based and is contrary to the provisions of the Treaty and the principle of proportionality . . . '). Reference should also be made to Article 87 of the Rules of Procedure as regards any order sought in the matter of costs.

2. In order to facilitate the drafting of the *Official Journal* notice provided for by Article 24(6) of the Rules of Procedure and to ensure that the subject-matter of the case and the pleas in law and main arguments contained in the application are clearly identified, it is advisable to annex to the application a brief outline of the pleas in law and main arguments together with a table of contents.

IV. PRODUCTION OF ANNEXES

1. Pleadings and procedural documents may be accompanied by documents annexed to them in order to substantiate or illustrate their contents. However, mere reference to an annex will be no substitute for including a summary of the facts, pleas and arguments in the body of the pleading or procedural document. Only annexes mentioned in the pleadings will be admissible.

2. A schedule of annexes must be submitted, as prescribed by Article 43(4) of the Rules of Procedure and Article 6(4) of the Instructions to the Registrar. Ideally, this schedule should set out the annex numbers, the date and nature of the documents annexed and the pages of the pleading on which reasons for the production of the respective annexes are given. In some cases, subnumbers will facilitate the identification of documents.

3. Lawyers and agents should ensure that the pleadings and evidence submitted are not made unnecessarily lengthy by the production of an excessive number of annexes and that the really important passages or information contained in annexes are still reproduced in the body of the pleadings.

Court of First Instance: Notes for the Guidance of Counsel at the Hearing of Oral Argument

These notes are intended to explain to Counsel appearing before the Court of First Instance the purpose of the oral procedure before it and the manner in which it is organised. The underlying concern is to reconcile in the best way possible the aim of maintaining the quality of judicial protection in the Community legal order and the need for proceedings to be conducted expeditiously and efficiently.

I. THE PURPOSE OF THE ORAL PROCEDURE

When the stage of the oral procedure is reached, the bench hearing the case and the Member of the Court performing the function of Advocate-General, if one has been designated, will already have a good knowledge of the case and will have carefully studied the formal claims, pleas and arguments of the parties. There is therefore little point in repeating orally everything that has been set out in writing or even in commenting on the pleadings or written observations.

The purpose of the oral procedure is:

— where necessary, to reiterate in condensed form the position taken by the parties, emphasising the key submissions advanced in writing;
— to clarify, if necessary, certain arguments advanced during the written procedure and to submit any new arguments based on recent events which arose after the close of the written procedure and which could not therefore be set out in the pleadings;
— to reply to any questions put by the Court.

II. THE HEARING OF ORAL ARGUMENT

1. Usefulness of oral submission

It is for Counsel for each party to judge, in the light of the purpose of the oral procedure as defined above, whether there is any real point in presenting oral submissions or whether it would be sufficient simply to refer to the pleadings or written observations. The oral procedure can then concentrate on the replies to questions put by the Court. If Counsel does consider it necessary to address the Court, he may always confine himself to making specific points and referring to the pleadings in relation to other points.

The Court would emphasise that if a party decides not to present oral argument this will never be construed as acquiescence in another party's oral argument if the argument in point has already been rebutted in writing, nor will such silence prevent that party from replying to an oral submission put forward by the other party.

In some cases, the Court may consider it preferable to start the oral procedure with questions put by its Members to Counsel for the parties. In that case, Counsel are requested to take this into account if they then wish to make a brief address.

2. Presentation and structure of oral submissions

In the interests of clarity and in order to enable the Members of the Court to understand oral submissions better, it is generally preferable for Counsel to speak freely on the basis of notes rather than to read out a written text. The reading of a written text makes simultaneous interpretation of oral submissions more difficult.

Counsel for the parties are also requested to simplify their presentation of the case as far as possible: a series of short sentences will always be preferable to a long, complicated sentence. It would also assist the Court if Counsel could structure their oral argument and indicate, before developing it, the structural plan they intend to adopt.

3. The constraints of simultaneous interpretation

Counsel are reminded that, depending on the case being heard, only some of the Members of the bench will be following the oral arguments in the language in which it is being presented: the other Members will be listening to the simultaneous interpretation. Although the interpreters are highly qualified, their task is a difficult one and in the interests of the better conduct of the proceedings Counsel are strongly advised to speak slowly and directly into the microphone.

If Counsel intend to cite verbatim passages from certain texts or documents, particularly passages not appearing in the documents before the Court, it would be helpful if they would indicate the passages concerned to the interpreters before the hearing. Similarly, it may be helpful to draw the interpreters' attention to any terms which may be difficult to translate.

As the courtrooms are equipped with an automatic sound amplification system, Counsel must press the button on the microphone in order to switch it on and wait for the light to come on before starting to speak. The button should not be pressed whilst a Member of the Court or another person is speaking so as not to cut off their microphone.

4. Duration of oral submissions

The Court is well aware that the time taken in presenting oral submissions may vary, depending on the complexity of the case and on whether or not new facts have arisen. However, having regard to the purpose of the oral procedure, there is generally little to be gained in allowing proceedings to exceed a certain length of time.

Counsel are therefore requested to limit their oral submission to 15 minutes or thereabouts for each party unless the Registry has indicated otherwise. This limitation applies, of course, only to the presentation of oral argument itself and not to time spent in answering questions put at the hearing.

If circumstances so require, a request for leave to exceed the speaking time normally allowed, giving reasons and indicating the speaking time considered necessary, may be made to the Registry at least 15 days before the date fixed for the hearing. When such requests are made, Counsel for the parties will be informed of the time which they will each have for presenting their oral submissions.

Where a party is represented by more than one Counsel, no more than two of them may normally present argument and their combined speaking time must not exceed the time-limits indicated above. However, Counsel other than those who addressed the Court may reply to questions from Members of the Court and give replies to the observations of other Counsel.

Where two or more parties are advancing the same argument before the Court (a situation which may occur where, in particular, there are interventions or where cases have been joined), their Counsel are requested to confer with each other before the hearing so as to avoid any repetition.

III. MISCELLANEOUS

1. Report for the Hearing

The Report for the Hearing is drawn up by the Judge-Rapporteur and provides an objective summary of the case. It does not set out every single detail of the parties' arguments but is meant to enable the parties to check that their pleas and arguments have been properly understood and to facilitate study of the trial documents by the other Members of the bench hearing the case.

The Court will make every effort to ensure that Counsel for the parties receive the Report for the Hearing at least three weeks before the date of the hearing. As far as the Court is concerned, the sole purpose of this document is to prepare the hearing for the oral procedure; the Court will not refer to it in its judgment and it will not form part of its judgment.

If the Report for the Hearing contains factual errors, Counsel are requested to notify them to the Registry in writing before the hearing. Similarly, if it does not correctly convey the essence of a party's argument, Counsel for that party may propose the amendments he considers appropriate.

If at the hearing Counsel submit oral observations on the Report for the Hearing, they should subsequently resubmit those observations in writing to the Registry.

2. Citing judgments

When citing a judgment of the Court of Justice or of the Court of First Instance, Counsel are requested to give all the references, including the names of the parties, and to state the number of the page of the ECR on which the passage in question appears.

3. Documents

Article 43 of the Rules of Procedure of the Court of First Instance provides that documents relied on by the parties must be annexed to a pleading. Save in exceptional circumstances and with the consent of the parties, the Court of First Instance will not accept documents produced after the procedural time-limits have expired, including documents submitted at the hearing.

Since all oral argument is recorded, the Court does not allow notes of oral argument to be lodged.

Appendix H

Court of Justice of the European Communities: Note for Guidance on References by National Courts for Preliminary Rulings

The development of the Community legal order is largely the result of cooperation between the Court of Justice of the European Communities and national courts and tribunals through the preliminary ruling procedure under Article 177 of the EC Treaty [new art 234] and the corresponding provisions of the ECSC and Euratom Treaties.[1]

In order to make this cooperation more effective, and so enable the Court of Justice better to meet the requirements of national courts by providing helpful answers to preliminary questions, this Note for Guidance is addressed to all interested parties, in particular to all national courts and tribunals.

It must be emphasised that the Note is for guidance only and has no binding or interpretative effect in relation to the provisions governing the preliminary ruling procedure. It merely contains practical information which, in the light of experience in applying the preliminary ruling procedure, may help to prevent the kind of difficulties which the Court has sometimes encountered.

1. Any court or tribunal of a Member State may ask the Court of Justice to interpret a rule of Community law, whether contained in the Treaties or in acts of secondary law, if it considers that this is necessary for it to give judgment in a case pending before it.

Courts or tribunals against whose decisions there is no judicial remedy under national law must refer questions of interpretation arising before them to the Court of Justice, unless the Court has already ruled on the point or unless the correct application of the rule of Community law is obvious.[2]

2. The Court of Justice has jurisdiction to rule on the validity of acts of the Community institutions. National courts or tribunals may reject a plea challenging the validity of such an act. But where a national court (even one whose decision is still subject to appeal) intends to question the validity of a Community act, it must refer that question to the Court of Justice.[3]

Where, however, a national court or tribunal has serious doubts about the validity of a Community act on which a national measure is based, it may, in exceptional cases, temporarily suspend application of the latter measure or grant other interim relief with

---

[1] A preliminary ruling procedure is also provided for by protocols to several conventions concluded by the Member States, in particular the Brussels Convention on Jurisdiction and the Enforcement of Judgments in Civil and Commercial Matters.

[2] Judgment in Case 283/81 *CILFIT v Ministry of Health* [1982] ECR 3415.

[3] Judgment in Case 314/85 *Foto-Frost v Hauptzollamt Lübeck-Ost* [1987] ECR 4199.

respect to it. It must then refer the question of validity to the Court of Justice, stating the reasons for which it considers that the Community act is not valid.[4]

3. Questions referred for a preliminary ruling must be limited to the interpretation or validity of a provision of Community law, since the Court of Justice does not have jurisdiction to interpret national law or assess its validity. It is for the referring court or tribunal to apply the relevant rule of Community law in the specific case pending before it.

4. The order of the national court or tribunal referring a question to the Court of Justice for a preliminary ruling may be in any form allowed by national procedural law. Reference of a question or questions to the Court of Justice generally involves stay of the national proceedings until the Court has given its ruling, but the decision to stay proceedings is one which it is for the national court alone to take in accordance with its own national law.

5. The order for reference containing the question or questions referred to the Court will have to be translated by the Court's translators into the other official languages of the Community. Questions concerning the interpretation or validity of Community law are frequently of general interest and the Member States and Community institutions are entitled to submit observations. It is therefore desirable that the reference should be drafted as clearly and precisely as possible.

6. The order for reference should contain a statement of reasons which is succinct but sufficiently complete to give the Court, and those to whom it must be notified (the Member States, the Commission and in certain cases the Council and the European Parliament), a clear understanding of the factual and legal context of the main proceedings.[5]

In particular, it should include a statement of the facts which are essential to a full understanding of the legal significance of the main proceedings, an exposition of the national law which may be applicable, a statement of the reasons which have prompted the national court to refer the question or questions to the Court of Justice and, where appropriate, a summary of the arguments of the parties. The aim should be to put the Court of Justice in a position to give the national court an answer which will be of assistance to it.

The order for reference should also be accompanied by copies of any documents needed for a proper understanding of the case, especially the text of the applicable national provisions. However, as the case-file or documents annexed to the order for reference are not always translated in full into the other official languages of the Community, the national court should ensure that the order for reference itself includes all the relevant information.

7. A national court or tribunal may refer a question to the Court of Justice as soon as it finds that a ruling on the point or points of interpretation or validity is necessary to enable it to give judgment. It must be stressed, however, that it is not for the Court of Justice to decide issues of fact or to resolve disputes as to the interpretation or application of rules of national law. It is therefore desirable that a decision to refer should not be taken until the national proceedings have reached a stage where the national court is able to define, if only as a working hypothesis, the factual and legal context of the question; on any view, the administration of justice is likely to be best served if the reference is not made until both sides have been heard.[6]

---

[4] Judgments in Joined Cases C-143/88 and C-92/89 *Zuckerfabrik* [1991] ECR I-415 and in Case C-465/93 *Atlanta Fruchthandelsgesellschaft* [1995] ECR I-3761.

[5] Judgment in Joined Cases C-320/90, C-321/90 and C-322/90 *Telemarsicabruzzo* [1993] ECR I-393.

[6] Judgment in Case 70/77 *Simmenthal v Amministrazione delle Finanze* [1978] ECR 1453.

8. The order for reference and the relevant documents should be sent by the national court directly to the Court of Justice, by registered post (addressed to the Registry of the Court of Justice of the European Communities, L-2925 Luxembourg, telephone (352) 43031). The Court Registry will remain in contact with the national court until judgment is given, and will send copies of the various documents (written observations, Report for the Hearing, Opinion of the Advocate-General). The Court will also send its judgment to the national court. The Court would appreciate being informed about the application of its judgment in the national proceedings and being sent a copy of the national court's final decision.

9. Proceedings for a preliminary ruling before the Court of Justice are free of charge. The Court does not rule on costs.

Appendix I

New Treaty Numbering: Table of Equivalences

TREATY ON EUROPEAN UNION

Previous numbering	*New numbering*
Title I	**Title I**
Article A	Article 1
Article B	Article 2
Article C	Article 3
Article D	Article 4
Article E	Article 5
Article F	Article 6
Article F.1 (*)	Article 7
Title II	**Title II**
Article G	Article 8
Title III	**Title III**
Article H	Article 9
Title IV	**Title IV**
Article I	Article 10
Title V (***)	**Title V**
Article J.1	Article 11
Article J.2	Article 12
Article J.3	Article 13
Article J.4	Article 14
Article J.5	Article 15
Article J.6	Article 16
Article J.7	Article 17
Article J.8	Article 18

(*)   New Article introduced by the Treaty of Amsterdam.
(**)   New Title introduced by the Treaty of Amsterdam.
(***) Title restructured by the Treaty of Amsterdam.

Previous numbering	*New numbering*
Article J.12	Article 22
Article J.13	Article 23
Article J.14	Article 24
Article J.15	Article 25
Article J.16	Article 26
Article J.17	Article 27
Article J.18	Article 28
Title VI (***)	**Title VI**
Article K.1	Article 29
Article K.2	Article 30
Article K.3	Article 31
Article K.4	Article 32
Article K.5	Article 33
Article K.6	Article 34
Article K.7	Article 35
Article K.8	Article 36
Article K.9	Article 37
Article K.10	Article 38
Article K.11	Article 39
Article K.12	Article 40
Article K.13	Article 41
Article K.14	Article 42
Title VIa (**)	**Title VII**
Article K.15 (*)	Article 43
Article K.16 (*)	Article 44
Article K.17(*)	Article 45
Title VII	**Title VIII**
Article L	Article 46
Article M	Article 47
Article N	Article 48
Article O	Article 49
Article P	Article 50
Article Q	Article 51
Article R	Article 52
Article S	Article 53

TREATY ESTABLISHING THE EUROPEAN COMMUNITY

Previous numbering	*New numbering*
PART ONE	**PART ONE**
Article 1	Article 1
Article 2	Article 2
Article 3	Article 3
Article 3a	Article 4
Article 3b	Article 5
Article 3c (*)	Article 6
Article 4	Article 7
Article 4a	Article 8
Article 4b	Article 9
Article 5	Article 10
Article 5a (*)	Article 11
Article 6	Article 12
Article 6a (*)	Article 13
Article 7 (repealed)	—
Article 7a	Article 14
Article 7b (repealed)	—
Article 7c	Article 15
Article 7d (*)	Article 16
PART TWO	**PART TWO**
Article 8	Article 17
Article 8a	Article 18
Article 8b	Article 19
Article 8c	Article 20
Article 8d	Article 21
Article 8e	Article 22
PART THREE	**PART THREE**
Title I	**Title I**
Article 9	Article 23
Article 10	Article 24
Article 11 (repealed)	—
Chapter 1	*Chapter 1*
Section 1 (deleted)	—
Article 12	Article 25
Article 13 (repealed)	—
Article 14 (repealed)	—
Article 15 (repealed)	—

(*)   New Article introduced by the Treaty of Amsterdam.
(**)   New Title introduced by the Treaty of Amsterdam.
(***)   Chapter 1 restructured by the Treaty of Amsterdam.

Previous numbering	*New numbering*
Article 16 (repealed)	—
Article 17 (repealed)	—
Section 2 (deleted)	—
Article 18 (repealed)	—
Article 19 (repealed)	—
Article 20 (repealed)	—
Article 21 (repealed)	—
Article 22 (repealed)	—
Article 23 (repealed)	—
Article 24 (repealed)	—
Article 25 (repealed)	—
Article 26 (repealed)	—
Article 27 (repealed)	—
Article 28	Article 26
Article 29	Article 27
Chapter 2	*Chapter 2*
Article 30	Article 28
Article 31 (repealed)	—
Article 32 (repealed)	—
Article 33 (repealed)	—
Article 34	Article 29
Article 35 (repealed)	—
Article 36	Article 30
Article 37	Article 31
Title II	**Title II**
Article 38	Article 32
Article 39	Article 33
Article 40	Article 34
Article 41	Article 35
Article 42	Article 36
Article 43	Article 37
Article 44 (repealed)	—
Article 45 (repealed)	—
Article 46	Article 38
Article 47 (repealed)	—
Title III	**Title III**
Chapter 1	*Chapter 1*
Article 48	Article 39
Article 49	Article 40
Article 50	Article 41
Article 51	Article 42
Chapter 2	*Chapter 2*
Article 52	Article 43
Article 53 (repealed)	—

Previous numbering	*New numbering*
Article 54	Article 44
Article 55	Article 45
Article 56	Article 46
Article 57	Article 47
Article 58	Article 48
Chapter 3	*Chapter 3*
Article 59	Article 49
Article 60	Article 50
Article 61	Article 51
Article 62 (repealed)	—
Article 63	Article 52
Article 64	Article 53
Article 65	Article 54
Article 66	Article 55
Chapter 4	*Chapter 4*
Article 67 (repealed)	—
Article 68 (repealed)	—
Article 69 (repealed)	—
Article 70 (repealed)	—
Article 71 (repealed)	—
Article 72 (repealed)	—
Article 73 (repealed)	—
Article 73a (repealed)	—
Article 73b	Article 56
Article 73c	Article 57
Article 73d	Article 58
Article 73e (repealed)	—
Article 73f	Article 59
Article 73g	Article 60
Article 73h (repealed)	—
Title IIIa (**)	**Title IV**
Article 73i (*)	Article 61
Article 73j (*)	Article 62
Article 73k (*)	Article 63
Article 73l (*)	Article 64
Article 73m (*)	Article 65
Article 73n (*)	Article 66
Article 73o (*)	Article 67
Article 73p (*)	Article 68
Article 73q (*)	Article 69
Title IV	**Title V**
Article 74	Article 70
Article 75	Article 71
Article 76	Article 72
Article 77	Article 73
Article 78	Article 74

Previous numbering	*New numbering*
Article 79	Article 75
Article 80	Article 76
Article 81	Article 77
Article 82	Article 78
Article 83	Article 79
Article 84	Article 80

Title V   **Title VI**

Chapter 1   *Chapter 1*

Section 1   *Section 1*

Article 85	Article 81
Article 86	Article 82
Article 87	Article 83
Article 88	Article 84
Article 89	Article 85
Article 90	Article 86

Section 2 (deleted)   —

Article 91 (repealed)   —

Section 3   *Section 2*

Article 92	Article 87
Article 93	Article 88
Article 94	Article 89

Chapter 2   *Chapter 2*

Article 95	Article 90
Article 96	Article 91
Article 97 (repealed)	—
Article 98	Article 92
Article 99	Article 93

Chapter 3   *Chapter 3*

Article 100	Article 94
Article 100a	Article 95
Article 100b (repealed)	—
Article 100c (repealed)	—
Article 100d (repealed)	—
Article 101	Article 96
Article 102	Article 97

Title VI   **Title VII**

Chapter 1   *Chapter 1*

Article 102a	Article 98
Article 103	Article 99

Previous numbering	*New numbering*
Article 103a	Article 100
Article 104	Article 101
Article 104a	Article 102
Article 104b	Article 103
Article 104c	Article 104
Chapter 2	*Chapter 2*
Article 105	Article 105
Article 105a	Article 106
Article 106	Article 107
Article 107	Article 108
Article 108	Article 109
Article 108a	Article 110
Article 109	Article 111
Chapter 3	*Chapter 3*
Article 109a	Article 112
Article 109b	Article 113
Article 109c	Article 114
Article 109d	Article 115
Chapter 4	*Chapter 4*
Article 109e	Article 116
Article 109f	Article 117
Article 109g	Article 118
Article 109h	Article 119
Article 109i	Article 120
Article 109j	Article 121
Article 109k	Article 122
Article 109l	Article 123
Article 109m	Article 124
Title VIa (**)	**Title VIII**
Article 109n (*)	Article 125
Article 109o (*)	Article 126
Article 109p (*)	Article 127
Article 109q (*)	Article 128
Article 109r (*)	Article 129
Article 109s (*)	Article 130
Title VII	**Title IX**
Article 110	Article 131
Article 111 (repealed)	—
Article 112	Article 132
Article 113	Article 133
Article 114 (repealed)	—
Article 115	Article 134

Previous numbering	*New numbering*
Article 116 (repealed)	—
Title VIIa (**)	**Title X**
Article 116 (*)	Article 135
Title VIII	**Title XI**
Chapter 1 (***)	*Chapter 1*
Article 117	Article 136
Article 118	Article 137
Article 118a	Article 138
Article 118b	Article 139
Article 118c	Article 140
Article 119	Article 141
Article 119a	Article 142
Article 120	Article 143
Article 121	Article 144
Article 122	Article 145
Chapter 2	*Chapter 2*
Article 123	Article 146
Article 124	Article 147
Article 125	Article 148
Chapter 3	*Chapter 3*
Article 126	Article 149
Article 127	Article 150
Title IX	**Title XII**
Article 128	Article 151
Title X	**Title XIII**
Article 129	Article 152
Title XI	**Title XIV**
Article 129a	Article 153
Title XII	**Title XV**
Article 129b	Article 154
Article 129c	Article 155
Article 129d	Article 156
Title XIII	**Title XVI**
Article 130	Article 157

Previous numbering	*New numbering*
Title XIV	**Title XVII**
Article 130a	Article 158
Article 130b	Article 159
Article 130c	Article 160
Article 130d	Article 161
Article 130e	Article 162
Title XV	**Title XVIII**
Article 130f	Article 163
Article 130g	Article 164
Article 130h	Article 165
Article 130i	Article 166
Article 130j	Article 167
Article 130k	Article 168
Article 130l	Article 169
Article 130m	Article 170
Article 130n	Article 171
Article 130o	Article 172
Article 130p	Article 173
Article 130q	
(repealed)	—
Title XVI	**Title XIX**
Article 130r	Article 174
Article 130s	Article 175
Article 130t	Article 176
Title XVII	**Title XX**
Article 130u	Article 177
Article 130v	Article 178
Article 130w	Article 179
Article 130x	Article 180
Article 130y	Article 181
PART FOUR	**PART FOUR**
Article 131	Article 182
Article 132	Article 183
Article 133	Article 184
Article 134	Article 185
Article 135	Article 186
Article 136	Article 187
Article 136a	Article 188

Previous numbering	New numbering
PART FIVE	**PART FIVE**
Title I	**Title I**
Chapter 1	*Chapter 1*
Section 1	*Section 1*
Article 137	Article 189
Article 138	Article 190
Article 138a	Article 191
Article 138b	Article 192
Article 138c	Article 193
Article 138d	Article 194
Article 138e	Article 195
Article 139	Article 196
Article 140	Article 197
Article 141	Article 198
Article 142	Article 199
Article 143	Article 200
Article 144	Article 201
Section 2	*Section 2*
Article 145	Article 202
Article 146	Article 203
Article 147	Article 204
Article 148	Article 205
Article 149 (repealed)	—
Article 150	Article 206
Article 151	Article 207
Article 152	Article 208
Article 153	Article 209
Article 154	Article 210
Section 3	*Section 3*
Article 155	Article 211
Article 156	Article 212
Article 157	Article 213
Article 158	Article 214
Article 159	Article 215
Article 160	Article 216
Article 161	Article 217
Article 162	Article 218
Article 163	Article 219
Section 4	*Section 4*
Article 164	Article 220
Article 165	Article 221
Article 166	Article 222
Article 167	Article 223

Previous numbering	*New numbering*
Article 168	Article 224
Article 168a	Article 225
Article 169	Article 226
Article 170	Article 227
Article 171	Article 228
Article 172	Article 229
Article 173	Article 230
Article 174	Article 231
Article 175	Article 232
Article 176	Article 233
Article 177	Article 234
Article 178	Article 235
Article 179	Article 236
Article 180	Article 237
Article 181	Article 238
Article 182	Article 239
Article 183	Article 240
Article 184	Article 241
Article 185	Article 242
Article 186	Article 243
Article 187	Article 244
Article 188	Article 245
Section 5	*Section 5*
Article 188a	Article 246
Article 188b	Article 247
Article 188c	Article 248
Chapter 2	*Chapter 2*
Article 189	Article 249
Article 189a	Article 250
Article 189b	Article 251
Article 189c	Article 252
Article 190	Article 253
Article 191	Article 254
Article 191a (*)	Article 255
Article 192	Article 256
Chapter 3	*Chapter 3*
Article 193	Article 257
Article 194	Article 258
Article 195	Article 259
Article 196	Article 260
Article 197	Article 261
Article 198	Article 262
Chapter 4	*Chapter 4*
Article 198a	Article 263
Article 198b	Article 264
Article 198c	Article 265

Previous numbering	New numbering
Chapter 5	*Chapter 5*
Article 198d	Article 266
Article 198e	Article 267
Title II	**Title II**
Article 199	Article 268
Article 200 (repealed)	—
Article 201	Article 269
Article 201a	Article 270
Article 202	Article 271
Article 203	Article 272
Article 204	Article 273
Article 205	Article 274
Article 205a	Article 275
Article 206	Article 276
Article 206a (repealed)	—
Article 207	Article 277
Article 208	Article 278
Article 209	Article 279
Article 209a	Article 280
PART SIX	**PART SIX**
Article 210	Article 281
Article 211	Article 282
Article 212 (*)	Article 283
Article 213	Article 284
Article 213a (*)	Article 285
Article 213b (*)	Article 286
Article 214	Article 287
Article 215	Article 288
Article 216	Article 289
Article 217	Article 290
Article 218 (*)	Article 291
Article 219	Article 292
Article 220	Article 293
Article 221	Article 294
Article 222	Article 295
Article 223	Article 296
Article 224	Article 297
Article 225	Article 298
Article 226 (repealed)	—
Article 227	Article 299
Article 228	Article 300
Article 228a	Article 301
Article 229	Article 302
Article 230	Article 303

Previous numbering	*New numbering*
Article 231	Article 304
Article 232	Article 305
Article 233	Article 306
Article 234	Article 307
Article 235	Article 308
Article 236 (*)	Article 309
Article 237 (repealed)	—
Article 238	Article 310
Article 239	Article 311
Article 240	Article 312
Article 241 (repealed)	—
Article 242 (repealed)	—
Article 243 (repealed)	—
Article 244 (repealed)	—
Article 245 (repealed)	—
Article 246 (repealed)	—

Final Provisions	**Final Provisions**
Article 247	Article 313
Article 248	Article 314

INDEX